IT Governance Policies & Procedures
2009 Edition

by Michael Wallace and Larry Webber

The role of IT management is changing even more quickly than information technology itself. The 2009 Edition of *IT Governance Policies and Procedures* is an updated guide and decision-making reference that can help you to devise an information systems policy and procedure program uniquely tailored to the needs of your organization. Not only does it provide extensive sample policies, but this valuable resource gives you the information you need to develop useful and effective policies for your unique environment. For fingertip access to the information you need on IT governance, policy and planning, documentation, systems analysis and design, and much more, the materials in this ready-reference desk manual can be used by you or your staff as models or templates to create similar documents for your own organization.

Highlights of the 2009 Edition

The 2009 Edition brings you:

- The latest on implementing IT governance methodologies such as ITIL, COBIT, and ISO 20000

- Actual sample policies on the enclosed CD that you can modify for your own use to enforce proper governance of IT within your organization

- New information on managing change within your IT organization

- New information on how to manage a virtual team

- New information on how best to implement the move toward ''green'' computing

- New worksheets on the enclosed CD you can use for planning and documentation of your critical processes

- New information on how a document management system affects your operation

- Tools and tips for mitigating the impact of events that can interrupt your business

- New information on data management and how to manage and protect your critical data

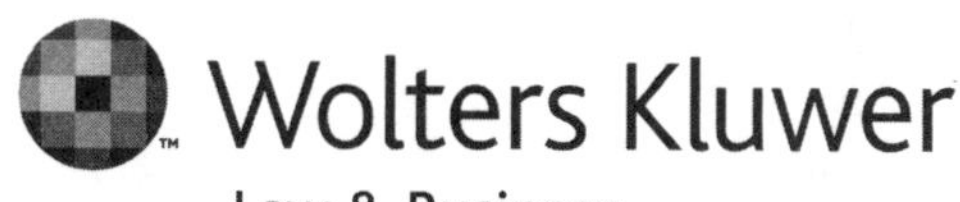

- Best practices on the management of instant messages and blogs

- Updated information on how to hire the right people

- The latest best practices tips updated for every chapter

- The latest information on web site usability techniques

- The legal issues surrounding the information your organization generates and your responsibilities for managing and safeguarding it (HIPAA, Sarbanes-Oxley, Gramm-Leach-Bliley, SEC, Committee of Sponsoring Organizations, Control Objectives for Information and Related Technology (COBIT™), Personal Information Protection and Electronic Documents Act (PIPEDA), Fair and Accurate Credit Transactions Act of 2003 (FACTA), ISO 17799, and Canadian Budget Measures Act (Bill 198))

- Updated information on testing your business continuity plan and keeping it up to date

- A significantly updated glossary with all the latest technology terminology and buzzwords

- Proposal templates, checklists, tally sheets, worksheets, tables, logs, questionnaires, and agreements for quick reference and adaptation to your particular needs

9/08

For questions concerning this shipment, billing, or other customer service matters, call our Customer Service Department at 1-800-234-1660.

For toll-free ordering, please call 1-800-638-8437.

IT
GOVERNANCE
POLICIES
& PROCEDURES

2009 EDITION

ASPEN PUBLISHERS

IT GOVERNANCE POLICIES & PROCEDURES

2009 EDITION

Michael Wallace ◆ Larry Webber

Wolters Kluwer
Law & Business

AUSTIN   BOSTON   CHICAGO   NEW YORK   THE NETHERLANDS

This publication is designed to provide accurate and authoritative information in regard to the subject matter covered. It is sold with the understanding that the publisher is not engaged in rendering legal, accounting, or other professional services. If legal advice or other professional assistance is required, the services of a competent professional person should be sought.

—From a *Declaration of Principles* jointly adopted
by a Committee of the American Bar Association
and a Committee of Publishers and Associations

ISBN 978-0-7355-7368-0

1 2 3 4 5 6 7 8 9 0

About Wolters Kluwer Law & Business

Wolters Kluwer Law & Business is a leading provider of research information and workflow solutions in key specialty areas. The strengths of the individual brands of Aspen Publishers, CCH, Kluwer Law International and Loislaw are aligned within Wolters Kluwer Law & Business to provide comprehensive, in-depth solutions and expert-authored content for the legal, professional and education markets.

CCH was founded in 1913 and has served more than four generations of business professionals and their clients. The CCH products in the Wolters Kluwer Law & Business group are highly regarded electronic and print resources for legal, securities, antitrust and trade regulation, government contracting, banking, pension, payroll, employment and labor, and healthcare reimbursement and compliance professionals.

Aspen Publishers is a leading information provider for attorneys, business professionals and law students. Written by preeminent authorities, Aspen products offer analytical and practical information in a range of specialty practice areas from securities law and intellectual property to mergers and acquisitions and pension/benefits. Aspen's trusted legal education resources provide professors and students with high-quality, up-to-date and effective resources for successful instruction and study in all areas of the law.

Kluwer Law International supplies the global business community with comprehensive English-language international legal information. Legal practitioners, corporate counsel and business executives around the world rely on the Kluwer Law International journals, loose-leafs, books and electronic products for authoritative information in many areas of international legal practice.

Loislaw is a premier provider of digitized legal content to small law firm practitioners of various specializations. Loislaw provides attorneys with the ability to quickly and efficiently find the necessary legal information they need, when and where they need it, by facilitating access to primary law as well as state-specific law, records, forms and treatises.

Wolters Kluwer Law & Business, a unit of Wolters Kluwer, is headquartered in New York and Riverwoods, Illinois. Wolters Kluwer is a leading multinational publisher and information services company.

ASPEN PUBLISHERS SUBSCRIPTION NOTICE

This Aspen Publishers product is updated on a periodic basis with supplements to reflect important changes in the subject matter. If you purchased this product directly from Aspen Publishers, we have already recorded your subscription for the update service.

If, however, you purchased this product from a bookstore and wish to receive future updates and revised or related volumes billed separately with a 30-day examination review, please contact our Customer Service Department at 1-800-234-1660 or send your name, company name (if applicable), address, and the title of the product to:

ASPEN PUBLISHERS
7201 McKinney Circle
Frederick, MD 21704

Important Aspen Publishers Contact Information

- To order any Aspen Publishers title, go to *www.aspenpublishers.com* or call 1-800-638-8437.
- To reinstate your manual update service, call 1-800-638-8437.
- To contact Customer Care, e-mail *customer.care@aspen publishers.com,* call 1-800-234-1660, fax 1-800-901-9075, or mail correspondence to Order Department, Aspen Publishers, PO Box 990, Frederick, MD 21705.
- To review your account history or pay an invoice online, visit *www.aspenpublishers.com/payinvoices.*

ABOUT THE AUTHORS

Michael Wallace has more than 25 years of experience in the information systems field. He began his career as a mainframe operator for Super Food Services and then moved to a programming position at Reynolds & Reynolds developing financial applications for automotive dealers.

He became a consultant after graduating magna cum laude from Wright State University (Dayton, Ohio) with a Bachelor of Science degree in Management Science. For eight years he was president of Q Consulting, a custom application development firm. Mr. Wallace has been an application developer, a business analyst, and a technical and business consultant and has assisted the state of Ohio in developing statewide IT policies.

Mr. Wallace has served on the board of directors of various information technology user organizations and is active in the local technical community. He is currently President of the Columbus Chapter of the International Association of Microsoft Certified Partners (IAMCP), is a Competent Toastmaster with Toastmasters International, and graduated from the Executive MBA program at the Fisher College of Business at The Ohio State University.

After working as a practice manager and director for the last few years, Mr. Wallace is now Vice President of Application Engineering at Result Data, which provides clients with guidance on IT strategy, application development, business intelligence, disaster recovery planning, and policies and procedures. He has also taught in the graduate programs at The Ohio State University and DeVry University Keller Graduate School of Management and has published several articles and books on business and technology topics.

Mr. Wallace can be reached by e-mail at *michaelw@columbus.rr.com*.

Larry Webber has more than 30 years of experience in the information services field. He began his career in the U.S. Marine Corps as a digital network repairman and then moved to a position as a COBOL programmer supporting the Marine's Logistics traffic management systems.

After his release from active service, he worked in Kansas City as a COBOL programmer, systems analyst, and IT manager at Waddell & Reed, Temperature Industries, United Telecommunications, and the law offices of Shook, Hardy & Bacon.

For the next 12 years, Mr. Webber held various systems engineering and data processing management positions with International Truck and Bus in Springfield, Ohio, where, among other achievements, he authored an extensive Disaster Recovery plan for the 2-million-square-foot manufacturing facility. He is currently a Senior Project Manager for Insight Corporation in Columbus, Ohio.

Mr. Webber has an Associate in Science degree from Darton College in Albany, Georgia, in Data Processing; a Bachelor of Science degree in Business Administration and an MBA both from Rockhurst College in Kansas City, Missouri; and an Associate in Science degree in Industrial Engineering from Sinclair Community College in Dayton, Ohio. He also completed a Master of Project Management degree from West Carolina University.

Mr. Webber is retired from the U.S. Army Reserve as a First Sergeant in the Infantry. He is a certified Project Management Professional by the Project Management Institute, Certified in Production and Inventory Management by APICS, Master of Business Continuity Planning by DRII, Six Sigma Black Belt, and ITIL Service Manager. Mr. Webber is a senior adjunct faculty member at DeVry University Keller Graduate School of Management, and has published several articles on disaster recovery topics. His published works include disaster recovery/business continuity, quality control, project management, and veterans benefits.

Mr. Webber can be reached by e-mail at *ljwljw88@hotmail.com*. Your comments and suggestions for improving this book are welcome.

CONTENTS

A complete table of contents for each chapter is included at the beginning of the chapter.

Foreword
Preface
Acknowledgments

1 IT GOVERNANCE: ALIGNING IT WITH THE BUSINESS
§ 1.01 Overview
§ 1.02 IT Governance Models
§ 1.03 IT Strategic Planning Process

2 ITIL AND ISO 20000: MEETING THE NEEDS OF BUSINESS
§ 2.01 Overview
§ 2.02 ITIL Service Support
§ 2.03 ITIL Service Delivery
§ 2.04 ITIL Certification
§ 2.05 ITIL as an Official Standard
§ 2.06 Criticism of ITIL
§ 2.07 Implementing ITIL

3 COBIT: MEETING OBJECTIVES
§ 3.01 Overview
§ 3.02 The Parts of COBIT
§ 3.03 COBIT Framework
§ 3.04 Implementing COBIT

4 BUSINESS IMPACT ANALYSIS: MEASURING RISK
§ 4.01 Overview
§ 4.02 Managing a Business Impact Analysis (BIA)
§ 4.03 BIA Data Collection Process—Get the Facts
§ 4.04 Crunching the Data
§ 4.05 BIA Results and the IT Department
§ 4.06 Evergreen

5 POLICIES AND PROCEDURES: SETTING THE FRAMEWORK

§ 5.01 Overview
§ 5.02 Organizing a Manual
§ 5.03 Setting the Standards for Responsibilities
§ 5.04 IT Policy Approval Process

6 PROJECT MANAGEMENT: GETTING IT OUT ON TIME

§ 6.01 Overview
§ 6.02 Project Management Fundamentals
§ 6.03 Important Elements of the Project Plan
§ 6.04 Executing the Project
§ 6.05 Project Closeout
§ 6.06 Project Management Office

7 BUSINESS CONTINUITY PLANNING: STAYING IN BUSINESS

§ 7.01 Overview
§ 7.02 Prepare to Plan
§ 7.03 Business Continuity Planning Basics
§ 7.04 Planning—The Next Step
§ 7.05 Writing a Plan
§ 7.06 Sources of Additional Information

8 IT AUDITS: STAYING IN COMPLIANCE

§ 8.01 Overview
§ 8.02 IT Management Audit
§ 8.03 IT Legal Mandates and Records Retention
§ 8.04 Resource Management
§ 8.05 Programming Activities Control
§ 8.06 Computer Operations
§ 8.07 Data Networks
§ 8.08 Disaster Recovery/Contingency Planning
§ 8.09 Workstation Audit Issues
§ 8.10 Strategies for Surviving an Audit

9 IT STAFFING: MEETING CUSTOMER SERVICE EXPECTATIONS

§ 9.01 Overview
§ 9.02 What Is This "Thing" Called Customer Service?
§ 9.03 Components of IT Service Staffing
§ 9.04 Metrics—IT's Measures of Success
§ 9.05 Why Use a Customer Survey?
§ 9.06 Translating Requirements into a Staff Level

10 HUMAN RESOURCES: IT'S POOREST MANAGED ASSET

§ 10.01 Overview
§ 10.02 Recruiting, Reassignments, and Promotions
§ 10.03 New Employee Orientation
§ 10.04 Performance Review
§ 10.05 Employee Development
§ 10.06 Managing IT Training
§ 10.07 Employee Communications

§ 10.08   Employee Burnout
§ 10.09   IT Employee Productivity
§ 10.10   Nontraditional Working Arrangements

11 VIRTUAL TEAMS: REMOTE CONTROL MANAGEMENT

§ 11.01   Overview
§ 11.02   The Virtual Company
§ 11.03   Becoming a Virtual Worker
§ 11.04   Virtual Workforce Strategy
§ 11.05   Leading a Virtual Team

12 VENDORS: GETTING THE GOODS

§ 12.01   Overview
§ 12.02   Vendor Management
§ 12.03   Play by the Rules
§ 12.04   Consulting and Temporary Personnel Services
§ 12.05   Requests for Proposal

13 DOCUMENTATION: GETTING EVERYONE ON THE SAME PAGE

§ 13.01   Overview
§ 13.02   Developing a Reference Documentation Policy
§ 13.03   Document Formats
§ 13.04   Document Management
§ 13.05   System Reference Instructions
§ 13.06   Project Documentation
§ 13.07   Systems Analysis Documentation
§ 13.08   Flowcharting Standards

14 COMPUTER SECURITY: PRACTICE SAFE COMPUTING

§ 14.01   Overview
§ 14.02   People Security
§ 14.03   Process Security
§ 14.04   Legal Issues

15 DATA BACKUPS—THE KEY TO A PROMPT RECOVERY

§ 15.01   Overview
§ 15.02   Data Recovery
§ 15.03   Data Backups—Major Responsibilities
§ 15.04   Designing for Backups
§ 15.05   Media Handling, Transportation, and Storage
§ 15.06   Workstation, Notebook PC, and Data Collection Station Backups
§ 15.07   Data Retention and Legal Mandates

16 SERVICE DESK SUPPORT: HANDLING DAY-TO-DAY HASSLES

§ 16.01   Overview
§ 16.02   Role of the Service Desk
§ 16.03   Establishing a Service Desk
§ 16.04   The Proactive Service Desk
§ 16.05   The Service Desk in a Disaster

17 MANAGING IT ASSETS: IDENTIFY WHAT YOU HAVE

§ 17.01   Overview
§ 17.02   Lay the Groundwork
§ 17.03   Conducting the Inventory
§ 17.04   Software Asset Management
§ 17.05   Software Assets

18 PERSONAL COMPUTERS: MANAGING THE DESKTOP SYSTEM

§ 18.01   Overview
§ 18.02   PC Coordinator
§ 18.03   PC Acquisition Procedures
§ 18.04   Operations Procedures
§ 18.05   End-User Technical Support

19 NETWORKS: THE GREAT FACILITATOR

§ 19.01   Overview
§ 19.02   Network Security
§ 19.03   The Network Coordinator

20 TECHNOLOGY RELOCATION: SUCCESSFULLY MOVING YOUR IT OPERATIONS

§ 20.01   Overview
§ 20.02   Business Issues
§ 20.03   Relocation Process

21 GREEN COMPUTING: EARTH FRIENDLY IT

§ 21.01   Overview
§ 21.02   A Time to Stop
§ 21.03   Put Energy-Hog Equipment on a Diet
§ 21.04   What Can You Do?
§ 21.05   Safe Disposal

22 DOCUMENT MANAGEMENT: CAPTURING CORPORATE KNOWLEDGE

§ 22.01   Overview
§ 22.02   Capture and Storage
§ 22.03   Retrieval and Collaboration
§ 22.04   Printing and Archiving
§ 22.05   Designing a Solution

23 THE INTERNET: MAKING IT PRODUCTIVE

§ 23.01   Overview
§ 23.02   Methods of Internet Access
§ 23.03   Internet Security Policy
§ 23.04   Internet E-Mail Use Policy
§ 23.05   Messaging and Blogging Policy
§ 23.06   Acceptable Use Agreement
§ 23.07   Software as a Service
§ 23.08   SAAS Vendor Selection Process
§ 23.09   SAAS Vendor Management

24 WEB SITE USABILITY: BUILD IT SO THEY WILL COME

§ 24.01   Overview
§ 24.02   Web Site Usability
§ 24.03   Web Site Usability Policies

25 DATA MANAGEMENT: TAKING CARE OF YOUR INFORMATION

§ 25.01   Overview
§ 25.02   Issues Relating to Data
§ 25.03   Access to Data
§ 25.04   Protecting Employee Data

26 END-USER SYSTEMS: DO IT YOURSELF COMPUTING

§ 26.01   Overview
§ 26.02   The Problems with End-User Computing
§ 26.03   Personal Computing vs. Corporate Computing
§ 26.04   Managing a Proactive End-User Computing Program
§ 26.05   End-User Policies

27 CHANGE MANAGEMENT: KEEPING EVERYTHING UP TO DATE

§ 27.01   Overview
§ 27.02   Change Management Policy
§ 27.03   Patch Management Policy
§ 27.04   Patch Management Tools

28 SYSTEMS ANALYSIS AND DESIGN: PLANNING FOR SUCCESS

§ 28.01   Overview
§ 28.02   Systems Development and Planning
§ 28.03   Systems Analysis
§ 28.04   Systems Design
§ 28.05   Systems Prototyping
§ 28.06   Systems Implementation
§ 28.07   Systems Maintenance

29 SOFTWARE DEVELOPMENT: SOLID PRACTICES

§ 29.01   Overview
§ 29.02   Software Development Process
§ 29.03   Programming Methodologies
§ 29.04   Programming Conventions
§ 29.05   Software Acquisition
§ 29.06   Program Testing
§ 29.07   Software Installation
§ 29.08   Program Maintenance

Glossary of IT Terms
Index

FOREWORD

IT governance is the idea of aligning the information technology strategy of the organization with the needs and overall strategy of the organization it supports. Whether the organization is large or small, public or private, proper IT governance ensures that the IT organization supports the strategy of the organization and helps the organization to meet its goals. IT governance also enables the organization to satisfy regulatory requirements and supports its disaster recovery efforts. Having worked with many different types of organizations in my career, I have found that effective IT governance is critical to the success of the organization.

The implementation of IT governance requires structure around how IT operates to ensure that the requirements of the business are being met, and helps to measure how well the IT organization meets those needs. This is best accomplished through the implementation of the appropriate IT policies and procedures. While most books on IT governance are theoretical in nature, Wallace and Webber have developed a practical guide that allows IT management to put the proper policies and procedures in place to support the organization quickly and efficiently. Rather than simply put together a "one-size-fits-all" book of policies, they clearly explain what goes into each policy area so that the IT manager can tailor each policy to their specific needs. I believe that IT management at any type of organization will find this book to be a useful guide in creating the policies and procedures that best fit their unique business needs.

Ben Blanquera, Director Applications Delivery
Progressive Medical, Inc.

PREFACE

While many of the basic principles of superior IT operations have not changed over the years—we still have to do backups, service business users, and so on—the Internet and an explosion of connectivity options have added new challenges to running an effective IT organization. Writing *IT Governance Policies & Procedures, 2009 Edition*, has been a challenge because of the explosion of IT technology. By the time you finish this book, technology changes are already being developed for the next edition.

WHAT THIS MANUAL WILL DO FOR YOU

No two information systems operations are alike, but many do share some basic elements, such as hardware, software, and personnel. This manual defines the common threads that link all information systems operations, providing for a variety of situations—not as a one-size-fits-all model but, instead, as an updated guide and decision-making reference that can help you devise an information systems policy and procedure program uniquely tailored to the needs of your organization. Rather than simply providing sample policies that will not encompass what is unique to your organization, this manual gives you the information you need to develop useful and effective policies for your unique environment.

ORGANIZED FOR QUICK ACCESS

"Simplicity is the ultimate design." Often, a multitude of forms are included in policies and procedures handbooks. This manual, however, provides a minimum of forms with the understanding that a well-written memo or e-mail message can take the place of a form and reduce the complexity of an IT operation. As an operation grows in complexity, the challenge to keep it running smoothly grows, and thus the need for a formal system of operations becomes a necessity. IT operations that have a formal systems and procedures manual in place are more efficient.

ADDED STRATEGIC VALUE

The role of IT management is changing even more quickly than information technology itself. Today the IT operation is no longer found in some obscure corner of the corporate organization. Instead, it plays an interactive role in global systems. This manual will help you to formalize policies and procedures that are needed to formally document the IT operation. Doing so will save both time and effort. This manual will help you identify standard operations and procedures, documenting as needed, but still allowing for special needs.

Reality check: End-user computer systems will grow with or without the guidance of corporate IT, but the two working together will provide synergistic dividends. This manual updates the policies and procedures that can expedite your objective.

Our research discovered many well-run information systems operations and some real disasters. The better ones had noticeably good management and practical documentation. Expensive consultants, fad innovations, and cutting-edge technology did not always produce the desired IT results.

IT Governance Policies & Procedures is a compilation of systems policies and procedures—the best practices within the industry—in current use. This manual is a process development tool that any seasoned information systems manager, working in a large or small IS operation, will find useful.

SAVING YOU TIME

In addition to the background information you need to create policies specific to your organization, sample policies are included with each chapter that you can use as a starting point for developing your own resource, by copying the sample policies from the included CD. Of course, you can also make needed changes and post the manual on a local area network or even a company intranet site.

ACKNOWLEDGMENTS

Michael dedicates this book to his teacher and mentor, George Jenkins, whose encouragement and support have been invaluable over the years, and to his wife and best friend, Tami, for all her support during his many projects.

Larry gratefully acknowledges the assistance of his wife, Nancy, in preparing this project.

Our extended thanks to Charles Godsey, who provided valuable information on information systems security, and to Scott Martin, for providing feedback and suggestions on document management best practices.

1

IT GOVERNANCE: ALIGNING IT WITH THE BUSINESS

§ 1.01   OVERVIEW
        [A]   Purpose and Scope
        [B]   Critical Policies to Develop Based on This Chapter

§ 1.02   IT GOVERNANCE MODELS
        [A]   Overview of Governance Models

§ 1.03   IT STRATEGIC PLANNING PROCESS
        [A]   Overview
        [B]   Policy and Procedures to Submit a Strategic Plan

§ 1.01 OVERVIEW

[A] Purpose and Scope

Information Technology (IT) departments have long struggled with providing the level of service that the "business" side of the organization has demanded. IT exists but to serve the rest of the organization, and yet customers always demand more. In addition, IT consumes a large share of the company's operating budget and has a voracious appetite for ever more resources.

To make matters worse, how often have IT users and business executives complained that the various IT teams seem to work at cross purposes? How often has one team completed something and "tossed" it to another IT group and walked away? How often has one IT team "slipped in" a change that no one else knew about, and that brought important IT systems to a halt?

Managing IT complexities, while maintaining customer satisfaction, is a difficult task. Companies typically do a few things well, a few things poorly and the rest falls somewhere in the middle. IT is typically not the core competency of the company, yet the very survival of the company may depend on how well its IT operation supports the goals and objectives of the business.

IT governance is an attempt to apply structure and control over how IT is managed within the organization. It includes proper controls over how resources are allocated, how change is managed, and how services are delivered. While IT has its own unique problems, applying basic management and governance principles to how IT is delivered allows the organization to get the most return for its investment in IT. IT governance can include the following activities:

A. Defining how money should be spent.
B. Justifying and prioritizing the investments in IT.
C. Defining the controls on spending.
D. Managing and controlling projects.
E. Deploying IT staff.
F. Using service level agreements (SLAs) to define appropriate levels of service from IT.
G. Managing the change control process.
H. Complying with regulatory requirements such as Sarbanes-Oxley.

While there are several different IT governance models to choose from, they all attempt to bring order to the chaos of IT by some combination of the following activities:

A. Measurement of results.
B. Justification of resources used.
C. Accountability and transparency.
D. Control of the work being performed.
E. Coordination of work being done in different areas.
F. Compliance with internal and external policies or regulations.
G. Ensuring that IT meets the needs of the organization.

IT governance becomes reality with the creation of the appropriate policies and procedures to ensure that the IT governance model used by your organization is being followed. With the right IT governance model and well thought out policies and procedures in place, you can properly control and manage IT to ensure that it brings the maximum value to the business.

[B] Critical Policies to Develop Based on This Chapter

Using the material discussed in this chapter, you will be able to create the following policies:

    A. IT governance model to be followed by the organization.
        1. Why the selected governance model is appropriate for the organization.
        2. IT policies and procedures must support the governance model.
    B. Developing a strategic plan.

Policies should always be developed based on the local situation. Successful managers cannot issue appropriate guidance if the policies are written with another company's or location's situation in mind.

§ 1.02 IT GOVERNANCE MODELS

[A] Overview of Governance Models

There are several different IT governance models that have been developed, some driven from a strategic viewpoint and others developed from tactical processes such as project management. Each has its strengths and weaknesses; the business and IT management must select the appropriate governance model based on the unique needs of the business. The following sections are a brief overview of the most widely used governance models.

    A. **COSO**—COSO (the Committee of Sponsoring Organizations) was originally formed in 1985 to sponsor the National Commission on Fraudulent Financial Reporting, which was a private sector initiative to study the causes of fraudulent financial reporting by public companies. In 1992, COSO established a framework for the proper authorization, recording and reporting of transactions. The Securities and Exchange Commission (SEC) officially recognizes the COSO framework as adequate for establishing internal controls over financial reporting. COSO is the basis for COBIT's professional standards for internal controls and auditing.

In COSO's framework, an internal control is a process. Internal controls only provide some assurance that something will occur, and not an absolute guarantee. Each internal control addresses a specific objective. COSO internal controls are measured in terms of:

    1. Control environment—processes for developing controls and a control-conscious work force.

2. Risk assessment—identification and analysis of risks of fraud and inaccurate financial reporting.
3. Control activities—policies and procedures for execution of management directives, such as management oversight, separation of duties, and audits by external organizations.
4. Information and communication—effective operation and control of the business.
5. Monitoring—ongoing activities or separate evaluations. Includes the feedback loop of reporting discrepancies and then promptly addressing them.

B. COBIT—COBIT™ (Control OBjectives for Information Technology™) is a framework of IT management best practices. It was originally released by the Information Systems Audit and Control Association (ISACA) in 1992 as an IT process and control framework for linking IT to business requirements. In 1998, "Management Guidelines" were added to COBIT providing management tools such as maturity models and metrics, making it more appropriate as a framework for IT governance.

COBIT utilizes controls that provide management and audit functions for IT departments and business process owners. This framework has 34 high-level objects that cover 318 control objectives in four domains:

1. Planning and organization.
2. Acquisition and implementation.
3. Delivery and support.
4. Monitoring.

Many companies use COBIT to fulfill Sarbanes-Oxley's 404 legal compliance requirements. It provides a proven solution to the current climate of corporate accountability and control. Rather than try to invent something new, they adopt portions of COBIT that fit their industry and situation. It also provides an entity-wide model of best practices to manage IT's contribution to the business. COBIT helps non-IT Managers understand their IT systems and set the level of security and control necessary to protect their company's assets.

C. ITIL—ITIL™ (Information Technology Infrastructure Library) is a collection of IT service management best practices developed by the government of the United Kingdom. It began as an effort to collect the best IT practices used by the most successful companies into one guideline for efficient IT Operations. An important aspect of this framework was that it be independent of any particular vendor.

ITIL contains nothing new. It is a collection of the proper way to do such things as change control, service delivery, running a service desk, etc. Most companies already do these things (or know that they should do them, and still do not). ITIL adds and clarifies the best way to conduct these processes.

However, its power is the way the ITIL framework glues these various functions into one coherent strategy.

D. **CMMI**—The Capability Maturity Model® Integration (CMMI) is a process improvement approach developed by the Software Engineering Institute at Carnegie Mellon University. It provides organizations with guidelines for developing effective processes at the project level, by a division, or by an entire organization. It helps connect business and IT functions, provides guidance on setting process improvement goals and priorities, offers advice for improving the quality of processes, and provides a mechanism for evaluating current processes. CMMI consists of the following models and reports:

1. CMMI for Development.
2. CMMI Acquisition Module.
3. Understanding and Leveraging a Supplier's CMMI Efforts: A Guidebook for Acquirers.
4. Adapting CMMI for Acquisition Organizations: A Preliminary Report.

CMMI's main value is in providing guidance on creating and acquiring quality software systems. CMMI uses a maturity model to determine the current state of the software development process and as a roadmap to improvement. The five levels of the maturity model are:

1. Level 1—Initial: The process is ad-hoc.
2. Level 2—Repeatable: Results are repeatable and basic project management is used.
3. Level 3—Defined: A set of standards is defined and followed.
4. Level 4—Managed: The process is measurable and controlled.
5. Level 5—Optimizing: Continuous improvements are being made to the process.

This idea of a maturity model can also be applied to the operation of the IT function as a whole. This can provide management with a measure of how well IT is meeting the needs of the business.

E. **PMBOK**—PMBOK (Project Management Body of Knowledge) was developed by the Project Management Institute (PMI) as 'the sum of knowledge within the profession of project management.' PMBOK documents and describes the current best practices for managing projects. While not specific to IT projects, it is heavily used in IT as a guide for managing complex IT projects.

PMBOK describes five basic process groups and nine knowledge areas that are typical for almost all projects. The basic concepts are applicable to projects, programs and operations. The five basic process groups are:

1. Initiating.
2. Planning.
3. Executing.
4. Controlling and Monitoring.
5. Closing.

The nine knowledge areas are:

1. Project Integration Management.
2. Project Scope Management.
3. Project Time Management.
4. Project Cost Management.
5. Project Quality Management.
6. Project Human Resource Management.
7. Project Communications Management.
8. Project Risk Management.
9. Project Procurement Management.

Following the best practices as outlined in the PMBOK can help ensure that resources used to complete IT projects are managed effectively for the benefit of the business.

F. PRINCE2—PRINCE2 (Projects IN Controlled Environments) is a project management methodology that provides a structured method for project management. It was initially developed in 1989 by the Central Computer and Telecommunications Agency (CCTA) of the United Kingdom government as a standard for information systems project management. It breaks projects down into the following four components:

1. Method—How will the project be organized and planned?
2. Procedures—Instructions on exactly what is to be done.
3. Techniques—The skills needed to get the work done.
4. Tools—Aids to completing the project.

PRINCE2 is a process—driven project management method which defines 45 separate sub-processes and organizes these into eight processes as follows:

1. Starting Up a Project.
2. Planning.
3. Initiating a Project.
4. Directing a Project.
5. Controlling a Stage.
6. Managing Product Delivery.
7. Managing Stage Boundaries.
8. Closing a Project.

Following the best practices as outlined in PRINCE2 can help ensure that resources used to complete IT projects are managed effectively for the benefit of the business.

G. TOGAF—TOGAF (The Open Group Architecture Framework) provides a detailed method and a set of supporting tools for developing an enterprise architecture. Developed by The Open Group in 1995, TOGAF is based on work done by the US Department of Defense. TOGAF defines four separate architectures that must be considered for the benefit of the organization:

1. Business (or Business Process) Architecture—The business strategy, governance, organization, and key business processes.
2. Data Architecture—The structure of an organization's logical and physical data assets and data management resources.
3. Applications Architecture—Defines how the individual application systems are to be deployed, their interactions, and their relationships to the core business processes of the organization.
4. Technology Architecture—The software infrastructure intended to support the deployment of core, mission-critical applications. This type of software is sometimes referred to as "middleware."

H.   TickIT—TickIT is a software quality assessment system developed primarily by the software industry in the United Kingdom and Sweden. Its purpose is to improve the effectiveness of the quality management process used to create quality software. TickIT is designed to improve quality of software by improving the effectiveness of auditors working in IT through training and subsequent certification. Software development organizations seeking TickIT Certification are required to show conformity with ISO 9001:2000.

A major objective of TickIT is to provide the software industry with a practical framework for the management of software development quality by developing more effective quality management system certification procedures. These include:

1. Publishing guidance material to assist software organizations in interpreting the requirements of ISO 9001.
2. Training, selecting and registering auditors with IT experience and competence.
3. Establishing rules for the accreditation of certification bodies involved in the software sector.

As with other quality processes, TickIT helps support the goals of the business by helping IT create high quality software that meets the needs of the business.

See Policy ITP-1-1 Establishment of IT Governance Model as an example.

POLICY ITP-1-1.   Establishment of IT Governance Model

Policy #:	ITP-1-1	Effective:	01/19/08	Page #:	1 of N
Subject:	Establishment of IT Governance Model				

1.0 PURPOSE

This policy recognizes establishes the IT governance model that will be followed by the organization.

2.0 SCOPE

The policy applies to all users of information technology within the company.

3.0 POLICY

The CIO must establish and provide governance for information technology policies, procedures, and best practices for the company's technology infrastructure in order to secure all IT assets and promote the most efficient use of technology resources.

The CIO will submit a report to the Board of Directors at its first meeting of each calendar year, and submit interim reports at the request of the Board, on the current status of the company's technology policies and procedures.

All operating units within the company that use information technology (IT) are responsible for:

A. Adhering to the IT policies issued by the CIO.
B. Developing and implementing, when appropriate, additional IT policies and procedures specific to their operating units.
C. Promoting IT policy adherence.
D. Complying with the requirements of the IT governance model adopted by the organization.
E. Ensuring the security of the IT systems and the network to which they are connected.
F. Informing the CIO if there are any problems with a policy or if inputs from other sources do not comply with the defined policies.
G. Providing new employees with instruction and/or documented procedures that relate to their job descriptions.
H. Providing an annual "refresher" for current employees highlighting the changes made or problem areas during the previous year.
I. Maintaining the functionality of the IT systems within their area.
J. Facilitating training and the dissemination of information.
K. Preventing unauthorized access to company information, personal files and e-mail.
L. Developing and maintaining a plan for recovery of mission critical data and systems if a loss is sustained.

The head of each business unit must designate an "Information Technology (IT) Coordinator" to ensure that these responsibilities are carried out and to serve as a contact person for that business unit with the CIO. This policy recognizes that different business units have different needs, IT resources, and levels of internal expertise. Hence, the needs and resources of a given business unit may not require the IT Coordinator to have an extensive technical background. Many business units also have "Technical Managers" who are responsible for the operation of the IT systems and with whom the IT Coordinator may share the responsibilities in this policy. Technical Managers are expected to have the technical expertise required to ensure the safe and reliable operation of their respective business unit's IT systems.

4.0 REVISION HISTORY

Date	Revision #	Description of Change
03/18/07	1.0	Initial creation.
01/19/08	1.1	Added support for IT governance model.

5.0 INQUIRIES

Direct inquiries about this policy to:

Tom Jones, CIO
Our Company, Inc.
2900 Corporate Drive
Columbus, OH 43215

Voice: 614-555-1234
Fax: 614-555-1235
E-mail: tjones@company.com

Revision #:	1.1	Supersedes:	1.0	Date:	01/19/08

§ 1.03   IT STRATEGIC PLANNING PROCESS

[A]   Overview

The IT strategic plan is the major vehicle for articulating the information systems needs of the business and the associated resource requirements. The entire business must be involved in the creation of the IT plan, as it will shape the IT resources available for delivering the objectives of the business. If left solely to the IT organization without business unit input, it will not provide maximum value to either part of the organization. The plan must reflect the business drivers for the organization, the relationship of those drivers to the intended IT activities, and the resources required to support those activities.

The head of the firm's corporate computer and/or PC operations takes responsibility for developing an effective IT plan for the organization. The corporate IT plan must integrate with the overall business strategies, goals, and objectives. Division-level plans also must be created, showing how the corporate objectives will be carried out. The head of the firm's corporate computer and/or PC operations reviews the division plans, ensuring these objectives are met, and provides support. Plans also will be reviewed to evaluate their technical feasibility and assess achievability of the planned benefits.

[B] Policy and Procedures to Submit a Strategic Plan

Each division within your organization should prepare an annual information technology strategic plan including strategies, goals, objectives, and performance measures. The division's plan must integrate with the overall business strategies, goals, and objectives. The plan also must consider the overall IT plan, developed at the corporate level if appropriate.

Submittal schedule. Department/division-level IT plans must be submitted at the beginning of each fiscal year to the head of the firm's corporate computer and/or PC operations. Each division should review its plan status quarterly and update corporate every six months.

Submittal procedure. The plan must be submitted to the head of the firm's corporate computer and/or PC operations in electronic format, PDF version, with one unbound paper copy.

The sections described below are required, with subsections or appendixes added, if necessary.

A. **Executive summary.** This is a 1- or 2-page summary that provides a general understanding of the division's IT plan and a frame of reference for understanding the overall objectives of the plan. It also may include information on who developed the plan and how the plan was created.

B. **Division mission.** This section discusses the mission of the division and how it fits into the organization. Each major functional area of the division and its role in fulfilling the division's mission should be discussed.

C. **Goals and objectives.** This section describes the major goals and objectives of the division and how they will be achieved. *Goals* are the long-term results that the organization will achieve as it fulfills its mission. *Objectives* are the near-term results that are attained as the organization meets its goals. Measurements used for determining whether or not the goals and objectives are met should be included in this section.

D. **External factors.** This section discusses the division's business drivers. The division's business drivers are derived from the mission, goals, and objectives and define how the division operates. Identify the external forces such as the economy, technology changes, and political environment and so on that drive the business.

E. **Internal factors.** This section identifies the factors internal to the division that affect the division's IT activities. This may include organizational structure, personnel capabilities, management strength, facilities, training needs, and financial resources. Describe the organization's strengths and weaknesses and how they affect IT programs and management. Include an IT organizational chart and personnel factors such as recruitment, retention, and training.

F. **IT architecture.** This section discusses how the division's IT planning supports its business drivers. A diagram showing the division's current architecture, including internal and external linkages, should be included. If there are plans to significantly change the architecture during the current year, a diagram of the proposed changes should be included. This section also should describe how the division's architecture fits in with the overall corporate architecture.

G. **Technology initiatives.** The major technology initiatives of the division are described in this section. Examples might include e-commerce programs, ERP implementations, wireless initiatives, etc.

H. **Business resumption plans** and the division's project management methodology also should be included in this section.

I. **Project plans.** A project plan for each major new or maintenance project should be presented in this section. Minor projects may be grouped together into one or more general support projects. Each project plan should include the following information:
   1. A brief statement of the project purpose.
   2. A reference to the goal or objective from the section above that the project supports. This section should describe the scope of the project, the expected benefits, the implementation time frame, the resource requirements for the project, and the expected impact the project will have on the organizational goals. Also, describe the impact on the organization if the project is not undertaken.
   3. Describe the success criteria for the project. What metrics (return on investment, service level, system performance, and so on) will be used to measure the success of the project?
   4. Describe the technical approach employed on this project. Include hardware needs, software to be used (including operating system and development tools), and any telecommunications requirements.
   5. List any additional concerns about the project, such as staffing and training needs, schedule, integration with other divisions, etc.
   6. Document the estimated costs by fiscal year for staffing, hardware, telecommunications, etc., needed to complete the project.
   7. Estimate any future maintenance costs for the life of the system once the project is completed.

J. **Project summary.** Document a summary of each project planned by the division in this section. This should list the project name, estimated costs, projected start and completion dates, and the estimated benefit in dollars.

2

ITIL AND ISO 20000: MEETING THE NEEDS OF BUSINESS

§ 2.01   OVERVIEW
    [A]   Purpose and Scope
    [B]   ITIL History
    [C]   ITIL Processes are Artifact-Centric
    [D]   ITIL as a Published Standard

§ 2.02   ITIL SERVICE SUPPORT
    [A]   Service Desk
    [B]   Incident Management
    [C]   Problem Management
    [D]   Configuration Management
    [E]   Change Management
    [F]   Release Management

§ 2.03   ITIL SERVICE DELIVERY
    [A]   Service Level Management
    [B]   Financial Management for IT Services
    [C]   Availability Management
    [D]   Capacity Management
    [E]   IT Service Continuity Management

§ 2.04   ITIL CERTIFICATION
    [A]   Training and Exams
    [B]   Foundations
    [C]   Practitioner
    [D]   Service Manager

§ 2.05   ITIL AS AN OFFICIAL STANDARD
    [A]   Standards—Why Bother?
    [B]   British Standard
    [C]   International Standards Organization

§ 2.06   CRITICISM OF ITIL
         [A]   ITIL as All or Nothing
         [B]   ITIL is not a Coherent Model
         [C]   ITIL Books are Poorly Written and Inconsistent

§ 2.07   IMPLEMENTING ITIL
         [A]   ITIL Changes Everything IT
         [B]   ITIL Implementation Leader
         [C]   Configuration Management Database (CMDB)
         [D]   Introduce ITIL to One Area at a Time

§ 2.01   OVERVIEW

[A]   Purpose and Scope

ITIL™ (Information Technology Infrastructure Library) was an effort spon-
sored by the United Kingdom's government to collect the best IT practices
used by the most successful companies into one guideline for efficient IT
operations. An important aspect of this framework was that it be independent
of any particular vendor.

ITIL contains nothing new. It is a collection of the proper way to do such
things as change control, service delivery, running a service desk, etc. Most
companies already do these things (or know that they should do, and still do
not). ITIL adds and clarifies the best way to conduct these processes. However,
its power is the way the ITIL framework glues these various functions into one
coherent strategy.

> **COMMENT**
>
> "ITIL", "IT Infrastructure Library" and "PRINCE2" are registered
> trademarks held by the United Kingdom's Office of Govern-
> ment Commerce. http://www.ogc.gov.uk/

[B]   ITIL History

ITIL began as a simple idea. How can the UK government improve its IT operations efficiency and perhaps share this "best way" with all companies? In the
mid-1980s, the Central Computer and Telecommunications Agency (CTTA),
an agency of the UK government, gathered the best IT management practices
used in major companies. This was intended to standardize government IT
operations as well as the many companies providing IT services to it. Another
goal was to avoid making the same mistakes over and over again throughout
the organization.

Over time, the success of this effort grew. In 2001, CCTA was merged into the
Office of Government Commerce (OGC) who promotes a wide range of best
business practices (such as PRINCE2™ for Project Management). OGC manages
the copyright for ITIL and the trademark for the name. It also promotes use of
best practices while maintaining control of them to ensure a high quality. This
control guarantees that ITIL remains independent of any one company.

ITIL is called a library because it consists of a series of books explaining how
it works. At one point, there were over 30 books in the set. There are currently
eight volumes in ITIL. These volumes include:

A. Service Delivery.
B. Service Support.

    C. ICT Infrastructure Management.
    D. Security Management.
    E. The Business Perspective.
    F. Application Management.
    G. Software Asset Management.
    H. Planning to Implement Service Management.

[C] ITIL Processes are Artifact-Centric

ITIL uses a series of processes and tools (artifacts) to tie the various practice areas together. For example, a key ITIL artifact is a configuration management database. This artifact contains information about everything in the IT organization that must be controlled. Some of the information in the configuration database might include:

    A. Software versions.
    B. Hardware standards.
    C. Every significant IT hardware item.
    D. Service Level Agreements with customers.
    E. Versions of internally generated documentation.
    F. About anything else that must be controlled to ensure the current version is always available and only changed by authorized persons!

Today, IT departments use a variety of home grown forms, processes, terminology and business policies that are implemented at the whim of a manager and quickly modified by that person's replacement. ITIL provides a standard set of terminology across the organization to ease the flow of information between the various functions.

COMMENT

ITIL does not come with a set of forms. It describes the information that is needed and how it will be used. The creation of forms and their exact content is open to the company implementing it.

[D] ITIL as a Published Standard

Most ITIL users are in the UK and the British Commonwealth. ITIL has made some progress in the United States, but has suffered from its "foreign birth." Also, each company, intentionally or not, applies its own twist to ITIL to accommodate its own business climate.

To standardize ITIL for wider acceptance, it formed the basis of British Standard 15000 (BS 15000). This published British Standard was useful for countries in the British Commonwealth, but full international acceptance was still lagging. ITIL has now been codified into ISO 20000, which focuses on IT Service Management.

ITIL is sometimes implemented alongside of other frameworks such as Capability Maturity Model (CMM) and Control OBjectives for Information and related Technology (COBIT). Microsoft's Operations Framework is based on ITIL. CMM is primarily focused on software and COBIT on regulatory compliance.

§ 2.02 ITIL SERVICE SUPPORT

[A] Service Desk

Most companies already have some variation of a service desk. It is a place to call for IT support on just about anything. Service desks run the gamut from an on-site staff, knowledgeable about local operations, to a call center in a remote corner of the world that takes messages and dispatches help. The goal is to provide a single point of contact for all users.

There are many types of "desks" that receive calls of IT system users and dispatch help. ITIL advocates a full service single point of contact for the IT department through a service desk. (Nothing new about that—they have been around for years.) However, an ITIL service desk provides assistance based on a catalog of service offerings. This catalog lists every IT service offered, the promised response times, the users it is offered to, the times of service covered, etc.

Service catalog creation and maintenance is controlled by Service Management. Its content is based on negotiated service level agreements (SLAs) between the IT department and the people IT supports. Internally within the IT departments, the SLAs are supported by Operational Level Agreements which act as internal SLAs. It may also include underpinning contracts with external service providers.

SLAs provide the details of what the users want to "pay" for. It will clearly describe the service wanted, and the cost for providing that service. The description includes the times of coverage (9 am to 5 pm, Monday through Friday or all day, every day).

The SLAs are then reviewed by the supporting IT organizations that either agree to provide that service using current resources or the cost to meet the requirements. For example, if a customer wanted a four hours response time to recover a lost PC file, during normal working hours and work days, then that may already be covered. However, if they want the same service and same response time 24 hours a day—seven days a week—including holidays (which they will ask for)—then they must bear the cost for someone to sit around all of those hours just in case they are needed (which they normally won't agree to pay for).

This exchange between IT and the rest of the company establishes an expectation of service level. Once the agreements are in place, then as long as IT meets the required times, they are fulfilling their part of the bargain. Over time, an SLA can be refined to reflect the true business need.

Previously, service desk calls were roughly assigned priorities (such as low, medium, and high). Calls were generally handled as First In–First Out. While this is simple to understand, user service delivery was uneven. Where one day a call was resolved in five minutes, on another the same problem took five days (due to other service issues).

Under ITIL, priority of calls is established in the SLAs. For example, if the SLA for password resets is four hours, then doing so anytime within those four hours is a success. If the users want to pay for someone to sit and wait for calls to come in—so a higher level of service is available—then, that option is available to their management also. Even if there is an "IT Technical Emergency," the four hour requirement must be met to fulfill the agreed service level.

[B] Incident Management

Any reported service disruption is known as an "incident." The service desk resolves whatever they can (within their local guidelines). If the problem still exists, then they refer to the SLA for a list of questions to ask the user that gathers initial diagnostic information.

Under ITIL, the analysis of reported problems is handled by the Incident Management team. The guiding focus of Incident Management is the prompt, cost-effective resolution of the problem. The Incident Management process begins by ensuring the problem is properly (and clearly) recorded. It is sometimes difficult for the service desk to gather the appropriate information into a clear document when users are adding information as it springs to mind. Also, if the phone lines are busy, there isn't time to step back and clean up the description.

The incident is matched to a SLA to verify that the user is entitled to this service. If not, then a change request is sent to Service Management to investigate a change to the service catalog. If the user is entitled to the service, then the SLA indicates how priority is assigned.

The incident is checked against other incidents to see if there is a pattern emerging in the problem reports. After that, the incident is assigned to someone to investigate. The result could be:

A. The problem is repaired and full service restored.
B. Problem resolution disrupts other IT services or cannot be immediately repaired. The incident is passed over to Problem Management for resolution. Meanwhile, a work around is created and made available through the Known Error database.
C. The problem is not considered cost effective to address (such as in a one time process).

As the incident progresses to resolution (or work around for a known error), Incident Management, through the service desk, keeps the user informed about progress. This reduces the number of calls to the service desk requesting updates.

COMMENT

ITIL version 3 was introduced in 2007. It shifts some of ITIL's emphasis from Service Delivery and Support to an integrated Service Management lifecycle. It also promotes planned, continual improvement in IT processes.

[C]   Problem Management

Incident Management is focused on the quick restoration of service and all that is needed for many service disruptions. However, the root causes of some problems are not so obvious—and the solution is not so soon to appear. These incidents are passed over to Problem Management.

Similar to Incident Management, Problem Management prioritizes the incoming work load to work on the most urgent, highest value tasks first. The incident tracking database is checked for similar problems in the past and possible connection to other recently reported incidents.

Problem Management will bring together the necessary technical skills to trace back the incident to its source. One tool commonly used is a fault tree analysis which details all the sequence of actions necessary to complete a technical task. The goal is to identify where the chain of events is broken. Another common tool is a fishbone analysis which details all of the factors required for something to work. This indicates what was missing that may have caused the failure.

Once the root cause of the incident is located, its classification is changed to "Known Error." If the problem can be easily repaired, then it is resolved.

However, if the problem will impact customer service levels, then a temporary work around process is created and provided to Service Management. The incident report is added to the Known Error Database (KED). Problem Management then submits a Request For Change (RFC) to Change Management to resolve the problem. Problem Management tracks the incident until the requested change is successfully completed.

The proactive portion of Problem Management is to address emerging trends before they impact customer service. An example might be a recurring problem that is quickly repaired by Incident Management, or a hardware item that is drifting toward an out of tolerance situation. Once reported or recorded by Problem Management, they are resolved in the same manner as requests from Incident Management, according to their priority.

[D] Configuration Management

Configuration Management supports the cost effective control of IT assets. (Historically, an IT asset was a chunk of hardware. Under ITIL, it is anything of value to the IT department.) It encompasses all aspects of IT to ensure that everything remains in sync.

The following are issues to address for support configuration management:

A. **Configuration Management Database.** Information about IT assets is gathered and maintained in the Configuration Management Database (CMDB). This database provides a significant amount of control for IT systems.

IT has long had an asset tracking problem. The tools it uses are expensive, are spread across the organization and they require regular maintenance or replacement. In the beginning, a configuration database began as a way to track hardware items (asset management). Many companies have these today to facilitate the maintenance of equipment. These same companies know how tedious it is to keep this database current.

Eventually, this tool was expanded to track software and its many versions. The logical extension was to tie the hardware and software files to a telephone listing. Now when someone calls the service desk, information on that person's equipment and software is available to anyone helping to resolve the problem.

ITIL takes the Configuration Management Database further. ITIL loads the database with *everything* used to govern IT. It includes:

1. Service Level agreements and version control.
2. End User documentation version control.
3. Change requests, active and historical.
4. Problem reports tied to the hardware or software that caused them.
5. Versions (and information about how that version is unique) for all mainframe/server and PC software.

The problem with this database is to know when to quit adding to it! Sure it is nice to know where all of the documentation (supposedly) is, so that in a version change it can all be collected and replaced, but is that necessary for every product?

B. **Keeping the Database Current.** Everything contained in the CMDB is called a Configuration Item (CI). A CI can be a single component (such as a telephone instrument) or an entire system (the PBX unit). Every configuration item is managed to a lifecycle. Initially, this is tied to the actual item. For example, a PC software package may have a useful life of three years. It is first entered into the database when it is purchased. The next entry might be when it is installed (which is linked to the hardware item where it resides) along with a maintenance agreement, if one was purchased. Every time it is patched, there is another entry for the last known good configuration (copies of both the old software and the updated module), etc.

Carrying this idea forward, a PC package typically creates and stores data. Given that different types of corporate data have different retention rates, it is conceivable that a company must maintain all of the various versions of its many software packages to ensure it can read archived data at some future point to defend itself in a legal suit. In theory, companies already do this . . .

> **COMMENT**
>
> Retention time for data depends on its content. Tax information must be retained for seven years, SEC information for a different time and then, medical records may have an indefinite retention. Always refer to your company's retention plan. The issue is, if the data is retained for a computer type, OS version and application software format that is no longer available, has the company fulfilled its retention requirements?

There is a cost for each element in the configuration database (and for that matter in any database). The costs include acquiring the data, entering it, storing it, and keeping it current. The more items there are to maintain, the higher the cost—the fewer items maintained, the less value the database adds to the organization! The key is to find the balance between costs and benefits.

C. **CMDB Holds the Last Working Configuration.** One benefit of the CMDB is that it contains the before and after images of software upgrades. This assists in rolling back failed patches and upgrades. Again, it is also useful for reloading software at a particular point. For example, some software is only used once per year for special tax generation, such as the program to print W-2 statements.

D. **Relationships.** A particularly time-consuming task is to identify, implement and maintain connections between the various configuration items in the database. Example relationships to track include:

1. User documentation that supports a specific generation of locally-written mainframe software. When an upgrade is made to the software, it is easy to determine who needs copies of the new documentation.
2. When someone calls for assistance, the connection between his or her workstation, its software and that person's server applications and authorization provides everything needed to address a wide range of problems.
3. Relationships between all of the hardware items supporting a specific application. For example, if a specific database server required an emergency shutdown, which applications use it and which users must be notified?

E.   Creating a Configuration Management Database. Many brave technical experts have tried to create their own database from scratch. However, as they worked through its many complex levels, they discovered how much easier it is to purchase one. There are several major vendors in the marketplace—and this software is not cheap.

1. The process for building a CMDB begins with developing a detailed implementation plan. Decisions must be made as to what is going into the database, what relationships will be tracked, etc.
2. Next comes locating and tagging everything. (If your asset database already includes asset tags, then this is the same process, except it covers many other things to track.) Given the wide range of items to tag, decisions must be made as to where tags go on a type of object (hardware, software media, software in storage, etc.).
3. After everything is loaded, additional complexity comes from establishing access rights so that only authorized personnel can change the configuration items. Further, a process is set in place to record all changes that are made.
4. Expect an immediate inflow of ongoing updates. As new configuration items arrive, they must be added to the database. As they are moved to (perhaps) a person's desk, another update is needed, etc. Software patches, new versions, repairs to hardware all require database updates.
5. Despite the team's best efforts, there will be something missed or incorrectly entered. An ongoing audit program samples data and identifies errors. A simple way to do this for something like hardware is to ask the caller the asset tag on his computer, etc. whenever he reports an incident.

[E]   Change Management

IT systems are massive and complex. There are servers, networks, applications, and workstations all interacting in many different ways. Individual IT items (hardware and software) may seldom change. However, when this is multiplied over the large number of items, the effect is a steady flow of changes and new installations across the entire technology spectrum (security, applications, hardware, software, etc.). Each change has the potential to disrupt customer service. The task of Change Management is to minimize the service disruption caused by installing these "improvements."

COMMENT

Change Management encompasses all changes to controlled items in the Configuration Management Database. However, each IT department must decide where to draw the line between a minor change (such as adding a person to the access list of a database) and a significant change that must be controlled.

To do this, Change Management works with everyone else to ensure that all changes to controlled items are made in a tightly controlled manner. Even those emergency changes that must go in *NOW* can be accommodated by the Change Management process. Change Management supports the organization by:

A.   **Ensuring that the Change Package Is Complete.** The Change Manager verifies that the package for implementing the change is complete before it is offered for approval. The CMDB identifies relationships between CIs to ensure that everything touched by the change has been addressed in the package.

The Change Manager ensures that the change package has been tested to verify that it alters what it is supposed to alter and nothing else. This may be done along with the package submitter or in a separate environment.

A Change Back-Out Plan is created and tested so that the change can be reversed if problems arise. The back-out plan must also be tested. This is the Change Manager's primary tool for minimizing the service impact of a change gone wrong.

The Change Manager's recommendation for approval of the change includes an analysis of the change's risk of failure or negative impact on IT service. It also includes a review of the resources required and a recommended slot in the change calendar.

B.   **Ensuring that Changes Are Scheduled.** Routine changes are scheduled in a published calendar known as the Forward Schedule of Changes (FSC). This plan is approved by both the various IT departments and the business it supports. Based on required availability, the calendar provides time windows for applying changes. As these windows fill up, everyone can see when a change can next be implemented. This involves the supported business in the discussion about priorities and change impact on availability (rather than IT making the call in a back room).

C.   **Ensuring that Changes Are Properly Approved.** Every change must be approved by either the Change Advisory Board (routine changes) or the Change Advisory Board Executive Committee (emergency or high impact changes). This board is an important hurdle for any change to pass.

Change Advisory Board members include business managers as well as the various technical disciplines. Everyone gets a chance to review the change package and comment on risks it might raise. This also provides advance warning to users so they are prepared for the change.

COMMENT

> Configuration items to be changed should be tied to SLAs which indicate which business managers must approve the change.

D. **Performing a Past Change Review.** After a change is implemented, the Change Manager reviews the results. The first check is to verify that the change provided the desired result. Inputs may be customer complaints (the service desk can provide this data), resource contention, adequacy of the back-out plan (if used), etc. The driving issue is to learn from every change ways to improve and streamline the change management process.

COMMENT

Change Management is an area where IT has consistently stumbled. It may be possible to sneak in 100 changes without the supported business realizing it was done—but that one change that flops will be the one remembered and repeated in meetings for months. This isn't idle complaining—business managers are trying to tell IT Management just how important stability is to their operations.

[F] Release Management

Release Management, as the name implies, controls the release of approved changes. It is closely linked to Change Management and, in some companies, is accomplished by the same team. However, in that case, care must be taken to ensure it does not dilute Release Management's role for ensuring that the change package is correct and ready for installation. It also works closely with Configuration Management to ensure that the released package's software is properly licensed and the CMDB is updated.

Release Management's testing procedures and pre-implementation checklists are IT's last defense against a poorly designed change. Procedures set up each release like its own small project. The details of Release Management include:

A. The resources required to ensure that people with the right skills are on hand or on standby as needed. For example, a network expert, a systems administrator, security technician, desktop repairman, etc. This includes contact information and if they will work on site or remotely.
B. A list of release implementation tasks to ensure that everything is completed in the correct sequence.
C. Times required for each task can be gathered during the release package testing.
D. An explanation of the changes made and how the service desk should handle calls concerning the changes (errors, complaints about the way the interface looks, etc.).

Release Management controls access to two important repositories:

A. The "Definitive Software Library" (DSL) of last known good copies. Release Management holds software licenses for purchased packages and validates licenses before installation. It is also the physical storage location of all software. The definitive copies of the software may be secured in the configuration management database.
B. The "Definitive Hardware Store" (DHS) is a secure area for storing emergency hardware spares. Items are used based on approved releases.

COMMENT

Release Management publishes a policy so that the IT department and the business users understand how the release of new systems (hardware, software, or a combination of the two) will be managed. The policy details various situations and how they will be addressed, such as emergency changes, required testing and documentation, how versions will be identified, etc.

§ 2.03   ITIL SERVICE DELIVERY

[A]   Service Level Management

Service Level Management is the primary interface between the customer and IT. It negotiates cost effective service level agreements with customers and then works within the IT organization and external vendors to ensure the desired level can be provided. The agreed services and support levels are detailed in the service catalog which is created and maintained by Service Level Management.

COMMENT

A customer is the person who has authority to describe and approve services to be provided to that business group. Users are the workers who use the services negotiated.

The Service Level Manager stands with one foot in the customer's world and one in IT. This person must speak both "business language" and "IT jargon." Service Level Management uses three different types of agreements to match requirements to resources:

A. Service Level Agreements (SLAs) are negotiated with customers to provide the level of service they desire, at a cost they can afford. By discussing these agreements in advance, the customer's service expectations can be set. SLAs are written using non-technical terms. They contain the "what" that will be provided and not the "how."

B. Operational Level Agreements (OLAs) are agreements between the various IT departments and Service Level Management to provide the types and levels of service requested by the customer. This might be response times, hours of support, etc. If the requested support involves additional cost (for example, Saturday support for a specific application), then that cost is provided to the customer to pay or to drop that requirement.

C. Underpinning agreements are made with external vendors to provide specific services, at a set cost, and within specified time frames. Typical examples are hardware repair, external network repair, pre-negotiated "best price" hardware purchase agreements, etc.

Service Level Management monitors the performance of the IT organization for meeting these promised levels to demonstrate to the customer how well IT is meeting its obligations and to demonstrate how well the IT internal organization provides its promised support. Reports on service quality are periodically reviewed with customers along with things that could be added or changed to improve service support.

[B] Financial Management for IT Services

IT is an expensive part of any business. Every aspect of its organization is expensive: equipment, technician salaries, maintenance agreements and a never-ending requirement to purchase upgrades. Without the proper level of funding, IT cannot operate. Without accountability for its expenses, there is no incentive to improve service and drive down costs. ITIL addresses this important area through the Financial Management for IT Services (FMITS) function. FMITS includes the following:

A. **Budgeting.** IT departments have long maintained budgets. A budget has many important uses:

1. Projects financial requirements for future periods. An approved budget sets a management limit on spending per time period (usually a month).
2. Provides a baseline for gauging performance (budget versus actual).
3. Ensures adequate funding will be available for when it is needed.

4. Projects major future purchases, such as mainframe software license renewal or major item replacement.

COMMENT

Budgets are a reflection of an operating plan. Once an IT department completes its annual operating plan, then the budget represents the cost to implement that plan. Sometimes, the cost is too high and the operating plan must be reduced to a financially acceptable level.

The IT budget funds support of its service levels. Based on the SLAs in place, the budget can be built from the ground up. Add in overhead expenses, salaries and long term commitments. The result is a month by month annual operating budget.

B.   Auditable Results. Once the budget is approved, the planned expenses are compared to actual expenditures. If something costs more than planned, then an analysis must determine if it was incorrectly estimated or if the cost exceeds expectation. ITIL emphasizes cost effective service. Over budget items may indicate a service issue that the IT Manager was not aware of.

Tracking of actual costs provides:

1. A process for generating financial reports, since the data to track actual versus budget is already maintained.
2. A historical tool for estimating future expenses.

C.   Cost Recovery. "To charge, or not to charge. THAT is the question!" Some IT departments charge the departments that they support for everything they do—and others do not. The value of charging is that those who use it pay for it. This rewards those who economize and use it the least. Charging for service implies there is a way to collect data on usage and a chart of how much each service charges. The hurdle for most organizations is building this data collection process.

Charging for services is a cost recovery issue. IT only exists to support the company and some departments use it heavily. Others do not. Some demanding executives can drive costs up requiring services that help them but whose costs far outweigh the benefits. However, if they paid for what they requested, the hope is they would moderate their demands.

Some companies implement an internal chargeback process without the intention of collecting any cash. It is used to demonstrate where the IT expenses are applied.

The ability to charge for a service can shape customer demand for it. Imagine a customer demanding service desk support on Sunday mornings. If two workers are scheduled to work in the office, should a service desk technician sit idle for most of eight hours just in case they are needed? Should the departments who do not work weekends pay for this person to wait for the telephone to ring?

[C] Availability Management

Availability Management focuses attention on ensuring IT services are active and available as required by approved SLAs. It works closely with the Change Advisory Board to minimize service availability impact whenever changes are implemented.

However, Availability Management is so much more. In addition to scheduling changes, it proactively roots out anything that reduces availability. It works closely with other ITIL teams to review technologies to make them quicker to change in a crisis or easier to maintain. Availability Management includes:

A. **System Resiliency.** Availability Management constantly scans the performance of systems to detect any that are drifting out of compliance. This might be a software application or piece of hardware that was designed for far fewer users than seem to be using it now. It might be the addition of a significant amount of online disk storage that requires longer to back up and is now encroaching on required uptime.

An important part of Availability Management is to review reports about problems that resulted in downtime. Availability Management may apply various tools to dig into recurring issues to identify the root cause of problems, such as Component Failure Impact Analysis.

Whenever new systems are proposed, Availability Management reviews the technical architecture for potential problems. This might be identification of single points of failure, the amount of load applied to equipment and the types of tests to be used prior to implementation.

Another systems resiliency issue is to improve the speed at which problems are detected. It is possible to detect and repair problems that result in down time, but that have no impact to the customer. The key is to discover them before the customer does, and repair them promptly.

B. **New Technology.** Availability may be enhanced by the introduction of new technology. The Availability Manager constantly scans the press looking for new technology that can improve the existing systems, in particular, new technology that reduces costs, increases availability or improves ease of maintenance.

[D] Capacity Management

Capacity Management is based on the concept of "enough"—will there be enough IT resources to meet demand? Capacity Management assists in the proper sizing of resources to meet desired service levels.

Capacity Management requires the constant monitoring of resource usages. Usage can be segmented by shift, by day of week, time of year, location in the company's business cycle, etc. It also monitors usage trends to detect threats to maintaining an adequate resource buffer. All of this information is maintained in the Capacity Database.

Capacity Management creates the Capacity Plan, which includes resource utilization for existing and planned systems. The Capacity Plan assists in the timely (and cost effective) purchase of additional resources (rather than a panic purchase when resources run out).

Demand for resources is rarely level. An important aspect of Capacity Management is to determine the peak usage times for each system and to encourage users to spread out their work. Demand Management seeks to reduce peak loads by shifting users to off-peak times. One way is to raise users rates for peak time (if internal chargeback is in place). The best way is to work with customers to demonstrate how the cost of their SLA will be lower by assisting in reducing the peak capacity requirements.

[E] IT Service Continuity Management

Despite the best planning efforts, something will go wrong. The fault may be due to human error, sabotage, severe weather, hardware failure—any number of things. To maintain service credibility, ITIL specifies IT Service Continuity Management (ITSCM). ITSCM includes:

A. **Business Impact Analysis.** Different IT systems provide different degrees of benefit to the company. A Business Impact Analysis is conducted with the business departments to identify their critical business functions, and the financial (or legal) impact of an outage over an hour, four hours, 24 hours, two days, one week and two weeks. The goal is to identify the true IT Vital Business Functions that ITIL focuses its efforts on supporting.

   In most organizations, this will be approximately 25 percent of their IT systems. This small set must be protected from interruption. If the remaining IT systems are interrupted, customers are annoyed but damage to the company is minimal.

B. **Disaster Recovery.** IT shops have long maintained some sort of disaster recovery plan—even if it was just a set of data backup tapes. Disaster recovery is a subset of ITSCM. Disaster recovery is activated after a disaster occurs whose damage is so extensive that the data center must be moved elsewhere (to another room or another town). This is a serious service disruption. Disaster recovery strives to keep the business alive, and is rarely invoked.

   Disaster recovery is the cheapest plan to implement but it is all cost since the benefits are not realized until there is a disaster. There are several ways to recover a destroyed data center:

   1. Do nothing in advance and figure it out later. This is a CIO gambler's position—it may never occur while I am in charge of IT, so why do it?

2. Cold site—renting a prepared data center shell (no computers) that is ready on request. The company must provide its own equipment to activate it.

3. Hot site—an expensive safety net where a data center and equipment is standing by for use when needed. This provides the quickest recovery.

C. **Business (Service) Continuity.** Business Continuity is the activity that most people think of when they say Disaster Recovery. Business Continuity risk reduction actions minimize interruptions from the many small disasters that occur in a typical work day. Examples are Uninterruptible Power Supplies (UPS) to avoid short term power outages, locks on the data center doors to prevent sabotage and RAID disks to recover if a disk drive fails.

A Business Continuity Plan contains a disaster recovery plan as one part of its recovery options. ITSCM works closely with Availability Management to keep vital systems running whatever the disruption may be.

D. **Keeping the plan current.** Keeping ITSCM plans current can be quite time consuming. The key is to be involved with project and resource expansions during the proposal stage to ensure that vital business system expansions include funds for the Business Continuity program. Otherwise, this funding must come later and creates considerable ill will in the organization.

E. **Testing.** Whatever plan is chosen, it is important that the plan is tested at least annually. Since it is unlikely that a data center or a significant amount of its resources can be turned off for a simulated disaster, testing is normally accomplished on related subsets of equipment. Testing not only debugs the continuity/disaster plans (pointing out errors and omissions) but it also trains the participants.

COMMENT

There are other ITIL books that deal with Information Security and ICT Infrastructure management, ITIL for Small Business. These are available through OGC.

§ 2.04   ITIL CERTIFICATION

[A]   Training and Exams

Mastering ITIL, like anything else, requires study. The surest way to learn about it is to attend formal training class and study the books available. Ideally, companies adopting ITIL will seed their organization with experienced, certified professionals who can mentor their coworkers and help them understand the ITIL study materials.

OGC has experience and qualification guidelines for companies offering ITIL training and licenses those who meet them. When selecting training, ensure the company is approved by OGC.

[B] Foundations

The Foundations certification demonstrates a familiarity with ITIL practice areas and terminology. IT professionals can self study for this certification or attend a training session (typically three days) which provides a deeper explanation. Passing the certifying exam is one way to measure the effectiveness of the training.

A Foundations certification is an excellent way to introduce all IT staff members to the ITIL way, as it touches on all service areas. Many companies send their entire IT staff to Foundations training so they will understand the basic terminology of ITIL and the different service management areas.

COMMENT

Foundations training is also beneficial to end users who work closely with their IT department.

The Foundations certification exam consists of 40 multiple choice questions and may be taken on line. There are no prerequisites to sitting for Foundations exam, but experience working in IT make the concepts much easier to understand.

[C] Practitioner

The Practitioner certification program focuses on a single area of ITIL Service Support or Service Delivery. The theory is there is one Practitioner exam for each ITIL Service Delivery or Service Support area. Some training companies offer combinations of several closely related areas, such as Incident Management and Problem Management, or Change Control and Release Management.

Classes for a single area typically run for three days (including the exam). Combination classes run for five days including the exam.

The prerequisites for sitting for a Practitioner exam are:

A. Possess a Foundations certificate.
B. One year general experience in an IT service management area.
C. Attend a course by an accredited training organization (self study is not an option).

[D]   Service Manager

The top ITIL certification is called Service Manager. The Service Manager training is broken into two parts, Service Support and Service Delivery. Each area has its own certification exam. A passing score on both exams is required to obtain this certification.

The ITIL Service Manager examination demonstrates a broad understanding of each service area as well as how they all work together. The prerequisites for sitting for a Service Manager exam are:

A.   Possess a Foundations certificate.
B.   Five years general experience in an IT service management area, with two of those years in a supervisory position.
C.   Attend a course by an accredited training organization (self study is not an option). During the training, the candidate must receive a positive assessment by the instructor for completion of class assignments.

§ 2.05   ITIL AS AN OFFICIAL STANDARD

[A]   Standards—Why Bother?

Companies engage in an ongoing struggle with their competitors. One area is in delivery credibility to their customers. How can a new customer without boundless time to investigate a company gauge if a supplier has the expertise and efficiency to reliably handle its business?

Conversely, how can companies stand out from among the crowd? What independent proof can they show that they are well-managed, efficient and dependable?

The concept of a standards organization is to identify the most effective and efficient way to run some aspect of the business and then to live up to that high mark. Further, an outside organization inspects the company to identify areas of improvement and to certify that they essentially meet the published standards.

[B]   British Standard

ITIL's wide acceptance in the UK and British Commonwealth led to its adoption as the basis for the official British Standard (BS 15000). BS 15000 was an attempt to establish an idea of what an efficient and effective IT organization would do. It focuses on:

A.   Service Delivery Processes.
B.   Relationship Processes.
C.   Resolution Processes.
D.   Release Processes.
E.   Control Processes.

[C]   International Standards Organization

Manufacturing companies have long sought ISO 9000 certification to demonstrate to prospective customers that they may be relied upon to deliver high quality products. But what about a company that sells data processing services? Or what if a company's products depend heavily on data systems? How may they demonstrate to prospective customers the high quality of such an intangible thing as IT service?

> **COMMENT**
>
> The International Organization for Standards can be located on the Internet at www.ISO.org.

Over the years, ITIL's appeal expanded worldwide to countries that do not recognize the British Standards within their own countries. (This may sound silly to some people, but to others it must be important! After all, a good idea is a good idea.) So BS 15000 was used as the basis for ISO 20000.

ISO standards have long been used as an indication of a well-run company. Many organizations have seen the benefits of adopting ISO practices to improve their operating efficiencies and product quality. However, there was a gap in the data processing part of the business—a part that drives the performance of the rest of the company.

An ISO audit begins with an initial assessment which provides a baseline from which to measure progress, and some ideas of where the greatest effort is needed. After a company has implemented all of the requirements, the auditors come through for a certifying inspection. This is a pass/fail review. Even companies who pass may have a long list of things that must be promptly addressed. To maintain their ISO certification, the organization must be re-inspected at least every three years thereafter.

Also, companies may not demonstrate their expertise by certifying as "ITIL compliant" since no such company certification program exists. However, companies may now be certified as ISO 20000 compliant. ISO certification requires an examination by a third party to certify the degree of conformance. Preparing for an ISO examiner forces a company to review and improve its internal processes to obtain or maintain certification.

ISO 20000 was recently updated to emphasize continuous improvement as an integral part of any IT activity. Often seen as after action reviews or "post mortems" after a serious incident, continuous improvement requires companies to examine and learn from their mistakes.

Conformance tells customers and company executives that the IT organization follows industry best practices.

§ 2.06 CRITICISM OF ITIL

[A] ITIL as All or Nothing

Purists sometimes seize on an idea and try to drive it to an extreme. This is a common problem with "Save the Company" solutions. TQM, Six Sigma and other quality improvement initiatives have experienced the same problem. The process is considered to be the solution and not the means to a solution. ITIL processes are useful but must be adapted to the local organization and to the local business situation. ITIL provides guidelines—not rigid laws that are all or nothing.

There is not one all-encompassing solution or one "best way" for every company in the world. ITIL provides a starting point. ITIL works best if the entire framework is adapted as its various parts are interconnected. However, the specific actions are left to the local organization.

> **COMMENT**
>
> The problem with ITIL is that companies see it as a "silver bullet" that will solve all of their problems. It is not. In most cases, the problem is not ITIL—it is mismanagement of IT departments. ITIL can provide many valuable processes and ideas, but if a company does not first address its management problems and internal politics, ITIL will just be another passing fad.

[B] ITIL is not a Coherent Model

IT departments have such a crushing need for an overall framework to glue all of their activities together that they read into ITIL things it was never designed to do. OGC has stated that ITIL was never intended to be an all-encompassing solution. ITIL expects organizations to incorporate their own processes based on their own business model.

However, ITIL can provide a basic framework for improving the efficiency of IT departments. It forces companies to examine their processes and, if they feel ITIL has skipped something, they are free to add it.

[C] ITIL Books are Poorly Written and Inconsistent

ITIL books are written by different authors. This equates to different writing styles, different approaches to problems and different focus for the chapters.

Read individually, they are very enlightening. However, taken as a set, there are problems:

A. They lack a uniform author "voice" where the approach to each subject is essentially the same.
B. The points where the different disciplines touch one another do not always line up exactly.

However, if ITIL is taken as a guideline and not as a verbatim mandate, this issue is not significant. ITIL version 3 is currently rewriting the ITIL library.

§ 2.07 IMPLEMENTING ITIL

[A] ITIL Changes Everything IT

ITIL is a unique way of running a business. Many companies do some aspect of it in some places, so some of the concepts are not new. What is new is how ITIL forces these disparate pieces to work together toward a common goal. Introducing ITIL is recognition that ad hoc processes of the past must give way to mature IT processes in the future.

IT departments typically evolve over time. There are people who were there from the first day to people who just walked in off of the street. Each of these persons has his or her own collection of ideas, motivations, and practices that worked successfully for him or her in the past. Implementing ITIL means overcoming the reluctance of many key IT participants to work closely together. Yet these same people will acknowledge the benefits if asked individually. Therefore, to overcome team members' reluctance, strong executive leadership is necessary. (A weak leader will lead ITIL to ruin in a few months.)

The first step is a clear vision of what you hope to achieve from implementing ITIL. Make a clear assessment of how the IT department provides services today.

A. How is the IT department functionally organized?
B. What does each function do?
C. What is each function's responsibilities to technology management, to customer service, to supporting internal IT processes?
D. What benefits does each functional group provide?
E. What service level agreements (SLAs) are in place?
F. What databases exist that describe IT assets, processes, or knowledge?

[B] ITIL Implementation Leader

Implementing a change in an organization requires overcoming the reluctance of the people within it. A heavy-handed approach may provide quick results but generate long-term animosity for the implementation leader and the new process. The concept of leadership is to guide people in the desired direction and to gain their willing cooperation.

The ITIL implementation leader provides the vision (used at the many decision points), provides encouragement, and breaks down the barriers to progress. The ITIL leader also acts as the team's cheerleader when the opposition seems to be insurmountable. IT executives can keep this person focused by tying his or her future bonuses and raises to that project's progress.

Some companies feel that the internal battles will be too bruising and damaging for an internal project manager to survive. Therefore, they bring in a consultant to manage implementation. This external resource lacks institutional knowledge and must refer to internal team leaders for information when adjusting ITIL concepts to local situations.

The leader must overcome reluctance through constant dialogue, listen to concerns, and address them promptly. Overcoming these concerns will remove some of the "fear of change" from the team.

COMMENT

An ITIL rollout may take up to two years depending on the size of the organization, its commitment to change, etc. An efficient rollout should proceed with minimum customer disruption. However, the longer a project takes to complete, the more likely it is to drift off course or to be cancelled uncompleted.

[C]   Configuration Management Database (CMDB)

A considerable amount of time is spent selecting a configuration management database. This tool can be rather expensive to purchase, to load with data, and to maintain. Many companies offer one, or a standard database tool currently in use can be adapted. However, establishing the many interlocking views of the data may make purchasing an already configured tool the best choice.

There are several important collections of data to load into this database. This is where the detailed analysis of existing databases, processes, and SLAs pay off. First, load all of the asset information into the database, including capacity planning information, information of the applications run on each server, and so on. There is quite a lot of information that likely must come from several sources.

Next create the tables necessary to begin using the CMDB's service management module for the service desk. To this add the SLAs with connections to the assets. This tells the service desk the priority for service calls as it includes the impact and severity for each item.

Creating a complete CMDB can take years. Each company must identify the point of diminishing returns and cut off adding more data elements. Each element has its own costs in maintenance to keep the data current, cost for disk storage, etc.

COMMENT

IT departments are heavily dependent on outside suppliers. Consider, who provides hardware maintenance for servers? Who provides patches for purchased software? The list can be extensive. For IT to meet its service- level objectives, these critical suppliers must meet theirs. Include key suppliers in the ITIL rollout process to ensure they do not become the weak link.

[D]   Introduce ITIL to One Area at a Time

For many companies, ITIL rollout begins at the service desk. They likely already have a Help Desk of some sort so this transition will seem easy at first. Also, better customer service is an easy sell to executives.

Rollout changes in a series of small tasks. Select the first few carefully for a series of quick successes. This helps to justify the ongoing expense and to build momentum for the changes. Carefully publicize ITIL's business alignment at every opportunity.

Training is essential to a successful rollout. Training for the IT staff tells them what needs to be done and how to do it. Training for IT executives helps them to identify decision points and make the trade-off decisions necessary to implement this process. Training for end users is also necessary if they are to understand their role in a successful operation.

Ideally, training is completed just before it is needed and provided in a classroom for all affected staff. In reality, this is very expensive both for the instructor and for the lost labor of the participants. Therefore, training is usually provided to a key few participants with the rest picking up their skills through reading, in-house newsletters, and one-on-one coaching.

3

COBIT: MEETING OBJECTIVES

§ 3.01   OVERVIEW
    [A]   Purpose and Scope
    [B]   History of COBIT
    [C]   ISACA & IT Governance Institute

§ 3.02   THE PARTS OF COBIT
    [A]   Overview
    [B]   Executive Summary
    [C]   Operational Framework
    [D]   Control Objectives
    [E]   Audit Guidelines
    [F]   Implementation Toolset
    [G]   Management Guidelines

§ 3.03   COBIT FRAMEWORK
    [A]   Overview
    [B]   Plan and Organize
    [C]   Acquire and Implement
    [D]   Delivery and Support
    [E]   Monitor and Evaluate

§ 3.04   IMPLEMENTING COBIT
    [A]   Overview
    [B]   Mind the Gap
    [C]   A New Way to Think

§ 3.01 OVERVIEW

[A] Purpose and Scope

IT departments exist solely to support the business that pays for them. Yet sometimes they become so preoccupied with trying to address a wide range of pressing customer requests that they lose a clear vision of what they should be doing. COBIT™ (Control OBjectives for Information Technology™) is a framework of IT management best practices that assists companies in maximizing the business benefits of their IT organizations.

COBIT utilizes controls that provide management and audit functions for IT departments and business process owners. This framework has 34 high-level objects that cover 318 control objectives in four domains:

A. Planning and organization.
B. Acquisition and implementation.
C. Delivery and support.
D. Monitoring.

Many companies use COBIT to fulfill Sarbanes-Oxley's 404 legal compliance requirements. It provides a proven solution to the current climate of corporate accountability and control. Rather than try to invent something new, they adopt portions of COBIT that fit their industry and situation. It also provides an entity-wide model of best practices to manage IT's contribution to the business. COBIT helps non-IT Managers understand their IT systems and set the level of security and control necessary to protect their company's assets.

COMMENT

"COBIT" and "Control OBjectives for Information Technology" are trademarks of the Information Systems Audit and Control Association (ISACA) and the IT Governance Institute.

[B] History of COBIT

Executives have proven they can manipulate their electronic accounting systems as well as their paper ones. Partially in response to this and legislative requirements, COBIT was developed in 1992 by ISACA.

A. **COSO.** In 1992, the Committee of Sponsoring Organizations (COSO) established a framework for the proper authorization, recording and reporting of transactions. The Securities and Exchange Commission (SEC) officially recognizes the COSO framework as adequate for establishing internal controls over financial reporting. COSO is the basis for COBIT's professional standards for internal controls and auditing.

> ## COMMENT
>
> The Committee of Sponsoring Organizations (COSO) can be found on the Internet at: *www.coso.org.*

In COSO's framework, an internal control is a process. Internal controls only provide some assurance that something will occur, and not an absolute guarantee. Each internal control addresses a specific objective.

COSO internal controls are measured in terms of:

1. Control environment—processes for developing controls and a control-conscious work force.
2. Risk assessment—identification and analysis of risks of fraud and inaccurate financial reporting.
3. Control activities—policies and procedures for execution of management directives, such as management oversight, separation of duties and audits by external organizations.
4. Information and communication—effective operation and control of the business.
5. Monitoring—ongoing activities or separate evaluations. Includes the feedback loop of reporting discrepancies and then promptly addressing them.

    B.   COBIT Today. COBIT is not a static statement. It is periodically updated and resynchronized with other world-class standards. COBIT describes what should be done instead of how to do it. It is designed to work well with other IT governance standards and best practices.

COBIT Version 4 was published in 2005. Version 4 is more closely aligned with ITIL and has a strong business orientation. It builds on and does not conflict with COBIT Version 3. Version 4 combines the main Version 3 books (Executive Summary, Framework, Control Objects and Management Guidelines) into a single volume.

> ## COMMENT
>
> A part of COBIT's appeal is that it is platform and vendor independent. The concepts apply equally to all types of IT technologies and situations.

[C]   ISACA & IT Governance Institute

The Information Systems Audit and Control Association (ISACA on the web at *http://www.isaca.org/*) was founded in 1967 to support professionals' auditing computer control systems. ISACA has since grown to a world-wide membership of over 50,000. ISACA provides training, professional development, and research into the fields of IT internal auditing, information security, and IT governance. ISACA's control standards are recognized worldwide.

ISACA offers training and internationally recognized certifications in:

A. Certified Information Systems Auditor (CISA)
B. Certified Information Security Manager (CISM)

ISACA sponsors a continuing series of technical and management conferences on contemporary issues as well as certification training. Many members consider the peer-to-peer contact during meetings to be a valuable benefit of their membership.

ISACA maintains a research organization called the IT Governance Institute® (ITGI) to continually research contemporary issues in IT governance. Among ITGI's published documents is COBIT. ITGI tools use non-technical language to improve executives' understanding of their company's information technology systems.

COMMENT

The IT Governance Institute (ITGI) advances international thinking and standards in directing and controlling an enterprise's information technology. It can be located at: *www.itgi.org*.

§ 3.02   THE PARTS OF COBIT

[A]   Overview

COBIT's comprehensive approach is divided into six major components. Each one complements the other and together they build a framework that executives can use for IT governance.

A. The Executive Summary describes the concepts of IT governance and the COBIT approach to achieving this. COBIT aligns IT strategies and performance with business objectives. This ensures the organization receives the full benefit of its IT operations.
B. COBIT Framework ensures that company executives have the information required to meet their objectives and control IT resources. This

      linkage is controlled by high level objectives organized into four domains.

  C. Control objectives are the desired results of implementing the 215 detailed control objectives found within COBIT's 34 IT processes.

  D. Audit Guidelines provide IT auditors with tools for evaluating the likelihood that control objects are not met.

  E. Implementation Tool Set is an overall process for implementing COBIT in an organization.

  F. Management Guidelines—an IT Process Maturity model for gauging an organization's current competency and planning to move it higher.

COMMENT

A complementary copy of COBIT Version 4 is available at *www.isaca.org/cobit*.

[B] Executive Summary

The COBIT Executive Summary is an explanation of COBIT's key concepts and underlying assumptions, presented in simple, non-technical terms. Companies spend massive amounts of time and capital creating an IT entity to support the business's goals. IT must be organized around the same sound management principles as used in the rest of the company.

Many executives feel comfortable debating the tradeoffs of "pull versus push" materials management, various ways of financing capital purchases or even the various aspects of accounting rules. However, when it comes to IT, computers are considered a black art, best managed by quirky people in a back room. Consequently executives see money go in and (hopefully) the answers come out, but they lack confidence about the effectiveness of their IT systems and their management. The COBIT Executive Summary details how COBIT breaks the "mysterious whole" of IT into much smaller and easier to understand components that can be understood and managed.

The COBIT Executive Summary links IT goals and metrics to business objectives, so the company can gain the full benefit from its investment. To accomplish this, executives should establish an IT internal control framework.

COBIT applies a maturity model against existing company standards to identify areas for improvement. This provides process improvement goals that are used to create a local plan for controls improvement.

Metrics, or performance measurements, are used by COBIT to monitor how well company processes fulfill a stated objective. This provides company executives with transparency into IT performance and how the money is spent.

The five IT Governance cornerstones are:

A. Strategic alignment between the objectives of IT and business.
B. Value delivery providing the service levels promised to support these objectives in an efficient and effective manner.
C. Resource management to ensure that resources (of all kinds) are efficiently used for maximum benefit.
D. Risk management to foresee problems and make decisions based on likelihood of success.
E. Performance measurement to monitor and report on delivery performance. A valuable tool for continuous improvement.

[C] Operational Framework

COBIT's operational framework and toolset links IT responsibilities to business management expectations. It describes the processes used to deliver promised levels of performance in each of the COBIT objectives. The framework's information is described in seven information dimensions:

A. Effectiveness.
B. Efficiency.
C. Confidentiality.
D. Integrity.
E. Availability.
F. Compliance.
G. Reliability.

Resources drive the cost of IT organizations. Resources must be carefully acquired and regularly refreshed to maintain optimal reliability and performance. COBIT describes resources as:

A. People—highly skilled individuals whose individual actions can cripple an IT process by accident or negligence. IT people plan operations, acquire expensive equipment of many types, support systems by monitoring operations, develop new solutions and implement them.
B. Applications are the software components of IT systems that gather, transform and report data as information.
C. Technology—the background equipment and underlying shared software such as operating systems, database management software, etc.
D. Facilities provide the secure, clean, climate controlled and cleanly powered environment for the technology to exist within.
E. Data concerns all forms of data elements that are captured, processed, and delivered by IT systems.

[D] Control Objectives

Control objects maintain control of some aspect of IT. It might be security access to customer data; it might be read access to the payroll file, the ability to manipulate data before or after processing, or even the ability to intercept data that should be confidential. COBIT has 215 specific control objectives.

The internal control of something involves some *thing* to control, a process for controlling it and a way to measure how well that object is controlled. The extent of this control is set by the company. After all, controls cost money to create and maintain. In addition, there is educating the appropriate personnel on the proper way to support or use that control. Multiply this across the entire organization and it is easy to see that completely secure controls and their maintenance are beyond the financial means (or interests) of most companies.

COMMENT

Nothing can be perfectly protected. For example, the US Bullion Depository at Fort Knox, Kentucky, is well protected along with a US Army armored division nearby for additional firepower. This may deter theft of the gold, but if someone dropped a large amount of radioactive material on the building (a dirty bomb), they might prevent the gold from ever being used, almost the same loss as if it were stolen.

Internal controls can be something simple, such as the lock on the computer room door or database security software that verifies permissions for that user ID to read that record. The costs here are:

A. To buy the computer room door locks, to provide a key to unlock the door to all authorized staff, to provide replacement keys, to recover keys from departing personnel, to escort guests in the area who do not have a key, etc.

B. To purchase, configure, and install the software that controls access to the database. Maintenance might include creating and updating the list of who is authorized to access what, and when.

A COBIT IT control objective provides reasonable assurance that the desired business objectives can be achieved. However, the control also provides detection actions to alert when undesirable actions occur.

[E] Audit Guidelines

It is one thing for someone to state that adequate controls are in place, but given the potential damages from a control failure, it is prudent for management to verify them. Audit Guidelines suggest activities for evaluating whether controls exist. Then the effectiveness and efficiency of each of COBIT's 34 high-level control objectives are tested. The risk associated with the control's current condition is reported to senior management. Properly applied, COBIT Audit Guidelines provide executives with a true sense of their IT controls.

[F] Implementation Toolset

The COBIT Implementation Toolset eases the transition to a COBIT framework. Moving to COBIT requires senior executives dedicated to improving their organization's effectiveness and efficiency. The implementation toolset includes:

A. Executive Overview.
B. Guide to Implementations.
C. Diagnostics for management awareness and IT controls.
D. Case studies sharing lessons learned by other companies implementing COBIT.
E. Frequently Asked Questions (FAQ)—to some extent, each COBIT implementation hits the same barriers.
F. Slide presentation for "selling" COBIT.

[G] Management Guidelines

COBIT provides an IT process maturity model that gauges existing controls and compares them to industry norms. This detailed information is used to identify the process maturity level of an organization, and allow management to select the level they desire to operate at. The difference becomes actions for improving processes and moving specific IT functional areas to higher maturity levels.

§ 3.03 COBIT FRAMEWORK

[A] Overview

COBIT provides benefits to managers, IT users, and auditors. Managers benefit from COBIT because it provides them with a foundation upon which IT-related decisions and investments may be based. Decision-making is more effective because COBIT aids management in defining a strategic IT plan, defining the information architecture, acquiring the necessary IT hardware and software to execute an IT strategy, ensuring continuous service, and monitoring the performance of the IT system.

IT users benefit from COBIT because the information controls and security assurance for gathering, processing, and reporting are in place throughout the processes. COBIT benefits auditors by identifying control issues within a company's IT infrastructure. It also helps them corroborate their audit findings.

An IT department encompasses a vast area of business. From the creation and maintenance of software to data communications security, and even to how the service desk works—IT involves many things. To address this broad range, COBIT uses 34 high-level objects that address 215 control objectives. These are organized into four domains:

A. Plan and Organize.
B. Acquire and Implement.

    C. Deliver and Support.
    D. Monitor and Evaluate.

Each high level objective in a domain uses a two letter prefix (e.g., "PO") and a number to uniquely identify it. For example, "Define a Strategic IT Plan and Direction" is identified as PO1, "Enable Operation and Use" is identified as AI4, and so on.

[B] Plan and Organize

Planning and Organizing recognizes that a successful IT organization is no accident. It requires a careful analysis of what is needed, how it is needed, and where it will be of most use. Then someone must translate these many needs into reality. Without a plan to guide the IT organization, it blunders forward day by day, expensive to operate and ineffective in its results. The Planning and Organization domain covers the use of technology and how best it can be used in a company to help achieve the company's goals and objectives.

    A. PO1—Define a Strategic IT Plan—It starts at the beginning—what benefits do the business managers expect the IT organization to provide? No organization has unlimited financial and time resources to throw technology out to see if any of it is beneficial. The plan identifies limitations and opportunities.

        1. *IT Value Management* identifies everything in the IT services portfolio and verifies it is supported by an approved business case (usually an approved Service Level Agreement). Metrics are in place to demonstrate that each service is both effective (delivers what is required) and efficient (does not waste resources).

        2. *Business-IT Alignment* integrates IT and business strategies to reflect corporate objectives in IT plan. This may require modifying business plans to reflect IT capabilities—or plan to expand IT capabilities.

        3. *Assessment of Current Performance* demonstrates how well existing IT systems contribute to business objectives. This includes an evaluation of their stability, costs, strengths, and weaknesses. This step helps to align services and to highlight vulnerabilities for inclusion in future capital plans.

        4. *IT Strategic Plan* defines how IT resources will be applied to support the company's strategic goals. Its measurements and deliverables must contain sufficient detail for creating supporting tactical plans.

        5. *IT Tactical Plans* are the many plans for turning strategic goals into reality. Many of the tactical plans will be programs with multiple related projects required to complete them. This is a considerable balancing act between funds, resources, contending projects, delays, and shifting business requirements.

        6. *IT Portfolio Management* is the management of all projects, pending and active, to ensure the organization obtains the greatest benefit.

Portfolio Management recognizes that organizations have limited resources and that every project provides equal benefit. Projects must be prioritized and started only when adequate resources are available.

B. PO2—Define the Information Architecture—a definition of the IT information (data) architectures, the standardized processes necessary to fulfill these service. Given the wide range of data repositories in a company, this objective attempts to standardize naming, description, etc., so that they are consistent and controlled to minimize redundancy. Data must be accurate, secure, and available to approved applications.

   1. *Enterprise Information Architecture Model* defines and maintains a company-wide information systems model consistent with IT strategies and tactical objectives. This model ensures that data is accurate, complete, and secure, yet still available for sharing as required.

   2. *Enterprise Data Dictionary and Data Syntax* mandates a company-wide data dictionary structure and standardized approved syntax rules. This reduces confusion and assists in the data rationalization process.

   3. *Data Classification Scheme* details data ownership, appropriate security levels, data retention, and data sensitivity. This standardizes management of the many "islands" of data across an organization to promote data integrity and to ensure obsolete data is purged according to data destruction procedures. This objective is the basis for access controls and encryption.

   4. *Integrity Management* is the approved processes, audits and validations used to ensure data integrity and consistency across all forms of electronic storage.

C. PO3—Determine Technological Direction—forward looking objectives to ensure that short term decisions about architecture, technologies, and information systems are positioned to take advantage of emerging technologies and not preclude their future use. In short, while everyone is looking at the next thing they need to do, these objectives are scanning the horizon for proven or emerging tools that will improve systems efficiency or effectiveness.

   1. *Technological Direction Planning* constantly monitors existing or emerging technologies to identify those that show the most promise for adoption. This requires a solid appreciation of existing architecture and projected requirements.

   2. *Technological Infrastructure Plan* creates a formal plan (document) that describes the organization's technical direction. It includes an analysis of the technology's competitive environment and potential impact on staffing and interoperability.

   3. *Monitoring of Future Trends and Regulations* is the process for monitoring changes in the entire business environment that might shape future technology decisions. This includes changes in technology, business practices, regulatory requirements, etc.

4. *Technology Standards* establishes and publishes organization-wide technology standards to guide future purchases and the retirement of existing technology.
5. *IT Architecture Board* publishes IT architecture guidance and audits its compliance.

AUTHOR'S NOTE

By now, the reader can see how comprehensive the COBIT objectives are. Nothing radical has been described, yet COBIT has gathered the essential activities necessary for effective and efficient IT operations. From this point forward, COBIT objectives are listed but not described.

D. PO4—Define the IT Processes, Organization and Relationships—a set of processes that ensure alignment of the IT organization to its strategic and tactical goals. It involves senior business executives as well as IT management, organized into a strategy committee determining IT resource priorities.
E. PO5—Manage the IT Investment—by creating a budget that reflects IT priorities. Collect data on actual costs and track ongoing operations against the budget acting to control variation. Ensure IT investments support published IT strategies and tactical plans.
F. PO6—Communicate Management Aims and Direction—All of the planning is worthless unless it is effectively communicated to the people who must execute or whose efforts are guided by these plans, standards, policies, etc. As these official directions change, the updates must likewise be effectively distributed. Additionally, everyone involved must be reminded annually about existing policies, procedures, etc. to improve compliance.
G. PO7—Manage IT Human Resources—A primary IT resource is its staff of skilled workers. People are much less predictable and require more ongoing maintenance than machines. To ensure the company obtains maximum benefit from this expensive resource, an ongoing program of performance evaluation, training and realignment of staff to fulfill strategic and tactical goals is needed.
H. PO8—Manage Quality—There are two kinds of quality management systems: the one where nothing is done until something breaks, which is characterized by chaos and a series of IT technology failures; the other involves a formal program to verify that new systems and system changes provide the requested result—and only the requested result. A robust quality management program includes staff support for ongoing continuous improvement in all aspects of a customer focused

IT organization. The quality program will include published processes and procedures to guide the IT staff.

I. PO9—Assess and Manage IT Risks—all business (and IT) activities entail a certain amount of risk. Risks should be foreseen, mitigated (or accepted) and monitored. Risk management is used in various forms throughout the IT organization.

J. P10—Manage Projects—A formal project management methodology is essential for an IT organization. It provides for a common language, common approach, common management and reporting techniques throughout the organization. IT project management includes coordinating efforts among various projects in execution and pending. Key elements of a successful project management program include resource allocation, quality control, proper control of schedule and costs, and finally, project closure that ensures all of the loose ends are tied up before the books are closed.

[C]   Acquire and Implement

The Acquire and Implement domain identifies IT requirements, acquires the technology, and implements it within the company's current business processes. This domain also addresses the development of a maintenance plan that a company should adopt in order to prolong the life of an IT system and its components. The high-level control objectives for the Acquisition and Implementation domain are:

A. AI1—Identify Automated Solutions—The requirements for an automated solution must be clearly defined before actual purchase or work begins. The potential solutions are evaluated in terms of risks, potential alternative solutions, effectiveness and efficiency of the solution, and a make or buy analysis. In some cases, a feasibility study is necessary to test the proposed solution and gather data for the final decision.

B. AI2—Acquire and Maintain Application Software—the design of applications (new and changes) to ensure they contain the appropriate controls and security, and meet published IT standards.

C. AI3—Acquire and Maintain Technology Infrastructure—a formal approach to adding to existing IT infrastructure to ensure it conforms to IT strategic direction in terms of technology, cost effective purchasing, recoverability, and vendor support.

D. AI4—Enable Operation and Use—the production of instructions to the ultimate users of all IT products to ensure they obtain maximum benefit from the company's investment and to reduce the calls for minor support. It also includes detailed technical and support team documentation for all current and previous technologies in a location and format that is readily available.

E. AI5—Procure IT Resources—the establishment, publication, and enforcement of processes to ensure the timely and cost effective purchase of all types of IT resources. This includes selecting vendors in a manner that is in the best interests of the company, negotiating and managing vendor contracts and obtaining the temporary services of skilled people.

F.   AI6—Manage Changes—IT assets (hardware, software, processes, etc.) are constantly changing. An individual item may only change two or three times in a year. However, spread this across thousands of IT assets and change is occurring all of the time. Software is patched; broken hardware is replaced, new systems installed, etc. Every change to the IT assets threatens the stability of some end user service. Therefore, every change must be controlled to ensure the potential negative outcomes are analyzed and steps taken to minimize the likelihood of occurrence. A formal change process must be created, published, and enforced.

G.   AI7—Install and Accredit Solutions and Changes—A formal testing and acceptance plan must accompany every change or new asset implementation. This plan must detail the desired outcomes and verify that anticipated undesirable outcomes do not occur. Such a test program requires a separate testing environment as identical to the target production environment as practical.

[D]   Delivery and Support

The Delivery and Support domain focuses on the delivery aspects of the information technology. It covers areas such as the execution of the applications within the IT system and its results, as well as the support processes that enable the effective and efficient execution of these IT systems. These support processes include security issues and training. The high level control objectives for the Delivery and Support domain are:

A.   DS1—Define and Manage Service Levels—predefined levels of IT service with end users sets an expectation for IT support. This approach makes the requestor jointly responsible for the service level and its financial support. SLAs ensure alignment of IT services with changing customer requirements. It also provides end users with a predictable level of support and assists IT through the predetermined priorities for each request, rather than on a first-in, first-out basis.

B.   DS2—Manage Third-party Services—defining a process to ensure that vendors are managed for the best long term benefit of the company. This reduces the risk of a vendor failing to perform as promised, which reduces IT services levels to its business users. Reliable vendors who consistently provide high quality goods at fair prices can be tracked and shared across the organization.

C.   DS3—Manage Performance and Capacity—the performance and capacity of IT assets is an important component of IT service support. This process describes steps for ensuring both are in adequate supply to fulfill customer demands. This includes forecasting demand, monitoring current requirements and projecting potential changes and initiating changes to maintain adequate service.

D. DS4—Ensure Continuous Service—the continuous on-demand services by a company's IT department are an essential part of its routine processes. An absence of IT service or a significant portion of it may create serious financial losses and regulatory compliance issues. IT departments must create and maintain adequate, tested disaster recovery and business continuity plans. These plans must be updated as the IT assets shift and tested periodically to verify plans work as well as to train the participants.

E. DS5—Ensure Systems Security—companies collect a massive amount of data about their operations, employees, suppliers, vendors, competitors, etc. This data must be safeguarded in a number of ways to ensure it is only accessible by authorized users and that it is not tampered with or intercepted during transmission. Everything that encompasses data security is included in this COBIT objective.

F. DS6—Identify and Allocate Costs—the most equitable way for IT to reflect the cost of its services is to charge those departments that use it for their assistance. This forces users to justify how they use IT and keeps IT focused on providing those services most valued by its business users.

G. DS7—Educate and Train Users—IT provides many useful devices and software. Business users must be adequately trained to maximize company benefits. As the technology changes, and as the user changes, this training must be updated and repeated.

H. DS8—Manage Service Desk and Incidents—objectives for the prompt response, problem identification and resolution of business user IT service requests. Requests are promptly recorded, categorized by priority and technology involved, and passed on to the appropriate seaport team (if the service desk cannot resolve it). The service desk analyzes call patterns to detect problem trends and report them for resolution.

I. DS9—Manage the Configuration—establish a central location for holding all IT asset configuration information for everything that may need to be tracked by its existence in IT, by its version, etc. This might be hardware, software, documentation, SLAs, vendor agreements, last known good configuration of a product, etc.

J. DS10—Manage Problems—serious IT incidents can be declared problems which have no immediate solution due to difficulties in installing a fix or identifying the root cause, or if the replacement item needs time to be delivered. This objective is to ensure that problems are tracked through to their resolution. Throughout the process, the customer is informed of its progress.

K. DS11—Manage Data—this provides for a formal plan for managing IT data, stored online, stored in archive and stored off site. All online storage must be backed-up and moved off site periodically. Stored data must be accessible within a reasonable amount of time and obsolete data destroyed (and not linger, occupying expensive storage space). This process works together with the security objective.

L. DS12—manage the Physical Environment—involves the many small things that companies do to keep people away from their computer room, and to ensure the inside of the computer room is an ideal technical environment. Physical security ensures that only a few people can touch (or accidentally turn off) the company's server farm or mainframe computer. Air conditioning and electrical power filtering ensure that the equipment is "fed" what it needs to maintain operations. Uninterruptible Power Supplies keep the power coming in an electrical outage. The key is to ensure that all of the shared servers or critical workstations not located in the computer room (such as PBX systems, departmental servers, servers in remote offices, etc.) are likewise protected.

M. DS13—Manage Operations—processes for ensuring that steps involved in data operation tasks are clearly documented, to include applicable policies and procedures. Jobs running on shared systems must be shared and sometimes re-sequenced based on time of month or to address unusual circumstances. In some companies, data operations are also responsible for monitoring systems performance and addressing issues. To ensure maximum hardware availability, equipment preventative maintenance programs are implemented with work scheduled during low usage periods.

[E] Monitor and Evaluate

The Monitoring and Evaluation domain deals with a company's strategy in assessing the needs of the company and whether or not the current IT system still meets the objectives for which it was designed and the controls necessary to comply with regulatory requirements. Monitoring also covers the issue of an independent assessment of the effectiveness of an IT system in its ability to meet business objectives and the company's control processes by internal and external auditors. The following table lists the high level control objectives for the Monitoring domain.

A. ME1—Monitor and Evaluate IT Processes—IT systems operations are subject to a wide range of interruptions from hardware failure to operating system failure to, well, about anything. These systems must be constantly monitored to detect problems before the customer notices them. This shortens the amount of time to resolution (in the customer's opinion).

B. ME2—Monitor and Evaluate Internal Control—separate from monitoring software operations is the monitoring of controls intended to ensure that safeguards are in place and not disabled, such as firewall rules, antivirus software, etc. All incidents are logged along with actions taken to resolve them. If third party services are on site, then a regular assessment of their controls is required.

C. ME3—Ensure Regulatory Compliance—requires an authoritative description of the necessary information to gather and the reporting format to comply with all regulatory reporting. These processes must be periodically audited to ensure efficient and accurate information.

D. ME4—Provide IT Governance—create and follow an IT governance framework that ensures the alignment of IT services with business requirements, present and planned. IT services are periodically checked to ensure they fulfill customer requirements effectively and efficiently, with minimal risk. Optimize resource utilization and measure service performance throughout the IT organization.

§ 3.04 IMPLEMENTING COBIT

[A] Overview

Implementing COBIT requires many independent-minded people to agree on what should be done, and to all work together in the same direction to accomplish something. The first step is to create a common vision of the benefits for a COBIT implementation project. In many cases, it will be promoted as a proven way to fulfill legal compliance of financial controls as mandated by law. Usually, this will be sufficient reason. However, this trivializes COBIT's other benefits. COBIT improves a company's business resilience by protecting its data from unauthorized or illegal compromise. It improves IT systems availability through the controlled changing of processes. Overall, COBIT forces IT professionals to specifically address IT governance actions that in many companies is accomplished informally or not at all.

[B] Mind the Gap

No company starts at zero. Every company has some aspect, some part of COBIT compliance process already in place. An audit of all processes will establish a baseline of "today." This identifies existing processes and the degree of their compliance. Next the IT leaders determine their goals from implementing COBIT. Usually there is some problem they are trying to address—from legal compliance to more resilient systems. These goals determine the sequence of implementation events, so they must be clearly defined. The difference between the audit and the goals is the gap—the areas that must be improved to achieve the goal. This sounds simple, but implementing COBIT involves people, and people take time to change their habits and preferences.

COMMENT

COSO provides a COBIT Implementation Toolkit. This valuable tool provides checklists and leading questions to guide leaders through the changeover process. Use this tool to guide your project.

The gap between the starting point of the COBIT project and where the implementation team is today demonstrates to executives the progress made and the work remaining to accomplish. One way to measure this progress is through Balanced Scorecards, which indicate improvements in key focus areas.

[C] A New Way to Think

All changes in an idea take careful preparation. The eventual objective is for everyone to internalize the COBIT values so they perform them without thought of doing something else. Changing attitudes takes patience. This is a long but worthwhile endeavor, so a project plan is necessary. Such a plan will establish the long term-goals and the incremental steps to achieve them.

Demonstrate to each department in the organization how it is in their own self-interest. Everyone wants to be on the winning team. Even if people acknowledge that their current processes leave something to be desired—they are familiar and their limitations are known.

Carefully select areas to apply COBIT principles. The selection criteria may be former audit discrepancies, management-identified emphasis areas, or which IT group has the team that is friendliest toward COBIT. In the beginning, keep your goals modest but clear so everyone can see the before and after results.

Learning a new way to perform an old task can be frustrating. Minimize this frustration through training. Training removes the distraction of working with something new and allows everyone to focus on the work at hand.

Finally, the last important element of implementing COBIT is persistence. If the project leader believes in the value of the COBIT model and in its benefits to the company, and has at least modest executive support, then slowly but surely most if not all of the COBIT standards will be adopted.

4

BUSINESS IMPACT ANALYSIS: MEASURING RISK

§ 4.01   OVERVIEW
    [A]   Purpose and Scope
    [B]   What is a BIA?
    [C]   Key Points in a BIA

§ 4.02   MANAGING A BUSINESS IMPACT ANALYSIS (BIA)
    [A]   A BIA is a Project
    [B]   Senior Executive Sponsorship Is Critical
    [C]   Building the Team

§ 4.03   BIA DATA COLLECTION PROCESS—GET THE FACTS
    [A]   The Basics
    [B]   Develop a BIA Glossary
    [C]   What to Collect?
    [D]   Data Collections Planning

§ 4.04   CRUNCHING THE DATA
    [A]   Gathering the Data
    [B]   Build Initial Reports

§ 4.05   BIA RESULTS AND THE IT DEPARTMENT
    [A]   Overview
    [B]   Recovery Priority
    [C]   Recovery Time Objective / Recovery Point Objective
    [D]   Recovery Point Objective
    [E]   Risk Analysis

§ 4.06   EVERGREEN
    [A]   Business Updates
    [B]   IT Updates

§ 4.01 OVERVIEW

[A] Purpose and Scope

IT executives face a basic problem. Their data systems encompass numerous programs, databases, and devices that span the company. If two data systems are dead at the same time, which one must be addressed first? What is the cost of downtime per system? Intuitively, some of these must be more valuable than others, but what is that value? How can this value be measured? In a time of scarce resources, which systems should be nurtured and which ones left to wither on the vine? In a major disaster, which systems are essential for the company's survival?

All of these questions are pertinent. Often, decisions are based on the perceived value of a particular data process when comparing two competing issues and the resources for only one of them is available. Capital spending, major improvement projects, and of course, support staff training often are decided by the perceived value that a data system provides the company. But what is this value based on? Where is the data that supports this value? How old is this data? Has the value provided by a process changed over time?

The problem with the business-as-usual approach to this is that it is based on a limited understanding or personal whim—not on the facts. A new IT Manager lacks the "institutional knowledge" of which system failures in the past have caused the greatest damage. Another caveat is that the business impact of a technology changes over time. Companies compete in an ever-shifting business environment. Yesterday's cash cow may be today's cash drain. Yesterday's cash drain may be today's regulatory compliance requirement and must be retained to keep the government at arm's length!

Unfortunately, few executives fully appreciate which of their technologies are truly critical. They draw on personal experience, but that is limited to the areas with which they are familiar. They can ask their peers, but each person sees the world through the narrow view of his own situation. The accounting department will identify all of their applications as critical since they handle the money. The materials management team will identify its technologies as critical since the company's assets are reflected in a fragile collection of materials. The engineering department will think this is the most critical since their technology holds the company's valuable intellectual property. To some extent, all of these people are right!

To determine where the true benefits lie, conduct a detailed analysis that breaks the business down by its major functions, and assigns value to each function in terms of cash flow and regulatory obligations. Then the data systems that support these functions are identified and the functions rolled up. Based on this data—based on these facts—an IT executive can more efficiently assign resources for the greater benefit of the organization.

[B] What is a BIA?

A Business Impact Analysis (BIA) is a systematic analysis of a company or business unit to identify its critical business functions and the impact to the company if these functions ceased to function. These business functions are linked to the IT systems that support them (lose the IT system, and that function cannot continue). Risks to the most valuable processes are identified along with mitigation actions to reduce the likelihood or impact of these risks. In the event of a disaster, the BIA indicates how much is lost per hour or per day for the length of the outage.

COMMENT

A BIA is a snapshot of what is currently in place. A major shift in business operations requires conducting a new BIA.

An organization's critical functions depend on its primary mission. For a charity, a BIA would focus on the key services provided to its target audience. For a factory, this might be the primary products created. A bank might identify the various services offered. An online store would value availability of its web page, speed of processing, and security of customer data.

[C] Key Points in a BIA

A BIA provides many benefits:

   A. Quantifies the financial and intangible costs of an outage.
   B. Identifies the Recovery Time Objective (RTO)—the length of time the organization can afford for that function to be disabled before severe financial damage is experienced.
   C. Identifies the people, software and vital records necessary for the function to recover.
   D. Through analysis, identifies the most critical functions to protect, which is input to a risk assessment.
   E. Identifies the sequence that IT functions must be recovered during an outage.
   F. Identifies vital records and the impact of their loss.

Financial costs of an outage might include:

   A. Lost revenue.
   B. Loss of shareholder confidence in company's executive management.
   C. Spoiled materials or finished goods.
   D. Penalties to customers for late shipments or lost services.
   E. Legal penalties for missed or inadequate reporting.

Intangible losses include:

   A. Loss of customer good will.
   B. Loss of marketplace confidence in delivery credibility.

C. Impact to employees.
D. Loss of local "good neighbor" image.

Based on the BIA report, the IT Director can determine:

A. Maximum Acceptable Outage (MAO) that IT can suffer before the company's finances are seriously harmed. In the case of a localized disaster, this is further broken down by application.
B. Recovery Time Objective (RTO)—the amount of time before a company is seriously financially damaged. This drives the disaster recovery strategy.
C. Recovery Point Objective (RPO)—the amount of data that can be lost before serious consequences. It is measured in time. This drives the data protection strategy.

§ 4.02 MANAGING A BUSINESS IMPACT ANALYSIS (BIA)

A BIA is best run as a formal project. The project definition and budget is approved at the highest company levels. With so many parts of the organization to talk to, people to meet with, a published project plan is essential.

In most companies, the Board of Directors is the authority ordering the study. Even if the BIA request originates in the IT department, its scope is so all-encompassing that it must have board approval to proceed.

[A] A BIA is a Project

A BIA must be a carefully coordinated effort. It is visible across the company. A well-run project builds credibility where a blundered effort raises defenses in every department. The key in any project's success is the selection of a skilled Project Manager.

The BIA Project Manager has a tough job. He must follow up and insist that the BIA questionnaires are promptly returned. He must moderate discussions among executives as to the true value of internal processes. He will touch on areas normally discussed behind closed executive doors. It is very easy for this person to bruise some executive egos and endanger his own long term career possibilities.

Therefore companies choose one of two paths:

A. Internal—An employee is appointed as the Project Manager. This person already understands the corporate structure, knows the personalities involved, where to find people, etc. This approach builds internal expertise.
B. External—bring in an outside organization to lead the project. This brings in someone without the internal ties and whose loyalty is to the executive paying their bill. The problem is that the company's inner business processes, finances and problems will be exposed to this third party.

The Project Manager is responsible for planning the BIA and executing the plan. In a large company, there are a lot of people to meet with. Meetings must accommodate executives' busy schedules. The Project Manager provides status reports to the executive sponsor.

[B] Senior Executive Sponsorship Is Critical

A BIA touches every part of a business. It asks probing questions that make many executives and manager nervous. They are concerned that the data may indicate that their work is not vital and that they may be cut from the company. They are concerned that the data may be misused in department infighting. They are concerned that the entire affair is a smokescreen for something nefarious that they cannot even guess at. Consequently, they will try to avoid the study or inflate their own importance.

To overcome the reluctance to participate, a senior executive is appointed. This person:

A. Appoints the Project Manager.
B. Approves the project's budget.
C. Issues executive directives mandating participation.
D. Addresses all objections raised by the various departments.
E. At the end, they approve the project's final report.

[C] Building the Team

A typical BIA project team consists of several business analysts. The analysts manage the data collection process to include:

A. Tuning the questionnaire to the local organization (many companies start with a standard form and modify for local use).
B. Providing training to small groups (usually a department at a time) on how to fill out the questionnaire.
C. Following up when data entered is illegible or incomplete.
D. Compiling the BIA data into a format for review by the various organizational levels.
E. Conducting peer review meetings with the participants to discuss the responses gathered by an entire department.

§ 4.03 BIA DATA COLLECTION PROCESS—GET THE FACTS

[A] The Basics

The goal of a Business Impact Analysis is to identify the most critical company processes. If ten different managers were asked what this might be, they would likely provide ten different answers—each slightly skewed toward their own departments. In the data collection phase of the analysis, the leaders of each important business function are asked for their opinion as to what is most critical. These functions are then reviewed in terms of financial and legal impacts.

A data collection plan addresses what to collect and from whom. Many other variables can be added to these basic items, such as when to collect, who must respond, etc. The guiding principle is that data should only be collected *once*. Time spent in preparation is saved later by only doing it one time.

The data collection plan is to:

A. Identify who will contribute information (based on the organization chart).
B. Create a questionnaire that reflects information required for the final report.
C. Roll out the questionnaires in a series of meetings.
D. Aggregate returned questionnaires into business units.
E. Review the aggregated data in meetings with the business units.
F. Review the total roll up with executive management.

COMMENT

Anyone who has been tasked with collecting data from a number of people knows the problem. The requirement seems so clear, just go find out the information from the various people. As the collection proceeds, each manager uses a slightly different term for the same thing. Each sees things differently and often throws in additional items or factors to consider. If accepted, these additional factors must be recollected from the people interviewed earlier, etc.

[B] Develop a BIA Glossary

The purpose of collecting data is to combine it into reports. It is important that responses are consistently described in the same way in every questionnaire. This speeds reporting, improves reporting consistency and makes obvious when something new (and unexpected) is encountered.

Electronic forms are very useful for this. Drop-down boxes confine the customer's answers to a set of categories or range of numbers to ease the consolidation of the data. However, always leave an "other" category where they can describe something and enter its value. Each of the other entries must be investigated but this keeps an analysis moving forward without pausing constantly to answer questions.

A glossary must be made readily available to all participants. This helps to standardize terminology across the study. When each department is briefed prior to filling in their questionnaires, the glossary can be reviewed with them.

[C]   What to Collect?

The easiest way to identify data elements to collect is to identify what will be used to create the final report. Start by defining what the result should be. Create a questionnaire that collects the data needed to answer these questions.

COMMENT

The BIA focus is on processes. A business process typically involves trained people, business records, and technology.

For example, consider the process of receiving material into a factory. The receiving clerk reviews the manifest and locates the purchase order number. Next, a data connection is made to the materials management software so that the shipment can be checked against the order to ensure everything was received. Then it can be marked as complete and undamaged which connects to the accounts payable system. Meanwhile, the person handling the material follows local procedures for storing it.

In this example, the manifest is a critical document (for claiming hidden damage), the software supporting the process is important along with the equipment used to run it.

A simplistic BIA questionnaire is found at the end of this chapter. It is presented here to explain its various parts. The sections of a BIA are as follows:

A.   Identification Block. A questionnaire begins with an identification block that indicates who filled in the data, and when. It also explains how to contact the respondent with further questions by telephone or e-mail. The function number is used by the BIA team to control the questionnaires and ensure they are all returned.

An important entry is the department name. Each department can have many business functions to report. Therefore, each department numbers their forms according to how many functions they are reporting. This reduces the chance of missing a report.

Department: ________________________________ Function # __________
Filled in by: _______________________________ Date: ______________
Phone: ____________________ Email: ___________________________

B. Describe the Business Function. The process name must be the one that it is most commonly known as. When the final report is reviewed, executives will question high values for something that no one can recognize. The process owner field will be used by the IT department as the contact person if any of this process's IT systems fail.

Business Process Name: ____
Business Process Description: ___________________________________
____
____
Process Owner: ____

C. Impact if This Business Function Is Lost. This matrix lists five categories across the top and a time scale along the vertical axis. It is the heart of the analysis and must be tuned to the local requirements. The impact categories for this business function are:

	Cumulative Financial Loss (Revenue lost plus costs incurred)	Legal Compliance Impact	Loss of Customer Confidence	Loss of Supplier Confidence	Damaged Public Image
1 hour					
4 hours					
1 day					
2 days					
3 days					
4 days					
5 days					
2 weeks					

1. Cumulative Financial Loss (Revenue lost plus costs incurred)—measured in dollars. This might include:
   a. lost revenues
   b. lost sales

    c. financial penalties
    d. wages paid for no work
    e. overtime wages paid to catch up
    f. spoiled materials and finished goods

2. Legal Compliance Impact—Yes or No. Space is provided later for an explanation.
3. Loss of Customer Confidence—Answers can be Low, Medium or High. Space is provided later for an explanation.
4. Loss of Supplier Confidence—Answers can be Low, Medium or High. Space is provided later for an explanation.
5. Damaged Public Image—Answers can be Low, Medium or High. Space is provided later for an explanation.

Rate each of the impact categories according to its impact over time. For example, what is the Cumulative Financial Loss for one hour of outage?

Example #1:
    If this was a busy online catalog, then a one hour outage might have a significant financial impact since buyers may look elsewhere for their goods.

Example #2:
    If this was the shipping department for a factory, then a one hour outage would mean that shipments would leave the dock late that day. A four hour outage might involve shipments arriving late to the customer. Beyond four hours, late shipments would be widespread and, depending upon the purchasing stipulations, may be refused by the customer. There may even be penalties for late deliveries. Also, at some point, the rest of the factory is shut down since finished goods are piled up with nowhere to go.

Example #3:
    If the payroll department was down for an hour, then the clerks can tidy up around the office or even leave early for lunch, and the cost is minimal.

However, if the same payroll department was inoperable for a week, the company may not have lost revenue but the employees definitely would be angry. If the employees belonged to a union, they might walk off the job.

Other categories to consider adding to the questionnaire include:

1. Shareholder Confidence.
2. Loss of Financial Control.
3. Employee Morale.
4. Customer Service.
5. Employee Resignations.
6. Vendor Relations.
7. Potential Liability.
8. Competitive advantage.

9. Health Hazard.
10. Additional Cost of Credit.
11. Additional Cost of Advertising to Rebuild Company Image and Reliability.
12. Cost to Acquire New Software and to Recreate Databases.
13. Damage to Brand Image.
14. Potential Reduction in Value of Company Stock Shares.

D.   Explain How the Non-Dollar Issues Will Impact the Company. The goal is to confine the answers within an easy to aggregate indicator, such as Low, Medium or High. Provide space so that the respondent can explain the factors that drove their answer.

<table>
<tr><td>

What Legal Compliance issues would be created: ______________________

Describe the Loss of Customer Confidence created: ______________________

Describe the Loss of Supplier Confidence created: ______________________

Describe Damage to the Company's Public Image: ______________________

</td></tr>
</table>

E.   Vital Records. Data retention and protection is a vital. Departments that originate, use or store vital business records must be identified. This information can be used to develop protection plans for this data. It can also identify documents that should be properly destroyed instead of stored on site.

<table>
<tr><td>

What critical documents are created, used or stored by this business function:

</td></tr>
</table>

F.   Vital Equipment. A BIA can identify weakness in processes that could bankrupt a business. In this section, respondents are asked to identify critical devices that may be difficult or impossible to replace. This can spawn a project to modify the project to eliminate these unique devices (and thereby reduce the chance of a business function outage due to a special machine).

<table>
<tr><td>

List the non-IT equipment vital to this business function:

</td></tr>
</table>

G. IT Applications Supporting This Process. This data is important for the IT department to determine the required recovery time for each application. For example, if a department claims that a one hour outage costs the company $10,000, then that is financial justification to purchase redundant equipment to reduce the likelihood or duration of an outage.

To ensure consistency among the answers, the IT department provides a list of all applications on all platforms (desktop, server, mainframe, on-line). The list is included in the instructions accompanying the form. Be sure to include both the official name and the commonly used name (if one is better known). Respondents can select from this list to minimize variation of system names.

COMMENT

This is one place where an electronic BIA data collection form is handy. An electronic form enables providing a list of all applications on all platforms (desktop, server, mainframe, on-line) in a drop-down box. Be sure to include both the official name and the commonly used name (if one is better known). This ensures consistency of data collection.

Tools	Impact							
	1 hour	4 hours	1 day	2 days	3 days	4 days	5 days	2 weeks
List of IT Applications								

[D]   Data Collections Planning

With the questionnaire complete, the plan turns to how to contact the various departments. The Project Manager must carefully sequence the BIA rollout and coordinate times to work with each department that minimizes disruption to its normal operations.

A.   **Who Will Receive a Questionnaire?** Obtain a current company organizational chart. This will be used to identify who will receive a survey and to break the organization into Business Units. Business Units are work groups with complementary functions that can be brought together for validating the data. Often, questionnaires are provided to the lowest level team leader in each department. Although it is nice to give everyone a voice in the BIA, it takes time to brief participants on the process, to review their responses, etc.

B.   **Stratify the Respondents.** Some people will expect more hand-holding than others. An effort to establish and maintain executive support in each department saves time in the long run. Enlist their support in their department's prompt return of completed forms.

Provide an advance copy of the questionnaire to the higher level executives (typically, the vice presidents). Meet with them to discuss its purpose and methods. They do not fill it out—just need to understand it. Their role comes later on when validating the data.

C.   **Run a Trial with a Single Department.** Before sending the form out to everyone, use one department to test. Walk through the entire process with them looking for places where the form is missing something or where the instructions are not clear. Often what is clear as day to the BIA team is obscure or has dual meaning to people who are less familiar with the material.

D.   **Issue the Questionnaires.** Meet with each of the department leaders and help them to draft a list of the major business functions within their domain. Provide a numbered stack of questionnaires. Assign a number to each person the department leaders indicate should receive one. An important management tool is a log of which form number went to which person. This is used to verify that all of the forms are returned.

Along with the questionnaire, provide written instructions. Explain how every field on the form will be used and what the respondent should fill in there. Ideally, include a telephone number for someone on the BIA project team to quickly answer questions. (The quicker questions are resolved, the greater the respondents will cooperate.)

COMMENT

Before issuing the questionnaires, be sure that person is not on vacation or a business trip—or about to leave on one.

E. Conduct Department Meetings. Passing out questionnaires to a list of people is not a good data collection plan. It will be stonewalled and sidetracked due to many questions as to what means what, etc. The best approach is to coordinate a series of meetings with the various work groups and departments. Yes, this takes time. Try to keep the groups smaller than 20 people. This provides opportunities to ask questions.

During these meetings:

1. Explain the purpose of the BIA and how it will help the company—*sell the concept to them!*
2. Provide copies of the executive support letter. This puts everyone on notice that they are expected to cooperate. If possible, ask this executive to drop by the meetings for a brief word of "encouragement."
3. Provide copies of the questionnaires along with a printed explanation of what each item means.
4. Walk through every item in the questionnaire and provide examples of how they might be filled in.

F. Special Handling. A few departments, such as the legal team, may be small and the workers all highly paid. In those cases, the BIA team may use interviews to fill in the questionnaires.

Selecting who gets a questionnaire (refer to the organization chart)

1. Traversing the hierarchy
   a. Start with the company on top. This is the CEO.
   b. The next level is for each Vice President.
   c. In this example, we enter the Accounting Department, and then Accounts Receivable.
2. Within Accounts Receivable, there are three Business Functions. A form is filled out for each of these functions.
3. Roll Up the numbers
   a. 1st Level
      i. Within the Accounts Receivable team, the Manager reviews the reports for each of the three functions.
      ii. As a team (facilitated by the BIA Project Manager), the three function workers and their manager discuss and agree on the recovery time required and costs for non-availability.
   b. 2nd Level
      i. Within the Accounting Department, the Vice President of Accounting reviews the reports for each of the five accounting teams.
      ii. As a team (facilitated by the BIA Project Manager), the five teams and their Vice President discuss and agree on the recovery time required and costs for non-availability.

EXHIBIT 4-1.   Example Organization Chart

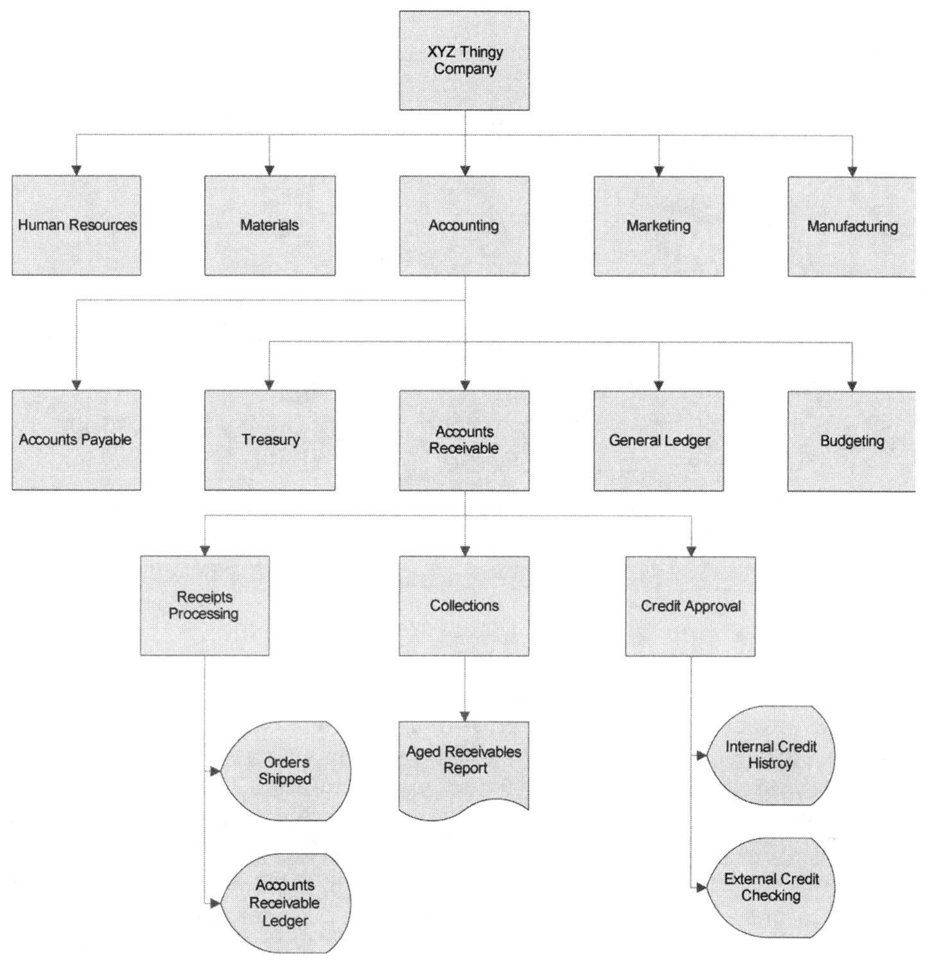

   c. 3rd Level
      i. All of the Vice Presidents, along with the CEO, review the reports for each of the five company departments.
     ii. As a team (facilitated by the BIA Project Manager), the five teams and the CEO discuss and agree on the recovery time required and costs for non-availability.

§ 4.04   CRUNCHING THE DATA

[A]   Gathering the Data

Most companies allow one work week to fill out BIA questionnaires. As the forms come in, be sure to check them off the questionnaire log. At the announced deadline, begin visiting anyone who has not submitted his form.

At first this is a friendly reminder. Most people just get busy and forget about it amidst their many daily crises. A few others won't do anything until the questionnaire becomes the daily crisis! After a few extra days, the crisis is created by alerting the various managers as to who has not complied with the data collection requirements. For the final few forms, a list must be sent to the sponsor who can reset their priorities.

COMMENT

Another way to improve the prompt return of questionnaires is to visit the respondents several days after handing them the form. Make it a friendly visit to see if they had any questions about the form, the process, etc. This reminds them about the due date. It also provides a one-on-one opportunity to answer questions.

As the forms come in, review them carefully. Look for:

A. Readability—handwriting can be a challenge to decipher.
B. Completeness. Incomplete forms must be returned with a request to complete the information. If only a few things are missing, the respondent likely did not know what to enter. A quick meeting can often fill in the gaps.
C. Review and address anything entered into an "Other" category. Some of the "Others" may fit into existing categories. Some of them may be unique situations that can become their own category.

COMMENT

There are two primary ways to analyze data:

- Qualitatively—represents the important but intangible values of something that is not easily measured.
- Quantitatively—or how many. Quantitative analysis presents summary data in terms of quantities, percentages or other mathematical terms.

To simplify data analysis, strive to frame qualitative questions such that they can be replied to quantitatively.

[B]   Build Initial Reports

Data from the questionnaires is compiled into a hierarchy of reports:

A.   Work Group. Groups of managers, supervisors, or team leaders who work in the same area. Each business function has a single form completed. As soon as all of the forms have been received from a department, proceed to create the department's roll-up reports. This example shows a rollout for a work group. Each business process is listed along the left side and along the top is the time range. This shows the impact of an outage of each function over time. In some cases, a financial loss is not listed since, at that point, the facility is shut down. There could be a financial loss value for that event—or just the idea of a forced shutdown may be serious enough to urge the group to do something.

COMMENT

Any business function that is required to fulfill legislative requirements is automatically treated as a high cost outage. In many cases, the daily fines could be used for the cost of outage.

B.   Department. The work groups are merged into a single entry. Conduct a meeting with everyone in a work group that completed a questionnaire—and their next level manager. The BIA analyst provides copies of the reports to all participants. If possible, project the spreadsheet so everyone can see it. One line at a time, the BIA analyst reads the business function title and asks the *entire group* if these numbers are valid. The BIA analyst is non-judgmental and only guides the discussion.

The group debates the data. In this way, the collective knowledge can point out existing manual processes and other efforts available to reduce potential losses and to lengthen the amount of time before the company incurs serious financial losses. The discussion may also point out overlooked business functions.

The amount of time a vital business function can tolerate downtime determines the disaster recovery strategy. The less tolerant that a business function is to an outage, the more expensive the disaster recovery strategy must be and more urgent that business continuity mitigation is implemented.

Every line in the report should be either validated or updated. In this way, the BIA report is the product of both the team and that work area's boss. The entire discussion is important, because this manager must defend the work group's consensus at the next level of data validation.

Work Group Report

Business Process	Cumulative Impact							
	1 hour	4 hours	1 day	2 days	3 days	4 days	5 days	2 weeks
Collections				$5k	$10k	$15k	$20k	$50k
Accounts Receivable	0	$1k	$5k	$20k	$40k	$80k	$160k	$500k
Sales-Major Accounts	$10k	$40k	$100k	$200k	$300k	$400k	$500k	$1.5M
Sales-Other Accounts	$1k	$40k	$80k	$160k	$240k	$320k	$400k	$800k
Shipping		$5k			shutdown	shutdown	shutdown	shutdown
Accounts Payable							$10k	$50k

C. Business Unit. The results of the departments are aggregated into a business unit-wide report. After all of the work group reviews are completed and the data approved, it is time to move up a level. Repeat the work group review at each level of the organization. As the teams meet, expect a lot of heated discussion as to what is vital, and how long the company can tolerate an outage of that function. For many executives, the discussion is an eye opener. An executive may discover important responsibilities and works areas under his control that he may not have been aware of.

COMMENT

When reviewing the data with higher levels of management, it takes too long to go through everything. Focus on the shortest time as these will drive the cost of the business continuity strategy. At the top level, the discussion may only hit on the impact of the first day's outage.

Executives are often surprised at the quantity of documents critical to a business function. Expect to uncover a lack of back ups for these documents and unmarked containers. This becomes an action item for those work areas to coordinate off site storage for archives, on site data security and a recovery plan if the on-site documents are destroyed. Be sure to pass all of this information to the company's Document Management Program.

§ 4.05 BIA RESULTS AND THE IT DEPARTMENT

[A] Overview

Once the business functions and amount of time an outage can be tolerated have been determined, the next step is to link that information to the application that supports those business functions. This provides the IT director with an idea of how long a data system outage for a particular application can be tolerated.

[B] Recovery Priority

For every business function, create a matrix that ties the IT systems required to support that function to a time frame. In this example, the applications are listed on the vertical axis and the timeline is across the top. Since different business applications have different times that they are critical, enter a number in the appropriate square for the number of applications. In this example, e-mail will impact three business functions on the first day, but one other will be seriously impacted within an hour.

Application	Impact							
	1 hour	4 hours	1 day	2 days	3 days	4 days	5 days	2 weeks
e-Mail	1		3	1	6	2	2	
Web Catalog	2	5	2	1				
EDI	4	1	2	4			2	
Sql Database	1	1	3	2		3		1
Payroll			1	1				
Remedy	3	1	2		2		4	

This information can be used by the Service Desk to identify restoration priorities when addressing multiple outages at the same time. Now, based on customer requirements, it is easy to see which system must be restored first.

[C]   Recovery Time Objective / Recovery Point Objective

Based on the required recovery time, the IT Business Continuity Manager can determine a Recovery Time Objective (RTO). This is the target time within which the IT department must have specific systems operational after a disaster. In their reviews of the BIA data, company executives settle on the required RTO. The IT department's task is to develop a strategy for fulfilling it.

In time long past, a set of back-up tapes stored off-site were considered the essential tool for data center recovery. However, with so much of a company's business stuffed away on computer disks, this is no longer practical. Consider, for a moment, how long it would take just to read a full set of data backups onto new disks. Added together to the unlikelihood that identical hardware would be available on short notice, the magnitude of the problem becomes obvious.

Leave the data center recovery discussion for the Business Continuity Manager. The point is that the IT staff must determine a strategy to fulfill management's mandated RTO. However, once they see the cost, they tend to soften how critical some business functions are.

[D]   Recovery Point Objective

The Recovery Point Objective (RPO) is the quantity of data that must be reloaded, or whose loss is acceptable in a disaster. This is a difficult concept to explain to end users.

Most companies make a full back-up of all disk drives every weekend. Every week night, they make back-up copies of what has changed that day, called incremental back-ups. So, if a disaster occurred in the night after the back-ups were made and sent off-site for storage, no data is lost. But if the disaster occurs in the mid-afternoon, then all of the data entered or calculated during that day must be re-entered or skipped over. This can be a significant amount.

> **COMMENT**
>
> Given today's internet ordering and many real-time systems, companies have invested in off-site data replication. This might be off-site journaling of data (similar to an incremental backup) or mirroring data at off-site locations. These expensive solutions are justified by the executives' RPO requirements.

[E]   Risk Analysis

With the BIA results in hand, the IT Director can initiate studies of the most critical systems, searching for ways to make them more resilient. Disaster Recovery is for recovering from a major disaster. However, a more common situation is a system outage. This analysis is to examine each critical system from end to end looking for:

A.   Single points of failure.
B.   Persistent problems with a piece of code or hardware.
C.   Old equipment that should be replaced.
D.   Critical third party software that is close to losing vendor support.
E.   Technologies where the IT staff lacks expertise.
F.   Quality of technical documentation.

Each of these can initiate a number of actions. These studies can provide input to the IT department's:

A.   Items for the upcoming capital budget to replace major hardware items.
B.   People and training for the upcoming training schedule and budget.
C.   Project proposals to rework unreliable software.

The risk analysis can also be general, such as the loss of electrical service or external network connection to the outside world. If the IT Department has a Business Continuity Manager, he should already have these worked out.

§ 4.06   EVERGREEN

[A]   Business Updates

After the BIA is completed, do not just toss it on the shelf. Although it is just a snapshot of the company, it can be updated whenever there is a major shift in the business. The BIA can drive so many parts of the IT department that it should be referred to regularly. In a dispute with an end user over priority, the BIA is the neutral expert that both can point to.

However, businesses change constantly. To keep the BIA in line with the business, perform mini-BIAs whenever a significant business change occurs. This might be the purchase of a new branch office, introduction of a new product line, replacement of a major IT system, etc.

COMMENT

BIAs should be completely redone every two years.

[B]   IT Updates

One of the more difficult parts of a BIA is keeping it in sync with IT changes. If the BIA identifies a data system as critical, and business continuity plans are created to support it, these plans must be updated whenever a significant IT change occurs. The best time to uncover these changes is during a project proposal. For example, if a new database server and additional disk is purchased to expand the company's ERP system, then this should be included in the project during the proposal stage, and not just prior to implementation.

5

POLICIES AND PROCEDURES: SETTING THE FRAMEWORK

§ 5.01 OVERVIEW
    [A] Purpose and Scope
    [B] Policies vs. Procedures
    [C] Critical Policies to Develop Based on This Chapter

§ 5.02 ORGANIZING A MANUAL
    [A] Manual Organization
    [B] Type Styles and Page Numbering
    [C] Printing Policies and Procedures
    [D] Page Layout

§ 5.03 SETTING THE STANDARDS FOR RESPONSIBILITIES
    [A] Who Has Management Authority?
    [B] Policies and Procedures Responsibility
    [C] Implementation

§ 5.04 IT POLICY APPROVAL PROCESS
    [A] Overview
    [B] Policy Creation Process
    [C] Policy Acceptance Criteria
    [D] Manual Maintenance
    [E] Annual Policy Review
    [F] Sunset Clause

§ 5.01 OVERVIEW

[A] Purpose and Scope

IT governance becomes reality with the creation of the appropriate policies and procedures necessary to implement the IT strategy of the organization. Comprehensive policies and procedures are critical for ensuring that your investment in IT is best used to support the overall strategy of the enterprise. They help ensure that all areas of IT are working toward the shared goal of supporting and enabling the mission of the organization. This chapter will show you the mechanics of creating effective IT policies and procedures. Each of the remaining chapters offers you examples using this format and templates to guide you in the establishment of comprehensive policies and procedures vital to the success of your IT organization. The goal of the remainder of this book is to suggest ways of developing, adopting, and distributing uniform IT policies and procedures that support the selected IT governance model.

The guidelines for policies and procedures contained in this book are appropriate for information systems functions at the corporate, division, local area network, and workstation levels. The guidelines are not intended to replace instructions by various vendors in the operation of their software or hardware. Although the examples used here can be adapted to fit your unique circumstances, there is no "one size fits all" solution.

A policy and procedures manual must be kept current, ideally by reviewing every section at least once a year. An out-of-date manual or one with too many gaps in it will not hold employee interest. After its review, the company executives should approve it and ensure it is properly presented to the relevant employees through presentations explaining its changes and by providing printed copies or online access.

The number of policies in effect should be minimal. The thicker the policy binder is, the less it will be read. However, there are times when it is necessary to include formal policies to inform employees and protect the company from legal entanglements.

[B] Policies vs. Procedures

Policies are general statements of direction. They provide guidance so employees understand the boundaries within which they must operate. Well-written policies provide freedom of action, promote initiative, and facilitate the delegation of authority throughout an organization. They also promote the efficient use of resources in the organization. Policies explain *what* and *why* things are done. They are not, however, a substitute for sound judgment and common sense.

Policies:

- Have widespread application.
- Change infrequently.
- Describe major operational issues.
- Usually are expressed in broad terms.

Policies represent management's guidance in the way that a situation is to be addressed. This framework empowers workers to make decisions and act on them without constantly referring to a higher authority.

Policies are effective only if they are enforced. If a policy no longer fits your business situation, cancel it. If it still fits, enforce it. All management personnel must know what the policies are and enforce them throughout their teams. If the managers do not understand them, they will be unable to explain them to others. Credibility is a powerful tool for managers. It permits issuing orders without reference to coercion. If credibility is lost, then only negative action will obtain results.

Policies must be applied equally to everyone. Selective enforcement damages the credibility of the policies and the management team as a whole. The few policies you fail to enforce will effectively cancel the remaining policies in the eyes of your employees.

Some policies are probably already in place through your human resources department. Where possible, do not overlap with any of them. Ambiguity between competing policies confuses the people they are supposed to be guiding.

Procedures, on the other hand, are specific statements designed to provide direction in actions necessary to support the policies of the organization. Procedures explain *how* things are done.

Procedures:

- Have a narrow application.
- Are prone to change as new systems are made operational.
- Describe process.
- Are usually very detailed.

[C] Critical Policies to Develop Based on This Chapter

Using the material discussed in this chapter, you will be able to create the following policies:

A. Document the lines of policy authority.
    1. How authority is derived.
    2. Responsibility for maintaining policies.
    3. How policies are implemented.
    4. How policies are enforced.
B. Policy approval process.
    1. How policies are created and accepted.
    2. Annual review policy.
    3. Policy expiration.
C. Policy to Submit a Strategic Plan.

Policies should always be developed based on the local situation. Successful managers cannot issue locally correct guidance if the policies are written with some other company's situation in mind.

§ 5.02   ORGANIZING A MANUAL

[A]   Manual Organization

A fundamental step to assigning structure is to develop a policies and procedures manual for quick reference and easy updating. This is true whether you create a paper version or post an electronic version to your corporate intranet. Building such a volume can be very time-consuming. The extent to which your company will benefit will be determined by how it is used. If the managers refer to it, so will the employees. If the managers ignore it, so will the employees. (Do you see a pattern here?)

If your organization does not already have a policies and procedures numbering and formatting policy, consider using the format of the chapters in this book. This book is divided into chapters as a "living example" of manual organization and style. Remember that, unlike a novel, a manual is not intended to be read from front to back. A manual must be organized for the quick location of pertinent information. Fortunately, this is made much simpler with word processing software, which can automatically build tables of contents and indices for you. Electronic and web-based versions can make searching for the appropriate information quick and easy. Make sure you use language that is appropriate for your organization to facilitate the use of automated search tools in finding suitable policies in a given situation.

A "chapter" in your policies and procedures manual might represent a subject area under which related policies are grouped. For example, all policies related to security should be grouped together in a "chapter." Each separate policy within a "chapter" is then numbered sequentially just as are the sections in a chapter of this book. The sections are subdivided into subsections, organizing the details of each policy. The manual opens with a table of contents displaying the chapters, sections, and subsections (just like this book). Contact information for the person responsible for the policies should be included in the front of the manual so users may request updates or get clarification, if needed.

Many organizations will use a two or three letter prefix for each corporate policy to denote the area responsible for the policy—"IT" or "ITP" are popular prefixes to use for IT policies. An example of the reference index for your policy manual (the format used for this book) is below:

        N. CHAPTER NUMBER
          N.N SECTION NUMBER
            N.N.N. Subsection number
              A. First-level subdivision
                1. Second-level subdivision
                a. Third-level subdivision
                  (1) Fourth-level subdivision
                    (a) Fifth-level subdivision

Using this format, a policy on covering the acquisition of peripheral devices might be designated ITP-12-1; "ITP" being the prefix you decide to use for all IT-related policies, "chapter" 12 containing all policies concerning non-PC devices, and '1' signifying that this was the first policy created in this "chapter."

[B]   Type Styles and Page Numbering

Most manuals use type styles to aid in fast information retrieval. For example:

[**CHAPTER** titles will be uppercase and bold.]

[**Section** titles will be bold.]

[The subsequent text's first character will be uppercase.]

Pages can be numbered sequentially like this book, or can be numbered within each section as page x-x. For example, if the last page of section six is four, it would be numbered 6-4. Whatever page numbering scheme you use, the placement of page numbers, headers, and footers needs to be consistent from section to section.

[C]   Printing Policies and Procedures

If the policies and procedures manual is printed, use 20-lb. white paper. Temporary policies or procedures should be printed on colored paper—light blue is a good choice—and should show the duration time in the "effective date" box at the top of each page (MM/DD/YY-MM/DD/YY).

[D]   Page Layout

A clean, uncluttered layout encourages one to read the material. Experiment with different formats to find the one that works best for you. Exhibit 5-1 shows some possible header and footer formats to use.

You should also develop standards for the sections to be contained within each policy. Determine whether all sections are required, or whether some are required and some are optional. Some sections you may want to include are:

A. **Purpose**—This section is where you document the purpose of this policy.
B. **Scope**—Document not only what this policy covers but also what it does not cover in this section.
C. **Reference**—If this policy references any other existing policies, document it here.
D. **Background**—This section is for background information on what brought about the creation of this policy.
E. **Policy**—The actual policy is documented in this section.
F. **Procedures**—Any procedures that were created specifically to support this policy are documented here.
G. **Revision history**—Document the lifespan of this policy.

EXHIBIT 5-1.   Headers and Footer

Headers

Policy and Procedure Manual		Page:	2 of 3
Chapter:	1. Organizational Responsibility	Issued by:	
Section:	2. Manual Organization	Approved:	
Effective Date:	03/01/2003	Supersedes:	

Subject:	Organizational Responsibility	Policy #:	1–2
		Page #:	2 of 3
Covers:	Manual Organization	Effective:	03/01/2004

Footers

Revision #: Revision Date:	Issued by:

Revision #:	Supersedes:	Date:

H. **Inquiries**—This section tells the reader where to go for additional information on this policy.

I. **Appendices**—Any material necessary to support the policy can be placed in this section.

You may need to add additional sections based on your individual situation. Exhibit 5-2 is a sample policy with suggested sections.

EXHIBIT 5-2.   Sample Policy Format

Policy #:	ITP-99-9	**Effective:**	03/18/08	**Page #:**	1 of N
Subject:	The title or subject of the policy				

1.0 PURPOSE

This is where you document the purpose of this policy.

2.0 SCOPE

The Document not only states what this policy covers but also what it does not cover here.

3.0 REFERENCE

If this policy references any other existing policies, document it here.

4.0 BACKGROUND

This section is for background information on what brought about the creation of this policy.

5.0 POLICY

The actual policy is documented in this section.

6.0 PROCEDURES

Any procedures that were created specifically to support this policy are documented here.

7.0 REVISION HISTORY

Document the lifespan of this policy using a table like the one here.

Date	Revision #	Description of Change
03/18/08	1.0	Initial creation.
08/12/08	1.1	Modified section X.4 to include new regulations.

8.0 INQUIRIES

This section tells the reader where to go for additional information on this policy.

9.0 APPENDICES

Any material necessary to support the policy can be placed here.

Revision #:	1.1	Supersedes:	1:0	Date:	08/12/08

§ 5.03 SETTING THE STANDARDS FOR RESPONSIBILITIES

[A] Who Has Management Authority?

Information systems policies typically flow top-down from the highest level of authority in the organization affected by the computer procedures. This person should designate a policy manager or team to develop and oversee the implementation of the policies. Note that imposing policies "from on high" without involving those affected can inhibit acceptance and compliance.

For consistency, it is important to designate a single corporate IT executive (usually the Chief Information Officer) with the authority to implement all companywide computer systems policies. This person will receive policy mandates from the firm's delegated operations policymakers. These policies will be defined in writing and dated, signed, and forwarded to the corporate operations manager who will incorporate these policies into the corporate operational policies.

> ## COMMENT
>
> The first policies developed for the organization should be to designate the authority for the establishment of IT policies and procedures. These policies should outline who has the authority, from what that authority is derived, explain the importance of compliance with the policies that are issued, and describe how policies are created and revised. They should be issued by the Chief Executive Officer and designate the top IT executive within the organization, the Chief Information Officer (CIO) as the person responsible for the care of all IT assets within the facility. This will include any assets purchased outside of the normal IT channels. See Policy ITP 5-1 as an example.

Financial aspects of the firm's computer systems may require the co-approval of the firm's auditors, both in-house and outside, if applicable. The responsibilities of the corporate IT executive are defined in the corporate policies and procedures manual.

The structure of the IT operation determines how local authority is derived and the scope of responsibility for the manager of the IT operation at the local level. Below are several common scenarios and the appropriate policy management structure.

Local network manager within corporate IT. The manager of a business unit using a local area network or individual PCs within a corporate information system operation is typically the authority for such systems. If the company has a corporate system with a network or PC policies and procedures manual in place, its maintenance will be the responsibility of the corporate information systems management. Policy enforcement will come under the authority of the manager of the business unit whose responsibilities are defined in the corporate information systems policies.

Where the manager of a local area network or individual PCs receives only policy guidance from the head of corporate information systems, he or she needs the flexibility to adapt these policies, as needed, into the PC policies and procedures manual.

Local network manager outside corporate IT. Managers of local area networks or individual PCs that are not part of the corporate system are the authority for the systems in their area. The company must create a combined policies and procedures manual formulated to carry out the firm's policies for the company network, local area networks, and stand-alone PCs. The manager of local area networks or individual PCs will be responsible for the procedure development, maintenance, and enforcement within his or her area of authority. The respective responsibilities for the PC policy and procedure manuals will be documented in the Corporate Policy and Procedures Manual. Any financial transactions or data access of the company's computer database systems by local area networks or individual PCs may require the co-approval of the firm's auditors, both in-house and outside, if applicable.

Local network manager with no corporate IT. Managers of local area networks or individual PCs in a firm that has no corporate information system will be the sole authority of the systems in their area. They are responsible for policy and procedure development, maintenance, and enforcement. The person approving will be so noted at the top right-hand side of each section's first page in the manual. This will be the same person who provides the policies or his/her designated representative.

POLICY ITP-5-1. Establishment of Policy Authority

Policy #:	ITP-5-1	**Effective:**	01/19/08	**Page #:**	1 of N
Subject:	Establishment of Policy Authority				

1.0 PURPOSE

This policy recognizes the authority and responsibility of the Chief Information Officer (CIO) to establish and govern technology policies, procedures and best practices for the company's technology infrastructure in order to support the company's business and IT strategies.

2.0 SCOPE

The policy applies to all users of information technology within the company.

3.0 POLICY

The CIO must establish and provide governance for information technology policies, procedures, and best practices for the company's technology infrastructure in order to secure all IT assets and promote the most efficient use of technology resources.

The CIO will submit a report to the Board of Directors at its first meeting of each calendar year, and submit interim reports at the request of the Board, on the current status of the company's technology policies and procedures.

All operating units within the company that use information technology (IT) are responsible for:

A. Adhering to the IT policies issued by the CIO.
B. Developing and implementing, when appropriate, additional IT policies and procedures specific to their operating units.
C. Promoting IT policy adherence.
D. Complying with the requirements of the IT governance model adopted by the organization.
E. Ensuring the security of the IT systems and the network to which they are connected.
F. Informing the CIO if there are any problems with a policy or if inputs from other sources do not comply with the defined policies.
G. Providing new employees with instruction and/or documented procedures that relate to their job descriptions.
H. Providing an annual "refresher" for current employees highlighting the changes made or problem areas during the previous year.
I. Maintaining the functionality of the IT systems within their area.
J. Facilitating training and the dissemination of information.
K. Preventing unauthorized access to company information, personal files, and e-mail.
L. Developing and maintaining a plan for recovery of mission critical data and systems if a loss is sustained.

The head of each business unit must designate an "Information Technology (IT) Coordinator" to ensure that these responsibilities are carried out and to serve as a contact person for that business unit with the CIO. This policy recognizes that different business units have different needs, IT resources, and levels of internal expertise. Hence, the needs and resources of a given business unit may not require the IT Coordinator to have an extensive technical background. Many business units also have "Technical Managers" who are responsible for the operation of the IT systems and with whom the IT Coordinator may share the responsibilities in this policy. Technical Managers are expected to have the technical expertise required to ensure the safe and reliable operation of their respective business unit's IT systems.

4.0 REVISION HISTORY

Date	Revision #	Description of Change
03/18/07	1.0	Initial creation.
01/19/08	1.1	Added support for IT governance model.

5.0 INQUIRIES

Direct inquiries about this policy to:

Tom Jones, CIO
Our Company, Inc.
2900 Corporate Drive
Columbus, OH 43215

Voice: 614-555-1234
Fax: 614-555-1235
E-mail: tjones@company.com

Revision #:	1.1	Supersedes:	1.0	Date:	01/19/08

[B]   Policies and Procedures Responsibility

The top IT executive for a company must be responsible for all computer operations, software, supplies, and supporting hardware for the firm. The authority to create and enforce policies and procedures should be defined in the manual. This person has the responsibility to approve and sign all issued and temporary policies and procedures and his or her name will be noted at the top right-hand side of each section's first page in the manual. The person writing the policies and procedures will be designated by the head of the company's information systems or he or she may elect to write it him-or herself. The writer is identified at the top right-hand side of each section's first page after the word "By" and under the name of the person noted as approving.

COMMENT

The higher up the approval authority, the more likely the policies will be followed. In addition, "buy-in" from users will help policies take root quickly. If the IT executive does not assign responsibility for enforcing a policy to someone, then it will not be enforced, as being the naysayer to someone is never a popular or rewarding task.

[C]   Implementation

All corporate and business unit managers using information technology are responsible for ensuring that the provisions set forth in the Information Technology Policies & Procedures Manual are complied with. These management persons:

A.   Ensure that all application standards are followed in their respective areas.

B. Inform the person in charge of approving the procedures if there are any problems with a procedure or if inputs from other sources do not comply with the defined procedures. This should be done in writing.

C. Provide new employees with instruction and/or documented procedures that relate to their job descriptions.

D. Provide an annual "refresher" for current employees highlighting the changes made or problem areas during the previous year.

All stand-alone PC operations will be covered by a user's procedure manual provided by the supervisor. This manual will contain all procedure information needed for the authorized PC user to be in compliance. Also, the service desk contact will be identified for any needed assistance.

§ 5.04   IT POLICY APPROVAL PROCESS

[A]   Overview

An official policy creation, review, acceptance, and update process should be created so that everyone in the organization understands and participates in the policy process. The life cycle of a policy is:

A. A policy need is identified.
B. A draft is created and reviewed.
C. The appropriate level of management approves the new policy.
D. The policy is distributed.
E. The policy may be revised.
F. The policy may be rescinded.

POLICY ITP-5-2.   Policy Approval Process

Policy #:	ITP-5-2	**Effective:**	03/18/08	**Page #:**	1 of N
Subject:	Policy Approval Process				

1.0 PURPOSE

This policy defines the policy approval process.

2.0 SCOPE

The policy applies to all users of information technology within the company.

3.0 POLICY

The following steps define the process for creating and approving a new policy:

1. A policy suggestion is made. Policy suggestions may originate from the policy manager, users, or management mandates.

2. The policy manager works with management to determine whether there is a need for a new policy (see Section 5.05[C], Policy Acceptance Criteria). If the suggestion is rejected, the requestor is notified of the reasons for rejection. Alternatives to a new policy should be suggested to the person making the request.

3. The policy manager assigns a priority to the policy. The policy manager works with management's input to assign a priority to the development of the new policy.

4. The policy manager or an assigned policy analyst researches the requirements for the new policy. This research includes reviewing existing policies, obtaining examples from outside the company, and conducting interviews with stakeholders affected by the new policy.

5. A draft policy is created. The draft policy is reviewed by others in the policy department, if applicable.

6. The draft policy is reviewed by management. The draft policy is sent to upper management and important stakeholders for review.

7. Revisions are made to the draft, if necessary. Revisions may be made after input is received from upper management and important stakeholders.

8. Is this a mandated policy? If management mandated the new policy, then go to Step 14. Mandated policies are typically those required by law or requested by upper management.

9. The draft policy is sent to all affected stakeholders for review and comment. This can be done by hardcopy, e-mail, or placement on the corporate intranet. The quality of the final policy can depend on the number of people who review the proposed policy.

10. Stakeholder comments are incorporated into the draft, if appropriate. Incorporating as many suggestions as possible from users will help in gaining acceptance of the new policy.

11. Determine if additional research is required. A large percentage of negative comments may suggest additional research is required.

12. Revised policy draft is sent to management for review.

13. The policy manager makes any revisions suggested by management.

14. Send the new policy to the CIO for signature.

15. The new approved policy is sent to stakeholders. This should include anyone affected by the existence of the policy.

16. Update the master policy manual.

4.0 REVISION HISTORY

Date	Revision #	Description of Change
03/18/07	1.0	Initial creation.

5.0 INQUIRIES

Direct inquiries about this policy to:

Harold Jenkins, CIO
2900 Corporate Drive
Columbus, OH 43215

Voice: 614-555-1234
Fax: 614-555-1235
E-mail: hjenkins@company.com

Revision #:	1.0	Supersedes:	N/A	Date:	03/18/08

Policy additions or revisions are communicated using the form shown in Exhibit 5-3, either as a hardcopy form or as a web page on the corporate

EXHIBIT 5-3.   Policy Suggestion Form

<table>
<tr><td colspan="4" align="center">Policy Suggestion Form</td></tr>
<tr><td>Name/Title:</td><td colspan="3"></td></tr>
<tr><td>Department:</td><td></td><td>Date:</td><td></td></tr>
<tr><td colspan="4">Manual Area:</td></tr>
<tr><td>Chapter:</td><td></td><td colspan="2">☐ New Policy</td></tr>
<tr><td>Section:</td><td></td><td colspan="2">☐ Change Existing Policy</td></tr>
<tr><td>Page(s):</td><td></td><td colspan="2"></td></tr>
<tr><td colspan="4">Suggested Policy/Changes:
Write the proposed needed revision. Attach any necessary details, along with supporting documentation.</td></tr>
<tr><td colspan="4">Rationale:
Describe the problem and how it is affecting the current operation or will affect future operations. How will the proposed revision resolve the problem?</td></tr>
<tr><td>Signed:</td><td></td><td>Date:</td><td></td></tr>
<tr><td>Approved By:</td><td></td><td>Date:</td><td></td></tr>
<tr><td>Approved/Disapproved:</td><td></td><td>Date:</td><td></td></tr>
<tr><td>Revision Completed By:</td><td></td><td>Date:</td><td></td></tr>
<tr><td colspan="4">Comments:</td></tr>
</table>

intranet. If a web page is used, a link to a web page showing the acceptance criteria should be included.

[B]   Policy Creation Process

The policy manager identified above is responsible for developing and following a standard process for creating new policies. This policy should define:

- Who can originate a policy suggestion?
- How the need for a new policy is determined.
- How is a priority assigned to the policy?
- Who develops the initial policy?
- The review process for the suggested policy (some firms have a formal policy review committee for review and change control; for others, this is ad hoc).
- How revisions are handled.
- Is this a mandated policy?
- Who approves the policy?
- How is the master policy manual updated?

[C]   Policy Acceptance Criteria

Policy suggestions are made either by filling out the Policy Suggestion Form (Exhibit 5-3) and delivering it to the policy manager or by filling out a form on the corporate intranet. The form must be filled out completely in order for the policy to be considered. The policy manager will use the following criteria to determine if a suggestion is accepted and a new policy is written or changes made to an existing one. Few suggestions will meet all criteria; the policy manager must balance strengths against shortcomings in evaluating each suggestion. Any of the following criteria may provide an overwhelming reason to accept or reject a specific suggestion. Policy suggestions made by upper management will be automatically accepted.

A. **Purpose.** The purpose of the policy suggestion must be stated clearly and be relevant to the mission, goals, and operations of the organization.
B. **Audience.** The suggestion must address and identify the intended users of the policy, and satisfy some real or perceived need of this audience.
C. **Authority.** The policy manager must have the authority to issue policy for the area in question.
D. **Currency.** The suggested policy must apply to current and/or future activities.
E. **Scope.** The scope of the suggestion must match the expectations of the intended audience.
F. **Uniqueness.** To avoid needless duplication of effort, the information contained in a new policy should not already be covered in any existing policy.

G. **Organizational impact.** A new policy suggestion should have a positive impact on the operations of the organization. Suggestions with a greater impact will have a higher priority than those with a lower impact. Impact assessments must address cost-benefit and forecast return on investment.

H. **Urgency.** Suggestions with a higher degree of urgency will have a higher priority than those with a lower one. Policy requests mandated by law or upper management will have a higher priority.

[D]   Manual Maintenance

Permanent manual revisions will be sequentially identified, after the word "Rev.," at the top right-hand side of each section's first page. Temporary policies or procedures supersede permanent policies and procedures. The permanent policies will remain in the manual; they can only be replaced by the issuance of replacement policies and/or procedures. In the event a policy and/or procedure is to be discontinued, an order will be issued by the person who originally approved the policy and/or procedure or by a successor or agent in writing. Requests for temporary or permanent policy and/or procedures will be handled as follows:

A. Any user, management person, information technology person, workgroup head, or manual holder may submit a request for a temporary policy and/or procedure or for a permanent revision to the Information Technology Policies & Procedures Manual.

B. Revision requests will be handled in the following manner:
   1. Request a revision using the Policy Suggestion Form in Exhibit 5-3.
   2. Submit one copy to the approving authority (or successor) for the policy and/or procedure.
   3. The final authority will review the request and approve or deny it, providing a reason for any action taken. The person assigned to investigate the request will be identified. The person assigned to determine the course of action necessary might also be the approval authority. The recommended course of action may result in a feasibility study if the required undertaking is large or expensive enough.
   4. If the initial request is denied, the person requesting the change may move up the chain of command to the appropriate level needed for resolution.

C. Revised documentation will be issued simultaneously to all affected manual holders using print or electronic means. The person responsible for maintaining the manual and any local area network or stand-alone PC policies will keep a current list of all manual holders with a partial or complete manual. Partial manual holders, who will have identified which sections they receive, will be cross-indexed by those sections. When a particular section is replaced, a list of appropriate manual holders may be provided for distribution. The lists may be maintained in a database and distribution lists printed as needed.

When permanent revisions are issued, all pages for the given section will be reissued. If corrections to current procedures are required and numbering is not affected, only the affected pages need be distributed. This applies to both temporary and permanent policies and/or procedures. All releases will have a cover memo noting:

A. The person issuing the release.
B. The effective date(s) of the release.
C. The reason for the release.

[E]   Annual Policy Review

Once per year, all policies will be reviewed by management for updating. These changes will follow the same review process as normal change requests except that they may be reviewed all at once. Following these updates, all policies will be reviewed annually with the IT employees. Some policies, especially those with legal ramifications, will be reviewed in their entirety (such as conflict of interest), while others will be reviewed by summarizing them in a simple paragraph.

[F]   Sunset Clause

Every policy has its day, and eventually, that day will pass. After a policy has been in effect for five years (or whatever time period you feel is appropriate for your organization), it should be closely examined as to its currency. Technology changes, people change, and business objectives change. Policies should also change. After five years, the policy should be rewritten to reflect current business needs.

6

PROJECT MANAGEMENT: GETTING IT OUT ON TIME

§ 6.01   OVERVIEW
    [A]   Purpose and Scope
    [B]   Critical Policies to Develop Based on This Chapter

§ 6.02   PROJECT MANAGEMENT FUNDAMENTALS
    [A]   Project Definition
    [B]   What a Project Is Not
    [C]   The Project Manager
    [D]   Creating the Project Plan
    [E]   Adding Resources to the Plan
    [F]   Essential Estimating Factors
    [G]   Hardware and Software Delivery
    [H]   Sponsor's Sign-off

§ 6.03   IMPORTANT ELEMENTS OF THE PROJECT PLAN
    [A]   Overview
    [B]   Risk Assessment
    [C]   Organizing a Project Risk Analysis
    [D]   Mitigation Plans
    [E]   Stakeholder Analysis
    [F]   Communications Plan

§ 6.04   EXECUTING THE PROJECT
    [A]   Managing the Project
    [B]   Scope Change
    [C]   Basic Rules for Managing Projects
    [D]   Task Completion
    [E]   Progress Measurement

§ 6.05   PROJECT CLOSEOUT
    [A]   Overview
    [B]   Sponsor
    [C]   Accounting Department
    [D]   Customer
    [E]   Team Members
    [F]   Contractual Issues and Contract Employees
    [G]   Final Project Report

§ 6.06   PROJECT MANAGEMENT OFFICE
         [A]   Overview
         [B]   How to Do It
         [C]   Establish a Tool Set
         [D]   Resource Management
         [E]   Executive Steering Committee
         [F]   Standardized Project Initiation
         [G]   Project Backlog Management
         [H]   Metrics

§ 6.01 OVERVIEW

[A] Purpose and Scope

Project management is the management of uncertainty. Through a series of analyses, large tasks are broken into their component parts, analyzed, and shaped into a plan. Project management is to a great degree the art of people management, as people are a project manager's primary tools. If someone moves a lever on a machine tool, they are a machinist. However, if they direct the people who work the tools in concert, they are a manager.

Project management is something everyone practices whether we realize it or not. Imagine planning a vacation. There was a destination to select and, for most people, a limit of how much could be spent. There was a time set to arrive at the airport, specific items to pack (a parka is not needed at the beach!), hotel and car reservations at the destination, and on and on. This scenario has all of the elements of a basic project plan.

The destination was the project's "goal," the budget was a resource constraint on activities, and traveling was a part of the action steps. With the goal in mind, a series of actions was identified, sequenced, and executed to successfully arrive at the vacation spot and to return. Resources, such as money and vacation time from work, were allocated and used to complete the project. An alternative to this scenario would be to decide at this moment to take a vacation, put everyone in the car, and drive off. Given the lack of preparation, it is doubtful that this would be a very happy experience.

> ## COMMENT
>
> For an in-depth explanation about project management and its many components, refer to *IT Project Management Essentials* by Aspenpublishers.com.

Project management is something that everyone encounters every day. Have you ever driven past a construction site? Are the workers busy or idle? Idle workers cost the builder money. How is the structure completed without bankrupting the builder's company in the process? If the workers are present and there are not any materials to use, they still must be paid for the day. If the materials are there but the workers are not, the materials may be damaged by the weather.

Another big user of project management is the military. They frequently organize the movement of large amounts of equipment and people, ensuring fuel, food, and water are available along the route. They station mechanics and tow trucks so that vehicles may be fueled or repaired at various points along the journey. As an added challenge, this movement may be through mountains or a jungle, or alongside a hostile population.

In short, project management is nothing new and quite widely used in government and business. From these examples, the essential elements can be identified:

A. **Sponsor.** Someone is authorizing this work and has a stake in its success. The sponsor is the project's "protector," keeping others from pulling it too far off course. The sponsor (or customer) is the one who "hired" the project manager and approves the bills. The sponsor ensures that the project has the resources necessary for success. The sponsor is kept informed of the project's progress and of any major decisions made about the project. Some sponsors seek to be actively involved with the project and others want to be left alone until it is finished.

B. **Goal.** What is this project trying to achieve? A clear vision of the project's goal makes it easier for everyone involved in the project to participate in its success. In the case of the vacation, the family can visualize the fun they will have at the beach and pack their own suitcases accordingly. Establishing a clearly defined goal is an important step in planning a project. A project creates *something*, such as a product or service. If the Project Manager cannot visualize the goal, it will be hard for him to explain it to others. Goals must be specific and measurable.

Often the goal is expanded as a list of success factors or requirements that must be achieved. For a data processing project, this might include reducing response time by half a second, the ability to search a specific web site, or requiring all technical documentation to be submitted before payment. A list of specific, measurable criteria is essential for clarifying what is often a vaguely worded goal.

C. **Scope.** Project scope defines the specific who's, what's, where's and timing of the project to the best knowledge of the project team. The project team must take into account constraints when defining the scope. How broad is this project? What are its boundaries? What departments are affected? For the vacation, one boundary and constraint was the amount of money available to pay for it. Another boundary was the number of vacation days that were available. All projects have boundaries whether they are obvious or not.

Establishing project boundaries reduces the likelihood of the project drifting off course and costing more than expected. Having a good handle on scope is necessary when estimating project resources and project schedules.

D. **Assumptions and Risks.** It is rare for a decision to be made with all of the necessary information at hand. This is especially difficult when writing plans for future action. Throughout the planning process, decisions are made based on assumptions. Often an assumption must be made as to when a specific resource will be available or how something will work in order to continue with the planning process. Maintain a list of each assumption and the decisions it affects. Review the list periodically with the sponsor. The project plan will be more realistic if errors in the assumptions are caught early.

Every project has risks. It is important to identify and periodically review the significant project risks. When identifying risks, include with each risk the conditions that trigger the risk, any risk mitigating actions that can be taken, and when the risk no longer affects the project.

E. **Start date and time.** Every project has a point in time where it began. Sometimes it is considered started when the boss says to set up a project to do something. Sometimes the start date is set in advance (e.g., beginning the project on the first day of the next fiscal year). However it is established, a project has not been properly launched until it has written goals and scope statements. They act as anchors to keep a project from drifting off course.

F. **End date and time.** A project must have an end. Sometimes the end is when the goal is achieved. Other times, an end is declared and whatever is completed must be delivered. There are two ways to establish an end date. The first (and often unrealistic) way is for the executives to mandate a completion date. However, sometimes this date is selected to meet a legal requirement and is out of their control. The second way is to develop a project plan that, based on the tasks, resources, and time estimates, indicates when the project should be completed and present that plan to executives for approval. Like most things in life, a project "takes as long as it takes," no matter what date executives may select.

G. **Resources.** Projects use resources to achieve their goals. Resources may be skilled workers for a construction company or cash for the vacation. Resources may be vehicles, fuel, food, and water for the military exercise. Resources are any item or person used to complete a project task. Identifying, quantifying, and coordinating resources is an important part of project planning. Resource requirements overlooked in planning will not be in the budget or project timeline and the project will assuredly go "off course."

COMMENT

Each resource has its own level of efficiency. Be specific when describing a resource. Using highly skilled resources, like master carpenters, will shorten a project but will add cost. Using an apprentice carpenter on a non-critical task may take longer, but be more cost effective.

H. **Predecessors.** Predecessors are tasks that must be completed before another task can begin, similar to prerequisite courses in school. Students cannot sign up for Algebra II until they complete Algebra I. A PC technician cannot load software onto a computer before it is purchased and delivered. The chain of tasks and their predecessors make up the length of time a project is expected to last.

> # COMMENT
>
> It is recommended that the Project Manager use some sort of project management software to organize project tasks into a plan. This software will automatically draw Gantt and CPM network charts, level resources, and recalculate the project schedule every time a date changes or a task is completed.

[B]   Critical Policies to Develop Based on This Chapter

Using the material discussed in this chapter, you will be able to create the following policies:

A.   Project plan requirements.
    1.   Required documents for starting a project and their format.
    2.   How resources are assigned to the project.
    3.   The role and requirements of the project sponsor.
B.   Project documents used to manage a project.
    1.   How risk assessments are to be performed and documented.
    2.   The requirements for communicating with project stakeholders.
    3.   Policy on frequency and format of project meetings.
C.   Project execution procedures.
    1.   How scope changes are processed.
    2.   How project progress is measured and reported.
    3.   Standards for managing a project.
D.   Project close out procedures.
    1.   Requirements and responsibilities of all project stakeholders.
    2.   Requirements for a final project report.

Policies should always be developed based on the local situation. Successful managers cannot issue appropriate guidance if the policies are written with another company's or location's situation in mind.

§ 6.02   PROJECT MANAGEMENT FUNDAMENTALS

[A]   Project Definition

Start at the beginning, the project's origination. Someone might think that an activity as expensive and important to a company as a project would include a formal beginning. Someone might think that, but often it is not the case.

In many companies, a project is verbally assigned by the sponsor—no formal goals are established; no clear description of the end product is given; no discussion is had of the resources required. There is just a single sentence order to make it happen.

However a challenge is assigned, the first thing to do is to ensure that the project manager's vision of the project is the same as the sponsor's. To do this, the project manager should recap notes concerning the project into a statement of the project's goals, scope, budget, start time, end time, and authority. All management parties involved must agree to these items, including user management and the project manager.

COMMENT

Projects are created to solve a business problem. A project description should state the problem, how it harms the company, how it will be solved, and the benefits derived from it.

A clear definition of a project's goal is essential. Sometimes the sponsor is intentionally vague. The sponsor may not be sure what the result should look like. In this situation, the project manager should help the sponsor to shape ideas and clearly define what the project is to achieve. Often, the sponsor is trying to solve a specific business problem. Keep asking the sponsor about the functions and features required in the product. Ask questions that begin with general subjects and then gradually narrow down to specific issues. Dig out the details. From this conversation, develop a list of requirements or "criteria of success" that describes the end object in some detail. It may help the sponsor to visualize the result if the project manager creates mock-up floor plans, computer screens, and reports.

All projects have boundaries. The project scope helps to define what is within the bounds of a project. Everything not detailed in the project scope is outside of the boundaries and should not be included in the project. For example, a data entry program is not intended to manage the controls on a building's air conditioning. It is not intended to run the monthly accounting reports that reconcile all accounts. Its only intended purpose is to enable the entry of data into a specific system.

Project scope should include such things as:

A. This program is to support the Dayton Assembly Plant. (No other facility.)
B. The data entry system will support the entry of Department 69's scrap material information. (No other department's requirements need to be accommodated.)

C. The data entry program will be written in Java, for use on PCs running LINUX. (This precludes using other languages or operating system versions.)

D. The data entry program will connect to the AS400 server via the corporate intranet. (This means the program will not use any other server or connection methodology.)

E. Systems installation will be transparent to users. (No downtime during normal working hours will be permitted.)

The project goals describe how the project's end product will look and function. Remember, *goals must be specific and measurable.* The project manager should create a memo of understanding that summarizes the project goals, including the criteria for success and the project scope, and then present it to the sponsor for approval. Before doing anything on this project, the project manager must clearly understand what the objective is and is not. This document synchronizes the project manager's vision of the project with the sponsor's vision. As the project progresses, "scope creep" will appear—where executives want to add features to the project, gradually spinning it out of control. The signed memo acts as the anchor to reduce the likelihood that this will happen.

[B]   What a Project Is Not

A project is used to create something that is unique. Milking a cow three times a day is not a project. It is an ongoing operation. Yes, the changes in the weather, the cow's attitude, the farmer's attitude, and the smell of the barn all make each milking a unique experience; however, essentially the same resources are used repeatedly to achieve the same goal.

If someone wanted to be argumentative, the discussion of what is or is not a project could go on for hours. In an IT setting, this means that making back-up tapes is not a project. Answering the service desk telephone is not a project, but developing a new data entry program is a project because it has unique tasks with start and end dates.

Projects do not have a defined size. For example, the department's barbeque may only take one person to plan and execute, but it still is a project. Some of the tasks include making a shopping list, starting the coals at the right time, etc. It has distinct start and end dates. The next time there is a barbeque, likely different resources will be used. "Personal" project planning is primarily a way to reduce the likelihood of missing an important item or appointment.

For most IT people, a project is something larger than a family cookout. It involves creating something that is complex, requires assistance from others, and is completed within a set timeframe. Well-run projects add value to the company and poorly-run projects drain cash without any return.

Overall, a project consists of four major areas:

A. **Project definition.** The goals, scope, assumptions, and risks are identified, thus defining the project. The project definition phase lays the foundation on which the project plan is built.

B. **Project planning.** An action plan is assembled to create what was described in the project definition. A good plan can be executed by a mediocre project manager—a bad plan is living hell from day one!

C. **Project management.** A military maxim is that all well-made battle plans go out the window after the first bullet is fired. Plans may look easy on paper, but bringing them to fruition may be difficult. This phase involves executing the project plan and ensuring the end product is true to its defined requirements. Executing a plan requires agility, good information, and the ability to work through adverse situations on short notice.

D. **Project closeout.** When the project is completed, the resources must be reallocated, the budget closed, and the project documentation gathered for later reference.

[C]   The Project Manager

A project's success depends on many factors, but the key element is the careful selection of a project manager. Project managers wear many hats:

A. Leader of team (not manager—a project manager must be a leader).
B. Negotiator with team members' home department managers.
C. Part-time accountant to track project budget.
D. All-around cheerleader and advocate of project's success. If the project manager does not believe in the project's success and work to convince others of it, then everyone will know the project is doomed. Workers will abandon a doomed project.

A project manager does not succeed by writing the code or turning a screwdriver. Success is achieved by coordinating the efforts of others to accomplish these tasks. A project manager lost in the minutia of details will not have the time to focus the efforts of others. Most technical professionals lack the administrative and interpersonal skills needed to function effectively in this position. With a bit of mentoring, they can rise to the challenge.

Selecting a project manager is the joint responsibility of the sponsor and the IT Manager. Choosing a candidate requires knowledge of attributes that have been proven to be universally successful. The only testimonial a person really needs is a successful track record with the company. However, a person selected as project manager for the first time requires special consideration.

[D]   Creating the Project Plan

With a top-notch project manager assigned and a clear vision of the project's objective, it is time to begin charting a course for the project's completion. Based on the criteria for success, the project manager has an idea of what is required to get from where the company is to where it wants to be. Based on an evaluation of the project goals, determine the technical expertise necessary to successfully complete the project and invite representatives from affected areas to a project-planning meeting. Included with the invitation should be a copy of the project's approved goals and scope. The people invited may be the ones who will work on the project or they may be subject experts who will help to define the skill set needed for the project. A representative of the people who will be using the final product should always be invited.

The planning meeting follows a simple format. First, the project's goals should be discussed to determine whether there are any major implied tasks that have not been foreseen. These could extend the project's timeline. Next, the scope should be discussed to ensure it is in line with the goals and addresses potential problem areas.

Now is the time to build a plan! It is a long journey from a blank piece of paper to a well-considered project plan. The first step is to draft an initial plan to build a framework for action and to fill in as many steps as possible. Once the initial plan is on paper, the remaining details can be identified. There are many ways to do this. Consider these basic approaches to drafting an initial project plan:

A. **Brainstorming.** This is a useful approach when the project flow is not immediately obvious. It is most useful when major parallel efforts obscure a clear vision of the plan, or the project is something the company has never done before.

One effective brainstorming method is to use "sticky notes" and a large whiteboard. Each sticky note is equal to a task on the project plan. Anyone can call out an action necessary to the plan, such as "build the data entry screen," "identify field edits," or "coordinate with the database administrators." The tasks do not need to be in any particular order. One person is assigned to capture the ideas onto large sticky notes and attach them to the whiteboard as they are called out. A second person moderates the discussion and keeps the conversation focused and flowing. All ideas are posted and no idea is criticized.

The team next selects group names and then indicates in which group each task logically belongs. Duplicate or overlapping tasks are consolidated or clarified. Group names might include "planning," "testing," "coding," and "documentation."

Finally, the tasks and groups are organized into a logical process flow from the beginning of the project to the end. The flow specifies which processes are predecessors to what tasks and represents the initial project plan. All of this information should then be written down and/or entered into project management software.

B. **Left to right, block diagram.** If the project is for something the team is familiar with, a list of tasks from start to finish can be made. A whiteboard should be used since there will be some modifications as the planning progresses. Left to right means that the tasks will be identified in the approximate order in which they will appear on the plan.

C. **Top down.** This approach starts with a very general task overview and then breaks each task down repeatedly until the lowest level tasks are identified. When dealing with a new idea, start by breaking the goals down one level at a time. Consider a five-block diagram where each block represents a phase of the project: "Define, Analyze, Code, Test, and Implement." Under each block, list the actions required to achieve these project goals. Next, break each block into its major components. On the lowest level of the breakdown (use as many as needed), identify any additional tasks. Then, organize the tasks into a logical flow and eliminate overlapping actions.

D. **Straw man.** Based on the project manager's experience, draft the project plan including as many tasks as the project manager can identify. Use previous project plans to help flesh it out. Present this plan to the group and ask them to critique its overall flow, content, etc. This approach is not for the thin-skinned as its purpose is to generate discussion by questioning every inch of the plan. It works best if the project manager already has a long-term positive project management relationship with the group.

For some people, this is the quickest way to develop a plan. When confronted with a blank page, many people simply stare at it unsure where to begin. On the other hand, if the team does not feel a personal stake in the project's success, they may rubber stamp the plan without suggesting any improvements.

With the tasks formed into a basic plan, the project manager should write a brief paragraph about each task to describe the meaning of the task name. For instance, if the task is to "build a data entry screen," it might be described as:

> "Write a Java program to build a visual screen to accept the 10 data fields on the Order Entry form. Edit every field for length and format, and validate against a table of acceptable values as required."

The project manager includes as much detail as necessary to describe the goals and scope for the desired task. These narratives will come in handy later when assigning tasks to team members. Some tasks, like the example on Order Entry, will highlight additional requirements. If the Order Entry screen is to validate against a table of acceptable values (such as in a drop-down box), then a way for someone to update the table must be provided. How is this table to be originally populated? When the narratives have been written, they should be sent with the plan to the planning team members, and a meeting scheduled to discuss it.

At the next meeting, each task should be discussed and validated. Discuss where the tasks most logically fit on the chart. This exercise, while tedious, should weed out most of the overlapping requirements and fill in any requirements that have been overlooked.

[E]   Adding Resources to the Plan

Up to this point, the project planning has been all theoretical. Adding resources to the plan throws the cold water of reality right into its face! A lack of resource availability when it is needed is a common factor in project delays. Highly technical resources are scarce. Often they are lined up at the beginning of the project and asked to be available for certain days. As the project moves forward, a small delay here and a brief setback there and pretty soon the entire resource plan will be askew.

Before estimating time on the project, detail the technical and business expertise level expected from each position. Technical skills can be identified by job title, such as "programmer." Level of expertise can be indicated by a title modifier, such as "senior" and "junior." (Some people prefer the suffixes I, II, III, or IV since being identified as a "junior" might be viewed negatively.) Assigning a task to an unqualified person can create delays and mistakes, while assigning the same task to an overqualified person wastes resources. When time permits, the manager should consider using project tasks to develop or enhance team members' skills.

Together with the team, add a time estimate and the resources required for each task. Break tasks into their components until they are small enough to estimate the time and resources required. When allocating task worker-hours, the project manager should note the worker's past record for finishing in the time allowed. The project manager should check with the assigned worker to confirm that the time allowed is reasonable. If not, a different time allowance should be negotiated. In addition, contingency time should be added, if needed, based on the worker's past performance record. If there is no previous record, time allowed should be more liberal. Ten percent above the original estimate is not unreasonable. The project manager should recalculate the project time based on this new information, rearranging the schedule as needed. When the project management software has analyzed this data, the project manager should complete the final staffing plans for the project.

[F]　Essential Estimating Factors

Estimating completion dates and the work-hours required become more accurate as the project advances. Unfortunately, it is most helpful to have this level of accuracy early in the project. If the organization has previously completed a similar project, the actual times required to complete tasks should be used to build time estimates.

COMMENT

Time Estimation Pitfalls

- Research has shown that project members who estimate their own performance for completion times are consistently optimistic.
- If a worker perceives that a task assigned to take three weeks will only require one week, then he is more likely to do something else for the first two weeks and then address the task. If the worker then realizes that the one week estimate was too low, he will blame the project manager!

> • To reduce the likelihood of workers misjudging the time required for a task, always schedule tasks tightly. If a task has slack time, move the due date that much closer and remove the slack. Only allow the worker the time required to perform the task.

Factors that affect the estimate accuracy and ways to minimize this distortion are:

A. **Project size.** The project size can affect the time and effort needed for completion. This in turn can affect the amount of calendar time needed and the final cost. Businesses exist in a very fluid environment. The longer the project takes, the more likely it is that the business sponsor will require additional changes. Changes that will be required for a usable product will also take additional time to install, which can justifiably lead to more changes. This is called the "snowball effect."

   To reduce this possibility, projects should be as small as possible. Changes made after project completion will then be maintenance changes to a tested system already in operation. This is preferable to making the same changes to a yet-to-be-debugged product. Large projects should be completed in phases with each phase ending in a working part of the product. Projects do not need to be an all-or-nothing affair.

B. **Project complexity.** The more project variables there are to manage, the more time and effort the project will take to complete. Complex projects are more difficult to estimate. They should be cut down into smaller modules for easier and more accurate estimation.

C. **Personnel productivity.** This is a universal problem with system and programming departments. In the IT data entry unit, the output minus the errors defines the person's productivity. If the source documents are simply input, the system for judging a worker's output is simple and fairly accurate. This is not the case with the systems and programming production estimates.

   A systems analyst's past performance can be a gauge for estimating future performance for similar tasks. The difference in the output of programmers has been estimated to be as high as 20:1 between the best and the worst. A person's activity level should never be confused with his or her results.

   When using in-house employees on the team, the project manager must take a hard look at their expertise. Some companies are willing to pay for good contract programmers, but not willing to pay competitive wages for better in-house programmers. A poorly performing programmer can reduce the group's total output. Consider contract programmers to help raise the expertise of their employees by mixing in-house and contract programmers in the project.

D. **Resources available.** Resources must have quality, but they must also be available in quantity. There is no assurance that the people promised for the project will be available when needed. The longer the duration of the project, the greater this problem can become. People leave, retire, are promoted, or are reassigned to other higher-priority projects.

If possible, the project manager should make sure funds are budgeted to hire outside contractors. It is better to have this money in reserve than to ask for it mid-project and be rejected.

E. **Resource technology.** The physical and technical resources available to the project team affect the time estimate as well. These items can include:

1. **Work area.** The team's work area can affect the productivity estimate. Is the project team housed together in a private area or spread out into different locations in noisy offices?

2. **Programming tools.** Are the programming tools familiar to the staff? If the tools are new, will training be available in time to be effective?

3. **Computer hardware.** Are the workstations fast and efficient or old and slow? Are notebook computers needed? Will everything be in place and ready to use when the notebooks arrive? What about e-mail and voice mail?

4. **Project management software.** Always use project management software. It will reduce the amount of administrative time and effort required.

When working through the project plan development process, the project managers should determine the level of detail desired in the plan. Should there be a single item for "Develop a Data Entry Program" or should it be a heading with task items under it for "Analyze," "Code," "Test," "Document," and "Deliver the Completed Package"?

Estimating time is tough. If possible, use the experience from past projects to estimate how long a step might take. Time estimates often depend on the resource. The difference in time it takes to accomplish tasks with specific resources can be compared to the time it takes to walk, run, or swim a quarter mile. Moving a person a quarter mile may be the task, but what a difference the resource of "movement choice" makes.

Create a resource calendar to indicate the availability of each resource. Be sure to include all company holidays. Ask prospective team members about their vacation/time-off plans. Include this information on the resource calendar for that person. Unfortunately, at the time the calendar is being established, some vacation plans may not yet have been scheduled and key people may already be lined up for other projects. The longer the project will be, the harder this factor will be to control. So again, the plan at this stage is still theoretical. Add to the growing list of assumptions the names of the resources expected to be available for this project and how much of their time will be needed. They may be full-time, half-time, or available on demand to help with a "spot" issue or whatever is needed.

At this point, tasks have been identified, resources assigned to each one, and an estimation has been made of the time required to complete each task. Assumptions have been stated as to which resources will be available and when.

Unfortunately, really good workers can be in short supply. It is not unusual for managers to "overbook" their best people to conflicting tasks. To smooth out the plan based on resource availability, use the resource leveling function in the project management software. This function will review every task and identify the resources overcommitted on the project. This will help the project manager to change work assignments, rearrange the sequence of events, or change their durations to smooth out the conflicts. This capability however depends on an accurate resource availability calendar.

Print the project plan diagram and highlight the time required to complete the longest path through the plan. This is the critical path. Most project management software will identify the critical path automatically. Reducing the time spent on tasks along the critical path will reduce the length of time required for the project—unless the changes create a new critical path!

Once again, review the plan with the project team. Review every assumption used to resolve resource conflicts and to reduce the critical path. Are they all still valid? This is the last review before meeting with the sponsor again. Make it good.

Next, roll up the costs identified with each task in terms of hardware, software, consultants, etc. These costs should be detailed on a month-by-month projection to show the cash flow necessary to sustain the project.

[G]   Hardware and Software Delivery

Identify the required dates for the project's software and hardware delivery. Use backward planning to place orders in time to have the items in-house when needed. Contact the vendor a week before the due date to ensure the material will arrive on time. Take appropriate action if it will be late. Key items should have extra lead-time planned to avoid project delays.

COMMENT

Backward planning means to assign due dates to tasks starting with the last task in the chain and working back to the first one. For example, if a company needs PCs ready to install software on the 30th of the month, then they must be in place on the 28th. Therefore, since they must be unpacked the week before (21st), they must be ordered two weeks before that (7th) and the purchasing document must be sent to the sponsor the week before that (1st of the month).

Delays may be caused for any of the following reasons:

A. Custom-fabricated hardware.
B. Custom-purchased software.
C. Shipping problems because of distance (delays are more likely when items are imported).
D. Items that have to be scheduled for processing (e.g., custom-printed forms).
E. Plants closed for vacation, holidays, or because of a strike.

Items should not be delivered too far in advance. If bulky items come in before they are needed, there could be a storage problem, incurring an unnecessary expenditure. IT hardware ordered too far in advance could become obsolete before installation or their costs could be lowered. If bulky items come in before they are needed, there could be a storage problem, incurring an unnecessary expenditure. IT hardware ordered too far in advance could become obsolete before installation or their costs could be lowered.

COMMENT

One nervous project manager was so afraid that his project budget would be cut that he purchased all the equipment the project required as soon as the project was approved. Due to programming delays, it was 18 months before the timekeeping system was ready for rollout to the customer. Meanwhile, the warranty had expired on the equipment that had yet to be unpacked! The project budget had to assume the burden for repair costs for any dead-on-arrival equipment. Even worse, most of the equipment consisted of PCs. By waiting 18 months to purchase the PCs, the equipment's capabilities would have almost doubled!

[H] Sponsor's Sign-off

Prepare a project review packet for the sponsor's approval. Schedule a team meeting where the project plan and budget are reviewed with the sponsor. Walk through the plan step by step and the budget item by item. Obtain final approval and a start date (which is usually dictated by resource availability).

The packet should contain a:

A. Cover sheet with an executive summary explaining how long the project will take and how much it will cost. A recap of the project's goal and scope should be included.

B. Printed project plan with Gantt chart.
C. Budget required to complete the project.
D. List of assumptions made when developing the project plan and budget.
E. List of the internal resources required to finish the project plan within the time stated.

With a bit of good luck, the sponsor's adjustments to the plan will be minor and the project can begin. With bad luck, the sponsor will slash the budget, slash the timeline, and threaten the project manager if the project is late. Such is a project manager's lot!

§ 6.03 IMPORTANT ELEMENTS OF THE PROJECT PLAN

[A] Overview

There are tools that will help to identify and avoid the various management pitfalls that may plague a project as the plan unfolds. These adjunct plans are very useful for small project plans but are essential for large projects. No project flows smoothly. The best of them are roller-coaster rides of problems and successes. The rest of them start as a disaster and speed rapidly downhill from there.

[B] Risk Assessment

A risk assessment looks at the project plan and identifies those areas where something might go wrong. It could be an incorrect assumption. It could be a resource that is not available until weeks after its scheduled availability date. It could be overlooked systems requirements that mean additional tasks for the schedule not in the budget or timeline.

A risk assessment is a review of the project in light of what could go wrong, how likely it is to occur, and how damaging it would be if it did happen. Based on these factors, a numerical score is assigned to identify those risks that should be reduced through a mitigation plan.

Certainties are things we know will happen. The sun will rise tomorrow. The risk of this not happening is zero percent. Risks dwell in the area of uncertainty. Risks are things that may or may not occur. Although anticipating good things is very uplifting personally, a project's risk plan mostly focuses on the risk of negative events. Making a risk assessment is easier for a pessimistic person.

Risks have their own characteristics, such as the likelihood of occurring. A meteor may one day fall from the sky and hit someone on the head, but the likelihood of that is very, very small. The likelihood of someone attempting to add on to the project's scope is fairly high. The likelihood of a risk occurring must be viewed within the context of the project.

A second risk characteristic is the impact of an event if it actually occurs. In the case of the meteor, the impact would be catastrophic. Normally something this dangerous would make someone want to walk around with a steel plate on his or her head to ward off falling space rocks. But given its low likelihood, the person would soon tire of the plate and it would be discarded.

[C] Organizing a Project Risk Analysis

The Risk Assessment form in Exhibit 6-1 is a good place to start building a project's risk analysis. This form will be the basis of the following discussion.

Identification section

A. Task is the name or identifier of the task under evaluation. This also may refer to a group of tasks or to all tasks under a milestone.
B. Risk is a description of the risk associated with the task.

Quantification section

A. Likelihood is an estimate of the probability that the risk will become a reality. Some risks are very real, but very unlikely to occur.
B. Impact is how badly the event would damage the project's scope, budget, or timeline if it occurred.
C. Warning is how much warning the team would have before this event occurred. In the case of a hurricane, someone could monitor the weather reports for days and plan accordingly. In the case of an earthquake, the team would likely have no warning before it struck.
D. Score is a numeric risk score based on the previous three values.

The scales for Likelihood and Impact are from 1 to 10, with 1 as extremely unlikely and 10 as a sure thing. Any consistent numbering system can be used for the scores, but if it includes a zero as a value, then that entire risk will be scored as zero.

The Warning column is scored the reverse from the other two. It is also rated from 1 (a lot of warning) to 10 (no warning). A risk typically accompanied with a lot of warning should be rated very low. A risk that could occur with little or no warning should be rated high since the project team would not have time to react.

A risk's Score is determined by multiplying the three columns (Likelihood, Impact, and Warning) together. The higher the score, the greater the attention that must be paid to that risk.

The Score is the key to the analysis. Once all of the risks are scored, the entire spreadsheet should be sorted based on this column in *descending* order. This brings the risks with the highest score to the top. At some point in the list, draw a line across it. Anything below this point will be monitored, but no further action taken. As the project progresses, review the risks below the line every milestone or monthly to see if they should be moved up the list or dropped all together.

EXHIBIT 6-1. Project Risk Management Plan

Project Risk Management Plan

WBS # / Description	QUANTIFICATION				Damage		Trigger	Risk Event Status	Actual Results	Mitigation Actions	Assigned To	Date	Comments
	Likelihood	Impact	Warning	Score	$ At Stake	Time at Slake							
				0									
				0									
				0									
				0									
				0									
				0									
				0									
				0									
				0									
				0									
				0									

Damage section

If this risk became reality, what would its impact be on the project? Damage is divided into two types: financial impact and timeline impact.

    A. Money at stake—How severely would this risk damage the project budget? For example, if the risk was that the task might overrun its schedule and incur additional costs for contracted programmers, how much would this be? Are there legal fines to pay or bonuses lost for being late?

    B. Time at stake—How long would this risk delay the project's completion? Use the same unit of time as used by the project plan (e.g., days, weeks).

These two factors describe the damage in various ways. For example, if a task is not on the critical path and it is late, it may not damage the project in either category, unless a change in the plan suddenly elevates that task onto the critical path. Some companies establish a risk guideline that the most a risk can put at stake financially is the budgeted cash outlay for that task.

Risk containment section

    A. The "Trigger" column describes events that would enable this risk to occur. The trigger column alerts the Project Manager that the conditions are right for this risk to arise. For example:
       1. A task becomes at risk of being late only after it has begun.
       2. The implementation phase of a project may be at risk of delay if the project is approaching the company's annual busy season.
       3. The project may be at risk of losing a sponsor's support if that executive is replaced or if the project falls significantly behind the plan.
       4. The project may be at risk if the company releases a financial report indicating excessive losses, which may signal an upcoming budget cut.

    B. The Risk Event Status column indicates if this risk is past, pending, or in the future. This column is useful for a quick review of risks looming on the horizon. The Risk Analysis spreadsheet is a valuable historical tool to review whenever new projects are started, and this column allows valid risks to remain on the document even after they pass. Valid values for this column are:
       1. Past—The task at risk is completed.
       2. Pending—The task at risk is in process or about to start.
       3. Future—The task at risk is in the future.

    C. Actual Results is the outcome of the risk once it has occurred or passed. Valuable project documentation for lessons learned and historical purposes can be pulled from this column. Did the risk occur? Were the triggers useful or incorrect? What was the impact? Which mitigation steps were the most effective? The least? Make the column as large as needed or use it to refer to a detailed document in the files.

D. Mitigation Actions are the steps to take to eliminate a risk or reduce its impact. Mitigation actions are key steps in proactive management of the project. Primary mitigation actions are avoidance, diminishment, transference, and acceptance. It is always cheaper to mitigate a risk than to repair the damage after it occurs.

Responsibility section

A. Assigned To is the name of the person assigned to monitor this risk. Instead of the project manager scurrying from desk to desk trying to monitor risks, he or she can be assigned to team leaders or the person working on the corresponding task. Although the project manager has the ultimate responsibility for the project, effective delegation spreads the workload around the team. The team member working on the task is close enough to it to see if the risk is becoming reality. If the team member is too close to the work to see the problems, the risk should be assigned to the team leader.

B. Date Assigned is the date the risk was assigned to this person to monitor.
   Comments are anything that would clarify the risk, its triggers, or its mitigation actions. When the risk is added to the list and analyzed, many details can be captured. Adding notes in this section will be useful when monitoring the tasks weeks later. This also provides valuable historical information for future projects. If the spreadsheet cell is too small to hold the pertinent comments, then refer to a detailed document.

[D] Mitigation Plans

Identifying what could go wrong is only the first step. Project management is not a passive job. It involves action! With the project risks identified, plans should be developed to eliminate them. These actions are called mitigation plans and fall into three primary categories:

A. Avoidance.
B. Reducing the impact/likelihood.
C. Transferal.

COMMENT

The alternative to mitigation is acceptance of a risk, where the project manager does nothing about it. An example is to not provide UPS support for developer PCs in an area that rarely experiences power outages.

Mitigation plans avoid the likelihood of a problem by planning around it. If the project involves accounting systems, consider scheduling the project to begin after the fiscal year books are closed and avoid the accountants' busy season. If the project depends on a new radio frequency (RF) network to support scan guns, avoid the impact of the RF network shakeout by waiting until it is installed and stable before beginning that portion of the project.

A second aspect of mitigation is to take steps to reduce the amount of damage should the risk occur. For example, if a network expert is not available to work on the project, consider hiring one earlier than needed to avoid being short one person at the last minute. This may cost more than necessary, but it reduces the likelihood of that risk occurring. Another example is with critical hardware. If one computer is crucial to a system's development, then arrange for a second one to be available on short notice or pay to have it available all of the time.

The third mitigation method is to transfer the risk to someone else. This is usually through insurance. Two easy examples come to mind:

A. A life insurance policy on the project manager or key technician could cushion the financial blow of a project delay because a replacement must be found and trained.

B. If the project depends on the timely arrival of new hardware at the facility, transfer the financial risk of freight damage by insuring the shipment.

[E] Stakeholder Analysis

Project stakeholders are people who will be directly or indirectly impacted by the existence of a project. They may try to influence a project's outcome or course of action based on their perception of how threatening the project is to them. To preclude these people from derailing the project, the project manager must identify who these people are and guide their perceptions toward the project in a favorable direction.

Stakeholders live in their own world in which the project may intrude. By understanding something about their work environment, their interests, and motivations, a plan can be charted for a win-win strategy between the project and each stakeholder.

The following are some of the project's stakeholders:

A. **Sponsor.** This person is normally very interested in seeing the project succeed unless he is transferred in the middle of the project and his successor hates him! In general, the sponsor is the project's guardian against executive interference. The sponsor also ensures that critical resources are available for the project. He often smoothes the way with other stakeholders.

B. **Executive management.** Typically, they view the project plan and budget as an agreement with the project manager as to when the project will be completed and at what cost. They cannot fathom why their meddling would ever change the completion date or the budget.

C. **Workers.** Cause them more work? Make their lives easier or a living hell? No matter how much they complain about their jobs, at least it is a known factor. They fear the unknown of the new project more.

D. **Team members.** They appreciate challenging assignments, working with new technology, etc. Do they view assignment to the project as an opportunity or a punishment?

E. **Union officials.** They may have other issues on their agenda and want to use cooperation with this project as a bargaining chip for something else.

F. **Project Manager.** Well, you'll just have to work on yourself.

G. **Accounting department** (if the project has a budget). Will they work with the project manager or complain about every nickel?

H. **Human resources.** This department provides the project with personnel. Are they forced to bring in technical consultants while, at the same time, they are laying off forklift drivers?

I. **Vendors.** Those who are providing contract programmers or making the result a showcase if they are installing their equipment.

J. **Shareholders.** If this project opens important new markets or results in major economies, then the shareholders will be very interested. If the project is a long-term or very expensive effort, then the shareholders will likewise be concerned.

K. **General public.** Will the end-product negatively or positively impact the company's public image?

L. **Regulatory agencies.** Does this project involve information regulated by the government, e.g., securities, taxes, employee information, patient records, etc.?

Managing stakeholder expectations is a difficult task. Each person exists in his own world with his own pressures and motivations. Accounting managers may push for the cheapest materials, the programmers may press for the latest exotic technologies, and some of the team members may enjoy the project more than their regular assignments and stretch everything out! The project manager must reconcile the differences between all of these influences and keep the project on track.

Determining which stakeholder to mollify and which one to stand tough against can be a difficult decision. Some people do not even want what they are asking for! When in doubt, decisions should be based on what is best for the customer. Accounting managers may be upset, but they may have to purchase the more expensive, but more reliable, hardware. The programmers may not be happy, but the project must be based on tried and true technologies, not the latest technology fashion.

To correctly gauge the impressions and attitudes of the stakeholders, meet with them separately. Review those parts of the project that most affect their workspace. It takes time for them to relax and hopefully spill what is on their mind about the project. Typical questions to ask:

A. What do you think about this project?

B. How do you envision the end-product?

   C. What features are important to include?
   D. How long should this take?
   E. Will this project interfere with the department's operations?

Organize this into a single document; consider using the Stakeholder Analysis Form in Exhibit 6-2. This form has the following fields:

A. Role: What role does this person play in the project? Typical roles are sponsor, team member, manager of customer department, union steward, and IT quality manager.

B. Stakeholder: List his name here.

C. Goals, Motivations, and Interests: What is their interest in this project? Did he suggest it? Will it reduce their operating budget? List all of his concerns (public and private) about the project here. Ask him what he thinks of the goals and assumptions. Ask his opinion about the timeline and listed tasks.

D. Power and Influence: This is a numeric score of 1 to 10. What is each stakeholder's ability to influence others for and against the project? What is his ability to speed along or hinder the project?

E. Importance to the Project: This is a numeric score of 1 to 10. How important is his active support to the project?

F. Impact on the Project: This is a numeric score of 1 to 10. He may or may not be powerful, but how badly could he delay or hurt the project if he chooses to? On the other hand, how valuable is his active support of the project?

G. Stakeholder Score: This is the product of the Power and Influence, Importance and Impact scores multiplied together. Sort this column in descending sequence to bring the most critical players to the top.

H. Role on Project: Are they cheering from the sidelines or players on the team? Stakeholders can be important to a project but indifferent to it. A stakeholder can have a small part on the team or be there from start to finish.

I. Win-Win Strategies: What can be done to address this person's concerns and still complete the project on time? Some people just want to be heard. Often, they have a single issue they feel is serious and must be addressed. The win-win strategy is the project manager's mitigation plan to keep this stakeholder on the team.

As is very obvious from the potential for personal opinions, this document is not for general distribution.

[F] Communications Plan

For a team to operate effectively it must communicate. Otherwise, it is just a collection of individuals. The communications plan should go beyond a weekly team meeting and determine the best way to keep each stakeholder apprised of the project's progress. If stakeholders do not hear what is going

EXHIBIT 6-2.   Stakeholder Analysis Form

Stakeholder Analysis Form

Role	Name	Goals, Motivations and Interests	Power and Influence	Importance to and Impact on Project	Role on Project	Win-Win Strategies
Sponsor						
Data Processing Manager						
Controller						
Plant Manager						
Employees						
Telephone Systems Manager						
Security Manager						
Facilities Manager						
Purchasing Manager						

on from the project manager, they may make their own assumptions that are based more on their worst fears than on the facts.

Drafting reports may not sound like much fun, but it is an important way to mold stakeholders' opinions. "Information is power" and no one has a better handle on what is occurring on a project than its manager. Keep the message simple and clear. Ambiguity is the enemy.

A good time to find out what the stakeholders want to hear about is when the project manager meets with them to gauge their views on the project. Ensure that the status of their specific concern is included in the status reports.

All projects have successes and setbacks. Accurate reporting should include all of this. The project manager was hired to detect and resolve problems. Normally, setbacks do not belong in status reports if they are under control and if they will not materially delay the project. On the other hand, if there is a serious problem, be sure to fully inform the sponsor and summarize the details for others. Follow up on the issue in later reports until it is resolved.

If a problem is going to cause a noticeable delay or affect the quality of the end product, the project manager should report it. Stakeholders may not enjoy the bad news, but they would prefer to hear it from the project manager rather than through office rumors.

Through all of this, remember that all reports must be truthful. The first time the project manager is caught in a lie, credibility is forever tarnished. Ambiguous statements are open to interpretation and can be considered as an untruth where no lie was intended.

When building the stakeholder communication plan, the following should be considered:

A. Executives may want a monthly summary indicating progress, budget performance, and any major issues. Some executives may want this face to face while others might be looking for an e-mail memo. If the reports include notification of problems, they may perceive that the project manager is asking for guidance or that the issues are beyond his or her ability to control.

B. Sponsor: The sponsor will want to be able to answer questions from his peers about the project. He may want a brief weekly summary along with a detailed monthly update.

C. Workers in the department: They will be interested in the final product's features and encouraged by how it will make their working environment easier. If workforce cutbacks are an intended result of the project, leave any information about this to the department manager.

D. Team members: They will want to know the progress of the project. This is important if their part of the project is coming up so they can prepare accordingly.

E. Union officials: They will want to know the project's progress. In some companies, this report is given to the human resources department who passes it on to them.

F. Accounting department: The accounting staff will want to chart the progress of the project in terms of overall cost and monthly cash flow. They may want to juggle the expenses a bit, paying something here and there in advance or a bit late. The project manager's job is to ensure accounting knows what is coming and what is pending.

G. Human resources: They will be primarily interested from a labor perspective. If the project needs more people or is releasing people, they will need to know in advance so they can plan accordingly.

H. Vendors: They will appreciate a heads-up on materials requirements.

I. General public: If the project is highly visible, the project manager must pass project progress information through the corporate communications office and often the legal office as well.

To assemble a communications plan, refer to Exhibit 6-3, Stakeholder Reporting Matrix.

A. Stakeholder: Name of the person to receive the report.

B. Reports to receive: Some people may receive multiple reports. The sponsor may want the accounting report, the progress report, risk assessment report, etc. Others may want only a brief summary.

C. Amount of detail: Brief or detailed?

D. Preferred format: Bullet points, narrative, Gantt chart?

E. Frequency: Weekly, monthly, at every milestone?

F. Delivery mechanism: Should this be delivered by e-mail, verbally, in an updated Gantt chart?

§ 6.04 EXECUTING THE PROJECT

[A] Managing the Project

The project plan is a road map for how the project should unfold. In reality, it is a rather fluid document that shows a general direction, but tasks can be completed early or late, the budget overrun, tasks omitted, etc. Even with these changes, the project plan represents the best communications tool to guide the team's expectations of what lies ahead. The team will use the project plan for a guide if the project manager refers to it and they will ignore the project plan if the project manager ignores it.

Project management is people management. Meet with the team at least weekly. Let them speak about the obstacles they have encountered and concerns about what is to come. The project manager can pass on information concerning the project's progress and any alterations to the plan. Remember that communications flow from bottom up (the team to the project manager), top down (the project manager to the team), and laterally (among the team members).

The project manager has a responsibility to use the resources of the project team in the most effective manner. This means that team members should be assigned according to their strengths and technical expertise, not on availability or the project manager's whim.

Project management requires that three important variables be in control: cost, quality (or scope), and time (or speed of completion). A project manager must have control over at least two of these variables to ensure project completion.

EXHIBIT 6-3.   Stakeholder Reporting Matrix

Stakeholder Reporting Matrix

Role	Name	Reports to Receive	Amount of Detail	Frequency of Reporting	Best Format	Delivery Mechanism
Sponsor						
Data Processing Manager						
Controller						
Plant Manager						
Employees						
Telephone Systems Manager						
Security Manager						
Facilities Manager						
Purchasing Manager						

Altering any one variable will affect the others. Generally, to improve quality (or to expand the scope), higher cost and, possibly, more time will be incurred. For example, a software project can be completed more quickly (time) if there is more money for overtime or to hire more contract programmers (money). Or, the project manager could cut the quality (scope) to increase the speed.

[B] Scope Change

The scope of the project is set by the sponsor before the project plan is drafted. All time and cost estimates should be based on the approved scope. Altering the scope will automatically alter both the timeline and the cost. As the project unfolds, some of the uncertainty will fall away and there may be pressure to adjust the project scope to better fit the current reality. This is where the project manager must stand firm.

Changes in the budget and the timeline are normally worked out between the sponsor and the project manager. The same holds true for the scope, except that sometimes it is changed without either the project manager or the sponsor being aware of it!

In their work on the project or in their contacts with the end users, programmers may sometimes make side agreements to include additional features to the system or alter the product design. They also may neglect to mention it to the project manager. This is known as "scope creep." Taken alone, each change may seem minor, but taken in aggregate, the changes can alter the project by loading it with additional code to test and maintain. Simple changes may prove more difficult than initially estimated with considerable time lost attempting to repair code that is not in the plan.

These unofficial agreements may be difficult to repudiate later. To contain scope creep, a formal process must be established to control all project scope changes. This should include a form to request the change and a log sheet to track it.

The form can be a basic memo stating what is wanted and why. The form should be presented to the project manager who will then analyze the request and identify its impact to the project in terms of time and money. This information is passed to the sponsor who should have the final authority to approve or deny the change. Approving the change also approves the project manager's estimated changes to the project timeline and budget.

[C] Basic Rules for Managing Projects

The following are basic rules for managing projects:

A. Plan the work—work the plan.
B. Resolve all issues brought to the project manager's attention as soon as possible. If the project manager delays, so does the project. If the project manager hesitates to make a decision or to raise an issue with the sponsor, so will the team.
C. Working with people takes time. Do not be in a rush when talking to the project team.
D. At every milestone, update the assumption list, risk analysis, and stakeholder communications plan.

[D] Task Completion

Projects that fall more than 15 percent behind schedule rarely finish on time. The project manager must press the project forward from the first day. As task milestones are reached, update the project plan. Assess completed tasks for quality, completion effort required, and effect on the project schedule. The hours estimated to complete a task effort should be compared with the actual hours, and the information retained for future estimates.

This task completion information will be used to identify the project status at different points in time, and will be discussed in status meetings. The following are some solutions that can be used to take care of project slippage:

A. **Overtime.** Working overtime, or hours in excess of the standard work day, should only be used to complete critical path tasks and only for a short time. If the need for overtime becomes routine, it can affect the personnel turnover rate. The best time for paid overtime is right after Christmas and the worst time is during the summer months.

B. **Assign more people.** Assigning people at the start of a project is less of a problem than adding more later. The worst time is at the end. As more people are added, the communications required between project members will reduce the output per worker. Using a skilled worker to break in a new coworker will further slow progress. The project effort may be less effective than if no additional people had been added.

COMMENT

Adding more people does not automatically speed up the result. If one woman takes nine months to make a baby, nine women cannot do it in one month.

C. **Pass on a task to a vendor.** This action has merit if the vendor has reliable skills in the appropriate area. For the best results, the vendor should be given advance notice to expect the project.

D. **Reduce the project scope.** If the sponsor is willing to reduce the project scope, this may be an effective solution to project slippage, helping to keep the quality of remaining project tasks intact.

E. **Reschedule module delivery.** Modules that may not be required for the finish date can be delayed. This can be a better solution than reducing the project scope; however, it can complicate resource planning.

F. **Request additional funds.** If the project is over budget, more money must be requested. The sooner this is done, the better, because as the end of the fiscal year approaches, money will become less available. If the dollars represent people cost, this is not so much of a problem. Salaried employees do not require overtime pay.

[E]   Progress Measurement

Items that must be controlled and managed should be monitored for both quantity and quality. It is harder to measure the quality of output than quantity at the time the work is being done, since the quality of the effort starts to show up only when the end product is tested and debugged. Therefore, testing should begin as soon as a major component is completed.

Employee time is usually the greatest cost of the project, and it should be closely monitored to gauge the results for effort exerted. Everyone must report the time spent working on the project—including the project manager. Some of the project management packages collect this data online and summarize it in a weekly report, automatically applying the time and dollar values to relevant project tasks.

To minimize the time and aggravation spent collecting this data, the project manager should:

A. **Explain why the data is needed**. Demonstrate the process used to record task time. Encourage the use of real numbers, not estimates. Stress that the information collected is for their benefit too.

B. **Simplify the recording**. Do not require too much detail. Let people know they may receive a telephone call from a spouse or go to the restroom. Typically allow workers 10 percent of their work day for personal time.

COMMENT

Have the time sheets entered into the project accounting system daily. Efforts expended on Monday morning are difficult to remember by Friday afternoon.

C. **Confirm time estimates**. Inform employees that the time estimates on which the project is constructed need to be confirmed. Estimates are only approximations and should be corrected if wrong. This cannot be done without keeping track of the actual time.

§ 6.05   PROJECT CLOSEOUT

[A]   Overview

Projects end for various reasons. Ideally, the project ends because the project's goal has been achieved and is ready to hand over to the customer. Sometimes executive management will decide that a project needs to stop. However the end of the line arrives, there are some steps the project manager should take to properly close out the project.

Planning to close a project is like planning for any other phase of a project. The only difference is that the goal is to end the project by closing off the various areas that support it. The project manager identifies the tasks to be completed, assigns resources, adds durations, and creates the plan. The projected financial requirements for the project closeout should be rolled into a budget for the sponsor's approval.

The project manager coordinates a planning meeting with the key stakeholders to identify tasks to be completed to close their involvement in the project. The key stakeholders for this phase are:

A. Sponsors: Hand over what has been completed and obtain their sign-off.
B. Accounting department: Assist in closing the project's budget.
C. Customer: Gather product documentation and provide training for usable products.
D. Team members: Reassign to company departments.
E. Contract employees: Release back to their companies.
F. Program office: Gather the project's records for storage and later use in research.

The closeout plan should include a document that identifies all company material purchased to support the project team and its location. The project sponsor should reassign these assets before they get lost.

[B] Sponsor

If the project was completed, the project manager obtains a written acceptance of the results from the customer. If the project ended before the goal was reached, the project manager should obtain formal written notice from the sponsor to close the project.

Designate a point of contact for any future project issues and transition key information to this liaison. This is usually the manager who will pick up support responsibilities for the product.

The project manager coordinates a closeout meeting with the sponsor to compare the statement of work and project scope against actual project performance. Identify any shortcomings and determine if they can be resolved prior to the project's end. Review the final project closeout plan and the timeline with the sponsor. After the sponsor has approved the closeout plan, publish it to all stakeholders.

[C] Accounting Department

Most projects have a budget to close at the end of the project. There are three major areas to address with the accounting department before the project can close:

A. Performance of the project—a comparison of the amount budgeted for the project to the amount actually required.

   B. Projection of budget requirements to implement the approved project closeout plan.

   C. A list of all pending invoices and open purchase orders. The list of pending invoices must include contract employees who are to be retained through the last days of the project.

[D] Customer

A clean handover of the products completed is critical to customer satisfaction. Coordinate training on finished products to acquaint users with their proper functions. Include a handbook to which users can refer and use to train new employees.

Coordinate the continued maintenance and support of the project product to include hardware servicing and service desk support. Both departments may require technical documentation as well as a copy of the users' manual.

This is an opportune time to gather some idea of the end users' impression of the project. Solicit and analyze feedback regarding project performance from business representatives, project team members, suppliers, customers, and management. Some companies create a customer satisfaction survey for distribution to pertinent stakeholders. If used, specify a deadline for its completion and return.

[E] Team Members

Taking care of the project team at closeout will have many benefits. As soon as project closeout planning begins, meet with the human resources department to discuss the redeployment of employees. The team members are counting on the project manager to "sell" their good work on the project to obtain desirable positions in the company. Word can get around a company pretty fast. If a project manager is known as someone who "takes care" of his team members, it will be easier to recruit people for future projects.

Schedule performance reviews for each person on the team. Discuss their involvement in the project to date, how well they performed to plan, and any new skills they acquired. Performance reviews completed during the project can be used to show trends of improvement. The result of these reviews can be used as justification for project bonuses or pay raises. Forward the individual's performance appraisal to the human resources department and the employee's new manager.

The project manager must try to keep people from jumping off the project early. Establish a range of release dates for team members based on the closeout plan. Add a week or two to the plan to ensure they will be available to address last minute questions. Do not let anyone leave the project early as it may start a stampede for the door!

When a project closes, it is important to take some time to celebrate its completion. Project closeout is a time of transition for many people—friendships as well as jobs are ending. To aid in this transition, most project managers throw a party where the contributions of the various team members can be recognized.

The event should be held off site and hosted by the project's sponsor or even the person to whom he or she reports. Disperse individual rewards such as gift certificates, bonuses, additional vacation days, trips, plaques, personalized certificates of accomplishment, items with company logo, and other tokens of appreciation. Do not forget to personally thank each person!

[F]   Contractual Issues and Contract Employees

Review all open contracts to identify terms that must be addressed before the agreement can be closed. There may be clauses concerning the number of days of notice required before releasing contractor-supplied employees back to their companies. There may be penalty clauses if the proper amount of notice is not provided to them. If in doubt, include the legal department in the contract reviews.

If the project ended early, look for penalty clauses for canceling materials. Common goods can be resold by the manufacturer, but custom materials often require the buyer to pay for at least a portion of the unit's price.

Review all work to date to ensure compliance with the current project plan and requirements documentation. This may require a review of all communications with the vendor, any work schedules, accounting data (invoices and payment), and inspection results. Audit completed work to ensure that it complies with the task specifications. Obtain written warranties from all subcontractors and vendors for completed work orders.

Complete updated performance evaluations for contract employees and forward them to their companies. Detail their accomplishments, task descriptions, strengths, and areas of improvement. Include letters of recommendation detailing their performance to assist them in securing their next engagement.

[G]   Final Project Report

An important part of closing a project is to gather all of the records and information about the project and file it with the Project Management Office (PMO). This information will be useful when planning for similar products or for making major changes to the end-product.

Compose a project completion report that highlights the achievements of the project and underlying reasons for any problems. Specify areas that added value for the customer. The report should:

A.   Identify which goals and objectives were fully or partially achieved.

B.   Identify which goals and objectives were not achieved and their impact.

C.   Identify any expected benefits that were not achieved and their impact.

D.   Indicate major milestones achieved with actual dates vs. planned dates and explain the reasons for any differences.

E.   Include guiding factors (objectives and constraints) that affected the project from the start.

F.   Include team members' opinions and perspectives of project successes and weaknesses as reported in the post-project review.

 G. Include documentation of the final scope, work breakdown structure, and the stability of the project's requirements.

 H. Include customer feedback and comments on the project as well as feedback from suppliers and other third-party suppliers.

A valuable section in the project report is a review of the lessons learned during the project. This section should review the challenges the team faced and how they were overcome. A "lessons learned" section can guide future project managers around the pitfalls of working with this type of product or in working with a specific department.

§ 6.06 PROJECT MANAGEMENT OFFICE

[A] Overview

An important function of the PMO is the control of projects. In times past, each department of the company might include in its strategic plans various types of projects to meet one business objective or another. These isolated projects were rarely coordinated to maximize resources. Sometimes they worked at cross-purposes or consumed resources for non-strategic objectives.

A PMO brings all pending and current projects together under a single office's control. By examining all projects side by side, the PMO is able to identify and resolve areas of overlap to the company's advantage. This framework optimizes the use of resources and minimizes mutually exclusive project goals.

[B] How to Do It

Establishing a PMO is like campaigning for any other cultural change in a company. An executive sponsor is essential. Often the sponsor is the executive to whom the PMO will report. A PMO cuts across department boundaries and shifts the control of individual project managers from various departments to a central office. Resistance to this shift in control can be minimized if the sponsor has sufficient executive stature to compel the change. Consolidating project managers under a single manager is essential to the PMO exercise of strategic oversight of projects.

The shift to a PMO eases workloads all around. Instead of dealing with individual project managers, each supporting department (e.g., accounting, purchasing, facilities, human resources) can refer to a single place when providing services. Instead of creating separate status reports for each concerned executive, project managers can submit a single document to the PMO who distributes reports to the interested parties.

A new PMO develops several fundamental documents to establish the scope of its actions and its strategy for implementing the office. Properly written, these documents will set an expectation of where the PMO fits into the company's organization and the value it adds to the bottom line.

 A. Mission Statement—A general statement that outlines what the PMO does, how it is to be done, and who the customers are. It establishes the scope of the PMO's authority within the company, such as IS-only, company-wide or support for a particular site.

B. Strategies are high-level directions on how the PMO will fulfill its mission statement and align the PMO with the company's business strategies. Strategies provide an overall framework for creating objectives as well as an anchor for PMO policies and procedures.

C. Objectives—A clear statement of what the PMO intends to achieve over the upcoming year. Objectives should be specific, measurable, achievable, and include a time duration. Typical objectives are:

  1. To hire and manage qualified project managers and support staff.
  2. During weekly project status meetings, to ensure that all customer commitments are documented and tracked to completion.
  3. On a bi-weekly basis, to track and maximize the use of resources (labor, cash, time, and equipment) for the greatest benefit of the company.
  4. To provide clear, summary information on all project status in a timely manner, on a scheduled basis or upon request from senior management.
  5. To provide mentoring, training, and assistance in the career development of the PMO's Project Managers.

D. Products and services created or offered by the PMO. Products are tangible "things" the PMO will deliver. Services are actions taken for the benefit of others. PMOs add value to the company through the combined application of their products and services.

See Policy ITP-6-1 Project Management Office Policy as an example policy for establishing a PMO.

POLICY ITP-6-1. Project Management Office Policy

Policy #:	ITP-6-1	Effective:	03/18/09	Page #:	1 of N
Subject:	Project Management Office Policy				

1.0 PURPOSE

This policy creates the IT department's Project Management Office (PMO). This office is to ensure the consistent, efficient, and effective implementation of projects across the IT department.

2.0 SCOPE

The policy applies to all users of information technology within the company. The Project Management Office is responsible for managing all IT projects of more than 20 hours, or that involve the purchase of hardware of more than $1,000.

3.0 POLICY

3.1 PMO Sponsor Duties

A. Create a Mission Statement that outlines the PMO's roles and responsibilities. The mission statement establishes the scope of the PMO's authority within the company.
B. Identify the primary strategies on how the PMO will fulfill its mission statement and align the PMO with the company's business strategies.
C. Develop a list of objectives for the PMO to achieve over the next 12 months.
D. Together with the IT Manager, appoint a person as the IT department's Project Management Office leader. This person is delegated to be responsible for implementing this policy.

3.2 PMO Leader Duties

A. Establish and maintain the tools and processes for use by the IT department's project managers.
B. Standardize project management methodology by consolidating status requests to flow through the PMO.
C. Manage the IT department's portfolio of pending projects:
   1. Create a standard form for requesting and analyzing projects. This ensures every proposed project summary has the same "look and feel" with a standardized format.
   2. Monitor contents of portfolio to combine projects where practical.
   3. Identify project goals that conflict with strategies or objectives of other projects.
   4. Develop guidelines for determining project costs and savings (tangible and intangible).
D. Standardize project management tools.
   1. Determine the strategy for selecting the PMO's tool set.
   2. Create a process for updating the tool set to meet changing situations.
   3. Ensure that the PMO staff is trained in their use.
   4. Publish a standard process for managing the changes to a project's scope.
E. Resource management.
   1. Coordinate the use of resources by the PMO to optimize utilization and minimize cost.
   2. Develop and maintain a positive working relationship with internal resource suppliers.

3. Identify external resources required by the PMO and pre-qualify major suppliers (internal and external).
4. Assign and reassign resources to projects.

F. Establish training and mentoring program.
1. Identify and train mentors for assisting new project managers.
2. Coordinate peer reviews for troubled projects.

G. Establish a project historical library.
1. Establish a library that contains the planning documents, status reports, and final report of all projects.
2. Publish rules for accessing the data.
3. Create guidelines for what is to be collected from each completing project.
4. Ensure that company confidential data is secured from unauthorized access.

4.0 REVISION HISTORY

Date	Revision #	Description of Change
03/18/09	1.0	Initial creation.

5.0 INQUIRIES

Direct inquiries about this policy to:

Tom Jones, CIO
Our Company, Inc.
2900 Corporate Drive
Columbus, OH 43215

Voice: 614-555-1234
Fax: 614-555-1235
E-mail: tjones@company.com

Revision #:	1.0	Supersedes:	N/A	Date:	03/18/09

[C] Establish a Tool Set

The heart and soul of the project management office is its tools and processes. These are variously called its "toolkit," methodology, or standard operating procedures. They include a set of processes and basic tools that ease the flow of projects through the organization. Some of the tools are:

A. Estimation guides for judging the time and expense for completing a task.

B. Resource-requirement projections to reserve technical resources for specific periods of time.
C. Standards for project scheduling and management to ensure others can assist with or take over a project.
D. Simplified equipment acquisition steps to reduce administrative overhead for the project manager.
E. Scope and budget change control processes to ensure control of these critical functions remains with the project manager.
F. Consolidated status reporting to present one "face" to executive management.

Standardized project management processes also make it easy for the PMO to provide oversight and mentoring of project managers. By using the same processes and tools for every project, team members spend less time orienting to a new project.

[D]   Resource Management

Ensuring that the right people will be available when needed is an important ingredient for project progress. Project managers use resources (e.g., skilled people, special tools, and cash) to move a project to completion. The more scarce or expensive these resources are, the more difficult they become to schedule since the company cannot afford to leave them idle for long. Also, the longer a project requires to execute, the more difficult it is to accurately project when a resource will be required later in the project. The PMO provides tools for project managers to estimate the timing of their resource requirements, consolidate them into a central requirements file, and resolve conflicts between projects.

To optimize resource utilization, the PMO must be established as the primary customer of these services—not the individual projects. This allows the PMO to request specific units of resources to support all projects and ensure their proper utilization. For example, the PMO might request 60 hours per week of Java programming support for project development. Instead of bombarding the Java programming team leader with requests from various projects, the team leader can identify the PMO resources available to support projects in advance and better plan work for the rest of the team. The PMO then can allocate the programmers to the projects that need them.

At the end of a project, there may be furniture, computers, or skilled people to reallocate or send on their way. The PMO leader's view over all projects makes the reallocation of resources easier and more efficient. Leaving this action to the very end of a project, skilled resources and expensive equipment may be idled, creating additional company costs.

[E]   Executive Steering Committee

To manage the project portfolio, many companies create steering committees of senior executives. This group reviews the progress of in-process projects to ensure they remain on track and focused on the company's strategic directions. Any projects that fall behind can be identified and corrective action taken.

Steering committees are not new. Companies have long used them for governing shared departments. In the case of the PMO, the committee provides executive perspective from a range of departments to ensure the PMO is not funded by all for the benefit of a few.

The steering committee reviews new project proposals to ensure they add value in proportion to their costs. The appropriate level of funding for a project requires executive support. The steering committee's approval for a project not only approves the funding, but also implies approval of the project across a number of departments. Along with funding, the committee assigns a priority to the project to indicate how quickly it should begin.

An important steering committee function is to set the overall priorities for the PMO and all projects. This is often a clearer restatement of the company strategy such as cost reductions, IS strategic direction for hardware, or for the promotion of specific business practices. The PMO's relationship with a powerful steering committee provides it with organizational power when overcoming internal resistance to proper project management practices.

Steering committees are not a project's sponsor. The sponsor is an executive who has a direct interest in the project and is often the person who requested it. Where the broad exposure of the steering committee is useful for guiding project selection, the sponsor is closer to the issues at hand and should be the one to make judgment calls on major changes in project scope or budget. Committees are useful but tend to be much less decisive than a sponsor who has a personal stake in the project's outcome.

[F] Standardized Project Initiation

A PMO is a lightning rod that attracts all incoming project requests into a central place for review. All project proposals must pass through the PMO's project proposal process. This ensures a consistent data basis for steering committee review and same-to-same comparison with other projects.

Keeping track of requests

Large PMOs use basic service request software as a tracking tool to ensure that requests are not lost in the shuffle of each day's "hot project." This is the same type of software service desks use to track service requests except that its purpose is to ensure that requests keep shuffling through the PMO bureaucracy. Service request management software provides metrics on how long each step in the process requires, an indication of whose desk the request's documents are resting on, and a measurable indication of the volume of requests.

Small PMOs can adequately track requests on a spreadsheet. Even small offices have a backlog of projects to be undertaken given the right circumstances, so some sort of ordered list is useful. PMOs that do not track outstanding projects will eventually find themselves reanalyzing the same rejected projects time after time.

Return on investment (ROI)

When a project request is received from a competent authority (generally someone authorized to spend the company's money), the PMO assigns a

Project Manager to review the proposal's costs and benefits. Few people requesting a project have a clear idea of how long a project will take or what it will cost to implement. In general, their experience has been to see or use the external aspects of the result, with little experience of the essential background effort or materials required. (If the project already has a complete and approved feasibility study, then base the ROI analysis on that information.)

The PMO creates a standard format for gathering the essential elements of a project. This includes a clear business case, a concise scope statement, a list of success criteria, anticipated costs and benefits, required completion dates, and a list of actions required to complete the project. Taken together, a reasonable bottoms-up cost estimate can be made for completing the project. However, the longer the project runs, the wider the tolerance for resource estimation must be. Estimates supporting a 90-day project should vary much less than estimates for a year-long project.

At this point, a minimal amount of time has been spent obtaining specific cost information. This analysis approximates a project's costs since most equipment and services quotes expire in 30 days. A complete costing of the project requires considerable analysis and that will be lost if the project is not promptly approved. Cost estimates at the "approximate cost" stage should be within ±25 percent.

With the cost estimate in hand, conduct an analysis of the project's benefits. As described by the project requestor, the project benefits can be inflated as much as the costs are deflated. Verify claims of project benefits. Labor savings are a particularly difficult area to calculate.

COMMENT

If labor savings are included, they must adhere to the company's labor accounting practices. For example, in most companies, a project cannot save one-half of a person. Either eliminate a position and someone is discharged (which reduces the company's payroll) or not. If no one leaves the company, then no payroll savings can be claimed—even though hours in the week are now available for other uses.

Project savings claimed for equipment departing the company is a different issue. Leased equipment may incur a penalty for early return. Equipment freed up as the result of one project does not become a "free" asset available for use elsewhere in the company. For a project to claim a savings for eliminating a device, that equipment must exit the premises.

Along with proposed ROI, the analyst will assess the risks surrounding the project. The risk of failure, that resource costs will skyrocket, of technical obsolescence, and all other risk dimensions must be included in the report. Some PMOs detail specific environmental and resource risks that must be addressed in proposals.

COMMENT

A variation of ROI is the cost of non-investment (CONI). CONI measures how much *not* doing a project will cost the company. This is common with legal compliance issues, such as mandatory environmental controls for air pollution, water pollution or disposal of toxic wastes. In some instances, the cost is measured in time instead of dollars—jail time!

Proper approval

After a project's costs and benefits appear to meet historically acceptable levels, the project can be added to the PMO's pending project list. This list is reviewed periodically with the PMO's executive steering committee to set project priorities and identify projects that must be executed immediately—even if outside project managers and resources must be used.

Some projects are pre-approved executive mandates and an ROI is not required. However, if time permits, an ROI review will provide considerable insight into the project's requirements and the resources necessary for its success.

[G]   Project Backlog Management

Today's non-urgent project can become tomorrow's hot topic. The PMO consolidates new project requests into a single file. Review each request periodically to determine if changes in its critical factors alter its payback time or its urgency.

The PMO monitors the projects in the backlog for opportunities to combine any of them with new projects. Opportunities also may arise to combine several of the backlogged projects into one. This would provide additional resource economies and potentially meet the company's ROI "hurdle rate."

[H]   Metrics

A popular management maxim is that a person cannot manage what cannot be measured. Create a consistent set of project performance metrics for executive oversight. Project metrics provide performance visibility to management in a common and consistent manner. They also permit the comparison of current project performance to historical levels.

There are two primary types of project metrics:

A. Product metrics pertain to the result or product created by the project. How closely does the result conform to the published specifications; how much better is it in identified key quality areas, etc.? How does the customer rate the final product's quality?
B. Project management metrics deal with how effective and efficient the project was in creating the result. Were unnecessary steps included? Were resources efficiently utilized?

Metrics provide a source of feedback into the PMO's performance and customer satisfaction. They ensure decisions are based on facts and not emotion. Metrics illustrate the result of changes made to processes and areas of potential improvement. Since metrics use numbers instead of pass/fail, smaller changes can be detected and monitored, such as a trend toward greater resource efficiency. Examples of metrics to track include:

A. Schedule performance.
    1. The number of tasks completed on time.
    2. The estimated hours to complete the project (as a percentage over or under run).
B. Financial performance—Actual expenses compared to budgeted expenses (as a percentage over or under run).
C. Customer satisfaction as measured by end-of-project or end-of-milestone surveys.
D. Percentage of tasks completed on time, sequenced by the resource used.

7

BUSINESS CONTINUITY PLANNING: STAYING IN BUSINESS

§ 7.01   OVERVIEW
    [A]   Purpose and Scope
    [B]   Critical Policies to Develop Based on This Chapter

§ 7.02   PREPARE TO PLAN
    [A]   Overview
    [B]   Hire an Expert
    [C]   Why Bother for Something That Will Never Happen
    [D]   Basic Planning Assumptions
    [E]   The Local Expert

§ 7.03   BUSINESS CONTINUITY PLANNING BASICS
    [A]   Overview
    [B]   Identify the Critical Processes
    [C]   Identify Risks (Threats)
    [D]   Other Risk Considerations
    [E]   Develop Action Plans to Reduce These Risks
    [F]   Executives' Business Continuity Plan

§ 7.04   PLANNING—THE NEXT STEP
    [A]   Use What Is Already Available
    [B]   Distributing Interim Copies
    [C]   Adding to the Plan—More Contact Information
    [D]   Keys
    [E]   Service Contracts—HELP!
    [F]   Vendor Contacts
    [G]   Walk-Around Asset Inventory
    [H]   Software Asset List
    [I]   Restoration Priorities
    [J]   Toxic Material Storage
    [K]   Employee Skills Matrix

§ 7.05   WRITING A PLAN
         [A]   Overview
         [B]   What to Write About
         [C]   Contents of a Typical Plan
         [D]   Which Processes Need a Plan?
         [E]   Testing
         [F]   Keeping the Plan Current

§ 7.06   SOURCES OF ADDITIONAL INFORMATION
         [A]   Publications
         [B]   Training and Certification
         [C]   Web Sites
         [D]   Business Continuity Plan Checklist

§ 7.01 OVERVIEW

[A] Purpose and Scope

Business continuity planning (BCP) is a lot like car insurance. If it is not in place when needed, then it is too late to get it. Most executives are optimists by nature. There are so many urgent, exciting, or challenging things to work on that it is hard to find time for something as doom-and-gloom as BCP.

Over the years, business continuity planning has evolved as the business environment has changed. Thirty years ago, it was primarily concerned with disaster recovery planning (DRP). DRP focused on recovery from catastrophic problems such as how to rebuild a flattened facility. An IT DRP was only activated if the damage required the displacement of the data center to another site. A DRP contained its own dirty little secret—that it was sometimes easier and cheaper to take the insurance check and walk away from the business rather than rebuild the facility. Examples of this might be a department store roof collapse, a factory fire, or even an accusation of selling less-than-wholesome foods.

> **COMMENT**
>
> Law mandates disaster recovery planning for financial institutions. It assumes that financial institutions hold assets belonging to others and closing up is not an option. Hospitals also have tested plans since a major crisis could open them to a slew of lawsuits. However, most industries do little disaster planning and only apply it to their data processing operations.

A major problem with DRP was testing the adequacy of the plans. Testing is expensive and company funds are always under pressure to address the day's immediate issues rather than a pessimistic future that may never happen. Testing, if ever done, usually occurred when the crisis was at hand with no time left to repair flaws in the plan. Still, the DRP concept survived.

Eventually disaster recovery planners recognized how important a company's customers and suppliers were to a long-term recovery. What good was recovering a facility if, in the process, neglected suppliers and customer relationships withered away? This led to the addition of BRP to the disaster recovery plan. A BRP addresses customers' concerns and explains to them any delays in their orders. It might also include explaining to customers where to find other suppliers in the interim. Supplier cooperation includes requests to help by taking back delivered goods not immediately required. A BRP keeps suppliers informed as the recovery progresses. BRPs made these two critical groups participants in the recovery efforts.

EXHIBIT 7-1.   Planning Scope Relationships

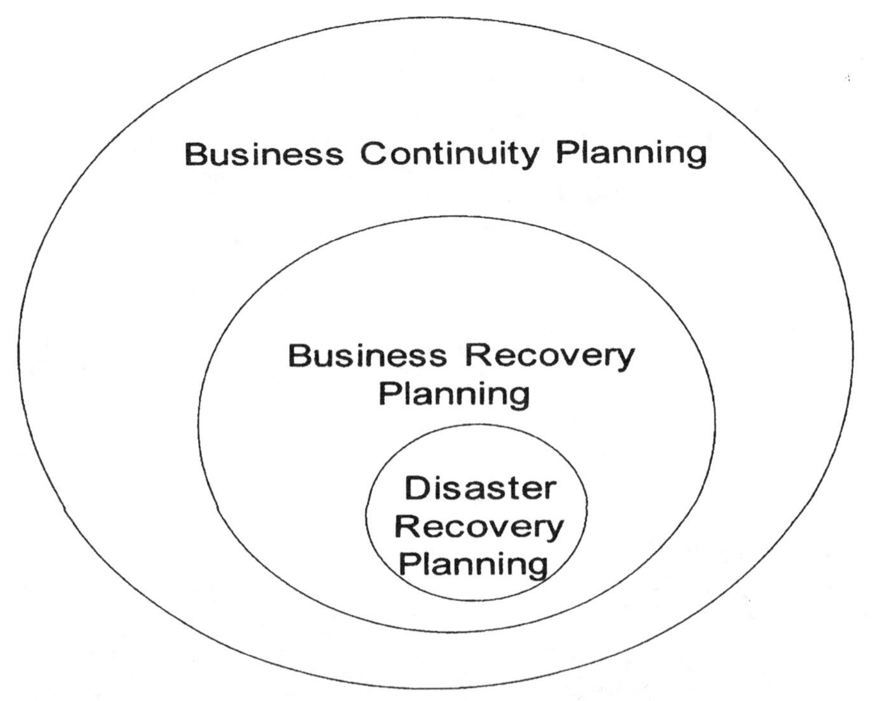

Time marches on and companies recognize the huge expense of holding materials inventories and large queues of work-in-process material. Impressed by the results of Japanese automakers, many companies have adopted lean production practices. Under the previous model, a factory might hold a 30-day supply (safety stock) of a key material to protect against interruptions to the supply chain. The assumption was that carrying extra inventory was necessary to protect the continuous flow of goods down the production lines. Multiply this carrying cost across all materials company-wide and the corporations were paying a lot of money to buy, store, and handle safety stock.

COMMENT

It should be a company policy that every critical business tool and process has a written and tested business continuity plan. The exercise of writing this plan will reap major business benefits as it forces managers to examine their processes and drive out their weak links.

Under lean production methods, companies realized this was not necessary and drastically cut their safety stock. In return, they became dependent on the reliability of their suppliers to deliver quality goods on demand. Many customers now rate their suppliers on the credibility of delivery promises. Late goods may idle in their own factory. On the other hand, keeping delivery promises in the face of adversity can be a major competitive weapon!

Taking this on-demand requirement even further, the Internet has made most companies 24 / 7 (24 hours a day, 7 days a week) sales centers. Interruptions to a company's operations cause customers to go elsewhere. Every company has charts that show the longer their customers must wait for their goods, the more the cancellation rate increases. Few companies can afford this.

So out of lean production and the around-the-clock world arose a need for BCP. BCP acts as the outer shell of disaster recovery planning. It addresses not only major tragedies such as burned warehouses but also the occasional major disruption such as severe weather, loss of electrical power, and even loss of a key machine. It is more than a set of dusty plans; it is a continuous proactive process of examining business processes to drive out problems and maintain workflow.

COMMENT

We all use business continuity every day. Consider a car. There is the risk of an accident. In this case, transfer the risk of loss to someone else (insurance company). This could be similar to disaster recovery if the insurance money was used to buy another car. If the car was severely damaged and there were difficulties making the journey to work every day on time until repairs were finished, a mitigation plan would inform your employer, family, and any other outside parties of potential delays. If a small, inexpensive "commuter car" was used for driving to work and a larger car for family outings, then the business continuity plan is to drive the larger car to work until the commuter car is repaired.

BCP is a broad topic. The goal of this chapter is to provide ideas for assembling a basic plan useful to an IT Manager. Start with the "10 Steps to a Basic Recovery Plan" in Section 7.04[A]. If planning stops after completing this list, then the plan is off to a good start. To obtain the full benefits, continue and write a full plan. If this appears to be too large a challenge, consider hiring a professional BCP consultant to develop it.

There is an even more important reason for IT Managers to develop a business continuity plan—keeping their jobs. Companies without plans waste time fighting crisis after crisis and never seem to run smoothly. This translates into higher cost of goods through overtime pay, airfreight for critical materials, and delayed customer shipments. Perhaps some people enjoy the chaos. Those companies are costly to operate and gradually fall by the wayside.

[B]   Critical Policies to Develop Based on This Chapter

Using the material discussed in this chapter, create the following policies:

A. Conduct a business impact analysis bi-annually.
   1. Company executives must sponsor and approve results.
   2. Conduct a facility-wide risk assessment of natural and man-made risks.
B. Assemble plans for every critical business function.
   1. Include supporting technologies.
   2. Develop and update annually.
   3. Test all plans at least bi-annually.

Develop policies based on the local situation. Successful managers cannot issue appropriate guidance using policies written with another company's situation or location in mind.

§ 7.02   PREPARE TO PLAN

[A]   Overview

A BCP is not a know-all book of how to recover from any potential problem. Such a tome would be far too large to be useful. Instead, it consists of a series of smaller plans that address specific risks. Each plan provides an overview of the technologies involved and guidance that can be applied to the problem at hand.

A disaster is an anticipated or unanticipated event that seriously disrupts critical business operations. Has the facility ever lost electrical power or telephone service? Has the data center ever run with half of the normal number of employees with the other half trapped by a major snowstorm? Most companies have muddled through these problems, so a lot of the plan already exists in the collective memory of the managers and workforce. **Write it down!**

A plan could contain many things. At a minimum, it explains the basic steps to take while waiting for key support staff to arrive. This immediate action (similar to the concept of first aid) addresses most of the common problems or stops the spread of the damage.

> **COMMENT**
>
> Disaster recovery is something of a misleading title. These plans do not detail how to rebuild a burned out data center, which would be a full recovery. Rather they explain immediate action steps to restore a business function to *minimal* usefulness so the company can resume its cash flow. (A minimal plan provides critical business functions at a labor, throughput, and/or quality penalty. It is "limping along.")
>
> Therefore, if a data center was burned out, the recovery plan, in this sense, would be to set up a temporary data center somewhere, with the minimal required equipment, as quickly as possible. The full recovery of a rebuilt room with new data center equipment, built for the long term, etc., is beyond the scope of these plans.

[B]   Hire an Expert

Creating a business continuity program requires expertise. Like learning anything else new to the company, a subject matter expert is essential to kick off and run a program. Some companies hire someone with this experience and others hire a consultant and then develop someone on their team to take over the program. An on-site expert ensures success and speeds the program over the small obstacles that regularly rear their ugly heads.

> **COMMENT**
>
> Cynical managers say that consultants must be dragged kicking and screaming to the door. Include an end date and exit plan in the consultant's scope of work so that, by the end of the engagement, they have trained someone in the company to carry on leading the program.

[C]   Why Bother for Something That Will Never Happen

There are many reasons to build Business Continuity plans. First, they are simply good business. Parts of them are likely already in place, such as a UPS electrical support system. Business continuity planning forces an examination of processes to determine the risks to their ongoing operation. As these risks are mitigated, business continuity is more ensured. As mitigation steps are prepared for catastrophic events, the Business Continuity plan takes shape.

However, there are other reasons. Disaster recovery plans are specifically required or strongly implied in a number of legal mandates:

A. HIPAA implies the need for a business continuity plan as personal health information must be readily available. A disaster recovery plan may delay availability for many days. In a crisis, a business continuity plan would make the information available within hours.

B. SEC Rule 17a-4 for records preservation. Without an adequate data system backup and recovery capability, this rule is violated.

C. Sarbanes-Oxley section 404 implies the need for a disaster recovery plan.

IT Governance models that require a documented, tested business continuity program include:

A. Information Technology Infrastructure Library (ITIL) standard for continuity management.

B. COBIT

C. BCP is mandated by the ISO 17799 standard for data security.

[D]   Basic Planning Assumptions

A list of assumptions to include in the plan:

A. **The primary objectives of all plans are the safety of people, and then the protection of company assets.** Always state that people come first, for both legal and ethical reasons.

B. **Problems arise in their own good time.** It could be in the middle of the day or in the dead of night on a holiday weekend. If a problem arises while key staff is on site, then they will take care of it. However, if it occurs in the middle of the night, or while they are away on vacation, would the staff on site have something to consult? What would the company do if the key people suddenly resigned?

C. **Major problems create major chaos.** Imagine the confusion caused by a loss of electricity in the building. Ideally, the support staff would know what to do, but just the loss of lights is enough to bring work to a standstill. Since their workstations are dead, employees will shuffle off to break rooms or congregate anywhere there is light. This reaction is normal. However, is it what the executives want?

D. **People are prone to inaction.** When problems arise, most people will just sit down to await the arrival of the "experts" as if there is nothing to do until they restore operations to normal. Is that what they should be doing? Is it true that these people are helpless?

[E]   The Local Expert

Most departments have someone that everyone turns to in a crisis—and it is rarely their boss. The "local expert" is often a long-time employee who has seen or worked through the most common forms of problems that arise in the department. Whatever the crisis, managers always consult this person.

The problem with the local expert approach is that everyone sits around until this expert appears on the scene. In addition, despite his air of confidence, the local expert's experience tends to be spotty and often the solution is something that others in the staff could have pulled together. It is time for a change.

There are many problems with the local expert approach.

A.   What will the team do if the expert is not available?
B.   It assumes this person is "all knowing" of business processes and technologies, including the latest ones.
C.   It makes the staff (and the IT Manager) dependent on one person (a single point of failure).

If an IT Manager would watch the local expert in action, he would witness someone with an informal continuity plan. He would have telephone numbers for vendors, help sheets for resolving problems (perhaps given to him by the original developers), and his own notes from over the years for what to do. A local expert has a mental index of where to find these fragments of information. A cynic would say that the local expert keeps the information dispersed to protect his status as the department's "wise one."

Rather than bet the company, and the IT Manager's job on this person, begin a plan by moving all of this information out of his area, off of the "sticky notes," and into a central department document. This provides at least something to act on in a crisis.

COMMENT

Most business initiatives begin with the assignment of an executive sponsor. This makes funding for the plan easier to obtain. However even without executive backing, IT Managers have a responsibility to the company and to their coworkers to develop a plan on their own initiative. Few modern companies can exist for long if their data system is out of service for an extended period. Reverting to manual processes or trying to rebuild everything from scratch is not an economically viable alternative.

§ 7.03 BUSINESS CONTINUITY PLANNING BASICS

[A] Overview

Assembling a plan is a long but valuable process. It will uncover weaknesses in processes to address before an actual problem occurs. Basic BCP involves three steps:

A. Identifying what is critical to the organization.
B. Identifying what risks (threats) these critical functions face.
C. Developing action plans to reduce these risks.

The IT recovery plan does not stand-alone. It exists alongside of the Facilities Recovery Plan and the Security/Safety department's emergency plans. By coordinating with these groups, the IT plans can focus on the technologies and leave those areas to the people who know them best.

For example, if a fire occurred in two offices, which also consumed the wire closet between them, the IT Manager would require quick access to determine the extent of the damage. Any recovery (and even access to the damaged area) must be coordinated with the facilities team. Therefore, knowledge of the facilities plans will help the IT Manager to establish coordinate points in the recovery process.

[B] Identify the Critical Processes

What are the essential few functions of the business? For some companies, delivering a high level of customer service is critical. For an electrical power supplier, it might be a high level of service. For a factory, it may be the on-time shipment of promised material to customers. In a crisis, there is not enough time to restore everything. Avoid diverting scarce resources to restoring low value functions. To focus resources and reduce the recovery time required, companies zero in on the essential few functions that keep the cash flowing in the doors.

> **COMMENT**
>
> Pareto's law indicates that roughly 20 percent of the business's effort (the critical tasks) provides 80 percent of its value.

These critical elements are the foundation of a continuity plan. They are what the company is trying to protect. Any functions that do not directly support these activities may still have a plan but are secondary in a recovery. It is an executive management responsibility to identify these critical few. If any critical function is having problems, then an IT Manager must expend whatever effort is necessary to resolve the problem.

> **COMMENT**
>
> The authors have worked for companies whose critical functions were "To build, ship, and invoice product on time." Another company's vital few functions were "To maintain 24 by 7 customer services, the ability to receive orders, and the timely shipment of goods."

In a small company, the executives identify critical business functions based on their experience. Larger enterprises conduct a business impact analysis (BIA) which identifies critical business functions based on their cash flow impact and their legal necessity.

A BIA involves a series of interviews with company executives to identify:

A. The origins of the company's cash flows, and the impact of losing them, over time. This might indicate that after one day's loss of a specific business function, the company would not lose any money at all. However, by the third day, the daily loss would be some large amount of money.

B. Potential negative impacts to the company, such as a contractual performance penalty for failing to perform a customer service. Another example is an inability to perform customer support or to deliver goods on time.

C. Actions required demonstrating legal compliance, such as air pollution monitoring systems.

D. The IT systems that support each of the critical business functions. This prioritizes them for IT recovery and drives the data center recovery planning. (Most plans assume that, in a crisis, office space could be found but the IT systems will be the most complex thing to restore.)

Taken together, the BIA quantifies the impact to the company of a total outage—or a partial outage affecting numerous business functions. The quantified impact is used to make trade offs between the risk of the loss versus the cost of mitigating actions. Therefore, the BIA justifies the BCP budget.

> **COMMENT**
>
> Beware of the "whining executive" who tries to inflate his importance by declaring all of his business functions as critical. It is up to the C level executives to arbitrate among the departments what is truly essential.

> Sometimes executives demand to restore everything immediately. Once they see the cost for immediate failover of just a few of the larger systems, they withdraw the request.

The BIA tracks the losses to the company over time. This is important as some companies cannot tolerate a single day of total outage (such as an online service) while others can tough it out with little more than some lost productivity and salary wages. The duration of a *tolerable* outage is the Recovery Time Objective (RTO) and drives the strategy of the data center recovery plan.

BIAs are time consuming and expensive to conduct but are valuable to the company in many ways. They benefit not only IT analysis but also the company's strategic planning processes. Based on the revenue loss of a disabled business function, the IT can rationally set system recovery priorities.

Most business managers lack a big picture perspective of their company. Even executives with long company tenure typically have a narrow view of departments other than the ones through which they advanced. BIA results are useful for allocating future capital and highlight the costs/revenues of marginal operations.

COMMENT

After the BIA identifies the critical functions, the IT Manager can review the staff's skills for supporting them and use any knowledge gaps to justify team training.

[C]   Identify Risks (Threats)

Every day the company's critical few functions face a series of risks. The first step is to identify these threats. The second step is to raise defenses against the more likely or damaging risks. To evaluate these risks, build a spreadsheet to sift through the threats and help identify the key ones to address. An example is found in Worksheet 7-1.

A risk, or threat, is the *potential* that something may happen. Although risks can be positive as well as negative, business continuity planning focuses on the damaging risks, or those that can go wrong. Risks have many dimensions.

The main four dimensions are impact, likelihood, warning, and recovery time.

A. First, examine risks based on their impact to company operations if they occurred. Impact is typically measured by lost revenue, and the time and resources required to restore normal function.

WORKSHEET 7-1.   Risk Assessment Form

Risk Assessment Form					
Date:				**Restoration Time**	**Score**
		Likelihood	**Impact**		
Grouping	**Risk**	**0–10**	**0–10**	**0–10**	
Natural Disasters					
	Earthquake				0
	Tornadoes				0
	Severe thunderstorms				0
	Hail				0
	Snow / Ice / Blizzard				0
	Extreme temperatures				0
	Floods / Tidal Surges				0
	Forest / brush fires				0
	Land Slides				0
	Sink Holes				0
	Sand storms				0
Man-Made Risks					
	Highway Access				0
	Railroad				0
	Pipelines				0
	Airports				0
	Harbors / Industrial Areas				0
	Chemical users				0
	Dams				0
	Rivers				0
Civil Issues					
	Riot				0
	Labor Stoppage / Picketing				0
Key Suppliers					
	(list your suppliers here)				0
					0
					0

For example, if the facility were located in Minnesota, the impact of a blizzard would be high due to problems of shipping raw materials in and finished goods out. Contrast the snowstorm with a department store fire. Damage from the flames is small. However, there is now an odor of smoke on all of the goods in the store. Recovery time to clean out all the smoke-damaged clothes and refill the building with fresh goods can be quite long.

A bank has a risk for robbery. The impact is high but the recovery is quick. The police are usually finished within a day and with a fresh stock of money the bank can reopen.

B. This leads to the second dimension of risk—likelihood. Many horrible things *might* happen, but realistically, what is the chance that they will? If the chance is very, very small, then ignore it. Yes, the sun might quit shining tomorrow, but its likelihood is too small to address. What is the likelihood that a crazed employee with a gun will rampage through the offices? What is the likelihood of an electrical outage? What is the likelihood that severe weather will shut the facility down for more than one day?

C. The third dimension of risk is warning. A weather report will warn about incoming severe weather. This allows some time to prepare. However, the theft of a server or a fire in the UPS unit arrives without any prior indication. Therefore, threats that can be anticipated allow more time to react. Threats that emerge suddenly allow no time to mitigate and are more damaging.

D. The fourth dimension is recovery time. For example, a critical device in a remote part of the facility may be susceptible to lightning strikes. Any outage of that device is a critical emergency. However, the recovery time is quick by exchanging it with an on-site spare. Another example is a server. If a server is physically destroyed, the recovery time is how long it takes to bring in a spare server and then reload it.

Refer to Worksheet 7-1 for some ideas of risks to consider. Use this example just to get the plan started. This process works best as a team exercise to gain many points of view. Change the list to address the local situation. Replace the section on natural risk with the ones in the local area. Carry on with this throughout the chart. Then working with other managers, assign scores (1 through 10) for likelihood (10 means almost certain), impact, and restoration time. The score for the warning column is 1 for the most warning and 10 for no warning at all. Multiply the scores together and sort them (descending) with the highest scores on top. Address these top risks. At some point, draw a line across the list and ignore anything below it.

A look at the risks shows that some of them would have the same recovery actions, such as a fire that gutted a building or a tornado that wiped it away. Two different risks, but essentially the same recovery plan.

[D]   Other Risk Considerations

Some risks are local. If a branch bank is robbed, that location will be out of service for the day but the rest of the company's banking branches are still operational. A bad day for that one branch office but the company as a whole experienced no disruption. Another localized risk is a tornado—terrible where it hits, but generally the rest of the area is fine.

> ## COMMENT
>
> It is essential that a company review the BCPs of its critical vendors. Otherwise, the vendor's disaster may become your own.

The opposite of a local risk is a wide area risk, such as the snowstorm in Minnesota. This risk may close roads across the state, keep employees away, and prevent the movement of materials on the highways. The factory is intact and may still be churning out goods but nothing is moving outside the facility's four walls. No fresh materials come in and no finished goods flow out until the highways reopen. Other wide area risks to consider are floods, hurricanes, and earthquakes. Wide area risks often hurt customers and suppliers.

Man-made threats come in many forms. There could be a terrorist threat against the company, a truck carrying toxic chemicals could crash outside of the facility and force evacuation, or an angry person with a gun could be looking for victims. Man-made threats tend to be localized.

Infrastructure threats would include problems with the things essential for the company to continue operating. Electrical power is an essential part of any company. Without it, there are no lights for the offices, desktop workstations fall dark, and the heating and air conditioning stop. Everyone has experienced electrical outages. Another infrastructure threat is to the telecommunications lines outside the building. These lines also carry data traffic, so this risk is a double whammy.

Possible subsets to the previously mentioned infrastructure risks are associated with the facilities. This includes roof collapses, interior electrical failures, etc. Many things can cause leaking water pipes and water damages spread quickly.

A very common risk facing companies involves the security of their assets and employees. Computers make attractive theft targets as do a wide number of things within a company's walls. The risk to this can be high as the PC stolen may be full of company secrets, confidential legal files, or the only copies of accounting records. A comprehensive internal security program is a key part of any business continuity plan.

> ## COMMENT
>
> In 2005, the Associated Press reported that a laptop computer stolen from the University of California, Berkeley, contained personal information of almost 100,000 alumni and graduate students.

Most companies have at least one disgruntled employee. As an insider, this person knows company processes and what would hurt operations the most if damaged. Employee sabotage may be difficult to stop. Alongside of this is employee theft. Sometimes a thief will try to cover his crime by setting a fire to destroy evidence. Address all of this through the company's security plan and policies.

[E]   Develop Action Plans to Reduce These Risks

After spreading "doom and gloom" to depress the brightest optimist, let's begin fighting back. Once we have stripped away the element of surprise from these risks, take steps to address them. There are three basic strategies to consider:

A. **Avoidance.** Are there any actions that can be taken to avoid the risk? If hurricanes interrupt operations, could the company move to Wisconsin? This move avoids the threat to the flow of work from hurricanes. Avoidance actions often introduce new threats to the company.

B. **Mitigation.** Unavoidable risks require steps to reduce the likelihood or impact of the threat. Examples of mitigation actions are all around. Consider the fire sprinkler system in the offices. A sprinkler does not stop a fire from starting. It requires the heat from a fire to activate it. A fire sprinkler contains and slows the fire's spread—reducing the damage it can cause. To reduce the likelihood of losing electrical power, some companies install instant-on generator systems. Another example is a car's spare tire. If needed, it reduces the delay caused by a flat tire by providing a way to return mobility to the car.

C. **Transference.** After trying to avoid and mitigate a problem, the third option is to transfer the risk to someone else. Transfer losses from a threat to insurance policies. For example, product liability insurance can protect a company in case someone was hurt using one of their products. Since a company cannot stop people misusing products, transfer that risk to an insurance policy. Reduce insurance rates through the introduction of well-written and tested business continuity plans. Insurance companies will often provide advice for writing a plan since it reduces their risk.

With these three strategies in mind, reexamine the list of threats to the company and see which strategy is best suited to each threat. The steps required to carry these actions out become the continuity planning action items. Some of these steps may have already been taken, such as the installation of fire sprinklers.

This third step of planning includes the development of specific plans to address threats to the critical few company activities. Start by comparing the risks to the list of solutions found in the notes of the local expert. Discussing this list in a staff meeting may also bring out some solutions used in the past.

To keep the planning efforts focused, constantly refer to:

A.   What are my critical processes and the critical assets that enable them to work?
B.   What threatens them?
C.   What actions reduce the likelihood of a threat becoming reality?
D.   What will minimize the damage if the risk does occur?
E.   What does the team do if a problem occurs?
F.   Where can more information be found on this?

COMMENT

If you cannot describe what you are doing as a process, you don't know what you're doing.

—W. Edwards Deming

[F]   Executives' Business Continuity Plan

In a crisis, most IT Managers want executives to be as far away as possible. However, they have a role to play. Rather than leaving them to their own imagination in a crisis, write an executive annex to the IT plan. This annex, a small plan in itself, describes the roles that executives must play during the crisis.

The executives' first responsibility is to assemble in a safe area as near to the disaster as practical. Practical means a room with telephones and data communication lines. Hotel rooms serve this purpose nicely. The executives will need this capability to communicate with customers, suppliers, news media, and shareholders.

During a disaster, these executives will receive the initial damage assessment from the facility manager and the security manager. If the IT Manager could safely enter the structure, then a quick damage assessment to the data system will be included. At this point, the executives must decide to restore service in a patched together structure or to restore IT services in another location. If this company has a hot site contract, they could declare a disaster and relocate to the hot site. Relocating a data center or activating a hot site is expensive, so executive involvement is essential.

The next executive action is to appoint someone to oversee the disaster management. The CEO and other top executives will be busy addressing external communications. This "Disaster Master" must be empowered to make purchasing decisions and to slice through paperwork to press the recovery forward rapidly.

See Policy ITP-7-1 Business Continuity Planning Policy as an example for starting the process at your organization.

POLICY ITP-7-1.   Business Continuity Planning Policy

Policy #:	ITP-7-1	Effective:	03/18/08	Page #:	1 of N
Subject:	Business Continuity Planning Policy				

1.0 PURPOSE

The purpose of this policy is to create and maintain a Business Continuity Plan (BCP) for the IT support of critical company processes. An effective plan allows the company to minimize the adverse effect of emergencies that arise. The Company has an ethical obligation to the organization's workforce, shareholders, and customer stakeholders to protect the continuing operations of the business.

2.0 SCOPE

This policy encompasses all IT processes and technology that supports critical business functions.

3.0 POLICY

The IT Manager is responsible for creating, maintaining, and testing the IT Business Continuity Plan. The following activities must be performed:

A. Identify Critical Processes.
   To identify the business processes critical to the company's financial and legal well-being, a bi-annual Business Impact Analysis (BIA) is conducted. The result is a Recovery Time Objective—that point at which company losses become intolerable (Recovery Time Objective—RTO). The IT Business Recovery Plan must ensure that critical IT processes (equipment and software) can be recovered at a remote site within the RTO.
   The CEO initiates and sponsors the BIA. The BIA will:
   1. Encompass all departments and areas of the company.
   2. Identify the point in time that the financial and legal issues seriously threaten the company's survival.
   3. Identify the processes required to meet all regulatory requirements.
   4. Include a risk assessment of natural and man-made risks to the critical processes.

B. Business Continuity Planning.
   The IT manager will assemble plans for every identified critical business function.
   1. Develop the plan.
      a. Develop plans for the recovery IT processes, equipment, and software for all critical business processes identified by the BIA. These plans must address steps necessary to reestablish the IT functions at an emergency recovery location.
      b. Based on the BIA, publish a restoration priority list of all critical technologies.
      c. Create an emergency notification program to ensure the prompt notification of executive management in a crisis.
   2. Maintain the plan.
      a. Perform a technical, natural, and man-made risk assessment annually.
      b. Identify mitigation actions to ensure the easiest and most timely recovery.
      c. Establish and maintain off-site storage of copies of all vital IT records, including a full backup of the disk storage media, updated daily. Ensure that the transportation and storage of media conforms to the company's data security policies.
      d. Update the IT Business Continuity Plan as technology supporting critical processes is changed.
   3. Exercise the plan.
      a. Test all IT Business Continuity Plans at least bi-annually to demonstrate the ability to achieve the BIA determined Recovery Time Objective. Conduct a lessons-learned session with all participants to capture and incorporate improvements into the plans.
      b. Report all test results to the CEO within 30 days of the test's completion.
   4. Training.
      a. Train all members of the IT department in their roles in supporting the BCP.
      b. Train all new employees on their roles within 30 days of joining the department.
   5. Coordinate with other company disaster plans. The IT manager will coordinate the IT BCP with:
      a. The Facilities Disaster Recovery plan and the Security/Safety department's crisis plan.
      b. The various business recovery plans of other departments.

4.0 REVISION HISTORY

Date	Revision #	Description of Change
03/18/08	1.0	Initial creation.

5.0 INQUIRIES

Direct inquiries about this policy to:

Tom Jones, CIO
Our Company, Inc.
2900 Corporate Drive
Columbus, OH 43215

Voice: 614-555-1234
Fax: 614-555-1235
E-mail: tjones@company.com

Revision #:	1.0	Supersedes:	N/A	Date:	03/18/08

§ 7.04 PLANNING—THE NEXT STEP

[A] Use What Is Already Available

Before writing the plan, check around to see what information is already available. Writing a plan can be time-consuming and yet much of the source material isn't far away. Assemble a basic community plan with a few calls and a notebook. *In most crises three keys are needed—key people, keys to the doors, and key support contract information.* Be sure to label the origin of any information collected, as there may be a need to go back for further clarification later.

Ten steps to a basic recovery plan:

A. **Start with the basics—whom do I call.** Obtain a current organization chart for the facility. This will show who works in what areas. Now get an organization chart for the entire company— specifically the key technical areas and executives. In a crisis, their help may be useful. For example, if there was a severe crisis with the data network, the IT Manager could call on the network experts from other company sites to come in on short notice and help for a few days.

B. **With these names in hand, match them to three telephone numbers.** This is very important for people directly supporting the facility and less so for people at other sites. Try to obtain the 24-hour contact information for at least one contact person for each of the other company sites (usually this is their IT Manager). For each person on the contact list, find their:
   4. Office telephone number.
   5. Home telephone number.
   6. Cellular telephone number.

C. **Check with the security staff to see if they keep a key to every door in a secure key locker.** Keys are easy to copy. It is impossible to know who has a key to what doors. If possible, use electronic locks on the critical doors. A report can be generated by the server controlling the electronic locks listing who has access to which doors protected by electronic locks. A part of this step is the identification of doors the individual IT staff members need access to.

D. **Build a spreadsheet of service contract information.** The sheet should indicate who to call for which items, the terms of service (24/7, Monday through Friday, etc.), how to call for help, and the contract expiration date. This could be a long list. A copy should reside at the service desk.

E. **Build a vendor list of anyone who supplies critical materials or who provides critical services.** This could be the company that prints IT's special forms (such as invoices and checks), the place from which the company buys backup media, etc. Service companies could be hardware repair services, the company that provides off-site storage of backup tapes, or companies that support software tools.

F. **Take a walk around asset inventory.** Walk around the entire facility and note every major piece of equipment and its location on an asset list. Which device is important to critical operations? Which device must always be available? Compare the asset list to the service contract list. Are all of the critical devices covered? Is the service coverage adequate?

G. **Talk to the systems administrators and make a list of software assets.** This includes purchased software as well as homegrown code. Do the purchased packages have service support agreements? Are these agreements included on the service contract list? Are the software licenses securely stored off site?

H. **Identify the various business functions that IT supports.** Make a list of them and then fill in the technologies that are necessary to support them. (This information is in the BIA report.) This is a big list.

I. **Establish a list of restoration priorities.** Base it on the list of critical business functions. Later on, review this list with executive management so planning efforts coincide with their expectations. In a crisis, the recovery team will use this to guide their actions.

J. **Build an employee skills matrix for the IT department.** This will give some idea of who to call on for emergency backup on a specific technology. It can also be matched against the critical equipment list and software asset lists to develop a staff training plan. Identify the skills gaps now and begin training the IT staff!

To complete these ten basic steps, the IT Manager probably spent a couple of days pulling the information together. However, now the staff has a lot of information for the service desk and other key people in this organization. Much more is needed, but this forms the nucleus of a formal continuity plan.

COMMENT

The essential ingredient for an IT recovery is the ready availability of readable backup media. Back up *all* files onto other media as often as possible, and store this media off site in a

> secure location. As media is rotated back to the data center, verify that it is still readable.

One way to see how ready the staff is (and to uncover any more hidden caches of information) is to make an unannounced visit to the support people and ask for their critical information. Some will reference the sticky notes that encircle their monitor; some will dig deep back into an address book for bypass codes, and some will bring out the cheat sheets. Others will give a condescending blank stare. Imagine the ball of energy they would become fumbling for this same information in a real emergency! Be sure to copy all of this information into the files, as it will be useful later.

COMMENT

Some people will declare that they already have a plan. Ask for a copy. In most cases it will lack many of the essential details. This shows they have already bought into the recovery plan concept. Make sure that the plan is executable by someone familiar with the technology, but who has not worked on that business process.

After organizing what has been collected so far, begin validating it with people other than those who provided the information. Crosscheck the accuracy, to see which employees are better organized than others. It is especially important if the notes copied were rather old and out of date. All information should be neatly typed (or copied) and placed in a three-ring binder, broken down by subjects with tabs to identify the sections. In an emergency, the tabs allow quick access to needed information without fumbling through a lot of pages.

Be sure to mark the binder and all sheets as "company confidential." Much of what is in the business continuity plan will be useful to mischievous people.

[B]   Distributing Interim Copies

There is now enough of a plan to make copies and distribute them to key people. This is an important step, as the project has now progressed from a one-person show to a team effort. Ask each of these people to help improve the book by filling in the gaps and commenting on what has been collected so far. The minimal number of copies is:

A.   One copy of the book at the plan administrator's office desk. (Use this when problems arise.)

B. One copy at the plan administrator's home to address problem calls when they come in (and in case something happens to the copy at work!).
C. One copy to the IT Manager.
D. One copy at the IT Manager's home.
E. One copy at the IT service desk.

At this stage it is best to keep the number of copies in circulation to a minimum since there will be many updates as the plan evolves. The IT Manager's copy and the service desk's copy may be skipped if they are stored on a CD and on the network as a read-only file.

[C] Adding to the Plan—More Contact Information

During normal work hours, it is easy to find people when problems arise. Rather than chase them down, obtain a facility telephone directory. The company's telephone technician likely has one. This list provides the daytime telephone numbers. However, emergencies have a habit of arising in the middle of the night, on holiday weekends, etc. Using the telephone list and the company organization chart, identify the key managers to call in the event of an after hours emergency. Ask these people for their home telephone and cell phone numbers.

These numbers are useful for advising people of IT problems during off hours. This forewarns them so when they come into work in an emergency, they are prepared for the situation. This might be to inform the materials managers that the warehouse management system has failed and will take many hours to repair. By calling them in the wee hours of the night, they can decide if their staff needs to come in early and work around the problem. The same situation holds for about every department: accounting, payroll, human resources, engineering, etc.

Respect the personal privacy of these home telephone numbers and never give them out to anyone. These personal numbers will likely be covered by the company's privacy policy, so do not leave them lying around. While on the subject, draft guidelines explaining the circumstances that are severe enough to call someone at home.

[D] Keys

An important step in BCP is keeping people away from critical equipment. Some people are curious, like to push buttons, and are intrigued about what will happen next. There is the occasional discontented person who wants to express his outrage by turning off a server or unplugging a network hub. It could be almost anything. So wherever possible, limit the ability of anyone to disturb the operation of equipment. Keep critical equipment in locked closets, hard wired into the electrical outlet, and away from the wondering masses.

After keeping everyone else out, make sure the IT staff can get in! Problems can arise at any hour of the day or night. If technical support staff is called in to work on something, can they get in? If there is a company security force, they should have a copy of the key to every door. If not, then establish an IT key cabinet. A key cabinet holds one copy of every key to every door or cabinet the IT staff needs to access. Be sure to attach a label to every key because in a small pile, they all look alike!

Some people are certain that the world is out to get them, and they will attach their own locks to doors and tool lockers. They typically forget to pass a copy to the key locker. Fortunately, a well-stocked key locker includes a master key named "Mr. Bolt Cutter." Whenever encountering a personal lock on one of the equipment room doors, introduce that lock to Mr. Bolt Cutter. If this is not done, valuable time will be lost in a crisis looking for someone to open a $2.00 lock that did not belong there.

COMMENT

The company's security policy should require the security office to stock and provide approved locks for doors and cabinets, or a process for the security office to obtain two keys to each. The same policy must prohibit the use of personal locks on anything other than company lockers. This together with an employee orientation should greatly reduce the use of personal locks on company equipment.

It is easy to copy physical keys without anyone knowing about it. No one knows for sure how many copies of a particular key are floating around. The security office should always sign out keys to people for ease of retrieval when the employee leaves the company. Otherwise, these keys may wind up with people who should not have them.

Physical keys can effectively keep out most people, but by far the best approach is the use of electronic locks. These are common in hotels. Instead of turning a key, an electronic key checks the database to see if that key should have entry through that door. It also maintains a log of who unlocked what door, and when. In addition, a record is available of who has propped it open.

Electronic keys allow the IT Manager to grant or remove access easily. Over time, some people forget their pass card and ask for a "temporary" one for the day. Then they forget to turn it back in. Some people will go through this frequently. It is doubtful they lose their car keys so often! When issuing a temporary card, always limit its access to one day. Otherwise, it is like the copies of physical keys floating around. It is impossible to be sure of who is walking through what door and what they might be carrying out!

Passwords are the logical keys to IT equipment. Just like a master key, a system administrator password is the golden pass to anywhere and anything on a computer system. Guard passwords closely. The problem is that, in a crisis, the support staff may need specific passwords to shut down or restart servers, mainframes, computers, etc. Establish a secure place to store them so they are available in an emergency.

[E] Service Contracts—HELP!

The company probably pays a princely sum every month for someone to be on call to repair its vital equipment. This is a common practice. However, paying someone to come in at any hour to fix something is useless if the support staff does not know how to contact them! Take the time to pull information on all service contracts and put it in the BCP book. This is important information for the service desk to have too.

Ask everyone in the department for a copy of their service contract information. This would include:

A. **Vendor's name.**
B. **What is covered.** Sometimes this is specific equipment (by serial number); sometimes the agreement is for everything on the premises.
C. **Hours of coverage.** The company pays one rate for service to cover normal working hours, and a higher rate for around-the-clock coverage. If the company pays for 24-hour coverage, do not let the service company off the hook if they try to defer until morning. Around-the-clock coverage is double the cost of normal service.
D. **Whom to call during normal working hours and after hours.** Every agreement must include a 24-hour number. Try to get an after-hours telephone number even for the companies only providing 8–5 service. It will be expensive to bring them in on a Saturday to help with a repair, but it might be worth it.
E. **When the contract expires.** This information should go on a calendar to reevaluate the service level before the contract expires. Reevaluate the importance of the covered equipment, its incidence of repair, and if the current service level is adequate.
F. **Any limitations or extra cost provisions.** Sometimes the agreement covers parts and labor; sometimes it only covers the labor cost of "best effort." Know what this is in case an emergency purchase order is required.
G. **Contract number.** The larger companies will check to see if the caller has paid his bills before sending anyone out. They will look up the contract number in their database to see if the item in question is covered. In some cases, they want the unit serial number as well.
H. **Company-appointed contact person.** Usually, a company designates one or two people the person(s) who can make the call. It helps to know who they are. Often, these are people who know how to make minor adjustments to the equipment and avoid service calls.
I. **Guaranteed response time.** How long will it be before they show up? Usually this is something like four hours or eight hours. If they do not show up on time, start escalating the requests!

There are five basic types of service agreements. Select the one that best suits that piece of equipment's failure rate, the degree of criticality of the equipment, and the availability of alternate devices until that machine is operational.

A. **Cold call for service.** This is where the IT Manager's fingers do the walking through the phone book and find someone to come out. The result will be a long service call since they know nothing about the site or its equipment. They may also take several days to get around to coming out.

B. **Time and materials.** The service vendor will come out for a set rate per hour and work until the machine is operational. They will also charge for the parts. Although the hourly rate is expensive, this may be cheaper than a service contract. This approach is good for equipment that rarely breaks and for equipment where there are on-site spares. Under the time and materials arrangement, there is an existing business arrangement so the service company should be somewhat familiar with the company's equipment and its business processes.

C. **Normal working hours.** This is usually 8 a.m. until 5 p.m. Under this agreement the service company will do what they can during these hours. If the job will run past 5 p.m., they will go home and pick up where they left off during the next business day.

D. **Full service.** This is 24/7 service. Unlimited calls at any time of day, for any day of the week. The contract includes all costs. Always use this type of service contract for mission critical equipment.

E. **Exchange.** This is a good approach for smaller items like bar-code scanner guns. Keep some spares on site and send in the broken ones for repair—usually at a set rate. However, it may take weeks to get the device back.

With this service contract information in hand, walk around and look at all of the critical equipment. Is it on the service contract list? Did someone forget to mention something or is there a gap in the service agreements? Does each critical device have the appropriate level of coverage? Business requirements change and often the service contracts do not keep pace with them.

After collecting all of this information into a spreadsheet, provide a copy to everyone who has the BCP book. The service desk will find this all very handy.

To ensure that everyone knows what to do, make up small cards with the service contract information on them. Attach the cards to the major devices like large printers, servers, etc. If possible, put it somewhere inside the machine where it is easy to find, such as under the dust cover of a printer. Be sure to remove any old service information. If there is a lot of equipment in a room, just post the collective information on the wall.

[F] Vendor Contacts

Like service contracts, the support staff needs to know who to call for a particular service or material. This is not an all-inclusive list. It should only include current vendors or someone the team may need to contact in an emergency. This list will do more than help in a major crisis; it can help with the more mundane emergencies that pop up everyday. Has an off-brand printer ever run out of toner at a critical business time? Knowing who to call could get the ball rolling.

A vendor list provides a single point of reference for everyone in the department who needs materials. (Of course they would still need to work through the usual approval process.) In addition, this list reduces the time required looking for vendors to bid on projects.

Include for each vendor the company name, account manager's name, daytime and after-hours telephone number, fax number, e-mail address, the company's address, and a description of what they supply. The vendor list should also contain every company on the service contract list.

When drafting the list, remember the "other" vendors such as the electric company, telephone company, water company, waste removal service, and local ambulance. These numbers may become very handy in a crisis. See Worksheet 7-2 Critical Vendor List.

[G]   Walk-Around Asset Inventory

Grab a pad and pencil and walk around the company areas. Begin in the IT department. Make a note of every major item found, like a server, network hub, major printer, etc. Do not try to do this from memory. In particular, look for equipment that has popped up in user departments. Indicate which of these items support critical company processes. Walk everywhere. Be curious and open cabinets and every closet.

Look everywhere—especially where equipment does not belong.

COMMENT

In a large factory, one of the authors found:

- Modems connected to antifreeze coolant tanks so someone could remotely monitor the contents!
- Old 8088-based PCs used to monitor PLCs!
- A copper pipe bender that used 8-inch floppy disks!
- IBM network controllers that used a 5-inch floppy for storage—a floppy so worn you could almost see through it!
- 8088-based PCs with a custom communications board!

At a different site, there was:

- A time clock server stashed under a desk in the payroll department!
- An electronic lock server in the security office!

WORKSHEET 7-2. Critical Vendor List

Critical Vendor List

Company Name	Contact Position	Name	Telephone Numbers				Email	Street Address
			Office	Cellular	Fax	Home		
	Sales							
	Tech Supt							
	Sales							
	Tech Supt							
	Sales							
	Tech Supt							
	Sales							
	Tech Supt							
	Sales							
	Tech Supt							

When walking through, note the location of disconnected equipment. Send someone out to pick it up for potential reissue. Likely some pockets of new equipment will be uncovered that someone keeps as a personal emergency spare parts stash. Check every closet! Arrange to have all of this equipment collected into one spot and lock it up. Repair and reissue the good material and scrap the broken ones.

Compare the asset inventory to the list of service contracts. Are all the critical devices covered? Is the level of coverage adequate? Sometimes the machine itself will have a sticker saying who to call for service. When in doubt, ask the operators whom they call with questions.

Include supporting equipment that enables other devices to work on the list. This might be an uninterruptible power supply or critical air conditioning unit. It may also include electronic time clocks or electronic door lock servers. An important goal is to identify "non-standard" equipment that is essential to a critical operation. (Often this equipment is too old to find replacement parts to repair.) The trouble with one-off equipment is that it can be impossible to replace in a crisis.

[H]   Software Asset List

With the easy part out of the way, move on to backup copies of software and data. A look around will reveal a vast proliferation of computers from departmental servers, to special client software that interfaces with other companies, to shop floor equipment controllers. Inside each of these is valuable and potentially irreplaceable software and data. The BCP must ensure that someone makes a periodic backup, or safety, copy of this data, clearly labeled and stored off site.

For each critical piece of equipment, make a list of its critical software. It is often easier to replace the hardware than the software. Some software is unique and almost all software has settings to customize it to the situation. The scariest machines are the ones that no one will shut off since they are not sure if they will ever start again.

Ensure that every device has more than one backup copy of its software and that they are stored separately (preferably off site). For equipment not maintained in the computer room (such as in offices or on the shop floor), store one copy off site and one copy in the data center's tape library room.

Some devices to include:

A. Telephone PBX, automated attendants, and voice mail system—these are simply special-purpose computers requiring data back-up in the same manner as a mainframe computer.
B. Programmable network devices.
C. Shop floor control systems, such as PLCs, robots, CNC devices, etc.
D. Special-purpose PCs that perform critical but highly specialized functions such as clearing credit cards.
E. Servers that control electronic door locks.
F. Copies of software source code locally developed.
G. Licenses for purchased software.

> ## COMMENT
>
> If the search uncovers software where the source code is lost, mark that system for replacement. If the source code cannot be found and that machine dies, then it may not be possible to use the replacement hardware without recompiling the software—which is kind of hard without the source code.

[I]   Restoration Priorities

With the list of the critical processes in hand (as identified by the BIA or by the company executives), the next logical step is to develop restoration priorities for specific technical systems around the facility. Keep this list in the service desk area so that they know which problem to dispatch a technician to first. Discuss it during departmental meetings so everyone knows what is expected. Now everyone knows which system outages require all hands to drop everything and run to the rescue.

For example, if the accounting system was dead and the network was dead, address the network first since it enables all other critical systems to function. Another example would be if both the e-mail system and the materials management system were down. Which system should the service desk dispatch a repair technician to first?

A valuable use for this list is to identify ways to keep these systems running even in the face of adversity. It might mean adding small UPS units to departmental servers or specific workstations. Another possibility is installing failover servers along with the active ones. If the primary system fails, then the shadow system automatically activates.

Use this list to identify areas where manual workaround instructions are needed until normal operations resume. Recovery from manual processing (which usually involves keying in all the data that was not captured) can be tedious but the facility can keep moving forward!

[J]   Toxic Material Storage

For safety's sake, everyone on the IT staff should know where toxic materials are stored and used within the facility. Technicians should take precautions in case whatever damaged the equipment also damaged the toxic materials containers.

Move or safely isolate equipment found in or adjacent to toxic materials storage areas. If moving this equipment is expensive, include it in the upcoming year's capital budget. This becomes a future planning item to isolate or move the equipment far away from the toxic storage area.

[K]   Employee Skills Matrix

If a key support person is on vacation in a far-off place, who will be called to fix the problems? The IT Manager can guess or ask around, but in the meantime, the problem is simmering and so is the boss. Save time by building an employee skills matrix before problems arise.

Begin with a list of the critical processes supported. Each of these processes uses a set of technologies (hardware and software) to accomplish their mission. Technologies exist within a business reference, so a degree of understanding of how they fit in the customer's operations is useful. The skills matrix breaks the critical system down into its components to identify support requirements. The components might be a programming language, specific hardware knowledge, and an understanding of the database management system. This list of components translates into a list of skills required to support them.

A spreadsheet makes an easy-to-use tool for building the matrix. The skills matrix lists the technologies along the vertical axis (which can be a very long list) and the staff names along the top (column headings). Rate each person according to skills at using each of these technologies.

Add a few more rows to this list to identify other useful expertise, such as who is emergency medical technician (EMT) qualified, who is a volunteer firefighter, etc. As an important added benefit, use this list to identify people for training over the upcoming year.

§ 7.05   WRITING A PLAN

[A]   Overview

Some people are reluctant to write recovery plans because they do not know where to start. Writing a plan is as simple as stating the basics of any story: who, what, where, when, why, and how. Base the format on what to do first, what to do second, etc. If the plan addresses these basic points, then it should be sufficient. The goal is to develop a set of instructions so that employees can take the right actions in a disaster. BCPs are intended as guidelines and advice. The technician on the scene should review the plan and then proceed as the circumstances dictate.

If there is a good risk analysis, then everyone has an idea of the various things that could go wrong. No one can predict exactly what will happen. However, a set of generalized actions fit in most situations. When working through the risk analysis, it is apparent that most plans contain the same details. Recovering a destroyed office is the same whether burned out in a fire or a snow-packed roof collapsed.

A plan is not a complete set of instructions to rebuild something. Typically, there are specific actions to repair something or contain the spread of damage to operations. Full recovery plans are created while the containment effort is still under way. When writing, always remember the target audience. Emergencies affect people in different ways. Emergencies are chaotic. A good plan reduces this confusion by providing guidance on what to do. Once the team is working on the problem, they will feel more in control and the chaos will diminish.

> ## COMMENT
>
> Cynics will say that a disaster will occur at the worst possible moment. For an accounting system, this might be when closing the year-end books, etc. Write plans as if the crisis erupted at the worst time in the annual business cycle, usually during the busy season.

Write each plan as if explaining the matter to someone. Think of the person likely to come in after hours to react to the emergency and imagine explaining it to him. Perhaps begin with a short overview paragraph that explains the business purpose of the process and essentially how it accomplishes this. Another way is to imagine the room during the emergency. What is the clearest way to address the problem?

A picture is worth a thousand words. Include pictures of hard to describe locations or drawings of how the major pieces work together. Use digital cameras to include some photos in the plan. Pictures can also shorten the narrative since who has time to read more than a few pages in a crisis?

[B] What to Write About

Every department should have a plan that addresses natural and infrastructure risks. People should not sit helplessly waiting for things to happen; they should be active participants in forcing the results they want. All department processes depend on some basic infrastructure support to be in place for them to be successful. This includes electricity, telecommunications, data communications, and data systems. Therefore, the facility-wide continuity plans should begin with supporting these areas.

Each plan should include three major sections:

A. **Immediate actions.** The first section is the "first aid" to be applied by the technician on the spot. This includes things like shutting off the sprinkler valve once the fire is out to minimize the amount of water damage to clean up. Another immediate action is to use employees' cell phones for communications during a telephone system outage. Many things are possible if thought out in advance.

B. **Containment.** The next section describes containment actions to reduce the spread of the damage until the primary support people arrive. This is not busy work. These are the same actions the "experts" would take when they arrive. In the fire sprinkler example, it would be to contain the water on the floor, picking up items from the floor to minimize water damage, etc.

C. **Establish minimal service levels.** The third major section of the plan contains the actions to return the process to a *minimal* level of service. A company cannot sit idle until a full recovery is completed. This could involve establishing a temporary office, shifting this process to a different company site, implementing manual procedures, etc.

With these three sections in mind, formulate a basic plan format. In this way, all plans at the facility will have a similar "look and feel."

[C] Contents of a Typical Plan

Base the plan's terminology and the level of explanation on the assumed audience. These plans are not targeted at the process expert who might use the plan to gather some ideas in the midst of chaos; an expert would typically just act. The plans are for others in the department who either were on site during the emergency or were the first ones in. Assume they are familiar with the technology but not with that particular business system.

Begin with how obvious the problem is. A building hit by a tornado is obvious. Magnetic damage to backup tapes is not. Hard to detect problems require detailed step-by-step instructions.

How much warning may there be before a problem hits? Some natural disasters, such as a hurricane, provide extensive warnings before they hit. Other disasters, like a lightning strike or blue smoke wafting from the back of a computer, provide little advance warning. Emergencies that have a warning time can trigger containment actions before they begin. Again, a hurricane is an excellent example of an emergency where action is warranted. This can range from covering all of the windows with wood to testing the emergency power generator.

The second consideration in writing a plan is how long the reader must hold out before expert help arrives. If they are fighting to contain a problem, can the expert be on site within an hour; two hours? They will need enough information to contain the problem and fight it until the expert arrives.

Finally, if a key process is dead, is there anything that can be done to keep the facility running? Could materials be shipped out of the front of the building until the network is restored to the shipping docks? Can the factory manually perform the processes that the dead machine used to accomplish? Can the payroll office issue "40 hour" paychecks until the payroll system is restored?

So in each plan, remember:

A. The target audience.
B. How obvious the problem is.
C. How much warning you will have.
D. How long until expert help arrives.
E. Are there any manual workarounds?

[D] Which Processes Need a Plan?

It is not practical to write a plan to cover every eventuality for every item. A plan is only required for critical processes (although a prudent IT Manager has a plan for recovering every process). The facilities department should have a plan to address all natural disasters and man-made disasters (as described in the previous risk analysis section). Other departments are also involved in these areas, such as human resources.

All infrastructure risks should also have a plan. This includes electrical service, data processing, and telecommunications. Even if the facilities department is handling the loss of electrical power, the IT department needs a plan for managing the UPSs for maximum availability, a power-shedding plan to relieve pressure on the UPS by turning off low value equipment, etc.

Most companies have a few other critical processes outside of the infrastructure area for which they should also plan. It might be an expensive and unique machine in the factory. It might be special equipment to route incoming calls to individual salespersons or even a very old machine that manages the finished goods inventory. Whatever specific critical processes are, they need a plan.

Even in our mechanical world, there are still some manual critical processes. They need recovery plans too!

Ensure that the manual processes are clearly documented.

[E]   Testing

Testing is a vital part of recovery planning. Often business managers view testing as time consuming, expensive, and a nonessential activity. This is completely wrong. An untested plan is a risk. Such a plan may provide a false sense of security if it misses the mark and no one takes the time to validate its contents.

Testing provides many valuable benefits:

A. **Testing a plan validates that it works**. It uncovers any gaps in the document. The author may have known what was meant by a passage but anyone reading the document would come to a quick halt.

B. **Testing ensures the document is up to date with the latest process it is supporting**. Keeping recovery plans in sync with process changes is a major challenge. With so much to do, busy people leave changes to the plan for last. Testing catches and updates plans with this problem.

C. **Testing trains the participants in their roles during a crisis**. It is one thing to read a plan but something different to do it. Involving people in a test helps to debug a plan as others interpret it. It builds confidence in the participants that they could fulfill their responsibilities in a crisis.

Preparing for a test requires considerable planning. People and materials must be gathered. A test scenario is required to provide a backdrop for the exercise. The primary types of tests are:

A. Walkthrough—The plan's author walks peers through the plan step by step. The goal is to identify omissions and difficult to understand passages.

B. Tabletop exercise—The plan is talked through by both the IT support team and the department they are supporting (such as Payroll). A disaster scenario is provided to make the plan more "real." An example might be a fire in the server room, a data security breach or a multi-day electrical blackout.

    C. Simulation—The IT team and the supporting departments act as if a real disaster has occurred. A good simulation places the teams in separate rooms (to complicate communications) and feeds information in a bit (or complication) at a time. Simulations require considerable preparation and many companies hire a consultant to develop and run the test.

    D. Wide area simulation—A company wide exercise. A worthwhile effort but rarely done due to expense. A simple example is a fire drill.

Few companies can afford to shut down their operations to conduct testing. Often it is accomplished in "slices," such as for an entire department, or a subset of it. The exception is for hot site testing. IT departments must test this at least annually. It is also a good idea to rotate the IT staff through the hot site. In a crisis, the team will be more familiar with the new location, its limitations, and rules of operation.

[F] Keeping the Plan Current

This is an ongoing struggle, especially in a large IT shop. There are several common approaches:

    A. BCP documentation must be updated within 30 days of upgrade installation.

    B. Additional hardware for the host site must accompany every request for system expansion (such as additional CPUs or disks).

    C. Make BCP updates a step in the formal change control process.

    D. Whenever a crisis erupts, check to see if someone pulls out the plan for reference. Whatever happens, after the emergency passes, require the team to review and update the plan with what worked the best during the recent problem.

The key to keeping the plan up to date is to train the team on the importance of current information in a crisis, and to require the various IT supervisors to enforce this requirement. In essence, push the responsibility as close to the source of the change as possible. IT supervisors tend to support this since they are the ones who scramble to repair systems when the primary support person is far away on vacation.

The support team must review plans not tested in the previous 12 months. The IT supervisor for that team will also review it and sign it as correct.

§ 7.06 SOURCES OF ADDITIONAL INFORMATION

[A] Publications

There are many books concerning this subject. Most of them are general in nature and a great place to start. As the planning program matures, look for something that is specific to your industry.

Some publications include a regular column about disaster recovery, such as Computerworld™ (*www.computerworld.com*). Two popular and free periodicals dedicated to Business Continuity are:

A.   Disaster Recovery Journal—*www.drj.com*
B.   Continuity Insights—*www.continuityinsights.com*

[B]   Training and Certification

Several organizations offer formal training on the concepts of Disaster Recovery and Business Continuity. Some colleges offer degrees and others only a few classes. These schools can be located by searching the Internet, and through the FEMA site (*www.fema.gov.*)

The most popular training organizations offering classes, certification, and ongoing professional information are:

A.   Disaster Recovery International—*www.DRII.org*
B.   Business Continuity Institute—*www.BCI.org*

[C]   Web Sites

The most comprehensive Web site on disaster recovery is run by the U.S. government's Federal Emergency Management Agency (FEMA) at *www.fema.gov*. This site contains information on training, developing plans, and links to many other useful sites. Take time and explore because the deeper into this site a person goes, the more interesting it becomes. It is the best site for all around (and free) information.

Another useful Web site for developing the risk assessment for your locations is also run by the U.S. government's National Oceanic & Atmospheric Administration at *www.NOAA.gov*. This site provides information about severe weather for your area, based on historical data.

[D]   Business Continuity Plan Checklist

A.   Is there a published policy assigning responsibility and guidelines for creating and maintaining a Business Continuity Plan?
  1.   Does it designate a person responsible for writing the plan?
  2.   Has an executive been assigned to oversee the planning effort? (Ultimately, the CEO is responsible for the plan.)
B.   Was a Business Impact Analysis conducted within the last two years? Does it identify:
  1.   Critical business functions.
  2.   Critical IT systems.
  3.   Recovery Time Objective.
C.   Was a risk assessment conducted to identify threats to the critical systems?
D.   Are mitigation actions assigned to the most serious risks?

   E. Does every IT technology that stores data have a current safety copy stored securely off site?
   1. Data.
   2. Software.
   3. Configuration tables.
   F. Is there a crisis communications plan for alerting the appropriate employees and executives at the appropriate time during a disaster?
   G. Is there a designated separate facility for the recovery of the IT department, such as a hot site?
   H. Does the BCP cover the prompt shipment of equipment in the event of an emergency?
   I. Is there a work area recovery plan for the business departments to continue work?
   1. Has this plan been tested within the last 2 years?
   2. Did the test include a sampling of departments?
   J. Are vital records securely stored on site, with safety copies securely stored off site? Usually this involves paper documents.
   K. Are there manual "workarounds" for every critical IT data system?
   L. Is there a crisis management plan in place for executive leadership?
   M. Is every plan tested at least every other year?
   1. Has every critical system been recovered at the alternate site?
   2. Does each critical system have its own set of recovery instructions?
   3. Can all of these technologies be recovered within the Recovery Time Objective?
   N. Is every person who might execute a plan trained in his role? Does this include new employee orientation?
   O. Is there a reliable process in place to update the BCP as the IT and business functions change?

8

IT AUDITS: STAYING IN COMPLIANCE

§ 8.01   OVERVIEW
    [A]   Purpose and Scope
    [B]   Types of Audits
    [C]   Critical Policies to Develop Based on This Chapter

§ 8.02   IT MANAGEMENT AUDIT
    [A]   Purpose
    [B]   IT Organization
    [C]   IT Controls
    [D]   Financial Analysis

§ 8.03   IT LEGAL MANDATES AND RECORDS RETENTION
    [A]   Overview
    [B]   Public Laws
    [C]   Records Retention
    [D]   Types of Records

§ 8.04   RESOURCE MANAGEMENT
    [A]   Scope
    [B]   Technical Resources
    [C]   Personnel Resources

§ 8.05   PROGRAMMING ACTIVITIES CONTROL
    [A]   Overview
    [B]   Standards for Systems Development and Programming
    [C]   Programming Activities Control
    [D]   Database Management
    [E]   Management Post-Implementation Reviews

§ 8.06   COMPUTER OPERATIONS
    [A]   Objective
    [B]   Computer Operations
    [C]   Computer Room Controls
    [D]   Computer Operations Management Reporting
    [E]   Data Library Controls
    [F]   Input Data Controls
    [G]   Output Controls

§ 8.07 DATA NETWORKS
[A] Overview
[B] Security Issues
[C] Network Audit Points
[D] Security Policies

§ 8.08 DISASTER RECOVERY/CONTINGENCY PLANNING
[A] Overview
[B] Data Center Contingency Planning
[C] Plan Updates

§ 8.09 WORKSTATION AUDIT ISSUES
[A] Objective
[B] Workstation Standards
[C] Workstation Environment

§ 8.10 STRATEGIES FOR SURVIVING AN AUDIT
[A] The Auditor Is Your New Friend
[B] Steps for a "Successful" Audit
[C] Using the Audit to Your Advantage

§ 8.01 OVERVIEW

[A] Purpose and Scope

"The auditor is coming!"—words that strike fear into the hearts of IT Managers everywhere. Employee attitudes toward audits depend on how the company uses audits. Well-run audits are not "witch hunts" devised to dig up real or imagined shortcomings with the IT department. They provide insights into departmental performance and suggestions for improvement. Only the incompetent fears these audits.

Audits are executive management's verification that the departments in their company follow proper management and financial practices. Most people are familiar with accounting audits—a review of financial transactions and procedures to ensure that money is not stolen or misused. This type of audit also verifies that appropriate checks and balances are in place to remove the likelihood or temptation to steal. An IT audit applies a similar approach to test and verify that funds are properly spent, appropriate process checks are in place, and resources are properly utilized.

An important aspect of an audit is to identify and address risks to the organization. Data systems are the heart of a company. IT audits look for risks that may be due to management or technical errors. More recently, audits have verified that IT departments are aware of and abide by laws concerning the management and retention of critical company information. The auditor must understand the workings of an IT department if he is to examine both aspects.

Auditors are best known through their military counterparts, Inspectors General, or IGs. The IG serves as an alternate conduit of information from members of the service upward (for reporting problems) and from the commander downward (by inspecting units). Anyone in the military can bypass commanders and obtain fast action by reporting a situation to the IG who answers only to the top unit commanders.

COMMENT

Department of the Navy Inspector General Web Site

"We are agents of change for the Department. We will highlight practices which deserve emulation and publicize pitfalls when we find them. We will help all DoN (Department of the Navy) activities and commands raise readiness while improving their business operations to ensure responsible stewardship of the resources of the DoN." (*www.ig.navy.mil*)

Executives in large companies have the same problems as their military counterparts. How can they gauge the true effectiveness of a department? They lack the time and the expertise to evaluate each one. Often layers of middle management filter out negative but important information as it moves up the reporting chain. Bad news causes upset executives and occasional loss of positions. The executives may think that reported problems mean the manager is incapable of handling the job and will replace him. Soon, everyone knows to tell them what they want to hear.

Unfortunately, this minimization of problems delays executive recognition until they are too big to hide. By that time, something simply solved in an earlier stage now requires a lengthy and expensive process.

To bypass the filtering of information by middle management, executives employ agents (called auditors) who report directly to them. The auditors inspect and evaluate company processes to ensure they provide the best return for the company's investment. Auditors sidestep the middle layers by speaking directly to the workers and examining their equipment. Audit reports go straight to top executives or the board of managers—making many a middle manager uneasy. A full audit of every practice in a department is a monumental task and a serious disruption to business. Typically, audits sample practices in a department based on their criticality, previous audit findings, or emerging risks to the company. These practices reflect priorities set by executive management and by changes in the business environment.

Auditors use personal expertise, checklists, and published policies and procedures to examine existing practices. A department's policy and procedure manual detail how employees are supposed to address specific issues. The auditor compares these documents to industry models to ensure that all of the appropriate steps are in place. Next, these documents are compared to employee interviews to determine how work is *actually* accomplished. Discrepancies between the policies and work practices are noted in the audit report.

Audits are necessary to ensure that IT departments operate on a solid foundation of policies and procedures. Careers sometimes advance by installing the latest software or cutting costs. Sometimes these changes are made at the expense of executive mandated business practices such as maintaining a current disaster recovery plan, shortcutting prudent security steps, or skipping technical support training. Audits ensure that these shortcuts do not occur behind the scenes.

Audits can be a bit disruptive but useful. If funding for important activities such as security upgrades has not been forthcoming, the auditor can report this as a potential problem. If funds are lacking for the replacement of antiquated critical hardware, or the funds diverted for other uses, this also is reported. On the other hand, if lazy IT Managers ignore their own policies, and generally run a halfhearted security program, then this also will be reported.

[B] Types of Audits

Corporate audits come in two flavors: management audits and technical audits. Management audits examine practices that are commonly used in all departments. The auditors are looking to see if the IT department is following company and commonly accepted management practices. Some of the areas examined might include:

A. Adherence to company policies concerning expense accounts, personnel management, performance evaluation, hiring/firing, and compliance with legal requirements.
B. Planning, both tactically and strategically.
    1. Is an IT technology strategy in place and current?
    2. Do the plans support stated company strategic directions?
    3. Are plans published (where appropriate)?
    4. Does the IT staff know and understand the plans?
C. Budgeting
    1. Do the head count, capital, and operating budgets reflect the plans they are designed to support?
    2. Are funds spent on what was appropriated?
    3. Are financial records retained and easy to find?
    4. Are all funds accounted for?
D. Are appropriate IT vital records maintained, such as software license files, purchase receipts for hardware, personnel records, etc.?

Technical audits examine technical aspects of the IT service offering. They include all sections of the department: management, operations, programming, systems programming, security, networking, and telephony. Often technical audits focus on system controls and audit trails.

Specific technical audit items sometimes reflect emerging threats such as virus protection and data security. Technical audits typically examine a few critical areas and a sampling of other areas. Most IT auditors have expertise in some aspect of technology and have checklists to examine the others. Some technical audit points will include:

A. Security review to include firewall and virus protection and the timely inclusion of updates. It may also include logs of intrusion attempts and actions taken.
B. Programming documentation and testing to ensure that proper controls are used to validate formulas used in financial reports.
C. Completeness of the department's business continuity plan and records of tests conducted.

[C] Critical Policies to Develop Based on This Chapter

Using the material discussed in this chapter, you will be able to create the following policies:

A. IT practices during an audit.
    1. Complete cooperation by the IT department.
    2. Managerial and technical audits.
    3. Auditing the financial aspects of IT.

   B. IT Manager responsibilities after an audit.
      1. Resolve each audit point to the satisfaction of upper management.
      2. Follow up 6 months after the resolved audit point to ensure it remains resolved.
   C. Ongoing IT practices.
      1. Establish and maintain audit trails for critical functions, such as user ID authorizations.
      2. Conduct IT Manager audits of policies to ensure compliance.

Policies should always be developed based on the local situation. Successful managers cannot issue appropriate guidance if the policies are written with another company's or location's situation in mind.

§ 8.02   IT MANAGEMENT AUDIT

[A]   Purpose

A management truism is to "inspect what you expect." If executives expect that specific practices are to be followed, then auditors will be eventually dispatched to verify that they are.

[B]   IT Organization

IT personnel are a major company expense. Proper utilization of personnel resources is important if the company is to receive the full benefit for its investment. Proper generally means that the level of expertise is equal to the assigned tasks—not too high or too low. The IT audit will verify that the company is receiving the maximum benefit for the money spent.

IT organizational charts should specify the following:

   A. Structure and the appropriate segregation of duties.
   B. Detailed job descriptions written for each type of position and reflecting the actual assignments and not a generic situation. Compare job descriptions to local job markets to gauge if the staff is over or under paid for the local economy.
   C. Maintenance of current employee resumes and employment records. The auditor can compare these to the job descriptions to verify that employee skills are properly employed.
   D. Positions that support critical data systems or infrastructure. Verify the resumes and employment records for the primary and backup support personnel to ensure they possess the expertise to support them.
   E. Provision of adequate continuing management and technical training, based on identified staff deficiencies and incoming technologies.
   F. Maintenance of an adequate staffing level, based on published service levels and industry norms.
   G. An adequate compensation program is in place for attracting and retaining qualified personnel.

Without a plan, an IT department is like a mob wandering the company's countryside without a road map. They may arrive somewhere but it will not be where their paymasters wanted them to be. The company's strategic plans are the road map that all departments are expected to follow. The IT department bases its strategic plans on the requirements it derives from the company strategy. This is broken down into technology updates, capacity planning, and support of changes to the various department plans. Identify future staffing level requirements by position and key skills to support these changes.

The IT department regularly participates in short- and long-term planning with its user community. The auditor verifies that the IT plans support the company's strategic directions and customer department improvement plans.

[C]   IT Controls

IT management requires controls ensuring the operation maintains adequate safeguards at all times.

A. **Management standards and procedure controls.**
   1. Secure personnel administration records, physical and electronic, to prevent compromise of company or personal data.
   2. Trace systems development audit trails to ensure that problems or system interruptions can be traced to their approximate source.
   3. Computer operations have adequate segregation of duties and limited access to file information. Only authorized personnel perform activities or obtain company confidential forms (e.g., checks).
   4. Networking operations permit only authorized personnel access to firewalls and network security systems.
   5. Contingency planning and disaster recovery procedures are current, published, enforced, and tested. Documentation of test efforts is available for examination.
   6. Logs are maintained and reviewed daily to ensure that backups are properly completed and stored, that intrusion attempts have been investigated, and that system errors are promptly addressed, etc.
B. **Reports on the effectiveness of IT.**
   1. Management performance metrics including employee turnover, budget performance, project budget, and schedule performance are gathered and tracked.
   2. Performance of critical company systems to include systems utilization and data accuracy.
   3. Performance and problem reports prepared by user groups. Items cited in these reports are reviewed for action.
   4. Internal and external audit reports of IT activities.
   5. Major hardware performance and load balancing to ensure maximum practical utilization of resources.
   6. Comparable performance norms available from similar sized companies in the same industry.

C. **Project performance reports.** To ensure control of projects, performance reports of selected projects are audited for management. These reports compare actual performance with project plans. Reasons for variances are determined and reported.

D. **Vital records management.** In the course of business, the IT department creates and utilizes vital records, both physical and electronic.

   1. **Identification.** Identify all records essential to the IT organization to include software licenses (mainframe and workstation) and warranties. Many of the vital IT records are electronic (e.g., security logs) and must be maintained to meet legal requirements.

   2. **Documents are properly completed.** Equipment warranties require identification of the date purchased to validate the warranty coverage. Incomplete personnel records may result in legal action and accusations of unfair discharge.

   3. **Document storage.** Documents of all type are stored for easy access (by the proper authorities) and safeguarded against the effects of heat, humidity, and insects.

[D]   Financial Analysis

Audits of IT financial records ensure that funds are properly requested and spent only for the equipment or services approved. This includes a comparison of IT operating costs to industry norms for a similar size and type of institution. Things to look for:

A. Ensure that documents used to request funds clearly state the intended purpose with a link to the company's strategic business plan.

B. Sample completed appropriations to ensure that funds were only used for the approved purposes and not diverted to other equipment or services.

C. Prices paid are appropriate.

D. Receipt of goods purchased. Often this involves inspecting the items and matching the serial numbers of the items to the receiving document.

COMMENT

When internally charging users for IT services, compare these costs with bids from outsourcing companies.

E. Obtain the credit ratings of critical vendors. Note those in danger of financial collapse so appropriate contingency steps can be prepared.

F. Ensure that vendor services include a written contract that specifies the type and level of service to be provided. The auditor verifies that the employees who can call for service understand what the vendor has agreed to provide.

G. Determine there is no conflict of interest between any IT employee and vendor. Company policies concerning conflict of interest and gifts from vendors are enforced.

H. Check vendor invoices against work done ensuring correct billing.

See Policy ITP-8-1-IT Audit Policy as an example.

POLICY ITP-8-1. IT Audit Policy

Policy #:	ITP-8-1	Effective:	03/18/09	Page #:	1 of N
Subject:	IT Audit Policy				

1.0 PURPOSE

This policy describes IT support for executive management mandated audits.

2.0 SCOPE

This policy encompasses all aspects of the IT department. Audits may be required to meet internal requirements or legal requirements. The IT Manager is responsible for implementing all aspects of this policy.

3.0 POLICY

This policy mandates IT management support to include:

A. IT practices during an audit.
  1. IT manager will brief all IT staff members on their conduct during the audit.
      a. Require honesty—employees are required to provide prompt, honest, and factual answers to all questions by the auditors.
      b. Opinion versus facts—employees will identify those answers that are their opinion and those answers they can substantiate as facts.
  2. IT managers will support all requests made by auditing officials.
      a. Making key employees available for auditors within a reasonable time.
      b. Providing records requested. If records are nonexistent, they will obtain whatever is available.
B. IT responsibilities after an audit.
  1. IT managers will carefully review the auditor's report and comment, within 5 working days, on each negative point:
      a. Concurrence—Include any clarifying facts and an action plan for resolving the point.
      b. Objection—Include reasons why the audit point is incorrect.

    2. Follow up the report after 6 months identifying:
       a. Audit points resolved—how they were satisfied.
       b. Outstanding audit points—must include an action plan for prompt resolution.
  C. Ongoing IT practices.
    1. Establish and maintain audit trails for critical functions, such as user ID authorizations.
       a. Identify records essential for auditing critical functions and all financial transactions.
       b. File critical records in secure storage.
    2. Conduct IT manager audits of policies to ensure compliance.
       a. Critical record completion and accuracy.
       b. Critical records storage.
       c. Critical files are complete.

4.0 REVISION HISTORY

Date	Revision #	Description of Change
03/18/09	1.0	Initial creation.

5.0 INQUIRIES

Direct inquiries about this policy to:

Tom Jones, CIO
Our Company, Inc.
2900 Corporate Drive
Columbus, OH 43215

Voice: 614-555-1234
Fax: 614-555-1235
E-mail: tjones@company.com

Revision #:	1.0	Supersedes:	N/A	Date:	03/18/09

§ 8.03 IT LEGAL MANDATES AND RECORDS RETENTION

[A] Overview

The IT department is, by far, the largest records custodian in the company. Accounting records, personnel records, mail, and a host of other records all reside under the control of the IT Manager. Numerous government regulations govern the control and retention of each of these record types. In the event of a legal action, the IT Manager must ensure that he is not personally liable for missing information.

This is not an area for IT Managers to "go it alone." The IT auditor can provide a wealth of information concerning the mandatory records retention for each type of data as well as prudent actions that can demonstrate "due diligence" by IT management. Do not hesitate to ask for assistance in this area. If "due diligence" compliance requires additional capital budget funding, then the auditor's opinion will speed executive approval.

COMMENT

In November 1986, Lt. Col. Oliver North, USMC, a national security advisory aid to President Ronald Reagan, began systematically deleting more than 5,000 e-mail messages from his account on the White House data systems. What he did not realize is that all of these electronic records were on backup media. Investigators later used these copies to reconstruct the Iran-Contra scandal.

[B] Public Laws

Many regulatory agencies place requirements on data management and retention. Some of these are specific to types of business but most touch every company in some way. Always refer to the company's legal counsel for a complete list. Examples of this are:

- The Sarbanes-Oxley Act ensures the integrity of the company's financial documents through the control and security of the financial system. The IT audit ensures that financial systems are accurate so that executives can certify their financial statements as reliable.
- OSHA—Records pertaining to company accidents and safety.
- EPA—Records pertaining to emissions and discharge monitoring and compliance.
- SEC—Securities and Exchange Commission's regulations governing the handling of non-public company information to guard against insider trading.
- Gramm-Leach-Bliley Act of 1999 concerning the safeguarding of customer information.
- Department of Labor and the Walsh Heasley Act concerning payroll data.
- HIPAA—regulations covering the handling of medical records.

> ### COMMENT
>
> Whenever making decisions about complying with legal issues, always consult your company's legal counsel. Do not waste time guessing—ask the people who should know!

[C]   Records Retention

IT Managers must be aware of the various types of data on their active and backup data systems and ensure they comply with all legal requirements. This will require some forethought when developing data backup strategies. Backup media automatically falls under the longest retention period of its contents. For example, to retain a single record on a tape indefinitely means retaining the entire tape.

Practically speaking, some segregation of backup data on media will create a need for more media but ease system restoration time. For example, if the accounting system lost a specific database or set of files, they may be quicker to locate. Some managers address retention requirements by backing up and retaining every bit of data indefinitely. This may seem the simplest answer but creates its own problems:

- The more data the company retains beyond its useful life, the greater the storage space requirements and costs.
- The more media that must be purchased but not reused.
- The more data that must be searched if the company is required to provide information during a legal "discovery" order.
- Retained media must be readable by current equipment. At some point, this mountain of data must be copied onto new media since backup tapes and microfiche decay over decades.

Retained records have many characteristics:

- The type of media, including tape, microfiche, paper, optical disk—both on site and off site.
- The length of time that a record has legal or historical value.
- The length of time that the record must be maintained in active storage.
- The method and proof of a record's destruction.

> ### COMMENT
>
> In December 2000, the Securities and Exchange Commission imposed fines of $1.65 million per firm against five major

> broker-dealer organizations for violations of SEC, NYSE, and NASD rules for failing to preserve electronic records for the mandated amount of time. Specifically mentioned is the retention of electronic communications.

[D] Types of Records

IT Managers should always refer to their company's legal counsel when establishing legal retention periods for records. Update these legal recommendations annually. File each written recommendation in a safe place to protect the IT Manager against potential legal action. It is important that the IT Manager knows which data elements are contained in each data system so he can determine the appropriate retention time. Examples of documents and data elements that require retention periods include:

* Personnel records.
* Insurance records.
* E-mail and internal memos.
* Instant messenger communications.
* Accounting and finance records.
* Tax records.
* Payroll records.
* Facilities and real estate documents.
* Research notes, patents, and copyrights.
* Customer credit applications.

§ 8.04 RESOURCE MANAGEMENT

[A] Scope

IT is one of the most expensive departments in any company. The people are expensive, the equipment is expensive, and there never seems to be enough of either! The IT Manager can be sure that, to some extent, the auditor will examine the resource management records of the department to ensure that expenditures are in accordance with company guidelines.

[B] Technical Resources

Technical resources encompass hardware, software, and all of the miscellaneous items required to keep them in operation. In essence, this includes all of the IT assets except the people. Technical resources are often long-term commitments. To guide purchases, the IT Manager develops a long-term strategy for hardware and software directions that minimizes the number of different technologies and maximizes their benefits.

> ## COMMENT
>
> Carefully designed technology strategies are seriously challenged by changes in technology that sometime burst onto the scene. Stand-alone PDAs became PDAs with wireless Internet, which became cell phone PDAs and, more recently, units with built-in cameras. All of this occurred in a few short years. From out on the fringe the simple PDA has evolved in a mainstream workstation with all of the security issues that go along with it. Auditors verify that IT strategies keep pace with technological change.

A. **Software inventory.** The software coordinator is responsible for developing and maintaining a list of active (in-house-developed and purchased) software.

1. A strategy to maximize the benefit of software products and minimize the variety of products supported. This is often based on functionality and interoperability.
   a. An overall plan that displays the "fit" for each product based on capabilities. Apply this to application development tools such as databases and programming languages.
   b. A process to identify obsolete products and then retire them. Adding new technologies without retiring the lesser used ones increases the expertise demands of the IT staff and increases costs.
   c. A strategy to eliminate products that duplicate functionality that is found in the "standard" company software products. The fewer products there are to support, the fewer the experts that are required and the lower the department's personnel costs.
   d. Publishing software development/acquisition method.
2. Purchased software information includes:
   a. Information protecting the company's licenses and proof of ownership to include the dates of purchases, the vendor's name, version number, and purchase price. License information must be organized for ready access according to the platform it runs on.
   b. Information on contractual vendor support both from the original purchase and for ongoing service agreements.
   c. Any internal audit reports that reconciled software licenses to the number of copies in use.
3. In-house-programmed software information includes:
   a. Information identifying when and by whom a data system was created. This includes the name of the authors, the date it was

implemented, and references to design documents used in its development.
   b. Major revision dates and explanations.
   c. User and technical documentation.
   d. Names of current support persons and their trained backup team.
B. **Hardware inventory.**
   1. A detailed technology strategy outlining the useful life of technologies in general and major installed items in particular.
   2. A listing of current hardware and attached components is maintained and grouped as follows:
      a. Mainframe or server computers and peripheral devices.
      b. Workstations and peripheral devices.
      c. Network devices.
      d. Telecommunications equipment.
      e. Expected future purchases of hardware.
   3. Identification and implementation plan to retire old hardware by migrating applications to other equipment over the next five years. Adding new technologies without retiring the lesser used ones increases hardware service expense and increases the potential of a forced hardware upgrade in a disaster.

[C] Personnel Resources

Maintain a published organizational chart of the IT department, both with names and with general responsibilities of each person. Identify lines of authority to ensure that responsibilities align with the authority to control them. This indicates an efficient use of delegation and improved productivity of the staff.

IT personnel expenses relate to the relevant expertise of the staff. To verify this, the auditor may follow a five-step process:

1. Identify the critical systems supported by the department.
2. Identify the technologies that these critical systems depend upon.
3. Identify the skills required by the IT staff to adequately support these technologies.
4. Compare the skills required to the skills found on the IT staff.
5. Note deficiencies in the audit report.

The auditor might check for an active training program based on the skills requirement data. The IT Manager should have a personnel skills inventory on file for each person. Compare these profiles to the job descriptions to identify training requirements for the staff. Personnel records should include:

A. Stated job descriptions.
B. Additional duties assignments.
C. Primary/backup persons identified for all critical systems.
D. Staff training plan, to include training for technical skills refresh.

    E. Skills assessments for each person completed by the individual and his or her supervisor.

    F. Salaries aligned to contribution to the department.

    G. Market check of salaries based on levels and types of expertise.

§ 8.05   PROGRAMMING ACTIVITIES CONTROL

[A]   Overview

In the absence of an official policy, technicians will make decisions they feel are most appropriate. Where policies have been created, a periodic audit ensures that these policies still serve the best interests of the organization.

Correct methodologies must be used to guide software management:

A. **Preliminary analysis.** The analyses required for a proposed system must state the business case for the system (or change) and the approximate cost to implement it.

B. **User service request evaluation.** The current system operation, including cost to user, has been assessed. Potential tangible and intangible benefits are detailed and ultimate objectives of requested services assessed. Demonstration that cost/benefit analysis is used to prioritize requests.

C. **Requirements and objectives.** Detailed definitions are assembled and descriptions of requirements and objectives are identified by the users. Requirements are approved by end users before work begins.

D. **System design** is based on IT standard processes and software tools.

E. **User nomenclature.** Explain customer specific terminology. Typically these are terms unique to their field of business, such as accounting, material management, etc.

F. **Computer programming standards** are followed permitting others to maintain the systems.

G. **Documentation.** Technical, operations, and user manuals are current and easily understood.

H. **Implementation.**
1. **Program testing.** Maintain test scripts in technical documentation along with sample data test cases.
2. **User, service desk, and operations training** is documented.
3. **A contingency plan** for a system rollback if the implementation fails.

[B]   Standards for Systems Development and Programming

Adequately define and follow standards for systems development, programming functions, systems development methodology, and program and system documentation. Controls should be implemented to ensure orderly software changes. The segregation of duties into application program development, cataloging of programs for production, and operating systems programming activities are in place.

An audit of the systems development area should look for the following items:

A. Written programming standards cover coding techniques, documentation, testing, acceptance, and data conversion and include:
1. Systems design and development.
2. Software package selection.
3. Program testing.
4. Systems implementation.
5. Systems and programming documentation.
6. Program change controls.
7. Quality assurance and cataloging.

B. Application systems design development standards including:
1. Project feasibility studies.
2. Project cost-benefit analysis.
3. Predetermined progress milestones and follow-up review of progress reports.
4. Documented user approval of systems design, program tests, user documentation, and user's final acceptance.
5. Documented post-implementation performance studies.

C. Programming standards such as:
1. Use of control totals, programmed audits, and validation checks of input before processing starts.
2. Audit trails and exception reports of uncommon transactions.
3. Standardized routines and modular coding.
4. Standards for reusable coding practices.
5. Involvement of users in major decisions affecting input, logic flow, and output.
6. Test plans that include all conceivable error conditions.
7. Documentation of user training before systems implementation.

D. Technical documentation standards that include:
1. Systems narratives.
2. Program narratives.
3. File layout schematics and output formats.
4. Database dictionary listings.
5. Descriptions of edit checking and programmed controls.
6. A chronological listing of program changes explaining what was charged, by whom, why, and when.
7. Naming conventions for data elements, software modules, files, etc.

E. Distribute current user manuals to all appropriate departments in the quantity required.
1. Program documentation library procedures are employed ensuring adherence to systems/programming standards.
2. Program documentation, including program changes, is complete.
3. Distribution of documentation to authorized parties.

[C] Programming Activities Control

To control programming activities and ensure uniformity and conformity, consider these guidelines:

A. Documents generated for new programs and after-program changes are reviewed and documentation contains the following:
1. A description of problem or reasons for change.
2. Name of programmer and date of change.
3. Signature and date of supervisor who reviewed and approved program change.
B. Sufficient numbers of persons with training and experience are available to provide support and backup for critical systems and programming functions.
C. Application programmers are denied access to:
1. Documentation and source listings for operating system.
2. Production program libraries.
3. Live data files.
D. Records of temporary program changes using patches or system utilities are maintained and periodically reviewed by supervisory personnel.

[D] Database Management

The database management system adequately meets audit standards when:

A. There is an appointed database administrator with a trained secondary support person.
B. Written procedures are employed for maintaining a data dictionary file.
C. Transaction logs and procedures effectively allow for recovery of the database.
D. Data security measures are employed to prevent unauthorized access of data and/or changes to it.

[E] Management Post-Implementation Reviews

Determine whether the IT management maintains post-implementation reviews and continued reviews of existing systems. Post-implementation reviews should compare the original time and cost estimates to the actual requirements to improve future project planning.

Compare the performance and benefits from the new system to the benefits used as a basis to approve the work. Inconsistencies may point out where unreliable data is used as the basis for expensive financial decisions.

Reviews should adequately determine that:

A. The resultant system designs are consistent with original objectives.
B. Audit trails and controls are satisfactory.
C. Program and system testing plans are satisfactory.
D. System and program documentation is adequate.

   E. Users are informed of changes in a timely manner and provided with revised user operation manuals.
   F. User training is adequate and timely.
   G. Synchronized source and object programs.

§ 8.06 COMPUTER OPERATIONS

[A] Objective

Data center operations are the enablers of the IT organization. Responsibilities vary between organizations, but in general, they encompass all of the routine efforts, such as backing up data, running a central print room, staffing the service desk, vital records storage, workstation and peripheral repairs, user IDs administration, security, etc. The primary goal of operations is stability—not optimal processes. A stable, predictable environment is more valuable to end users than an optimal but erratic service. Computer operations provide the environment in which the more complex tasks can run in the background.

The data center operations manager is the "landlord" for all of the central computer and network rooms and has control over the equipment within them. This control includes physical security, logical security access, environmental controls, fire safety, operator training, and anything else necessary to keep the back room stable. This enables the manager to control items placement and to ask people to leave the area.

[B] Computer Operations

Computer operations procedures auditing points may include:

   A. Performing equipment maintenance and maintaining records of equipment problems.
   B. Maintaining controls over access to information systems hardware, files, and production program libraries.
   C. Maintaining a proper separation of duties among input batches, computer operations, and output distribution.
   D. Ensuring business continuity and disaster recovery plans are documented, tested, and in effect. Training the staff on the individual roles for contingency actions addressing anticipated problems such as loss of electrical power, loss of data networks, loss of a key-shared system, loss of air conditioning, etc.

[C] Computer Room Controls

Control the computer room environment to ensure safe computer operation. The following safeguards are appropriate for a wide range of room sizes:

   A. Establish adequate procedures ensuring only authorized persons are permitted in the computer room.

B. Restrict operation and repair of computer hardware to authorized personnel.
C. Adequately protect the computer room facility with:
   1. Housekeeping procedures to minimize the accumulation of paper and other flammables in and around the computer room.
   2. Heat, smoke, and water detectors.
   3. A suitable fire control system with the appropriate type of fire extinguishers.
   4. Temperature and humidity control equipment.
   5. Alternate power supply and emergency lighting.
D. Adequate on-call personnel and maintenance agreements covering all equipment are up to date.
   1. Recall rosters for critical personnel are readily available.
   2. Instructions for summoning service for each item covered by a service agreement are readily available.
E. Perform preventive maintenance according to a posted schedule based on the manufacturer's instructions. Maintain a log of all maintenance performed.

[D]   Computer Operations Management Reporting

Computer operations reporting for feedback and control might include:

A. Detailed hardware problem logs.
B. Computer-generated reports that include:
   1. Proper program identification.
   2. Job processing times.
   3. Rerun times.
   4. Downtimes.
   5. Operator identification.
C. Machine utilization and performance reports.
D. Review console logs for unusual activity such as reruns, halts, and failed accesses.

[E]   Data Library Controls

The data library (also known as the tape vault) requires its own audit readiness procedures. Some of the core duties/procedures requirements are:

A. Librarians' responsibilities are prohibited to anyone with conflicting duties.
B. Only authorized personnel have library access.
C. Use external labels to identify removable data storage media.
D. A removable media locator database includes:
   1. File name or description of contents.
   2. Storage location.
   3. Volume serial number.
   4. Creation and expiration dates.

> **COMMENT**
>
> A major expense during the Year 2000 conversion was the lack of source code at many sites. Organizations could not find the current version of code to change, forcing major rewrites of programs.

E. Live media in off site storage is never used to restore data. Copies must be made by the off site storage facility and the copy sent to the data center. This reduces the chance of losing the backup copy in transit or during the restoration process.

F. Periodically test backup media in the library to ensure that each type of media can be read.

G. Store data storage media in a closed, fire-resistant, and limited-access vault.

H. Provide controlled storage for blank payroll and accounts payable checks. Maintain a beginning and ending control number log.

[F]   Input Data Controls

Control input data for any computer operation. The systems and operations audit must ensure that the following procedures are followed:

A. Reference manuals, including examples (copies) and illustrations (drawings) of source documents, are available for each data entry operator.

B. All data received by the data entry unit is accompanied by pre-numbered transmittal batch forms and posted control totals.

C. A log is maintained of input received by source.

D. Retain batch control documents received with the input data in an orderly and logical manner for final balancing.

E. All transactions, such as item counts, are subject to controls similar to those used for monetary transactions.

F. Require monetary totals and item counts for data entry systems.

G. Supervisory personnel regularly review exception and reconciliation items.

[G]   Output Controls

Output controls cover physical materials created by IT operations, such as CDs, printed, network-accessible, and microfiche output. Typical procedures that the auditor might follow include:

A. Review all reports for print quality prior to distribution.

B. Control procedures are in place to ensure reports are produced and delivered as scheduled.

C. Procedures are published for the control of signature stamps.

D. Locked output distribution boxes for pickup of company controlled documents, such as checks.

§ 8.07 DATA NETWORKS

[A] Overview

Data networks are the lifeblood of modern computer systems. Through them, programs exchange information, customer orders are received over the Internet, and long distance telephone communications is economically provided. A single malicious person who penetrates a network can undo all of these wonderful things.

IT auditors will verify that the company's data traffic is secure from intrusion, interruption, or interception. As with other IT areas, the auditor will check that policies and procedures are in place, that they are adequate, and that they are enforced.

People from both inside and outside of the company threaten networks. Outsiders may be attempting entry simply to say they have accomplished it—or to access confidential company data. Disgruntled employees or competitors may attempt to disable a competitor's network and temporarily paralyze the company.

All network security plans should address:

A. **Physical security**—Barriers that separate unauthorized people from the network equipment, such as locked rooms and wire closets.

B. **Network security**—Isolate network segments, packet encryption, and password protection.

C. **Platform security**—Isolate and control administrator functions, intrusion protection, and detection monitoring tools.

D. **Application security**—Authentication, privilege management, electronic commerce.

[B] Security Issues

The network team is the linchpin of a company's data security effort. Intruders bypassing their defenses can roam at will among the files and programs. To be effective, the network security team must diligently examine every potential entry point and apply the appropriate security measures to screen incoming traffic.

A. **Internal threat**

The primary threat against the network is from inside the company offices. Company insiders commit 80 percent of computer crime. Insiders may be motivated by malicious intent or financial gain. They know exactly where to look for specific data or how to gain access.

Insiders may be familiar with the network defenses and know how to bypass them. Even adequately defended systems may be attacked through the misuse of access authorization. An insider criminal's situation is analogous to a fox running loose inside the hen house. Once past the exterior defenses of the walls and bolted doors, he can easily lay hands on many things of value—unless there are adequate internal safeguards.

IT auditors will be looking for several basic internal management practices:

1. Separation of duties divides critical steps in a process among several people, often in different departments. Just as employees processing incoming funds are separated from those who audit these accounts, network security administrators are separate from system administrators who control file access and separate from programmers. Although separated duties can be defeated by a conspiracy, it is much harder to disguise.

2. "Least privilege" restricts users to the minimum functions required to perform their duties. This includes physical access to special data center items such as signature stamps or blank checks. Server restrictions include the ability to read, write, or delete files. Managing an effective "least privilege" program is time consuming and auditors will be checking for ill-advised short cuts, such as blanket privileges to classes of users.

    An adjunct to this defense is to educate users about securing their data files. Many users (including executives) leave confidential data unsecured in shared network directories unaware of how many employees surf the systems looking for files of interest.

    Individual accountability is most effective when it is continually publicized. User IDs leave traces in transaction and system logs. Attempts to bypass network security can be detected and traced back to the originator. By publicizing this capability, end users with security access will be less likely to leave their workstations logged in and unattended since they will be blamed for the access attempts.

    Typical internal defenses are network segmentation through virtual LANs and firewalls, a vigorous program of password management with regular changes, and the tight control of internal access to data. Unfortunately, such measures will face internal resistance. Executives must balance the degree of threat and possible harm against the inconvenience required to adequately secure their data systems.

B. **External threats**

A great deal of the network defenses are focused against external threats. Given the global nature of the Internet and data networks, the potential number of attackers is immense. In general, network attackers look for weaknesses in systems and exploit them. Companies should identify the threats to their systems and tailor defenses to address them.

Defenses against external attacks depend on layers. The first layer is access to the network. If a company's networks are internal, and not physically connected to the "external world," then an attacker must find a way to tap into the physical network connection. This does not always require cutting into a wire. Improperly secured wireless networks make this as simple as sitting with a wireless notebook in a car outside of a building.

The second layer is to isolate the networks into segments so that access to one does not automatically open the door to everything. Few companies can afford to isolate themselves from the Internet and easy access by their customers. Firewalls must separate services intended for external use from those intended exclusively for internal use.

A third level of security is to restrict the access to data files. Do this at the server, directory, or file level. By admitting only specific user IDs, some external attackers are excluded.

A fourth level is the security to execute specific programs, such as to print checks or to read payroll records. Some programs contain code granting the authority to access secured files and must not be available for general use.

In addition to screening out undesired users, firewalls often screen out undesirable traffic. Computer viruses arrive in a variety of guises and the firewall must be ready to screen all of them out. Message attachments, browser controls, and applets all have the potential to harbor virus software. Malicious denial-of-service attacks have also blocked Internet commerce for extended periods of time.

[C] Network Audit Points

Data network audit procedures ascertain that the following are in place:

A. Publish a thorough written data security policy covering all telecommunications and network systems hardware and software.

B. Network firewall systems are in place and updated at least daily.

C. Configure firewalls to protect the company by filtering undesirable Internet sites such as pornography.

D. A strong password program that forces password changes at least quarterly. All passwords must contain a combination of letters, numbers, and uppercase letters. This includes any system that uses password protection—especially network devices.

E. Data systems that access funds also use a double authentication process such as an access card along with a password (something you own and something you know). This improves security since knowledge of a password will not provide access.

F. Virtual private network (VPN) access to servers and services are tightly controlled.

G. Authentication of dial-in access through hardware tokens or dial-back technology.

H. User access to critical data is periodically reviewed to determine if it is still warranted.

I. Tightly controlled temporary employee access through unique ID identifiers and an ID expiration date.
J. The human resources office promptly notifies the IT department when someone leaves the company so that all access can be immediately disabled.
K. Control access to network systems.
L. Control physical access by locking doors and closets.
M. Control digital access to network control programs by identification and passwords.
N. Maintain logs for all transactions performed remotely.
O. Monitor and record unauthorized access attempts to all critical systems. Logs gather sufficient data to track the attempt back to the source. Review logs daily.
P. Incorporate alternate processing procedures into disaster recovery plans.

[D] Security Policies

Security policies guide the network staff in the proper way to approach given situations. They must contain sufficient detail to provide clear staff guidance but not enough to aid an attacker. Policies must be published and periodically reviewed with the staff to ensure they are aware of them and to provide information on improving them. Policies should be in tune with the network's topology and capabilities.

A. **System logs.** A proactive security policy guides installation and use of technology to prevent intrusions and to detect attempts. The investigation of entry attempts will require specific data elements to place the attempt into context. Policies must identify what these data elements will be, such as date, time, user ID, etc. Collect data into secure system logs. The handling, review, and retention period of system logs must be detailed in the policy along with their proper storage location. Data from logs may be used in litigation so advice from the company's legal advisor on data collection and handling will be useful.

Safeguard system logs since they may contain sensitive company data. They must be properly stored and destroyed.
B. **System administration.** This policy guides the people who are watching everyone else. It details the circumstances and required approvals before a network or system administrator can examine a user's account, monitor a person's network traffic, read his or her files, or open his or her mail.
C. **Successful break-in.** This policy and accompanying procedures detail actions to take when an intruder has successfully breached security. Often this is detected after the intruder has departed. The policy will guide whom to inform, information to gather for potential prosecution, etc. It must specify the point at which law enforcement agencies are to be notified.

§ 8.08 DISASTER RECOVERY/CONTINGENCY PLANNING

[A] Overview

An essential audit point is the adequacy of the IT department's business continuity and disaster recovery preparations. The terror attacks on September 11, 2001 not only destroyed several large buildings, but interrupted a great number of surrounding businesses in the New York City area. This event forced companies to scrutinize their own disaster contingency plans and many were severely lacking. Few auditors today will pass through an IT department without carefully reviewing portions of their plans.

There are two distinctly different plans to review:

1. Disaster recovery involves actions to contain and recover from a major disaster, such as the loss of a data center or a portion of a building. IT plans tend to focus on the data center but must also look at the company's use of technology as a whole. IT disaster recovery plans include the ability to restart the data center at a distant "hot site" using backup media. The key to a rapid recovery is the availability of complete and readable system backups.
2. Business continuity plans address the more common but shorter duration problems, such as loss of electricity, loss of data network, loss of a server, etc. These plans identify risks and detail mitigation plans to reduce the likelihood of an occurrence and its impact if it occurs.

[B] Data Center Contingency Planning

The data center disaster and recovery contingency plans should include:

A. Complete data and software file backups according to a published schedule.
   1. Critical data systems are identified. Few companies can afford to deal with everything in a crisis. Critical systems are identified by executives and typically involve cash flow and regulatory requirements.
   2. Restoration instructions are tested and available for rapid use at the hot site.
   3. The recovery team tests portions of the recovery process annually at the hot site.
   4. All back-up media is tested periodically to ensure it is still recording properly.
   5. Off-site storage location should:
      a. Closely control access to stored media.
      b. Provide a stable environment for maximum media life.
      c. Be organized to rapidly locate specific backup media for quick dispatch.

    B. A method of transporting materials to and from the off-site storage facility with the same high level of environmental and physical security as employed at the data center.
    C. A written emergency plan addresses:
        1. Physical security of the computer installation.
        2. Actions to be taken in specific emergency situations, such as the loss of electrical power, the loss of external network communications, etc.
        3. Contingency procedures required to recover from a disaster or server failure.

[C] Plan Updates

Data systems evolve over time. They emerge and eventually they fade away. In between are changes to the software, to the technical documentation, and even to the platforms used. It is critical that when new systems are implemented or changed, the impact on their disaster recovery processing be considered. In some cases, this will require a modification to the hot site support contract.

An important part of a systems analysis will be the impact on the system's recovery plans. The subsequent change control meeting must ensure that as system changes are implemented, the recovery plans are likewise adjusted. Auditors must verify this process and compare sample recovery plans to system changes.

In a crisis, time is in short supply. Under the best of circumstances, it may take days to reestablish a data center in a hot site. Incomplete or inaccurate plans will increase recovery time. Issues that may arise include:

    A. The upgrading or addition of servers to the computer room means that additional servers must be available at the hot site.
    B. Reflecting changes in network access at the recovery site.
    C. Plans for restoring retired systems will delay the recovery effort by working on something no longer needed.
    D. Security measures may have changed inhibiting the recovery team's ability to restore an application.

§ 8.09 WORKSTATION AUDIT ISSUES

[A] Objective

Workstations have changed dramatically over time—from shared terminals to PCs and now include Web-enabled cell phones. IT auditors will ensure that workstation policies and control have kept pace with these changes.

[B] Workstation Standards

Policies and procedures for the appropriate control and use of company workstations must be in place. To be effective, orientation sessions with end users must be conducted to explain workstation policies. The goal is compliance rather than punishment.

To control workstation assets, the IT department will maintain an inventory of hardware and software owned by the company. This will aid in the detection of theft and unauthorized copying of software.

A. Hardware and software relocation will be controlled by the IT department. This will assist in maintaining asset database accuracy.

B. Neither software nor hardware shall leave the facility without an approved pass by the IT department. Anything removed without this pass is theft.

C. Company workstations shall only be used to conduct company business and not for personal use. This includes the Internet.

D. The IT department will maintain an organized and accessible software license file in a fireproof environment.

E. The loading of software by anyone other than the IT department is prohibited (and restricted by the operating system if possible).

F. The IT department will approve all purchases of workstation hardware and software to ensure compliance with published standards.

G. Employees using company owned notebook PCs, PDAs, or cell phones outside of the facility:
   1. Are responsible for the safe return of company property. If these items are lost, the employee must promptly file a theft report with the local police authorities. Otherwise, the employee will be suspected of theft and the cost of the replacement item deducted from his pay.
   2. Shall only use these items for company business.
   3. Shall obtain a properly approved property pass before the item can leave the facility.

Policies governing the proper use of workstations:

A. All company critical files are stored on network drives and not on personal workstations.

B. Restriction of network access to Internet and e-mail to business use only.

C. Software developed on company time and/or using company assets is company property.

[C] Workstation Environment

Environments where workstations are used do not require the same degree of control needed by IT computer operations. However, their users are usually unfamiliar with IT operation requirements and must learn those that are applicable. The following are standard environment requirements:

A. **Workstation security**
   1. Physical security maintained by key locks on the hardware.

  B. **Access controls required**
    1. Passwords for access.
    2. Encryption of classified data.
    3. Use of password protected screen savers.
  C. **Power supply**
    1. Computer hardware must not share its power outlets with any other devices.
    2. Plug all hardware into surge protectors.
    3. Areas that may have power supply problems must have uninterrupted power supply (UPS) backup supply units capable of providing power for the full time required to bring down the system properly.

§ 8.10 STRATEGIES FOR SURVIVING AN AUDIT

[A] The Auditor Is Your New Friend

Audits are unavoidable. The more managers squirm to avoid them, the more the auditor believes that there is something to uncover. "If you can't beat them—join them!" Take advantage of the auditor's visit to improve the department's operations. Yes, there will be deficiencies noted for the department, but that is to be expected. If nothing is reported, the auditor's boss will think he did not do his job. Make the auditor's job easy by assisting him in uncovering and reporting problems.

This is not as radical as it sounds. Again, the auditor must report *something* is wrong to justify his existence. The key is to influence what is reported and how it is reported. Is something a sweet-smelling long-stemmed rose, or is it a dead red thing on a green stick with thorns? The difference is all in the wording! Most auditors will appreciate some assistance with the specific technical details.

By guiding the audit, the IT Manager is less likely to be stuck with the worst curse imaginable—the vague audit point. Every citation in an audit must be resolved before the next audit—maybe immediately. A vaguely worded audit citation may require unnecessary extraordinary effort to satisfy. Ensure that all citations are clear and as specific as possible.

[B] Steps for a "Successful" Audit

The rest of this chapter explains what an audit is and how it functions. Audits are useful tools for both the company's executives and the IT Manager. Do not hide in an office! Dodge the bullet by managing the audit to everyone's benefit.

Step 1—Did anyone pay attention to the last auditor? Begin with the last several audit reports.

  A. Has everything cited on the reports been resolved? If this involves a report, pull it out and read it. If this involves equipment, find it and personally verify that changes were made and are still in effect. Do not take someone else's word for it.

B. Can anything from previous reports that has not been addressed be resolved before the upcoming audit? It is never too late to address an open issue. If the task is too large, but will be attempted, then an in-process effort will often satisfy the audit point.

C. Is there an audit point that is impossible or a very bad idea to do? Write an explanation of what the audit point is *really* asking for and why it is impossible or illogical to attempt. It is possible that the audit point was poorly written. This will verify the citation. Auditors make mistakes too! When the audit begins, discuss this issue with the auditor to clarify or satisfy the citation as misguided.

Step 2—Prepare for the visit. Appearance of records is half of the battle.

A. If the policy manual looks ragged and dusty, it will be closely scrutinized.
   1. Ensure the document shows dates from within the last 12 months.
   2. Ideally, review, update, and re-authorize each policy.

B. If the financial documents are occasionally missing or the signatures are illegible, the auditor may dig deeper.

C. If documents are difficult to find or take a long time to produce, the auditor may suspect sloppy bookkeeping practices. Clean up all file systems and ensure that all financial and performance records for the period being audited, and the period before, are readily available.

D. Pull the department together to explain what an IT audit is and why it is important to the team. Do not assume that they understand the purpose or process of the audit. State your expectations to them.
   1. Treat requests from the auditor as high priority.
   2. Require everyone to answer questions truthfully. (It is too difficult for an entire department to remember the same lie.)
   3. Explain the importance of providing information the auditor requests and no more. Excessive information is like a half truth that raises more questions than it solves.
   4. Separate opinions from facts. Label opinions as such. If they become audit points, much time may be wasted to prove that a problem did not really exist.
   5. Attempting to slip personal attacks into data as a fact may result in disciplinary actions.
   6. Identify important but under-funded activities. Sometimes prudent technology purchases are sidetracked by middle managers for more career enhancing activities.

E. For an IT department, audits can be a bit disruptive but useful. If funding for important activities such as security upgrades has not been forthcoming, the auditor can report this as a potential problem. If replacement of antiquated critical hardware has not been funded, or the funds diverted for other uses, this also is reported. On the other hand, if the IT Manager is lazy, ignores his own policies, and generally runs a halfhearted security program, then this will also be reported.

Step 3—Perform a pre-audit audit. Walk around and play auditor. See what can be found and cleaned up before the "real article" arrives.

A. Make a list of things to check in each IT department.
B. Ask the managers for each department to verify the accuracy of their policies and procedures, and that the appropriate workers know and follow them. After the managers confirm that this is done, play auditor and verify this is done.
C. Check all security procedures, system logs, maintenance logs, inventory records, management metrics, etc. for completeness, currency, and accuracy.
D. Check records for previous executive mandates over the past two years. Ensure they are in place.
E. Ask the legal department for an updated chart of legally mandated data retention periods.

Step 4—During the audit. Appearance is the other half of the battle.

A. Be candid. It is far easier to provide honest answers than to try and remember a string of lies. Remember that part of an audit is to meet individually with the IT staff members—away from the management. If their story does not match the manager's, then everything the manager says may become suspect.
B. Show an interest in the audit process. Like most people, auditors are overworked and under-appreciated.
C. Open records freely. Hiding information at worst raises suspicion and at best indicates incompetence at critical recordkeeping. If the auditor later learns of intentional obstruction, the IT Manager's credibility will be shattered.
D. Stay close to the auditor and write down comments—pro and con. Openly take notes and allow the auditor to read them at any time. If the auditor requests a copy, provide one at every request. Use these notes to identify items that will appear on the report.
E. As the audit proceeds, the auditor may mention or communicate in some fashion points that are below standard. If any of these items can be resolved quickly—immediately do so. This saves time later and may keep them off the report. Track all of these quick changes to ensure they are permanent.
F. Do not be shy about clarifying audit points! Any audit point should be clear enough that action can be taken or a response provided. It is possible that the auditor is mistaken. A vague audit point will be very difficult to address later.
G. If an audit point cannot be quickly satisfied, find out why. It may be possible to form a reasonable action plan for addressing the problem before the auditor leaves—even if the solution will not begin for some time.
H. Explain why a situation is as it is, but never argue with the auditor. No matter how the argument ends, they have the last word in their report!

I. Ask the auditor's opinion about the department's toughest problems. An outsider's perspective may be very insightful.

Step 5—After the audit. Answering the audit citation is the rest of the fight.

A. Begin preparing for the audit report to hit the executive council. Immediately follow up on any items cited in the report. Do not wait for publication of the final report. Report small tasks as they are finished. Either large tasks should begin or a proposal should be developed for the next capital funding cycle.

B. Begin preparation for next year's audit. Analyze the IT audit process. Write down what went well during the year and what went poorly with the audit. Bring together everyone who participated in the audit.

C. Which records were requested but were hard to find? Change the filing system to capture this data and make it easy to find.

[C] Using the Audit to Your Advantage

Sometimes urgent requests for technology go nowhere. If the old equipment is still running, then purchasing the newer models is just an exercise in "computer envy." This may be the accounting manager's opinion but is not always the case. Properly maintained data systems can run for decades—far longer than their reasonable useful life.

Sometimes the purchase of essential technology is shuttled aside by middle managers pursuing their own objectives. The auditor can provide executive support for these purchases if they can be included in the audit report.

The auditor will decide to include or exclude an item from his report based on the description the IT Manager provides to him of the items in question. If their purchase is tied to compliance with a legally mandated action, it will be difficult for the purchase to be rejected. It is all in how it is described. Once an item is included in an audit as critical to legal compliance, no manager will sign on as the one who obstructed it.

Use this logic to:

A. Drive out obsolete equipment, such as servers, printers, and punch card equipment.

B. Improve data backup equipment (which may reduce staff and storage expenses).

C. Support additional staffing or training requests in key areas.

9

IT STAFFING: MEETING CUSTOMER SERVICE EXPECTATIONS

§ 9.01   OVERVIEW
    [A]   Purpose and Scope
    [B]   Critical Policies to Develop Based on This Chapter

§ 9.02   WHAT IS THIS "THING" CALLED CUSTOMER SERVICE?
    [A]   Opinion vs. Fact
    [B]   Level of Service
    [C]   Operational vs. Development Activities
    [D]   Perceptions Color Both Sides of the Issue
    [E]   Communications
    [F]   Voice of the Customer

§ 9.03   COMPONENTS OF IT SERVICE STAFFING
    [A]   Overview
    [B]   Stand-by
    [C]   Technical Experts
    [D]   Separation of Responsibilities
    [E]   Applications Support
    [F]   Overhead

§ 9.04   METRICS—IT'S MEASURES OF SUCCESS
    [A]   Overview
    [B]   Critical to Quality
    [C]   What to Measure
    [D]   Typical Customer Service Metrics

§ 9.05   WHY USE A CUSTOMER SURVEY?
    [A]   Overview
    [B]   The Survey
    [C]   Determining a Service Level Baseline
    [D]   The Survey Form
    [E]   Evaluating the Survey Results
    [F]   IT Team Performance

§ 9.06   TRANSLATING REQUIREMENTS INTO A STAFF LEVEL
    [A]   Overview
    [B]   Establish a Service Level Performance Goal
    [C]   Staffing Ratios
    [D]   Allocating the IT Staff

§ 9.01   OVERVIEW

[A]   Purpose and Scope

IT departments have a problem. Their customer base is "captive" and generally forced to use their services. In a free market, inefficient businesses disappear since no one will pay for their services. Companies lack this ability of weeding out poorly performing departments. Too many IT departments blunder along as personal fiefdoms until they are outsourced by frustrated executives.

However, proactive IT Managers can address this problem head-on by constantly seeking their customers' feedback on the team's performance. Some managers even seek employees with reputations of complaining. These people will tell you what others are too polite to mention.

[B]   Critical Policies to Develop Based on This Chapter

Using the material discussed in this chapter, you will be able to create the following policies:

A. Service level management.
    1. Policy for establishing acceptable service levels.
    2. Collection of service level metrics.
    3. Identification of the service levels critical to quality factors.
    4. Root cause determination of critical or systemic problems.
    5. Establishment of staffing ratios.

Policies should always be developed based on the local situation. Successful managers cannot issue appropriate guidance if the policies are written with another company's or location's situation in mind.

§ 9.02   WHAT IS THIS "THING" CALLED CUSTOMER SERVICE?

[A]   Opinion vs. Fact

Customer service is a combination of opinions and facts. From the customer's perspective, the level of customer service is an opinion. From the service provider's perspective, the level of customer service is demonstrated by performance statistics. The trick is to align the two perspectives so that expectations equal performance.

The "opinion" perspective is whether the person receiving the service is "satisfied" with the end result. This satisfaction is very difficult to measure as it is affected by a wide range of factors from the day's weather to the number of other problems plaguing the person that day. Evaluating a series of events rather than a single occurrence provides a general perception of service. For example, we have all experienced the reliability of telephone and electrical service we use every day. Our experience has been that it seems to be always ready for use, so that the only times it is commented on is when it is absent.

We generally perceive it to be a high-quality service, yet we have all experienced times when these services were absent.

The "fact" perspective is represented in the performance statistics generated by the service provided. When confronted with complaints about poor service or when trying to add more staff members, the IT Manager will provide sheets of customer service statistics. These would include the average response time for a call, problem resolution rate, etc. Although these make a compelling, data driven statement, in the mind of end users, they rarely change a complainer's opinion.

[B] Level of Service

An important factor in the size of an IT department is the level of service it provides to the company. Although a large staff does not automatically translate into a high level of service, it does indicate the potential. Service levels seek to provide the right number of workers, with the right mix of skills, available at the right time. Customer service is the single biggest determinant of IT staff size in most companies.

An IT department's customer service level is a collection of expectations by the various departments that it supports of how quickly the IT team can provide solutions to their technical problems. From the end user's perspective, customer service is everything that the end user expects the IT department to provide to them. The closer that this expectation matches reality, the higher the customer's satisfaction will be. Some of its components are:

A. How quickly a clear and accurate service request can be conveyed from the requestor to the IT department.
B. How promptly a solution is provided.
C. The correctness, completeness, and permanence of the solution.
D. Communications during the process of problem resolution and follow-up with the requestor after the solution is provided.
E. Reliable and predictable service from each of the IT areas.

Traditionally, IT departments led the way in introducing technology to the various business units. As computers became common home appliances, the need to drive technology into the workplace was greatly reduced. This, together with economic downturns, has evolved many IT departments into a "keep the lights on" mode rather than maintaining their leadership role. This follows the theory that IT is a utility and is expected to provide a service on demand. Such a passive stance results in executives noticing IT departments only when things go badly and not crediting things that go well.

To nurture or reestablish this leadership role, everyone in the IT department must work to establish and maintain positive working relationships with all areas of the business. In this sense, the IT department is a de facto member of each department's staff since most process changes require its involvement. This linkage will not occur by itself. It requires a consistent flow of communication between IT and each of the departments concerning expectations, service issues, and performance. This open channel of two-way information flow will positively enhance the perception of IT's service levels and contribution to the company's overall success.

This discussion is important to staffing and skills because service levels influence the number of people and the mix of skills required in an IT department. Given unlimited time, the staff would only need enough people to have a single expert for every technology. Each problem would be addressed in its own turn, depending on workload and the IT Manager's priorities. Anything occurring overnight would be addressed in its own good time. With only one expert per technology, some problems may wait weeks until they are addressed.

Unlimited time for a task is definitely not something IT departments possess. The level of skill a person possesses and applies has a direct impact on the speed of reaching the solution and customer satisfaction.

A comprehensive staffing formula that determines team size does not exist. A formula can only work with the factors that are provided to it. Miss a single factor and the answer will be wrong. Every company and every company branch has its own unique customer service requirements, and one size does not fit all.

When evaluating the quality of the IT department's services, consider this test. If the people calling for assistance had a choice to call the IT department or call anyone else, who would they call? If they had to write a check to the IT department every time they used it, would they do so or send the check elsewhere?

[C] Operational vs. Development Activities

An IT department provides two basic types of services: operational and developmental. Operational services are those activities used to sustain existing activities, such as printing reports, maintaining existing programs, or troubleshooting desktop computer problems. Developmental services are those one-time activities that require additional labor to complete, such as rolling out desktop software updates or writing new application programs.

Factors driving operational services:

A. Degree of standardization of IT products.
B. Number and dispersal of users and servers.
C. Number of sites supported.
D. Skill levels of end users.
E. Stability of the end-user workforce.
F. Stability of the business applications.
G. Age and stability of infrastructure.
H. Whether applications are developed internally or are vendor supplied.
I. Degree of automation installed.
J. Criticality of applications.

Factors driving development services:

A. Business growth rate.
B. Business environment stability.
C. Number, complexity, and urgency of pending projects.
D. Planned technology migrations.

[D]   Perceptions Color Both Sides of the Issue

Customer service is a complex concept that means different things to different people. It has many different facets based on the person seeking assistance (perspective) and what he is requesting. To the IT Manager, it may mean responding to requests in a reasonable amount of time by applying the correct solution. Most business managers would agree with this on the surface. If only life were this simple.

Let's break this down further. In all companies, there are multiple users requesting a wide variety of services, from quick jobs to major efforts. They may request a new report, urgent program changes, a PC file restored, or a new user ID established. Some of these requests may be ill-conceived or a duplication of existing services. Others may lack approval of the department's manager or specify actions that are the wrong solution to the problem. The request may even be a tool in a departmental "power struggle" and not at all an important company task.

Complicating this situation are the people in the IT department who are delivering these services. Each has his own set of priorities, biases, skills, and product knowledge. Given these uncontrollable factors, providing a consistent level of service can be quite a challenge. Each IT support person has assigned tasks that are interrupted by service requests. They also have personal opinions or feelings about the requestor that may hinder the speed of their response.

[E]   Communications

The key to managing expectations is communications. Customers must know that their issues are understood, being worked on, and what progress has been made. They should also understand the nature of the solution if it will require a change in their processes. Allow external time pressures to distract the IT support team from these important discussions and the customer's anxiety will rise and opinion of the group's service fall.

Ongoing communications allow the customer to shape the problem's description. If a particular deadline is missed, they may say that the urgency is now lessened until the next time the weekly program runs. They may explain a work-around they have used in the past or that they have used now, so again, the urgency is still high, but has dipped below the crisis level. They may even say that the problem has "gone away."

An important customer service communication is to alert end users of planned outages. Emergency outages can be very frustrating to the business units juggling their workload to meet deadlines. Most users can plan their work around a data system outage if they receive enough advance notice. Whenever possible, planned outages should be scheduled during the time of day and day of the week when the data systems are least required. If this is unavoidable, then ensure that everyone is provided at least one working day to reshuffle their work plans—or to suggest a less painful time.

A variation on planned outages is the early detection of a problem. Monitoring data systems availability and network performance can provide early warning of system components failure, such as a network circuit. Instead of waiting for someone to call and report a problem, valuable time can be saved by immediately dispatching the repair person and notifying the impacted departments of the problem. They will not welcome the news, but it is better to hear that IT is aware of the problem and work has begun to repair it rather than find out at an inopportune time that a critical system is dead.

[F]   Voice of the Customer

It is easy to guess at what end users might be looking for in terms of customer service and just try to meet that. However, this could lead to wasted effort fulfilling low priority requirements while the true customer "needs" are left unfulfilled. Guessing is the fastest and easiest way to address the identification of customer service issues—and also the wrong way.

Everyone has some expectation of service when they conduct business. When entering a fast-food restaurant, each person has an expectation of how long it should take to receive the food, how warm it should be, its flavor, even the condiments like ketchup that should accompany it. All of these combine to create an overall experience of the transaction between the customer and the restaurant.

People who contact the IT department likewise have expectations about timeliness, accuracy, ease of communications, and a range of other things they expect to see when dealing with the IT staff. Taken together, they form a level of service in the eyes of the customer. To focus the IT team's customer service efforts, analyze the customer's expectations.

The "voice of the customer" is easy to find. Letters of complaint (or compliment) on the company's products and services, calls to the service desk, and the volume of services used or avoided are all signals by customers that they are satisfied or dissatisfied with what is being done for them.

§ 9.03   COMPONENTS OF IT SERVICE STAFFING

[A]   Overview

Customer service is the single biggest determinant of IT staff size in most companies. IT departments tend to think in terms of positions such as the weekend network support person or the second shift service desk technician. Consider these same positions according to their contribution to the customer service efforts. Every position in IT has the following five characteristics to one degree or another.

[B]   Stand-by

Stand-by—this person sits and waits for something to occur. This is analogous to a security guard. They may have other duties to perform, but if a problem arises, their top priority is to respond quickly. Examples of this are a service desk technician waiting for the telephone to ring or the person monitoring the flow of network traffic. Their primary responsibility is to be immediately available in case an event occurs. If nothing requires their attention, they provide value by their availability to respond.

Factors driving stand-by requirements:

A. Volume of calls for end-user support. Reduce this by increasing end-user training and repairing/replacing unstable technologies.
B. Desired speed of response for problem calls. For example, supporting a real-time securities sales and purchasing system requires instantly addressing problems during the hours that the stock market is open.
C. Correctly determining the urgency of the problem reduces the number of technicians that must be immediately available. If an issue can wait for an hour to be addressed, then the normal support staff can be assigned to it instead of requiring someone to stand by at all hours of the day, ready to act on a moment's notice.
D. The number of critical technologies requiring instant support. The impact of downtime must be evaluated for each system.

Undoing a well-thought-out stand-by strategy:

A. Upper management wants the fast response but has little tolerance for the sight of these expensive people sitting idle waiting for the telephone to ring. Often they will try to assign them to other tasks, thereby reducing their instant availability.
B. Technical people like to be challenged and will be bored during the slow work periods. They will appreciate the value of immediacy but find "excuses" for doing something other than sitting by the telephone. At times, the manager must personally enforce the scope of the work and the location of their place of work.
C. The law of inertia will take hold where objects (people) at rest tend to remain at rest. When the call volume again picks up (the whole reason they are all there), they will be slow to react. The authors recommend slightly understaffing to overcome this.

[C]   Technical Experts

Technical experts—these folks are too difficult to find or pay for on a temporary basis. Often they are employees who were trained on the job. Examples of this are system administrators or network engineers. At a minimum, there will be one person assigned for each of the skill areas identified, even if they are not fully utilized.

Factors driving technical expert requirements:

A. The degree that the company's systems are standardized. If the company utilizes a wide range of vendors and technologies, then more experts are required since not all technology expertise is easily transferable.
B. The stability of the technology is a major factor in the number of experts required. Unstable hardware and software must be repaired or replaced. A variation is to provide standby equipment for critical hardware so that when a failure occurs, the alternate device is used until the primary unit is repaired by the expert (instead of the expert standing by to address failures).

C. There is a degree of "stand-by" for technical people such as a network expert always on station for companies that rely on the Internet for customer order entry.

Undoing a well-thought-out technical expert strategy:

A. Some executives feel that if they deny the funds for a sufficient number of experts, the IT Manager will be forced to find other ways to provide this service. Indirectly, this approach "wishes away" the offending technologies. Although there is some merit to this approach, the dark side is the failure of a major system with no one available to repair it for hours.
B. Introducing critical, nonstandard technology without adding adequate resources or training to support it. This might be from an executive who purchased something at a "bargain" rate that no one knows how to repair.

[D] Separation of Responsibilities

Sometimes it is not prudent management to place all of something into one person's trust. Checks and balances are essential inhibitors for removing temptation from the weak, for example, the security team that watches over confidential files and firewalls. It is important to separate the people who secure data from the ones who manipulate it. Otherwise there is a case of the fox guarding the henhouse. Security team members ensure that confidential data is identified, secured from unauthorized access, and that access is enabled as required.

Factors driving IT security requirements:

A. A security team requires a minimum of two people since someone must always be available in a crisis (covering vacations, sick days, etc.). Also, the more security staff that a company uses, the harder it is for a single security person to violate the security undetected.
B. The greater the number of technologies that must be protected (hierarchical databases, relational databases, different manufacturers, different OS architectures), the more experts that will be required. Standardization will minimize the staff requirements.
C. The greater the amount of data that is secured, the more staff that may be required. Break confidential data such as credit card numbers into linked tables and secure those tables, leaving the remainder of the fields with normal security.
D. The geographic dispersal of the facilities supported.

Undoing a well-thought-out security strategy:

A. A successful program will seem as if it is addressing a nonproblem since there are not any security breaches! If the time requirements permit, these people can work part-time in other areas as long as it does not compromise the separation of security and other IT functions, such as applications.

[E] Applications Support

Applications support—the classic IT position. These employees maintain existing data systems and develop new ones. Often they are grouped by their primary programming language skills, but are assigned to support entire application systems, such as accounts payable, EDI, etc.

Factors driving IT applications support requirements:

A. Dissimilar user interfaces require training classes for each application. It is unlikely that a single software package will suit all areas of the company (the secretaries will not want to use a spreadsheet for word processing), so standardizing on a single software package is unlikely. However, using an ERP with a standard user interface across multiple applications can ease customer training. If the underlying software likewise uses a standard set of software tools, then fewer technicians are needed.

B. Standardization of development tools such as programming languages, databases, operating systems, etc., will permit the IT Manager to rebalance work between the staff members.

C. The extent that end users can create or modify their own reports will decrease applications requirements.

Undoing a well-thought-out applications support strategy:

A. Non-IT executives "discover" new applications solutions that are inconsistent with the standard software tool set and implement them without the appropriate level of technical support training.

B. Rushing the development and implementation of new systems based on vague and shifting specifications.

C. Lack of clear, published, and enforced system development practices.

[F] Overhead

Overhead—the positions that drive up the IT head count. Overhead positions are the ones that facilitate the work of the other areas, such as specialized IT purchasing, contracts administration, and, of course, management. Overhead processes often seem to grow on their own into a paper shuffling bureaucracy. IT Managers must avoid this as it decreases the department's flexibility.

Factors driving IT overhead requirements include:

A. Many IT departments approve the purchase of all computer technologies within the company. This contributes to standardization by guiding requests to approved products, but it takes a staff member's time. The more tasks such as this that the department takes on, the greater the staffing requirement.

B. The span of control for a manager is four to seven subordinates. If the subordinates are motivated toward the same goals as their leader, and if they are technically competent, then a larger ratio of workers per supervisor is possible. If they are new to the company or require considerable mentoring, then fewer workers can be effectively managed.

C. IT service contracts and their performance clauses are best administered by someone familiar with the technologies, department priorities, and support of end users rather than a distant clerk in the purchasing department.

D. The geographic dispersal of the facilities supported.

E. A well-thought-out, clear, and published IT strategic plan will broaden the span of control across the department.

Undoing a well-thought-out overhead strategy:

A. Previous management attempts at "flattening" an organization by removing middle management have reduced personnel costs but allowed the workers to inefficiently drift in whatever direction they wished.

B. Using an accounting clerk to administer IT contracts generally results in payment for a level of service that is never delivered since the accounting clerk lacks the knowledge or inclination to enforce the terms—thereby causing more work for the IT staff!

§ 9.04 METRICS—IT'S MEASURES OF SUCCESS

[A] Overview

IT staffing is driven by customers' service requirements. It is important to establish a process for gathering these requirements from the customers and measuring the team's performance at delivering them. End users exist in an ever-changing business environment. By periodically polling customers, the IT department's efforts can stay tuned toward the tasks most relevant to the company.

IT Managers are not unbiased judges of their service levels. They are too close to the efforts made by the department. Their view is colored by their intentions to provide a high level of customer service. However, a customer service level is not an intention. It is the opinion of the customer that counts (what was done—not what was meant). The best way to find out the customer's impressions is to ask them!

Identifying customer requirements is a five-step process.

1. Determine what the department's customer service levels are believed to be today.

2. Poll customers as to their opinion of the team's service performance. The difference between steps one and two often results in action plans to improve specific components of the service offering.

3. During the previous poll, ask the customers to determine the service levels they want to see.
4. Publish an improved service level goal for the department. This may not be all the customers want to see but is based on staffing and technical realities. This will establish an expectation in the minds of both the customer and the IT staff.
5. Draft a plan to focus the team and improve processes to achieve the new service goal.

To compare the different levels of customer service, a set of standard measurements is needed. These measurements, or "metrics," must be based on objective data. Customer service is very much a perception and we all perceive the same situations differently. Perceptions must be quantified by measuring their individual components.

[B] Critical to Quality

Customer service has many different aspects. Trying to track them all would be time consuming and not provide sufficient payback. The task at hand is to identify those aspects that are *critical* to the quality of the service offering.

Critical to quality (CTQ) characteristics are the most important parts of service. They are the basic elements of service offerings and vary somewhat between customer segments. In general, they follow the consumer CTQs characteristics of speed, cost, and quality. Changing any one of these changes the others. For example, increasing the speed (reducing the response time) costs more money for more people, or results in decreased quality.

A. Speed is how quickly something is delivered. In IT services, this might be how quickly a correct solution is provided, or how quickly someone answers the service desk phone. Lack of urgency is the most common IT services complaint.
B. Cost is something that all companies struggle with. Some companies use a direct charge-back for IT services while others use a simpler overhead allocation to all departments. Cost is also a consideration when the IT department estimates the cost of technical components for capital projects.
C. Quality is sometimes defined as conformance to specification. In customer service, this is how well the service conforms to what was wanted. For example, if an end user ordered software, just delivering the package to the requestor's desk fulfills what was asked for. Installing and configuring the software is implied since what the person actually wanted was use of the software. A high-quality delivery might additionally include an hour of desk-side assistance navigating through the product, assistance migrating files into the new format, and information on locally available training.

[C]   What to Measure

The trick to customer service metrics is to correctly identify what to measure. Gathering data takes time. A properly planned data collection effort minimizes this time. The management axiom that a manager gets what he rewards is very true. If the reward is for the number of calls closed, then the same problem report may be closed and reopened a number of times until a satisfactory conclusion is found. If the reward is for the speed with which calls are answered, then calls will be answered by inexperienced staff who will take messages for later action when the customer wanted the answer from the first person he spoke to.

Customer service factors are measured to demonstrate performance and to identify problems within the IT service offering for improvement. Performance factors might include the amount of time a call waits before it is answered, the elapsed time between when a problem is reported and when it is resolved, etc. Service offering problems are metrics gathered to uncover problems with technologies that cause these problems, such as an unstable program or piece of hardware. These metrics are used by the IT Manager to improve the data services offered. Each of these issues can be broken down into a number of smaller issues.

COMMENT

Uptime of 99.99 percent is worthless if the server crashes when it is needed most. Metrics must make sense and be relevant to IT's customers. Tracking the uptime during Saturday third shift when no one is around and the system is quiet is not something to crow about.

[D]   Typical Customer Service Metrics

If the service desk is already in place, metrics should be readily available. Ideally, this would include a problem tracking database that indicates who is calling, what they called about, when they called, and the time elapsed before the problem was resolved. These four key pieces of information will provide most of the data needed.

1. **Who is calling?** It is important to know who is using the service desk services. Some end users are more skilled than others. They call less frequently but the problems may be more difficult to resolve. Some end users are more inclined to call for smaller issues rather than try to figure them out themselves.

   Just as important as who is calling is who is not calling. Some departments have an official or unofficial person that everyone goes to with their technical problems before they call the IT department. In other cases, the departments have bypassed IT altogether by hiring such a person into a position with a clerical title but with actual responsibilities for IT support.

A large volume of calls from a department may also be indicative of its future requirements. If a project is under way to expand that group, then what does that add to the IT department's support requirements?

2. **What they called about.** The types of problems being serviced directly affect the staffing mix. Some problems are simply resolved such as resetting passwords for people with short memories. Others are more time consuming such as tracking down why a report has a given value in one of its fields. Repeated calls for the same problem point to unreliable equipment, unstable programs, or end users in need of further training. All of this is addressed by proactively identifying repeat issues and addressing them.

3. **The time of day and the day of week that they called.** Calls for help tend to come in waves and at about the same time of day every week. Many problems are first realized in the morning when workstations are restarted and people attempt to log into their applications. By tracking the time when calls come in, staffing levels can be augmented to ensure that someone can take the calls as they arrive. Comparing the type of problem to the time of day further helps to determine the skills required for these work surges.

4. **Time elapsed before the issue was resolved.** Simple calls can be quickly addressed where difficult problems may require days to address. Comparing this value to when a call was received indicates, from the customer's point of view, responsiveness of the IT department. The longer the interval between the report and solution, the more follow-up calls the team receives from the requestor urging quicker action.

If service requests are categorized according to the IT department it was assigned to, then an average resolution time per request to a department can be calculated. Is this average time satisfactory? The service desk is a logical place to gather data, but is there any other? If the department's data covers these four areas, the IT staffing and skills mix can be approximated. If so, then the service survey will validate and expand on the results. If the department lacks data on its IT support, then a process must be developed to consistently and accurately gather such data.

See Policy ITP-9-1 IT Staffing Metrics Collection Policy as an example.

POLICY ITP-9-1   IT Staffing Metrics Collection Policy

Policy #:	ITP-9-1	Effective:	03/18/09	Page #:	1 of N
Subject:	IT Staffing Metrics Collection Policy				

1.0 PURPOSE

This policy mandates the metrics to be collected by IT to track the use and performance of the help desk.

2.0 SCOPE

This policy encompasses all calls made by users to the IT department for support. The IT manager is responsible for implementing all aspects of this policy.

3.0 POLICY

The IT department must collect metrics on the operation and use of the IT help desk. These metrics must include:

A. Who is calling? This must be tracked by user and by department.
B. What the user called about. Calls must be tracked by system and application being used when the problem occurred.
C. The time of day and the day of week that the user called. The type of problem should be compared to the time of day to help determine the skills required for work surges.
D. Time elapsed before the call was resolved. This value must be compared to when a call was received to measure the responsiveness of the IT department.
E. The IT manager who was assigned to resolve the problem. The average resolution time per request to a department is then calculated.

Help desk metrics must be updated monthly and made available on the corporate intranet.

4.0 REVISION HISTORY

Date	Revision #	Description of Change
03/18/09	1.0	Initial creation.

5.0 INQUIRIES

Direct inquiries about this policy to:

Harold Jenkins, CIO
2900 Corporate Drive
Columbus, OH 43215
Voice: 614-555-1234
Fax: 614-555-1235
E-mail: hjenkins@company.com

Revision #:	1.0	Supersedes:	N/A	Date:	03/18/09

§ 9.05 WHY USE A CUSTOMER SURVEY?

[A] Overview

The IT Manager may already have a clear idea of the department's service level, or may never have thought about it. After all, whenever executives call on anyone in the department, they always receive a prompt response. But are all callers treated with the same urgency as the IT Manager? Not likely! In this section we will establish the department's service level as seen by IT's customers.

Customer service exists to fulfill customer requirements. However, the business environment is constantly changing. As business shifts to keep pace with the competition, the mix and timing of IT services must also change. The survey is one tool for maintaining the alignment between the IT department and its customers. The survey indicates a general sense and not a statistical certainty. Therefore, it does not require a rigorous statistical sampling analysis.

[B] The Survey

The intent of the survey is to gauge the level of service provided by the department—based on the customer's point of view. Unfortunately, most IT Managers "guess" about their level of service and do not ask for their customers' opinions. They provide several unsatisfactory reasons for this.

A. Asking for an opinion resurfaces many of the customer complaints for actions denied due to company policy or lack of funding. This is an error since educating end users about department capabilities and limitations is important for setting expectations in their minds. Irreconcilable issues should be reevaluated for inclusion in the future service level.

B. The IT department is already overloaded with work requests and does not want to stimulate a new pile of work orders (the "let sleeping dogs lie" approach). Again, if the current IT Manager does not address these issues now, then the next IT Manager will! If there is an excess of pending work to be done, then the general service level will fall below customer expectations.

After reviewing the survey results, a desired customer service performance level is identified based on end-user expectations and funding. This desired level may include the IT Manager's perception that the team can achieve better results with the same resources. The performance metrics used for both the survey and the desired service level should be the same for easy comparison. The IT Manager's task is to develop a plan for moving the team's performance from the survey's baseline service level up to the desired level.

> ## COMMENT
>
> When someone picks up a telephone to dial it, there is an expectation, based on personal experience, of when to expect to hear a dial tone. After the number is entered, there is another expectation of when to expect to hear the telephone ring on the receiving end. When the time to hear the dial tone or the ring at the other end exceeds the customer's expectation, a problem is suspected.

The customer opinion survey will gather seven types of essential data, each of which drives customer service staffing levels:

A. Hours of operation, both normal and foreseeable additional hours. This is to validate alignment between customer work hours and IT support staff.
B. A detailed list of critical applications. This expands on the hours of service by assigning "experts" to specific support times.
C. A visual inspection of the hardware actually in use. During the interview, take a long look around. This is to uncover equipment slipped in without the IT department's knowledge or that was scheduled to depart, but never did. It would be valuable to also gather an inventory of software in use, but it would be very time consuming.

> ## COMMENT
>
> Several years ago, one of the authors was trying to drive out from the facility all of the old model workstations. New units were purchased and the service contract covering the old units was dropped. Meanwhile, a programmer at corporate headquarters was "saving" money by using the headquarters' old model workstations for a project to be installed in the same facility. Watch for someone else's junk slipping in the back door!

D. The department's staff turnover rate. New employees need some sort of orientation to the data systems. The higher the turnover, the greater the training need will be.

E. Any pending technical or process changes that impact IT's ability to support them.

F. Any ongoing IT problems. Some people hold back their frustration until they "explode." Find out if there are any simmering IT support problems and address them promptly. This one action will greatly enhance the perception of the service levels.

G. Collect a perception of service levels as they are delivered now, and how the customer would like to see them in the future.

COMMENT

Be wary of the "squeaky wheel," the person who attempts to dominate others through a stream of complaints and half-truths. Throughout all discussions, take care to educate managers and end users about the IT service priority system and why it is important to prevent low payback actions from delaying more important ones.

[C] Determining a Service Level Baseline

Surveys can be very time consuming to conduct. A 100 percent survey will allow everyone to contribute, but how much more will be learned than if only a sample of people were surveyed? The goal of the survey is to gather a general picture of the service levels. If there are complaints, now is the time to bring them out and address them. A sample service level survey is provided as Worksheet 9-1 Service Level Survey.

Who are the department's customers? This may sound like examining the obvious, but it helps to identify who the IT department is supporting. Sometimes, it may be more than the IT Manager has directed. A statement of the scope of work for the IT department anchors its service offering by establishing boundaries to guide the IT team. Trying to be all things to all people inevitably leads to failure as more and more work (and expectations) will be added to the workload without a corresponding increase in staff resources.

So who are the department's customers? Like many simple questions, the answers may be complex. Of course, customers are fellow workers within the company. These are the ones normally concentrated on. Other customers might be temporary workers or contract technical staff. This technical staff may be auditors, regulators, or contract technicians. Some companies provide equipment, software, and expertise to key suppliers or customers either to help them or to ensure they can keep up with the company's pace of operations.

WORKSHEET 9-1. Service Level Survey

<table>
<tr><td colspan="6" align="center">Service Level Survey</td></tr>
<tr><td>Department</td><td></td><td></td><td>Date</td><td></td><td></td></tr>
<tr><td>Interviewed</td><td></td><td></td><td>Interviewer</td><td></td><td></td></tr>
<tr><td>Number of workstations</td><td></td><td></td><td></td><td></td><td></td></tr>
<tr><td>Normal workdays</td><td></td><td colspan="3">Normal work hours</td><td></td></tr>
<tr><td>Additional workdays</td><td></td><td colspan="3">Additional work hours</td><td></td></tr>
<tr><td colspan="6" align="center">Critical Applications</td></tr>
<tr><td>Application Name</td><td>Platform</td><td>Max Outage</td><td colspan="2">Days of Week</td><td>Hours</td></tr>
<tr><td></td><td></td><td></td><td colspan="2"></td><td></td></tr>
<tr><td></td><td></td><td></td><td colspan="2"></td><td></td></tr>
<tr><td></td><td></td><td></td><td colspan="2"></td><td></td></tr>
<tr><td></td><td></td><td></td><td colspan="2"></td><td></td></tr>
<tr><td></td><td></td><td></td><td colspan="2"></td><td></td></tr>
<tr><td></td><td></td><td></td><td colspan="2"></td><td></td></tr>
<tr><td colspan="6" align="center">Staff</td></tr>
<tr><td>Turnover rate</td><td></td><td colspan="2">Average longevity</td><td></td><td></td></tr>
<tr><td>Department trainer</td><td></td><td colspan="2">Super user</td><td></td><td></td></tr>
<tr><td colspan="6">Pending system changes:</td></tr>
<tr><td colspan="6">Ongoing problems:</td></tr>
<tr><td colspan="6">What would you like to see done differently:</td></tr>
</table>

Side A

WORKSHEET 9-1.   (Continued)

Service Level Survey Matrix							
	Operations	Programming	Desktop	Help Desk	Networking	Telephone	Applications
Availability to receive request							
Understand what is requested							
Accurate priority							
Promptness of solution							
Correctness/completeness of solution							
Follow Up							
Helpfulness							
Attitude							

Place these statements into a sequence of one to ten with ten being the most important and one being the least relative importance.

— Ease of contact – how easy it is to contact someone to report a problem.

— Hours of support – hours when support is available

— Speed of 1st response – elapsed time to responder to call and discuss problem.

— Speed of solution – the elapsed time between first notice and providing solution.

— Correctness of solution – problem is solved and stays solved

— Completeness of solution – problem is solved and cannot surface again.

— Follow up call after solution

— Courtesy – even in tense situations

— Communications – listens politely and explains in non-technical terms

— Understanding of the business environment surrounding the problem.

Side B

> ## COMMENT
>
> One of the authors managed a service desk for a large company and regularly explained to callers that the service desk was not a substitute for the facility's telephone directory and did not redirect calls from outside salespeople. This was especially a problem with outside calls routed to the service desk by other employees since the company lacked a telephone operator. If the service desk had accepted this work by servicing these calls as they came in, assigned tasks would have been delayed and a new expectation would have been established in the minds of the customers that this was a part of their job. The service desk also fended off calls for supporting employees' home PCs and dispatching the facility's maintenance staff.

Separate customers into support groups. There are several easy groupings for end users. From a staffing perspective, the easiest group is shifts. The requirements of the third-shift employees are typically different from the first shift, etc. It is a rare company that does not have someone in the facility at all hours of the day—often every day of the week. There are security guards, custodians, 24-hour call centers, off-hour teams for international, East Coast, or West Coast support, etc.

Another common grouping is company influence leaders. Not all customers are created equal, so the customer base should be segmented at least into priority customers and everyone else. All IT departments do this already. A request from the CEO is always treated as a high priority while a similar request from a clerk might wait several days until it rises to the top of the list. Aside from keeping their job, IT Managers do this because of impact. Most of the executive's actions impact a number of people, whereas the clerk's actions will impact a much smaller aspect of the company. Taken from another angle, an idle executive (no jokes, now) costs the company more per hour than an idle clerk. This may seem harsh in a society where everyone is considered equal, but it is true. From a survival standpoint, executives' opinions as to the IT department's service levels and competence have an impact on future funding and staffing.

Pros and cons of priority executive support. Arguments for executive priority service: Executives are paid more "per hour" than other workers. If they cannot complete their work due to a data system problem, then the company has lost more "labor expense" than if a clerk's system was broken. Executive systems should always work as fast as they can think so as to not hinder the forward movement of business. A disruption of work at the top ripples down through the organization, causing multiple delays for other workers. Also it is important for the IT department to generate "good will" with key decision makers.

Arguments against executive priority service: Since executives do not receive the same level of support as everyone else, they cannot appreciate the service level that others must live with. Priority treatment of executive requests presents an illusion that all is well when it is not.

To simplify the process, focus the survey on:

A. **Executives and department managers**—These are the influence leaders whose opinion counts more than that of others. Also, as a central point of contact for their teams, executives and managers can pass on any issues raised by their department in the past. Survey every one of these people.

B. **Key end users**—Usually more technically oriented than their peers, they would have a more realistic idea of the complexity of their requests. They often have insights into the true causes of long-term IT problems. Survey every one of these people.

C. **A random sampling of end users from each department and each shift**, to gather their perception since each touches the technology in different ways. Be sure to randomly survey at least 10 percent of this group. If the sampling is not random, then the results of the survey may be skewed.

D. **Vocal critics**—Survey every one of these people. Many people in our society feel it is rude to speak negatively of anything but the most serious of faults. The critics may point out areas of friction between IT and its users—and they won't be shy about telling the interviewer about it!

[D]   The Survey Form

To consistently gather this data for later analysis, create a survey form that reflects the situation. An example form is provided to illustrate this discussion. This form is intended to gather a "broad brush" customer opinion and not a statistically rigorous response. That would require a different form and different sampling technique.

Forms allow for a consistent collection of data since each respondent is asked the same questions. This is important if more than one person will be conducting the data collection interviews. The sample form is a two-part document that should be copied to two sides of the same page to keep everything together.

Front side of the form

The first section is information used to verify for the service desk's records and the IT department's basic statistics:

A. **Number of workstations**—The more workstations in a department, the likelier that someone will call with an issue. This is normally provided by the department manager. Determine what will be counted as a workstation. Is it a terminal, a PC, a server dedicated to a single user, a PDA? Include work-from-home users.

B. **Normal work days and hours**—The department's normal working hours must be covered by on-site IT assistance with the appropriate skills. This is the key to customer service. If the IT staff has the right skills at the wrong hours, service levels will be considered to be low.

C. **Additional work days and hours**—Many departments schedule special days during the year when weekend or late evening support is important. Examples include inventory update counts, year-end closing for accounting, etc. These days and times also require on-site IT support, with the correct skill sets.

Critical applications. A critical application is any system that halts a company process that has been identified as critical to company operations. In a factory, this is a process that halts the assembly line. In a sales office, this might be an inoperable telephone system that prevents customers from calling in orders. This is important because the support of every critical application must be assigned to someone in the IT staffing plan. Some departments will claim that every system is critical, but this means that requests for new user IDs would be just as important as an inoperable payroll application. If the IT Manager cannot convince the customer to identify which systems are critical, then try ranking all of them on a list from 1 to whatever. Draw lines across the list to indicate which ones are critical, important, useful, etc. Critical systems should be between the top 10 percent and 25 percent of the applications.

Fields on the form for critical applications:

A. **Application name**—The name this application is commonly known by.

B. **Platform**—Does this application run on a server, a mainframe, or a workstation? If multiple critical systems are concentrated on a few platforms, it may be prudent to spread them around.

C. **Max outage**—What is the maximum amount of time this application can be unavailable before the department's workflow is severely impacted? This is a key driver to staffing since a low value here means that a technical expert must be provided on standby during working hours.

D. **Days of the week**—What days of the week is this process normally used?

E. **Hours**—What hours of the day are most important for this process?

Staff. This section focuses on the department's staffing practices. Cheaper labor can be obtained if fewer skills are required. So while the hiring manager's budget looks good for hiring unskilled workers, their increased requests for technical assistance represent a cost shifted to the IT department. These workers will generate a greater number of support calls. Such workforces must be trained by either the IT department or the department hiring them, prior to providing them the IT support telephone number.

Pending system changes. If a department has major data systems or process changes near to implementation, the IT department should be alerted to shifts in support requirements. A chilling statement by an end-user department manager is, "Gee, I thought you knew. . . ."

Back side of the form

The reverse side of the form must be modified to reflect the department structure of the IT team. The intention is to elicit from the interviewee their opinion and impressions of the different IT groups' performance. Remember that someone calling the operations department to reset a user ID (perhaps requiring a few minutes) has a different expectation for task completion than they would for requesting a new business data report (probably requiring several days). Also, if someone is bypassing the service desk and calling their friend in IT operations for assistance, then the department's metrics would not reflect this.

Along the top of the matrix is a list of the various IT departments. Along the left side are a series of questions concerning this person's experiences working with these groups. A scale of 0 to 10 is recommended, where a 0 represents minimal or no contact with that IT team and 10 represents absolute perfection in all encounters.

A goal of this portion of the survey is to detect how often the various departments are contacted directly. Users should route their calls through the service desk. Secondly, a single IT team may be undoing all of the goodwill that the IT Manager is working hard to create. This may highlight who is doing this to which customer departments.

[E]   Evaluating the Survey Results

The results of this survey are evaluated in several ways.

A. **Total the number of workstations.** Assume that each one is loaded with the company standard software. The ratio of workstations to support persons is one gauge of IT efficiency and is useful when planning company expansions.

B. **Confirm hours of support to critical applications.** Service levels vary according to the hours of the day and the day of the week. During those hours when the majority of the workers are present, the service level should be at its optimum. During evening hours, weekends, and holidays, any workers on the job may have an expectation and a requirement for support.

Another issue for support times is special days when long hours are expected in the department. These might be during the annual reconciliation and closing of the accounting files, during a materials inventory verification, or to receive orders in support of seasonal sales (such as Christmas for a retailer). Each of these would change the normal support hours. A sample of hours or support matrix is provided as Worksheet 9-2.

WORKSHEET 9-2. Hours of Support Matrix

Weekday Processing																								
	00	01	02	03	04	05	06	07	08	09	10	11	12	13	14	15	16	17	18	19	20	21	22	23
Payroll									×	×	×	×	×	×	×	×	×	-	-					
Accounts Payable									×	×	×	×	×	×	×	×	×							
Accounts Receivable									×	×	×	×	×	×	×	×								
Materials - Inbound		×	×	×	×	×	×	×	×	×	×	×	×	×	×	×	×							
Shipping Notices	×																×	×	×	×	×	×	×	×
Production Schedule																								

Saturday - Weekend Processing																								
	00	01	02	03	04	05	06	07	08	09	10	11	12	13	14	15	16	17	18	19	20	21	22	23
Payroll																								
Accounts Payable																								
Accounts Receivable								×	×	×	×	×												
Materials - Inbound																								
Shipping Notices																								
Production Schedule																								

Sunday - Weekend Processing																								
	00	01	02	03	04	05	06	07	08	09	10	11	12	13	14	15	16	17	18	19	20	21	22	23
Payroll																								

Accumulate the list of critical applications identified by each department. When laid alongside the vertical axis of the desired support hours, it is easy to see the technical skills required to be on site for optimal support. The survey asked for the days of the week and hours of the day each application is needed, but the current support person can identify any behind the scenes action required for an application to be available for workers first thing in the morning.

The list of critical applications must be compared to the IT staff organization to ensure that every critical application has someone assigned to support it. While developing the skills database, the IT department offered what they thought the critical applications would be. The survey's intention is to ask the customers what they believe the critical applications are.

A. Critical applications in the database but not on the survey list should be evaluated to determine their current significance to the company. Their importance may have faded and IT did not realize it.

B. Critical applications on the survey list but missing from the database should be examined to determine their underlying technologies and added to the list. Someone in the IT department should then be assigned to support the application. (Will this identify further training requirements?)

Use a spreadsheet to track when critical systems need support. Use one column for each hour. Down the left column, list all critical applications. Place an "X" in the column for each hour that a particular critical application is needed based on the customer survey, and based on the IT Manager's knowledge of when critical systems and their supporting software run. Include overnight processing for these systems.

Compare the spreadsheet requirements to the staff's work hours. Should any of them begin their work day earlier to provide better coverage? The focus of customer service levels is on the availability of skills and timeliness of a solution.

A. **Turnover rate and planned system changes.** This will provide planning estimates for future service requirements. Both will temporarily require additional technical support. If a department experiences a high degree of turnover, then their data systems must be greatly simplified to reduce the amount of time expended on training. Another side of this is company "downsizing" where experienced users will be reassigned and suddenly using systems new to them.

B. **Pending system changes.** These are to catch any upcoming system or process changes that may require additional staffing support, usually temporary. These occur in branch offices when the corporate headquarters may be creating applications specific to a department. In some companies, communications between departments can be somewhat lax. Use this list to initiate discussions with each department to understand the impact of any change on IT support planning.

[F]   IT Team Performance

On the reverse side of the survey form are ratings for each of the IT teams. The goal of this matrix is not statistical. It is to uncover indicators of problems. The purpose is to:

A. **Identify which user departments are directly calling which IT departments.** In some cases, this may be appropriate. In other cases, it must be stopped and refocused through the service desk. Otherwise the support and problem identification metrics will not be accurate.
B. **Identify any negative customer experiences with IT.** This will provide some idea of the type of problem and the department.

These questions could be further developed to obtain some clear statistical inference, but that is beyond the scope of this study.

§ 9.06   TRANSLATING REQUIREMENTS INTO A STAFF LEVEL

[A]   Overview

Many companies have a "head count" budget as well as a capital and an operating budget. This is one way that a large company seeks to control their employment benefits and pension expenses. The IT Manager has a responsibility to provide the optimum customer service for the minimal cost. The ideal trade-off is rarely achieved but managers try to do the most with the resources at hand.

[B]   Establish a Service Level Performance Goal

Once the department's baseline customer service level is established, the next step is to identify what the department's service level should be. The gap between reality and the goal identifies the staffing and skills necessary for the department to deliver this service. To identify the desired service level, use the same approach as with identifying skills by starting with nothing and imagine building the department from scratch. This helps to reduce the "filters" of corporate culture and a "business as usual" attitude.

Establish a level of service agreement with the executives for the responsiveness they require. (We exist but to serve!) Ensure that the proper number of people with the correct skill sets is available to meet that level. Keep in mind the previously discussed characteristics of standby, separation of responsibilities, etc. Note that staffing levels should be set to something less than peak requirements. (Otherwise, when a work surge arrived, there would be no "slack" time to address it.)

[C]   Staffing Ratios

Major IT industry pollsters have asked companies about the number of people they use to service a set number of end users. The ratios vary by many factors such as the industry, the technical sophistication of end users, etc. Companies of less than 500 people may have a ratio of 18 end users per IT person while companies with more than 10,000 people may have a ratio of 40:1. A part of this is the spreading of IT staff overhead. A small shop would need a minimum of one expert per major technology (network, programming, operations, systems administration, manager, telephone system, etc.). In a lean organization, the manager may be one of these experts as well as the team leader. Large organizations can spread their technical specialists over a wide range of equipment. To estimate the service desk size in a large environment, figure at least 30 minutes per desktop, per year, for support if upgrades are addressed centrally. Allow another half hour, per year, if upgrades are applied individually.

Some industries are more IT intensive and have a low tolerance for delays. For example a stock brokerage may have a ratio of one IT person per 11 end users. In a manufacturing environment, the ratio may be 33 workers to one IT technician because shop supervisors are more than likely to be the only ones using PCs, and they require less support than most employees in the shop who do not have PC workstations.

Factors driving the staffing ratio:

A.   Technology stability and reliability. Standardizing systems on proven technologies will require fewer support people rather than chasing the latest technologies—or limping along with the oldest ones.

B.   An active preventative maintenance program that cleans, lubricates, and adjusts moving components on critical devices such as high-volume printers.

C.   Timely replacement of obsolete equipment. Some companies purchase their technologies with three-year warranties and dispose of the equipment after the warranty expires.

D.   Some companies will never upgrade their desktop units. New units are purchased with the latest software and peripherals which are expected to suffice until the hardware warranty expires. Then they are replaced with new units.

E.   Variety of technologies being supported. It is easier for one person to support a large number of desktops with standard software than trying to support a few workstations with everything that anyone can install.

F.   Frequency and complexity of technology refreshes. Variation in technology carries with it its own learning curve.

[D]   Allocating the IT Staff

There are three typical ways to determine the staffing organization and size of an organization: The "warm body" approach; the "magic staffing" formula; minimal staff, tweak and adjust. Each approach has its own merits and deep pitfalls—yet the IT Manager may recognize his own organization within one of these frameworks. The task at hand is to balance and periodically rebalance the work between the IT teams and the individual staff members so that the appropriate level of staff is present—but no extra. Remember, all decisions are driven toward improving customer service.

Expect considerable resistance to shifting work among the team based on current requirements. Over time, employees become familiar with their responsibilities and are loath to exchange them for the unknown. Work expands to fill the time allotted to it, so a vigorous program to root out low-value tasks is essential. Otherwise, everyone will state that they are too busy with this or that, and that the IT department does not understand their customers.

Also remember that end users dwell in a dynamic business environment. To provide a high level of service, the IT organization must periodically reconfigure itself to meet changing requirements.

The warm body approach. One author spent a considerable amount of time in the Marines where the term "warm body" was used to indicate a "living, breathing" person of any type. The implication is that whoever was in charge of the task would ensure the person provided would know how to accomplish the task (usually something simple). The person in charge would further provide the "direction and motivation" to ensure it was properly accomplished. This rather direct approach to people management is common in most IT shops. A set number of people (warm bodies) are assigned to vaguely described staff positions and then expected to perform the work. This approach results in the assignment of people based on their primary skill and/or availability at the time the opening appeared—not on the total skills necessary.

The warm body approach begins with a nod toward customer focus but always ends with a focus on finding "a place" for the existing staff. Its essential elements are:

A. **Identify the major task assignments within the department.** This might range from watching a high-speed printer in the data center to development of systems enhancements for a major data system. Sometimes the task is just to be immediately available, such as answering calls at the service desk.

B. **Write job descriptions that describe the responsibilities as imagined by the IT Manager.** A set of job descriptions ensures that the department's work is accounted for among the various positions.

C. **Assign each job responsibility some general quantity of time required to perform it.** Use a weekly or monthly timeframe. This time may have some basis in history but we are estimating future requirements. The time is totaled until a full-time equivalent (FTE) of a person (40 hours in a week) is arrived at.

D. **Assign existing staff members to these positions.** Do this according to the best fit between their perceived skills and the estimated requirements for each position. This step is often complicated by in-process projects.

For example, the IT Manager assigns:

A. One programmer for each major business area supported to include all major and minor programs, reports, etc. This includes all end-user generated programs used within these departments. This is a general estimate that says each major system requires a full-time person. It does not address the full range of technologies those data systems depend upon.

B. One computer operator per shift, three shifts by five days per week. In this situation, a person must be standing by even if there is no work. Routine tasks could be shifted from someone else to this person, if they are technically capable of completing them.

C. One service desk person for first shift minus two hours, and another one for the second shift plus two hours. Computer operators handle the rest of the calls. This again indicates a "watch stander" who sits and waits for the telephone to ring. The job requirement is immediate availability. It also shows how routine tasks such as the third shift service desk can be shifted to operations since the call volume is low to none.

D. One network support person and one server administrator. These two people provide backup support for the other. In these cases, the skills required are so unique that it is cheaper to hire someone to perform them rather than to always bring in a consultant—even if they are idle from time to time.

One IT administrative manager should manage the IT budget, licensing, contracts, and any other paperwork.

The warm body approach is often used when reorganizing existing IT staffs to address existing requirements without hiring more people. In these cases, its focus is workload shifting.

Some pitfalls of this approach include:

A. All workers are not equally productive as this approach assumes they are. Their inclination to work or learn new technologies varies widely among the group.

B. Few IT Managers have a clear idea of what is required for each position and how long each responsibility will require. Their guesses are normally too low.

C. Workers settle in the role they are assigned and are reluctant to "clean up" the tasks not completed by others.

The magic staffing formula. Many companies are intimidated by the amount of work required to conduct a detailed customer expectations survey and seek a mathematical approximation for a staffing level. Such a formula may provide a quick answer, but it does not address such essential elements as individual expertise level, dispersion of the work sites, complexity of tools, etc. It is called a "magic" formula since many IT Managers seek it but are never satisfied with the result. The best use of a staffing formula is as a guideline for a theoretical staffing level.

> ## COMMENT
>
> The magic staffing formula starts with an estimate of the work required, which in turn leads to the job descriptions. The warm body method approaches the issue from the other direction by building a task list with its implied work requirement as the job descriptions are built.

An example of a formula is provided. It requires the IT Manager to make assumptions about work requirements so that full-time equivalent positions can be determined. A quick glance at the formula shows that it must be adjusted to address local conditions. If multi-shift operations are supported then this should be accomplished for each shift, with likely different factors for each shift (assuming the majority of nonemergency support is completed on the first shift).

Calculate each of these points and add up the total number of people required.

A. Desktop support—The number of workstations in service divided by a factor representing the number of stations that a single person can support. This might be anywhere from 100 to 1,000, depending on the degree of hardware standardization and end-user technical sophistication.

B. Server support—The number of servers in service divided by a factor representing the number of stations that a single person can support. This might be anywhere from 10 to 100, depending on the degree of standardization. There should be at least two server support people (primary and backup).

C. Network support—The number of ubs and major network switching devices in service. Consider one person for every 20 devices. Add another person for backup support.

D. Telephone service—Typically two people can support a facility, with one acting as the backup. This has increased with the elimination of office switchboards and the shift to IVR technology for routing calls.

E. Programming—One person per major data system or customer department.

F. Security—Two or more people. This responsibility may be split among a part of the staff. More than one person reduces abuse, but too many people permits circumvention.

G. Operations—A minimum of one per person per shift. Add more based on specific workload. This may be the same person that works the service desk.

H. Administration—At least one supervisor for every ten IT people plus one department administrator.

The caveats to this model are the age of the equipment, how widely it is dispersed, the degree of standardization, and the technical sophistication of the users. These factors may vary the results of the formula by as much as 30 percent.

Minimal staff. The minimal staff scheme is to identify the bare minimum number of people required to achieve the desired level of service. Then as service deficiencies are identified, grow the staff slowly to cover them. This creeping approach will initially result in some customer dissatisfaction but will ensure that the IT staff is tightly focused on its goals. The steps are:

A. Establish an initial service level. If the service desk already has metrics for the number of calls and the response time by urgency level, track the number of calls over time, by priority to get the average response and resolution times.

B. Identify the minimal staff required to provide a basic level of customer service. This is generally someone to answer the phones during normal business hours and a single technical expert for each major technology supported. Staff to this level and monitor service level performance.

C. After a 60-day break-in period to allow the team to settle into their new roles and determine the fastest way to address problems, review service response and determine if additional staff are needed, and where.

D. Add new staff members incrementally and allow another 60 days to determine the impact before hiring any more.

The result of adding a new person (after the break-in period) should be an improvement in the service level statistics. If there is no change, then the problem is something other than the number of people assigned to customer service. The 60-day delay also allows time to absorb the person's efforts into the metrics before adding the next one.

The major drawback to this approach is that each person added requires some shuffling of responsibilities among the staff. Although this is manageable, it is disruptive to productivity until everyone settles into their new roles.

The level of customer service the IT department provides has a direct impact on the staffing of the department. Higher service requirements generally translate into more people. The trick is to provide an acceptable level of service with the minimal employee costs. Given that the service the department is providing is to meet ever shifting customer needs, good luck!

Flexible assignments make it easier to shift people to address work surges. If grocery stock clerks are called to the front of a store to run a cash register, this is flexible staffing at work. Instead of rigid job requirements, the entire staff should consider itself as a labor pool to assist wherever they have the skills to do so.

If the IT budgets limit the number or quality of the people that can be hired, then reduce the published service levels, usually by cutting support to lightly used systems, or systems with few users. This will focus the team on the mainstream requirements.

See Policy ITP-9-2 IT Staffing Levels Policy as an example.

POLICY ITP-9-2   IT Staffing Levels Policy

Policy #:	ITP-9-1	Effective:	03/18/09	Page #:	1 of N
Subject:	IT Staffing Metrics Collection Policy				

1.0 PURPOSE

This policy mandates the staffing levels required to support each division with the organization.

2.0 SCOPE

This policy encompasses all divisions within the organization. The IT manager is responsible for implementing all aspects of this policy.

3.0 POLICY

The staffing of IT personnel within each division of the organization will follow the formulas listed below.

A. Desktop support—There will be one desktop support person for every 150 desktop workstations.
B. Server support—There will be one server engineer for every 15 servers. There should be at least two server support people (primary and backup) for each server.
C. Network support—There will be one network support person for every major network switching devices in service. There must be at least two people in each division to allow for backup support.
D. Telephone service—Typically two people can support a facility, with one acting as the backup.
E. Programming—One person per major data system or customer department.
F. Security—Two or more people. This responsibility may be split among a part of the staff.
G. Operations—A minimum of one per person per shift. Add more based on specific workload. This may be the same person that works the help desk.
H. Administration—At least one supervisor for every 10 IT people plus one department administrator.

Exceptions to these staffing levels require approval of the division head and the corporate CIO.

4.0 REVISION HISTORY

Date	Revision #	Description of Change
03/18/09	1.0	Initial creation.

5.0 INQUIRIES

Direct inquiries about this policy to:

Harold Jenkins, CIO
2900 Corporate Drive
Columbus, OH 43215

Voice: 614-555-1234
Fax: 614-555-1235
E-mail: hjenkins@company.com

Revision #:	1.0	Supersedes:	N/A	Date:	03/18/09

10

HUMAN RESOURCES: IT'S POOREST MANAGED ASSET

§ 10.01 OVERVIEW
    [A] Purpose and Scope
    [B] Critical Policies to Develop Based on This Chapter

§ 10.02 RECRUITING, REASSIGNMENTS, AND PROMOTIONS
    [A] Overview
    [B] Creating a Clear Job Description
    [C] Establishing Clear Selection Criteria
    [D] Internal Opportunity Posting
    [E] External Opportunity Posting
    [F] Using Offshore Staffing
    [G] College Recruiting
    [H] Student Interns
    [I] Notes on Interviewing
    [J] Some Prudent Checks

§ 10.03 NEW EMPLOYEE ORIENTATION
    [A] First Impressions
    [B] IT Orientation Package
    [C] Mentor Assignment

§ 10.04 PERFORMANCE REVIEW
    [A] Overview
    [B] Conducting a Review
    [C] Periodic Performance Reviews
    [D] Peer Performance Reviews
    [E] Documentation
    [F] Preparing the Way for Employee Termination

§ 10.05 EMPLOYEE DEVELOPMENT
    [A] Overview
    [B] IT Skills Inventory
    [C] Continuing Education and Training
    [D] Plan for the Future
    [E] Training and Consultants

§ 10.06 MANAGING IT TRAINING
    [A] Developing a Training Strategy
    [B] End-User Training
    [C] Keeping Records of Training
    [D] Employee Recognition
    [E] Education Information Booklet
    [F] Outsourced Training
    [G] Annual Reporting

§ 10.07 EMPLOYEE COMMUNICATIONS
    [A] Overview
    [B] Staff Meetings
    [C] E-mail and Memos
    [D] Rumor Board

§ 10.08 EMPLOYEE BURNOUT
    [A] Responsibility
    [B] What Causes Burnout?
    [C] Company Assistance
    [D] Signs of Burnout

§ 10.09 IT EMPLOYEE PRODUCTIVITY
    [A] Overview
    [B] IT Management Productivity
    [C] IT Employee Productivity

§ 10.10 NONTRADITIONAL WORKING ARRANGEMENTS
    [A] Telecommuting Policy
    [B] Job-Sharing Policy
    [C] Flex-Time Policy
    [D] Rehiring Former Employees

§ 10.01 OVERVIEW

[A] Purpose and Scope

Imagine purchasing a new server for the IT department. It would be a large powerful server that might cost somewhere in the range of $90,000. What would an IT Manager do to prepare for this major investment? Ensure there was an outlet on the UPS? Find rack space or even buy a new rack? Assign an administrator to set up and ensure the machine runs smoothly? Purchase an equipment maintenance agreement to cover required repairs for the next four years? Create a project plan to ensure that everything was done to make the device quickly available and productive? Likely they would do all of these things—and more.

So why when it comes to staffing an IT department is so much left to chance? The salary and overhead for the average IT professional is about $90,000 (salary plus 50 percent for overhead). Yet how often are new employees haphazardly introduced to an IT department? The ongoing maintenance of these people is only an afterthought. Their work environment is based on whatever is available—even if it is noisy and distracting.

The old saying that an IT staff is the department's most valuable resource is quite true. A quick look at the department's budget will show where the costs are. Staffing is always near the top of the budget of most IT departments. For an IT Manager to be effective, this resource must be carefully nurtured.

Management of the IT department's human assets must be a proactive effort. Through daily conversations, staff meetings, and performance reviews, the IT Manager must strive to identify and address issues before they become major problems. People don't want a manager. They want a leader. Leaders know that they set an example in all they do—good and bad.

Human Resources policies governing IT personnel are focused on:

A. Obtaining the best workers with the required skills.
B. Continually motivating the workers for high productivity.
C. Improving skills sets through training.
D. Retaining employees through fair treatment and fair compensation.

IT personnel policies only augment corporate personnel policies. On close examination, they are simply good management practices. The difference between IT and other departments is that highly skilled technical people are expensive and difficult to find. They can more readily depart for other companies if they believe they are not fairly treated.

It is time consuming to train a replacement for a competent employee in any department. Training requires both the new person and a skilled person to teach him or her. Replacements must be trained and allowed time to learn their new responsibilities. This may delay scheduled projects. New personnel often cost more than current employees creating a pay imbalance in the department.

IT jobs attract a certain personality type. Studies indicate that IT workers are motivated more by personal fulfillment and growth than money or job titles. Other research indicates they tend to be more loyal to their profession than to their firm. IT personnel policies and procedures must accommodate these differences for the department to function effectively and to minimize turnover.

[B]   Critical Policies to Develop Based on This Chapter

Using the material discussed in this chapter, you will be able to create the following policies:

A.   Recruiting.
   1.   Pay a bonus for employee referrals.
   2.   Verify candidate claims of skills and education.
   3.   Verify a candidate's character through a police background check and drug screening.
   4.   Policies for posting and interviewing.
   5.   Guidelines for hiring relatives.
B.   Performance reviews.
   1.   Reviews are conducted at a frequency determined by the company.
   2.   Reviews follow a prescribed format.
C.   Training for new employees.
   1.   Orientation policy.
   2.   Mentoring policy.
D.   Developing staff.
   a.   What the IT training strategy is.
   b.   Who authorizes training.
   c.   What types of training are appropriate.
   d.   Recordkeeping requirements.
   e.   Identify skills in employees.
   f.   Identify future skills requirements.
   g.   Aligning employees with future needs through training.
E.   Nontraditional working arrangements.
   1.   Working from home.
   2.   Flex time.
   3.   Job sharing.
   4.   Rehiring workers.

Policies should always be developed based on the local situation. Successful managers cannot issue locally correct guidance if the policies are written for some other company's situation.

§ 10.02   RECRUITING, REASSIGNMENTS, AND PROMOTIONS

[A]   Overview

Recruiting is the responsibility of the Human Resources department. Based on the information provided by the IT Manager, the Human Resources recruiters attempt to match resumes with an open position. However, without a detailed understanding of IT technologies and local requirements, this is a poor way to find people. If the IT department cannot obtain a dedicated Human Resources recruiter to learn about their specific needs, then they must screen all incoming resumes themselves.

Workers vary widely in productivity and their inclination to work harmoniously with others. Through its experience in hiring and disciplining workers, the Human Resources department strives to ensure that new employees are as "trouble free" as possible. Human Resources professionals know that less than 5 percent of the employees cause over 95 percent of the problems. It is essential that the company's interviewing and screening processes identify problem people before they join the organization.

COMMENT

IT management professionals also learn over time that the most productive 5 percent of all IT people get 95 percent of the work done. Corporate compensation plans rarely take this into account.

A common pitfall of recruiting is hiring relatives of valued company workers. In theory, this becomes a further reward for successful service. In practice it can lead to a wide range of problems. Because of the controls needed for an IT operation, hiring relatives causes nothing but problems. Relatives tend not to abide by the same rules as nonrelatives. They tend to cover up more errors and have higher rates of orchestrated thefts. Very large companies can successfully overcome this by requiring large separation in facilities, subsidiaries, or other company subdivisions between related workers.

[B]   Creating a Clear Job Description

It all begins with a clear idea of the job. A job description, as the name implies, describes a job. Some managers try to shortcut the process and substitute vague boilerplate descriptions that are generic and not specific to the actual job. This is a big mistake. A well-written job description details the type of tasks that the employee is expected to perform. It communicates an expectation from the employer to the worker as to the skills and duties expected for that position. Job descriptions are the foundation for setting a position's pay range.

How detailed should a job description be? Some will argue that more than a page is too much detail. Much of the description can be "standard" but some must be specific. For example, the "standard" part might be a description for a C++ programmer. Essentially, all of this class of workers has about the same technical requirements. The "specific" part of the description is that this person will be supporting the materials management department and must understand the business side of that department.

Some managers do not like detailed job descriptions. They feel it hinders their flexibility when assigning work. This is not true. Work is assigned as required. Well-written job descriptions include a final statement that the person will perform any additional duties as assigned. A well-written job description includes:

A. **Primary responsibilities** are the expectations that justify the existence of this staff position. This list is used to determine who will be chosen for this position, so it must be carefully written. The primary responsibilities detail what is wanted and how much. Any candidate that does not meet *each* of the primary responsibilities is automatically excluded from consideration. Since the list of primary responsibilities narrows the list of potential candidates, it should be 10 items or less.

   An example of a primary responsibility might be a requirement that the candidate possess at least "5 years of project management experience." Just asking for project management experience would open the position to someone with insufficient background. Often the requirement would even more specifically require "web software design project management."

   Technical skills may be the same as with other positions within the department. An example might be two Java programmers sitting side by side with different business knowledge requirements. When listing skill requirements, think specifically about what this person will be assigned to do rather than sticking to generic tasks. This person's software application might include coding access to a non-standard database, it may interface with some antique equipment or software, or it might require extensive travel.

   Sometimes skill levels are indicated by professional certifications, such as PMI's Project Manager Professional or Microsoft Certified Systems Engineer. Certifications indicate an understanding of technical specific principles but are not a reliable indicator of the person's ability to translate these principles into action.

COMMENT

Project Management Institute (PMI)'s Project Management Professional certification can be found at *www.pmi.org*. Microsoft's MCSE (Microsoft Certified Systems Engineer) can be found at *www.microsoft.com*.

B. **Secondary responsibilities** are the non-critical functions assigned to this person. Candidates are evaluated by how well they fulfill these requirements. However, not meeting a secondary responsibility will not disqualify them from consideration. This might be expertise with technology outside of their normal responsibility but would be handy for the department. It might be knowledge of a specific foreign language or experience working for the government.

C. **Standard boiler plate** is a list of company-wide expectations that are sometimes tacked onto the bottom. This runs the gamut from "supports company EEO initiatives" to "works well with others." Usually these are already covered in company policies and are stated here to highlight them to all applicants.

Job descriptions can be misused. They can be tailored to only fit a single person or to require an inflated salary. Examples of how job descriptions can be misused include:

A. **Tailored job descriptions** are written in such a way as to exclude as many people as possible (usually all internal candidates). An alternative is to write in such a way that only one person could plausibly qualify. Both will backfire on the IT Manager. It exposes the job posting system as a phony management practice and not fairly applied for promotions or transfers. The implication is that, to be promoted or transferred, the employees must leave the company.

B. **Inflated job descriptions** add nonessential requirements and technical skills to inflate the position's pay scale. Examples would be to require a Masters degree, expert level expertise in a technical area, or a significant number of years experience.

C. **Hiring someone who lacks the primary requirements** applies a standard for excluding some employees and not others. Like the tailored job description, this one is hard to disguise and demoralizes the rest of the employees.

COMMENT

It is always interesting to see an advertisement in the newspaper asking for more years of experience working with a hot new technology than that technology has been in existence.

[C]   Establishing Clear Selection Criteria

All new cars are nice. The same goes for interviewing job applicants—they all seem so suited for the position. To select the best candidate for a position, and to be fair to all applicants, the hiring IT Manager must establish the criteria for rating all candidates before speaking to the first one. These criteria become the "yard stick" against which all candidates are measured.

The criteria should be written and are usually maintained in a "score sheet" form created just for filling this position. The first section is for primary responsibilities. Each of these is weighted according to its importance. Candidates may barely meet a requirement or be an expert in that skill. Their degree of compliance should be indicated. Any candidate that does not minimally fulfill all of the primary requirements is automatically disqualified.

> ## COMMENT
>
> One trick to help keep your biases in check is to force yourself to be harder on candidates you immediately like, and to give those you don't like at first the benefit of the doubt.

Secondary requirements include: education, industry experience, personal characteristics, and future growth potential. They reflect characteristics of present employees who are happy and successful in the same type of position. Again, the degree to which someone meets these skills should be noted.

[D]   Internal Opportunity Posting

One of the most difficult things to gauge is an IT professional's degree of institutional knowledge. An understanding of how a company actually works is not available from any textbook—it must be gained through experience. Personal relationships built over time make implementing technical change much easier. For these reasons, it is preferable to fill open positions with qualified internal candidates.

Most companies post job openings internally for at least two weeks before looking outside of the company. This allows time for people to return from business trips and vacation to see them. However, this is also abused by posting for only one week during holidays or peak summer vacation season. When an exciting opportunity appears, some employees will see that they lack a primary requirement and not apply for it. Imagine the discontent when someone else lacking the same skill is hired! (If a primary responsibility is moved to the secondary column because sufficient candidates cannot be found, then the job *must* be reposted internally.)

A major benefit of internally posting jobs is to open opportunities for all and to break up some of the "buddy" system of promotions. Using a "buddy" system to select people opens the door to a discrimination lawsuit. Posting positions may reveal latent talent and skills within the department. Whenever hiring or promoting people, management is open to accusations of gender or race bias. An open posting of positions makes them equally available to all.

Managers get what they reward. If "friends" are rewarded with promotions that their performance does not rate, then the hard-working employees will shift their efforts from technical results to being the manager's "buddy," since that is what is rewarded. Other workers will become demoralized by their unfair exclusion from consideration and "retire on the job."

Some large companies rate their IT managers on the number of positions filled internally. Although it is not possible to find someone internally that is a good fit for every job, a high internal fill rate is indicative of managers "growing" their staff and improving their skills. Managers who "protect" their team by preventing anyone from leaving need to be replaced—before everyone on their team does!

[E]   External Opportunity Posting

Locating the right person for a position is an expensive and time consuming process. There are many places to post open position notices and many ways to receive resumes. Unfortunately the ones most used by IT professionals are the ones that are the hardest to make effective. The most used external posting opportunities are:

A. **Employment agencies.** Using an employment agency hands the responsibility of finding good candidates to a third party. An employment agency is not cheap and typically charges a fee that is equal to 20 percent or more of the candidate's first year salary.

   Employment agencies have the advantage of disguising the company that has an opening. Sometimes a company does not wish its employees to know a search is underway, such as when they are replacing a key employee, or if all internal candidates are obviously not suited for the position.

   An agency is most useful if hiring someone whose expertise is not already in-house. Without knowledge of the subject, the hiring company cannot ask pertinent questions to determine the depth of a candidate's knowledge. A well selected agency assumes the task of validating the candidate's technical qualifications.

B. **Employee referral.** A popular program is to pay a bonus to employees who recommend someone from outside of the company for an open position. Proven personnel usually recommend qualified persons like themselves. The person recommending someone has a personal stake in "bringing in a winner."

   An immediate benefit is that the company saves time and money over using an employment agency. Other expenses saved include newspaper advertisement and Internet posting costs. Bonuses for finding a candidate who is hired should be no less than $1,000. Smaller bonuses will result in fewer recommendations. See Policy ITP-10-1 Recruiting Bonus Policy as an example.

POLICY ITP-10-1.   Recruiting Bonus Policy

Policy #:	ITP-10-1	**Effective:**	03/18/09	**Page #:**	1 of N
Subject:	Recruiting Bonus Policy				

1.0 PURPOSE

This policy is designed to encourage employees to recommend someone from outside of the company for an open position within the IT department. Proven personnel usually recommend qualified persons like themselves. The person recommending someone has a personal stake in "bringing in a winner." An immediate benefit is that the company saves time and money over using an employment agency or using other recruiting methods.

2.0 SCOPE

This policy applies to all IT staff members.

3.0 POLICY

Subject to the conditions described below, it is corporate policy to compensate employees that recommend someone from outside of the company for open positions within the IT department. Employees will be compensated in the amount of $1,000 for each referred employee under the following conditions:

A. The referred candidate cannot have at any time been employed by the company or any of its subsidiaries.
B. Payment will be made on the pay period following the 3 month anniversary of the new employee.
C. The new employee must remain employed in good standing with no reprimands during the initial 3 months of employment.
D. The referring employee must be employed at the company and in good standing at the time the referral bonus payment is due.

4.0 REVISION HISTORY

Date	Revision #	Description of Change
03/18/09	1.0	Initial creation.

5.0 INQUIRIES

Direct inquiries about this policy to:

Harold Jenkins, CIO
2900 Corporate Drive
Columbus, OH 43215

Voice: 614-555-1234
Fax: 614-555-1235
E-mail: hjenkins@company.com

Revision #:	1.0	Supersedes:	N/A	Date:	03/18/09

C. **Internet posting and search.** Posting jobs on the Internet has been a valuable tool for human resources staff. Prior to this, just getting the word out about an open position was difficult. Creating advertisements for newspapers had to hit certain deadlines and were expensive. If the best candidates did not read the paper that weekend, then they would not know of the opportunity. Cost is based on newspaper space, and small ads may fail to adequately describe the opportunity and how exciting it is.

Posting open positions on the Internet makes them immediately available to a wide audience. Job applicants near and far can learn about openings, qualifications desired, and in some cases, the salary range offered. There is usually space for including the entire job description, plus information on the company.

Unfortunately, this openness has led to abuses. In days gone by, candidates would print their resumes and mail them to individual companies. Even if they tried to send resumes to all companies within an area, it was time consuming and expensive to create the letters and post them. The ease with which the Internet can create and mail resumes has changed this entirely. There are now companies that will blast resumes to hundreds of companies at once for little cost and irrespective of the candidate's qualification. This in turn has inundated companies with more resumes than they could possibly review. (Large companies could receive hundreds of resumes per day.) As a defense, most human resources departments now use text databases to receive and store resumes. Candidates are screened through key word searches.

The result is that resumes are now peppered with "buzzwords" that indicate some specific skill. Supposedly these buzzwords will fool the search process long enough for the resume to be read by someone. Unfortunately, this means that many valuable resumes are never reviewed since they did not use the appropriate phrase.

COMMENT

Popular Internet job sites for technical professionals include *www.monster.com*, *www.dice.com*, and *www.computerjobs.com*.

D. **Temporary-to-permanent hiring.** Some companies prefer a "try before you buy" approach where open positions are first filled with temporary employees. The company then evaluates their performance over time and determines if they are suitable candidates for employment. If they do not work out, then their contract (usually 6 months) is allowed to expire, and a replacement is brought in. This approach sounds safe but it is also expensive.

First, time is required to orient the new person to the duties required, the peculiarities of the local operations, who on the team does what, etc. This requires the efforts of an existing employee. Second, the person's temporary agency will charge a fee in addition to that person's salary. Finally, the temporary employee may be offered a permanent position elsewhere and leave on short notice.

[F] Using Offshore Staffing

For years, companies have been "outsourcing" work to other companies. These companies submit either fixed bid or time-and-materials contracts and deliver whatever service is desired. Service desk support and PC repair were some of the first services to be widely outsourced. The idea was that by using a company focused on delivering this type of service, they could do it better and sometimes cheaper.

A natural follow-up was the still cheaper labor overseas. Offshore companies can be located anywhere in the world. Labor overseas can be cheap and, with inexpensive worldwide telecommunications, it makes little difference if the contractor is down the street or around the globe.

This type of arrangement works well with some IT tasks and is a failure in others. Work that is clearly defined, such as the specifications for programming a new accounting system, is well suited for offshoring. However, tasks that require interaction with customers have had mixed results.

Companies feel a greater sense of security for their trade secrets and program code if it is within the same borders. Some of the pitfalls or important considerations when offshoring include:

A. Poorly defined work can result in extended times to complete it. Tasks must be clearly understood—even through the filters of language and culture.

B. Language/cultural interpretation differences. English is a highly nuanced language. An understanding of proper English may not help when speaking to someone with a thick regional dialect.

C. Contracts may be interpreted under the laws and customs of the offshore country. This is important in terms of who owns the code, who owns the design and other intellectual property rights.

D. Contract workers may be more inclined to test the company's security limits and, if they are weak, download confidential material.

E. Sending work offshore adds the complications of communicating across multiple time zones, cultural, and language barriers.

F. Some of the more technical offshore companies have high employee turnover.

G. The technical infrastructure of these countries may not be as stable as in western countries. Electrical and telecommunications outages, civil unrest, and disrupted communications due to natural disaster are factors that make offshore contracting more complex than hiring someone down the street.

> ## COMMENT
>
> One author worked for a company that offshored individual technical support positions. At one point they tried to offshore a project manager position. Unlike a technical support person who dealt primarily with machine issues, project managers deal primarily with people and normally face-to-face since 80 percent of communication is nonverbal. Problems immediately arose with time zones, cultural communications, and a lack of understanding about the client's product. It was not long before the job was brought back into the building.
>
> Like all things, offshoring must be the right tool for the right job and is not always the correct answer.

[G] College Recruiting

Colleges are an excellent source of entry-level IT employees. A degree in computer science is just that—training in the use of computers. Graduates know how to code a program but not how to convert business requirements into usable code. Hiring graduating students implies a requirement to train them in common business processes.

Hiring new graduates into the department can be something of a culture shock. The new employees will be bright, energetic, and highly enthusiastic. It is important to harness and direct this energy into positive directions and not let it be crushed by cynics. All newly hired graduates need their own mentor. Some companies prefer mentors of nearly the same age (big brother/sister), while others go for a generational difference, sort of a father/mother figure.

Keep in mind that most new graduates have few of the domestic obligations that "force" other employees to stay. If they are not challenged by their work and reasonably well compensated—or advanced as they improve—then they will quickly depart for another company.

College recruiting requires a person with the enthusiasm to match that of the candidates. Often the IT department is tasked to send "someone" to explain their programs and technology to graduating seniors. Be sure to pick someone knowledgeable about the company, its processes, and who can tell a positive, compelling story about its technological environment and achievements.

[H]   Student Interns

A common "try before you buy" approach is to hire college students as part-time employees, generally referred to as interns or co-ops. These students schedule their work around their classes and are usually available for a few hours a day, several days each week. They may also work full-time during their school breaks.

Internships enable a company to get to know the prospective candidate. The student not only has to perform, but also "fit in." If hired by the firm after graduation, they will already know the IT operation and corporate culture. A student intern program is an excellent recruiting tool. However, it must be properly managed. Unlike experienced employees, interns require a structured work situation and should not be assigned to work without a mentor. Assign an intern to shadow and assist a senior worker who will take the time to explain what is happening and why.

A successful intern program requires planning. Interns are very useful for assisting the IT department with many routine tasks—once they are trained on how to do them. However, to gain the full benefit from the program, interns should be attached to major projects where they can observe and learn how the IT team works.

Including interns in interesting projects that tax their skills is important for the company's recruiting efforts. Interns do not automatically accept a company's offer upon graduation. Some interns reject offers if they felt the IT team was boring, dysfunctional, or a dead-end opportunity.

[I]   Notes on Interviewing

Interviewing candidates is a very important responsibility. The demeanor and professionalism of the interviewers will be the candidate's primary impression of how desirable a company is to work for. In this sense, the interviewers are "selling" the company as a great place to work. It would be unfortunate if the style and actions of the interviewers scared away the best person for the position.

Whenever speaking to candidates, there should always be two interviewers in the room. This provides multiple perspectives on the candidates and their answers. It also reduces the likelihood of a candidate claiming improprieties during the discussion. Sometimes a representative of the company's human resources department wants to be present to ensure that the questioning follows company and legal requirements.

A consistent way to collect interview data is through use of a standard form. This form is filled out by each interviewer when meeting with the candidates. Record all impressions, since sometimes nonverbal responses expand on the candidate's verbal answers. At the conclusion of each interview, the hiring manager collects all forms and keeps them secured until time to select someone for the job. After the position is filled, the forms are retained by the hiring manager or forwarded to the human resources department according to company policy. *Never* throw these forms or interview notes away. Disgruntled candidates have been known to file lawsuits months later claiming all sorts of discrimination.

During the screening process, there was something on the candidate's resume that stood out as a reason to interview this person. Discuss it in detail. Never accept a claimed skill at face value. If they claim to have written Java programs, ask them to describe the programs and the systems. When they touch on a technology or process that the hiring company also uses, ask them to explain in fuller detail. Take time to drill down to a level of detail that illustrates the depth and breadth of their knowledge.

The goal of these questions is not to find someone who can answer 100 percent of the technical questions. Often interviewers optimistically take claimed skills at face value and do not gauge if these skills are at novice, expert, or nonexistent levels.

COMMENT

When discussing a candidate's work experience, make sure to ask for specific details such as who else worked on the team, the candidate's specific role, what worked well and what didn't on projects, etc. Asking for specifics makes it more difficult for the candidate to embellish his experience.

[J]   Some Prudent Checks

Sometimes it becomes necessary to discharge an employee. This can be a long-term, time consuming process. There isn't much to be done with the people already on the team, but the IT Manager must take care when inviting a new person to join the team. The likelihood of future problems can be reduced by thoroughly checking the candidates before they are hired.

IT personnel, by the nature of their work, have many opportunities to play havoc with company information. They might be able to expose personal information, company confidential information, or even steal money from the company. They can poke around company confidential files and reveal information that may breach legal disclosure regulations.

Prior to extending an offer, verify:

A. Any claim of formal education that was a qualifier for this position, such as college degrees.
B. Comments by previous employers.
C. References provided by the applicant.
D. Character by running a criminal background check to ensure there have been no felony convictions.
E. Character through a drug screening (at the company's expense).
F. Judgment, by running a credit check to determine if the candidate employs good judgment in his or her own affairs.

> ## COMMENT
>
> The best advice when dealing with employees is to be slow to hire and quick to fire. What that means is to be diligent in the hiring of new employees, and realize that problem employees rarely turn into desirable team members.

§ 10.03 NEW EMPLOYEE ORIENTATION

[A] First Impressions

First impressions are lasting, and in time, those employees reacting negatively may depart for another firm. To create a positive, lasting impression during the employee's first few days, the IT department follows two simple procedures. First, designate a mentor. Second, give the employee a "welcome aboard" education package.

> ## COMMENT
>
> An insurance company in Ohio thinks so highly of this training that they developed and carefully follow a detailed procedure for new employee indoctrination and education.

[B] IT Orientation Package

This package is a compilation of useful information for the new IT employee. It should contain the following information:

A. **Organization description.** At a minimum, the organization description includes an explanation of each unit's function and identifies those in charge. An organizational chart is useful for large departments. Include a short chronological history of the information systems operation. This provides the new employee with information about promotion tracks, areas of vested interest, and fast-track employees. Note IT's position within the organization.

B. **Equipment and facilities.** List all the hardware in use and its locations. Identify personnel authorized to use the equipment. A facilities map should include the locations of the restrooms, dining areas, and restricted facility areas.

C. **Telephone numbers.** Provide an up-to-date telephone directory of the firm. Include a supplementary list of numbers for frequently called IT units, personnel, and services.

D. **E-mail listing.** Indicate the proper way to address e-mail to other employees.

E. **Mail.** Note when and how the employee will receive his or her mail. This covers both interoffice and outside mail (U.S. Postal Service, UPS, FedEx, etc.).

F. **Forms.** Include a listing of all important forms required by IT personnel, providing the name and number of each form, its source and destination(s), purpose, and any other special information. Include samples used by the new employee's unit. The needs of computer operators are not the same as systems analysts, so packages for new employees may contain different forms.

G. **Schedules.** Include schedules of operations in the procedure package. These can be daily, weekly, or monthly. For daily schedules include begin and end times of normal activities, such as breaks and lunch hours. The weekly, monthly, and annual schedules contain paydays, holidays, vacation scheduling, and meetings. Some IT departments publish monthly listings of employees' birthdays.

H. **Glossary and practices.** This section contains a list of common terms and acronyms used by IT and the firm. Note practices that are extremely important or different from the industry norm.

I. **Unit procedures.** This section contains a listing of all IT procedures and where they are explained. Use a checklist for each type of IT procedure. Check off and date as new employees read the material.

COMMENT

A firm in Michigan, for its own reasons, does not run a slash through the character zero. They place the slash through the alpha character O. There were problems because a new programmer was unaware of this practice. Emphasize unusual department practices to minimize difficulties.

J. **IT project descriptions.** New programmers, systems analysts, and other staff personnel should be provided a list of current and pending IT projects. Note a short description of the objective, as well as target dates, along with the Project Managers' names.

[C] Mentor Assignment

Joining a company can be a personally traumatic situation. New employees feel disoriented since they do not know where basic services in the facility are located or how to make requests for simple support. At the same time, they are striving to make a good first impression on the new coworkers.

New IT personnel require a "personal touch." Each new employee is assigned a mentor, someone to give a permanent positive impression of the firm. The selected mentor should be personable, someone who the new employee feels comfortable about asking questions concerning procedures.

The mentor must also be patient. Often a simple question answered calmly by a mentor is critical for a new employee. The mentor should not be condescending, which only makes the new IT employee nervous and doubtful about his or her future. A mentor program allows new employees to become productive much more quickly since all of the new employee's questions can be answered directly.

The mentor is responsible for ensuring that the new employee is given a tour of the facility to see where basic services are located, and is properly introduced to his or her coworkers. The mentor ensures that a work area is ready when the employee arrives for the first day of work. The work area should include a telephone, a workstation, a desk containing basic office supplies, log-on passwords, voice-mail password, and in some cases, their new business cards.

Remember that first impressions are lasting. A new IT employee joins the department with high hopes, and a mentor's positive attitude can become infectious, reinforcing these high expectations. Make them feel welcome and a member of the team. See Policy ITP-10-2 New Employee Mentoring Policy as an example.

POLICY ITP-10-2.   New Employee Mentoring Policy

Policy #:	ITP-10-2	**Effective:**	03/18/09	**Page #:**	1 of N
Subject:	New Employee Mentoring Policy				

1.0 PURPOSE

This policy mandates that all new IT employees shall be assigned a mentor during their probationary period.

2.0 SCOPE

This policy covers all new IT employees and any rehires that have been gone over 24 months. The IT manager is responsible for implementing all aspects of this policy.

3.0 POLICY

Every new IT employee will be assigned a mentor during their probationary period by the IT manager. The mentor is charged with doing the following:

A. Give the new employee a positive impression of the firm.

B. Make the new employee feel comfortable about asking questions concerning procedures.
C. Be patient and answer questions calmly.
D. Take care not to be condescending, which only makes the new IT employee nervous and doubtful about his or her future.
E. Give the new employee a tour of the facility to see where basic services are located, and to be properly introduced to his or her coworkers.
F. Ensure that a work area is ready when the employee arrives for the first day of work. The work area should include a telephone, a workstation, a desk containing basic office supplies, log-on passwords, voice-mail password, and in some cases, their new business cards.
G. Make them feel welcome and a member of the team.

The mentor must report weekly to the IT manager on any issues or concerns with the new employee throughout the new employee's probation period.

4.0 REVISION HISTORY

Date	Revision #	Description of Change
03/18/09	1.0	Initial creation.

5.0 INQUIRIES

Direct inquiries about this policy to:

Harold Jenkins, CIO
2900 Corporate Drive
Columbus, OH 43215

Voice: 614-555-1234
Fax: 614-555-1235
E-mail: hjenkins@company.com

Revision #:	1.0	Supersedes:	N/A	Date:	03/18/09

§ 10.04   PERFORMANCE REVIEW

[A]   Overview

Performance reviews are an important management tool for adjusting employee behaviors and productivity before these issues become major problems. Managers who do not properly use this tool invariably complain about the people on their team not cooperating or being disruptive.

In our culture it is considered discourteous to mention people's shortcomings or to recommend ways to improve unless they first ask. However, a good leader knows that this "fine tuning" is an essential part of a team member's development. Performance reviews open a channel of communication between the manager and the team members.

There are many fine books available on the subject of conducting employee performance reviews. Your company may have specific details on how they want the program to be conducted. Points provided here only highlight some of the basics. The key is to open and maintain a flow of feedback between the team members and the manager so that issues can be resolved before they turn into a crisis.

[B]   Conducting a Review

Before beginning the interview, be aware of your own state of mind. If it has been a bad day, it is not a good time to review team members. The same is true for the person to be reviewed. However, many people "steel" themselves for a slew of bad news at these reviews so in most cases, the reviewer has a slight psychological advantage at the beginning of the review. Take care not to waste it!

A performance review is a *two way* conversation that takes place within the supervisor/worker context. The manager must be aware of this and choose his or her comments carefully. It is important that (in most cases) these reviews be held in a nonconfrontational manner. They must be conducted in a quiet place and completely out of hearing of others.

It is a rare employee who has not earned some positive feedback to begin the conversation with. A bit of well directed praise does much to place people at ease. If the employee has no positive actions since the last review, then the manager must be at fault for assigning him or her to tasks beyond the employee's ability.

The performance conversation flows two ways—the manager's appraisal of the worker and the worker's appraisal of the manager. Both people must be open to discussing performance and behaviors. It is possible that the problem is with something done by the manager. Often it is easier for the person to absorb some of the recommended improvements if the manager also acknowledges his or her own faults and asks the worker how he or she can improve.

Some pitfalls of performance reviews are:

A.   Saving up everything negative and dumping it all at once on someone who was unaware there was a problem. If something needs corrective action, bring it up at that time and do not "sit on it." Reviews are not a time to spring surprises.

B.   Arguing, as it indicates people are taking defensive positions and are resistant to change.

C.   Allowing the discussion to sink into a "battle of wits" which, like arguing, is more focused on winning than on learning from the conversation.

D.   Manager nitpicking and micromanaging minor details.

    E. The worker manipulating the wording to try to push all faults on the manager and none onto him or herself to address.

Performance reviews should end on a positive note. Last impressions are the most enduring ones. Many managers leave training, new assignments, and career discussions for the end of the conversation. This is a good time to look ahead with positive expectations of what is to come.

[C]   Periodic Performance Reviews

In this context, performance is a comparison of what has been accomplished to what was expected to be accomplished. Performance reviews compare assignments to results. Therefore, the review begins with a recap of the assignments made at the previous review and any interim changes. This is another chance to emphasize the positives. It is easy to judge something long past and ask why it took two weeks to accomplish it—but without the context of the situation, the judgment may seem flawed. During this session, time must be set aside to identify the manager's expectations for worker performance during the upcoming review period. This can be specific tasks to be accomplished and any actions that would improve this person's interaction with the rest of the team.

A good starting place for discussing technical expectations is the job description. The incumbent should be working toward mastering all of the requirements. The second step is the job description of the next level up so that the person is working toward promotion. (Not everyone will want to do this, but it should be offered.) By stepping through each assigned responsibility and discussing performance, the workload on a particular person can be evaluated and adjusted. It also indicates which skills need improvement.

Keeping the review positive does not mean that the manager should avoid offering constructive criticism. This should be worded carefully and clearly. "Hinting" at a problem may seem polite to the manager but is ambiguous to the team member. Speak plainly, discuss the problem with the team member until you are sure he or she understands and then move on and do not belabor the point.

At times during a discussion, assignments will have been delayed due to lack of tools or training. If valid, these act as performance reviews of the manager's results in providing everything needed for success. Take note of these and set a performance goal of when they will be delivered to the team.

> **COMMENT**
>
> A variation on the performance review is a monthly one-on-one meeting between the manager and the team members. These half-hour meetings are free form and provide an uninterrupted conversation.

[D]   Peer Performance Reviews

Some companies use Peer or 360 degree reviews. This allows critiques by coworkers as well as the supervisors. These must be conducted so that they do not cross any company guidelines for "personal comments." Peer review can be valuable because team members interact in a manner differently than when the manager is present. This also allows team members to vent their interpersonal frustrations before they become too deeply held.

Peer reviews are time consuming. They must be carefully controlled or they can turn into outright fights. After all, the people are evaluating someone they are competing with for pay raises and promotion. When they think there is money at stake, objectivity may suffer. If a peer review sinks into personal attacks, then cut it off immediately. See Policy ITP 10-3 Peer Performance Review Policy and Worksheet 10-1 IT Staff Peer Performance Form to help develop your peer review process.

POLICY ITP-10-3.   Peer Performance Review Policy

Policy #:	ITP-10-3	Effective:	03/18/09	Page #:	1 of N
Subject:	Peer Performance Review Policy				

1.0 PURPOSE

The peer input policy is a mechanism for IT staff members to receive important feedback from their team members about their performance. Peer input is to be obtained through a means that it is both fair and respectful of IT staff members. Peer Performance Reviews must occur annually and should be completed before the end of the fiscal year. Peer is defined as an employee's coworkers or individuals other than the employee's supervisor who are familiar with the employee's performance, work products, and/or services. Peer input should be done independently of the evaluation being conducted by the employee's supervisor.

2.0 SCOPE

The policy applies to all IT staff members within the IT department.

3.0 POLICY

The following steps define the process for performing a peer evaluation:

A. Peer selection is made using the following steps:
   1. Employee selects one peer.
   2. Supervisor selects one peer.

   3. Employee and Supervisor jointly select one peer.
  B. For purposes of peer input, the employee will be rated on demonstrated values and customer service utilizing the following rating scale:
     1—Employee's performance is consistently below expectations.
     2—Employee's performance sometimes meets expectations and needs.
     3—Employee's performance consistently achieves expectations improvement.
     4—Employee's performance often exceeds expectations.
     5—Employee's performance far exceeds expectations.
     NA—No longer applicable/unable to determine.
  C. Each of the selected peers will evaluate the employee using the appropriate form.
  D. The evaluation forms are turned into Human Resources for scoring and aggregation of comments.
  E. Human Resources delivers the evaluation results to the employee's supervisor.
  F. The supervisor reviews the results with the employee.

4.0 REVISION HISTORY

Date	Revision #	Description of Change
03/18/09	1.0	Initial creation.

5.0 INQUIRIES

Direct inquiries about this policy to:

Harold Jenkins, CIO
2900 Corporate Drive
Columbus, OH 43215

Voice: 614-555-1234
Fax: 614-555-1235
E-mail: hjenkins@company.com

Revision #:	1.0	Supersedes:	N/A	Date:	03/18/09

[E]   Documentation

Comments made during every review must be carefully documented. In the event that an employee must be formally disciplined or terminated, these contemporary accounts make the action easier to arrange. To ensure that the essential information is captured during these sessions, many companies

WORKSHEET 10-1. IT Staff Peer Performance Form

IT Staff Peer Performance Form		
Employee Name:		
Position:	Evaluation Period:	

Performance Rating Scale:

      1 – Employee's performance is consistently below expectations
      2 – Employee's performance sometimes meets expectations and needs
      3 – Employee's performance consistently achieves expectations improvement
      4 – Employee's performance often exceeds expectations
      5 – Employee's performance far exceeds expectations
      NA – No longer applicable/unable to determine

Value Expectations	
Employee will demonstrate, model and reinforce the company values listed below. The employee should demonstrate these values in interactions with coworkers, supervisors, and customers; in personal contributions to work assignments and projects; and when representing the IT department or the company.	

Personal Values	1 – 5 or NA
Honesty – displays integrity in work and interactions with others	
Fairness – treats others equitably	
Attitude – maintains a professional attitude	
Respect – is considerate of others	
Business acumen – demonstrates proper business behavior	

Team Values	1 – 5 or NA
Excellence – strives to create a high performing work environment	
Cooperation – participates and shares information within the department and the company	
Commitment – performs in accordance with the vision and mission of the organization	
Teamwork – willingly collaborates with other team members	

Competencies	1 – 5
Employee is expected to demonstrate the following technical competencies based on the requirements of the position.	
Enter competency #1	
Enter competency #2	
Enter competency #3	

Notes:

Adding the score from each rating and dividing the sum by the number of ratings assessed will provide the employee's annual peer rating.

This form should be submitted to the Human Resources department when completed.

use a standard form. Copies of review documentation must be filed with the human resources department promptly after the session.

Notes made during performance reviews must remain confidential (as must the conversation). Failing to do this will result in some very reticent team members.

Notes made during previous performance reviews make an excellent starting point for the next review. Any commitments made by either party can be evaluated and discussed. Using notes in this way provides continuity between the sessions.

[F]   Preparing the Way for Employee Termination

Discipline and termination policies fill a special need in every department. Discipline should not jeopardize any future relations between employees and the firm, and must be fair.

Discipline establishes the boundary of acceptable behavior. Although unpleasant, it is preferable to leaving a festering problem that may erupt into a crisis. IT workers are free thinkers and will not be productive in a restrictive environment. However, from time to time, someone's behavior may create a negative imbalance in the team. The IT Manager owes it to the company and to the other team members to firmly and fairly establish the boundaries of acceptable behavior.

Termination of an IT employee requires careful treatment. Procedures must be in place and followed precisely ensuring no further trouble from a departing employee. Security access must be severed and company property recovered. Worksheet 10-2 is a termination checklist you can use to make sure all procedures are followed.

Terminations send ripples of uncertainty through a department as people pause to consider whether their own employment is in jeopardy. It is critical the IT Managers use this as a last resort and, when practical, explain to the remaining employees why termination was required.

To protect the company, information systems managers use special termination procedures. Departing IT employees have many opportunities for destructive activities. As the termination process gets underway, the IT Manager must remove the person from the potential of harming company systems and reassign him or her to an area of low risk—usually as a "special assignment."

WORKSHEET 10-2.   Employee Termination Checklist

Termination Checklist			
Date:		Department:	
Employee Information			
Name:		Number:	
Department:		Business Unit:	
Last Official Day:		Last Day On Site:	
Physical Access			
Access		Date Access Terminated	
Building Access			
Office Access			
Desk/cabinet keys			
Software Applications			
Application		Date Access Terminated	
Accounting System			
CRM			
Payroll			
Remote Access			
Email			
Instructions for existing and new emails:			
Office Equipment			
Equipment		Date Recovered	
Office Phone			
Voice Mail			
Long Distance Access			
Calling Card			
Conference Call Access			
Pager			
Cell Phone			
Laptop			
Home Equipment			

WORKSHEET 10-2.   (Continued)

PDA	

Electronic Communications	
Medium	Date Terminated
Dialup Account	
VPN Access	
LAN/WAN Account	
Access to Special Files	
Home Internet Access	

IT Employees	
Item	Date Terminated
Access to Computer Room	
Access to Hosting Facility	
Access to Development Servers	
Passwords	
Servers	
Routers	
Systems	
Listed as Technical Contact	
Applications	
Network Management	
Remote Monitoring	
Software Distribution	

Other	
Item	Date
Non-compete agreement	
Confidentiality agreement	
Notice to security	

§ 10.05 EMPLOYEE DEVELOPMENT

[A] Overview

An important management responsibility is to prepare team members for new technologies and their next promotion. Selfish managers try to build walls around their most valuable people and prevent them from advancing, since if they leave the team, the manager would be forced to train a replacement.

The flip side of this is "stagnant" and passive people. Often they have retired on the job. They know just how little they need to do to get by. Such departments are typically led by weak leaders who complain they must do everything themselves.

Training must be tied to an assignment. Classes only provide familiarity—not expertise. Expertise only comes with experience. Since classes are "shallow," they must be immediately followed by several assignments to reinforce the knowledge gained.

[B] IT Skills Inventory

Information technologies are never static. Programming languages more in tune with current requirements seem to appear every four years or so. In the interim, many other skills emerge and recede—from batch oriented procedural languages to event driven programming to Artificial Intelligence to database systems. All of these have emerged, shot to popularity, and gradually became an ordinary part of the IT landscape. Unless IT management prepares the team for these changes, the company will be burdened with low productivity legacy team members and paying a premium to bring in new workers with the latest skills.

To establish and maintain a correlation between employee skills and the skills required by the department, a "Skills Assessment" is done. This compares the skills in the team to the skills required by the department. The gap then becomes the training requirements for the IT department. Skill assessments are normally scheduled to be completed in time for adding training costs into the early stages of the annual budget cycle.

The department's skill set is the sum of the team members. A skills inventory is maintained for each employee and updated at least annually. A file of this type might contain:

A. Person's name and ID number.
B. Date the person started with IT.
C. List of technical skills and their skill rating on a scale of 1 (novice) to 5 (expert).
D. Formal education received.
E. Other training received.
F. Certifications received.
G. Current job title.
H. Future education plans.
I. Future training plans.
J. Hobbies or interests that could benefit firm.
K. Next goal/promotion objective within firm.

[C] Continuing Education and Training

Many IT departments assign to someone the part-time duty of coordinating the team's education and training. Often this is the same person who maintains the skills inventory since the two responsibilities are clearly related. This person is both an advisor to and an information source for those seeking education or training information. He is familiar with the company's policies and paperwork involved in training. The coordinator must also know the various sources of training available.

[D] Plan for the Future

Refer to the asset management list of hardware and software. List every hardware and software tool used by the company. Add to this list every critical process. Use the department roster and build a spreadsheet. (See Worksheet 10-3 Employee/Process Matrix as an example.)

WORKSHEET 10-3. Employee/Process Matrix

	Employee/Process Matrix								
	AS/400					Shop Floor Systems			
	OS		Applications						
	Queue Mgmt	Admin	Order Entry	Payroll	Warehouse System	VOC Tracking	Waterjet Cutter	Paint Line Robots	Tank Farm
Abraham Lincoln									
William McKinley									
Theodore Roosevelt									
Ronald Reagan									
Bill Clinton									

Using Worksheet 10-3, list the names down the left side of the page and the technologies across the top. Rate each employee from 1 to 5 (5 being an expert) on how skilled he is in each area. Do the same thing on a different spreadsheet for critical processes. Are there any gaps? Are there two (preferably three) people in a high skill level for every technology or critical process? If not, then assign someone as the backup person for the technology and schedule him for training.

Combine this information with whatever new technologies are anticipated for the upcoming year and a complete set of data necessary to build a training plan is at hand.

Repeat this same evaluation process, but this time let the team members rate themselves. Compare how they rate themselves to how their manager rates them as additional input into the training plan.

[E] Training and Consultants

The development or installation of a major new technology is always an exciting time in an IT department. Often, temporary technical employees (consultants) are brought in since no one in the company has experience with this technology. It is a prudent policy to match one employee to every one or two consultants. This allows the employee to gain valuable experience with the new product and provides a path for the eventual departure of the consultants. Otherwise, the consultants could become a permanent fixture.

For this to be effective, the IT Manager must monitor and ensure this training is being accomplished. Eventually, a "stake in the ground" is set—a date when the consultants will leave. The person being trained will see that he will soon be on his own and must gather as much understanding as he can before the experts depart.

COMMENT

IT managers at a major truck manufacturer complained that their ERP consultants often cost $200 per hour, and that many were needed to support the product. When asked why they didn't train their own employees to support the product, they said that if they did, the employees would just leave to be consultants!

§ 10.06 MANAGING IT TRAINING

[A] Developing a Training Strategy

A training strategy is not hard to develop. The purpose of training in an IT department is to prepare someone to provide a level of support for a technology. Strategy development involves identifying areas of weak or non-existent expertise and then preparing someone to fill that gap. The basic steps for developing a training strategy include:

A. Identifying the expertise gaps.
B. Identifying training requirements for projects planned over the upcoming year.
C. Identifying non-technical training essential for the department to function optimally.

Identifying the expertise gaps. The first step is to identify existing gaps between the requirements to support existing systems and the IT department's current expertise. To accomplish this, we will assemble a matrix that compares the technologies to be supported to the employees on staff. To do this:

A. Begin with an inventory of the hardware and software necessary to be supported. The foundation of your training plan is an understanding of what skills the department should possess to effectively maintain the existing hardware and software. These skills may be confined to how to use it (hardware—we do not repair the circuitry) or how to repair it (such as Java or SQL training classes).Create a list of every hardware model and variation you support. This can be quickly obtained from your asset management database if one exists. If not, then talk to the various people in the IT department and create a list. If you have a service desk, their problem-tracking database could be a resource to identify hardware items. Only include model variations on the list if they are significantly different from the base model. When creating your hardware list, be sure to include hardware supported by every team in the IT department. This includes the mainframe computer, the network components, desktop units, engineering workstations, data collection devices such as scanners, printers, notebook PCs, etc.

B. Remove from the list any hardware items that may not require any team training. Some hardware categories such as monitors may not be a training issue because they are normally repaired by exchanging them for new units. Other hardware categories such as mainframe computers are serviced by the manufacturer and we do not intend to change that. The goal in building the hardware list is not to train people to repair the equipment but rather to show them how to determine if it is broken or misused. Enter the list of hardware supported along the left side of a spreadsheet. We will be doing more with this later.

C. With the hardware list in hand, create a similar list for software. Some software will be obvious, such as the programs that run on your desktop PC. Some software may require some digging, such as the specialized programs used in network routers. List all of the software you can find in all of the various computers and technologies supported. Next, identify the programs that are purchased and the ones developed in-house. Purchased programs are usually supported by the company that created them. Their in-house support component is often the system administrator. Many of the mainframe programs are purchased but they should still be on the training list. There could be some fine tools available for use that only a few people understand how to use. The program's author usually supports in-house developed programs, although in some cases, that person may have moved on and a different person is saddled with the job. The list of in-house developed programs can be quite long. Refer back to the spreadsheet created for the hardware. Open a second workbook in the same spreadsheet. Enter the list of software supported along the left side of a workbook using the same format as was used for the hardware.

D. Identify which of these products support critical business functions. The IT Manager must identify which hardware and software items are used to support the facility's critical business functions. To do this, refer back to the critical systems identified in the IT business continuity plan or base this on experience in the department. Mark each of the critical items by shading in their columns on the spreadsheet.

E. Identify the basic technical skills required by everyone in the department. These are the fundamental technical skills that the IT Manager expects everyone in the department to possess. Ask the IT Manager to mark the hardware and software with which everyone should be proficient. Use a different-colored column. This might include the company standard word processing program, the standard desktop PC operating system, etc.

F. Identify the basic skills required for everyone on a specific team (applications development, operations, network support, etc.). Each of the functional teams within the IT department depends on its own basic technologies that each person on the team should know. Schedule a meeting with the IT Manager and the team leader for each section to identify these skills.

G. Survey employees to determine their expertise for supporting each of these functions. Create a survey form for the employees to use. Along the left side, list each of the hardware and software technologies. Do not mention anything about the technologies identified as essential. Ask each person to evaluate their skills for each technology in terms of zero to five: 0–No experience with the product at all. 1–Novice—has started the product and reviewed some documentation. 2–Familiarity—has successfully used the product but would need some time to prepare before using it again. 3–Competent user—has successfully used the product before and ready to use it again. 4–Expert user—has used the product a number of times and explored many of its options. 5–Complete mastery of the product. This is a great time for the team members to also indicate those technologies for which they have primary or secondary support responsibilities. When the surveys are complete, enter them into the spreadsheet. An optional exercise is to ask the team leaders to fill out their own skill assessments for each team member. Later the team leader can compare them with the team member's self-evaluation to better understand the team's perception of itself.

H. Identify those areas where support is required but employees are not at the expert level. Identify training required.

   1. Based on the items on the matrix that are required, are there any team members who are not at least rated as "competent"? Make a list of these people and the technologies involved. If someone indicates that they are a key support person for a technology and they do not rate themselves at least "competent," then their training should be scheduled immediately. If a critical technology does not have anyone listed as its primary or secondary support technician, then the IT Manager must designate someone. Again, check to see if they are at least competent at supporting that technology. Identify potential instructors.

   2. Anyone claiming to work at the expert or master level of a product is a likely instructor for that technology. Before asking for their assistance, verify this competency claim with their supervisors.

I. Develop training plans to fill these gaps. Review your list of technologies. Make a note of how each item will be trained now and in the future. Some tools are easily taught one-on-one between the new employee and his or her mentor. Other tools must be taught in off-site classes. Each technology should have a training strategy for instructing IT employees on how to maximize its value. Based on the matrix of technologies supported and the skills in-house, develop a training plan to bring each person in the IT department up to the desired technical level.

Identify training requirements for projects planned over the upcoming year. Every year, companies plan their operating and capital budgets for the upcoming year. A part of this process is to identify new initiatives to be undertaken. The training manager must be involved in this planning to identify technologies that are not covered in the current skills assessment and to project training required.

Often the technologies to be used are not clearly defined this far in advance. The training manager is at the same disadvantage as the people lined up to support these projects. Maintain open communications with the facility planning staff so that as a project prepares to begin, the training manager can begin lining up the requisite training.

Identify non-technical training essential for the department to function optimally. There is more to an IT department than bits and bytes. Other job skills are important for the department to function smoothly. The training manager must keep these training objectives equally to the front of the planning discussion to prevent them from becoming lost in the shuffle of programming classes.

A. Time management. Technical people are generally not the best practitioners of time management. If an IT Manager wants to improve the productivity of the department, he or she should schedule training for the employees to optimize the use of their workdays.

B. Project management. This is an important part of information technology management. Just about everyone in the department can benefit through improved skills at organizing their work and coordinating with others to complete tasks. On a larger scale, this becomes a stepping-stone for developing people for increased responsibilities.

C. Organizing and running effective meetings. No person or system in IT exists in a vacuum. We all interact with our peers and end users to maximize benefit to the company. A common method of this is through meetings. Meetings can be useful events or boring wastes of time. Well-organized and productive meetings do not occur by accident. Training the IT staff to effectively plan and execute meetings will not only provide improved productivity but also raise the end user's opinion about the competence and professionalism of your entire operation.

D. Stress management. The IT staff can be worked hard and under immense pressure when critical systems fail. Stress management training involves teaching techniques for relaxation to avoid IT burn-out. Technicians working in high stress environments tend to make more mistakes and take risks they would not normally consider.

E. Effective writing. Some technicians are quite articulate and some can barely write their own name with a crayon. Effective writing again improves the productivity of the author, the reader, and raises the company's opinion of the IT department as a whole.

F. Negotiation skills. Some IT people would be very happy if left to themselves in the corner. Unfortunately for them, IT is a service department that must interact with the people who use its services. Effective communications with these people often involves tradeoffs between the work necessary to accomplish something technical and the benefit to be derived. It also involves obtaining cooperation during times of short deadlines. Negotiation skills help the IT technician to identify areas of agreement so they can focus on areas to resolve for quick results.

G. Training presentation. The IT staff represents a ready team of instructors (whether they know it or not). They know their users, they know their technologies, and they are often called on for impromptu instruction for using one feature or another. In this class, teach them how to teach. You explain how to break complex thoughts and processes down into bite-sized pieces of information and explain it to others.

[B] End-User Training

The need for computer operation training is not limited to the IT department. Make company-wide training available to all computer users. This not only provides needed training, but also helps to create goodwill between IT and the rest of the firm. The charge-back for these services depends on corporate cost accounting procedures.

Request for training may be initiated by a user or an IT project leader. A user's request should be in the form of a memo from the user's management, directed to the IT trainer. If a project leader desires the service, make it part of the formal project effort.

Furnish a list of users completing each course to the employee's supervisor(s) by a memo from the manager of the IT training unit. All persons completing the program receive certificates of completion forwarded to the employee's supervisor for presentation.

End-user training is critical for the success of any business system. Without proper training, the benefits planned from the system will not be realized.

A. **New System Rollout.** Implementing new technology is an exciting part of working with computer systems. But all computer systems depend on human interaction to reach their maximum potential. People must be trained on ways to maximize the effectiveness of a tool. Without this training, the best tools in the world will sit and not be used.

The training department should become involved with a new system project well before it is ready for installation. The training department's role is to present the system to the users and explain how to make it work. To do this, the trainer must become familiar enough with the tools to be installed to write an explanation of them. This explanation becomes the outline for the training class.

Training for new systems should be completed and tested prior to presenting the technology to the users. The training can be provided immediately before the product rollout. Developing booklets with explanations of what to do in a given situation can provide a ready reference for the occasional user and the service desk. It can also be used later to train new end users.

B. **Ongoing Training.** Another source of end-user training requirements comes from the service desk problem logs. The service desk can identify problems that seem to generate multiple calls. Information on how to address these issues can go into the next training class (and immediately in the facility's newsletter). The service desk can also identify individuals who seem to be struggling with using a product. This can be addressed by one-on-one instruction or by offering them the next class scheduled. This training will reduce end-user frustration and reduce the number of calls to the service desk.

A well-stocked technical library is an important adjunct to your training room. Often technical staff members need to know how to do a specific action using your company's technical tools. A library provides a central source for them to research problems. In addition to the library, provide a list of the manuals that different people keep in the work areas. This will maximize the use of manuals, many of which the company must purchase.

[C]   Keeping Records of Training

Each IT employee file contains education and training information, including training the employee brings to the department and recommendations for future training. All additional training received is posted to a file that is part of the IT skill inventory. (See § 10.05, "Employee Development" for more procedure information.) Starting a file is simple; keeping it up to date is a more challenging task. Do not neglect this.

IT employee training files contain the following information.

A. **Education and training before joining the IT department**
   1. Degrees received, courses taken, dates, and grades.
   2. Dates of noncredit courses taken.
   3. Type of work-related material read.
   4. Dates of certifications received.
   5. Listing of professional memberships and any offices held.
   6. The hardware type and software used if the employee owns a personal computer.

B. **Future education and training benefiting the employee.** Establish the training needs of each employee. This information can justify a training program and give the people on record first choice. Priority is as follows:
   1. Training or education that helps develop personnel for current positions:
      a. Areas of weakness.
      b. Areas that require training to stay current with new technology.
   2. Training or education needed for promotion.
C. **New education or training received**
   1. Upon completion of training not provided in-house, each employee forwards to the IT department a memo containing the following to be included in the employee's file:
      a. What training was received.
      b. Who provided the training.
      c. What grade was received, if any.
      d. When the training was received.
   2. Upon completion of in-house programs, the overseer of IT training programs forwards the necessary information for inclusion in the training record files. For non-IT people, a memo will be sent to each supervisor listing which of their employees has completed the training and indicating the following:
      a. What training was received.
      b. When the training was conducted.
      c. Personnel who are to receive credit for completing the program.

[D] Employee Recognition

When an employee completes an in-house course, his or her supervisor should present a certificate for course completion. Certificate forms are available from most office supply firms and should be completed and signed by the manager of training and also the IT Manager.

Certificates provide a visual acknowledgement of achieving the course completion and are often found decorating a person's work area with pride. They also provide backup proof of course completion if training records are not properly kept.

[E] Education Information Booklet

The IT education unit provides an "education information booklet" to all new IT employees as part of an orientation package. Revised editions are distributed to all current IT employees. It should contain the following information:

A. **IT outside education policy and procedures.** Outline the type of support the firm provides for outside education and training, and the procedures required to apply for sanctioned education outside the firm. Copies of any required reimbursement forms are included.

B. **Scheduled courses offered by the training unit.** Detail the courses offered, including dates and times, requirements for admission, and procedure for enrolling in courses and/or programs.
C. **A list of self-paced training packages available.** This list is available from the IT training unit and includes videotapes, self-teaching texts, and PC self-instruction programs. Include an explanation of how to request this material.
D. **Publications available.** A list of books and journals should be available in the IT training department and/or computer store.

[F] Outsourced Training

Because not all information systems departments have resources available for in-house IT training, it is common to use outsourcing firms for professional IT training at the firm's location. (See Chapter 12, "Vendors: Getting the Goods," for more information.)

Recordkeeping of outsourcing personnel training is still done by the IT department for IT personnel. A person delegated by the manager of IT provides user training. Costs will be paid from the IT training budget. User training can be charged back to the user's budget and prorated if need be. This is all dependent on the internal accounting practice of the company.

Training evaluation is performed by a person from the IT department at the end of the course or program. Payment may be governed by the results of the evaluation. If so, inform accounts payable of this procedure before the outside firm bills for the service. The follow-up three- to six-month evaluation, also performed by the IT training department, is particularly important to alter future training if needed. The evaluation also is an effective way to judge the provider of the outsourced training.

[G] Annual Reporting

The IT training unit should submit an annual report of activities, including cost. Cost justification (relating dollars to return on investment) of training dollars spent can be a problem because most of the returns are intangible. Any input from user management can help. However, intangible items contribute to the company's bottom line and should be listed in the annual report. There is a worldwide fast-food chain known for its training programs and even more for its success story.

Time required to produce instruction packages is often more than anticipated. Preparation time rule of thumb for a lecture presentation with simple slides can be as much as 15 hours for each lecture hour. Producing a 30-minute video presentation can take up to 200 hours. General planning, setup, reporting, and equipment repair will consume time. All these hours are reported. Treat each new program as a project with individual cost of materials and time cost reported. Compute time cost as hourly cost plus benefits.

> ## COMMENT
>
> Be aware that training and education evaluations can be subjective. People tend to give higher appraisals when they are entertained.

Both students' and trainers' time is a cost factor. With new technology, training and preparation time can be reduced. Therefore, the training department should house an array of software and hardware tools to be effective. Drop ineffective resources. Include plans for the coming year, as well as current year results, in the annual report. The report also should contain activities of the training unit for the year. The following items are reported:

A.   Number and size of classes conducted.
B.   Number of self-study programs completed.
C.   Number and purpose of new programs developed.
D.   Total number of people served by training unit.
E.   List of participant evaluation comments with any supervisor's comments or memo information.

§ 10.07   EMPLOYEE COMMUNICATIONS

[A]   Overview

A common complaint from employees is that they find out more about what is happening in their own department from other groups than they hear from their managers. Use all available tools to push a steady stream of information to employees. They will feel more like a team and less like isolated islands. This will also reinforce the manager's authority as the primary source of information about the department.

There are many avenues for employee communications: e-mail, memos, newsletters, rumor boards, telephone, voice mail, information meetings, and work meetings. More than one method should be used to communicate important employee information. The best tool for the job depends on how dispersed the team members are.

[B]   Staff Meetings

The best way to pass and receive information to and from the team is a regularly scheduled staff meeting. Team members may have heard a rumor about this or that, but a statement by the manager about the same issue makes it an official announcement.

Preparation is the key to a successful meeting. Staff meetings should be kept to one hour or less and follow a standard agenda. One approach is to hold the meeting the day after the team submits status reports. In this way, only exceptions need to be discussed. Any discussion that runs more than five minutes must be set aside for a later meeting so that it does not derail the meeting. Focused meetings are appreciated, rambling time wasters will be avoided!

[C]   E-mail and Memos

When the IT Manager has a message to get out fast, or even routine announcements, an e-mail sent to every team member is an easy way to do it. Written messages allow everyone to see the same message worded the same way. They can be drafted in advance and sent when the time is right.

However, written announcements must be carefully worded. Unlike face-to-face communications, the reader cannot see any body language that accompanies the message. They will fill that in based on their own experience. For this reason, the message must be clear and not ambiguous.

Written communications are a great way to maintain the flow of communications to the team. Did someone do a great job that everyone should know about? Has a new employee joined the team? An e-mail is a great way to introduce a new employee to the team.

[D]   Rumor Board

In times of uncertainty, rumors can sweep through a department and disrupt productivity. To minimize their impact and reassert the department's leaders as the primary source of factual information, IT Managers must address rumors immediately. Rumors often reflect the deepest fears of a group and will grow in magnitude on their own. Rather than wishing them away, the IT Manager can eliminate this distraction to the workday by decisively and clearly answering with the true situation.

If rumors are a factor in a company, establish a rumor control box where anonymous messages can be left. A rumor control box works as follows:

A.   A person concerned about a rumor writes it on a slip of paper and places it in a locked box attached to the department bulletin board.

B.   Management reads the slip of paper and places a response on the bulletin board.

Rumor boards require judgment on the IT Manager's part to ensure that veiled personal attacks are not treated as legitimate questions. The anonymity of the locked box encourages participation but may be used for negative purposes.

§ 10.08   EMPLOYEE BURNOUT

[A]   Responsibility

IT support requirements can place a great deal of pressure on skilled and caring team members. It is the manager's responsibility to watch for signs of overwork (or burn-out) and address the problem immediately. Exhausted employees make mistakes both with the company's systems and in their own personal safety. Overworked employees are a sign of failed IT leadership.

There are times when a great deal of time and stress are a part of a project. Major product rollout, year-end closing, flash cutovers of major changes all can be stressful times. However, in these cases, IT Managers can anticipate the upcoming events and rest the team before the major effort begins. After it is over, time should be allowed for the team to decompress.

No employee should suffer from burnout. Any supervisor responsible for pressure and time demands resulting in an employee's experiencing burnout should be reprimanded, and the details of the reprimand placed in their personnel folder. This will also include Project Managers or project leaders.

[B]   What Causes Burnout?

Often, employees bring burnout on themselves. Some people just cannot say "no" to a request. Some spend hours building a paperwork jungle around their assigned work—all work not assigned or desired by the manager. Some feel that if they show any sign of weakness, their position with the company may be eliminated.

Sometimes, unknowingly, the IT Manager asks for more than workers can reasonably deliver and they scramble to fulfill the request by working long hours. If a worker is susceptible to making major projects out of simple assignments, the IT Manager must take the time to ensure the person understands the true assignment before starting. The worker must understand that in the eyes of the IT Manager, a lot of activity does not equal a lot of value or productivity.

[C]   Company Assistance

It is in the company's best interest to care for burned out employees. They should first be given paid time off. When they return, the IT Manager must determine how they ended up in the state they were in and address it. Did they take on too much work? Were they over-assigned by the manager? Did the worker misunderstand the scope of a simple project?

Other actions to address the issue include:

A.   Provide the person with someone to share the workload.
B.   Encourage the person to take a seminar somewhere that will reduce the strain and include a weekend "on the house" for some fun time. No contact between company and employee will be allowed during this time.
C.   Periodically rotate IT tasks.
D.   Allow for telecommuting and more flexible work hours.
E.   Limit overtime.
F.   Limit on-call demands.
G.   Reassign workloads.
H.   Encourage feedback.
I.   Schedule team social activities for meeting project milestones.

[D]   Signs of Burnout

The signs of burnout are everywhere—if the IT Manager is inclined to look. Irritability, a harried look, and late assignments are all signs that something is not right. Other signs include:

  A.   Extreme dissatisfaction with work.
  B.   Notice of drinking or substance abuse during lunch or after work.
  C.   Reduced productivity.
  D.   Panic attacks.
  E.   Marital problems.
  F.   Problems with coworkers.
  G.   Persistent eating, sleeping, and fatigue disorders.
  H.   Noticeable signs of depression.

§ 10.09   IT EMPLOYEE PRODUCTIVITY

[A]   Overview

Productivity is the goal of every IT team. Managers spend hours trying to identify ways to improve it. New IT tools are purchased, training is provided, incentives handed out and even a few sharp rebukes. Still, it seems as if nothing can force the lethargic mass of IT flesh to move one way or the other!

IT productivity requires both management and leadership skills. A leader works with the team members to identify problem areas as early as possible and deals with them before they become irretrievable disasters.

[B]   IT Management Productivity

There are several indicators of good management: low employee turnover and absenteeism, no employee sabotage, good productivity, and a reliable employee suggestion system. The signs may look good but must be confirmed. Some ways to confirm this in information systems are:

  A.   Projects are finished when planned.
  B.   Completed projects are finished within budget.
  C.   End users have faith in information system reports.
  D.   Most IT job promotions are filled from within the company.

IT Managers must actively work outside their offices. Do not depend on memos and the telephone to understand IT productivity. Leadership is a people business, and there is no better way than face to face. Some things the IT Manager can do to help actively promote IT production:

  A.   Encourage participatory management.
  B.   Ask what can be done about problems, and listen.
  C.   Set realistic norms and goals.
  D.   Use real quality circles.

E. Employ time management.
F. Delegate and follow up.
G. Learn when to say no.
H. Set deadlines.
 I. Finish what is started.
J. Do difficult jobs during the more productive time of day.
K. Make a daily timetable.
L. Do unpleasant things first.
M. Realize employee behavior may be due to weak supervisors or disruptive coworkers.

[C] IT Employee Productivity

It is more difficult measuring IT personnel's productivity than production jobs. Areas particularly hard to monitor are systems and programming. Programmers are too often measured on how hard and long they work, and how many lines of code they write. The ignored programmer is often the one who could do the same program in much less time with half the lines of code and no test data errors.

To discover the level of a programmer's productivity, survey other programmers about how they would rank their colleague's skills. Do this at employee review time. The feedback could be informative. Other ways to get feedback are:

A. End users speak well of the service desk and other IT assistance by programs and systems. The flip side of this is when users specifically ask that a certain person not be sent to their department again.
B. Use work simplification studies for programmers and systems people.
C. Compare performance with other projects and tasks.
D. Have all project work effort ranked regarding each member's contribution to the project's completion.
E. Notice who is the most helpful and who people go to for help.
F. Review how systems conversions are made. Are the end users satisfied with the assistance, training, service desk response, and the presence of project members during and after the conversion?
G. Find ways to have employees work together in teams—they will quickly discover who is productive and who is not.

§ 10.10 NONTRADITIONAL WORKING ARRANGEMENTS

[A] Telecommuting Policy

Telecommuting is an alternative to the traditional office-bound work practice. Telecommuting benefits both the employee and the employer. Given the low cost of high speed Internet lines, it is now practical for more people to work from home.

Telecommuting, however, brings its own set of problems. There could be problems with hourly workers' time records and overtime problems, but none with salaried personnel. Work with human resources management to craft policies and procedures that protect the company when using telecommuters.

Some of the benefits of telecommuting include:

A. Marked employee productivity.
B. Greater job satisfaction.
C. Less job turnover.
D. Lower absenteeism.
E. Lower company worksite expense due to:
   1. Annual office floor space cost.
   2. Reduced employee parking requirements.
   3. Reduced janitorial service costs.
   4. Less need for utilities.

Some workers with physical challenges would prefer to work at home. Others could work from remote sites or even out of the country. Employees could benefit from the following:

A. Lower day-care costs.
B. Lower transportation costs.
C. Less travel time and fighting traffic.
D. Less time spent getting ready for work.
E. Reduced eating-out costs.
F. Reduced wardrobe investment.
G. Less need for a second car.
H. More flexible lifestyle.
I. Can have the radio on while working.

[B] Job-Sharing Policy

Job sharing can benefit both parties. Two different skill levels, not necessarily equal, can fill one full-time position. It does not require each to have half of the same job. Divide this position as flex-time responsibilities or even telecommuting. Flexibility can attract higher skilled talent than more traditional routes for IT specialties. Fill the position with salaried employees.

Pay for job-shared positions will not require equal pay for equal time. The employee benefits package may not be the same for both parties. The cafeteria benefit plan provides for a more equitable distribution of benefits. Paid vacation time as part of the benefit program should resolve the vacation question. Policy about taking unpaid vacation time should be determined in advance for this arrangement.

This policy attracts better talent to the IT department. It assures a backup is available. It is better to lose a half-person specialty than a whole, if that position is the only one IT has. This provides for safer backup than if that talent is being vested in one person. Depending on the responsibility, the job sharing may be done by related people, as long as one of the individuals, upon giving notice of leaving the firm, would not affect the other member, too.

[C]   Flex-Time Policy

Flex time is commonly used as a "free" company benefit. It is free since flex time is valued by the employees and it costs companies nothing to implement it. Flex time is defined as open windows of time to arrive or leave work provided an 8-hour day is completed. It also applies to telecommuting and job-sharing positions.

Most companies establish a core time when all employees are required to be present: for meetings, training, etc. This is normally no less than a 4-hour window. Core time is sometimes at the discretion of the IT Manager. Anyone abusing this will be placed back on the standard work hours the IT operation maintains. See ITP-10-4 IT Staff Flex-time Policy as an example.

POLICY ITP-10-4.   IT Staff Flextime Policy

Policy #:	ITP-10-4	Effective:	03/18/09	Page #:	1 of N
Subject:	IT Staff Flextime Policy				

1.0 PURPOSE

This policy is intended to respond to the needs of full-time IT staff members for whom the standard corporate work schedule is not ideal. Some of the reasons that an individual may wish to work an alternative schedule include:

- A. Need for before or after hours system maintenance
- B. Car pooling arrangements with spouse or fellow employees
- C. Avoiding traffic congestion problems
- D. Coordinating schedules with a working spouse
- E. Child care issues
- F. Coordinating work schedule with a limited bus schedule

2.0 SCOPE

This policy applies to all IT staff members for whom there is no business requirement to adhere to the standard work hours.

3.0 POLICY

Within the guidelines described below, it is corporate policy to provide all full-time IT staff members the opportunity to request the hours of work that consistently suit their individual needs. However, it is recognized that it will not be possible to accommodate all such requests for alternative schedules.

The standard corporate schedule is from 8:00 a.m. to 5:00 p.m. Monday through Friday, and it is expected that all offices will be open during regular corporate hours.

Guidelines

1. Under flexible working hours, daily hours totaling 8.0 per day, 5 days per week, may be selected during the time 7:00 a.m. through 7:30 p.m.
2. A fixed schedule should be selected for at least three months at a time.
3. Some departments may be unable to offer flexible hours for some positions and/or during certain times of the year.
4. All employees must take at least half an hour for lunch each day.
5. A request for an alternative schedule (i.e., other than 8:00 a.m. through 5:00 p.m. with one hour lunch) must be discussed and confirmed in writing with the individual's supervisor and any others who are directly affected by the individual's work.
6. The individual selecting an alternative schedule must see that at least one other person is available to handle issues that arise during his or her absence from standard working hours.
7. Hours actually worked must be recorded on each non-exempt employee's time reporting form.
8. Staff members in their first six months in a new job may expect to be asked to work the standard 8:00 a.m. to 5:00 p.m. schedule to ensure appropriate training and interaction with others in the department.
9. Flexible working hours are not available to bargaining unit employees unless it is so stated in the governing labor agreement.

4.0 REVISION HISTORY

Date	Revision #	Description of Change
03/18/07	1.0	Initial creation.

5.0 INQUIRIES

Direct inquiries about this policy to:

Harold Jenkins, CIO
2900 Corporate Drive
Columbus, OH 43215

Voice: 614-555-1234
Fax: 614-555-1235
E-mail: hjenkins@company.com

Revision #:	1.0	Supersedes:	N/A	Date:	03/18/09

[D]   Rehiring Former Employees

Many organizations have a firm policy against the rehiring of former employees, usually citing security concerns about still angry laid-off employees. For IT Managers, there are many good reasons to consider rehiring ex-employees. These reasons include:

A. Lower training costs. Former employees have already been trained in the technologies used, and may have picked up additional valuable skills while at another firm.

B. Shorter learning curve. Former employees are already familiar with the company's systems and processes.

C. Return of vital expertise. When senior people leave, they take valuable experience and skills with them.

D. Possibly greater loyalty. If the employee left voluntarily due to feeling that "the grass is greener on the other side of the fence," he or she may appreciate more what the firm has to offer upon returning.

Any rehire policy must be clearly documented and understood by all employees. The policy must clearly state:

A. Who the policy applies to. Does it apply only to full-time staff, or also to part-time employees and consultants?

B. Guidelines on when the former employee will not be considered for rehire. This typically is applied to employees terminated for serious offenses, such as theft, workplace violence, breach of security, felony conviction, etc.

C. The period of time from the employee's separation for which they are eligible to return without going through the normal hiring procedures.

D. How severance pay is handled when the employee returns.

The exit interview is a great place to identify departing employees who would be eligible to return. See ITP 10-5 IT Staff Rehire Policy as an example.

POLICY ITP-10-5.   IT Staff Rehire Policy

Policy #:	ITP-10-5	**Effective:**	03/18/09	**Page #:**	1 of N
Subject:	IT Staff Rehire Policy				

1.0 PURPOSE

This policy outlines the process and conditions for the rehiring of IT employees. Some of the reasons that the IT department may wish to rehire a former employee include:

A. Lower training costs. Former employees have already been trained in the technologies used, and may have picked up additional valuable skills while at another firm.

B. Shorter learning curve. Former employees are already familiar with the company's systems and processes.
C. Return of vital expertise. When senior people leave, they take valuable experience and skills with them.
D. Possibly greater loyalty. If the employee left on their own due to feeling that "the grass is greener on the other side of the fence," they may appreciate more what the firm has to offer when they return.

2.0 SCOPE

This policy applies to all IT staff members that have previously worked for the company and wish to be rehired. It covers former fulltime employees, part-time employees, and individuals who have worked at the company as consultants.

3.0 POLICY

Within the guidelines described below, it is corporate policy to allow for the rehiring of IT staff who have previously worked for the company.

Guidelines

A. Only employees who left in good standing are eligible for rehire. Employees who were terminated for violation of any corporate policy or for illegal activity are not eligible for rehire.
B. Previous employees who have been separated from the company for more than 6 months must go through the normal hiring procedures. This includes background and credit checks and drug screening.
C. If the employee is rehired for a different position than the one held previously, the rehired employee must go through the standard probationary period for the new position.
D. An employee who has received severance pay and who returns to work in a position with the company at the same or higher salary as the position held at the time of separation shall repay to the company any portion of severance pay received that is in excess of the time the employee was separated from the company.

4.0 REVISION HISTORY

Date	Revision #	Description of Change
03/18/09	1.0	Initial creation.

5.0 INQUIRIES

Direct inquiries about this policy to:

Harold Jenkins, CIO
2900 Corporate Drive
Columbus, OH 43215

Voice: 614-555-1234
Fax: 614-555-1235
E-mail: hjenkins@company.com

Revision #:	1.0	Supersedes:	N/A	Date:	03/18/09

11

VIRTUAL TEAMS: REMOTE CONTROL MANAGEMENT

§ 11.01 OVERVIEW
    [A] Purpose and Scope
    [B] Policies and Objectives
    [C] Critical Policies to Develop Based on This Chapter

§ 11.02 THE VIRTUAL COMPANY
    [A] What's in It for the Company?
    [B] What's in It for the Worker?
    [C] What's in It for Society?
    [D] Virtual Pitfalls

§ 11.03 BECOMING A VIRTUAL WORKER
    [A] Overview
    [B] Work Area
    [C] Communications
    [D] Home Office Security
    [E] It Takes a Special Person
    [F] Career Management Is Just a Bit Different

§ 11.04 VIRTUAL WORKFORCE STRATEGY
    [A] Places Where Virtual Workers Fit Best
    [B] Organizing Your Business for Virtual Workers
    [C] Acquiring Virtual Workers
    [D] Not Suitable for Virtual Work

§ 11.05 LEADING A VIRTUAL TEAM
    [A] Virtual Team Manager
    [B] Virtual Team Members
    [C] A Little Bit of Help
    [D] Virtual Support Processes
    [E] "Pumping Up" the Virtual Team
    [F] International Issues

§ 11.01 OVERVIEW

[A] Purpose and Scope

A virtual worker is someone who is virtually in the office. Virtual workers work on their assignments, meet objectives, and participate in meetings. Virtual workers can meet with customers, create software, and even troubleshoot technical problems. They can do all of this without ever physically being there.

Previously, these workers were called "telecommuters" because they used telephones to connect to their office. Instead of driving to the office, they set up a work area in their home. Telecommuting is one tool companies used to retain their talent with conflicting family responsibilities. Today, it is not unusual for an office worker to occasionally work remotely from home during bad weather or perhaps one day per week to eliminate the commute. All of this has been made possible by modern data and telephonic communications.

Company culture plays a significant role in the success or failure of a virtual workforce. If the company respects its employees as skilled workers motivated to succeed and complete their assigned tasks promptly, then virtual workers may be the answer. If the company believes workers are lazy and untrustworthy, and must be watched at all times, then virtual workers are not for them.

COMMENT

Long ago, "virtual" was something that a computer did. For example, virtual memory was where the computer's Random Access Memory (RAM) was artificially expanded to a portion of a fixed disk. If more RAM was needed, some of the code in RAM was "rolled out" onto a special area of disk and managed by the CPU as if it were a part of the computer's RAM. Virtual teams are similar to this. People working from home—nearby or far way—act is if they were in the office, laboring alongside everyone else to accomplish the company's goal. Given how glued people are to their office's monitor and telephone, their coworkers may as well be miles away!

[B] Policies and Objectives

Virtual team policies provide guidance to everyone involved with the program. The objectives may be to reduce company costs and improve team member satisfaction while reducing the amount of greenhouse gases emitted by workers (as they no longer commute daily to work). These policies must be well considered, approved, and distributed to everyone affected by them.

Working out-of-sight of the boss makes companies uneasy. Companies that determine that virtual teams are appropriate to their business situation must establish measurable goals so that even though no one sees the team working, its results validate the team's efforts. Typical work includes data entry or program development, both of which provide tangible results.

[C]   Critical Policies to Develop Based on This Chapter

Using the material discussed in this chapter, you will be able to create the following policies:

A. The appropriate type of work for virtual workers.
B. Support policy for virtual work teams:
    1. Virtual workers are provided with standard tools to use and are trained on their use.
    2. Virtual workers need home office support for administrative issues and to expedite routine actions.
C. Conduct guidance for virtual team members' conduct:
    1. The work product of virtual workers must be measurable. Evaluations focus on delivered results.
    2. Virtual team members must be readily available for business communication between specified hours.

Policies should always be developed based on the local situation. Successful managers cannot issue appropriate guidance if the policies are written with another company's or location's situation in mind.

§ 11.02   THE VIRTUAL COMPANY

[A]   What's in It for the Company?

Traditionally, a company hires people, provides them with tools and a place to work, and assigns them things to accomplish. Throughout the workday, supervisors walk about the office to see who shows up for work, who is working hard, who is working little, and so on. Managers can see the progress and gauge how close a task is to completion. A virtual workplace changes all of this.

Companies that use a large virtual workforce may realize other savings. As location becomes of secondary importance to the labor pool, smaller offices can be closed and their servers merged into the primary data center. Workers all connect to the central office via high-speed Internet. Alternatively, smaller offices can be opened far from the large (expensive) cities. This may provide a pool of lower-cost virtual workers. Benefits to the company include:

A. **Avoid the high cost of office space.** In the early days, a prime driver for data processing was the way it decreased costs by automating massive manual processing. Once considered a radical idea, data processing today is the norm. So what about the high cost of office space? Just the cost of floor space alone can run $50 per square foot, per month (depending on location). Add in office furniture/cubicle walls for several thousand dollars, plus parking, networking, telephone equipment, utility costs, and more—and it is easy to see that providing employees an adequate place to work is expensive. Imagine cutting this cost to almost nothing!

Just as computers eliminated many manual jobs, why not use them to dramatically reduce the high expense of office space required by a company? Virtual teaming is a money saver.

B. **Scalable workforce.** Virtual workers enable a company to scale its labor pool. Instead of limiting the amount of attempted work by the number of local workers, a temporary work surge can be shared with a virtual workforce from across the entire enterprise. As work increases, virtual workers are assigned from the various locations. As it is reduced, virtual workers are turned to other tasks.

People prefer to reside where they wish rather than where the centers of employment are located. For example, consider the situation where Colorado has an excess of expert Java programmers while Boston is critically short. In years gone past, the only way to use these Java programmers was to move them to where the work was (or move the work to them). However, if they did not want to move, then the out-of-balance situation remained. Using a virtual work arrangement, the Colorado workers can be employed in Boston while still enjoying the western mountain sunsets.

COMMENT

Using virtual teams around the globe permits rapidly developing software. A team in one time zone writes the code and the team on the other side of the world tests it that same day—feeding results back to the coding team the next morning.

[B] What's in It for the Worker?

Workers have a lot to like about working virtually. It simplifies their life and saves them money. However, it trades these advantages for other complexities that the typical worker never needed to deal with. Benefits to the workers include:

A. **Think green—no daily commute.** Imagine all of the hours spent every workday driving to and from the office? How many hours is this per week, per month, per year? Imagine recapturing all of that time for other uses. Instead of leaving at 7:00 a.m. to arrive at work before 8:00, just be seated at the virtual work place by 8:00 a.m.—another precious hour of life is recaptured! The same benefit arises again at the end of the workday.

Not driving to work also means savings in fuel. How much is saved by not filling a car just to drive to work? This is like an immediate pay raise as daily expenses visibly drop. Does it cost to park near the office? Not anymore. Wear on vehicles is also saved, making them last longer and stretching the time between required mechanical services. When cars last longer, fewer are needed and you are even greener than ever.

COMMENT

Is it snowing outside? Is a major storm raging? No problem—it is warm and dry inside! Start work on time, safe at home.

B. **At home to handle simple issues.** Working from home improves employee attendance. Often, domestic issues and responsibilities combine to pull workers away from work and back into the home. If people normally worked out of their homes, these issues could be resolved without missing work and disrupting the efforts of all who depend on them. For example:
   1. Let a repairman in. Sounds simple, but it requires a round trip from the office or, just as frequently, skipping a day of work altogether because repair services rarely say when they will drop by.
   2. A mild illness that makes it too uncomfortable to be in an office with others but fine to work from home.
   3. Staying home to tend sick children or children homebound by a school "snow day."
C. **Save on business attire.** Typically, women are more fashion minded than men and tend to spend more on clothes for work. Yet, an office that requires all men to wear suits incurs the daily cost for pressed and starched white shirts. In short, some jobs require the purchase and maintenance of expensive clothing. This is not an issue when working from home where you can wear a robe and fuzzy slippers.

[C] What's in It for Society?

Some people have a lot to contribute but have physical mobility difficulties, child care responsibilities, elder care requirements, or any number of reasons. Virtual jobs enable these people to do to work around their home responsibilities (or limitations). Companies that reach out to homebound people may find loyal and dependable employees.

[D]   Virtual Pitfalls

With such a rosy outlook, why would anyone want to tramp through rain and snow to work in an office? There are several reasons:

A. Lack of direct contact with boss. Many find it harder to be promoted without daily personal contact with their managers—daily contact lets them know that everything is okay.

B. Consciously and subconsciously, people use a considerable amount of nonverbal communication. Without visual contact during conversations, communications are not complete and part of the message is lost.

C. It is more difficult to find quick answers to simple questions. Remote workers trying to contact someone in an office spend more time trying to establish communications—especially if the individual they are trying to contact will not respond to electronic requests. Who hasn't worked with someone who screened all of their calls and ignored most of their e-mail?

D. Virtual workers may feel socially isolated because their coworkers are just a disembodied voice. They may spend a considerable amount of working time trying to find out "what is going on" in the virtual workspace, rather than working. There are many visual cues found in an office—on bulletin boards, the way people decorate their work areas, etc., that are missing when working from home.

E. There are too many distractions when working at home. Dogs want out, family members want errands run, and other domestic responsibilities may lure the worker away from their employer's assigned tasks.

F. Absence of a coworker support network make taking the tough times more difficult.

G. It is more difficult for companies to cultivate a corporate culture and loyalty.

§ 11.03   BECOMING A VIRTUAL WORKER

[A]   Overview

Working at home takes more than a telephone line and a corner of the kitchen table. A home office requires essentially the same floor space and furniture as an office cubicle. Office workspaces are configured as they are because that is the optimal layout for that type of work. Before volunteering to work from home, be sure enough dedicated space is available.

COMMENT

Virtual workers maintaining a home office incur expenses normally borne by the employer in a traditional setting. A prime example is office supplies—pads of paper, paper for a

> printer, toner, etc. Companies may provide each virtual worker an allowance to cover these expenses—or should not be surprised when virtual workers refuse to pay for these things with a corresponding loss of productivity.

[B]   Work Area

A typical office cubicle is about 6 feet wide by 8 feet deep—about the size of a crypt vault. Minimally, the desktop space must provide room for a keyboard, a monitor (and computer if it must sit on top), a telephone, and a writing area. Ideally, there will be enough room for several writing areas to accommodate the paperwork sprawl, as well as some shelves to hold reference manuals. Because no one is at hand to answer quick process questions, reference manuals are important for working through problems.

The work area must be in a quiet part of the house. If no one else is home all day, then this is easier. If children come home from school, they may be disruptive for the last few hours of work unless a door can keep their noise out. Other interruptions to avoid:

A.   Noise from outside such as busy streets, railroad crossings, noisy neighbors, etc.

B.   "Sounds of the home," such as chiming clocks, cuckoo clocks, squeaky chairs or doors, sounds from televisions in adjacent rooms, etc.

C.   Demanding pets such as barking dogs, cats who must sit on keyboards, loud birds, etc.

The work area must include storage for files. These documents provide background materials and cross-references to business issues. If the worker is someone who must see things on paper, he or she must also obtain a laser printer (cheaper to use than an inkjet printer) to print documents and drawers for filing these documents. Ideally, the virtual workers store documents electronically which minimizes the need for file cabinets.

COMMENT

A quick way to gain weight is to sit all day. In a normal office, there are regular ups and downs out of the chair to attend meetings, discuss things, etc. In a home office, the work effort is to sit by the PC and telephone (with the occasional trip to the refrigerator). Home workers must plan exercise into their day the same as they plan their work.

[C]   Communications

Teamwork is based on communications. In the office, this is through spoken words, gestures, memos, meetings, casual encounters, and so on. For the virtual worker, the two main vehicles of communication are data and voice (telephonic). If either of these is out of service, then the virtual worker is "speechless."

> **COMMENT**
>
> Companies employing virtual workers should always provide them a complete electronic setup: a workstation loaded with software, a cell phone (with the bill paid by the company), and ready access to high-speed Internet. Companies must also devise a process to rapidly replace broken hardware.

Critical communications tools required by the virtual worker include:

A. **Personal computer and software.** Some companies provide telecommuting workers with computers and network connection devices. The advantage of this is that they know what is on the working desktop and can provide prompt tech support for issues. The company's VPN (virtual private network) client can be included with the basic workstation image. This standard office setup ensures that documents can be easily exchanged among team members. Telecommuters using their own personal computers may introduce problems with virus transmission, inconsistent software, software version interfering with document exchange, and so on.

Providing company-owned PCs also enables the company to control its software efficiently. All patching is accomplished by the home office to ensure seamless data exchange.

However, many companies dislike spreading their hardware assets all over the country. It is too easy to lose them. It is hard to ensure that the equipment is properly safeguarded and easy to recover when someone separates from the team. An alternative is to require virtual team members to purchase their own equipment. These workers should be provided applications over the web, such as Software as a Service (SaaS). However, this only works for employees with the financial resources to do so before receiving their first paycheck.

> ## COMMENT
>
> Home workers' PCs also require an Uninterruptible Power Supply (UPS) to filter electrical power and protect it from data losses and damage during a power outage. Because data are stored on the local workstation, some method of backing up the workstation's disk storage is also essential. Backing up local data to a server in the company's data center also provides control of documents in case an employee must be separated.

B. **Broadband network connection.** The primary enablers of virtual workers are the widespread availability of broadband communications and cheap long-distance telephone service. Dial-up data communications (similar in function and speed to a dumb terminal) can be used for data entry or e-mail but lack strong security and are limited by telephone equipment speeds. Dial-up communications barely keep up with the pace of work. Broadband is the enabler of video conferencing, webinar training, and groupware to share documents. Access to a high-speed data connection must be a qualification when hiring virtual workers (just as reliable transportation to work is a requirement for office-bound workers).

A high-speed data connection enables the use of video. This allows you to mount a camera on your PC and exchange live video with the other members on your team. A high-speed line also opens the opportunity to use Voice over IP (VOIP) and save on long-distance connection charges.

C. **VPN.** A virtual worker's PC requires a secure connection to the company's network. The most common approach is a VPN connection through the Internet. This safeguards the company's data from interception. A VPN requires software and some authentication mechanism for the operator. VPN software may use a client program on the workstation or establish the connection through a sign-on screen over the web.

A VPN connection uses "something you know and something you own." This is a combination of an authentication device, such as a number-generating token or fingerprint reader and a password. Successfully logging on through the VPN authenticates someone as the real thing. Once the VPN connection is established, that workstation acts as if it were located within the company's office walls.

D. **Groupware for team collaboration.** Many documents are the result of collaboration between team members. Groupware provides a virtual workplace for sharing team documents, sharing ideas, and submitting ideas or prototypes for team review. For example, the "team description" document is drafted by the virtual team manager and then passed around to virtual team members who each add to it or correct some part of it. By posting it in a shared area, each team member can update it without playing round-robin with the e-mail.

Groupware is also a valuable way to collect all of a team's files into a central repository. When a new person joins the team, he or she can review the files to learn about the team's issues and progress to date. If someone leaves the team, his or her documents are still in storage. Also, all company data stored in the repository are backed up.

E.   **Telephone.** Most homes use a single telephone line. Transforming a simple home phone to a business line takes a bit of effort:

1.   A virtual worker is heavily dependent on reliable telephone service. Because calls can come in at any time, it is not advisable to use the family's home number as your official business number. If family members tie up the line with local calls, some of the workday may be lost. Consider using the family telephone line only for outgoing calls.

2.   A second telephone line is useful for incoming calls. This is the number that will be spread around the company for anyone to contact you. A cell phone is handy for this as it usually comes with a voicemail feature to catch missed calls. Some companies provide virtual workers with a cell phone and pay for all of the charges. This provides an added benefit to the team in that this person's replacement will have the same telephone number.

3.   A connection for low-cost, outbound, long-distance calls is essential. These can be purchased by the month for a standard telephone line or included on a cell phone account.

4.   The home worker's telephone needs a speakerphone (and/or headset) and a mute button. The speakerphone or headset reduces the fatigue of holding a telephone handset to an ear (many meetings will last an hour or more). The mute button reduces the amount of noise passed over the line when listening to a meeting over a bridge number. It is also nice to have hands free to look things up on the computer or to shuffle documents during the call.

F.   **Telephone bridge number.** Companies frequently provide a "bridge" number for team meetings. This is a toll-free number (available from the telephone companies) where anyone can dial in and join a virtual conversation. Issue a bridge number to each virtual worker. Documents can be distributed by e-mail prior to the meeting or an online web service can be used where everyone can log into and see the documents under discussion as they are changed.

COMMENT

Because the bridge number is toll free, consider dialing out on the house line and save the cell phone minutes for other calls.

G. **Electronic mail.** Electronic mail delivers documents and memos to team members. It allows for quick distribution of the same message to many people. Many companies maintain their telephone directories in the same place as their e-mail addresses. E-mail provides a way to fill in forms, pass on friendly notes—and many other things that an office worker takes for granted but that are vital to a virtual worker.

Most e-mail systems also include a calendar function for scheduling meetings. This is very important for virtual workers who may be assigned part time to various assignments. Rather than trying to catch someone by telephone in their free moment, time can be set aside on everyone's calendars for a quick chat.

H. **Instant messaging.** Instant messaging is the virtual worker's prized tool. It is the vehicle for informal communications with coworkers and acts as the quick question over the cubicle wall. Many people can respond to a quick instant message when they don't have the time to answer a telephone. For instance, a virtual worker sitting in on a long telephone meeting and listening to the discussion can respond to a quick question that appears at his or her workstation—without ever leaving the meeting.

[D]   Home Office Security

If you work in an office building, security is provided for all workers. Doors are locked, entrances monitored, equipment safeguarded against theft. Not so a home office! All of this security is now the responsibility of the virtual worker. Managers of virtual teams must provide a new-hire orientation that explains:

A. **Safeguarding equipment.** Sorry if a burglar carries off the hardware, but no work can be done until it is replaced. So, if no work is done, should a salary be provided? Not only must the virtual worker report theft of the equipment to the police, they must promptly report theft of the data to the company!

B. **Communication connections must be secure at all times.** This requires use of a VPN.

C. **Company documents no longer needed on site must be shredded.** This reduces the likelihood of the company's documents scattering across the lawns when a trash can is accidentally overturned.

D. **CDs containing company data must be shredded.** (Be sure to purchase a shredder that chews up CDs as well as paper.)

E. **Data backups of the virtual worker's PC must be protected as well as the computer.** Stealing a backup provides a criminal the same information as stealing the computer and its data.

[E]   It Takes a Special Person

Working virtually is quite different from sitting in the midst of a sea of cubicles. It is easy to be distracted when the work is tedious or boring. Virtual workers must be self- disciplined to focus on their assignments without constant supervision. Even people who work well by themselves feel adrift without the traditional office boundaries,

Virtual workers must be skilled communicators. Without visual cues from others on the team, they must pick up conversational nuances and react appropriately. The tone of voice and rhythm of the conversation fills in somewhat for the lack of body language. They must also not read dark inferences into hasty or poorly worded messages. Virtual work is a tough job for pessimists.

Finally, virtual team members must not require a lot of social interaction during their workdays. Telephones, e-mail, and instant messaging all provide some sense of community to the isolated worker and a chance to build friendships. However, people need more than a distant voice to feel accepted within the team and to take the drudgery of work to a higher level.

[F] Career Management Is Just a Bit Different

Virtual careers must be managed slightly differently than in-office careers. Virtual workers may have multiple bosses as assignments roll in. This makes it difficult to build a track record of solid performance. Ask for a performance evaluation whenever working on an assignment for someone for more than 80 hours. Things you might do to help your career along include:

A. Provide an online resume that details the types of work successfully completed in previous projects.
B. Volunteer for specific projects that would benefit most from your skills.
C. When work is slow, take some time to develop your contacts with co-workers. A wide support network of coworkers is one way to learn more about the inner workings of the company's virtual organization.
D. Send a monthly status report to your many bosses—but send all of them the same one. It lets them know what you are working on to show what you are capable of in the future.

§ 11.04 VIRTUAL WORKFORCE STRATEGY

[A] Places Where Virtual Workers Fit Best

Successful virtual workforces are the result of careful planning. Companies considering a virtual workforce must allow adequate time and money for planning and implementation. These costs are easily offset by the savings in floor space, furniture, and so on. Prior to embarking on this journey, develop a strategy of how this workforce will be created, supported, and applied to available work.

Virtual workers are ideal for assignments that have a definable deliverable, such as a code module, a document, or a users' manual. When an assignment is made, a time estimate to completion is also submitted. This approach allows virtual workers to set their own deadlines.

Virtual work is also suitable for data entry. This works well with the local workforce. A web-enabled screen with VPN access is provided for all workers. This removes the variability of the equipment used at home and minimizes company investment. Virtual workers can be compensated by the page or the hour.

Another successful virtual strategy is for companies with many offices across the country (or even around the world). Typically, as work tapers off in one region of the country, it usually picks up in another. This allows rapid scaling of resources according to the local requirements, while still maintaining control over workers in the offices.

COMMENT

Virtual workers are more successful if their efforts do not require close coordination with others. Save those jobs for a traditional work environment.

[B]   Organizing Your Business for Virtual Workers

A successful virtual worker program requires the establishment of a support structure. The following steps are critical for the success of your virtual worker program:

A. **Select a leader.** Even if it is only part time, someone must be assigned responsibility for the proper use of virtual workers. Companies that outsource projects or an entire segment of their organization must assign a single person to monitor the results. The virtual workforce leader ensures that everyone keeps up with their administrative tasks, such as submitting timesheets, properly submitting expenses, and so on. The leader also provides performance reviews for each person.

    If virtual teams are something new for your company, make the first virtual team leader someone who has virtual teamwork experience. This may avoid some of the learning problems of new teams.

B. **Human resources support.** Assign a human resources clerk as an advisor to the virtual workforce manager. Sooner or later some issue will arise where the manager must deal with poor performance (not everyone can handle working at home).

C. **Technical support.** Arrange for technical support for virtual workers. They may have a special line into the service desk to provide quick answers. If company equipment is provided, it may be necessary to quickly ship a replacement workstation to the virtual worker's home.

[C] Acquiring Virtual Workers

Virtual workers can be found in many places:

A. Company sites that are closing
B. Freelance contract technicians
C. Employees who are unable to come into the office
D. Employees who want to work from home several days per week

A great place to find virtual workers is by asking other virtual workers to locate them. This type of work is not suitable for everyone, but current virtual workers may know of others who have worked well in the past. Also, the team will come together quicker if some of the people are already acquainted.

[D] Not Suitable for Virtual Work

Sending work outside the office to employees working at home is not always a good idea. Critical business functions should not be to be assigned to virtual workers. The key to work that must be kept onsite lies in the types of virtual workers you use. If they are long-time employees, they can be trusted with more. If they are hired off the street to work from home, their motivations may be less aligned with those of the company.

Consider this when selecting work to distribute offsite:

A. Keep the responsibility for the effectiveness and overall success of a business function in the office where it can be closely monitored.
B. Prior to assigning a process to virtual workers, ensure that the process is operating effectively and efficiently. Sending a broken process offsite can, at best, provide no better results than it does using onsite staff.
C. Never use virtual workers for any part of your company's unique business processes. Once these processes are offsite, they are easier for a competitor to learn about.
D. The IT department should always own the customer relationship with either in-house or external customers. Much valuable feedback information is lost when passing this off to others.
E. IT legal compliance and security controls must stay in-house.

§ 11.05 LEADING A VIRTUAL TEAM

[A] Virtual Team Manager

The challenge in leading a virtual team is in the increased reliance on verbal and written communication. Trust is the basis for all communications. Workers and managers lacking trust in their coworkers will be defensive, will be less willing to share their ideas, and may withhold information.

Leading a virtual team takes patience and trust. Patience is needed because virtual tasks may take more time to complete than to do the same work in an office where advice and assistance are readily available. Trust is needed in that the manager is confident that team members will meet their assignments.

Virtual team members need more "care and feeding" than a typical team. In a traditional setting, a manager might walk around and visit each team member sometime during the day to quickly see if there are any issues or obstacles with their assignment. Without the nonverbal communications, they feel uncomfortable about their status in the team and the team manager's true attitude toward them. In a virtual team, the same thing can be done with short instant messages. The difference is that when this is done in person, there is the personal message, "we're both OK." An instant message must be cheerful and carefully worded not to sound mechanical or micromanaging.

Everyone, whether sitting in an office or working from the beach, has a preferred way to receive electronic information. This may be through an instant messenger service, by e-mail, by telephone, and so on. Managers who can determine the best way to communicate with each individual team member will encounter fewer problems. Some options are:

A. **Make frequent, short visits.** As team members are out of direct contact with their boss and teammates, they may feel out of touch with the organization and peer opinions (which might be more obvious in body language were they standing before you). During conversations, the manager must determine if a virtual worker is struggling and needs some assistance. The tone of voice and rhythm of the conversation fills in somewhat for lack of body language.

COMMENT

A sense of isolation is the primary reason people drop out of virtual teams and return to traditional office positions.

B. **The online break room.** Create an online message board and open chat room where virtual workers can swap ideas and stories and generally learn more about others in their virtual workspace. The team manager uses this space to ensure that all pertinent company information—both big and small—is provided to everyone. Include a knowledge base for addressing the administration problems of virtual workers. Permit anyone to add to it.

    However, managers must monitor everything posted to these spaces for inappropriate comments or confidential company information. Otherwise, it is a wide-open exchange between virtual and office-bound workers.

C. **Managing someone you will never meet.** It can be uncomfortable for managers working within a tight deadline to depend on someone when they cannot even see if that person is working or playing. One approach is to break deliverable results into one week increments. Organize and specify work in terms of results so that it can be accomplished without detailed management supervision. In this way, the results validate the work time required.

> ## COMMENT
>
> When someone has a computer problem in the office, he or she calls the local service desk. However, a virtual team member generally does not have anyone local to turn to. The virtual team manager must have a plan for supporting virtual team member equipment. If the company owns the equipment, then keep a spare cell phone and a PC loaded with software and ready for immediate shipment. In a crisis, it can be sent out for overnight delivery to exchange for a broken unit. Otherwise the worker sits and waits while time drags on.
>
> If virtual team members provide their own equipment, ensure they have prearranged for local tech support including hardware repair.

Leading a virtual workforce of independent-minded IT experts is a demanding task. It is made easier by establishing a framework for data collection and sharing through a set of standard forms and processes. Use Worksheet 11-1 Virtual Team Checklist to help manage your virtual team.

[B] Virtual Team Members

A strong focus on goals and task completion keeps virtual teams working without someone nagging them for action. Team members prefer that the virtual team manager clearly define their assignments and reward them according to their performance.

A. **New team members.** New virtual team members require time to orient themselves to their new surroundings. Bring them into the virtual team support office to pick up their equipment, learn how to use the tools and to walk through the team processes. This also allows them to meet the support staff—putting faces to the voices.

New employees should clearly understand what is expected from them. Use a checklist to review such things as availability during

WORKSHEET 11-1.   Virtual Team Checklist

Virtual Team Checklist	
Manager's Checklist	**Date Completed**
Create a place to share team documents	
Standardize document naming conventions	
Company policies and forms for reference	
Create, update and frequently publish up-to-date contact lists for team members, support staff and key customers	
Document procedures to	
Submit expense statements	
Submit time sheets	
Submit status reports and the standard format	
Ordering office supplies	
Publish updated contact information monthly	
How to report data loss to the company	
Document practices to	
Reply to all team messages within 24 hours	
Availability during published working hours	
Virtual Team Member Checklist	
Data	
Workstation	
Standard office software	
Standard communications software	
High speed data line	
Camera for video conferencing	
Laser printer	
Telecommunications	
Outbound line with unlimited long distance time (usually a cell phone)	
Inbound line	
Fax machine	
Voicemail	
Headset & mute button	

WORKSHEET 11-1.   (Continued)

Work area	
Desktop, chair	
Office supplies	
Shredder for paper and CDs	
Publish work hours	
Publish resume with work skills	
Supporting a Virtual Team	
Always keep a back-up workstation loaded with software and ready to ship.	
Use a national carrier for company supplied cell phones so that repairs and exchanges can be completed locally.	
Arrange a process and time for online patching of company owned workstations used by virtual team members.	
Create an online repository for team documents and require its use. Reference material can be stored here for team use.	
Create a standard document naming convention for the team to facilitate the exchange of documents.	
International Issues	
Pick an official language	
Research local business cultures	
Project Leader:	**Date:**

working hours, submission of timesheets, document requirements, and so on. Break in new virtual employees with a few easy assignments until they become accustomed to the company's processes and software tools.

B. **Team etiquette.** Virtual teams develop their own social rules governing communications. Team managers can force the issue early in team forming by providing simple guidelines for communications:

1. Carefully prepare all participants for meetings. Distribute documents for advance review. These meetings will result in fewer follow-up discussions.

2. Always debate points over the telephone and not through e-mail. If more than three e-mails are exchanged to clarify a point, it is easier to call and explain it than to write pages explaining things in detail.

3. If something someone says rubs you wrong, wait a while and then call him. Don't let misunderstandings fester. Be sensitive of others. It is easier to work patiently with someone courteously than to fight and create enemies.

4. Respect the normal working hours of others. Keep time zones in mind when scheduling meetings or calling. However, emergencies take priority.

5. Always return messages promptly. Do not build delays into the team.

6. There is no shame in not knowing how to do something—but there is in not asking for help. Never hesitate to ask other team members for help but spread out the requests to various team members because everyone is busy.

7. Be careful when using humor, as the body language aspect is not present. Also, humor does not translate well across cultures.

Because the team is dependent on messaging and prompt responses, the manager must ensure that the team promptly responds to requests from other team members. (In an office, a person can check to see if someone is on the telephone. Virtual workers cannot see that far, so they leave their message and move on.) Team members slow to respond (for whatever reason) to a question will cause the team progress to lag. Further, if the slow responder is intentionally delaying an answer, the team will develop mistrust and considerable dissention. Disaffected team members can choose to ignore messages or leave them for other times. This increases team stress.

C. **Meeting minutes.** Virtual meetings are a bit different from the typical business meeting. The meeting leader cannot look around to see who is attentive and who is sleeping. Be sure that the high points of the discussions are recorded and passed out to the participants. Meeting minutes are a valuable source of information to managers for the early detection of problems. Also place a copy in the central team document store as a historical record of what did (or did not) happen, and when.

Schedule regular meetings to assess needs, give feedback, discuss problems, and just catch up. If you hold regular meetings to set timetables and assess progress, employees will have deadlines to keep them on target. Every meeting must be formally documented because, unlike a face-to-face discussion, no one can see if anyone else is writing anything down. Also, without eye contact around the room, the team manager may experience difficulty bringing a meeting to an emotional conclusion.

COMMENT

If practical, bring all virtual team members into the home office quarterly for a day or more of face-to-face discussions. This goes a long way in building team cohesion as faces are added to the voices.

[C] A Little Bit of Help

Virtual teams need administrative assistance to complete their assignments. Assign a core group of administrators in the virtual workforce office to provide advice and answer questions. This might be assistance with routine clerical tasks, expediting purchase orders through the approval process, following up on nonresponsive team members or customers, or fulfilling requests for materials and supplies. Sometimes, they might just need a friendly voice to chat with.

If the virtual team is supporting a customer, either place one of the team members onsite with the customer or arrange for the customer to provide a "go-to" person to assist the team. This "feet on the street" can chase down answers, look at things, and represent the team to the customer. A motivated onsite team member can make the toughest assignment seem (somewhat) easy.

[D] Virtual Support Processes

The virtual workforce office must have clearly documented and published processes. This reduces confusion when virtual team members are working part time for multiple managers. Processes to support your virtual workers include:

A. **Store all documents in a central repository.** Virtual teams have a higher attrition rate than normal teams. To ensure a smooth transition, require that copies of all key documents are sent to the virtual workforce office for storage in a central server. This includes:
    1. Design notes explaining trade-offs considered and the reason for the one selected.
    2. Customer contact reports.
    3. Status reports—Like any office, the customer will expect performance metrics. Ensure that status reports contain the essential information that can be rolled up into a summary report.
    4. Meeting minutes.
    5. Customer approvals—provide contact lists so that workers don't lose time trying to find out how to contact someone. Provide up-to-date contact lists in a central location.

B. **Standardize document naming conventions.** Provide a standard document naming convention to reduce confusion. Typically, this is the time charge account number, followed by the official team name, followed by the title of the document. If the document is revised, then a version number is appended onto the end. For example:
    QC-1234 Team Manager's Compensation Study—Meeting Minutes 1 Apr 09 v13.0
    - Time charge account number: QC-1234
    - Team name: Team Manager's Compensation Study
    - Document title: Meeting Minutes 1 Apr 09
    - Version number: 13

C. **Communications and response.** Communications overload can be an issue. Set a standard priority for communications among the team. The sender of a message is responsible for setting its priority and including it in the first part of the message title line. Each level of priority corresponds to the number of business hours within which it must be replied to. Example levels:

- Hot! Must have an immediate response
- Urgent—answer within four hours
- (no urgency listed) two days

Always use e-mail subject lines that describe the subject. Then place the key part of your message in the first few lines of the message. Skip slang as it may mean different things in different regions of the country—or to international team members. When in doubt, be more formal rather than less.

COMMENT

Everyone has experienced arguing through e-mail. The results satisfy no one. The virtual team leader must carefully chose comments to avoid accidental offense, especially when pressing an issue on a reluctant team member.

D. **Create a common virtual workforce vocabulary to minimize misunderstanding.** The meaning and intent of communications are easier if everyone uses the same terms in a consistent manner. Definitions must be clear and understood by the entire team. This is particularly important for cross-cultural teams. Any two people can disagree about the same term. Complicate this with regional or international cultural backgrounds and avoidable problems can be addressed.

COMMENT

Another communications issue is to ensure that messages are sent within their context. A simple way to do this is to forward responses to messages that include the original questions. Another way is to repeat the question along with the response.

E. **Team members must post their normal working hours on the contact list.** Team members must be readily available at agreed-upon times. In the United States, this is normal working hours for the local time zone. International workers must be available for at least half of the normal U.S. working hours, even if it forces them to work the night shift. European workers are usually available early in the North American morning.

By posting hours, it is easier to separate work time from family time. There will be times when workers will cut into their normally off-work hours to attend a meeting, but the manager must ensure these times are few. Otherwise, team members may stop accepting virtual assignments.

[E] "Pumping Up" the Virtual Team

Take time to celebrate the team's successes at milestones. Everyone can use a pat on the back sometimes. With a virtual workforce, it just requires some new ideas. One way is to plan a virtual team party. Schedule the event in advance. Send out gift cards for national restaurants and ask the local team to pick up something to share at the same time (lunch is tough to schedule across many time zones).

The manager can help to reduce team member stress by instituting a continuous improvement program. Team members note the top things that get in the way of completing their work. The manager strives to eliminate these obstacles—even if it means standing up to the customer (something many managers seems afraid to do). Progress is reported to the team every other week. As one of the tasks is completed, the team can nominate another for that spot.

The second part of the continuous improvement program is a list of things impossible to change. In the long run, nothing is impossible. The manager must also whittle away at this list, although successes here take much longer.

[F] International Issues

Communications between people sitting together are sometimes challenging, but communicating across time zones, educational backgrounds, and cultures complicates this significantly. Language nuances, different holidays, or even different workdays can disrupt team communications. The way that team members relate can be drastically different. Even the meaning of basic terms such as when a task is "finished" can mean different things to different cultures. In some cultures, it is shameful to admit when someone is unsure of the task or how to complete it—so workers from such cultures may not ask for help.

English is the modern language of business, so finding someone who can communicate with you is not the trick. The issue is to ensure that the meaning of what you are asking for, and what is being said to you, is the same as if talking to someone across the room. Different cultures have different rules of etiquette. Violating these local norms may create ill will where none was intended. Also, different cultures have different expectations of what a normal workday should be, how hard to drive tasks to completion, and how to handle interpersonal conflict.

The key to minimizing your cultural missteps is doing your homework. Where possible, have an advisor who is well versed in the business customs of the country you are using, to include the regional nuances.

A. **Offshore workers.** Some virtual teams include members from outside North America. This is an extension of the idea that virtual workers can live anywhere. Whoever engages these workers must make clear to them the hours they must be available for communication with the customer and the team. Typically this is 8:00 a.m. to 5:00 p.m. wherever the customer is located.

Depending on their origins and cultural background, it may be difficult to understand what the various team members are saying. Accents, language skills, and possession of a technical vocabulary are important requirements of offshore team members. As with all team members, the use of graphics helps to share ideas.

Take time to carefully interview prospective team members. Are they claiming an expertise that they know little about? Do they speak English but lack a technical vocabulary? Do they have experience working with North Americans and therefore understand something of the local business culture and customs?

B. **Cultural sensitivity.** We are all a product of our cultural background. It is reflected in our values, our customs, our habits, and our language. Much of what we do is a product of this culture and we don't even think about it. Someone from a different culture can easily understand some things ("do unto others as you would have others do unto you," for example, is universal). Other business customs are neither so obvious nor easily discovered from books.

Some cultures hold corporate position and age in high respect and feel it is rude or unacceptable to question higher-ups. This can stifle team discussions. If technical discussions seem to lack usefulness, it may be that some of the participants have a problem expressing a contrary opinion to those offered by others.

Even if they do not understand, foreign team members may say "yes" to whatever you tell them. In their culture this may mean "I am listening to you" (but do not understand a thing you have said), whereas you culturally filtered this to mean acceptance and understanding of what was said. After explaining something to foreign team members, engage them in a conversation of its finer points or choices to gauge their depth of understanding.

C. **Building a cross-cultural team.** Building a cross-cultural team is a lot like building any other team. It begins by finding some neutral topic that everyone can join in with, taking sides, and expressing opinions without offense. Sports are a great international topic. Pick up information on local or national teams for every participant. Toss it out as an icebreaker to get the conversation started. Stand by to rein in the discussion if it gets too heated.

Another important tip is to take the time to clearly pronounce basic terms, such as "thank you," "please," good work," "excellent," "I do not understand," and so on, in each international member's home language. Also learn about international members' foreign nuances, as their language may not translate exactly into what they mean in your own location.

D. **Pick the team's official language.** Usually, the official team language is the one spoken by the sponsoring organization. However, if a significant number of team members speak a different language, consider using that one for meetings. Discussions will run faster and smoother. If you do this, select a group leader to report back with a translation of meeting results.

Using translators is expensive and prone to problems. Words must be translated within their context as well as by their literal meaning. Always meet with a translator prior to a meeting. Discuss with the translator what will be covered and the message you want to convey to the team. This will allow the translator some time to work the message into the correct context.

See Policy ITP-11-1 Virtual Workforce Policy as an example of a policy covering virtual workers.

Policy #:	ITP-11-1	**Effective:**	03/18/09	**Page #:**	1 of N
Subject:	Virtual Workforce Policy				

1.0 PURPOSE

This policy creates the IT department's Virtual Workforce program. It ensures the consistent, efficient, and effective implementation of virtual workers across the organization.

2.0 SCOPE

The policy applies to all information technology departments within the company that want to employ virtual workers. This program encompasses all employee programs where the employee is not physically working in company owned offices, to include remote workers, part-time remote workers, and contract labor.

3.0 POLICY

The type of work sent out of the office depends to a great degree on who the virtual workers are. If they are long-time employees, or employees at remote sites, then more sensitive work can be assigned to them. If the virtual workers are new to the company or contracted labor, then their work must not reveal sensitive internal company processes.

A. Types of work suitable for virtual workers

Virtual work is ideal for assignments that have a definable deliverable, such as a code module, a document, or a users' manual. It can also be used to provide data entry of documents (which also has measurable results).

Virtual work can be assigned to under-utilized company employees in remote offices. They can remain in their offices while supporting other company sites.

Also, ensure that a process is working optimally prior to assigning it to virtual workers.

B. Types of work not suitable for virtual workers

Critical business functions should not be assigned to virtual workers.

1. Keep the responsibility for the effectiveness and overall success of a business function in the office where it can be closely monitored.
2. Never use virtual workers for any part of your company's unique business processes. Once these processes are off site, they are easier for a competitor to learn about.
3. Customer facing processes must remain in house and only use virtual workers for selective assignments. All customer contact must be handled by the IT staff.
4. IT legal compliance and security controls must stay in house.

C. Virtual workforce leader duties

1. Is responsible for implementing this policy.
2. Create a Mission Statement that outlines the virtual workers' roles and responsibilities within the IT department. It also establishes the scope of the policy.
3. Identify the primary strategies on how the virtual workforce will fulfill its mission statement and align with company business strategies.
4. Establish and maintain the tools and processes for use by the IT department's virtual workers.
5. Establish processes for prompt technical support of virtual worker issues.
6. Manage the IT department's portfolio of pending virtual assignments:
   a. Create a standard form for requesting virtual worker support. This ensures every request has the same "look and feel".
   b. Monitor contents of portfolio to combine assignments where practical.
7. Standardize virtual worker tools.
   a. Set processes
   b. Create tools
   c. Establish ground rules
8. Resource management.
   a. Coordinate the use of virtual resources to optimize utilization and minimize cost.
   b. Develop and maintain a positive working relationship with internal resource suppliers.
   c. Identify external virtual resources required and pre-qualify major suppliers (internal and external).
   d. Assign and reassign resources
9. Establish training and mentoring program.

       a. Identify and train mentors for assisting new virtual workers.
       b. Coordinate peer reviews for troubled assignments.
   10. Establish a virtual worker document repository.
D. Worker responsibility
    1. Posts their normal working hours (as approved by the Virtual Workforce Leader)
    2. Promptly responds to communications by telephone, electronic mail, and instant messaging.
    3. Provides a high-speed data connection and telephone line into the work area.
    4. Provides physical security for company equipment and data.
    5. Provides a weekly status report for every current virtual assignment in process.

4.0 REVISION HISTORY

Date	Revision #	Description of Change
03/18/09	1.0	Initial creation.

5.0 INQUIRIES

Direct inquiries about this policy to:

Tom Jones, CIO
Our Company, Inc.
2900 Corporate Drive
Columbus, OH 43215

Voice: 614-555-1234
Fax: 614-555-1235
Email: tjones@company.com

Revision #:	1.0	Supersedes:	N/A	Date:	03/18/09

12

VENDORS: GETTING THE GOODS

§ 12.01 OVERVIEW
    [A] Purpose and Scope
    [B] Critical Policies to Develop Based on This Chapter

§ 12.02 VENDOR MANAGEMENT
    [A] Overview
    [B] Vendor Selection
    [C] Personnel Augmentation
    [D] Acquiring Goods and Services
    [E] Purchasing—The Magic Three Factors
    [F] Recognizing the Key Vendors
    [G] Commodity Vendors
    [H] Low-Volume Vendors

§ 12.03 PLAY BY THE RULES
    [A] Overview
    [B] Maximizing the Purchasing Department's Expertise
    [C] Legal Review of Contracts
    [D] Receiving the Goods
    [E] Accounting's Role in Positive Vendor Relations
    [F] Budgets Drive the Purchases

§ 12.04 CONSULTING AND TEMPORARY PERSONNEL SERVICES
    [A] Overview
    [B] Types of Temporary Personnel Organizations
    [C] Utilizing Temporary Personnel
    [D] Ground Rules for Engaging Temporary Staff
    [E] Outsourcing

§ 12.05 REQUESTS FOR PROPOSAL
    [A] Overview
    [B] Project Startup
    [C] Preparing Requests for Proposal
    [D] Developing RFP Evaluation Criteria
    [E] Bidder's Conference
    [F] Evaluating the Bids

§ 12.01   OVERVIEW

[A]   Purpose and Scope

Problems! An IT Manager's desk is covered with problems. Fortunately, for every problem at hand, there is a long list of vendors standing by to help solve them. The key is to locate and engage the vendors who provide the right product, at the right time, and at a fair price.

When properly selected and managed, purchases will solve problems. Poorly selected and unmanaged purchases will create far more problems than they solve. However, IT Managers do not have time to sit and entertain every salesperson who wishes to visit. It is essential that the company identify those vendors who are the most important to its ongoing success and develop them as valuable members of the team.

Some IT technologies represent long-term investments for the company. The IT department normally directs the purchase of servers, major software packages, and desktop units. The IT department's future success depends on the success and direction of future products of these companies. The IT Manager must include the plans of these vendors into the department's budget to minimize "surprises."

A positive working relationship between IT and the purchasing department is important. Both groups want what is best for the company. A positive working relationship will allow members of each department to address issues as they arise and minimize battles over "turf" and personalities.

COMMENT

All companies are buyers of goods and services—and all companies are vendors. Treat vendors with the courtesy that you hope your own company receives from its customers.

The best policy for dealing with outside vendors is exercising good business practices based on sound moral and ethical codes. Depending on its dealings with vendors, a company can lose or gain respect from other vendors, employees, and the industry at large. Remember that the company needs reliable suppliers and suppliers need reliable customers.

[B] Critical Policies to Be Developed Based on This Chapter

Using the material discussed in this chapter, you will be able to create the following policies:

A. Vendor management.
   1. Nondisclosure agreements.
   2. Focus efforts on critical vendors.
   3. Verify financial health of critical vendors.
B. Vendor selection.
   1. Require disclosure of family or business connections with vendors.
   2. Limits on gifts from vendors and reporting requirements.
   3. Legal review for all agreements.
C. Temporary workers.
   1. Selecting suppliers.
   2. Work agreements approved by legal and human resources departments.
   3. Ownership of intellectual property.

Policies should always be developed based on the local situation. Successful managers cannot issue appropriate guidance if the policies are written with another company's or location's situation in mind.

§ 12.02 VENDOR MANAGEMENT

[A] Overview

The second most important task an IT Manager faces is the timely purchase of high quality goods at a fair price. (The most important IT Manager task is the leadership and care of the IT staff.)

Vendors can be a time saver or a source of constant irritation. In most cases, this reflects their relationship with the IT Manager. If the IT Manager's attitude (or the company's culture) is to "beat up vendors," then vendors will be defensive and passively resist concessions. Pressing vendors may bring results in the short-term but will create long-term animosity if the treatment persists. An aggressive approach may result in the IT Manager not knowing how badly the vendor takes revenge in pricing and delivery or the IT Manager may be forced to spend a considerable amount of time researching technology to ensure the vendor cannot push back on price or features.

Such adversarial relationships are unnecessary and wasteful. If the IT Manager lacks trust in a key vendor, then that vendor should be replaced. Key vendors should be treated as partners who are looking out for their own interests. However, they also may be allies who will work hard to protect a valuable business relationship. The trick is to keep them close enough to benefit the company, but distant enough that they keep working to earn the company's business.

Not all vendors are of equal importance to the company. Some vendors provide critical technology whose well-being is vital to the IT department's success, while other vendors are only needed occasionally. Most IT Managers make this distinction subconsciously.

Good vendor management is a key to successful IT management. Vendors can be a source of information about technologies and their industries. They can provide quick solutions to vexing problems and make a manager's job a lot easier. They can also get a manager fired.

Vendor management is managing the relationship between the IT department and its vendors to the company's long-term advantage. Long-term advantage means that the IT Manager protects the company by driving down the vendor's prices, and increasing the vendor service levels. However, vendors that lose money to a customer cannot afford to do so for long. They cease to either sell to that customer or become insolvent. Therefore, the IT Manager must keep prices down while allowing for a fair return to the seller.

The buyer-seller relationship is an agreement between two consenting parties to exchange one thing for another. In this case, the exchange is money for goods or services. The amount of money exchanged for goods depends on the relative power of the two parties:

1. **Power of the Purchaser** is most evident when acquiring goods and services that are commonly available. The purchaser has multiple sources readily available to provide the desired materials. This increases competition and drives down prices. Examples are paper for printers, network cables, and long-distance carriers.

2. **Power of the Seller** is when there is a single or very few suppliers. This occurs often in IT when there is a unique product such as a major database package or specific network equipment. The seller dictates the price and the buyer must accept it or go through greater expense to implement an alternative (which may also be a competing unique product). The IT Manager selects products that, wherever possible, avoid this situation. Examples of products where the seller has a great deal of power to set the price are enterprise resource planning (ERP) software systems and local telephone companies.

In the end, the IT Manager needs the vendor as much as the vendor needs the IT Manager. The vendor wants to sell and the IT Manager wants to buy. The key is to find the middle ground that meets the requirements of all parties concerned. IT Managers most appreciate the vendors who solve problems and do not create any new ones. See Policy ITP-12-1 Vendor Management Policy as an example.

POLICY ITP-12-1.   Vendor Management Policy

Policy #:	ITP-12-1	**Effective:**	03/18/08	**Page #:**	1 of N
Subject:	Vendor Management Policy				

1.0 PURPOSE

IT spending represents a large portion of the company's annual expenses. This policy provides guidance on the development of positive vendor relationships. It is a supplement to existing company policies covering the purchasing of goods and services, and for the payment of invoices.

2.0 SCOPE

This policy encompasses all IT purchases of materials and services, from the recognition of a procurement need through the delivery of the final product.

3.0 POLICY

A. The IT department will provide the technical requirements to the purchasing department. The designated company purchasing agents will conduct all price and terms negotiations with vendors.

B. The goal of the IT vendor policy is to ensure the department obtains the best quality and delivery at the lowest practical price. To accomplish this, the department will divide its materials into:

1. Critical materials and services—essential for continued critical IT operations, or consumes at least 10 percent of the IT annual operating budget.
   a. Cultivate at least two primary vendors.
   b. Maintain close strategic alignment through annual discussions of mutual strategy and nondisclosure agreements.
   c. Annually compare prices to alternative vendors.
2. Non-critical materials and services.
   a. Provide specifications for acquisition by Purchasing department.
   b. Assist in the evaluation of products by new vendors.

C. The IT Manager will work closely with the Purchasing department to qualify reputable vendors for use by the IT department. As technologies change and new companies enter markets, it is beneficial to understand the materials and prices available in the marketplace. Based on IT trade information, the IT Manager may recommend new vendors for qualification by Purchasing.

D. All vendors will be selected in a fair and public manner. When submitting the purchase request to Purchasing the IT manager will:

1. Disclose family or business connections with the requested vendor by *anyone* in the IT department.
2. Disclose any gifts from that vendor to any IT employee during the previous 12 months.

E. The Legal department will review all agreements with external organizations prior to submitting them to executive approval. This includes:

1. Nondisclosure agreements.

    2. Terms of purchase.
    3. Ownership of intellectual property.
  F. When time permits all major purchases will be conducted through the Request for Proposal process.
    1. A clear and technical description will be provided to a list of at least 5 qualified vendors for their bid.
    2. Conduct a bidders conference to clarify the requirements and hear objections to specifications.
    3. Predetermine a scorecard for evaluation proposals prior to receiving the proposals.

4.0 REVISION HISTORY

Date	Revision #	Description of Change
03/18/08	1.0	Initial creation.

5.0 INQUIRIES

Direct inquiries about this policy to:

Tom Jones, CIO
Our Company, Inc.
2900 Corporate Drive
Columbus, OH 43215

Voice: 614-555-1234
Fax: 614-555-1235
E-mail: tjones@company.com

Revision #:	1.0	Supersedes:	N/A	Date:	03/18/08

[B] Vendor Selection

How can an IT Manager select a supplier who will actually deliver what is wanted, when it is wanted, and at the agreed upon price? Acquire vendor services based on the optimal solution for the IT department and not just on price. To avoid any form of collusion that would influence selection or inflate price, there must not be any familial or close personal relationships between a vendor and person with selection authority within the company. Never accept gifts from a vendor as they imply a favor to be reciprocated later.

Steering the company through the minefield of vendor incompetence is only half of the challenge; the other half is to understand the purchasing company's culture. An unrealistic internal culture can spell disaster for any undertaking even when employing the most competent service organization.

> ## COMMENT
>
> What is wrong with buying from the lowest bidder? Nothing—if the item is a commodity that is exactly the same no matter where it is purchased. However, consider specialty and build-to-order items. Once airborne, cynical military transport pilots like to remind their passengers that their aircraft was built by the lowest bidder.

An IT Manager should take care not to create enemies when negotiating vendor services. Information systems personnel are mobile; their paths cross in unexpected ways. Today's salesperson may be tomorrow's boss. While a person may try his or her best to avoid problem situations, many discoveries emerge only after the contract is signed.

[C]   Personnel Augmentation

IT departments typically hire the services of two types of outside personnel—consultants and temporary workers. Hire consultants to work on a specific project. They may work off site and only appear for meetings. Temporary workers may be on the job indefinitely.

The key to hiring consultants is to have a clearly defined objective for them. Vague objectives may consume the IT budget before the work is completed. Recriminations may pass back and forth, but the project is still incomplete. A clear vision of the scope and deliverables in the beginning will provide the most efficient use of consultants.

Another important task is to assign someone on the IT staff to work closely with consultants to ensure they understand what is being done and why. Otherwise, all of the knowledge required to support the final product may walk out of the door in the consultant's head!

Unlike consultants who are on-site for the duration of a project, temporary employees are just that—workers acting like employees for a limited amount of time. Temporary workers are assigned tasks in the same manner as regular employees, but serve at the convenience of the company. Some people support a short-term surge in work while others may linger for years. When their contract expires or when the company no longer requires their assistance, they can be terminated on short notice.

A variation on this is bringing in prospective new employees on short-term contracts. This permits the managers to evaluate the employees' performance before hiring them.

[D]   Acquiring Goods and Services

IT uses a variety of materials to support its operations. This runs the gamut from laser printer toner to network cables, workstation repair parts, monitors, paper for printers, and software manuals. Most IT materials are commodities purchased based on price and supplier reliability.

Companies closely watch their cash outflows. Acquisition of material is made through the purchasing or supply management departments. These departments ensure all purchases adhere to company policies and accounting rules. Where possible, IT should funnel their purchases through the same few purchasing agents. This will save time by eliminating the need to explain the same basic requirements for every purchase.

The purchasing department will provide information about vendors with which the company deals and verify the financial health of key suppliers. (What good is a warranty if the company has vanished?) Purchasing also will check with other customers to ensure the vendor fulfills its promises.

The legal department will review all contracts before approval. Just as the IT staff is expert in building and delivering quality service, the company's legal team is expert at monitoring current legal developments and protecting the company's interests in its agreements.

A critical management maxim is to "inspect what you expect." Even the most honest vendors sometimes make mistakes and the dishonest ones will consistently try to bid low and then deliver less. Most companies have a procedure to confirm upon receipt that an item meets purchase order requirements and to start the payment process for the invoice or bill received. A delay of payment can force an obstinate vendor to be cooperative in meeting contract obligations.

[E] Purchasing—The Magic Three Factors

The magic three factors in purchasing a product are how well it meets the need, the promptness of delivery, and its price. A product that meets the need but is not available when needed is not of much use. On the other hand, if it is available but highly priced, then questions also will be raised as to the wisdom of completing the purchase.

A. **Fits the need.** To purchase the right product, the buyer must have a clear understanding of what is wanted. Often this is not the case. The IT Manager may want to buy a certain item (e.g., LTO2 tape drive) but does not have the detailed understanding of all of the options available, the trade-off between these options, and which one best fits immediate and anticipated requirements. Further, the IT Manager rarely knows the same information about leading competitors of the technology.

It is always prudent for the IT Manager to check with several organizations that review the performance and features of the types of equipment in question. Many of these resources are available online, but may be biased. However, to save time, most companies align with their key vendors to provide these specifications and solutions. This is a lot like "the fox watching the hen house" since the vendor can specify items far more expensive than required. This is where the long-term key vendor approach comes in. The tradeoff is a bit of money lost to a less-than optimal-price against time saved by the company.

The IT Manager can reduce the vendor's temptation to overcharge by spreading the business among several similar companies. In this way, the threat of further competition will help to keep them focused on the account. It also provides multiple viewpoints about the same problem. Lazy IT Managers who hand blank checks to vendors will eventually be disappointed and probably replaced by the company.

B. **Can I have it when I need it?** The timing of product delivery is important. Companies do not want to pay for equipment before it is ready to use. On the other hand, they do not want workers to be idle while waiting for a key component to appear. It is important, when ordering complex material or hiring skilled temporary workers, that the vendor identify an expected delivery date. The purchase should be contingent on the vendor meeting that date.

Some IT Managers wait until the last minute to push through purchase requests for vital goods and services. They expect the salesperson to scramble and deliver the material on time. The miraculous delivery may not seem so when charges for express shipments appear on the invoice. (This would be where the vendor quotes the purchase price plus shipping.) If an urgent purchase is anticipated, the IT Manager should ask the desired vendor about availability. The vendor may order the required item and hold it at the warehouse until receiving the order.

Delivery also depends upon the goods ordered. While a factory may be able to afford to keep machinery in a finished goods warehouse for a while, it is difficult to do the same with people. Unlike equipment sitting in a warehouse, qualified personnel are rarely sitting around doing nothing. Lead-time is essential for locating and hiring skilled temporary workers. This becomes more complicated when hiring a large number of skilled people.

As with all things, there is a twist to the timing of purchases. It pays to know the vendor's fiscal cycle. Most sales forces strive to meet a sales quota. Accelerating a major purchase to fall within the current sales year may help the sales representative (and his manager) to meet sales objectives and possibly secure bonuses. In this situation, the IT Manager will gain additional price and feature advantages by accelerating the purchase.

COMMENT

The biggest cost driver in IT is standardization. It reduces the costs of support, training, and price per unit. Wherever practical, IT Managers should "fit" requests into the context of a standardized product before considering a different technology. However, a square peg is still square and a round hole is still round. If a standard product does not

> meet the requirements, the manager should not waste hour
> after hour trying to force the square peg into the round hole.

C. **How much will it cost?** Acquiring goods or services "at a fair price" requires an understanding of the suppliers' costs for what is being purchased. This is easier for commodity items than for specialty items. Determining the "fair" price begins with a comparison between products supplied by different companies. Calculate costs over a five-year useful life span. This includes the cost of a maintenance agreement, the cost of materials and consumables, and the expense of any required supporting devices.

A caveat of this is the "spot" market. Sometimes vendors carry much more inventory than their financial condition will bear. They may occasionally run a "sale" with special pricing to cut their inventory in a short time. Low-volume vendors generally offer these deals. Vendors of premium priced goods would rather scrap them than admit that they could have sold them at a lower price. Therefore, if there is flexibility in the goods or services wanted, and if the item will not significantly alter efforts to standardize products, the IT Manager should check the spot market before making a purchase.

IT Managers must take the time to learn about the things that motivate the vendor. Is it volume? Is it maintaining an ongoing sales relationship? Is it the protection of existing service contracts? Knowing what the vendor prizes most will provide the buyer with a negotiating advantage. Another important thing to understand is the vendor's cost structure. Ask the vendor what aspect of a purchase is driving its costs. They cannot sell goods at a loss unless they expect to recoup those funds later. Forcing a vendor into a money-losing situation will hurt the buyer in the end.

The lowest price is not everything. It is advantageous for the company to deal with the fewest number of vendors possible. It also is ideal for IT staff to have as few products as possible to learn and support. Therefore, if one of the company's "key vendors" is within 10 percent of the lowest price, buy it.

On the other side, vendors will reduce their marketing expense if they know they can pitch their best price up front. Vendors save time and labor haggling over pricing. Their understandings of the purchaser's company will help them to understand what is required to fill the company's needs.

[F]   Recognizing the Key Vendors

Key vendors are those who provide critical technology to the company. This could be the supplier of the "standard" IT server or network hub. It could be the company that provides the database management software, the operating system, or even the standard programming language.

Another way to identify a key vendor is one that is allotted a large portion of the IT budget. This might be any company that provides more than $1 million in goods and services or that is assigned more than five percent of the budget. Key vendors for an IT department rarely number more than a dozen. Keeping this number low is important because the IT Manager will spend time working with these companies to ensure their alignment with the department's direction.

IT Managers have a responsibility to train their critical vendors in how the company purchases materials or services. They need to understand such processes as the paperwork flow of purchases, who to call for accounts payable questions, and the name of the buyer for IT. This will allow them to address their own problems rather than pass them on the IT Manager. Some steps to take when working with key vendors include:

A. **Letting them in on the company's plans.** Key vendors are long-term partners. This creates an opportunity to work together and strategically align the company's IT plans with their product offerings. To some extent, this reduces the IT Manager's negotiating power, but it also increases price reductions and improves service since the seller spends less time on "selling" and more time on "servicing" the account.

   Before exchanging insights into strategies, both companies should enter into a nondisclosure agreement (see Worksheet 12-1 Mutual Non-Disclosure Agreement as an example). This document (approved by the legal department) assures the parties that neither will disclose to anyone else the confidential insights provided to the other. The vendor wants to keep its product changes under wraps and the company does not want the vendor to disclose its plans to competitors.

   With the nondisclosure agreement in hand, the IT Manager can share the company's three-year technology strategy with key vendors to explain the direction of the IT department and its anticipated requirements for goods and services. Often the vendor can provide explanations of technical trends that will work with the company's plans and indicate areas of technical opportunity.

   In turn, the vendors should share with the company their technical directions over the next several years. This might alert the IT Manager as to when the vendor intends to drop support for an old technology or make a change in pricing. The vendor also may provide some recommendations and cost estimates when the IT Manager is creating the annual budget.

WORKSHEET 12-1.   Mutual Non-Disclosure Agreement

MUTUAL NON-DISCLOSURE AGREEMENT

THIS NON-DISCLOSURE AGREEMENT (this "Agreement") is entered into this _______ day of ____________, 20 _______ and made effective the _______ day of ____________, 20 _____ by and between XYZ Company, Inc., a [name of state] corporation ("First Party"), and [name of client] ("Second Party"), an [type of entity] with offices at [address].

A. **Purpose.** Both parties, during the term of this agreement, will have access to and become familiar with various trade secrets, confidential and proprietary information, technology, data, computer source code, designs, development concepts, plans and know-how of the other party and heretofore known only to its employees, agents, and independent contractors. These trade secrets and confidential or proprietary information, including without limitation, client data, client information, company data, software, related products, information relating to software or technology provided by first party to second party for use in consultation regarding and in the design and development of the software and/or related products, first party's operations or the financial conditions or results of its operations, its marketing or business strategies or plans, the names, addresses, case histories or specifications of any of its customers or prospective customers, the types of goods or services sold or proposed to be sold to any customers or prospective customers of first party, the names, addresses, training, background or information regarding any person who is or was an employee, agent or independent contractor of first party and other compilations of information, which are owned by first party and which are regularly used in operation of its business (all of the foregoing shall be referred to collectively as "confidential information"), are the result of large amounts of time, effort and expense of first party in developing such information and in recruiting and training such employees, agents and independent contractors and are essential to the success of first party.

B. **Covenants of Non-Disclosure.** Absent receipt of express written consent from the other party, each party shall:

   1. Not use any confidential information for his own purposes other than in connection with his activities for or on behalf of the other party and shall refrain from, either intentionally, directly or indirectly, during the term of this agreement or after termination of this agreement, using, disclosing, disseminating, or publishing, to or with any person, firm, company or entity, or knowingly making available to any others, for any use other than in connection with the transactions contemplated hereby, any confidential information; and

   2. Restrict disclosure of such confidential information only to others as may reasonably be necessary in the conduct of the other party's business; and

   3. Advise all such persons of the strict obligations of confidentiality hereunder; and

   4. Take such steps to protect the confidentiality of confidential information as required by the other party's policies and procedures and such additional steps as would be taken by a reasonably prudent person to protect confidential materials.

C. **Public Knowledge.** Notwithstanding the foregoing, information provided to the undersigned shall not constitute confidential information if such information (i) is or becomes generally available to the public other than as a result of a disclosure by or through the undersigned or the undersigned' partners, directors, officers, employees or affiliates in contravention of this agreements, (ii) was already available to, or in the possession of, the undersigned prior to its disclosure by, or at the direction of, the Second Party in connection with the undersigned's evaluation of a possible transaction, or (iii) is or becomes available to the undersigned from another source.

This Agreement shall be construed in accordance with [name of state] law. The parties hereto agree that any action concerning, relating to or involving this Agreement must be filed in [name of county] County, [name of state] and the parties hereby consent to the jurisdiction of the courts in [name of county] County.

First Party: XYZ Company, Inc.	Second Party:
Signature	Signature
Title	Title
Print Name	Print Name
Date	Date

B. **Negotiating a national pricing agreement.** The sales process is very expensive for vendors. Vendors closely aligned with the company may offer a national pricing agreement. This is a schedule of the company's best price based on the company's historical purchasing volumes. A price list reduces costs for the vendors and allows the buyer to compare prices without calling for quotes.

C. **Reviewing their business continuity plans.** Once a vendor becomes an important part of the company's future success, it may be important to inspect its business continuity plans. Close alignment means that if the vendor has a problem, the IT department also has a problem. Written and tested business continuity plans demonstrate a corporate commitment to minimize the impact of disasters on the vendor-company and therefore on its customers.

D. **Being careful not to trust too much.** The IT Manager must always be on guard against allowing the convenience of a critical vendor relationship to overshadow good business decisions. Vendors definitely watch out for their own interests. They may attempt to preempt IT's purchase of a competitor's product by alluding to a nonexistent product or features on a product (commonly known as "vaporware").

A recurring sales pitch vendors make is that they want to be the company's sole supplier of a given product or service. Of course they do! They want to inflate their prices! *Sole suppliers are never a good idea.* Whenever they exist due to unique products, consider adding similar technologies or moving to a commodity technology. Although key vendors are convenient, compare their prices to their main competitors to ensure they are not slowly inflating their prices.

E. **Monitoring the financial health of key vendors.** Companies need their key vendors to be financially healthy and to remain in business for as long as the IT department needs them. The company's purchasing agent must periodically verify the financial viability of key vendors to provide early warning of a collapse or serious problems. If problems are detected, the IT Manager should create a plan of action to implement if the supplier is in danger of insolvency.

COMMENT

An awkward situation is the "captive" customer where a sister company provides goods or services. One author worked for a company that owned a chain of PC stores. Every purchase was required to pass through them; however, the sales representative was not paid any commission for these sales. Other companies were anxious for the business, but the company was forced to use this "in-house" supplier. Consequently, prices were high, service was poor, and deliveries late.

[G] Commodity Vendors

A commodity is an item that is essentially the same no matter where it comes from. A sealed copy of Microsoft Windows is the same no matter where purchased, yet prices may vary. Items identified by the IT Manager as commodities can be procured through the normal purchasing processes since where it is purchased is primarily a matter of price and delivery.

The goal of the purchaser is to drive for products that are commodities. Commodities markets are highly competitive and the prices tend to be cost based. Commodity suppliers strive to drive down their costs since margins are already thin. In a commodity market, the company with the best managed supply chain will typically be the lowest cost supplier.

The goal of a commodity vendor is to establish that its product is somehow not a commodity and superior to other like items. The intention is to widen margins. The vendor achieves this with a high level of customer service, product "branding," or the additional features.

[H] Low-Volume Vendors

Low-volume vendors provide small quantities or on-demand materials. They are not welcome to "drop in and chat" with the IT Manager. Low-volume vendors make up the bulk of the IT department's vendors. Typically, the IT Manager will not spend a lot of time cultivating the relationship.

The advantage of low-volume vendors is that they will work to become key vendors. This may naturally occur when the company migrates from one technology to another. The vendor also may provide special pricing in the "spot" market—when a company must unload some of its inventory and is willing to do so at a reduced price.

§ 12.03 PLAY BY THE RULES

[A] Overview

Every company has its own processes for spending money. The purchasing of materials should not be the IT Manager's responsibility. It should be the province of the company's purchasing or supply management department. Leave it this way. Otherwise, the IT Manager will drown in a raging sea of administrative detail. To minimize the amount of time spent in this area, the IT Manager should learn all facets of the company's purchasing processes, policies, and procedures to ensure the smoothest flow of requests. It is easier to learn the purchasing department's processes than it is to fight a losing battle against them.

COMMENT

It is far cheaper for a vendor to "wine and dine" an IT Manager than it is to lower its prices. This could include expensive dinners, free tickets to sports events, occasional gifts or even paid vacations. IT Managers may feel that it is just a perquisite of their position. Such a rationalization is wrong and unethical. Vendors only spend this money in the expectation of future favorable treatment. IT Managers know that the "gifts" will stop if purchases cease. It is the vendor's way of bypassing the company's safeguards against wasting money.

Some companies have a policy that prohibits the acceptance of gifts from vendors (including free meals) over a certain amount (often $20). Other companies only require the prompt reporting of these activities. Otherwise the purchasing agent may find the IT Manager demanding a high-priced item from a specific vendor for "technical" reasons.

[B] Maximizing the Purchasing Department's Expertise

The purchasing department ensures that the company obtains the best goods, delivery, and price combination for all procurement. Just as IT Managers are the experts in their field, treat the purchasing department likewise. After sending the appropriate paperwork to the purchasing department, the IT Manager should relax and wait for the goods to appear.

Although everyone has been cheated by someone at some time, employees in the purchasing department have likely encountered it much more often. Their procedures weed out fraudulent vendors before the company's funds are at risk. They go through several steps to qualify vendors, including:

A. Confirming the financial "health" of the vendor through a financial rating review.
B. Verifying the status of the vendor in the community, through such things as the Better Business Bureau and customer referrals.
C. Drafting the purchase order, which will include the company's standard terms and conditions for purchasing goods. Modifications to these terms are between the purchasing department and the vendor—and not the concern of the IT Manager.

Due to the complexity of the specification for purchasing IT products, most companies leave it to the IT Manager to select the desired product and vendor. While this may save time, IT-controlled purchasing decisions may be reviewed by internal auditors.

Purchasing departments must not succumb to sales representatives bypassing the IT department. Just because they claim their product is a low-cost alternative to the item specified by the IT Manager, that does not make it true.

[C] Legal Review of Contracts

IT Managers will encounter several vendor management documents on a regular basis. The first is the company's purchase order. A purchase order is a legally binding document. The company's legal team carefully reviewed the terms in these documents. The IT Manager must never alter them. Vendors who have any complaints must work them out with the purchasing department.

For example, before a temporary worker can work on site, a workers' compensation insurance policy is required, usually for a set amount. This will be included in the terms of the purchase order but rarely discussed during negotiations between the IT Manager and the employment agency. Large companies routinely provide this, but small companies cannot—especially on short notice. Only the company's purchasing agent can approve exceptions to required terms.

Another legal document is a service contract. These can run the gamut from repairing servers to staffing the service desk. The terms of the agreement may drive up the vendor's cost, which in turn will drive up the price to the company. When negotiating these agreements, request only the minimum services. However, once approved by all parties, never excuse the vendor from performing to the level specified in the agreement. If the vendor promised to provide something at a set price, then it must deliver or renegotiate the contract at a lower price.

The company's legal team should always review contracts for goods or services. Agreements may seem straightforward until added clauses contradict the contract's original intent. The company's attorneys can make sense of these complex documents and protect the company.

COMMENT

When hiring consultants or temporary employees, IT should always review the agreement with the human resources department to ensure adherence to all relevant laws and company policies.

[D]   Receiving the Goods

Many things can go wrong with an order, and the receiving dock is the company's first line of defense against incorrect shipments. Materials can be damaged in transit or even the wrong item shipped. The receiving dock clerk should be required to match the purchase order to the item received to ensure that the correct item has arrived before accepting the material.

In most companies, materials must be "properly received" before an invoice can be paid. This provides a "check and balance" because the payment cannot be processed until the person who ordered the materials approves the receipt. In a crisis, IT materials and parts might come in the front door by express delivery and bypass the receiving clerk. In those cases, the IT Manager must properly submit the paperwork so the vendor can be paid.

For services, the IT Manager must verify to the accounts payable department that the services billed on the invoice are correct. Compare copies of contractor and temporary worker time sheets to the invoice to validate the expense.

[E]   Accounting's Role in Positive Vendor Relations

Once the correct goods arrive, the IT Manager should timely pay the vendor. This is one area IT Managers often overlook because they do not consider it to be their responsibility to ensure prompt payment. Yet, this action can greatly raise their value in the vendor's eyes. Orders are nice to receive, but all vendors need a cash flow to remain in business. Do not let the company's Byzantine accounts payable processes ruin a carefully nurtured vendor relationship.

Sometimes paperwork gets lost, is incomplete and shuffled into a pending basket, or held by an accounts payable clerk for other reasons. IT Managers can pass the invoice off to a faceless clerk or help the clerk to work through issues that arise. Just as a high level of service is expected within the vendor's organization, the vendor will be pleased to receive the same courtesy.

[F]   Budgets Drive the Purchases

Budgets are a company's way of projecting costs against anticipated revenues. The drawback is the need to forecast major purchases far in advance of their actual purchase (if they are even purchased at all). The challenge for the IT Manager is to predict what will be needed and the price of each component.

Before the annual budgeting cycle for the upcoming year, the IT Managers should visit with each of the key vendors. Ask them what products will come to market in the next year. Ask them about prices for the new technology and projected price reductions for existing equipment. If this is a true partnership, they can provide most of this information. All of this is fodder for assembling a budget.

§ 12.04   CONSULTING AND TEMPORARY PERSONNEL SERVICES

[A]   Overview

IT departments occasionally require the services of nonemployees. This may include supplemental technical support for a specific project or temporary staff augmentation. In either case, temporary technical workers are an expensive purchase. Unlike a machine that delivers something tangible, much of an IT worker's output is intangible. The IT Manager ensures that these workers deliver the value for the price the company is paying.

A distinction is drawn here between consultants who are brought in to assist with defined tasks of a fixed duration and temporary employees (temps) who are integrated into the department and assigned tasks like any other team member. Temps may work on a range of assignments and remain on site for an indefinite length of time.

Consulting services are often justified because in-house skills are unavailable, extra personnel are required, or the firm is seeking an unbiased, objective opinion. Many of these personnel are well paid, ambitious individuals who enjoy the variety of challenging assignments that a consulting firm offers.

Outside consultants can be objective because they are not embroiled in the organization's political struggles. They should render professional judgments based on the facts. Unfortunately, whoever hired the consultant may have influenced the selection of a "cooperative" consultant, thereby losing objectivity.

Sometimes the workload is such that the company will arrange for temporary workers to supplement the staff. Unlike consultants who are engaged for the duration of a project, temporary employees are just that—workers acting like employees for a limited amount of time. "Temps" can be very useful during seasonal workload surges. They are useful during the long-term absence of an employee.

Highly skilled temps are similar to contractors except their tenure is not tied to a contract. In some cases, they linger for years. Some companies use highly skilled temporary employees on a large scale to push the responsibility of maintaining a workforce onto the employment agency (e.g., service desk, PC repair). Based on their agreement with the employment agency, this allows the company to rapidly scale back the number of temps on site. (Rapidly scaling up the workforce is difficult due to finding and training a large number of people at the same time.)

It is a good management practice to locate and prequalify consulting services before the company actually needs them. In some cases, the agreements and pricing can be determined far in advance. Later, if a staff increase is required on short notice, the agreement can be referenced, which will shorten the acquisition cycle.

Referrals are the best way to find reliable contractors. The IT Manager should maintain memberships in IT professional organizations to develop these contacts. By discussing the performance of various vendors with peers, the manager can learn which ones to avoid as well as which ones to hire.

[B] Types of Temporary Personnel Organizations

Consulting firms can provide a range of services or focus on a select few. Choosing the right organization to supplement the IT department is a very important task. Often the size of the company selected depends on what is needed. Companies tend to fall into the general categories of small and large.

Small organizations are usually local and may have some idea about the buyer's company and its services. They will work hard to build a long-term relationship with their customers. Small companies typically focus on a single technology (such as UNIX) or are broad-based but technically shallow.

Small companies may be financially unstable and no longer in business when needed problems arise—even if under a warranty period. The loss of one large customer can force some small companies to fold.

Large professional services organizations try to provide "one-stop shopping." In a sense, the IT Manager drops the staffing problem on their door step and they provide all of the answers (for a fee). If the large company does not have the required expertise on hand, it will sub-contract it to someone who does.

The dark side to large companies is that, from time to time, they have workers not currently hired out to customers. These "off-the-bench" workers are sent to customers as experts in something they know little about. To prevent this, IT Managers must personally interview and approve every consultant assigned to a project.

In addition, contract workers might make work for themselves to extend their employment. The old saying that good contract workers must be dragged kicking and screaming from the building is not too far off the mark. Always document contract workers' exit plans before hiring them.

[C] Utilizing Temporary Personnel

Many of the reasons for acquiring contracted temporary personnel are the same as for contracting a consultant. In addition to being less expensive than consultants, temps offer other benefits to the company.

Because employers compete in a market for skilled talent, it is best to avoid designation as a company that hires and quickly fires. Just as the firm compares job candidates when hiring, job seekers compare the merits of different employers. One of the major reasons that job candidates do not accept positions is a company's unstable employment profile.

COMMENT

> Some companies use temporary technical staff as a "try before you buy" approach. Prospective employees are hired through an agency as temporary employees for a set period—usually six months. At the end of that time the company can hire them as regular staff or release them with no further obligations.

On the other hand, there are some valid reasons for not employing temporary workers. One involves the learning curve—the time needed to master a job or learn a firm's processes. The more complex the job is, the larger the learning curve will be. When a temp leaves the company, the time spent training that person will be lost.

Another reason is that temps may not be very loyal. If a better opportunity arises, they will leave, and all of their training time is lost. While this is a valid concern, many contract workers are comfortable with temporary employment and commit to the task. The more professional the responsibility, the greater the loyalty that person will exhibit to the profession than to the firm. This may account, in part, for the turnover of skilled personnel who feel their employers are not giving them opportunities to gain professional maturity.

[D] Ground Rules for Engaging Temporary Staff

Consultants can be valuable assets if a proper relationship is established. It is imperative to maintain proper conditions for maximum benefit while minimizing the cost. There are several procedures to follow when acquiring the services of an outside consultant.

A. **Define specifications and scope.** This will give the consultant a clear understanding of what to do and what not to do. The IT Manager should clearly state what is expected as far as specifications and have this confirmed in writing. A major mistake when using a consultant is to hire the consultant before clear specifications are developed and then complain about the cost. If the IT Manager cannot clearly articulate which services are required and the desired product to be created, then how can the consultant provide an accurate price? Any wasted effort will be included in the bill even if the firm does not get what it wanted. Imagine a giant taxi meter sitting on the consultant's desk. As long as the consultant is on site, the meter runs whether the taxi is moving or not. IT Managers should manage consultants just as any other employee—except that they should be used for the expertise for which they were hired. Do not drop them at a desk and walk away without instructions or there will be a bill for a lot of wasted time!

B. **Clearly define what is needed.** The IT Manager should provide a written job description to the contracting company whenever requesting workers. This helps them to establish the appropriate billing rate for each level of expertise. Whoever works on the project, the IT Manager should ensure that person remains on it for its duration. The consulting company should not be allowed to change personnel without IT's approval.

C. **Required documentation.** The documentation left behind after the completion of a project may be the only future source of reference for that job. Documentation is expensive and often ignored to save time or money. This type of savings will only create more expenses later. When defining documentation requirements, the IT Manager should make certain the consultant adheres to the company's standards.

D. **Monitor the consultant's progress.** Outline a monitoring procedure for the consultant in the contract. Obtain feedback on the status of the consultant's work at predetermined time intervals by defining efforts in the smallest measurable units and relating them to percentages of the total time. As progress is reported, the cumulative percent of progress completed can be compared to the cumulative dollars spent. These two values should be in accord to ensure dollars budgeted will not be depleted before the project is completed. Use a Gantt chart to compare these values. The effectiveness, or lack thereof, of the consultant's performance should not be a surprise at the end of the project. Consultants are self-directed persons; they must be to survive in the profession. However, they may be sidetracked by extending their scope or misinterpreting directions received from more than one source. As with any newly employed person, do not leave consultants alone for long periods. Nor should there be any misunderstanding as to the status of an in-process project. Document this in a clear, easy-to-understand, written, dated, and signed report.

E. **Always pair a consultant with an employee for development projects.** If consultants work alone, when they walk out of the door, all of the project knowledge will go with them. True, there may be system documentation, but experience provides so much more. Pairing an employee to work alongside the consultant builds in-house expertise. Additionally, it is a good way to infuse a different technical perspective into the IT staff. Ignoring this step may require the company to have to rehire the consultant for a high fee to provide ongoing system maintenance.

F. **Know who is being hired.** When hiring a consultant, the services of a company or a specific individual are employed. When hiring a specific individual, it is easier to estimate the time and cost for a project based on that person's proven expertise. However, will that person be available when he is needed? This is difficult if the purchasing paperwork is held up by budget politics. If a large number of people are required, then a consulting company will select and "validate" the credentials of the people provided.

G. **Ensure that intellectual property remains the property of the company.** All contract employees must sign an agreement that all intellectual property created while contracted by the company is the property of the company (see Policy ITP-12-2 Ownership of Intellectual Property Policy).

POLICY ITP-12-2. Ownership of Intellectual Property Policy

Policy #:	ITP-12-2	**Effective:**	03/18/08	**Page #:**	1 of N
Subject:	Ownership of Intellectual Property Policy				

1.0 PURPOSE

It is critical to protect the intellectual property rights of the company. This policy provides guidance on protecting the intellectual property of the company when engaging outside IT consultants.

2.0 SCOPE

This policy encompasses all work performed by IT personnel that are not employees of the company. This policy shall apply to intellectual property of all types, including but not limited to any invention, discovery, trade secret, technology, scientific or technological development, research data and computer software regardless of whether subject to protection under patent, trademark, copyright or other laws.

3.0 POLICY

All services provided by outside vendors shall be considered "work for hire", and all intellectual property rights that may apply to that work shall belong to the company. All vendors will be required to sign an intellectual property rights agreement before any work can be done for the company.

4.0 REVISION HISTORY

Date	Revision #	Description of Change
03/18/08	1.0	Initial creation.

Direct inquiries about this policy to:

Tom Jones, CIO
Our Company, Inc.
2900 Corporate Drive
Columbus, OH 43215

Voice: 614-555-1234
Fax: 614-555-1235
E-mail: tjones@company.com

Revision #:	1.0	Supersedes:	N/A	Date:	03/18/08

[E]   Outsourcing

At some point, a company may decide that an outside company can more effectively manage a portion of its IT operations. The idea is that a company focused on a single aspect of IT, such as PC repair, can do it better than a company that does it as one small part of its operations. Some IT Managers believe contracting for this service is similar to contracting for electricity or other essentials that a company could but does not provide for itself.

Outsourcing agreements typically provide for a company to deliver a specific service for an extended period such as:

A. Service desk services.
B. Database operations.
C. Hardware maintenance.
D. Network operations.
E. Training.
F. Web site operations.
G. Programming.
H. IT computer operations.
I. Systems analysis.
J. End-user computing support.

Replacing an existing business function brings with it major training issues about local processes, personal contacts, local technical issues, etc. To overcome this, the outsourcing company normally hires the employees whose function is being outsourced. This presents several opportunities as well as problems:

A. It reduces operating cost through (hopefully) better management. Outside management with no internal loyalties may be needed to make necessary staffing changes.

B. Consider using outsourcing to start up a new operation. Once a professional facilities management service starts up an operation, the department can be turned over to internal operations management. The outside service can stay on temporarily to ensure everything is up and running, while permanent employees have a chance to develop skills necessary to run the department.
C. It can be a step toward avoiding unionization or for breaking up a union shop. Using an outside management service or outsourcing will convert the facilities to a nonunion operation without going through a difficult decertification process. If this is the company's intent, it must consult with legal counsel prior to proceeding.
D. Outsourcing may provide temporary technical services where no in-house talent is available, such as to conduct an asset inventory.

There are some issues to be aware of when using an outsourcing service operation. The operating responsibility shifts away from the firm's own controlled management, and the outside management may not understand the firm's particular needs. Also, implementing an outsourcing agreement may impact employee morale. Information systems personnel may resent reporting to an "outsider." This can be a greater problem when there is an expected reduction in the workforce. Problems can escalate to sabotage.

The IT Manager should never enter into this type of arrangement without an agreed-upon exit plan for the contractor. Relationships can sour over time and once a contractor has all of the expertise in its control, it may be very expensive or difficult to eliminate. The agreement should allow that, at a minimum, the company can hire the contractor's on-site employees for no penalty.

Outsourcing to offshore companies introduces other complications. Areas with low labor costs tend to be in developing countries. The technical infrastructure in these places is less fault-tolerant, civil order is more fragile, and the company may lack an adequate, tested business continuity plan. Once these and other factors are considered, the IT Manager should be able to determine whether the benefit of the low-cost service outweighs the potential loss of service to the company's customers.

§ 12.05 REQUESTS FOR PROPOSAL

[A] Overview

Selecting vendors for major purchases can be a tedious process. Like any large endeavor with many details, it is best managed as a project. Few people begin a major purchase with crystal clear ideas of what is needed down to the fine details. They begin with a general idea, such as to hire a vendor to provide on-site workstation support. The request for proposal (RFP) process can help clarify many of the lesser details through discussions with the vendors. In this sense, the vendors help shape the solution as they bid for the business.

The RFP process is normally run by the purchasing department with technical advice from the IT Manager. However, in some companies, the responsibilities are switched with IT running the process under the purchasing department's guidance. In either case, purchasing is the team that should oversee the final selection.

A well-run RFP process is a tedious process for both the company and the bidders. It should only be used for major purchases of services or technology.

[B] Project Startup

As with any major endeavor, a well-executed start is critical to the project's success. The following steps will help ensure a good start to any project:

A. Conduct a kick-off meeting with the project team.
B. Confirm project plan, scope, approach, and schedule.
C. Identify and schedule key interviews with staff and management.
D. Collect, review, and summarize background materials.
E. Identify project templates to be used.

[C] Preparing Requests for Proposal

To begin the process, a formal RFP letter should be sent to all possible candidates. The RFP should define the format of the proposal to ensure a responding vendor can be evaluated and compared with others.

The RFP must contain several essential elements:

A. Technical specifications of the hardware, software, or services desired. This may include CPU speeds, disk capacity, or working hours for contract personnel. These details will drive the cost of goods and services, so they must be clear and request the minimum reasonably required. Any unstated (but necessary) specification provides an opportunity for the bidder to underbid the price knowing that a later expansion will be required.
B. Mandatory requirements should be clearly separated from the "nice-to-have" requirements. Vendors must know early in the process the minimum qualifications for the bid.
C. A statement that selection will not be based on price alone and that the company has the option to reject all bids.
D. Any required terms and conditions for the purchase. This should be the same as the boilerplate on the back of a purchase order.
E. The due date for submitting all proposals. This is normally 30 to 60 days after the bid is published.
F. The date of the bidder's conference.

COMMENT

One author bid a workstation support agreement for three full-time PC technicians to support a major factory. Bringing in a substitute technician to cover vacations was awkward because the facility encompassed several buildings and 2 million square feet. Instead, the vendor was required to schedule technician vacations during the factory's annual summer maintenance break when the workers were away. This negated the need for trained vacation substitutes and lowered the vendor's cost.

About four months into the agreement, the vendor pushed hard to be relieved of some of the required deliverables. This is a form of bait and switch where the vendor bids low to gain the business with the intent to reduce service after a settling-in period. After several calls to the vendor reminding them they must fulfill what they agreed to, the purchasing department gave the vendor 30 days to fully comply or the agreement would be terminated.

Never write an RFP that is clearly skewed toward a single vendor or when the vendor has already been selected. Either action will tarnish the company's reputation leading fewer vendors to bid in the future.

When writing specifications for the bid, it helps to understand what drives the vendors' cost. If an optional item is identified as a mandatory requirement, the price might be driven higher. One way to understand the vendor's cost structure is to look at it from their point of view. What material needs to be purchased to meet the agreement? How many skilled people need to be involved to fulfill the agreement and for how long? What should they cost? If you were the bidder, what sort of budget would you need to fulfill these customer requirements?

[D] Developing RFP Evaluation Criteria

After the RFP is approved by the company and before submitting it to vendors, the evaluation criteria for bids should be determined. An easy way to accomplish this is by assigning one of two value types to each specification:

A. A mandatory requirement without which the bid will be automatically rejected. This might include a required service level, a minimum CPU speed, or a firm delivery date.

B. Optional-but-important factors. Each of these should be assigned a weight to indicate which specifications are more important than others.

Evaluate the costs and expandability of hardware and software purchases over a three-year period. This should include mandatory supplies (some companies sell the equipment cheap and then overcharge for expensive supplies), service contracts, and service level agreements.

Training, documentation, conversion, performance, and acceptance are all optional items that can be included in the bargaining process. Some general items to consider include:

A. Delivery or start dates.
B. Finish or completion dates.
C. Vendor responsibilities vs. customer responsibilities.
D. Pricing methods for purchase, lease, or rent.
E. Annual cost escalators for multi-year contracts.
F. How and when the vendor will bill.
G. Removing the vendor's disclaimers.
H. Provisions for equipment, software, and personnel backup.
I. Emergency and preventive maintenance.
J. Provision for detailed specifications for hardware, software, or service performance.
K. Realistic launch dates for implementations.

In addition, IT should avoid long-term contracts with new or unproven vendors. All contracts also should include performance clauses and penalties for nonperformance or late delivery times.

The compilation of weighted factors is best done using the Delphi method. The IT Manager should have seven people who are familiar with the proposal independently list those factors important to the purchase and their corresponding weights. Then those seven send the lists to a person who was not involved with the selection to compile. This person will make a list of all the factors and return the new list to the seven participants. They will once again go through these factors, choosing and weighting their choices, and new lists will go back to the person to compile the list of most prevalent factors and their weights. Those items assigned low-weight values or only mentioned once should be discarded. This process should continue until a general consensus is reached.

COMMENT

An important mandatory requirement for any long-term agreement is that the vendor possess a documented, tested business continuity plan. An IT Manager does not want someone else's disaster to impact local operations. The continuity plan of the successful bidder should be reviewed and approved before placing an order.

[E] Bidder's Conference

A bidder's conference is a meeting between the company and all vendors bidding for the contract. This important meeting helps to identify overlooked specifications and may drive the price. The open forum allows all bidders to hear the same answer to questions. The purchasing department normally conducts the bidder's conference.

The format for the meeting should be as follows:

A. All bidders sign in as they enter so they can later receive an updated RFP that includes changes made during the meeting.

B. All representatives of the company introduce themselves and explain their roles in the RFP development.

C. A representative of the company reads the RFP line by line. At the end of each section, the company representative asks the bidders if there are any questions or suggestions for improving it.
   1. Every suggestion or question is written down for later evaluation.
   2. Clarifications can be agreed to on the spot.

D. A representative of the company asks the bidders if there are any specifications in the RFP that prevent them from bidding on the proposal. If there are, the company should consider whether that item is essential to the bid or can be moved to the optional category.

E. At the end of the reading of the RFP document, open the meeting for questions from the bidders.

F. Within a week the updated RFP is reissued to all bidders.

[F] Evaluating the Bids

Reject all submissions received after the cutoff date for submitting bids. This is only fair to the companies who submitted bids on time.

Review bids as a team, which should include at least one IT person familiar with the technology and a purchasing agent. The team should begin with the completeness of the bids. Remove from consideration any bid that does not fulfill all of the mandatory requirements. If the bidder's response to a mandatory item is ambiguous, the company may choose to ask for a clarification or not. Use a form similar to Worksheet 12-2 Bidder Analysis to help you rank the bidders objectively.

Vendors who provide clear and complete information asked for in the RFP and meet preliminary evaluation standards should be selected for more detailed analysis. Those who do not should be removed from further consideration. Bids should address the specification elements noted in the RFP. The goal is to narrow the field to the final five candidates for close evaluation.

The final vendors may be required to demonstrate their ability to perform as promised in the bid. This includes demonstrations of equipment, customer recommendations, and specific tests used to prove performance benchmarks. Validate every critical requirement in the RFP by testing or through a performance demonstration.

WORKSHEET 12-2.   Bidder Analysis

Bidder Analysis							
Good and Services			**Bidder 1**	**Bidder 2**	**Bidder 3**	**Bidder 4**	**Bidder 5**
Mandatory Requirements	**Meets**						
Deliver 20 units by April 1							
3 GHz CPU							
1 TB Disk							
Optional Requirements	**Rating (1 to 10)**	**Weight**					
Expandability – Technical							
Expandability – Price							
Training Cost							
Training Availability							
Service Agreement							
Financial Analysis							
Purchase Price			8				
Service over three years			8				
Materials over three years			8				
Training			6				
Installation			8				
Vendor Analysis							
Customer References			10				
Dun & Bradstreet Report			10				
Better Business Bureau search			8				
Internet search			6				

If the bid includes a service agreement, the bidders should present the resumes of the people they are proposing for the assignment. Each person should be "locked in" to the account for at least one year to stop the vendor from presenting top-notch people and switching them for novices.

The company should keep all bids and notes pertaining to the evaluation process. Unhappy bidders who did not win the contract may file complaints about the process later. All records should be stored by the purchasing department and available for review by the company's auditors. The legal and accounting departments will determine the ultimate retention period for this material.

An evaluation of the vendor is just as important as the response to the RFP. Is it financially viable enough to deliver as promised? Is it known for ethical business practices or just the opposite? Verify this in several ways:

A. Financial health.
B. Annual 10-K reports for publicly held companies.
C. Ethical business practices.
D. Customer reports (ask for and verify references).
E. Web searches for "I hate" Web sites.
F. Searches of news archives for published problems.
G. Local Better Business Bureau reports.

COMMENT

The IT Manager should contact the vendor's customers to make a final evaluation before signing an agreement. Ask if they would recommend the vendor's product or service. If they do, set up a site visit. Be sure to talk to the project manager who would be familiar with the details—not the upper executives who do not hear about the routine problems.

Visit the operation to see anything reflecting the vendor's accomplishment. Since most people are reluctant to offer negative information, ask the following:

A. Would you use the same vendor again? If so, why? What has been the major problem with the vendor? Do you know other users of the vendor's product? Are they generally happy? If so, why? Who are the other users? What are their names and telephone numbers?
B. How long does it take for the vendor to respond to issues? Are the people who respond knowledgeable and friendly? Has the vendor ever lied? Has the vendor had the resources to resolve your problem(s)?

C. Does the hardware/software satisfy your needs? Follow up with questions about how long they have had the system and how often it has gone down. Ask about its expandability and upgrading possibilities.

D. Do the users like the system or service? Ask to talk to users to confirm this. Ask users their likes and dislikes about the system or service and why.

E. Ask how long it took to put the hardware/software into operation. Did they receive adequate training? Are the user manuals easy to understand and follow?

F. Is the operation or service provided better than what they could do themselves? If so, why? Is the service worth the cost?

G. Were there any unexpected or hidden costs? What was the nature of these costs? Were the costs reasonable? Was the vendor confronted? If so, what was the reaction?

H. Were the vendor's employees easy to work with? Did their salesperson follow up after the sale? Does the vendor exhibit a genuine interest in the success of the service or product?

I. If you were starting all over, what would you do differently?

13

DOCUMENTATION: GETTING EVERYONE ON THE SAME PAGE

§ 13.01 OVERVIEW
    [A] Purpose and Scope
    [B] Critical Policies to Develop Based on This Chapter

§ 13.02 DEVELOPING A REFERENCE DOCUMENTATION POLICY
    [A] Overview
    [B] Policy Objectives

§ 13.03 DOCUMENT FORMATS
    [A] Overview
    [B] Know Your Audience
    [C] Readability

§ 13.04 DOCUMENT MANAGEMENT
    [A] Overview
    [B] Enforcing Quality
    [C] Storage and Access
    [D] Version Control

§ 13.05 SYSTEM REFERENCE INSTRUCTIONS
    [A] Process Overview
    [B] End-User Reference Documentation
    [C] Operations Reference Documentation
    [D] Service Desk Reference Documentation
    [E] Technical Reference Documentation
    [F] Program Testing Reference Documentation

§ 13.06 PROJECT DOCUMENTATION
    [A] Overview
    [B] Identification and Responsibility

§ 13.07 SYSTEMS ANALYSIS DOCUMENTATION
    [A] Overview
    [B] Systems Documentation Binder
    [C] Scope

[D]   Product Specifications
[E]   Schedule
[F]   Risk Assessment
[G]   Stakeholders
[H]   Recommendations

§ 13.08   FLOWCHARTING STANDARDS
[A]   Purpose
[B]   Global System Flowcharts
[C]   Enterprise System Flowcharts
[D]   System Flowchart
[E]   Procedure Flowchart
[F]   Dataflow Diagrams
[G]   Supplemental Dataflow Conventions
[H]   Program Flowcharts
[I]   Unified Modeling Language™
[J]   IDEF

§ 13.01 OVERVIEW

[A] Purpose and Scope

The purpose of documenting IT processes and procedures is to save money. When installing or creating processes, programs, and hardware, someone analyzed the requirements, planned the solution, and created it. This analysis, creation, and implementation all took a considerable amount of time, thought, and planning. Yet, often this knowledge is not captured and slips away into distant memory. IT Managers have the choice between paying a bit more to capture this information during implementation, or paying someone else later to go through the same tedious process of analyzing and learning about a process so they can address a problem. When the next problem occurs, they will again pay someone to analyze and learn about the process, and on and on.

Why is this lesson so difficult to learn? Well-written reference documentation for all IT processes pays for the time required to develop it, over and over again. The IT Manager's task is to provide policies and processes to make this documentation easy to write and yet capture the essential information useful in the future. To accomplish this, they must publish a policy guiding when to document a process and the information this document should contain.

Processes that must be documented include business critical systems, processes where no deviation is permitted (such as data backups and security measures), and processes that rarely fail. Omit from this requirement processes that are one-time data systems and ad hoc reports.

The quality and comprehensiveness of IT reference documentation is an important determinant in the size of an IT staff. If all technical knowledge is in the head of a programmer, then how many systems can that person adequately support? If that person left the company or even took a vacation, then what materials are available to train the next person? A thorough program of IT technical documentation allows a smaller staff to support more technology than maintaining a larger staff of experts with the details locked inside their heads.

It is rare to encounter an IT Manager who does not believe in good system documentation, but it is just as rare to find one that consistently ensures its completion in a timely manner. A management maxim is that "You get what you reward." Management support is the key to this program. Without the visible and ongoing management support of a documentation program, it will quickly fade. Make the team believers and the IT Manager will not need to nag them—they will do it on their own!

Creating reference documentation, like anything else in the IT department, is a matter of time and labor. Often it requires the involvement of some of the department's more expensive technicians. A standard format focuses the writers on providing the essential information without losing time determining how to organize it. Standard document formats become simple fill-in-the-blank answers to a series of questions. Whoever a document's target audience may be, the text must answer the "5 Ws & H": Who, What, Where, When, Why, and How. By keeping these in mind at all times, the reference material will always be on target.

[B] Critical Policies to Develop Based on This Chapter

Use the material discussed in this chapter to create the following policies:

A. Determine what should be documented and what can be ignored.
   1. Identifies what needs documentation created for IT.
   2. Mandates compliance.
   3. Describes the essential elements of information to include with documents.
   4. In the case of technical documentation, assumes the reader is familiar with the technology described.
   5. Describes when the documentation should be delivered, such as within 30 days of implementation, before rollout.
B. Standardize documentation overall formats.
   1. There may be different formats for different types of documentation, such as technical, end user, and project.
   2. Allows for finding the same types of information in the same places in all documents of that type.
   3. Establishes a "readability" level target for documents, such as the "fog index."
   4. Requires that all error messages created by a program are listed as to what causes them and where they occur in the program.
   5. Provides a standardized naming convention for identifying documents.
C. Develop a policy guiding document version controls and retirement.
   1. Ensures the most current information is always available.
   2. Explains which changes in a document requires a new version number and how it is applied.
   3. Any document older than 12 months must be revised—or reviewed and re-approved as up to date.
   4. How documents will be stored.
   5. Limitations on availability of sensitive systems documentation.
   6. Requires all documentation to be reviewed and re-approved annually by the team leaders to ensure it includes all updates.
D. Develop a policy guiding the development of standardized flowcharts.
   1. Standardized symbols and their meaning.
   2. Identification blocks for all flowcharts and what goes into them.

Develop policies based on the local situation. Successful managers cannot issue appropriate guidance using policies written with the situation in another company or location in mind.

§ 13.02 DEVELOPING A REFERENCE DOCUMENTATION POLICY

[A] Overview

This chapter identifies the essential elements of IT documentation and formalizes them into a policy to guide the department. A key consideration in the development of any document is how the reader will use it. For example, technical documentation is for quick reference. The reader will scan it in an emergency for the essential information. End user documentation tends to be step-by-step actions that are explained in terms and in relationship to the end user's processes—not IT jargon.

IT documentation policy formalizes the requirement and format for the various types of reference materials. Among the benefits:

A. Minimize the time lost reanalyzing processes when troubleshooting or during new development. Technical documentation of a system's internal workings is the starting point for programmers to investigate problems or to make system changes.
B. Reduce IT staff training costs since knowledge is available when needed.
C. Reduce the number of service desk calls by providing users of IT processes with clear, adequate instructions on how to use the systems and what to do if specific error conditions appear.
D. Standardize reference document formats to ease cross training and to allow a wider range of people easier access to technical details.
E. Standardize storage and handling of reference documentation to ensure that the current version is always available.

COMMENT

Developing and maintaining accurate and complete systems documentation is an important part of a company's disaster recovery and business continuity plan. Over the long run, the identification of obscure or unstable technologies can lead to capital spending to replace them.

Good data systems documentation makes everyone's job easier. The cost of document development is "up front" in technician time building the documents. Payoff occurs repeatedly whenever someone needs to research the features of a system or to address problems in a crisis.

How often does a data system fail while the primary support person is on vacation? Has an important system failed at night when the after-hours support staff must be called on to address the issue? Has a key employee ever departed from the company taking all of the knowledge of the system along with him?

A consistent documentation program helps an IT Manager to provide guidance to employees. It reduces the variations in customer service from "the way we have always done it" to a well-considered approach. In essence, it details how to implement processes and then audits performance to enforce compliance.

> ## COMMENT
>
> Does your IT department support a complex system that is critical but stable? In the beginning, the person who developed it knew how the technology worked. However, since this application has not failed in years, the next time it had a problem, they had to start over from the beginning since the knowledge of the data flows has faded. Good documentation in this case would serve as a refresher when isolating a problem. Be sure that the documentation includes *all* technology in the system chain, including hardware and software.

Some managers require a review of system documentation before implementing routine changes or new systems. Another procedure is to schedule an annual management review of system reference materials for those "stable" systems that never seem to need changes. Do not be afraid to audit. A principle of sound management is to "inspect what you expect."

Documenting data systems highlights the chain of technology that is critical to the application's operation. From a business continuity planning standpoint, documentation helps to identify process weaknesses and single points of failure. The identification of a single point of failure calls for several immediate actions by the IT Manager—all aimed at better serving the customers:

A. Document any actions that would work around the problem until it can be resolved. Often these are manual processes.

B. Install duplicate equipment, if possible, so that the process can be shifted to the alternative hardware and work can promptly resume.

C. Ensure that all technical documentation pertaining to the process is current and understandable.

D. Ensure that personnel assigned to support that process are properly trained and aware of all of the aspects of the process.

[B]   Policy Objectives

The IT documentation policy has several objectives. It mandates compliance, provides some measures of what adequate reference documentation is, and provides guidance for a department librarian to ensure the availability of the latest versions. The IT documentation policy objectives include:

A. The IT documentation policy is all-inclusive of processes and technical systems supported by the department.

B. IT documentation will follow specific standards defining the content, approach, and objectives. Standard formats allow all readers to focus on the content of the document and not waste time trying to decipher different document layouts.
C. The IT librarian maintains all reference documentation in the appropriate format.
D. All documentation will be updated whenever a system change or enhancement is implemented.
E. Every year, each IT supervisor will review, update, and certify the accuracy of the documentation that supports their operations.
F. Submit technical, end user, operations, and service desk instructions prior to the rollout of all new systems or updated processes.

See Policy ITP-13-1. IT Documentation Policy as an example.

POLICY ITP-13-1   IT Documentation Policy

Policy #:	ITP-13-1	**Effective:**	03/18/08	**Page #:**	1 of N
Subject:	IT Documentation Policy				

1.0 PURPOSE

This policy identifies the essential elements of IT documentation and formalizes them into a guide for the IT department. Well-written reference materials communicate a clear, accurate picture of the process or system. This policy mandates the creation and maintenance of reference materials, and provides guidelines on what they should contain.

2.0 SCOPE

This policy encompasses end-user instructions, technical flow explanations, project documents, systems analysis studies, and all of the various reference documents created to provide ongoing support to an IT activity. Excluded from the policy are typical memorandums and e-mails.

IT functions requiring policies and procedures documentation include, but are not limited to:

A. Software development.
B. IT internal processes.
C. End-user instructions.
D. Help desk troubleshooting steps.
E. Systems analysis and reports.
F. Project plans and supporting historical documents.
G. Disaster recovery actions.
H. Security procedures.
I. Network logical and physical architectures.

3.0 POLICY

3.1 Know Your Audience

Write all documentation to a specific audiences' background. Technical documentation assumes that the reader has a fundamental understanding of the technology. End-user documentation assumes they know the basics of using the equipment.

A. **Technical reference documents.** Use technical references to locate a piece of information. What information elements would you want to see in a document if tasked to fill in for an absent programmer? At a minimum, it should include an overall diagram of the system modules and data flows; a list of all file layouts; a list of where major inputs come from, what the primary outputs look like, such as reports; and a narrative of how it all fits together.

B. **End-user documentation.** End-user reference material follows the process flow from the user's perspective. It includes the screens they would step through, the menus, and an explanation of all options. Use this type of reference for training and for looking up answers. The text of each section will be narrative but there should be an outline format table of contents along with an index—both of which are easily created using the tools in most word processing programs.

3.2 Types of Documentation

A. **Informational documents.** Detail all of the steps in performing a function that allow latitude on the part of the operator. For example, if an overnight process normally ends by 4:30 a.m. and it is still running at 5:00 a.m., the instructions may require the operator to call the supporting programmer. However, if the operator is aware of earlier issues with the overnight processing that delayed the start of this program for two hours, provide the option to exercise judgment and wait before calling.

B. **Directive document.** Follow these steps exactly. The process steps are a directive from the IT manager. An example might be a step-by-step process to be followed by the help desk technicians to verify a caller's identity before resetting a password. No one may deviate from this process. Another directive type process is a precise explanation of the proper handling, shipping, and storage of data backups.

3.3 Text Standards for All Documents

A. Use 12-point type using an Arial or Times Roman font.

B. Each document should read from major topic to minor topic—or broad view to narrow view. The beginning of the document deals with actions that would affect the entire process, and then deeper into the document addresses specific issues.

C. On the first page, include a brief narrative of the business function that this particular process supports.
D. Be concise. Limit each sentence to less than 25 words, each paragraph to one topic, and each sentence to a single idea. This avoids swamping a person's short-term memory. Concise text respects the reader's time and reduces ambiguity.
E. Write in a neutral tone and avoid humor, personal opinion, inspirational statements, and popular slang.
F. Define any unusual technical or business terms that are used. Reader comprehension is improved by writing longer statements that work around "insider" code words. Common technical or business terms are acceptable.
G. Use graphics to provide supporting information, not to repeat what was already written.
H. Always write in the active voice. It is easier to understand than the passive voice.

Use simple, direct sentences and leave the large words for the dictionaries. Simple sentences are not an insult to anyone's intelligence. No one looks to IT documentation as a source of fine literature; they appreciate finding what they want to know as quickly as possible.

3.4 Document Identification
A. Set the page footers to include a page number in the center, and the current date in lower-right corner. This date will help to indicate which files are the latest.
B. Include the phrase "Company Confidential" in the heading for every page along with a small version of the company logo.
C. Every page must have the date approved in the lower-left corner. When updating individual pages and sections, this date will change, so there may be more than one "approved on" date in the same document.
D. Every document more than 5 pages long shall have a table of contents. This should include all section headings in the document for quick reference.
E. Section headings group together similar information and assist the reader with quickly locating the topic he or she seeks. Use these guidelines when writing section headings:
   1. Use a "level-one" heading to start a broad subject area. Level-one headings are typically generic titles, such as "Hardware", "System Justification," or "Immediate actions for system crashes." Level-one headings should contain one distinct type of information subdivided by lower level sections.
   2. Use level-two, level-three, and level-four headings to progressively subdivide information into easy-to-identify sections. The titles should succinctly summarize the information contained in that section.
   3. Do not use more than four heading levels. Instead, subdivide the level 0 (zero) section into its major sections.

4.0 REVISION HISTORY

Date	Revision #	Description of Change
03/18/08	1.0	Initial creation.

5.0 INQUIRIES:

Direct inquiries about this policy to:

Tom Jones, CIO
Our Company, Inc.
2900 Corporate Drive
Columbus, OH 43215

Voice: 614-555-1234
Fax: 614-555-1235
E-mail: tjones@company.com

Revision #:	1.0	Supersedes:	N/A	Date:	03/18/08

§ 13.03   DOCUMENT FORMATS

[A]   Overview

Documentation is institutional knowledge, permanently recorded for ready reference. It includes procedure development, design, implementation, operation, and revision data that successors can follow. It incorporates policies, rules, and information for distribution to all users associated with information systems operations.

Documentation tells a story about how something works or how to use it. It is a shame to spend days writing a document that is useless to the intended audience. One of the problems is the variety of writing styles and formats used by various people. People write in the way most comfortable to them. Some seem to get quickly to the point and some explain every small action in tedious detail.

However, each type of document requires its own format. Technical documents are for troubleshooting, so highlight the essential facts in the front, and do not bury them deep in the text. Examples of this might be the name of the server, software, and various technologies used. End-user documentation would skip all of this as the customer does not care if hub #7 supports a particular peripheral. Something works or it does not. Therefore, end-user documentation looks at the same process, but from the end-user's perspective. Technically, this is only as deep as their desktop monitor will reach. Beyond that, the end-user's interest is minimal.

Creating documentation, like anything in the IT department, is a matter of time and labor. Often it requires help from the department's more expensive technicians. The establishment of a standard format helps to focus their efforts to provide the essential information in a minimal amount of time. No time is lost trying to discern the layout of a document. All effort focuses on locating what was wanted. Technical documentation that follows a standard format will ensure that whoever is called up to address a problem will at least not waste time fumbling through page after page looking for basic details. The information will be in the same place in all documents.

The manager's task is to remove the roadblocks (real and imagined) and develop an easy to follow writing methodology for the staff to use. This should include standard document formats, naming conventions, and word processing guidelines.

Many technicians will tell you they are not "writers." (Of course, they were not technicians until they learned what to do, either.) Like any technical skill, it needs a bit of explanation, a few examples to demonstrate the basics, and a lot of practice.

Writing good reference documentation is no more difficult than telling a story to someone. Good documentation is easier to read when written conversationally. Start at the beginning (where the process originates) and then explain the flow of data through to the end. Use simple, direct sentences and leave the large words for the dictionaries. Simple sentences are not an insult to anyone's intelligence. No one looks to IT documentation as a source of fine literature; they appreciate finding what they want to know as quickly as possible.

[B]   Know Your Audience

Before writing the first word, consider who will be reading this document and how they will use it. Each audience has its own set of requirements and expectations. Documentation is useless to a technician if it is too wordy, useless to end users if it is too technical, and useless to the service desk if it is too long. If the authors focus their efforts on how the audience will use the document, they can save themselves a lot of time writing it.

When writing the technical explanation, a general rule is to assume the reader understands the basics of the technology. Likewise, when explaining an accounting program, it is unnecessary to explain the accounting rule as to why to debit to a particular account.

The best judge of the usefulness of documentation is the people who will be using it. Often, developers write the documentation for code they have personally written. In general, the technical explanation they write is not for them; it is for their supervisor and their backup person. The supervisor and backup support person should judge whether it is appropriate to the requirements. Likewise, the end user for that document should approve it. Otherwise, it is likely to be set aside and the users will call for every small problem.

A. **Technical reference documents.** Use technical references to locate a piece of information. Everyone approaches technical debugging in his or her own fashion. What information elements would you want to see in a document if tasked to fill in for an absent programmer?

At a minimum, it should include an overall diagram of the system modules and data flows; a list of all file layouts; a list of where major outputs come from, such as reports; and a narrative of how it all fits together. The section of the policy covering technical reference documentation should require that an explanation of a data system's use and internal workings be an integral part of any new system implementation.

Funds for the development of reference materials are a part of each project. Write technical and end-user reference materials during system implementation to capture a fresh understanding of how the system works. See Exhibit 13-1 as an example.

EXHIBIT 13-1   System Document Format

Process Title: Bill of Lading System	
Written by: Larry Mosshammer	Approved by: Jim Webber
Document Number: S-13-001	Date Approved: April 1, 2008

System Objective:

To provide accurate Bills of Lading so that finished goods are routed to the correct destination with the correct optional accessories.

Word-Around Steps in an Emergency:

This system is classified as <u>CRITICAL</u> to this facility. If it totally fails, then the shipment of finished goods from the factory is halted.

A. If the scanner gun fails, then use the keyboard at the shipping office to enter the job number into the workstation. This functions the same as the scanner and creates a Bill of Lading. It is important to enter the correct job number. A spare scanner gun is located in the office.

B. If the scale or its interface fails, continue shipping and call for service by the scale company.

C. If the data download from the mainframe fails, continue shipping until it is resolved. The workstation has 48 hours of shipping information stored on it, but any corrections to this information will not be included on the Bills of Lading.

D. If the workstation fails, replace it with the stand-by unit sitting in the office. Download the data from the mainframe and continue shipping. The download may require an hour to receive and load the database.

E. If the printer fails, a spare printer is located in the shipping office.

F. If the "product shipped" transaction to the mainframe fails, then the job number's status remains built-not-shipped until it is scanned by the receiving warehouse.

Process Steps During Normal Operation:

A. The day before a product is scheduled to be assembled, the shipping information is extracted from the mainframe's Production Master Table and copied into a generation dataset called "aaa.bbb.HeresYourStuff(0)." Changes to the shipping information fields on the Production Master will flag that record for the next download. Extracts are scheduled to run at 0530, 1130, 1730, and 2330.

B. At 0600, 1200, 1800, and 2400 the shipping office workstation automatically requests a copy of the mainframe extract.
C. This file is loaded into the SQL database called ShippingData.sql. The job number is the record key and is unique to each finished product. If the record exists, it is replaced. Otherwise, it is added.
D. When a finished item is ready to ship, its ticket is scanned to obtain a Bill of Lading. The job number is looked up in the database. If it exists, then Crystal Reports is used to format a Bill of Lading and print the document. If the job number is not found, then Crystal Reports formats and prints a rejection ticket.
E. After a Bill of Lading prints for a job, it is flagged as shipped in the PC's database and a single transaction file is sent to the mainframe to change the job's status.
F. This file is sent as xxx and is picked up by the mainframe program xxxx which executes every 90 seconds.
  1. <u>Production Scheduling</u> for reporting actual versus scheduled built.

Technologies Used:
A. Hardware.
  1. PC at shipping station.
  2. Special serial interface board connecting to scale.
  3. Personal UPS on shipping PC.
  4. IBM Mainframe.
  5. Bar code scanner gun.
  6. Scale Interface Box.
  7. HP Laserjet.
  8. Internal facility network.
  9. External network to data center.
B. Software.
  1. Visual Basic version 7.
  2. Crystal Reports 7.
  3. SQL Server version 7.1.

Files and Interfaces:
C. Mainframe.
     aaa.bbb.HeresYourStuff(0).
D. Workstation.
     ShippingData.sql.

Operator Routine Maintenance Actions:
A. Properly shut down and reboot the shipping workstation once every workday.
B. Once per week, run the database cleanup function using the process outlined in the operator procedure.
C. Clean the printer per the manufacturer's instructions every time the laser toner cartridge is replaced.

B. **End-user documents.** End-user reference material follows the process flow from the user's perspective. It includes the screens they would step through, the menus, and an explanation of all options. See Exhibit 13-2 as an example.

People will read this type of documentation to gain some overall understanding on how the system works or to look up solutions to problems. The better the user instructions are, the fewer the calls for help! Use this type of reference for training and for looking up answers. The text of each section will be narrative but there should be an outline format table of contents along with an index—both of which are easily created using the tools in most word processing programs.

User instructions should include illustrations of screens, reports, and lists of valid edit codes. Explain any error messages used by the program that the end user may see. This is true even if the response is to report the error to the service desk since end users often are the first to encounter software problems.

An important factor in end-user materials is to avoid the use of technical jargon—unless it is in common use in that department. In this case, the text should avoid bits and bytes discussion about network devices but would appropriately include business terminology used within that department such as scrap reporting and automated shipping notices.

EXHIBIT 13-2   End-User Document Format

Process Title: Creating New User Accounts Written by: Larry Mosshammer	Approved by: Jim Webber
Document Number: P-13-001	Date Approved: April 1, 2008

Process Objective:

This procedure is for approving and creating new user IDs. User IDs are the first line of security defense against unauthorized access to company data. This process assures that only authorized personnel are provided user IDs.

Responsibilities:

A. Service Desk Technician—ensures the form is properly and completely filled in, creates the new account, and stores forms in the file.
B. Service Desk Supervisor—works with other departments to obtain advance notice of major changes that would require the creation of new user accounts. Ensures that this procedure is followed by training new technicians in its use and by periodically monitoring the creation of new accounts.

Supporting Materials:

A. New User ID request form #F-0100-001.
B. Restricted supervisor authority to create new accounts.

References:

A. Process P-0100-020 for background checks on all personnel able to create new user accounts.

Technologies Used:

A. Hardware.
   None
B. Software.
   None

Process Steps:

1. The Service Desk Technician verifies at the beginning of each shift that there is an adequate supply of new user ID request forms in the hopper outside of the Service Desk Door.
2. New ID request forms are sent through the interoffice mail or picked up from the hopper outside of the door.
3. Forms are completed according to the instructions on the back of the form.
4. Completed forms are sent to the Service Desk via interoffice mail or dropped off at the Service Desk window.
5. The Service Desk technician reviews incoming forms for completeness, ensuring that both the employee and supervisor signature blocks are completed.
6. A call is logged in the Service Desk trouble tracking system to set up the user ID.
7. The Service Desk technician uses the AS400 xxx to establish a user ID following the company's ID pattern.
8. A standard password of "Christmas" is set for the account. The account is set to require that the password be changed the first time it is used.
9. The Service Desk calls the user based on the telephone number on the application to inform them of their new account ID and password.
10. The ID request form is filed in the Service Desk cabinet under "User ID Requests," in alphabetical order of the user's last name.
11. The trouble call to set up the ID is closed.

C. **Service desk or operations documents.** Service desks are often an extension of the data systems operations team. Both sit in Service back rooms and address routine issues that arise. The documentation needs for both are similar. Service desk and operations documentation comes in two basic forms, informational and directive. Each is appropriate in certain circumstances.
   1. **Informational documents.** List the steps that allow latitude on the part of the operator. For example, if an overnight process normally ends by 4:30 a.m. and it is still running at 5:00 a.m., the instructions may request the operator call the supporting programmer. But if the operator is aware of earlier issues with the overnight processing that delayed the start of this program for two hours, he

or she will have the option to exercise judgment and wait before calling.

2. **Directive documents.** Follow these steps exactly. The process steps are considered a part of a directive from the IT Manager, for example, a step-by-step process to be followed by the service desk technicians to verify a caller's identity before resetting a password. Deviation from this process is not permitted. Another directive type process is a precise explanation on the proper handling, shipping, and storage of data backups.

[C] Readability

There is a "score" that can be determined for a document that indicates its readability called a "fog index." Most word processors include some sort of reading level gauge to identify the audience's difficulty in understanding a document's text. IT documents are dry and definitely not recreational prose. At least try to make them easy to read.

A fog index for technical documentation is somewhat skewed by technical terms. Technical writing should be simple and easy to understand. Readers have a responsibility to understand the common technical terms used in their specialty and by the company. If in doubt, add a glossary to the document. Rather than repeat glossaries in every document, consider establishing a single library-wide glossary of technical and company-unique terms. To calculate the fog index:

A. Count the number of words in the document or passage under review.
B. Count the number of sentences.
   1. Divide the number of words by the number of sentences and save this number.
C. Count the number of words with three or more syllables.
   1. Divide the number of words into the number of big words to obtain a percentage. Treat this percentage as a whole number and save it.
D. Add the two saved numbers together (as whole numbers) and multiply the results by 0.4. The result is the fog index.

Most IT documents will have an index rating of between 11 and 13, but the lower the rating is, the easier the information is to read.

§ 13.04 DOCUMENT MANAGEMENT

[A] Overview

Every IT department keeps some sort of reference library. In some cases, it is in a dusty bookcase. More often, manuals and system documentation are scattered around the various work areas and programmer cubicles. All of these documents vary in how current they are. In many cases, no one knows what material a coworker may have on the shelf and must search around the department looking for an old manual.

A well-maintained reference library will provide an IT Manager with ready access to the latest information, savings on storage space since so many copies of so many things are not floating around, and greater agility for responding to user problem reports. Most hardware and software vendors would be very happy to provide their documentation electronically (on a disk or via an Internet link) since printing mounds of manuals only distracts them from what they do best.

> ## COMMENT
>
> Well-written software documentation is a service-desk's most valuable tool. When users call, service-desk analysts can answer most questions if they have access to current user documentation and can look up detailed questions in the technical reference materials. The more information the service-desk has, the fewer distractions passed on to the technical staff. Oh yes, and the callers appreciate the quick answers to their questions!

An IT reference library is a tradeoff between restricting the flow of materials and widely dispersing them. Its goal is to ensure that current information is readily available when needed. An IT library should use a variety of methods to provide information to those who need it.

For reference material generated by the IT department, or provided electronically by vendors, the library should use an intranet Web page. This reduces the number of paper copies and the likelihood of using obsolete information.

Using an outdated document may hinder or misdirect troubleshooting efforts and deepen the crisis of the moment. The IT librarian ensures the latest version of all documents is readily available.

Some technicians find it easier to purchase new books instead of checking into what is already in the IT library. Perhaps they feel more secure if they possess their own copy or they are casually interested in something new and would like to research it further. The IT library's inventory provides the IT Manager with data for controlling this cost.

[B] Enforcing Quality

The librarian establishes a schedule that spreads the revalidation of documents throughout the year. This minimizes the workload on the IT staff and allows them to schedule this task into their slack periods. The librarian ensures the annual audits are performed on each document and follows up with supervisors for document reviews that are past due.

> **COMMENT**
>
> To minimize the drain on the librarian's time, consider using an electronic document management system, such as Microsoft SharePoint software (*www.microsoft.com/ sharepoint/*).

[C] Storage and Access

The librarian must devise a filing system to readily identify documents. Often this involves using the names and code numbers already assigned to the various data systems. Most IT staff members think of the various data systems by their common names. Use these when possible.

IT reference material is normally stored in one of three places.

A. **Materials needed at the workplace to accomplish the job.** These reference materials are what a worker needs immediate access to in the normal performance of his job. Individuals may keep essential reference materials by their workstations. Examples are programming language reference materials at the desk of each programmer. Keep a copy of documents that must be readily available in the individual work areas. In most companies, each developer has basic manuals at his desk. Work should progress as fast as the developer can think so a basic set of manuals should be readily available in his work area.

   A computer operator might need step-by-step instructions for performing a specific action, etc. Material such as this should be available at his point of application. For example, attach the documentation explaining the operation of a tape backup device to its side.

B. **Electronic materials.** Much of an IT department's technical documentation are developed locally. Rather than print and track who has copies, a central location for review is needed. Reference materials created by the IT staff should be stored on a shared network drive that is accessible through a secured intranet web page controlled by the librarian. Read access to this directory is generally available to the IT staff while write access is restricted to the librarian.

   Whenever publishing a newer version, the intranet link points to the newer version. As problems arise, the troubleshooter looks up the documentation on the network instead of searching for his (possibly outdated) copy of the documentation. For this reason, printing copies of reference documentation off the network is discouraged, but not prohibited.

> **COMMENT**
>
> Several software vendors provide tools that make it easier to collect policy and procedure information and make it available over the corporate intranet. Some packages to check out include Zavanta from Comprose, Inc. (*www.zavanta.com*) and onGO DMS from Uniplex Software (*www.uniplex.com*).

C. **Physical reference materials stored in the central library.** To save on storage space and to minimize the cost of lightly used manuals, many companies collect them into a central library for review (or borrowed for a short time). The intention is to make documents and manuals available for use and yet minimize floor space requirements. These resources are accumulated into a central location and loaned as needed. Log in a "due back by" date so that the next person requiring the material will not need to search for it. Few materials are required beyond a week, so this encourages storing them in the library instead of on a cubicle shelf.

Previously, manuals were purchased as desired with no control over versions, location, or verification that the book was not already on the premises. A central repository saves on shelf space and ensures the maximum benefit from the company's investment in manuals. The trick for the librarian is to ensure the materials get maximum use while maintaining control over their location. In a pinch, it is better to lose track of a book for a short while than to hinder the troubleshooting of a critical issue.

> **COMMENT**
>
> Librarians must balance the savings realized by reducing the number of manuals floating around against ensuring they are readily available for use. Do not let the library become a place where manuals enter and never see the light of day again! Make it easy to take out books and gently remind people to return them.

[D]   Version Control

Reference materials have a problem. How can the support staff determine if they are reading the latest information on the topic? Some data systems are in constant flux while others may remain static for years. A document may be four years old but still be the latest word—or one week old and obsolete. It is difficult to keep current multiple copies of documentation. Page replacements, pen changes to text, and maintaining a locater of each document can be a massive undertaking. Multiply this by the number of systems in a large company and it is easy to see why some companies do not even bother to try.

There are several ways to address version control. The first is that only the current documentation is available via the Web page. Printing personal copies is discouraged. Second, the "date approved" provides an indication of currency. Finally, if the data system uses a version number in its name, then that can be included in the document title. Although a large IT shop may devise some sort of version or serial number for documents, many companies will find this more effort than required.

A goal of version control is for the librarian to weed out and destroy obsolete manuals. "Obsolete" is a strange term in IT since there may still be hardware and software in operation that might be considered long past its prime yet the company still depends upon it for daily service. It does not matter how old a document is, only whether it is the best available reference for that technology. Tracking manuals eases the problem of gathering up old manuals when a newer version is issued. See Policy ITP-13-2 IT Documentation Management Policy as an example.

POLICY ITP-13-2   IT Documentation Management Policy

Policy #:	ITP-13-2	Effective:	03/18/08	Page #:	1 of N
Subject:	IT Documentation Management Policy				

1.0 PURPOSE

This policy establishes a central repository of technical information in the IT department to ensure that the latest version is readily available to the IT department. It also provides guidance on ensuring the current version of documentation is readily available when needed.

2.0 SCOPE

This policy includes the management of all IT documents, whether purchased, received from outside organizations, or originated within the department. Documents supplied by other company departments, such as Human Resources are excluded.

3.1 Central Repository of Reference Material

All IT manuals, technical instructions, process instructions, etc., are to be managed centrally. IT reference material is normally stored in one of three places:

A. **At the point of application.** Reference materials required frequently will be stored at their point of use. Examples are reference materials for programming languages at the desk of each programmer or systematic instructions for a Help Desk technician.

B. **Electronic materials.** The IT librarian will establish a network file share and a collection of manufacturer provided CDs for ready use by the department. Reference materials created by the IT staff are to be stored on a shared network drive accessible through a secured intranet Web page controlled by the librarian.

C. **Central library.** To save on storage space and to minimize the cost of lightly used manuals, they are to be collected into a central library for review as needed or short-term borrowing.

D. **Purchasing new manuals and reference material.** The IT librarian will check the list of existing documents to ensure that the manual requested is not already on the premises.

3.2 Restricted Access

A. **Company confidential materials.** Some of the department's technical documents could be used against the company. Examples are documentation of security systems, manuals detailing the accounting and payroll systems, etc.
   1. The IT librarian will safeguard these materials and only permit access by those whom the IT manager approves.
   2. The IT librarian will segregate these materials so that access is only granted to the appropriate information. For example, the IT security team does not need access to the payroll system documentation, etc.

B. **Monthly access list review.** The IT librarian will submit to the IT manager a list of employees that have access to the confidential documentation. The IT manager will note any changes, approve, and return it for the IT librarian's file.

3.3 Document Management

A. **Department librarian.** The IT manager will assign a member of the IT department as the official keeper of all reference materials. This person will be referred to as the IT reference librarian. Before adding anything to the library, the librarian will ensure:
   1. The documents conform to department policy for reference materials.

2. The documents are stored in the proper location. This may include archiving old versions on the same subject.
3. Authorized personnel have the appropriate security to access or update confidential material.
4. The documentation custodian should maintain a copy of all documents on CDs for times when the online system is not available.

B. **Document's author.** A process's developer is responsible for writing the documentation and providing it to the librarian in an acceptable format. If the document conforms to the reference documentation policy, it should contain all of the required information. The librarian will reject vague or poorly written documents.

C. **Author's supervisor.** The developer's supervisor ensures the documentation is technically correct and reviewed annually to ensure it is still relevant.

3.4 Version Control

Version control is a process for ensuring that the department uses the most current information. The IT librarian will maintain a list of all library controlled documents along with their version numbers. The librarian will also include the location of each document, such as those kept at the workplace (programming manuals).

The IT librarian will weed out and destroy excess copies of obsolete manuals (always keeping at least one on site).

A. **Electronically stored reference material.** Only the current version of documentation is available via the Web page. Print copies as needed.

B. **Central library.** To save on storage space and to minimize the cost of lightly used manuals, collect them into a central library for review as needed or short term.

C. **Old versions.** The IT librarian will maintain a storage area with older versions of manuals. The IT librarian will also maintain an online storage area for older versions. In both cases, the IT librarian controls access to older versions.

3.5 Annual Documentation Review

Every month the IT librarian will check through the locally created IT technical and end-user documentation for documents not updated in the past 12 months. The IT manager responsible for that system must validate that the documentation is still correct.

4.0 REVISION HISTORY

Date	Revision #	Description of Change
03/18/08	1.0	Initial creation.

Direct inquiries about this policy to:

Tom Jones, CIO
Our Company, Inc.
2900 Corporate Drive
Columbus, OH 43215

Voice: 614-555-1234
Fax: 614-555-1235
E-mail: tjones@company.com

Revision #:	1.0	Supersedes:	N/A	Date:	03/18/08

COMMENT

End users tend to keep printed copies of documentation for quick reference. Use a different color of paper for the different versions of end-user documentation (or at least for the cover). This will make it easier to spot out-of-date copies.

§ 13.05   SYSTEM REFERENCE INSTRUCTIONS

[A]   Process Overview

Most data processing systems will require the same major sections in their documentation. In essence, each section is like a chapter of a book since each addresses a different audience. Each section tells the story of the same system or process from the perspective of the various groups. Write sections to stand on their own without reference to the others. Insert a "page left blank" page in the place of unneeded sections. This demonstrates that the section is not missing, just not required. Most systems documentation will follow the format outlined in the following sections.

The narrative section should briefly explain the business context of a process and, in general, how it functions. It should describe the benefits provided by the process to the company and its day-to-day business/technical environment.

The narrative should identify the upstream and downstream data flows as well as the primary intended functions of the process.

[B] End-User Reference Documentation

Most departments experience some measure of employee turnover and absence. Well-written end-user documentation is useful for training new employees or as a valuable reference for occasional users. It provides the reader with a "big picture" perspective of a system. The weakness of pop-up help screens is that they are context sensitive. They may be used for support or training.

Write this stand-alone section for printing and for use in the end-user's department. User procedures should be easy to read and follow (written at an eighth-grade level for nontechnical personnel).

On-screen help and tips pop-ups can be a source of helpful instructions as they provide assistance in context of the problem. They are a valuable supplement, but not a replacement for end-user documentation.

Well-written end-user documentation should contain:

A. Program or hardware operating instructions.
B. Corrective action for error messages.
C. The texts of all on-screen help messages and when they can be invoked.
D. Steps for accessing tutorial information.

[C] Operations Reference Documentation

The operating procedures include everything necessary to initiate, schedule, process, control, and restart all phases of the system(s) while it is in operation. An operator may need to monitor the job's progress, set up high speed printers for special jobs (like printing customer bills for a utility company, or payroll checks), or restart failed programs.

The types of information to be included are:

A. Input/output requirements.
   1. Scanning instrument instructions.
   2. Removable disk and/or CD instruction.
   3. Special printer setup instructions.
   4. External labeling.
B. Data management is an important part of operations. Files must be mounted, broken programs restarted at the correct file generation, and a wide range of actions required in given circumstances. Operations data management actions include:
   1. Data retention period.
   2. Data security level.
   3. Number of backup generations required. If more than one, they should not all be stored in the same location.
   4. Any special recovery instructions to ensure data consistency.
   5. How to verify that recovered data is properly in place and the program is processing it.
C. Program job instructions should include the following:
   1. Job setup instructions.
   2. Sources of originating data.

3. Report setup and disposition.
4. Sample output forms.
5. Corrective action to take for error messages.
6. Expected job run time.
7. Process restart procedures.

[D]   Service Desk Reference Documentation

Service desk technicians refer to the reference materials provided by the other IT departments. Sometimes end users "forget" to read their documentation and the service desk walks them through a system action. Sometimes the service desk uses the technical documentation to see if a reported problem indicates a more serious issue or is something they can resolve.

The service desk requires access to the instructions provided to all departments (except for information held back for security reasons). In some cases, they will need a subset of the instructions to address frequently asked questions.

[E]   Technical Reference Documentation

Maintain information about hardware and software for each data system. They contain:

A.   **General information.** This section identifies the technology and its objectives. Each program and major hardware device should have a unique identification number or name.
B.   **General objectives.** The general objectives include a brief narrative statement of each program's purpose or use. It also addresses what passes data to it, how the data is transformed, and what passes out of it.
C.   **Program's systems specifications.** Vendor-supplied information also will be included.
D.   **Program flowcharts.** Flowcharts will be drawn using American National Standards Institute (ANSI) symbols.

COMMENT

Visio from Microsoft is a popular program for creating a wide range of business and technical drawings. Contact Microsoft at *www.microsoft.com.*

E.   **Written program documentation.** Software reference documentation serves various functions. Pay back for the time and expense required to document software includes reduced maintenance costs, faster response to user requests, and possibly management job security.

COMMENT

A key aspect of object-oriented programming is the reuse of code. If the purpose, inputs, and outputs of a software object are vague, then how can someone reuse it? Establish a standard format for all reusable objects as soon as possible and ensure all future documentation conforms to it.

Software reference documentation should include:

A. Overall flow of program showing data going in, how it is transformed, and to where it is passed.
B. Source code listings.
C. Source and format of input data, to include all combinations of data strings into and out of each module.
D. System naming conventions—needed for variables, database, inputs, outputs, and controls.
E. Report layouts.
F. Screen layouts displaying control buttons, text boxes, and screen labels.
G. List of all validation edits and tables used by the program.
H. List of error messages that can be generated by this code and what causes them (do not include ones generated by the operating environment).
I. Formulas used in any critical calculations.
J. Index of table field names—names used in databases, programs, and input/output locations (useful when programming and doing maintenance later).

[F] Program Testing Reference Documentation

The proper testing of software is a formalized process. Test data takes considerable effort and time to develop. Always retain test data and scripts along with a narrative explaining how it exercises the program. Keep it in a CD attached to the technical documentation. Test data will require modification to follow changes to the programs; it will save the developer a considerable amount of time if it remains in sync with the programs.

Keep listings of input used for testing and the resulting outputs in the program test file. Screen-print or draw screen displays for documentation.

§ 13.06 PROJECT DOCUMENTATION

[A] Overview

The history of previous projects, both successful and incomplete, provides invaluable assistance in gauging the risks, costs, time duration, and task identification of future ventures. Important project documents are the initial plans (which are estimates for work) and the project's results (actual task duration, actual resource utilization, etc.). Project documentation also includes instructions, charts, correspondence, and other material dealing with a specific project. It provides a permanent record of the decisions made, along with a short list of the problems encountered and the methods used to resolve them.

Create a project binder at the start of a project to provide an ongoing record of pertinent information. It should include all related material throughout the life of the project. It is important to know which document supersedes another, so date each one before placing it in the binder.

[B] Identification and Responsibility

Project managers are responsible for initiating and maintaining their project binders. Binders can help ensure the required documents are accumulated and forwarded to the IT library. Do this at the conclusion of every project milestone.

The IT librarian is responsible for ensuring that all of the project documents are collected at the various stages of the project:

A. Initial plan when the project begins.
B. An in-progress "snapshot" of the plan at each milestone.
C. Final results at the end of the project.

The librarian organizes all materials to facilitate future reference. Typically, a project's materials are stored in a hard copy filing system.

See Policy ITP-13-3 Project Documentation Policy as an example.

POLICY ITP-13-3. Project Documentation Policy

Policy #:	ITP-13-3	Effective:	03/18/08	Page #:	1 of N
Subject:	Project Documentation Policy				

1.0 PURPOSE

The purpose of this policy is to collect documents used for managing a project for use in later review and analysis. These documents can be reviewed for information on improving the quality of the project management effort. It also provides insights into design tradeoffs and the logic behind them for team members later supporting that system.

2.0 SCOPE

This policy encompasses documents used in the management of a project. It excludes routine memos and working papers not directly related to the project analysis.

3.0 POLICY

3.1 Project Binder Contents

The project binder will contain any analysis used to justify the project plan. The size and complexity of these documents will vary according to the size and complexity of the project. The project binder should contain:

A. **Table of contents or index.**
B. **Basic project documents.** The basis for the project may be in the form of a feasibility study or a systems design. The project proposal should include:
   1. **Project charter.** A document describing the project's scope and key objectives. It also provides the authority for the project manager to commence the project. This should include the project's criteria for success.
   2. **Major project tasks.** An outline of the steps necessary to complete the project.
   3. **Estimated costs and benefits.** Compute estimated costs for each major task and/or material. Identify costs as "estimates" obtained at the time the proposal was written and subject to revision. List all assumptions made in determining these costs.
C. **Project plan.** The schedule includes:
   1. Systems concept. A brief narrative written for non-technical, management-level personnel that provides a detailed overview of the project objectives.
   2. List of tasks, and their sequence.
   3. State all assumptions made about resources, features, and timelines made during the planning process.
   4. Risk assessments.
   5. Stakeholder analysis.
   6. Communications plan.
   7. Initial budget.
   8. Resource list and work calendar.
   9. A copy of the feasibility study is included if available.

3.2 Project Progress Folders

Project progress documentation, maintained during the life of the project, contains the history of the project and copies of all relevant correspondence filed by date. These documents provide a source of information when writing the project completion report, and should reflect any agreements between the project group and users or vendors. These documents include:

A. **Minutes of project status and problem-solving meetings.**
B. **Labor utilization record.** Post the estimated "hours per task" versus the "actual hours per task" to the project schedule.
C. **Project documentation checklist.** To ensure that documentation for the in-progress project is fully collected, refer to the project documentation checklist (Worksheet 13-1).
D. **A final report that illustrates the actual course of the project.** Compare this to the initial documents to improve task identification and estimates of budget and time duration.
    1. Final project plan showing the actual duration and sequence of tasks.
    2. Final budget, indicating the actual project expenses.
    3. Final risk assessment plan along with a list of mitigation actions taken during the project.
    4. Scope change log detailing all proposed and accepted changes to the project scope.

4.0 REVISION HISTORY

Date	Revision #	Description of Change
03/18/08	1.0	Initial creation.

5.0 INQUIRIES

Direct inquiries about this policy to:

Tom Jones, CIO
Our Company, Inc.
2900 Corporate Drive
Columbus, OH 43215

Voice: 614-555-1234
Fax: 614-555-1235
E-mail: tjones@company.com

Revision #:	1.0	Supersedes:	N/A	Date:	03/18/08

Use Worksheet 13-1 Project Documentation Checklist to track project costs and progress.

WORKSHEET 13-1.   Project Documentation Checklist

Project Documentation Checklist		
Description of Project		

Major Project Tasks (Use only those applicable to this project.)

	Start Date	Finish Date	Estimated Cost
Preliminary Analysis	MM/DD/YY	MM/DD/YY	$999,999
Systems Analysis/Design	MM/DD/YY	MM/DD/YY	$999,999
Programming	MM/DD/YY	MM/DD/YY	$999,999
Data and File Conversion Costs	MM/DD/YY	MM/DD/YY	$999,999
System and Program Testing			$999,999
Training Costs			$999,999
Hardware Purchase			$999,999
Software Purchase			$999,999
Administrative Costs			$999,999
Miscellaneous			$999,999
TOTAL COST			$999,999

Estimated Annual Operation Cost	
Data Entry	$999,999
Processing	$999,999
System/Program Maintenance	$999,999
Administrative	$999,999
Other (specify)	$999,999
TOTAL ESTIMATED ANNUAL OPERATIONS COST	$999,999

Project Staffing

(Name the project leader and state the estimated number and competence level of personnel assigned to work on the project.

Personnel to Contact

(List names of people best able to answer pertinent questions about the various tasks within the project.

§ 13.07 SYSTEMS ANALYSIS DOCUMENTATION

[A] Overview

Systems analysis is the technical and business review of a proposed change or addition to a data system to determine the extent of the time required and the approximate cost. IT Managers use the results of the study to establish the cost to benefit ratio of the proposed changes. The documents also provide much of the initial information.

A systems analyst establishes a scaled down version of a project plan to ensure that the true impact of the request is considered. The analyst formalizes the request's scope and reviews the technical and business processes involved to identify all of the tasks required to make the change. The result is a time and direct cost estimate for management consideration. If the proposal is accepted, the systems analyst's report will provide the basic information for the project's charter.

Include rejected proposals in the library. Business conditions may change on short notice and yesterday's "nice to have" request becomes tomorrow's urgent requirement.

[B] Systems Documentation Binder

Maintain a systems documentation binder for each assignment. This is a scaled down version of a project plan. Combine some of these items onto the same page depending on the complexity of the issue. All binders should include:

A. **Title page.** The title page contains the project name and identification number, effective dates, and the lead analyst's name and title, names and responsibilities of all other persons assigned to the project on the second page.
B. **Table of contents.** This reflects the specific contents in the systems binder.
C. **Revision sheet.** Included in every systems binder (see Worksheet 13-2), it contains columns for:
   1. **Number of revisions.** Revisions are numbered sequentially starting with 1.
   2. **Revision date.** Effective date of the revision.
   3. **Portion revised.** The specific part of the system under revision, including all areas of documentation such as procedures, flowcharts, reports, etc.
   4. **Name.** The name of the systems analyst making the revision.
   5. **Authorization.** The name of the person authorizing the revision.

WORKSHEET 13-2.   Revision Sheet

Revision Sheet				
Project Name:			Project Number:	
Revision #	Date	Item Revised	Revised By	Approved By
Project Leader:			Date:	

[C] Scope

The scope of the assignment is the boundaries of the request. Vague requests result in vague estimates. It is the analyst's responsibility to translate the business-based request into a succinct technical description. The scope anchors the analysis to minimize drift. On occasion, the analysis is broken into several requests and may require several different scope statements.

Expand the succinct scope statement by listing the criteria for determining if the change has been successful. This is where the specific requirements are detailed, such as items to be added to reports, required validations, etc. This section also includes a statement on the business issues that justify the request.

[D] Product Specifications

What is to be created or changed because of this activity? Will it be a new report or a new database? Perhaps a new subsystem added to an existing function. Systems specifications provide a means of communication between the designer and the implementation team, who may be in-house programming staff or outside contract workers. The systems specifications provide a record of the structure, functions, flow, documentation, and control of the system and include:

A. **System narrative.**
   1. Descriptive title of system.
   2. Source, expected schedule, and volume of input data.
   3. Size and characteristics of the data.
   4. Sample exhibits of input documents.
   5. Outputs indicating volume and due dates. (This may be a monitor display or hard copy.)
   6. Sample exhibits of outputs.
   7. References to material or organizations that may furnish additional information. (This may include vendor-supplied information.)
   8. Samples of interactive screens.
B. **Data system and business process flowcharts** identifying the steps in the processes performed and illustrating their sequence.
C. **Program specification requirements** defining the environment within a system in which a subsystem or a single program operates. They describe the data inputs and outputs, including source, format, disposition, and retention method. They include the time when the process will run, process controls, functions, and limitations. The specifications include any security issues that may arise.
D. **File/database specifications** used in the system are identified.
E. **A test plan** based on existing test data and previous test plans for this process.

[E] Schedule

To determine the cost and timeline of a system change, the analyst should develop a basic project plan. This plan should list the tasks involved and apply time and cost estimates to each task.

All plans are projections of the future and created in the context of assumptions. There is an assumption that all of the required people will be ready, willing, and able to perform when called upon. There is an assumption that the computers and network will be operational, provide adequate response times during development, etc. Trying to build a schedule without making assumptions is not practical. An assumption list, however, should skip basic items such as the example about system performance and identify other assumptions that are essential to the schedule.

One result of the task breakdown is a resource plan that identifies all of the people and special equipment required to make the change. This might be additional workstations, new software packages, etc. This breakdown helps to identify costs and the lead time for ordering materials and services from outside of the company.

[F]   Risk Assessment

Even small changes have risks and a brief risk assessment will detail the potential problems with the change. At a minimum, every item on the assumptions list should be on the risk assessment sheet along with its mitigation actions. Potential problems include:

A. End-user resistance.
B. Incorrect specifications.
C. Critical days to avoid due to the business cycle (in the end user's department or in IT).
D. Unproven technologies.
E. Planned changes to upstream systems.
F. System performance from existing poor design.

[G]   Stakeholders

It is important to identify all of the groups involved with the change so they can assist in its development and approval. The systems analyst would likely have interviewed each of them during the analysis, and this is a good place to capture who they are, their attitude toward the changes, the abilities or inclination toward helping to develop, test, or implement them, etc. This is also the place to identify those against the changes. Typical stakeholders include:

A. Requestor.
B. Users.
C. Union officials.
D. Business department manager.
E. Network analyst.
F. Systems security analyst.
G. Service desk.
H. Operations.

[H]   Recommendations

After the analysis is completed, make recommendations both in summary and in detail. The summary recommendation includes a recap of the request, major time and cost drivers uncovered, and a total requirement in time and money.

The detailed report would provide all of the supporting information that totaled to the time and cost estimates. The detail is important in case any assumptions were flawed. If a proposed project is rejected, always record who denied the request and why.

§ 13.08   FLOWCHARTING STANDARDS

[A]   Purpose

Flowcharts pictorially explain how data flows through a system. They illustrate the relationships between modules and decision points and make it easier to understand its accompanying narrative. Flowcharts perform several functions in the systems investigation, analysis, design, development, and installation phases. They provide a visual overview of a process so that you can quickly locate the part of the process of greatest interest. There are several good software flowcharting programs available for PCs. Using a software package to draw flowcharts allows them to be easily and neatly changed.

Flowchart diagrams range in complexity from global system flowcharts to procedure step detail. Often software flowcharts begin with a "big picture" view and then display finer levels of details on additional charts.

The flowchart exhibit(s) should be on a single page. The manner in which the flowchart is illustrated will depend on the IT technical skills of the viewers. Such charts are most valuable when rendered in the simplest terms for the whole group.

[B]   Global System Flowcharts

A "global system" is an interaction of systems, with one or more systems outside the organization. One example would be a travel agent's system, interacting with both an airline ticket reservation system and the various credit card systems. The reservation and cost information must be approved before the travel agent can issue a ticket and charge the customer's credit card account.

[C]   Enterprise System Flowcharts

An "enterprise system" is an interaction of two or more data systems within the organization, which requires all participating systems to function. One example occurs when the production control system interacts with the incentive payroll system of manufacturing, which then interacts with the inventory system for inventory control. The payroll is affected by the worker's scrap rates, which affects inventory and scrap rate report counts. The production unit count credits the worker's pay, but also affects the preventive maintenance schedule, etc.

[D]   System Flowchart

The system flowchart shows how the information flows through a data system or process. It is all on one page. If greater detail is required for any area of the system, a subsystem or lower-level flowchart, which illustrates only the desired detail, is drawn for that purpose.

System flowcharts are not governed by any national standard. Intended for a diverse audience, from top management to programmers, flexibility is necessary to be able to target a presentation appropriately. While programmers can follow a system flowchart drawn for top management, top management may have a problem with one drawn for a project team of systems analysts and programmers because it will often utilize standard programming flowchart symbols.

[E]   Procedure Flowchart

Procedure flowcharting is useful for illustrating manual office procedures and is easy to follow, even by people outside the data-processing area. It confirms to the operations personnel that the systems analyst has recorded the procedure correctly. It also gives the systems analyst an easy-to-follow source of information when writing procedures.

Six symbols are used to draw the procedure flowchart. They represent:

1. Original information placed on document.
2. Addition of information to document.
3. Physical handling of document.
4. Document inspection to render a decision.
5. Document holding or storage.
6. Document leaving procedure area.

These are illustrated in Exhibit 13-3. A sample procedure flowchart is shown in Exhibit 13-4.

EXHIBIT 13-3.   Procedure Flowchart Symbols

Process or Element	Symbol
Original operation, the first time information is placed on a document.	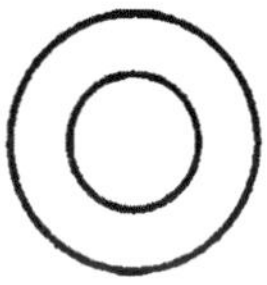 ◎
Adding information to a document in a later procedure step.	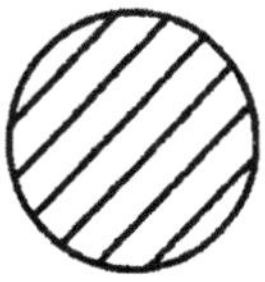 (hatched circle)
Handling the document, such as sorting, matching, separating, or stapling.	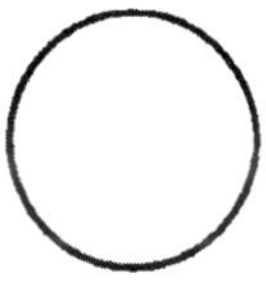 ○
Inspection of a document for a decision to be made. Two or more courses of action will follow.	□
Storage of document(s) as inactive, delayed, filed, or held. Also used as a destroy symbol.	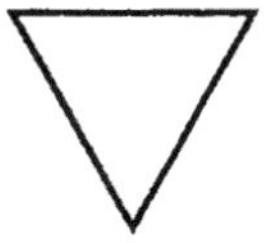 ▽
Sending or moving the document from one area to another. Also used to show document being sent outside.	 ○

EXHIBIT 13-4.   Sample Procedure Flowchart

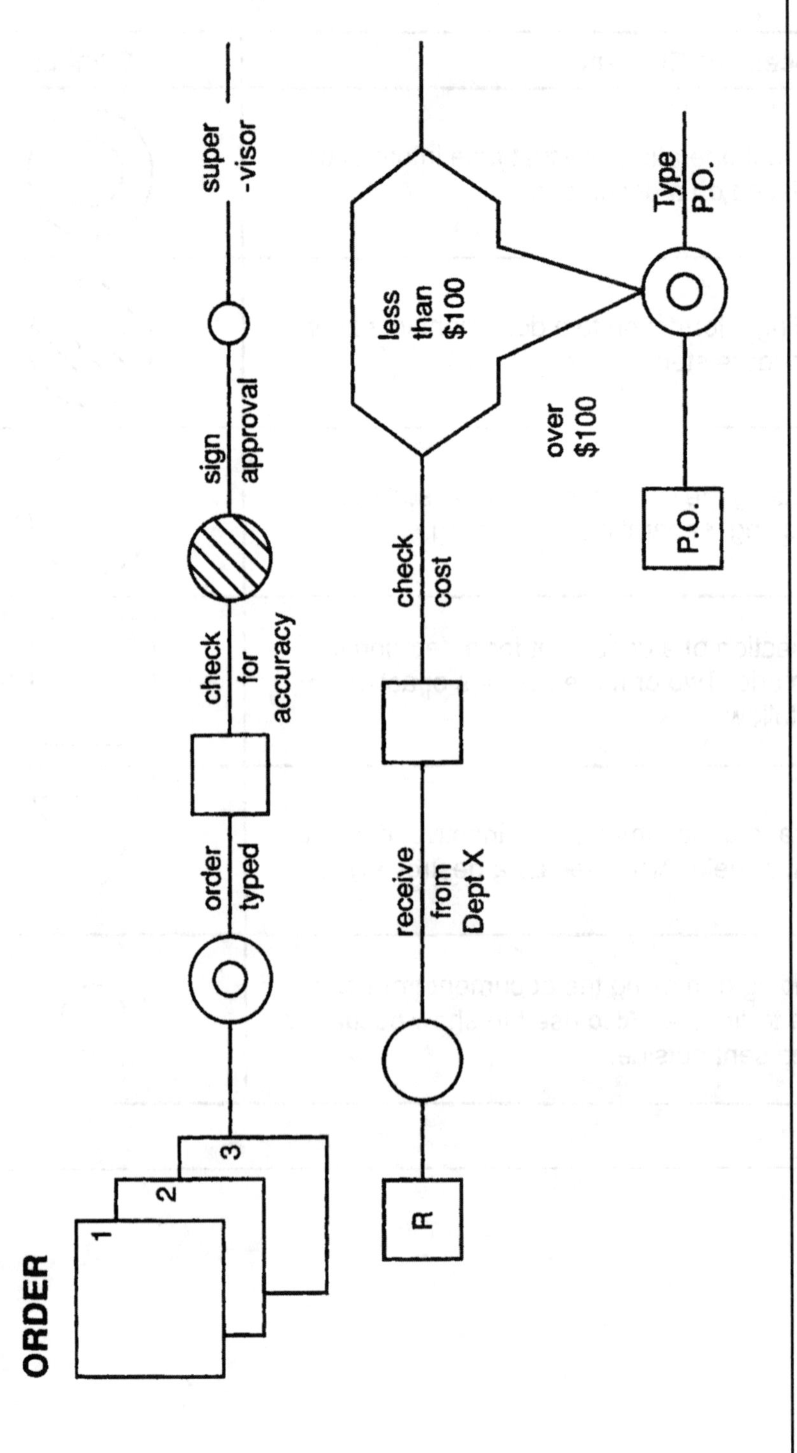

If a new, changed procedure contains manual operations, draw it as a procedure flowchart. When preparing a procedure flowchart, consider the following:

A. The direction of flow is left to right—and from top to bottom.
B. Identify the procedure flowchart in the lower left-hand corner with the following:
    1. Project name.
    2. Project number.
    3. Date.
    4. Name of person who produced flowchart.
C. All input documents have a receiving point, a starting point, and a disposition. Documents may be sent to a file, disposal, or to someone else.
D. Each line represents a data element flow.
E. Describe process steps briefly by printing the information to the right of the symbol.
F. When a multiple copy form, the parts are illustrated by the inspection symbol and the form title or number is printed inside the square.
G. When the same activity affects two or more documents simultaneously, it is shown by drawing a vertical rectangle around a symbol indicating the activity. Draw the flow lines to meet the rectangle.
H. Indicate the charting of one document affecting or creating other documents on the line of the affected action. A "V" line coming from the original document is dropped or inverted to meet the affected document line. After the action shown by a symbol is completed, the last leg of the "V" returns the document to its original level.

[F] Dataflow Diagrams

Dataflow diagrams are replacing the more traditional systems flowchart. Like the systems flowchart, they have not been guided by any one national standard. There is more than one proposed set of symbols, but all share the same concept and objective. The four diagramming symbols used in this text are based on work by C. Gane and T. Sarson. Their book, *Structured Systems Analysis and Design Tools and Techniques,* is the source of the concept and symbols represented here.

Dataflow diagrams, which have been around for some time, are familiar in the academic environment. They have many advantages over traditional systems flowcharts when presenting graduated levels of overviews for both current and proposed systems. Because the documentation system is so simple and employs so few rules and symbols, there is little variation between textbooks illustrating its use. Its simplicity provides for a uniform pictorial presentation of systems by systems analysts, programmers, operations personnel, and most users.

Refer to Exhibit 13-5 for the dataflow symbols. The standard programming flowcharting template may be used with some minor substitutions. The auxiliary operation symbol can replace the dataflow environmental element symbol. The process symbol can replace the dataflow process or procedure symbol. Use the programming or procedure flowcharting templates to draw the data storage symbol.

EXHIBIT 13-5.   Data Flowchart Diagram Symbols

Process or Element	Symbol
Entity, an environmental element, can be the source or destination of data to or from the system or subsystems.	
Process system or procedures that act on data being received from an external source or an internal file (hard copy or computer database or file).	
Data storage. This can be a computer file or database, hard copy, microfilm or COM, reference lists or tables, even the back of a tablet.	
Data flow. This can be in many forms, such as LAN or WAN systems, direct computer communications, the U.S. mail, UPS, courier, or what have you, between the process system (symbols) and data storage or external source. An arrow will be drawn at the contact point of the receiving symbol to denote the recipient of the data.	

The diagramming symbols used for data flow diagrams are based on work by C. Gane and T. Sarson, *Structured Systems Analysis and Design Tools and Techniques*, Prentice Hall, Englewood Cliffs, NJ, 1979.

The dataflow diagram illustrates the system's flow and transformation process all on one page. Draw subsystems requiring more detail at the next level, also in their entirety, one per page, with an identification number linking them to their source. This is shown in Exhibits 13-6, 13-7, and 13-8. Repeat this procedure until the final, lowest subsystem level. The complexity and number of subsystems within the undertaking determine the number of levels that may be "exploded." The dataflow diagram levels may be defined as follows:

A. **Context diagram.** The total system concept is the "large picture," illustrating all data flows into and out of the system. The processes themselves remain unnumbered and not described in this general overview. The context dataflow diagram would be the one most likely considered for use in a management presentation (see Exhibit 13-6).

EXHIBIT 13-6. Context Dataflow Diagram

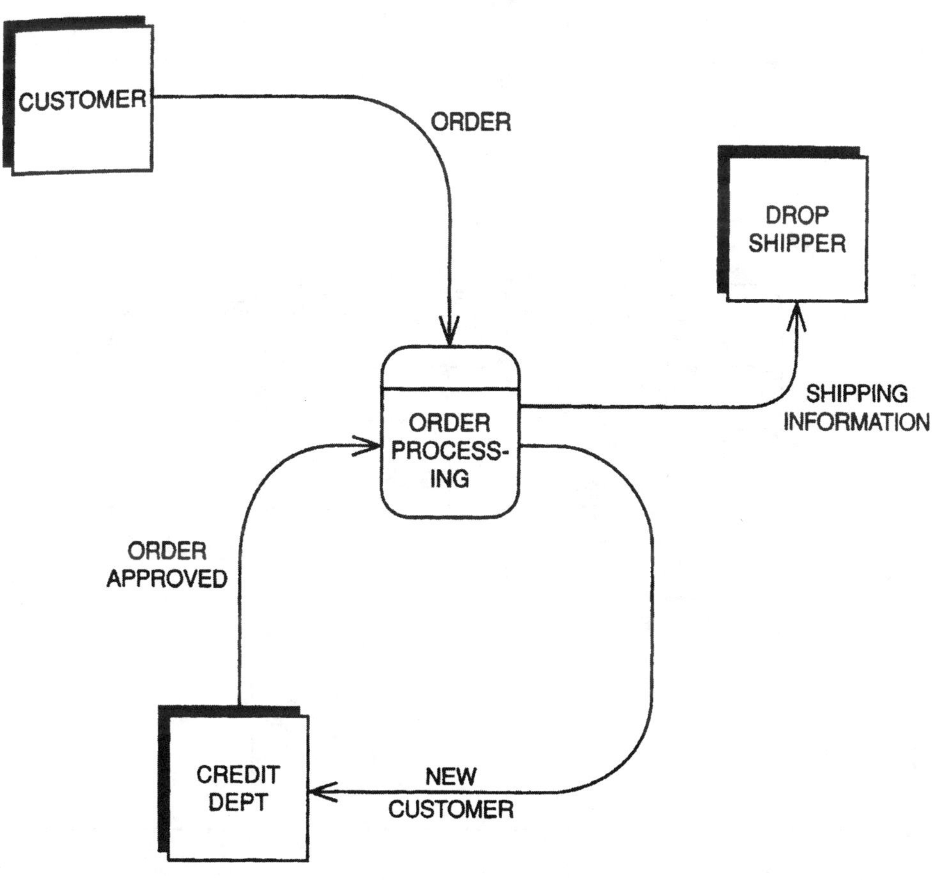

B. **Level 0 (zero) dataflow diagram.** This level represents the total system, numbering and describing each process. Data storage symbols depict the movement of data to or from storage (see Exhibit 13-7).

C. **Level 1 dataflow diagram.** This level represents one of the processes or procedures found at the zero dataflow level exploded into its own subsystem detail (see Exhibit 13-8).

D. **Level 2 dataflow diagram.** This level represents the further exploding of a given process found at level 1 into its own subsystem detail.

EXHIBIT 13-7.   Level Zero Dataflow Diagram

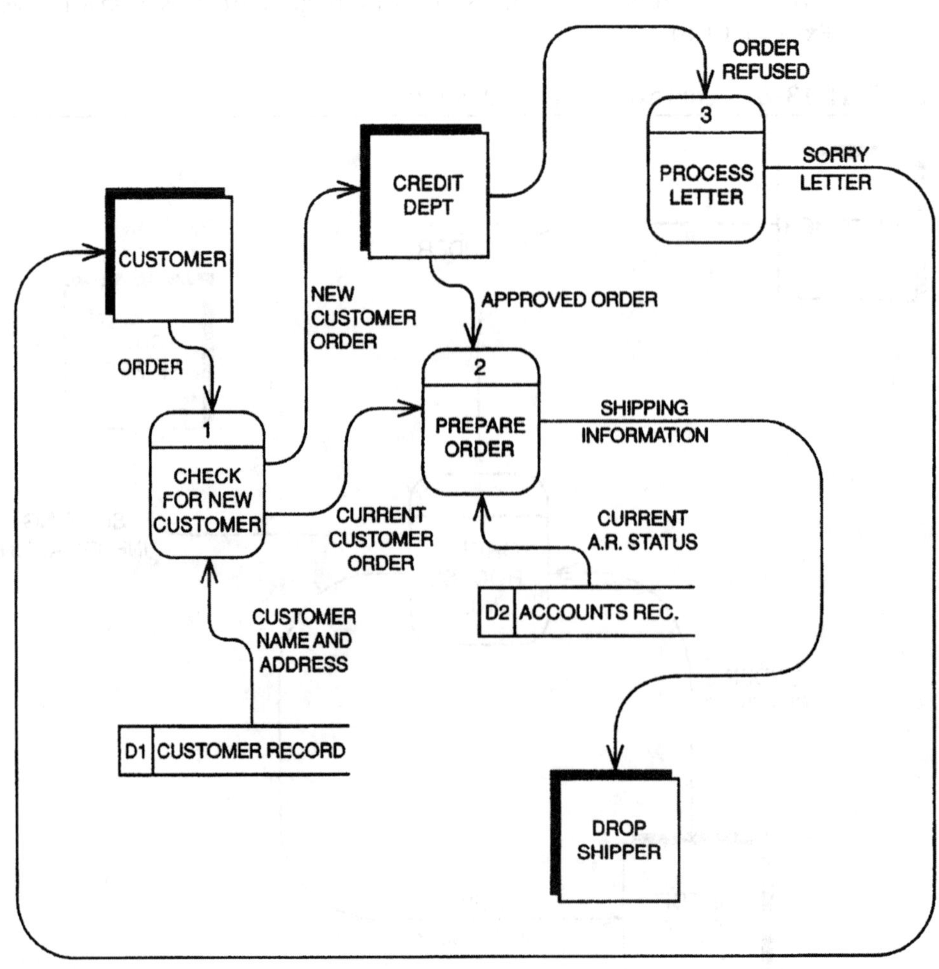

EXHIBIT 13-8.   Level 1 Dataflow Diagram

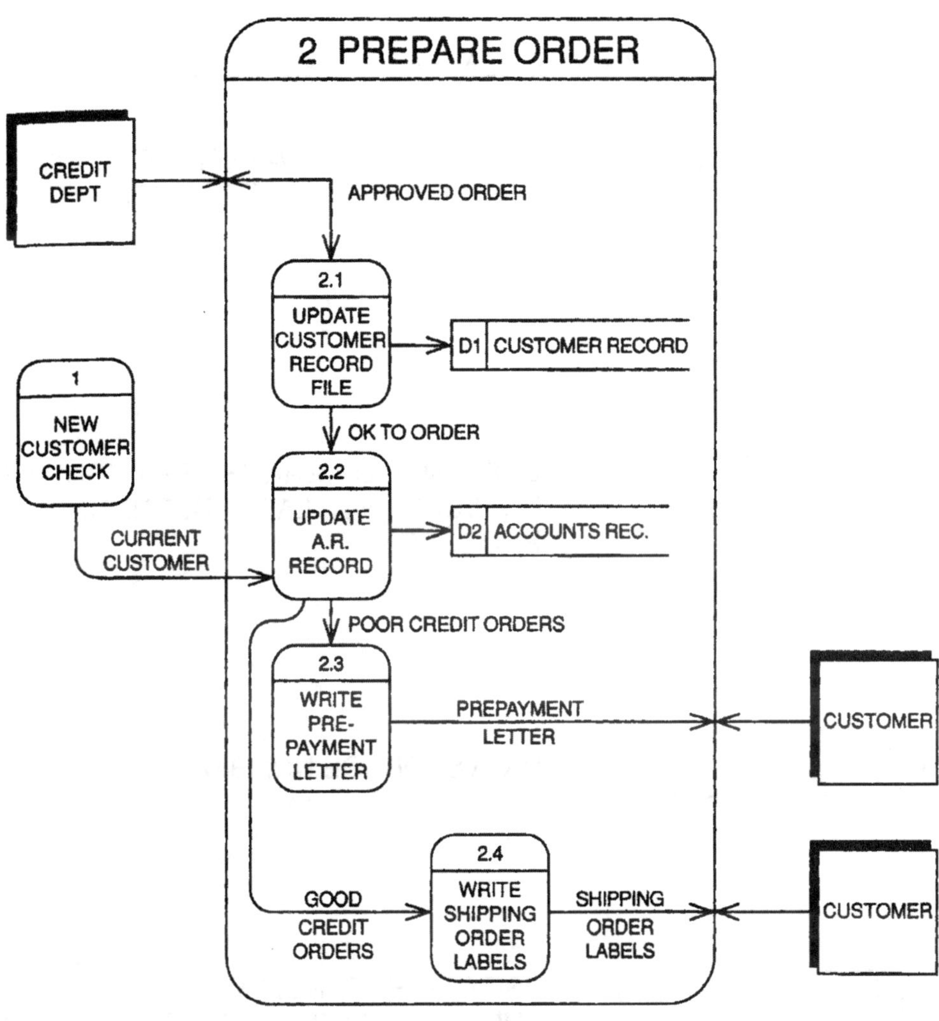

[G]   Supplemental Dataflow Conventions

The dataflow diagramming procedure can get complex with successive levels of explosions. To help clarify the diagram, each of the four symbols employed can use supplemental conventions. Refer to Exhibit 13-9. Following are additional conventions that may be of help:

A.   Duplicated entity symbols contain a diagonal slash in the bottom right corner. This can reduce the complexity of dataflow lines.

B.   Process symbols contain the process number in the top part of the symbol. When a diagram is exploded, append a decimal representing the current level to the process number to provide for an audit trail of the related detailed processes (see Exhibit 13-9).

EXHIBIT 13-9.   Supplement Dataflow Conventions

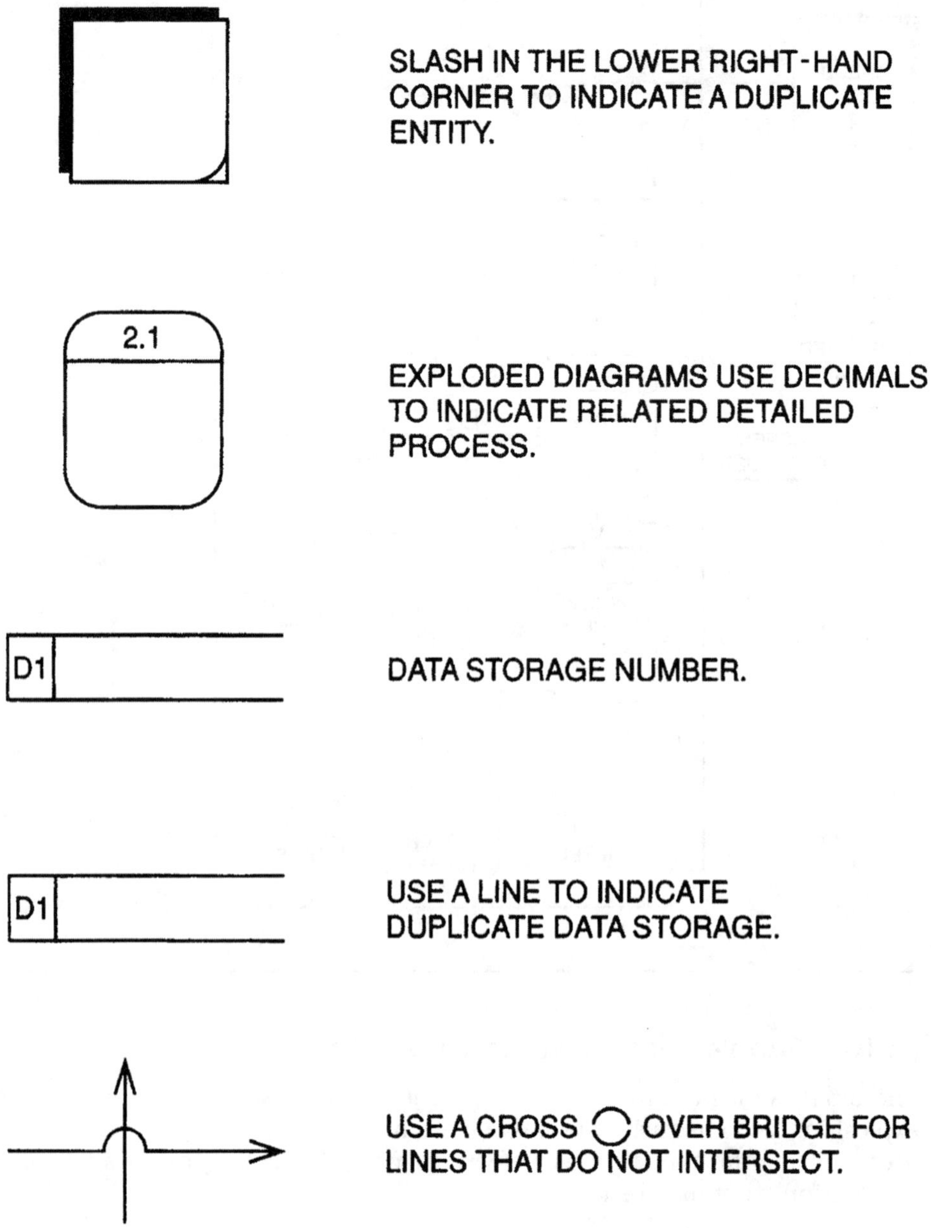

SLASH IN THE LOWER RIGHT-HAND CORNER TO INDICATE A DUPLICATE ENTITY.

EXPLODED DIAGRAMS USE DECIMALS TO INDICATE RELATED DETAILED PROCESS.

DATA STORAGE NUMBER.

USE A LINE TO INDICATE DUPLICATE DATA STORAGE.

USE A CROSS OVER BRIDGE FOR LINES THAT DO NOT INTERSECT.

   C. Data storage symbols have a boxed area on the left side of the symbol in which to write the data storage ID. A vertical line drawn to the left of the ID indicates a duplicate data storage location.

   D. When dataflow lines cross each other, one of the lines may use a small crossover bridge to illustrate that the lines do not intersect.

Using dataflow diagrams is good for both documenting a current system and developing a proposed system.

   A. Develop a freehand context diagram. This can start with on-hand user input.
      1. List external entities, data flows, and processes.
      2. Determine scope of system being charted.
      3. Draw context diagram.
   B. Develop a level 0 (zero) dataflow diagram.
      1. Apply detail to each process or procedure.
      2. Identify and post data storage. Note data storage types such as hard drive, tapes, optical disk, file drawer, etc.
      3. Identify process exceptions and post to diagram.
      4. Draw the diagrams with the aid of a template. Relabel any symbols requiring meaningful text and clean up the arrangement of the symbols.
      5. Explode to the next level and repeat 1, 2, and 3 above.

[H] Program Flowcharts

A program flowchart shows operation steps and logic decisions followed by the computer for a given program in the processing sequence. All the symbols employed should conform to the ANSI standards. Refer to Exhibit 13-10. Follow these rules in preparing the flowcharts:

   A. The general direction of flow is top to bottom, and left to right.
   B. Whenever increased clarity is desired, use arrows to indicate the direction of flow.
   C. Identify each page with:
      1. Project name.
      2. Project number.
      3. Name of person who produced the flowchart.
      4. Date.
      5. Page X of Y.
   D. Identify the terminal connector showing that a line continues to a following page with an uppercase alphabetic character in the center of the connector symbol. The line continued on the following page starts with a connector symbol and the same character in its center as the departing connector. If that line does not continue on the following page, post the page number to the right of the connector symbol and post the departing page number to the right of the receiving connector.

E. Describe process steps briefly by printing the description within the symbol. If necessary, print additional information next to the symbol to clarify a step.

F. Later, when changing the flowchart, updates should be noted, dated, and signed by the person making the change.

EXHIBIT 13-10.   Common Flowchart Symbols

Data Store Used for hard disk storage.	
Process Represents a processing function or activity.	
Decision Represents a decision step, with one or more alternative paths to be followed.	
Preparation Represents the modification of a program.	
Document Represents a printed document input or output (i.e. reports).	
Sequential Data Used for sequential data, such as tape input or output.	
Manual Operation Shows a manual operation which is limited to the speed of a human being.	
Data Represents data that is available for input or resulting from processing.	
Off Page Connector Used to indicate that the flow continues on another page. The page number is written inside the symbol.	
On Page Connect Used to indicate that the flow continues elsewhere on the page. A number is written inside the symbol to match up with the target connector.	
Flow Lines Used to connect the symbols and show the process flow.	

EXHIBIT 13-10.   (Continued)

Annotation Used for adding comments to an operation step.	
Predefined Process Used to illustrate a process that is defined elsewhere.	
Display Used to show output on a display (looks like a CRT screen).	
Manual Input Used from manual input (i.e. keyboard input).	
Terminal Point Used to start or stop a flowchart.	
Online Storage Represents any type of storage that is directly accessible by the system.	

[I]   Unified Modeling Language™

The latest method being developed for documenting object-oriented systems is the Unified Modeling Language™ (UML). Rational Software Corporation (now part of IBM) developed UML, with contributions from other leading methodologists, software vendors, and many users. UML is based on extensive use of the Booch, OMT, and Jacobson methods to document business processes and objects, and for component modeling. UML provides the application modeling language for:

    A. Business process modeling with use cases.
    B. Class and object modeling.
    C. Component modeling.
    D. Distribution and deployment modeling.

The Object Management Group (OMG) is developing UML into an industry standard. OMG is an open membership, not-for-profit consortium that produces and maintains computer industry specifications for interoperable enterprise applications. This standard is still in the process of being developed; for the latest information on UML, go to the OMG Web site at *www.omg.org,* or the IBM web site at *www-306.ibm.com/software/rational/.*

[J]   IDEF

Integrated Definition, better known as IDEF, was originally crated by the US Air Force as a series of modeling methods that can be used to describe operations in an organization. It is now being further developed and maintained by Knowledge Based Systems. IDEF was originally developed for use in manufacturing environments, but has been adapted for wider use and for software development in general.

There are sixteen different modeling methods, each of which is designed to capture a particular type of information through the modeling process. IDEF methods are used to create graphical representations of various systems, analyze the model, create a model of a desired version of the system, and to aid in the transition from one to the other. The following is a list of IDEF methods either currently used or in development. IDEF0 through IDEF4 are the methods most commonly used.

A. **IDEF0**—Function Modeling
B. **IDEF1**—Information Modeling
C. **IDEF1X**—Data Modeling
D. **IDEF2**—Simulation Model Design
E. **IDEF3**—Process Description Capture
F. **IDEF4**—Object-Oriented Design
G. **IDEF5**—Ontology Description Capture
H. **IDEF6**—Design Rationale Capture
I. **IDEF7**—Information System Auditing
J. **IDEF8**—User Interface Modeling
K. **IDEF9**—Scenario-Driven IS Design
L. **IDEF10**—Implementation Architecture Modeling
M. **IDEF11**—Information Artifact Modeling
N. **IDEF12**—Organization Modeling
O. **IDEF13**—Three Schema Mapping Design
P. **IDEF14**—Network Design

More information about the IDEF methods can be found on the Internet at *www.idef.com.*

See Exhibits 13-5 through 13-10 for sample flowchart materials.

EXHIBIT 13-11.   Common IDEF Symbols

Process Represents a processing function or activity.	Process Name A0
Label Used to label an input, output, control or mechanism.	Label
Connector Used to connect processes.	

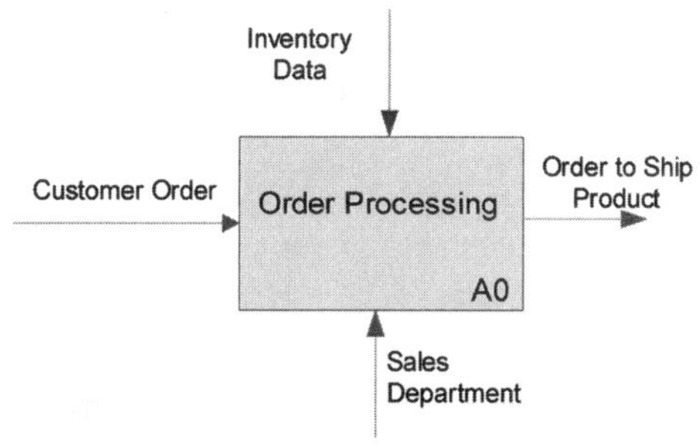

IDEF0 Example Process

14

COMPUTER SECURITY: PRACTICE SAFE COMPUTING

§ 14.01 OVERVIEW
    [A] Purpose and Scope
    [B] Security Objectives
    [C] Critical Policies to Develop Based on This Chapter

§ 14.02 PEOPLE SECURITY
    [A] Internal Threats
    [B] Social Engineering

§ 14.03 PROCESS SECURITY
    [A] Threat Analysis
    [B] Process Security Planning
    [C] Software Development
    [D] Network Design
    [E] Passwords
    [F] Physical Security
    [G] Disaster Recovery Planning
    [H] Testing
    [I] Instant Messaging (IM)

§ 14.04 LEGAL ISSUES
    [A] Overview
    [B] Health Insurance Portability and Accountability Act (HIPAA)
    [C] Sarbanes-Oxley Act (SOX)
    [D] Gramm-Leach-Bliley Act
    [E] SEC Rules
    [F] Committee of Sponsoring Organizations (COSO)
    [G] Control Objectives for Information and Related Technology (COBIT™)
    [H] Personal Information Protection and Electronic Documents Act (PIPEDA)
    [I] Fair and Accurate Credit Transactions Act of 2003 (FACTA)
    [J] ISO 17799
    [K] Canadian Budget Measures Act (Bill 198)

§ 14.01 OVERVIEW

[A] Purpose and Scope

A company's computer systems are the lifeblood of its ever-changing, complex operations. The investment in computer systems is more than a question of resources and cost. It also is a question of remaining competitive. Properly implemented and secured computer systems can give a company a competitive advantage by multiplying the effectiveness of its workforce. Poorly designed systems act as a drag on the business. To protect this investment, the company must have clearly defined policies to stipulate that all computer systems are properly secured and protected from improper use. A well-implemented security system provides integrity, confidentiality, and availability.

Implementing and supporting computer systems is expensive, and a company that employs its own support staff has invested a considerable amount of money into processes to support its business. All of this is lost if confidential and critical company and customer data is compromised to the world. If you have internal staff or hire a computer security consultant, insist on a CISSP certification. This certification proves a well-rounded scope of knowledge and knowledge of current new threats.

[B] Security Objectives

Computer security is often perceived as elusive and costly. The reality is that strue security is a myth. Any security system will yield at some point if the attacker has unlimited time, money, access, and intellectual capacity. So the magic question that every CIO wrestles with is how much security do we need? How much money, manpower, and time should be committed to security?

The answer: A company only needs to buy one second of security. The challenge is to invest enough to exceed the tenacity, creativity, and resources of an attacker plus a safety factor of that one second. All information systems will yield under varied, sustained, and tenacious attacks. The ideal system will protect unauthorized use of information systems for one second longer than the maximum limits of frustration and tenacity of the worst hacker or until the information is no longer of value. The "art" part of security planning is in choosing the correct time when your protective systems will yield. All information has a "value lifespan," which is the point where its value reaches zero. For example, the combination to my middle school locker was 24-18-46. This information no longer has any value to anyone.

So, how do you get to that second? The answer is to go through a three-step process that looks under all of the rocks, fills in all of the potholes, and paves the road to remaining employed and sleeping well at night.

> Step One—Identify the protection needed and for how long.
> Step Two—Select the methods to protect.
> Step Three—Pre-plan detection, recovery, and response.

> Make time your ally!

Step One. This is often the hardest step because it requires senior management to acknowledge they are willing to sacrifice certain areas of their business to focus maximum protective activities on the most critical assets to the business. Often these can be identified by legal requirements, contractual requirements, trade secrets, patents, research and development, brand protection, sensitive materials, or other items that if compromised, altered, or stolen would have a significant impact on the business. Examples include:

- Banks—Transaction queues, accounts payable, accounts receivables, and securities records.
- Hospitals—Medical records, accounts receivables, accounts payables, and logistics.
- Manufacturing—Processes, marketing, accounts payables, accounts receivables, and logistics.
- Retail—Client information, marketing plans, accounts payables, accounts receivables, and logistics.

Step Two. The key to selecting the most appropriate and cost-effective methods to protect the critical assets is to create a fabric with a diverse multidimensional framework. Four areas that must be considered:

- Internal personnel and profiles of external attackers.
- Operational procedures.
- Electronic barriers and honey pots.
- Time.

Step Three. The final step is to carefully pre-plan a response to an attack. This planning can be the most important part of successfully defending the entire organization. A plan must be developed for three things:

- Detection and identification of the intent of the attacker.
- Recovery.
- After-an-attack response.

An attack can be detected in many forms, including poor network performance, altered information, deleted information, or public disclosure of internal documents. Recovery may be as simple as restoring information from a back up or as complex as comparing a production database with a backup copy table by table, record by record, field by field, and then manually identifying and correcting any fraudulent entries.

COMMENT

The IT staff should be trained on providing an immediate response to an attack. One company used red cable for their

> interconnection to the Internet and had a relay so they could interrupt the connection remotely from various locations. One large company used an inline intrusion detection system (IDS) that would automatically detect many types of attacks and block those attempts while simultaneously allowing normal traffic to flow.

Remember, time is an ally. The longer the system can withstand an attack, the more likely it is to exceed the patience or resources of an attacker. Many companies like to buy all of their network hardware from one manufacturer because it reduces the amount of spare parts that they must keep on site and reduces the amount of training for their support personnel. The problem with this is that once a hacker penetrates the network, he or she will know where a weakness exists that will allow them free access to the entire network. By using equipment from more than one manufacturer, time is gained and an attacker is frustrated.

[C]   Critical Policies to Develop Based on This Chapter

Using the material discussed in this chapter, you will be able to create the following policies:

A. Proper actions to protect systems against people.
 1. Internal threats from employees and partners.
 2. External threats from competitors, former employees, etc.
B. Security must be integrated into your business processes.
 1. Change control guidance to ensure all software changes are properly tested for security issues prior to implementation (all changes proposed, including a detailed back-out plan).
 2. Network design to ensure a secure network.
 3. Physical asset protection.
 4. Integration of security into the disaster recovery plan.
 5. Security as it relates to regulatory requirements.

Policies should always be developed based on the local situation. Successful managers cannot issue appropriate guidance if the policies are written with another company's or location's situation in mind.

§ 14.02   PEOPLE SECURITY

[A]   Internal Threats

Companies employ many people. The issue is: can these people be trusted? Nontechnical employees perform 85 percent of all fraud using authorized systems. This internal fraud costs businesses an estimated $660 billion in 2003.

Does the company employ anyone who has been convicted of embezzlement or blackmail? Are the employees loyal to the company and its leaders? Was anyone discharged from the military with anything other than an honorable discharge? Are there any employees who maintain close personal contacts with employees at competitors? Is anyone exhibiting signs of financial trouble, such as gambling, working multiple jobs, abusing alcohol or drugs, or spending well beyond his or her salary? Is anyone taking judgment altering prescription drugs?

COMMENT

One employer noticed that the administrative assistant to the vice president of sales, a single mother of two, began driving a new Porsche to work and then asked for vacation time so she could vacation in the Cayman Islands with her new boyfriend. Upon further exploration, it was discovered that her boyfriend was connected to a major competitor.

Policies to protect against employee security threats include:

A. Having all employees sign a confidentiality and "noncompete" contract. This at least gives legal recourse to recover the economic cost of damages. Labor laws of your country or locale may restrict the structure or scope of what you can include.
B. Running routine security checks on all company officers every year or two to make sure there are no significant changes in their background.
C. Running routine security checks on critical technical people.
D. Developing a written policy on automatic prosecution of anyone caught in the theft, unauthorized destruction or unauthorized use of company data.
E. Limiting who has access to very sensitive information, such as mailroom workers, administrative assistants, file clerks, marketing staff, and external printers.
F. Compartmentalizing sensitive information so that few employees know the entire picture until it is about to become public knowledge.
G. Having all systems administrators and key network people write down their passwords and provide them to a trusted party in sealed envelopes. One company used a safe with two locks to secure the passwords so it required two officers of the company to access the information. An alternative to this **elaborate procedure** is to make sure that you have fully qualified and cross-trained key staff members who have fully equal capabilities.

H. Ensuring that all contracts with external companies include confidentiality and noncompete clauses and assign ownership rights to the company.

Another area that is critical to the protection of computer systems from internal threats is computer and network account management. Always ensure the number of people that have the authority to grant access to IT resources is small and that there are routine audits or cross checks. Disable guest accounts on all systems. Make sure the number of accounts with full control is limited to a small number of people that is proportional to the size of the organization.

COMMENT

One company had production programs and databases located in individual personal accounts. When one systems administrator left the company, no one could delete or disable the account because of the number of production processes that were running there. Separate development, test, and production accounts that mirror each other should be created and the number of IT people with access to the production accounts restricted. One company even had a completely independent group that just handled the deployment of software changes and thus no developers were allowed direct access to production systems.

Separations can be a major source of computer security issues. When an employee leaves the company, it can be a challenging experience for everyone involved. Are there clear written procedures on the actions to take when an employee leaves the company? Are there additional steps if the person is an IT person, such as inventorying all of the systems he or she had access to and transitioning all in-progress work to knowledgeable staff? Are there clear written procedures on the actions to take when temporary employees or contractors leave the organization? Are e-mail accounts reviewed for improper activity and future traffic rerouted to a successor or manager?

Keys to managing internal threats from people include:

- Management at all levels must be aware of IT security risks and procedures. Security should be a mandatory requirement in every person's job appraisal.
- Eternal vigilance by everyone.

- Training should be periodic and updated. Small training sessions every month or two will keep security fresh in everyone's mind. By covering a different topic each time, the training can be made comprehensive and relevant.

[B] Social Engineering

Social engineering is the use of nontechnical means to get information about a company or computer system that allows unauthorized access. Movies often show a female spy extracting secrets from a scientist. While such scenarios are fictional, true sting operations like this are performed every day. It usually involves the use of interpersonal telephone skills to convince unsuspecting victims to provide sensitive information over the telephone. These "social engineers" can be hackers, prison inmates, or someone from the competition. The most common scheme is for the caller to call in to a receptionist and ask for someone in technical support. When connected to that person, the caller gets a name and then claims that the receptionist has sent him to the wrong number. He then asks the person to transfer him to his intended victim, and then proceeds to convince the victim that he is from tech support and needs his password due to a system problem. Once he has the password, all he needs is an external connection to the network and he is in.

Malicious attackers know that the easiest way to break into a system is through the people that use it. Important information can be found in the trash (Do you know who empties your trash?), in e-mails (many login IDs are the same as a person's e-mail prefix), and by just asking. Social engineering depends on the ability to persuade people to divulge information that is useful to the attacker. Many times each piece of information by itself seems harmless, but put together can give attackers the tools they need to get into your system. An old invoice or company directory can give the attacker enough information to convince his victim that he is part of the team. Much of the information needed is available on the Internet or in company brochures and other publications.

Attackers use the following general steps in performing their attack:

A. Gather information: There are many sources of information that can be used to develop a relationship. These include old phone lists, company documents such as invoices, the Internet, trash bins, eavesdropping at social events, etc.

B. Develop a relationship: Once the attacker has enough information, he or she can then begin to develop a relationship with someone at the target company. This can be done in one day with a single phone call or over the course of several weeks. The attacker exploits the natural tendency of most people to be trusting.

C. Take advantage of the relationship: Once the attacker has gained the person's trust, he or she can trick them into revealing additional information needed for the attack.

D.   Attack: Now that all the needed information has been collected, the attacker proceeds with the attack.

So how do you protect your company against social engineering attacks? It starts with a clear, comprehensive, and communicated security policy. The security policy must be trained, enforced, and compliance monitored regularly. The policy must be relevant and easy to use by the employees. A policy that is hard to follow and not clear gets in the way and encourages employees to work around it. Other guidelines to protect your company include:

A.   Forbid the exchange of passwords between employees for any reason. A technical support person should never ask an employee for his password. Use automated password reset tools to eliminate human intervention in changing passwords.
B.   Use password authentication questions to ensure that requests to reset passwords come from authorized users.
C.   Avoid using password authentication questions that are easy to answer with just a little research. Mother's maiden name, children's names, addresses, pet names, etc. can all be found without too much difficulty.
D.   The use of biometric devices or security tokens can significantly reduce the chances of a successful attack using social engineering.
E.   Background checks of all employees with access to sensitive systems can identify employees who might be susceptible to divulging information in exchange for money.

While you cannot and do not want to turn your company into Fort Knox, securing the information inside your company may just be the most important job in your company. This information in most cases is the most important asset in your company. Securing your systems from internal and external threats is not a one-time activity, but requires continuing vigilance and commitment to keeping your data safe.

§ 14.03   PROCESS SECURITY

[A]   Threat Analysis

Conduct a vulnerability analysis to determine how the company's systems may be attacked and when they may be attacked. When studying how the company's systems may be attacked, the IT Manager must consider internal threats, external threats, accidental disclosures, deletions or alterations, and denial-of-service attacks. One technique is to take the perspective of one of the company's competitors and write a plan on how they would take apart the company. This can provide great insight into the company's weaknesses. Look for the holes in people, processes, and technology. Review the audit checklist in Worksheet 14-1 and customize it for your company.

WORKSHEET 14-1   Security Audit Checklists

SECURITY AUDIT CHECKLISTS—DESKTOP

1. Do you have multiple layers of security including several layers of door locks (keyed differently) as well as network and application passwords?
2. Do you have limits on who gets CD-RW or DVD-RW drives?
3. Do you disble USB ports where not needed so that memory stick devices cannot be used?
4. Is anti-virus software kept current mechanically?
5. Is another brand of anti-virus software on hand to be used in the event of failure of the primary?
6. Is Internet access limited?
7. Do you limit employee's ability to download and run executable files over the Internet?
8. Do employees understand that they should treat company data the same way they would treat cash?
9. Are screens viewable from open doors, windows, or common areas?
10. Are screens that are visible by noncompany employees maintained to the highest level of security?
11. Are passwords changed frequently?
12. Are passwords required to be strong (i.e., composed of A–Z, a–z, 0–9, $.;*^#@!)?
13. Are common area computers disabled when not in use?
14. Are the owners of notebook computers and PDAs taught to carefully guard them?
15. Is the loss of a notebook or PDA immediately reported, removed from network access lists, and have all security privileges been revoked?
16. Is the amount and sensitivity of information stored on notebooks or PDAs limited to the minimum necessary?
17. Do people know how to encrypt files and are the proper tools available for use?
18. Do people know to never share their passwords with anyone including internal staff and technical staff?
19. Do you have testing criteria, procedures, and equipment to evaluate any new software and upgrades for malicious activity?
20. Are all systems maintained with a secure version of the operating system and all necessary security patches applied?
21. Are computers turned off during evenings, weekends, and holidays?
22. Is a hardware key or user authentication required?
23. Once a user is authenticated, how is access to authorized materials contained?
24. Does the operating system provide the necessary secure environment?
25. Does the operating system keep each application in restricted memory space?
26. Does the operating system purge passwords from memory?
27. Does the operating system wipe files that are deleted?
28. Does the operating system lock the screen and keyboard when not in use?
29. Do you use terminal servers instead of PCs?

SECURITY AUDIT CHECKLISTS—NETWORK

1. Do you still have hubs or mini-hubs on the network or have they all been replaced with switches?
2. Does the number of wired connections in switches match the number of devices? Are spares bundled and disabled?
3. Are there nonsecure wireless network access points?
4. Is dial-in access used? Does it require VPN software to function? Can dial-back modems be implemented?
5. If modems are on the network, are they separated from the network by a firewall device?
6. Is sensitive information being sent over the Internet unencrypted?
7. Are network cables properly labeled and bundled?
8. Do routers block unauthorized traffic?
9. Do you have a firewall to block unauthorized access attempts?
10. Do you restrict who can send data to outside destinations (FTP)?
11. Are all satellite offices given the same level of attention and protection as the home office?
12. Do satellite offices use the home office firewall security for Internet access?
13. Are there limits on who has dial-out modems on the network?
14. Are there tools that can identify all equipment on the network?
15. Are network cables bundled separately from telephone cables and clearly marked?
16. Do trustworthy personnel install network cabling?
17. Is fiber optic cable used where possible?
18. Do other trading partners who provide data have the same emphasis and level of commitment to security?
19. Do you have two telephone truck cables providing service to the building via different routes and telephone exchanges (POP)?
20. Have the points or equipment in the network where a failure of that one item would disrupt service been identified? Is there an alternate route or stand-by equipment plan?
21. Are encryption devices necessary and, if so, are they in use?
22. Is there an intrusion detection system in-line with the Internet interface?
23. Are intrusion detection systems logically located immediately before the servers with no routers between them?
24. Has the network been reviewed by a certified ethical hacker for security holes?
25. Are server logs checked on a regular basis for security violations?
26. Are all system administrators and network people trained that in the event of a successful attack they are to capture all evidence to CD-ROM as soon as possible?
27. If cryptography is used, are the people using it properly trained in its use?
28. Is there a honey pot system to automatically attract attacks?

Security Audit Checklists—Computer Room

1. Are your major systems on an uninterruptible power supply (UPS) system and not on a stand-by (SPS) system?
2. Does a stand-by generator back up your UPS?
3. How long can you go without commercial power?
4. Is maintenance routinely performed on the UPS and generator? Are they tested regularly?
5. Are backups performed routinely?
6. Are your computer room people happy?
7. Are the working conditions safe and comfortable?
8. Do you have a fire suppression system?
9. Does your fire suppression system work automatically?
10. Does your fire detection system automatically report it to the fire department?
11. Does the air conditioning system automatically shut down when a fire is detected to deprive it oxygen?
12. If you have a Halon system, do your people understand how it works and the dangers of it?
13. Is the computer room door locked, with a limited number of people having access?
14. Are computer rooms located in the core of a building with no outside windows?
15. Does the computer room have emergency lighting?
16. Are there flammable materials in the computer room (including carpet)? What about adjacent rooms?
17. Are all cables routed overhead or under the floor?
18. Can servers detect unusual activity during evenings, weekends, and holidays and page someone?
19. Can servers track unusual activity and provide a complete log?
20. Can unusual activity be reversed?
21. Who has night, weekend, and holiday access to the computer room and why?
22. Is the location of all keys known?
23. How long has it been since the locks were changed?
24. Is a hardware key or user authentication required?
25. Once a user is authenticated, how is his or her access contained to authorized materials only?
26. Does the operating system provide the necessary secure environment?
27. Does the operating system keep each application in restricted memory space?
28. Does the operating system purge passwords from memory?
29. Does the operating system wipe files that are deleted?
30. Does access to the main system consoles provide extra physical security?
31. Do your systems have remote control software such as PCAnywhere?

SECURITY AUDIT CHECKLISTS—PEOPLE

1. Can your people be trusted?
2. Has anyone been convicted of embezzlement, theft, or blackmail?
3. Are your people loyal?
4. Has anyone received a discharge from the military with anything other than an honorable discharge?
5. Are your people motivated and do they have goals that are consistent with the company's?
6. Do you employ anyone who is working multiple jobs and may be in financial trouble?
7. Do you employ people who maintain close personal contacts with employees at competitors?
8. Do you employ people that gamble a lot?
9. Do you employ any alcoholics or illegal drug users?
10. Do you employ anyone on prescription drugs that could alter their judgment?
11. Do you employ anyone that is spending well beyond his or her salary?
12. Do you employ confidentiality contracts with all employees?
13. Do you limit who has access to very sensitive information?
14. Do you take good care of your systems administrators and network engineers?
15. Do you have a policy to refer for prosecution anyone caught in the theft of company data?
16. Are routine security checks run on all VPs and above and critical technical people every year or two to verify that nothing has significantly changed?
17. Is new account creation limited to a small number of people and cross-checked?
18. Are guest accounts removed from all systems?
19. Is the number of accounts with full control limited to a number of people that is proportional to the organization's size?
20. Do your system administrators and key network people write down their passwords and provide them to a trusted party in sealed envelopes?
21. Is security a mandatory requirement in every person's job appraisal?
22. Do your employment agreements with software developers assign ownership rights to the company for anything developed on company time or with company assets?
23. Do you have clear procedures on the actions to take when an employee leaves the company? What if he or she is an IT person?
24. Do you have clear procedures on the actions to take when temps or contractors are used and then leave?
25. Is your service desk person and other technical people trained to detect social hacking?
26. Are sensitive documents shredded beyond recovery?

Security Audit Checklists—Processes

1. Do you have policies regulating games, freeware, and shareware?
2. Are sensitive documents shredded beyond reconstruction?
3. Is internal code thoroughly tested before it is moved into the production environment?
4. Are there periodic code reviews that examine all custom source code for potential damaging problems?
5. Is code scanned for future dates, login IDs, passwords, copy or FTP commands?
6. Are there safeguards in place to preclude wrongful alteration of data?
7. Do you have a response plan to address hacking attempts? Does it include contact phone numbers for technical and law enforcement resources?
8. Are your network people trained on identifying a denial of service attack? How fast can they isolate and thwart the access route?
9. Do you have a response plan for a virus attack?
10. Are standard software products pre-selected and their use enforced?
11. Is the security impact given consideration with all technology purchases?
12. Do you keep a list of the security risks that have been considered and approved with the approval manager's name and date?
13. Do your e-mails and faxes have confidentiality footers?
14. If you have security people, do they have clearly written instructions? Do they include inspecting outgoing boxes?
15. When new equipment is purchased, does it come from a trusted source?
16. Is new computer equipment locked up until it is placed in service?
17. Is access to mainframe ODBC datasets read-only and password protected?
18. Is access to mainframe ODBC datasets limited to a need-to-know basis?
19. Are common passwords blocked from usage?
20. Does someone maintain a notebook of all of the software license numbers and the agreements? Is there a periodic internal audit to verify that no unauthorized copies have been made and that all licensing requirements are met?
21. If unauthorized copies are found, are they immediately removed or purchased?
22. Are the company's intellectual property rights guarded on internally developed software and products?
23. Is a standard security checklist (ISO 17799) used and maintained?
24. Are there built-in mechanical checks of financial data to detect alterations or out-of-tolerance numbers?
25. Is there double entry of critically important pieces of information?
26. Is there an audit trail that can detect all adds, changes, and deletions?
27. Do your people know how to search the audit trail?
28. Does the audit trail assign responsibility for the action to a person or unique process?
29. Can the auditing be disabled? Who knows how to do it?
30. Is company-confidential information clearly identified or marked? Do screens have the word "Confidential" on them?
31. Is sensitive information on your web site? Who checks your web site and how often?

32. If competitors wanted to find out information about your company, how would they do it?

33. How do you deal with data integrity issues? Who is responsible for correcting them and identifying their point of origin?

34. Do you have a feedback mechanism that blocks the reoccurrence of data integrity problems?

35. Are remote control applications used such as PCAnywhere or VNC? Are they properly secured?

36. Do the introduction screens of all systems clearly state ownership and confidentiality of the information they contain and the prosecution policy?

37. Is there a diversity of equipment and operating systems so that a successful penetration into one machine does not allow access into other more secure machines?

38. Do your internal web applications use CGI instead of Java?

39. If you supply sensitive or proprietary data to other companies, do they have the same level of commitment to security that your company does?

40. Do your contracts with suppliers or third-party companies provide recourse if their network is hacked and the hacker gains access to your data?

41. Do you periodically physically inspect your trading partners that handle sensitive information?

42. Do your trading partners have any personnel problems that could compromise your data?

43. Have you ever had your main conference rooms, boardroom, HR, marketing, purchasing and executive offices checked for unauthorized clandestine listening devices?

SECURITY AUDIT CHECKLISTS—RESOURCES

Hacking Exposed
www.hackingexposed.com

AntiOnline
www.antionline.com/index.php

Yahoo! Security and Encryption
d4.dir.dcn.yahoo.com/computers_and_internet/security_and_encryption/

CERT Coordination Center
www.cert.org

Center for Information Technology, National Institutes of Health
www.alw.nih.gov/Security/security.html

National Institute of Standards and Technology, Computer Security Resource Center
csrc.nist.gov/

Computer Security Institute
www.gocsi.com/

U.S. Department of Energy, Office of Cyber Security
www.ciac.org/ciac/

TruSecure
www.trusecure.com/

ITSecurity.com
www.itsecurity.com/

Ovitz Taylor Gates
www.ovitztaylorgates.com/TheITSecurityEssentialsGuide.html

Security Intelligence Technologies
www.spyzone.com

A threat analysis should answer three major questions: Who, what, and why? Who the attacker is may include U.S. competitors, foreign competitors, foreign governments, disgruntled employees, or independent attackers. What the attack may target includes critical assets such as financial and logistical systems; business functions required to sustain normal operations; business assets that are valuable, rare, and difficult to imitate; customer and medical information; and future business plans. Key IT resources also can be targets. Why the attacker does it usually involves a transfer of wealth, denial of service, retaliation, fun or challenge, or corporate espionage.

In thinking about when the company's systems might be attacked, consider the following.

A. U.S., foreign, and religious holidays.
B. Significant dates in history in this country and others.
C. Peak business hours locally and in time zones where competitors are located.
D. After-school hours (3 P.M. EST).
E. Foreign governments that may be interested in your company's protected assets, trade secrets, or future research.
F. After significant corporate events such as:
   1. Layoffs.
   2. Outsourcing.
   3. Mergers and acquisitions.
   4. Public knowledge of increase in liquid assets.
   5. Shortly after a new operating system is released.
   6. When key people are traveling.
   7. Corporate events (social hacking).
   8. Happy hour.
   9. Right after a patent is issued.
   10. Right after a joint venture or partnership is formed (bleeding through).
   11. After implementation of new hardware, software, or applications.
   12. Retirement of senior security personnel because junior staff may not detect the attack.

A threat analysis should answer three major questions: Who, what, and why? Who the attacker is may include U.S. competitors, foreign competitors, foreign governments, disgruntled employees, or independent attackers. What the attack may target includes critical assets such as financial and logistical systems; business functions required to sustain normal operations; business assets that are valuable, rare, and difficult to imitate; customer and medical information; and future business plans. Key IT resources also can be targets. Why the attacker does it usually involves a transfer of wealth, denial of service, retaliation, fun or challenge, or corporate espionage.

[B] Process Security Planning

Once the threat analysis is completed, the IT Manager should have a clear understanding of the security risks so the following questions can be answered:

    A.   What needs to be protected?
    B.   Who does the protection?
    C.   When should it be protected?
    D.   How is the best way to protect it?
    E.   What should be in the response plan?

In the IT world, key resources such as passwords, laptops, servers, networks, databases, and proprietary information often require protection. The IT Manager should clearly assign responsibilities to design and implement security to protect the company's critical assets. Any company person that is traveling must be aware that he or she becomes a moving target and any information on a laptop computer can be stolen.

> ## COMMENT
>
> All employees must be taught to treat sensitive company information like it was cash!

When should security be considered in the design process? Any time new IT equipment is being selected, security should be considered. Any time new applications are designed or significantly altered, security should be considered. Security should be reviewed in response to new threats. When new employees are hired, security access should be reviewed. Mergers, acquisitions, or the sale of a division of the company provide significant holes where sensitive company information can grow feet.

The security plan must:

    A.   Be in writing.
    B.   Be taught to all employees.

C. Require when and who has received the training to be documented.

D. Outline the IT Manager's accountability for accepting all known risks.

E. Ensure quality, focused time be set aside on a periodic basis to develop and review the plan.

In addition, the security plan must include:

A. Prevention.
B. Detection.
C. Recovery.
D. After-action response.
E. Criminal prosecution.

The response plan must be a written document! Detection and how to develop an audit trail for evidence collection and preservation should be included. It should focus on recovery and the uninterrupted continuance of business operations. It should include the phone numbers of technical personnel and law enforcement officials.

[C] Software Development

Just like any software development product, it should be built to last the first time. Too many applications are written as one-time, short-lived projects that seize roots and last forever; security was rarely considered in the initial design. Security should be considered on every project no matter how small. A one-time application that is left on the production system can accidentally be executed again at some point in the future by someone on your staff or a hacker.

COMMENT

Could It Happen to You?

Overvalued house goofs up city's budget.

Value erroneously changed to $400 million may lead to municipal layoffs.

The Associated Press Updated: 5:42 p.m. ET Feb. 10, 2006

VALPARAISO, Ind.—A house erroneously valued at $400 million is being blamed for budget shortfalls and possible layoffs in municipalities and school districts in northwest Indiana.

An outside user of Porter County's computer system may have triggered the mess by accidentally changing the value of the Valparaiso house, said Sharon Lippens, director of the county's information technologies and service department. The house had been valued at $121,900 before the glitch.

County Treasurer Jim Murphy said the home usually carried about $1,500 in property taxes; this year, it was billed $8 million.

Lippens said her agency identified the mistake and told the county auditor's office how to correct it. But the $400 million value ended up on documents that were used to calculate tax rates.

Lippens said the outside user changed the property value, most likely while trying to access another program while using the county's enhanced access system, which charges users a fee for access to public records that are not otherwise available on the Internet.

Lippens said the user probably tried to access a real estate record display by pressing R-E-D, but accidentally typed R-E-R, which brought up an assessment program written in 1995. The program is no longer in use, and technology officials did not know it could be accessed.

URL: *http://msnbc.msn.com/id/11278451/*

When developing software, use the model and process shown in Exhibit 14-1. Each developer should write new code in his own personal account space. If he is modifying code, then he should check out the most recent version from a code library. There are many code library management systems. If the company does not have one, buy one. The code library should have source code and compiled code. It also should be used to move commercial code to the production environment. Once the code is developed and tested at the individual level, the developer should move the code to the acceptance testing area. This allows it to be tested for interactions with code and environment that replicates the production system. Once it passes testing, then it should be moved into the code library. Operations personnel should be informed by an approval document that testing and management have completed. Operations personnel should then move the code from the library to a staging area. A mechanical process will then move the code to the production area during a quiet period in operations, usually early morning or on a weekend.

Some key points to keep in mind:

A. Shred sensitive scrap documents beyond reconstruction.
B. Thoroughly test code before it is moved into a production environment.
C. Periodically review all custom code for potential damaging problems.
D. Scan all code for future dates, login IDs, passwords, copy, or FTP commands.

Exhibit 14-1.   Software Development Process

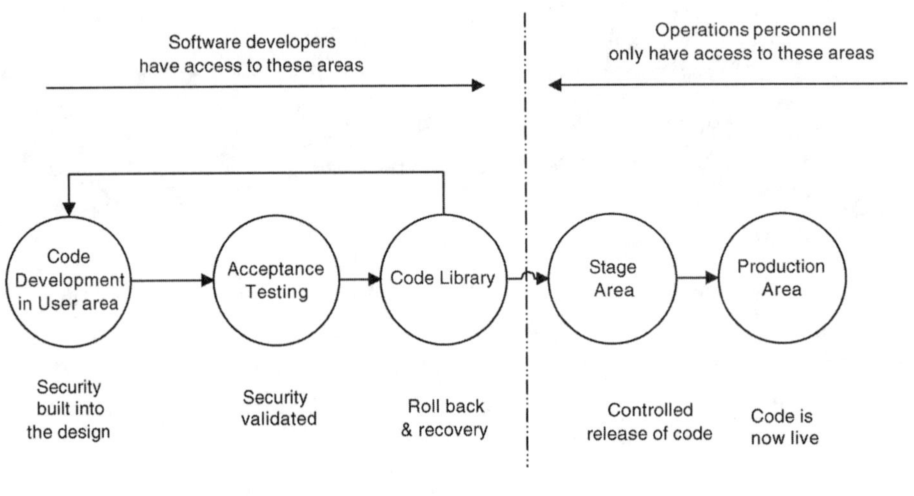

E. Always have a rollback plan.
F. Implement safeguards that will preclude wrongful alteration of data.
G. Make all ODBC and OLE access to your critical databases read-only and password protected.
H. Designate one person to maintain a notebook of all software license numbers and agreements. Systems should be audited periodically to identify any unauthorized copies. Read and have legal staff approve all license terms and agreements before integrating commercial software into your business processes. Make sure that your company owns all work products developed using commercial or open-source products.
I. Protect internally developed software as intellectual property just like a patent or copyright.
J. Clearly mark screens, documents, and e-mails as confidential if they contain sensitive information.
K. Implement a feedback process that identifies data integrity issues and traces them back to their points of origin.

A company has the most control over internally developed software, but it also offers the greatest possibility of containing defects that can improperly alter data or allow a hacker to access data. Databases that provide data to web screens is best served from a replica of the production databases. Any data entry from the web can be fed as transactions to the production database, so they can be logged, validated, and reversed if necessary.

[D] Network Design

In the ideal network, every authorized user can access what they are authorized for and the other three quadrants of possibilities are blocked and attempts logged. The company should have a single portal to external data sources that is guarded by an inline intrusion detection system, while all internal systems should be masked and invisible to outside sources. Servers such as web servers are placed in a middle controlled-access zone sometimes referred to as the DMZ. Satellite offices should be given the same level of security attention as the home office.

> ## COMMENT
>
> Automatic discovery tools should be used to identify all the devices on the network. You will probably be surprised at what you will find at some point, especially evenings, weekends, and holidays. This brings up a key point; if a server containing sensitive information is not needed during non-business hours, it should be disconnected from the network. The software that manages sensitive data should record unusual activity and alert the proper individuals. When diagramming a network, any place where the failure of one piece of equipment can disrupt operations should be identified. Alternative methods, routes, or equipment should be planned to mitigate these single points of failure.

One of the most common errors in network design is to look beyond the touch points with your business-trading partners. If their network is hacked, then your interconnection can become compromised. Even if you only send them a data file, if their system is compromised then your data file can be stolen. Make sure that your trading partners have at least the same level of commitment to security as your company.

[E]   Passwords

The most common approach to securing data systems access is through a User ID/Password combination. A "User ID" is a name for identifying to the computer the person (or entity) who is seeking access. Authentication is the method to prove to the computer system that the user is one and only correct user with that ID. The best authentication uses at least two of three techniques: something that someone knows, possesses, or a personal physical characteristic, such as biometric measurements. A password is one of the most commonly used methods because it is the least expensive to implement and, when paired with a user ID, authenticates that the person requesting access is really that user. Passwords are an important aspect of computer security. They are the front line of protection for user accounts. A poorly chosen password may result in the compromise of the entire corporate network.

The choice of rules for passwords that people are required to follow is significant in blocking unauthorized access. If you look at Exhibit 14-2 you can see that the longer the password and more options that can be used to construct it, the longer it will take to break the password using brute force attacks. For example, the move from seven to nine characters dramatically improves the protection level. Note that the time to crack is based on a single computer attempting the attack. Attackers now resort to hijacking a grid of computers to conduct an attack and thus may harness 1,000 or 10,000 computers to break passwords. There also are most frequently used word lists that yield a useful password much faster than running through all possible combinations sequentially.

Exhibit 14-2. Password Security

Number of characters in password	Possible Combinations A–Z	A–Z, 0–9	Estimated time to crack 1.5 GHz PC
1	26	36	
2	676	1,296	
3	17,576	46,656	
4	458,976	1,679,616	
5	11,881,376	60,466,176	
6	308,915,776	2,176,782,336	5.8 hrs
7	8,031,810,176	78,364,164,096	8.8 days
8	208,827,064,576	2,821,109,907,456	321 days
9	5,429,503,678,976	101,559,956,668,416	31.4 years
10	141,167,095,653,376	3,656,158,440,062,980	

See Policy ITP 19-1 as an example of password policy.

If encryption is used for network traffic, the largest key possible should be used. For example, in Exhibit 14-3, the use of a 128-bit key to encrypt communications would require a significant amount of money and resources that would normally only be available to a government. If your company operates completely inside the United States, you are highly encouraged to use 128-bit encryption with one of the high security algorithms that are available in the United States. If your company does business inside and outside the United States, then you have to consider and comply with the laws, including import and export laws, in all of the countries in which the company operates. This makes choosing a security product a challenge.

COMMENT

InfoSysSec is a good Web site to explore for help (*www. infosyssec.net/index.html*).

Sometimes it is advantageous to choose a standard that is in use in the countries outside the United States and then implement it in the United States. The reason is that the United States has restrictions on exporting some encryption products, but no limits on importing them.

Exhibit 14-3.   Encryption Key Security

Power/Cost–Time for brute force attack	40-bit key	56-bit key	64-bit key	128-bit key
$2K – 1PC	1.4 min.	73 days	50 years	10^{20} years
$100K – Company	2 sec.	35 hours	1 year	10^{19} years
$1M – Government	0.2 sec.	3.5 hours	37 days	10^{18} years

[F]   Physical Security

Physical security is simple but often overlooked. A lost notebook or PDA should be reported immediately so that it can be locked out of the network and any passwords changed. All key security patches should be checked for updates daily, automatically if possible. The amount of information stored on PDAs and notebook computers should be maintained at the minimal level necessary, and notebooks should be backed up to a protected server. There are security devices that encrypt the contents of a notebook computer or destroy sensitive files when hacking attempts are detected. Some high-end PDAs can read a fingerprint to verify owner identity before granting access. If your building has security guards, they should have written instructions on identifying packages and identifying data theft methods.

Many executives and managers love to have windows in their offices. If their computer screens can be seen through the window, then they can be read from a distance. Reflective window coating and polarized screen filters can limit outside observation. If you have any computers in an area accessible to nonemployees such as a public lobby, they should be given intensive security protections.

> **COMMENT**
>
> When Holiday Inn centrally computerized their reservations, they were so proud of their computer system that they built a round building with floor-to-ceiling glass on all sides in front of their corporate headquarters to show it off.

[G]   Disaster Recovery Planning

All businesses should have a written disaster recovery plan (DRP). It can be as simple as a couple of pages for a small company to several hundred pages for a large multi-national corporation. One way to determine how much effort should be invested in the DRP plan is to determine the cost per minute of total loss of a company's computing capacity. This should include the salaries of idle employees, average revenue, and a projection of lost customers and the gain to your competitors.

> ## COMMENT
>
> One very common mistake is not having your backup data far enough away from the primary site. If you think about drawing a circle around each site at the maximum range that a disaster could reach from that site, the circles should not touch between your primary and backup site. Some major companies have put their backup sites in the same city with the primary site to share training; however, the entire city was in an earthquake fault zone. Earthquakes, hurricanes, and volcanoes can cause damage up to 300 miles away.

Organize the DRP so that selected parts can be implemented if required. Keep it rich in details on key contacts, decision makers, and phone numbers—especially after hours. If the plan calls for augmentation by contractors, ensure that the vendors are preselected and prequalified. Some contingency contracts may need to be in place before a disaster, since several companies may be demanding the same support resources at the same time. Get first priority. Have a contingency fund or quick access insurance plan in place. Finally, test your plan!

> ## COMMENT
>
> Security policies written with teeth are legally defendable. Some companies have a notebook with more than 20 one-page policy statements that every new employee must read and sign. Policies need to address people, processes, and technology issues. Training time should be used to refresh people about policies. Great policies are one of the layers in designing a secure, multi-layer fabric to protect corporate assets and your job.

[H]   Testing

This is the one area where you really want to be from Missouri—Show Me! Testing software to validate that it does what it was designed to do is frequently done. Testing software to verify that it does nothing else is rarely done. Test commercial hardware and software for malicious activity before it is allowed on your production network. Internally developed software testing should include a code review for dates, passwords, account names, and copy or FTP commands. You might consider a special "firewall" that will allow any program to read from the database but log all write attempts without committing the transactions. This technique allows a review to verify transactions before they are allowed in the production environment.

What questions should I be asking my technical staff? The best questions are: Where are the holes and weaknesses in our organization? How can scams, spoofing, viruses, and worms damage our company? How can an attacker disrupt or deny our ability to use our computing and network resources to conduct normal business? Do we have multiple and diverse protective barriers? Do you have an inline intrusion detection and prevention system that alerts your technical staff when specific attacks or attempts occur? Do these systems automatically adapt and respond to different attacks? Do they detect unauthorized locations, activities, connections, and IDs? See Policy ITP-14-1 Anti-Virus Policy as an example.

POLICY ITP 14-1.   Anti-Virus Policy

Policy #:	ITP-14-1	Effective:	03/18/09	Page #:	1 of N
Subject:	Anti-Virus Policy				

1.0 PURPOSE

The purpose of this policy is to prevent the infection of company computers, computer systems and other digital devices by computer viruses and other malicious code. This policy is intended to prevent major damage and loss of information to hardware, applications, and user data.

2.0 SCOPE

The policy applies to all corporate computers and devices that store corporate information. It applies to all users of the organization's network, using any device that has access to the network.

3.0 POLICY

All corporate computers and devices that store corporate information and that at any time connect to the corporate network must have approved and supported anti-virus software correctly installed, configured, activated, and updated with the latest virus definitions. Any devices infected with a virus or other malicious code (collectively referred to as "malware") must be immediately disconnected from the corporate network until the infection has been removed. Directions for procuring, installing, configuring, and using anti-virus software are posted on the corporate intranet.

If a particular operating system or computing platform does not have anti-virus protection available, use of a device using such an operating system must be approved by corporate IT security, who shall determine the operating procedures necessary to minimize the possibility of malware infecting the corporate network. If anti-virus software becomes available for an operating system or computing platform previously lacking such software, it must by installed as soon as possible on all such devices.

When an enterprise-wide malware attack is in progress, corporate IT security must notify all corporate users via the best available method. After such an attack has been identified, all storage devices must be scanned using the latest virus definitions available.

Any exceptions to this policy must be approved in advance by the corporate IT security department.

4.0 REVISION HISTORY

Date	Revision #	Description of Change
03/18/09	1.0	Initial creation.

5.0 INQUIRIES

Direct inquiries about this policy to:

Harold Jenkins, CIO
2900 Corporate Drive
Columbus, OH 43215

Voice: 614-555-1234
Fax: 614-555-1235
E-mail: hjenkins@company.com

Revision #:	1.0	Supersedes:	N/A	Date:	03/18/09

Have you tested your recovery plan? Do your systems produce audit logs and how are they reviewed? Is your staff trained on how to respond to intrusion activity involving theft, alteration, deletion, or insertion of Trojan horses? Review the audit checklists in Worksheet 14-1 and customize them for your company.

If you are the victim of an attack, it is critical that you and your staff collect the information you need to identify the attacker and prevent future attacks. Is your staff trained in legal evidence collection requirements? Some things you and your staff should know include:

A. Evidence should be collected as soon as possible after an attack.
B. Evidence must be preserved in a permanent form (e.g., printed, CD-ROM).
C. Collection and preservation of evidence should be witnessed by more than one person.
D. Evidence must be maintained in a pristine, unaltered state.
E. Evidence should be collected by trained experts.
F. Original evidence should be surrendered to law enforcement officials while copies should be maintained by corporate attorneys.
G. A log must be maintained identifying the chain of custody of all evidence materials.
H. Each person involved should write a memorandum outlining dates, times, and activity as soon as possible.

COMMENT

Prosecution of security violations is necessary!

[I] Instant Messaging (IM)

It is hard to stop an idea whose time has come. "Instant Messaging" technology allows users to quickly send messages to coworkers or family over the Internet and has become a fixture on most PCs. However, this new tool has the potential to unravel carefully built network security defenses.

Many of the messages are short. IM is a great tool for obtaining quick consensus from coworkers on an issue. A prime example is its use by stockbrokers who need fast decisions during a rapidly shifting market. Others find the tool faster than walking over to a coworker for an answer. Many workers keep their IM window open during the day to communicate with family members.

Instant messaging can cause big problems. The SEC has already levied multimillion dollar fines for stock broker/dealers that use IM to arrange illegal sales advantageous to their clients. A company's IM acceptable use policy should be consistent with its policies for other communications, such as e-mail. It must refer to other company policies on appropriate language and disclosure of confidential information.

As an uncontrolled communications technology, IM introduces new problems into a company such as:

A. Instant messages are unrecorded company communications. They take place on third-party servers and are not collected in the company archives, potentially enabling collusion for illegal purposes.

B. Companies have long published guidelines for acceptable language and content in e-mail. IM messages are shorter and may seem to the correspondents to be more personal. However, they must still follow company guidelines avoiding forbidden references to race, gender, religion, etc.

C. IM provides yet another path for a virus to enter the company system.

D. Even if a company blocks IM tools from loading onto its workstations, they are still available through other means. For example, cell phones and wireless communications PDAs can carry IM traffic and then link to a workstation.

COMMENT

IM conversations are like e-mail and must be saved like any other official company document to fulfill the many regulatory data retention requirements. For example, the Securities and Exchange Commission (SEC) rules views IM as correspondence with the public.

Policies must focus on prevention, education, acceptable use, and continual enforcement. Companies have tried to contain the situation in several ways:

A. Forbid all IM use on company equipment. This is a short-term fix to allow time to determine a long-term solution. IM is available on so many different devices that this option will not be effective for long.

B. Use an internal IM tool. This puts the security team back in the picture with virus filtering, content monitoring, and the ability to record conversations. However, personal cell phones and other rapid communications devices (like Blackberrys™) make this difficult. Also, most people already have accounts on third-party providers.

C. Publish a policy on acceptable use. Such a policy should require all company business to be conducted using the company provided tool but permits the use of third-party tools for purely personal use. This compromise does not address the issues of appropriate language and content, but does recognize that current technology does not enable full filtering of third-party IM communications.

Educating users is the key to a successful IM security program. Many of the same security guidelines can be reused to address IM issues. Inform all users about security problems, such as using IM to trick people into downloading infected files, unknowingly permit access to their equipment, etc. See Policy ITP-14-2 Instant Messaging Policy as an example.

POLICY ITP 14-2.   Instant Messaging Policy

Policy #:	ITP-14-2	**Effective:**	03/18/09	**Page #:**	1 of N
Subject:	Instant Messaging Policy				

1.0 PURPOSE

This policy guides employees on the acceptable use of Instant Messaging technologies.

2.0 SCOPE

The policy applies to all users of all Instant Messaging technologies used to conduct any aspect of the company's business whether the device used is owned by the company or is provided by the employee.

3.0 POLICY

3.1 Technology

Employees are required to use the Instant Messaging tool provided by the IT department to conduct all company business. This includes casual contacts with coworkers during the day. Third-party instant messaging technologies are not to be loaded or enabled on company desktops, PDAs, cell phones, or other communication devices.

Instant Messaging technologies loaded onto personal cell phones, PDAs, or other technologies are not to be used for contacting coworkers, customers, suppliers, or anyone else connected with the company.

3.2 Acceptable Use

A. Employees are reminded of the company's policies on acceptable language in the workplace including derogatory references to gender, race, national origin, religion, etc. Instant Messaging traffic must conform to these guidelines at all times.

B. Third-party Instant Messaging technology:
   1. Is only permitted on personally owned equipment.
   2. May never be used to conduct company business, including informal contact with customers, suppliers, and other company stakeholders.
   3. May never be used to send confidential company information.

3.3 Information Technology Manager

A. Provide a company controlled Instant Messaging tool that conforms to the company's information security program.

B. Identify, block, and disable third-party Instant Messaging software on company owned equipment and networks.

C. Screen Instant Messages to identify content that conflicts with company policies on acceptable use and report offenders to the Human Resources Manager.

D. Record and archive all Instant Messages to conform with legal mandates.

E. Provide annual training to all employees on the content of this policy.

F. Provide ongoing communications and reminders using posters, newsletters, and management meetings on the appropriate use of Instant Messaging.

4.0 REVISION HISTORY

Date	Revision #	Description of Change
03/18/09	1.0	Initial creation.

5.0 INQUIRIES

Direct inquiries about this policy to:

Harold Jenkins, CIO
2900 Corporate Drive
Columbus, OH 43215

Voice: 614-555-1234
Fax: 614-555-1235
E-mail: hjenkins@company.com

Revision #:	1.0	Supersedes:	N/A	Date:	03/18/09

§ 14.04   LEGAL ISSUES

[A]   Overview

The data stores of companies have long been under siege by people who wish to exploit them for criminal purposes. Over the years, the repeated loss of data by various companies has led to a series of regulations that directly affect the daily efforts of IT departments. It is essential that IT Managers know about these legal issues as they may become personally liable for failing to follow these laws.

As with all legal questions, IT Managers must refer to their company's legal counsel for *written* guidance on what they must do to comply. Furthermore, IT Managers must monitor changes in the legal landscape to ensure their policies, procedures, and strategies do not lead the department into activities outside of the limits of these laws.

In general, recent laws address:

A. Ready availability of critical information such as medical records. This has required moving some archived data from tape (stored off site) to online disks.
B. Records availability through data retention. These laws mandate how long specific data elements must be retained. The complexity is that data is often mixed up on storage devices, forcing the retention of entire pieces of media (such as an entire backup tape) for as long as the longest period for each data element on that media.
C. Data accuracy through software controls. Companies must now identify their internal control processes and verify that they provide adequate safeguards for the accuracy of financial reporting. These controls must be in place and monitored regularly to identify tampering.
D. Security of data records. Companies must safeguard from disclosure specific types of data. This data has long been protected by companies but now there is a legal requirement to ensure compliance. Examples are customer data and health records.

[B] Health Insurance Portability and Accountability Act (HIPAA)

The Health Insurance Portability and Accountability Act (HIPAA) requires securing and maintaining personal health information (PHI) for specific retention periods (depending on the type of information). While organizations possess this data they must safeguard it from unauthorized access. Although this information may be on a wide range of media (x-ray photographs, paper records, electronic records), the primary challenge to the IT Manager is electronic availability, security, and retention.

Consideration for implementing HIPAA is similar to any other data security issue. Common practices include:

A. Password protection and authorization controls.
B. Hierarchies of security based on need to know. A doctor might need different information than a nurse.
C. Backup and retention of data and ensuring 100 percent data reliability.
D. Forms and releases must be scanned, saved, and available.
E. Health records must be retained for at least six years.
F. Automatic audit trail.
G. A business continuity plan is mandated as necessary to ensure records are readily available.

The process for safeguarding data is moving toward the increased use of fixed disks. DVDs and CDs create a security and control problem both because of the nature of the media and the ease of copying it. Such portable technologies bypass physical and electronic security measures. This will drive up online storage costs over time.

HIPAA's reach is long. Many professionals believe it extends to electronic mail and IM communications that discuss patient conditions or that include other medical data. Such messages must use encrypted communications to avoid interception. These communications, in turn, must match the retention levels for that type of information.

A good place to start researching a compliance program is the National Institute of Standards and Technology's (NIST) HIPAA Resource Guide. These standards provide a general requirements framework that should be a part of any compliance program.

[C] Sarbanes-Oxley Act (SOX)

Several cases of major corporate accounting fraud have led to the enactment of the Sarbanes-Oxley Act (SOX) requiring the safeguarding of sensitive corporate data. The act contains many sections. The part generally applicable to IT Managers is Section 404.

Section 404 requires that the Securities and Exchange Commission (SEC) publish rules governing internal controls to ensure that a publicly traded company's financial data is accurate. Since all companies rely on information technology to create this data, IT falls squarely in the middle of this law. Companies must now be able to certify IT processes annually as secure, comprehensive, and repeatable.

Rather than fight SOX-required changes, implement them as part of an overall IT process improvement initiative. Well-run IT shops have many of these safeguards already in place such as change management and information security, so the task is to identify and plug the gaps. IT must demonstrate that it has emplaced appropriate internal controls to manage any changes to software that play a significant part in financial controls or reports.

Special attention must be paid to:

A. Financial record retention systems and policies that manage them. They affect information collection, validation, analysis, and storage.
B. Data mining, scrubbing applications, and analysis systems because they jeopardize data integrity.
C. Data and systems security, because unauthorized access could severely and negatively impact the quality of reported information.
D. Ensure that all IT policies and procedures are documented and current. Include an annual review plan for all.

SOX constantly refers to "controls." A control is a checks-and-balance process ensuring that new systems or changes to existing systems function properly. This is present in most companies as their change control process. However, in most companies there is a way to bypass the process or it is just an automatic approval. Correctly done, the change is properly tested, verified by others, and then verified again after implementation.

SOX requires an annual audit of all controls to verify their effectiveness. This implies keeping records during the year. Common control concepts encountered when implementing a SOX program include:

A. Documentation of each control and how it is supposed to work. IT Managers can perform their own audit and regularly compare how the documented process compares to reality. For example, the software development process, from inception to development standards to testing program to finally change control of installed modules.

B. The separation of responsibilities between the person requesting a change and the one approving it. People cannot approve their own documents. A list of who is authorized to approve what changes must be published.

C. The most common approval control points are change prioritization, test result approval, and rollout. All approvals must be written and recorded. Keep these records in a safe place. In most cases, there will be multiple people authorizing changes (IT Manager, IT quality technician, requestor, manager of department affected, etc.)

D. Audit and verify that controls are still in place and effective. The details are important. Event logs, audit trails, and reporting are key to meeting this goal.

E. Periodically test critical financial business processes to ensure they still work as planned. Keep records of all such checks along with what was checked, how it was verified, who did it, when, etc. Use a formal test plan and record the results.

COMMENT

SOX compliance does not end at the four walls of the company's offices. They include any outsourced functions as well. Be sure that any outsourced support (or contract labor) that touches any of the company's controls or controlled objects, also is compliant with the company's SOX program.

Key indicators of a well run SOX compliance program are:

- Repeatable processes.
- Change management.
- Consistency of control testing and documentation throughout the organization.

- Ongoing management emphasis through employee training and refresher training.
- Proper authorization of changes.

There are several models to choose from when selecting a roadmap for compliance. Each has its own strengths and costs. All models overlap in important areas.

- ISO17799—International standard for information security.
- COSO—An SEC approved internal controls framework.
- COBIT—A business focused framework based on COSO.

COMMENT

An ironic twist is that SOX Section 404, the one that causes IT management the most problems, has the same identifier as the HTTP 404 error.

[D]   Gramm-Leach-Bliley Act

The Gramm-Leach-Bliley Act covers any business significantly engaged in financial activities. It addresses the confidentiality of customer data. Responsibility for protecting the data from disclosure remains with the company even when the data is passed to a third party for use. Ensure all third parties are required by contract to secure the data at all times.

The Gramm-Leach-Bliley Act has two areas of emphasis:

A. The financial privacy rule governs collecting of customer's personal and financial information. It also applies to companies who receive this information.
B. The safeguards rule requires the design, implementation, and maintenance of safeguards to protect this data.

The act encourages the encryption of data in storage and in transit. It also recommends destroying data that is not needed, since this ultimately protects it from disclosure.

A criticism of the Gramm-Leach-Bliley Act is that it is more descriptive than prescriptive. The act leaves the definition of "protecting the security and confidentiality of information" up to each company.

> **COMMENT**
>
> More information is available from the Federal Trade Commission at: *www.ftc.gov/privacy/privacyinitiatives/glbact.html*

[E]   SEC Rules

SEC rules have long mandated the collection and retention of financial records and anything pertaining to a securities transaction. More recently, the rules were updated to include electronic mail and instant messaging. The SEC found that these communications were involved in communicating to customers and between securities employees and yet the records of these communications were not made or retained.

Specifically, SEC Rules 17a-3 and -4 have implications for IT Managers and for IT securities team members. Companies now require comprehensive, auditable, and legally credible policies, practices, and systems to manage e-mail. Typically, these records must be retained for six years.

[F]   Committee of Sponsoring Organizations (COSO)

In 1992, the Committee of Sponsoring Organizations (COSO) established a framework for the proper authorization, recording, and reporting of transactions. The SEC officially recognizes the COSO framework as adequate for establishing internal controls over financial reporting. COSO is also the basis for COBIT's professional standards for internal controls and auditing.

In the COSO framework, an internal control is a process—a way to approach an issue. It is about what people do, not what manuals say they ought to do. Internal controls only provide some assurance that something will occur, and not an absolute guarantee. Each internal control addresses a specific objective.

COSO identifies internal controls as processes designed to provide reasonable assurances regarding objectives in three areas:

A.   Effectiveness and efficiency of operations.
B.   Reliability of financial reporting.
C.   Compliance with applicable laws and regulations.

The COSO framework measures five internal controls for each of the three areas:

A.   Control environment—processes for managing and developing people in the organization and delegation of authority systems.
B.   Risk assessment—identification and analysis of risks to achieving assigned objectives.

C. Control activities—policies and procedures for execution of management directives.
D. Information and communication—effective communication for running and controlling the business.
E. Monitoring—ongoing activities or separate evaluations.

[G]   Control Objectives for Information and Related Technology (COBIT™)

COBIT was created by the Information Systems Audit and Control Association (ISACA) and the IT Governance Institute (ITGI). It describes a set of control objects for maximizing the benefits derived from the use of IT. It also describes appropriate IT governance and control. (COBIT is a trademark of the Information Systems Audit and Control Association and the IT Governance Institute.)

COBIT uses COSO definitions as the basis of its control objects, but extends the notion of control throughout the enterprise. It also makes the COSO principles and objectives applicable to the IT function. The COBIT control objectives provide a working document for IT management and staff, the control and audit functions, and business process owners. The conceptual framework includes:

A. Information criteria.
B. IT resources.
C. IT processes.

COMMENT

COBIT version 4 was announced in late 2005.

The COBIT framework focuses IT process on the company's business. It strives to ensure IT resources are used responsibly and appropriately. IT Managers appreciate COBIT because it helps them to understand their IT systems and decide on the level of security and control necessary to protect their companies' assets through the development of an IT governance model.

While the full COBIT framework exceeds SOX Section 404 requirements, companies should consider customizing the applicable portions of COBIT for their own compliance requirements.

COBIT has 34 high level objectives that cover 318 control objectives in four domains:

A. Planning and organization.
B. Acquisition and implementation.
C. Delivery and support.
D. Monitoring.

> ## COMMENT
>
> The IT Governance Institute (ITGI) advances international thinking and standards in directing and controlling an enterprise's information technology. It can be contacted at: *www.itgi.org*.

The COBIT Control Objectives within these four domains are:

A. Planning and Organization.
   1. Define a strategic plan.
   2. Define the information architecture.
   3. Determine technological direction.
   4. Define IT organization and relationships.
   5. Manage the IT investment.
   6. Communicate management aims and direction.
   7. Manage human resources.
   8. Ensure compliance with external requirements.
   9. Assess risks.
   10. Manage projects.
   11. Manage quality.
B. Acquisition and Implementation.
   1. Identify automated solutions.
   2. Acquire and maintain application software.
   3. Acquire and maintain technology infrastructure.
   4. Develop and maintain procedures.
   5. Install and accredit systems.
   6. Manage change.
C. Delivery and Support.
   1. Define and manage service levels.
   2. Manage third-party services.
   3. Manage performance and capacity.
   4. Ensure continuous service.
   5. Ensure systems security.
   6. Identify and allocate costs.
   7. Educate and train users.
   8. Assist and advise customers.
   9. Manage configuration.
   10. Manage problems and incidents.
   11. Manage data.
   12. Manage facilities.
   13. Manage operations.

    D. Monitoring.
        1. Monitor the process.
        2. Assess internal control adequacy.
        3. Obtain independent assurance.
        4. Provide for independent audit.

A criticism of COBIT is that it describes what needs to be done, but never states how to do it. COBIT helps define processes for identifying and managing IT risk. Other existing standards must take up where COBIT leaves off. While every control objective is applicable to every organization, few companies are able to implement the entire COBIT process.

[H] Personal Information Protection and Electronic Documents Act (PIPEDA)

Canada has enacted the Personal Information Protection and Electronic Documents Act (PIPEDA). Among other things, this legislation governs the collection, use and disclosure of information in commercial activities. Personal information is factual or subjective information in any form about an identifiable individual.

PIPEDA addresses ten principles for protecting gathering, retaining, and destroying information about people.

    A. Accountability—an organization is responsible for protecting both personal information in its possession or that it transfers to a third party. Accountability for PIPEDA rests with individuals designated in a commercial enterprise.
    B. Identifying purposes—an organization must identify the reasons for which personal information is collected either prior to or at the time of collection.
    C. Consent—an organization is responsible for collecting, using, or disclosing personal information only with the individual's knowledge and consent. This requires an organization to document and retain all consent given and withdrawn.
    D. Limiting collection prohibits organizations from collecting personal information indiscriminately or through deception. Each data element must have an identified purpose.
    E. Limited use, disclosure, and retention means organizations must use or disclose personal information only for the purposes for which it was collected. Retain personal information only as long as necessary to fulfill the identified and consented-to purpose.
    F. Accuracy—organizations must ensure that personal information is correct, complete, and up-to-date. The validity of the data is the commercial enterprise's responsibility. Implied is a process for identifying and correcting errors, and cross validating data.
    G. Personal information must be secured against loss, theft, or unauthorized access. Safe destruction of the data is required when it is no longer needed. Always document destroyed data.

   H. Organizations must publish their information management policies to employees and customers. Make it easy to find and understand.

    I. Individuals can request access to their personal information, determine its appropriate use, and learn the names of third parties to whom it will be disclosed.

    J. Legal guidelines exist for challenging a company's compliance with this act. Individuals dissatisfied with a company's collection or use of their data have a legal process to correct it.

[I] Fair and Accurate Credit Transactions Act of 2003 (FACTA)

FACTA (Fair and Accurate Credit Transactions Act of 2003) governs records disposal. Consumer information is any record about an individual (paper or electronic) such as credit worthiness, reputation, characteristics, etc. It applies to companies that possess or maintain consumer reports for business purposes, regardless of industry.

FACTA reduces the risk of consumer fraud created by improper disposal of any consumer report record. FACTA requires that anyone that possesses or maintains covered consumer information take reasonable measures to protect against unauthorized access or use in connection with its disposal.

[J] ISO 17799

ISO 17799 is the International Standard Organization's standard for information security. It is an adaptation of an earlier British Standard BS-7799. In the future, ISO will change the numeric designator to ISO-27002 as the ISO-27000 series has been set aside for information security.

ISO 17799 provides best practice recommendations on information security management for initiating, implementing, or maintaining information security management systems. The 2005 version of the standard contains the following 11 main sections:

   A. Security policy.
   B. Organization of information security.
   C. Asset management.
   D. Human resources security.
   E. Physical and environmental security.
   F. Communications and operations management.
   G. Access control.
   H. Information systems acquisition, development, and maintenance.
    I. Information security incident management.
    J. Business continuity planning.
   K. Compliance.

[K] Canadian Budget Measures Act (Bill 198)

Drafted in response to major corporate accounting scandals in the United States, the Canadian government enacted a law similar to the U.S.

Sarbanes-Oxley Act (SOX). The Budget Measures Act increases the level of executive responsibility and accountability in Canadian companies. The law describes certification requirements, disclosure controls, and internal control requirements.

The law requires an annual certification by executives that their filings are true and do not omit facts. Like the SOX legislation, this means that the IT processes that contribute significantly to these reports must be tightly controlled to avoid accidental or purposeful manipulation. Internal controls must be established, tested, and used. Controls encompass the collection of information, its processing and summation.

These controls will significantly impact the design of data management systems. Records retention, security and overall management will force IT Managers in Canada to examine all of their existing systems for gaps.

A legally defensible records management system is an important part of a Budget Measures Act compliance program. Consistency in process across all IT systems is essential. This includes procedures, data retention schedules, policies, data disposal methods, etc. An important tool in consistency is clear documentation explaining what to do, how to do it, and when deviations are permitted.

15

DATA BACKUPS—THE KEY TO A PROMPT RECOVERY

§ 15.01　OVERVIEW
　　[A]　Purpose and Scope
　　[B]　Critical Policies to Develop Based on This Chapter

§ 15.02　DATA RECOVERY
　　[A]　Types of Backups
　　[B]　The Data Backup Lifecycle
　　[C]　Recovery Time Objective (RTO)
　　[D]　Recovery Point Objective (RPO)
　　[E]　Recovering Data

§ 15.03　DATA BACKUPS—MAJOR RESPONSIBILITIES
　　[A]　Overview
　　[B]　IT Operations Manager
　　[C]　Database Manager
　　[D]　Software Manager
　　[E]　Network Manager
　　[F]　Shop Floor Systems Manager
　　[G]　Telecommunications Manager

§ 15.04　DESIGNING FOR BACKUPS
　　[A]　Overview
　　[B]　Data Mirroring
　　[C]　Journaling
　　[D]　Data Retention

§ 15.05　MEDIA HANDLING, TRANSPORTATION, AND STORAGE
　　[A]　Overview
　　[B]　Marking Media for Ready Identification
　　[C]　Periodic Inspection
　　[D]　Destroying Old Media

§ 15.06　WORKSTATION, NOTEBOOK PC, AND DATA COLLECTION
STATION BACKUPS
　　[A]　Overview
　　[B]　Identifying the Problem
　　[C]　Separating Data from the Software

§ 15.07   DATA RETENTION AND LEGAL MANDATES
     [A]   Overview
     [B]   Legal Mandates
     [C]   Do Not Overdo It

§ 15.01 OVERVIEW

[A] Purpose and Scope

Data can be stored on a range of media. Paper, CD, and magnetic tape all hold data of some sort. Data backups are "safety" copies of data for use if the original data medium is destroyed or damaged. A backup can be a copy made on carbon paper, copy machine, or more typically, a non-volatile storage disk. The potential cost to the company if data was lost justifies the time and expense that goes into making and handling backup copies of computer data.

The IT world handles massive amounts of data. Where even 30 years ago the bulk of the company's data was stuffed in file cabinets and dusty boxes, it is now spread across a wide range of computers and servers. The task of the IT Manager is to ensure that data is safeguarded, available, and readable in the event that the company requires it again.

Computers are rather fragile devices. Environmental factors—such as extreme temperatures, dust, magnetic radiation, and moisture—can cause them to fail suddenly. Add to this the chance of hardware failure such as a disk head crash or even a stray voltage surge that disables some components, and it is easy to see the harsh climate in which computers exist.

To protect computers, or at least the larger, less portable ones, secured and filtered rooms called data centers are built. These rooms have filtered air, filtered electricity, thick walls, a secured entry, and a long list of safeguards to protect the equipment.

As a further safeguard, copies of the data should be periodically made and stored off site in a secure location. This off-site storage should be updated often (usually daily). Once the data departs the cozy safety of the data center, it must again be protected from threats to its integrity until it is safely and properly stored at the offsite facility.

Data backups are the key to any disaster recovery plan. Equipment can be replaced. Buildings can be leased. However, the expense of recreating corporate data from scratch is far more than most companies can support. If an IT Manager misses this point, his or her long-term employment outlook is bleak.

The challenge for the IT Manager is to find the best way to ensure this is done properly. In the past, data was stored in a computer room on the mainframe computer and IT had complete control to shut it down (usually on Saturdays at midnight) to make full backups. For some companies, this is still the best method.

Most companies however cannot backup their data this way. Their customers expect around-the-clock service every day of the year. This includes hospitals, web-based enterprises, and virtual companies whose employees are located around the world. Web applications must be available 24 hours per day—every day of the week. This means those files can never be closed.

Complicating matters is that data is collected and distributed among a variety of locations. The increased use of notebook PCs means important company data is floating around and probably not being backed up regularly, if at all. Consider for a moment the company CEO's PC. What might be stored in it? How well protected from theft or a harsh environment is it, and how likely is it to have a daily data backup stored safely away?

[B]   Critical Policies to Develop Based on This Chapter

Using the material discussed in this chapter, you will be able to create the following policies:

A.   Mandate a program for data backups.
  1.   Assigns responsibility to IT Operations Manager.
    a.   Requires active support.
    b.   Requires written and approved procedures.
  2.   Includes all files on all servers.
    a.   "Idle" and "never changing" files are backed up weekly.
    b.   Software is backed up weekly.
  3.   Includes telecom and network.
  4.   Types of data.
    a.   Personal.
    b.   Legal compliance data.
    c.   Business critical data.
    d.   Noncritical data.
  5.   Data backup frequency.
    a.   Full backups weekly.
    b.   Incremental backups daily for changing data.
    c.   Identifies data for off-site journaling.
B.   Workstations, notebook PCs, and other data-creating/retaining devices.
  1.   Only backs up data—not programs.
  2.   Normally collected once a week.
  3.   Requires process for segregating data from programs.
  4.   Do it yourself program.
C.   Off-site storage.
  1.   Daily pick-ups.
  2.   Controlled transportation.
  3.   Inspect semiannually.
  4.   Verify returning media.
D.   Data retention.
  1.   Know what data is stored where.
  2.   Retain media for greatest period.
E.   Legal mandates.
  1.   Policies that detail the data retention rules that apply to the company.
  2.   Company policies for data retention, such as retaining accounting records for seven years.

Always develop policies based on the local situation. Successful managers cannot issue appropriate guidance if the policies are written with another company's or location's situation in mind.

§ 15.02   DATA RECOVERY

[A]   Types of Backups

The frequency of data backups depends on how much the data changes over time. Files containing purchase orders and employee attendance records probably change daily, while files supporting end-of-the-year accounting reports probably only change once per year. Rather than tediously evaluating and tagging each file, most data backups copy the entire contents of a disk volume to tape.

Typically, companies make many types of data backups:

A.   Weekly (or full) backups are time consuming but everything on every server or mainframe disk is copied to the backup media.
B.   Daily (or incremental) backups copy only those files where something has changed since the last full or incremental backup.
C.   Mirrored disk where a copy of the data is always up to date and available. A variation is for the mirrored data to reside in a distant data center.
D.   Journaling transmits transactions to an off-site storage facility as they occur. This is also known as a continuous backup.
E.   Create special backups when specific files must be transported.

COMMENT

Although this chapter refers to backups as copied to magnetic tape, they can just as easily be stored on any other nonvolatile media such as optical disk or a disk pack located a significant distance away.

[B]   The Data Backup Lifecycle

An interesting aspect of data backups is the belief that once the backup media is full, the job is done. The purpose of data backups is not to make copies. The goal is to have something readily available and technically readable when needed. Therefore the task of making a backup does not end until that copy is reused for a future backup or destroyed. The implication is that the person responsible for creating the data backups is responsible for it throughout its "life cycle," including transportation for off-site storage and its safekeeping in the facility. This requires establishing a chain of custody throughout the media's "lifetime."

Once filled with data, move the media promptly off site. Data backups sitting in the data center will protect the company against damaged files, but if the data center is destroyed, the company will not be protected. To achieve its full potential, the backup must be transported to the off-site storage facility and securely locked.

Inspect the off-site facility periodically. Take nothing for granted. Companies change, priorities shift, and new people come onto the job. What was well done in the past may now be in a shambles. Verify that the climate control of the vehicle transporting the media keeps it within an acceptable range. Ensure that media is closely protected during transit. Verify these same issues inside the storage facility itself.

COMMENT

IT Managers in small companies sometime take their backup tapes home for safe keeping. Although these people mean well, this does not address the issue of protecting the tape while in transit and storage. Few houses or cars are climate controlled or as physically secure as a data center. A backup only has to fail once—and can do so at the worst possible time.

[C]   Recovery Time Objective (RTO)

One of the critical considerations for data backup planning is the company's recovery time objective (RTO). RTO is the cornerstone of a disaster recovery plan. The RTO identifies how long the company can afford to wait after a disaster to recover its critical data systems. (See Exhibit 15-1.) This time includes locating a facility, obtaining equipment, preparing it for use, and recovering the data/software from the media. In the meantime, money will be flowing out of the company with very little flowing in. Few firms can survive this for long.

Because the RTO identifies how long the company can wait for the backup data to be restored, by implication it determines the backup strategy. A company that can afford a long term outage (such as a Minnesota golf course in the dead of winter) can wait for as long as it takes (well, at least a few weeks) until alternate equipment is installed and the backup tapes methodically loaded. A company that cannot tolerate anything but the briefest outage might demand instant recovery. Instant recovery requires an always-on remote data center that mirrors the active data center's activity. When the primary data center fails, then the back up operation kicks in. However, this means twice the cost (dual servers, dual disks and redundant high speed data connection between them). Instant recovery requires a "hot" backup with the alternate servers always on and data mirrored from the primary system. As is obvious, the faster the data recovery, the more expensive it is.

EXHIBIT 15-1.   The Recovery Time Objective Identifies How Long a Company Can Afford to Wait to Recover Its Data Systems

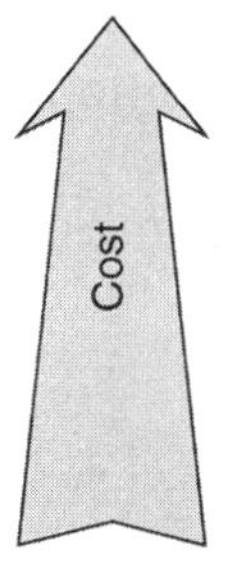
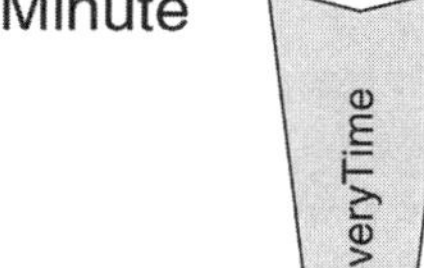

Magnetic tape can only spin so fast; it takes time to restore servers. To shorten this time, some companies establish shadowing data centers, use hot site contracts, or disk-to-disk backups. The solution selected will often be as unique as the company's data requirements. RTO should be a major consideration whenever evaluating any data backup changes.

COMMENT

The Recovery Time Objective focuses on the recovery of critical files, not everything in the data center. (Critical files are identified by the Business Impact Analysis.)

[D]   Recovery Point Objective (RPO)

The recovery point objective (RPO) is the amount of data that must be added to the recovered files to bring the business records back up to date. For example, in a company that only operates from Monday through Friday, a full data backup is made every Saturday and stored off site. Incremental backups are made each workday night of any files changed that day. If the data center was destroyed on a Sunday, then no data would be lost because the full backup was made on Saturday and no files had been changed since. However, if the disaster struck on late Monday afternoon, then all of the data that was added to the files that day would be lost (anything changed between the Saturday morning full backup and the point of incident).

Consider what this data might be: online transactions, data keyed from documents, or real-time database corrections. What could be used to recreate these adds, changes, and deletes? Think of a company with 100 people in the accounting department and all of the data they change in a day. Would it be possible to recreate all of their work from a single day? How much of a data loss can the company survive?

RPO is important because it indicates the tolerable time between data back-ups. After the backup is restored, the data lost from the Monday transactions must somehow be recreated. If this loss is not tolerable, then a real time backup strategy may be required. Source documents are rarely retained and many trans-actions are now entered online without a paper trail. One solution to this is to "journal" or record every transaction that occurs throughout the day and then discard the file after the next good backup. However, this may only cover a small part of the many transactions that pass through a data center in a day.

COMMENT

The Recovery Point Objective determines the frequency and type of data backups. For example, medical records or stock transactions cannot lose many hours of backups so a mirror-ing solution is required. However, a grocery store's inventory can lose point-of-sale connection for several hours. The cost of recounting the shelves once every several years is less than paying for real time data mirroring.

[E]   Recovering Data

Backups are only made so that, if needed, the data on them can be reloaded onto another machine. Typically this means recalling the backup media from off-site storage and then reloading the file. Of course, this means the support person must know which tape holds the desired file. Often the software that manages the backup provides this file list.

A problem with this scenario is that users seldom want to wait to recall a tape from off-site storage. Many people think "When was the last time the data center was flattened?" and consequently do not send their backup tapes off site until the next backup is made. However, this means the tapes going off site are at least one week old. While this method provides a higher service level, it pushes the RPO to at least one week—which is too much time for any company to recover from.

COMMENT

Few IT Managers personally verify their data backup and off-site storage process. Never take for granted this is exactly as it should be. Pull out the documented backup and off-site storage process and walk through it.

Some companies reach a compromise by making two copies of the weekly backups. One set is stored off site the next day and the other set is retained for prompt file restores. See Policy ITP-15-1 Data Backups and Retention Policy as an example.

POLICY ITP-15-1.   Data Backups and Retention Policy

Policy #:	ITP-15-1	Effective:	03/18/09	Page #:	1 of N
Subject:	Data Backups and Retention Policy				

1.0 PURPOSE

This policy guides the frequency and type of data backups. It also addresses the length of time that backups must be retained.

2.0 SCOPE

The policy applies to all devices that hold or accumulate data in the support of company operations, to include telecommunications, network applications, desktop units, notebooks, PDAs, etc.

3.0 POLICY

The IT Manager is responsible for making and retaining an adequate number of data backup "safety" copies. To accomplish this, the IT Manager may create further policies and procedures and delegate authority to implement them.

3.1 Devices
Data backups will be made of all devices that contain or collect data, to include at a minimum:

    A. Servers and their internal disks.
    B. Storage Area Networks.
    C. Telecommunications switches (PBX).
    D. Network Controllers.
    E. Desktop PCs.
    F. Notebook PCs.
    G. Programmable Logic Controllers.

3.2 Types of Data

    A. Personal data is not to be stored on company equipment.
    B. Legal compliance data—must be identified. The label on the backup media must include what data it contains and the appropriate

retention period. Care must be taken to ensure the data is securely stored.

C. Business critical data—must be identified. The label on the backup media must include what data it contains and the appropriate retention period. Quick access to this data is required in the event of a disaster.

D. Non-critical data—must be identified. Non-critical data is not legally required to be retained for a period of time. Typically this data is deleted after 13 months. The label on the backup media must include what data it contains and the appropriate retention period.

3.3 Data Backup Frequency

The frequency of data backups is determined by how frequently and how much a data storage element changes.

A. Full backups weekly—*all* data is backed up weekly and retained for 13 months.

B. Incremental backups daily for changing data. These are retained for 30 days.

C. Off-site journaling is used for immediate backup of critical data that cannot be reconstructed from daily backups.

3.4 Data Retention

The company's Records Management Office determines data retention. The retention period is determined by the data element with the longest required retention period on that backup media. If the contents of the media are not known, then the media must be retained for a minimum of 7 years.

3.5 Off-site Storage

A. Data backups will be transported off site every morning after the backups are created.

B. Once every calendar quarter, the IT Manager will audit the off-site storage process to ensure that:
   1. Media is kept in a climate-controlled environment during transit.
   2. The storage facility is secure.
   3. The storage facility is climate controlled.
   4. The data center security is appropriate for media going out and for media coming in.
   5. There is a documented chain of custody for backup media from the point it leaves the data center until it is returned.

3.6 Data Destruction

Data that has outlived its usefulness to the business, and whose age exceeds the legal limits for retention, must be properly destroyed.

A. The media must be rendered permanently unreadable. This is primarily accomplished through physical destruction. Paper documents are

shredded, burned, and the ashes pulped. CDs and magnetic media are shredded.
   B. When data is destroyed, it must be documented as to whom, by what means, when, and what the data consisted of.

3.7 Legal Mandates

   A. SEC Rules 17a-3 and -4. Brokers and dealers must retain records for 6 years.
   B. Gramm-Leach-Bliley Act—Financial institutions must ensure confidentiality of customer data.
   C. HIPAA—Health records must be retained for a minimum of 6 years.
   D. Sarbanes-Oxley—Public company accounting records must be retained for 7 years.

4.0 REVISION HISTORY

Date	Revision #	Description of Change
03/18/09	1.0	Initial creation.

5.0 INQUIRIES

Direct inquiries about this policy to:

Tom Jones, CIO
Our Company, Inc.
2900 Corporate Drive
Columbus, OH 43215

Voice: 614-555-1234
Fax: 614-555-1235
E-mail: tjones@company.com

Revision #:	1.0	Supersedes:	N/A	Date:	03/18/09

§ 15.03   DATA BACKUPS—MAJOR RESPONSIBILITIES

[A]   Overview

A basic management rule is that if no one is responsible for an action, then nothing will happen. The policy for data backups must clearly identify the person responsible for ensuring that all data backups are properly made, transported, and stored off site. Delegate this person authority to ensure the cooperation of all IT staff. In most companies, the person appointed to this responsibility is the IT Operations Manager.

A comprehensive data backup program encompasses many areas:

- Telecommunications switches are simply special-purpose computer servers. Should the voice-mail system be backed up? How often should this be done and would the recovered data be worthwhile?
- Network devices take time to configure and are set to specific firmware versions. Yet in the end, is it easier to spend the time periodically backing it up rather than recreating the data?

Each of the IT Managers should have a role to play in a successful backup program. Any one of the individuals could inadvertently undermine what the company believes to be a comprehensive and reliable program.

[B]   IT Operations Manager

Traditionally, the data center operations manager is responsible for managing the company's data backups. This is an outgrowth of the old data center days when all of the company's computer data was stored in the fixed disks drives in "the glass house." Over time, the world has changed from a single mainframe to multitudes of servers proliferating across the company. What was once nearby and manageable is now spread out of sight and in some cases, its existence known only to a few.

COMMENT

Like all IT processes, backing up data to tape can create a log of errors that must be monitored and investigated to avoid partially backing up—or skipping—critical files during a back up.

Appointing the IT Operations Manager to manage backups is easy since most of the disk and tape backups still reside in the data center. Once appointed, make sure the person appointed is clearly responsible for the success of the *entire* program. This person must create policies and procedures to ensure safeguards are followed. He must then drive these processes throughout the company to ensure they are followed.

Responsibilities for this position might include:

A.   Ensuring that all data center disks are protected with off site data backups. It is possible to rationalize which parts of which disk volumes should be backed up, but the time saved would be more than lost in the ongoing management of such an arrangement.

B. Educating the company on the importance (and limitations) of data backups and the many places they need to be made (e.g., network devices, telephone PBX, voice mail, PC, remote servers).

C. Contracting for an off-site data backup storage facility or arranging for storage at a distant company-owned facility. This includes a secure courier service to protect media en route.

D. Periodically inspecting the security, handling, and storage of media stored off site. Document each inspection for later reference.

E. Validating that media returning from the storage facility is still readable. Often testing is not necessary as it is accomplished with every successful file restore. The Operations Manager must ensure that all media types are verified, not just the troublesome few.

F. Establishing and publishing standards for marking backup media. A consistent naming approach makes media management much easier.

G. Establishing a program to "retire" media that has been used so many times that it may be unreliable. This ensures the media is properly destroyed and not just tossed in the trash (where it might be read by an enterprising thief).

H. Actively seeking out and ensuring that company servers located outside of the data center are properly backed up.

I. Ensuring that a copy of all company software (written in-house and third party) is maintained off site. As software is patched, this must be kept current. (In some environments, software must be reloaded and cannot be directly restored from media.)

COMMENT

One of the authors was the Operations Manager at a data center but was locked out of the data management functions of one section of the servers. They were managed by one of the systems administrators. That person decided, without telling anyone else, that it was not necessary to back up some of the servers since they were for reference and never changed. Over time, the backup tapes for these servers rotated through and were overwritten with a different backup. When a disk crashed on one of the "reference" servers, active production files were discovered running on that machine. There was no way to recover either the files or the production data.

[C] Database Manager

Not every backup is a simple copy out and then back in. Some database systems will not work this way. The method for making database backups depends on how the data will be later reloaded, such as a dump/rebuild or a direct copy. An important person in the development of a backup program is the database administrator (DBA). With around-the-clock service now the norm, the DBA must ensure that the architecture of the systems enables the timely backup of all databases and supporting files.

In addition to being backed up, the database must be able to be recovered quickly. Often this exercise is performed during version upgrades or during a small crisis. Approach each database management system separately as each may have its own unique recovery requirements.

[D] Software Manager

Wages for software developers are expensive. The loss of code created by a major development effort can not only set back a company's progress but also create a major financial loss. Software managers must ensure that the data backup strategy is considered for each new system developed.

COMMENT

Sometimes applications servers are not backed up regularly, as they are constantly changing the code. This is wrong. If that server disappeared tomorrow, how many man-hours of labor are lost, and how much more is required to recreate the code. Always back up development servers by the same schedule as the production data—even if they are located on a server disconnected from the main network.

There are files other than databases that support applications. Parameter files and other fixed reference files may be essential to software operation. These files must be closed or copied for backup. In addition to copies of source code, software often depends on third-party programs. The source code and license keys for these programs must also be stored off site for recovery during a disaster.

COMMENT

One of the major problems with updating software for Y2K compliance (converting year fields to four digits) dealt with

> lost source code. Many programs could not be updated because no one knew where the original code was. Some companies felt it was cheaper to simply upgrade to a new system.
>
> Also, store a copy of each purchased software package off site along with the licenses proving the number of copies purchased.

[E] Network Manager

Network devices are essentially special-purpose computers. They contain configuration and software versions that are important to the company's continued operation. If a firewall, router, or bridge were physically damaged, it could be replaced and reconfigured. However, once the replacement device is in place, where are the configuration data and logic rules to reload? If this information must be reconstructed from memory or old documents, how long will this prolong the outage? With backups and documentation (paper backups) of configuration information, network devices can be recovered more quickly.

The network manager must identify all devices that contain data and arrange to back them up. Network data is not normally large. For disaster recovery purposes, it is usually printed in documents for reference in rebuilding the network. For recovering individual devices, it is often backed up to the data center—over the network! Sending the data to the data center allows it to be backed up along with the normal systems backups and the network team avoids handling tapes. Paper copies of network configuration information should be maintained in the off-site storage facility and updated as devices change or at least monthly.

[F] Shop Floor Systems Manager

Servers spring up like weeds in the most unusual places. Time and attendance servers may be found in a payroll office cabinet. Servers controlling electronic locks may be under a desk in the security office. Shop floor monitoring servers may be cached away all across a factory. Each of these represents important company information that should be copied and stored off site.

Sometimes these orphan servers are isolated from the corporate network. Locating them is the first challenge. Backing them up is the next one as the users may resist anything that threatens their total control. This is where the company policy is handy to establish the requirement for backups. The key is to teach them how an IT backup protects them. Often this will deflate most of their arguments.

The first option is to back these devices up over the network. This will eliminate the handling of media by the users. If that is not possible, then it may be necessary to purchase additional hardware. Leave nothing to chance. Provide preprinted labels using the company's standard media marking format along with a supply of the media. Create a time-controlled program that will automatically make the backup during a scheduled quiet period. A process for delivering the backups to the data center for inclusion in the off-site storage containers must be provided.

Some servers, such as shop floor control servers, only need the software backed up. The data can be reloaded from the main computers. However, if the server collects historical data that is essential to the company, then that data must also be backed up.

[G]   Telecommunications Manager

Telephone switches and their supporting devices are special-purpose computers. They use configuration files for switching, voice-mail files for holding messages, and automated attendant files for routing calls. All of these should be carefully recorded on backup media and, where appropriate, in print.

Some data systems do not recover well. Installing a new telephone switch may take just as long as configuring the backup. It all depends on if a small part of the switch was damaged or the entire telephone switching room is gone.

Voice-mail systems and automated attendants are good candidates for restoring from backups. Current and old voice-mail messages may be important to conducting the company's business. They also may fall under the legal data retention of such laws as the Sarbanes-Oxley Act or various SEC regulations. (When in doubt about data retention, always consult the company's legal advisor as requirements vary based on the industry the company serves.)

§ 15.04   DESIGNING FOR BACKUPS

[A]   Overview

Designing for backups balances the competing requirements of several groups—each with a legitimate business concern. It sounds simple, yet it is quite complex. Consider these three contending parties:

A.   **Operators** who are pressed by management to minimize the number of tapes used and the amount of time required to make backups. Tapes are expensive, so the fewer that are used, the lower the cost. From a labor perspective, this translates into fewer tapes to handle. Operators will use software to compress data onto tapes and use a backup method that selects volumes for backups based on how quickly they can be backed up.

B.   **System administrators** are most interested in the availability of files for restoration when they need them. Decompressing a tape to find the desired files takes time, so they prefer uncompressed media. Also, they might prefer the tapes to correspond to disk volumes rather than from across a variety of storage devices. Further, they want the tapes to remain readily available on site for prompt file recovery.

C.   **Disaster recovery managers** want the critical files segregated from the rest of the files so that in a disaster, only the files required for a recovery are on the tapes to be loaded. This greatly reduces recovery time and helps the company to meet its recovery time objective. In addition, tapes must be *immediately* moved off site after backups are completed.

COMMENT

A complicating factor is the legal retention for a piece of data. A piece of backup media must be retained (and not reused) for as long as the longest legal retention time for a single data item. Therefore, it may save a company some expense by separating data into long term and short term retention when creating backups instead of mixing them.

This illustrates just three of the primary contending groups who use data backups. Three different requirements, three different technical strategies, and all address some business requirement. It is up to the IT Operations Manager to determine which approach is best suited for the company.

If the equipment allows, two copies of the full backups can be made. This requires a tape loader with sufficient capacity to hold the media or someone to refill it. In this case, one set of tapes should be retained on site for use in recovering files and the other copy is promptly sent off site for disaster recovery.

Backing up an open file can be a challenge. Backup software typically skips an open file since it is possible that an update will occur halfway through the copy, which would make the file unreadable later. Yet if the file is critical to the company, it is all the more important to make a backup of it. Software developers must ensure they do not design their systems so files cannot be backed up. If 24/7 availability is required, an alternate backup strategy must be in place prior to the "go live" date.

[B]   Data Mirroring

Data mirroring is a set of on-site disks that are exact duplicates of the primary production file. The process for keeping the two copies in sync vary, but the idea is that as updates are made to one file, it is reflected in the other almost instantaneously. When it is time to back up the database, the mirror connection is "broken" leaving the primary database to continue running while the mirror becomes a snapshot of the database at the moment the connection was shattered. The tape backup is made of this snapshot. After the backup is completed, the mirror is reconnected and reconnected with the primary disk bank. Of course, like all technology based solutions, this approach depends on expensive hardware to implement.

There are several issues with this approach:

A. Expense—since the amount of disk required will be double.
B. Data mirroring addresses high availability but not disaster recovery. Backups must still be made and moved off site.
C. A corruption in the primary file will likely be reflected in the mirror, making them both unusable.

A variation on this is data vaulting where the "mirror" is maintained in a distant off-site, secure facility. This provides several advantages to the company. It eliminates the need to make backups for emergency recovery since the data is already loaded off site and ready to attach to a recovered server. (However, this does not fulfill legal data retention requirements since the mirror is always changing and sometimes backup media is retained as a data "snapshot" for many years.)

Vaulting requires a high-speed data line from the data center to the vaulting site. An alternative is to send it through a virtual private network (VPN) over a high-speed Internet line. The transmission media selected will depend on the size and frequency of transactions to be recorded.

[C] Journaling

Some companies have a very tight recovery point objective. They cannot recreate or afford to lose any of their data. Examples include stock trading, banking, and credit card transactions systems. For these companies, restoring to yesterday's backups is not an option.

To support these environments, a journaling process can be used. This records every transaction onto a backup system, often located off site. These micro-incremental backups can be used to recreate all transactions up to the point of failure.

[D] Data Retention

How long should data backups be kept? It depends on what they are being made for. If the backups are made for local business reasons, then they are kept for as long as they satisfy these reasons. If they are kept for legal reasons, then the laws will say how long to keep them.

To build a history, a series of archives was established. Daily backups (incremental) were kept for seven days and then recycled. Weekly backups were retained for a month. The last weekly backup of the month was retained for 12 months as the monthly backup. The last monthly backup was retained for seven years as the annual backup. At that point, seven years was how far back a tax audit could reach.

In times long past, backups were made so that files could be restored. Once per week, a full set of backups was made. Every weekday after that, incremental backups were made. Incremental backups only copy files that were changed that day. At the end of the week, usually on Saturday night, the next set of full backups was made.

Of course, there are gaps here. If a file is created one day and deleted the next, it would never show up on the annual backups. Some companies addressed this by keeping weekly backups for a year. This still did not fully address the problem, but it was a compromise between coverage and the cost of the tape media.

Those days are gone. We now live in the world of Sarbanes-Oxley, HIPAA, and others. It is now imperative that the IT Manager obtain from the company's legal advisor a written statement of how long to keep each type of data to fulfill legal mandates.

COMMENT

Some companies strive to maintain the smallest amount of backup data possible. The less data there is available to search, the less the company must provide for a litigant during legal "discovery." This is especially important for e-mail and instant messaging archives.

§ 15.05 MEDIA HANDLING, TRANSPORTATION, AND STORAGE

[A] Overview

It is always interesting to watch people unfamiliar with backups. They believe the job is done once the tape is filled. That is only the beginning. The backup media must be properly stored in shipping containers and safely conveyed to the storage site. The vehicle transporting them must be climate controlled and protected from dirt, magnetic influences, etc. It would not be appropriate for the tapes to sit in the back of a car while the driver stops for lunch in the middle of the Arizona summer (or the depths of a Montana winter). Throughout its "life" (from creation to its later reuse in the data center), the media must exist in the same type of secure environment as found in the data center.

To ensure that this is the case, the courier service used to transport the media must be evaluated periodically to ensure it correctly handles the media both going to the storage facility and returning from it. Tapes must be climate controlled and controlled through a "chain of custody" to avoid compromise.

A further check is to verify the extent of the courier's liability if the data is lost. If the courier is reputable, this potential loss helps to sharpen their attention for proper handling of backups. If the courier service is the "low bidder," then it may be the weak link in the data security chain.

> ## COMMENT
>
> In April 2005, the Associated Press reported that a major discount broker lost one of its backup tapes while in transit. The company began informing 200,000 people of the potential data compromise.

[B] Marking Media for Ready Identification

If there were only a single tape to send off, life would be simple. In most companies, there is a series of tapes to store. Clearly identify each of these. In some manner, this identification must be cross-referenced to a list of the files on the media. Files should be able to be located both electronically (the fast way) and manually (visually scanning a list of which files are on which tape).

Data centers using automated tape loaders take advantage of bar-coded serial numbers on the tapes. The operator loads the machine full of tapes and returns when they are full. The media management software (which controls the tape loader) keeps track of which file is on which tape.

However this is done, a standard process for marking media should be included in the data backup policy. This will allow the media for remote sites, telecommunications, network and any other users to be readily identifiable as to where it came from and when it was made.

> ## COMMENT
>
> When writing the policy, develop a set of markings and where the label should go for all types of media used. The telephone system may use one type, the network machines another, etc. Typically this includes tape cartridges (each type may be different), CDs, floppy disks, etc.

[C] Periodic Inspection

IT Managers spend a considerable amount of effort establishing and maintaining a secure environment for their equipment. Snug within this cocoon sits the company's data. Once that data is copied to backup media, effort must be made to ensure it stays safe. As the media is handed over for transportation to the storage facility, ensure it is guarded every step of the way. Follow a package through the entire process from end to end. Critical areas include things that would make the data less secure and things that would harm the media, making it less reliable to read.

> ## COMMENT
>
> The data Operations Manager should audit the off-site storage process at least twice per year. Visit the storage space and look for lax security, structural problems, etc. Be sure to stand in front of the company's containers on the rack and then look around. Don't accept a tour through "the nice section" and not see where the company's valuable data is actually kept.

The policy for data backups should include mandates for the IT Operations Manager to verify the security of backups. This includes ensuring:

A. Media is delivered for off-site storage in a locked, labeled container.
B. The media leaving the data center is handed directly to the courier. (Identification is required—every time.)
C. The courier does not make unauthorized stops along the way.
D. The media is secured in a controlled climate during the entire trip.
E. The media is received at the storage facility and promptly locked away.

Things to look for include:

A. Media is not kept in a climate-controlled environment during transit. This might mean tapes deforming in a hot car trunk while the courier takes a leisurely summer lunch break. The same would be true for a bitterly cold day while the media is left in an unheated space.
B. The storage facility security is insufficient.
C. The storage facility is not climate controlled.
D. The data center security is lax for media going out and for media coming in. Examples would be unattended data containers lying about or containers sent to the wrong customer.

[D] Destroying Old Media

At some point, backup media may be damaged, no longer usable or needed. These items cannot be casually tossed into the trash as some enterprising thief may still read them—even if the data is past the legal expiration date. Media must be destroyed in a controlled manner.

> **COMMENT**
>
> The custodian of the backup media may be legally liable if data is willfully destroyed to obstruct an investigation.

Most companies use a third-party service to shred or burn expired media. Before the media is shipped off site, it should be logged as to what items were shipped for destruction and when. The third-party company should provide a report detailing which items were destroyed, on what day, by whom, and the method used. Refer to the company's legal advisor for how long to keep data destruction records.

Why is this important? If a court order arrives for a legal "discovery" and specific data files are included, a list of destroyed media will identify which items are no longer available. Otherwise the company will be uncertain as to what is available and spend a considerable amount of time chasing down something that may no longer exist. In addition, the researching party may suspect that any media that is not produced may have been hidden.

> **COMMENT**
>
> Some companies offer on-site destruction. The IT Manager can carry the container of obsolete media to the truck and watch its destruction to be sure it is unreadable.

§ 15.06 WORKSTATION, NOTEBOOK PC, AND DATA COLLECTION STATION BACKUPS

[A] Overview

Workstations, notebook PCs, and other data collection devices, by their nature, create, process, and collect data from many sources. This data may be of great value to the company. It also may be difficult or impossible to recreate. The problem is how to capture this data and back it up.

Making a data backup is not that hard. Connect the PC to the company's data network and copy everything from the disk to the data center. At some later point, copy this data to backup media. Take a moment to consider what data has been copied. How much space was required to copy the operating system (which is not needed for a recovery)? How much space was required to copy the application programs which likewise are not necessary? All that is needed is the data! How can it be separated?

[B] Identifying the Problem

The issue is how to back up the data without also copying the programs. Microsoft's Windows program is on most corporate PCs. It requires about 2 GB of storage to run. Copying this over to backup media not only wastes time but also creates unneeded copies of software.

Over the years, many ways to accomplish this have been attempted.

A. In the early days of PCs, companies tried backing them up to a roaming tape drive. This unit sat on a cart and stopped by to back up the PC's disk while the owner went to lunch. However, the cost of the tape controller cards (required for each PC) kept the number of users small.

B. Another way was to minimize the hard disk size on the workstation to be just sufficient to support the software thereby forcing users to save their data on network drives. These drives would be backed up along with the rest of the company's data. The problem was that network storage was much more expensive than desktop storage so the company ended up buying additional PC disks.

C. More recently, notebook PCs and desktop units have come equipped with CD writers. On the surface this seems like an easy way for individuals to back up their own data. The problem is that data that was secure behind passwords and other security devices is now floating around on uncontrolled CDs that are stuffed into drawers or lying on desktops.

[C] Separating Data from the Software

The first step is to separate the data from the software. Most PCs are backed up to a server in the data center over the corporate data network. Although not a big deal for one unit, it can stress the network if 500 PCs all dump at the same time on a Friday afternoon.

Copying files can take one of two approaches: inclusive or exclusive. The inclusive approach copies all of the files. It is simple to implement and trades ease of administration for a heavier load on the resources.

Exclusive copying examines the file suffix of every file being copied. It excludes copying any file with an .exe or .com suffix. Other file types also can be added to the "stop list." A variation on this is to not copy any files from specific directories that are found in the company's standard PC image, such as the operating system or applications software.

Another approach is to require all users to store their PC data in one master directory, such as "My Documents." Anything in this directory is backed up and everything else is not. This can be implemented with a bit of user training. Also, any software installed by the company that saves files should be set to default their storage somewhere under the data directory.

§ 15.07 DATA RETENTION AND LEGAL MANDATES

[A] Overview

Companies retain data for their own historical uses. Beyond that, from a business standpoint, this media can be recycled or destroyed. In reality it passes from data retained for a business need to data retained for legal purposes. Many laws dictate the length of time certain types of data must be retained. During this retention period, the data must be safeguarded in the same manner as any other important, confidential data.

[B] Legal Mandates

Legally, different types of data have different retention periods. Legal mandates must be based on opinions provided by the company's legal representative. Legal requirements must be written and included in the backup policy. This will prevent people along the chain of custody from claiming ignorance. These legal mandates should be reviewed and updated at least annually.

The longer media is retained, the greater the storage costs will be. Backup media equipment evolves. It requires the company to retain old media reading equipment or to contract with a company that can provide this service.

This is complicated by how the media backup was made. If all of one type of data was saved on one backup device, that retention period is based on what the data is. Since most companies mix all of their data together, all of the media must be kept for as long as the retention period of the data with the longest time.

The balance to this is to keep no more data on hand than is necessary. In a legal investigation, there is no need to leave pieces of information that may inaccurately paint a picture of something illegal. When media has passed its legal expiration date, it should be properly destroyed, and that destruction recorded for future reference.

A list of legal mandates and how they apply to a company should be provided by its legal advisor. With the fast pace of technical innovation, these laws are somewhat open to interpretation. Some of the current laws that impact the retention of data include:

A. The Sarbanes-Oxley Act of 2002 (SOX), which applies to publicly traded companies. The Act requires IT, accounting & finance, and legal to collaborate on the implementation of a published records management program.
   1. Section 404—Discusses internal controls on information technology for financial control.
   2. Section 302—Effective internal controls are designed and maintained to ensure officers are aware of all material information.
B. The Health Insurance Portability and Accountability Act (HIPAA), which details how personal health information can be electronically maintained or transmitted.
C. The Gramm-Leach-Bliley Act, which protects consumers' personal financial information being held by financial organizations.

    D. Various tax and accounting rules, which require the retention of accounting data for seven years.

[C] Do Not Overdo It

A fool's approach to data retention is to try and keep everything and in that way hope to miss nothing. This is foolish because storage requirements would grow and grow until the expense bankrupts a company. Data retention is a cost like any other and appropriate strategies are required to meet all legal and business purposes for data retention and then to properly dispose of it.

    A. Make an inventory of the data created by the company (yes, it is a big task).

    B. Categorize the data into groups of the longest retention time. When in doubt about which category to use, choose the one that has the longest retention period.

    C. Review this plan with legal counsel since one of its primary purposes is legal compliance. Be sure to obtain a written answer.

    D. Publish these guidelines to all employees.

16

SERVICE DESK SUPPORT: HANDLING DAY-TO-DAY HASSLES

§ 16.01 OVERVIEW
  [A] Purpose and Scope
  [B] Critical Policies to Develop Based on This Chapter

§ 16.02 ROLE OF THE SERVICE DESK
  [A] Voice of the Customer
  [B] Staffing
  [C] Working Under Pressure

§ 16.03 ESTABLISHING A SERVICE DESK
  [A] Overview
  [B] Establish a Service Level
  [C] Which Products Will the Service Desk Team Support?
  [D] Building a Service Desk Team
  [E] Service Desk Staffing Issues
  [F] Service Desk Problem Tracking Database
  [G] Communicating with Customers
  [H] Other Handy Service Desk Tools

§ 16.04 THE PROACTIVE SERVICE DESK
  [A] Overview
  [B] Managing by Metrics—Nothing but the Facts!
  [C] One Call—One Success
  [D] Training End Users
  [E] Carry the Message to the Masses
  [F] Hail and Farewell
  [G] Knowledge Base
  [H] Power Users—The Service Desk's On-Site Helpers
  [I] Customer Surveys—Closing the Feedback Loop

§ 16.05 THE SERVICE DESK IN A DISASTER
  [A] Overview
  [B] The Service Desk's Role in the Crucial First Few Hours
  [C] The Service Desk as the Emergency Command Center

§ 16.01 OVERVIEW

[A] Purpose and Scope

Most IT departments have established a service desk to support their user communities. A service desk acts as a lightning rod to attract all of the calls for IT assistance into one central point and away from the rest of the department. The service desk is where users of the company's technology assets can turn for help.

In times gone past, whenever someone wanted support from the IT department, they would call whomever in IT they worked with last. This was a positive thing since in times of trouble they were falling back on the people who had helped them before. It represented a relationship based on confidence in that person's expertise (or else they would not call them). Often the user took pains to maintain a positive one-on-one relationship with these secret contacts.

There were just a few flaws with this approach. First, what would they do if the person that they were looking for were absent or ill? The caller would leave a message and wait for a response. They had no way of knowing how long their wait would be unless they walked over looking for them. What if the person they called was not inclined to help that day? In addition, there is not a record made of each call so persistent problems were not visible to IT management. Without this critical feedback, the manager might be sitting in the midst of a crumbling house and not even know it. In addition, most of the support calls were about very basic issues. These calls pulled expensive IT staff away to handle simple tasks. These interruptions prevented the manager from focusing the staff on the most pressing business issues.

So over time, service desks evolved as a tool that kept all of the good in the previous example and addressed all of the bad in a positive way. Service desks function as a single point of contact for anyone calling with an IT question or problem to report. Instead of "knowing who to call" and hoping they will be available, people seeking assistance can call the service desk and be sure of obtaining a prompt answer. The service desk in turn takes ownership of reported problems until they are resolved.

[B] Critical Policies to Develop Based on This Chapter

Using the material discussed in this chapter, you will be able to create the following policies:

A. Creating a service desk.
   1. Establishing the level of service to be provided.
   2. Which products will be supported.
   3. Communications procedures.
B. Service desk operations.
   1. What metrics are to be collected and how they will be calculated.
   2. Procedures for handling different types of calls.
   3. The service desk's role in a disaster.

Policies should always be developed based on the local situation. Successful managers cannot issue appropriate guidance if the policies are written with another company's or location's situation in mind.

§ 16.02 ROLE OF THE SERVICE DESK

[A] Voice of the Customer

The service desk receives calls from a wide range of people. It is the IT director's "public face" to the company. The folks answering the service desk telephones will spend far more time talking to the end users than the director will. If they present a positive, helpful attitude, then the IT department's image will shine. If they are impolite and cannot communicate effectively, then the department's reputation will suffer accordingly.

In their conversations with the service desk, callers will also provide valuable feedback on the service the IT organization is providing. Sometimes they may say this is a repeat call because the problem persists. Sometimes they may say "Please don't send so-and-so over from IT because they are rude, incompetent, etc." There is a lot of valuable information coming across these lines so IT Managers should periodically take turns on the phones. Always act on complaints. The old rule is for every complaint made, 10 more were never reported.

Encourage a constant flow of customer feedback on the service desk's services. Ensure customers know they can call the service desk manager or the IT Manager if they experience any problems with the service desk staff. It is better to hear a bit of bad news from them than to have it amplified by flowing through the executive channels. In casual conversations with end users, ask them specifically about their experiences with the service desk. Some people are too polite to call the IT director about a problem but may raise the issue if prompted. Managers may also hear some good things that can be opportunities for publicly praising or rewarding the staff.

[B] Staffing

When staffing the service desk, select people carefully for attitude and patience as much as for technical knowledge. During its busy times, the service desk is a hectic place. Patience is essential to calm down a situation while the problem is resolved. Often callers are in a panic and can at times be quite brusque. Cool-headed service desk personnel can defuse the heated emotions and work toward the technical solution. Hotheaded ones will get the IT director in trouble as well.

Before extending an offer to a service desk applicant, always run a background check. Service desk technicians will soon find their hands deep in a broad range of tools. If this person is to hold a position of trust, they must be of sound character. A criminal background check is essential if they will be responsible for changing user passwords and setting up accounts.

Service desk manager

The service desk manager's attitude, work ethic, and demeanor will establish the tone of the service desk staff. Choosing the right person makes all of the difference between a successful service desk and a mediocre one. The service desk manager should plan from the beginning to be a hands-on leader who pitches in when the telephone queue gets too long. He must be dedicated to customer service and ensure that everyone connected with the service desk is likewise minded.

The service desk manager must have the authority to drive calls to completion within the IT department. He personally follows up on calls that are unresolved after 48 hours. Usually, these were escalated to a programmer or network technician to address. If they are unresolved for a second 48 hours, escalate them to that person's manager. This action will not gain them any friends, but a truly service oriented service desk manager would not trust this task to anyone else.

The service desk manager is the "lightning rod" to take all of the complaint calls about the service desk. Sometimes the caller just wants to unload his frustrations onto someone. Sometimes he has a valid point that will improve the service desk's service. Other times the service desk manager must educate him as to why his request violates company policy. Taking these calls and listening carefully is important. Otherwise they will flow through the management chain, growing ever uglier until surfacing in an executive staff meeting.

The manager represents the service desk at IT change control meetings. As new systems roll out, the service desk manager ensures that developers provide the end users with training and documentation. (This is a defensive move since, without something to refer to, end users will all call the service desk with the same questions.) The service desk manager further ensures that the developers provide adequate desk support documentation and reviews it for adequacy. Proofread all documentation for clarity, accuracy, and pertinence to the support the service desk will be providing. It is important that the service desk be informed in advance about any impending changes so they can answer user inquiries about changed screens or know who to call if the change is failing.

COMMENT

If the service desk knows a data system change has been implemented, they can judge from their calls if the change has failed and can provide the programmer with a quick "heads-up" about the problem.

The manager also acts as the service desk "tool master" by reviewing problem resolutions entered in the problem tracking system. These resolutions are candidates for the service desk knowledge base. Search this repository when confronted by tough problems. Offer the same knowledge base for user self-help through the service desk's intranet web site.

Another important task is to assemble metrics of the problems encountered during the previous reporting period. Use this to uncover trends, identify marginal equipment, and even users who need further training on their software.

Metrics are valuable tools for the IT director to demonstrate the high quality of support they are providing to the company.

Service desk technicians

Most service desks employ at least two technicians to cover the telephones—one to come in early and one to stay late. These technicians should be very patient people who can sympathize with the caller while calming them down and gathering the pertinent information.

The early shift person begins work at least one hour before the bulk of the employees arrive. This person uses a start-of-day checklist to verify that the network and servers are functioning properly. This allows a bit of time to address any system problems and to call for technical support on the problems before they are uncovered by the users.

Accompany start-of-day checklist by a list of action steps required to check each device and explaining what the proper response would be. Sometimes this involves linking to each server to verify they are operational. It also requires checking each print queue to detect printer jams or other problems.

COMMENT

Just as some people are slow to wake up in the morning, so are some computers! Calls seem to peak sometime before the morning break and then slack off until almost quitting time when they make one final surge. Of course each site is different but the morning seems to be when most calls come in. Adequately cover the telephones during this peak time.

The late shift person covers from some point later in the day until about an hour or so after normal business hours. This provides help assistance for people working late. If additional hours of coverage are required, schedule them through the service desk manager in advance. This reduces the likelihood of abuses. The service desk manager can carry an after-hours pager if night coverage is required, or this pager can be rotated through the IT staff. Many companies cover their third shift service desk with the late night computer operators.

During normal business hours, make sure the service desk staff takes their breaks. They should leave the telephones behind and walk around. They should not be visiting users during their breaks. Breaks allow them to mentally decompress and be ready to jump back into the fray!

> # COMMENT
>
> Encourage the service desk staff to take their breaks away from their workstations. Visiting users will not understand that a technician is reading the newspaper while the telephone is ringing. The technicians should relocate to the company break area, or to a designated spot in the office.

[C] Working Under Pressure

Sometimes the callers are so angry that they take out their frustrations verbally on the technician. Although this may give them some measure of personal satisfaction, it is not acceptable business practice. Everybody has the right to respect and human dignity, both the caller and the service desk technician. The goal is to defuse the situation, identify the facts, and quickly move the problem to resolution. If achieved, then these callers can turn into appreciative customers. There are some basic steps the service desk can take for addressing abusive callers.

In both types of calls, record the facts as they unfold. If the caller makes specific insults or accusations, then record them. When the call ends, immediately pass on notes of the discussion to the service desk supervisor who can determine if there is sufficient cause to complain through the Personnel Office channels. It is a violation of human resources policy in most companies to verbally abuse an employee with references to their gender, their race, etc. People who call in anger may find themselves in a company disciplinary situation if their remarks are not business-like and focused on the issues.

Angry callers. Angry callers are disturbed about something and rarely was it caused by the service desk. Something set them off before they called and as unfair as it sounds, the service desk technician was just the first person they could unload it on. These callers feel compelled to share their frustration verbally, and often forcefully, with the service desk. Angry callers spew out their complaint and usually run out of steam. They then settle into asking for help with a problem.

Steps for addressing this type of call:

- Try to separate the facts out of the midst of their emotion. A small bit of information here and there gradually turns the conversation toward the problem at hand.
- Overlook the angry words (if they are not abusive) while shaping the problem definition.
- Slow down the tempo of the call. If necessary, apologize, make an excuse, and quickly put the person on hold for 15 seconds or so to let them cool down.
- Empathize, agree with them that the situation is regrettable, and ask for their help in resolving it.

Abusive callers. Abusive callers are an entirely different matter. They gain some sort of personal gratification from the exchange. Abusive callers are as much (or more) interested in irritating or intimidating the service desk technicians as they are in having their problem resolved. A call is abusive if the language and word selection of the caller are personally derogatory or make the service desk technician feel uncomfortable.

Steps for addressing this type of call:

- If they get the service desk technician angry or argumentative, then they have achieved their personal goal. Give them a few moments to run out of steam and always respond calmly to their tirade. Remember, the service desk technician is in control and can end the call at any time. Answering angrily or meekly encourages more of the same caller behavior.
- If the telephone has caller ID, call the person by name, which may slow him down (unless he is using someone else's telephone).

COMMENT

Never argue with a fool. They will drag you down to their level and beat you with experience.

- Take charge of the calls. No matter what they are focusing on, bring the conversation back to the issues at hand—a description of the problem, when it first began, etc. Keep the tone of the call firm, even tempered, and unflappable.
- Whether it is true or not, inform the caller that all calls into the service desk are recorded.
- If the abuse does not stop, tell the caller that either the abuse ends or the call does. Only state this once and feel free to hang up if they continue their abuse. Immediately report the situation to a supervisor.

§ 16.03 ESTABLISHING A SERVICE DESK

[A] Overview

There are at least six major decisions to make when establishing a service desk. Some of them, like staffing, cannot be determined until all of the questions have been addressed and a picture emerges of what the service desk service offering will look like. If a service desk is already in place, consider how these factors stack up against local operations:

A. Establish a service level.
B. What products will the service desk support?

    C. Building a service desk team.
    D. Service desk problem tracking database.
    E. Communicating with IT customers.
    F. Other handy service desk tools.

COMMENT

ITIL provides an excellent model for a service desk. However, it requires executive commitment to be put in place. An ITIL based service desk creates a catalog of services based on negotiated service level agreements, providing specific services (and resolution times) for specific customers (usually an entire department). If a customer wants a higher level of service, then they must fund it. For example, the service desk may offer a four hour resolution for password resets on Monday through Friday. If a department requires a one hour resolution, then they must fund staff for that additional service.

See Policy ITP-16-1 Service Desk Policy as an example.

POLICY ITP-16-1   Service Desk Policy

Policy #:	ITP-16-1	Effective:	03/18/09	Page #:	1 of N
Subject:	Service Desk Policy				

1.0 PURPOSE

This policy establishes a central Service Desk as the initial point of contact for all IT service requests.

2.0 SCOPE

The policy applies to all users of information technology within the company.

3.0 POLICY

The Service Desk is the IT department's first point of contact with all end-user service requests. The Service Desk resolves those issues within its capability and passes on to higher levels of technical support those requests requiring their services.

3.1 Hours of operation

At least one Service Desk technician will be at the desk from 0500 until 0200 the following morning. The goal is always to provide someone on site to address urgent issues.

3.2 Scope

The Service Desk provides first-line support on all IT hardware and software purchased by the company. The Service Desk does not:

A. Support equipment that is not purchased and used for the company's benefits. This includes equipment belonging to employees, on-site contractors, or other non-company equipment.
B. Answer questions about or dispatch the maintenance team.
C. Provide telephone directory assistance or forward outside calls to inside employees.
D. Take messages to pass on to others later.
E. Take absence-reporting calls from IT employees.

3.3 What to support

The Service Desk provides support for all hardware and software on the supported item list. As time permits, the Service Desk assists with nonstandard IT hardware and software support.

3.4 How to support

A. A major value of the Service Desk is the immediacy of someone answering the telephone at all hours the Service Desk is open. Even if the telephone is quiet, at least one of the Service Desk technicians will remain at the desk (unless on scheduled breaks, etc.).
B. The Service Desk does not visit customer sites to address problems. The Service Desk dispatches desktop support team members to visit customers.
C. Walk-in customers will wait until all of the incoming calls have been addressed.

3.5 Password reset procedure

A common user issue is for the Service Desk to reset passwords. The Service Desk will follow the user validation process in the password reset procedure step by step with no deviation.

3.6 System status

A. The Service Desk will monitor the infrastructure-monitoring software and notify the appropriate technician if a problem occurs.
B. The Service Desk will notify the IT Manger immediately in the event of any severity 1 or 2 problems.

3.7 Information security

At all times, the Service Desk is on alert for attempts to breach the company's information security defenses and immediately reports all attempts to the IT Security Coordinator.

3.8 Metrics

The Service Desk technicians will track all incoming calls. Simple calls are tallied on a sheet with "tick" marks. Calls that take longer than three minutes to resolve or that are referred to someone else will be entered into the Service Desk database.

4.0 REVISION HISTORY

Date	Revision #	Description of Change
03/18/09	1.0	Initial creation.

5.0 INQUIRIES

Direct inquiries about this policy to:

Tom Jones, CIO
Our Company, Inc.
2900 Corporate Drive
Columbus, OH 43215

Voice: 614-555-1234
Fax: 614-555-1235
E-mail: tjones@company.com

Revision #:	1.0	**Supersedes:**	N/A	**Date:**	03/18/09

[B]   Establish a Service Level

Once a decision is made to establish a service desk, the first thing is to determine what level of service is to be offered. This translates directly into how much user assistance the service desk will provide before the call is escalated up the IT support chain. This decision will drive the size and expertise level of the service desk staff.

A.   What days of the week and hours of the day will the service desk be manned? An office that runs from 9 a.m. until 5 p.m., Monday through Friday, may want a service desk available from 7 a.m. until 7 p.m. That allows time for the service desk technicians to change the backup tapes, verify that the network and servers are ready for the day's work, etc.

If there is enough of a need for Saturday support, staff that day also. Always bring in the service desk early enough to verify that critical systems are operational before the bulk of the employees arrive. This allows time to address system problems before the employees arrive.

COMMENT

Publish the service desk's normal hours of service. It sets an expectation in the users' minds so they will not be shouting because no one answered the telephone on a Sunday morning.

Some departments will appreciate extra support at different times of the year. The accounting department will work late when they are closing the fiscal year books. The materials department may need help during a weekend inventory count, etc. The IT director must understand the events scheduled in the facility and provide the appropriate level of service desk support. Eventually, the other departments will see the benefit and notify the service desk of upcoming events.

Another staffing issue will be the peak times of the day. After a few weeks, the peak demand times will be obvious. There will also be peak days of the week. During those times, extra help answering the telephones is always appreciated. During times of peak demand, rotate the rest of the IT staff through the service desk a few at a time. Taking service desk calls from time to time might open their eyes a bit.

B. Time to answer incoming calls. How long is too long for the telephone to ring? Thirty seconds may seem like eternity if the person is calling with an urgent request. It takes people to answer a surge in incoming calls. The service desk's telephone equipment must allow multiple calls into the same telephone number so others can answer the phones.

However, when the calls drop off or there is a lull before the next barrage, the service desk staff is just sitting and waiting. This is the difficult part of staffing, balancing between enough people to answer the telephone and people sitting around since the phones are quiet.

Tracking the time to answer and the number of calls that give up and stop waiting are both important metrics to track. They will be useful for identifying peak times and shifting the service desk's staff around to meet it. If possible, provide a way for people to leave a voice-mail message when the call wait times are high.

C. Call to resolution time. How much time will elapse between receiving a call and the resolution for an average request? The more skilled the service desk staff is, the more calls they will address while the customer is still on the line. We all would like to have our issues resolved with a single call. It is a helpless feeling when a caller is told that "someone" will call us back "later." Not everyone can remain chained to a telephone waiting for "someone" to call back at some vague point in the future.

COMMENT

Resolution time, by product, is another metric to track. When analyzing the service desk performance data, this will indicate which devices on the primary support list take longer per call to support.

D. Substitutes. A trained substitute must be on hand to cover the service desk while the usual people go to lunch, take restroom breaks, are absent due to illness, etc. Do not just park someone in front of the telephone to answer it. It is unfair to them and the callers will not receive the level of service they have come to expect. The trained substitute should also be available to handle call volume surges. These usually come at the beginning of the day with a smaller surge toward the end. In most cases, the service desk manager sits in during the breaks and to cover sick days.

[C] Which Products Will the Service Desk Team Support?

What technologies will the service desk support? Even if the service desk staff is skilled, there is a limit to what can be supported. Use a copy of the last hardware and software asset inventory list. Mark each item that will be fully supported as "Green," each item that assistance can be somewhat provided as "Yellow," and those items that you will be helped with as time permits as "Red." Publishing this list is an important part of the IT department's stated service level.

Just as important as determining what the service desk will support, the service desk staff must clearly understand what they will not support. Beware of people dumping their support responsibilities onto the service desk. Good service desk technicians hate to not provide assistance with anything that they can. Do not become the facility's source for telephone numbers. They need to get directory assistance elsewhere. Understand where the other points of dispatch are within the facility, such as facility maintenance and the security office. Refer callers to them. If the questions do not involve IT, do not try to help. Ensure that the service desk technicians understand that only the service desk manager can approve taking on any additional support tasks.

> ## COMMENT
>
> Make a policy to cover the items the service desk will support and to what level. Changes to this list are up to the IT director (typically quarterly). Otherwise, the IT director will one day find the service desk staff supporting the televisions in the cafeteria!

Typically, "Green" level items are the IT standard products. This should be the majority of the calls. This also implies that as new items are added to the "standard" list, the service desk must be among the first to be trained. Copies of these products should be available on the service desk computers so they can see what the caller sees. In addition, classify any item that is a component of a critical business function as "Green."

Green items have additional value to end users. These are the ones the IT department will hold training classes on, provide tips on their use in the company newsletter, and provide third-party books on how to use them. This positive approach strategy is intended to "pull" users toward the standard items instead of "pushing" them off the Red ones.

The "Yellow" items are usually the previous standard items. Over time, the staff can easily handle these calls also since they previously supported them as Green. The Yellow list tends to hold all of the legacy equipment that just keeps on running despite its age. Every year at capital budget time, be sure to propose eliminating these technologies.

Red level items are items the team gives their best effort to support after all of the Green and Yellow level calls are resolved. Some sites disavow any help for this category, but the company has already spent the money to buy them so the service desk may as well try to keep it going—after the other categories are addressed. Red level items often require picking up a manual and trying to determine how something works. Red items are those that are too old to repair or "renegade" systems that somehow appeared in the facility despite all policies against them.

> ## COMMENT
>
> Try as it might, the IT department will never be able to fulfill all of the demand for data processing services. Renegade (or "stealth") systems can pop up in any department. Eventually, someone finds a way to circumvent the IT acquisition policies. This can be by political strength or by finding a

> way around controls of the purchase of hardware and software. They may even have a vendor that rents them hardware and software to support their products.

Some people will never give up their tried and true hardware and software, but these same people are the ones still driving their old brown Studebaker to work. A few people may be emotionally attached to something but what they value most is its predictability. A few may be afraid of change but if the IT department makes it easy for them, and proves that the new system is reliable, then most people will cooperate. Make the transition easy by loading their data into the new software, and providing training and support until they settle in with the new products. Important (business-wise or politically) Red level items can also be supported by arranging for third-party support. Be sure to make the requesting department pay for this. If they feel the pain, they will be interested in replacing it and will be reluctant to do this again in the future.

COMMENT

> At one time, one of the authors had a public affairs team that demanded to use a specific brand of software to create the facility's newsletter. "Politically," this purchase could not be blocked. Technically, there was not anyone on the staff who knew how to support it. The expense to train someone to answer the occasional question was not cost justified. Instead, a company was contracted to provide on-site training and support for the product, and the cost was billed to the user's budget.

Hardware—End-user hardware is usually supported by dispatching repair technicians to the users' site. In the case of small items, such as keyboards or bar-code scanner guns, end users may also bring broken items to the service desk to exchange for working units. Resolving hardware issues takes time, so consider how many devices there are out there that could break. Also, the service desk needs documentation on what to ask and what to do when troubleshooting each class of item. Clear, complete documentation will help to determine the proper person to dispatch and the tools they should bring along.

Green level hardware items should have a pool of on-site spares. When one of these items breaks, the spare unit is exchanged for the broken one. The broken unit is sent out for repair and, on its return, becomes the new spare. This provides a high level of support and the least downtime. If the hardware is too large to exchange, then a service contract and "work around" contingency plans must be set in place.

Typically, Yellow level items are not repaired unless they would be expensive to replace. Yellow items will use up their spares until they are gone and then be replaced by equivalent Green level units.

Red level hardware items are not supported. If they can be replaced by a Green or Yellow item, they should be. But if they must be repaired, then send them out for repair or have an on-site repair technician called in. However, if the item is that critical, then it shouldn't be in this category.

Software—There is a wide world of software on the market. However, most companies focus their efforts on a carefully selected list of products. How much help should the service desk provide before dispatching someone to address the problem? Software problems can often take a considerable amount of time to address. Some users cannot adequately (or truthfully) explain what they did that led up to the problem. It can try the service desk's patience to dig out the facts without making a desk-side visit.

Unlike hardware, software lives in a "matrix" world. The operating system interacts with the network on different levels and the many applications running on a PC interact with both. The fewer variations there are, the better. To avoid the subtle problems that can be caused, most companies configure their workstation operating systems to restrict users from loading their own software.

Network devices—The service desk supports network availability by watching a network monitor. This monitor indicates when traffic ceases in a network segment or is excessively high. In either case, they immediately notify the network manager to investigate.

Telephones—Telephone adds/changes/removal requests are often controlled through the service desk. Telephone instruments sometimes break, employee offices are moved, and voice-mail accounts must be established. All are routine requests for service. The service desk adds value by asking the next set of questions. In the case of a departing employee, where should their calls be routed to? (Usually this is whoever is taking on that job responsibility or his or her supervisor.)

For departing employees, the same questions apply to their e-mail and data files. The service desk can dispatch one request to close someone's accounts and ensure the flow of information is picked up by their department.

Servers and mainframes—Usually this involves user IDs and passwords. The service desk either sets up new users or collects incoming ID applications and passes them to the appropriate system administrator. Another routine request is for access to specific files or databases. These requests must be checked against a table that details who can authorize access to whom and then the access request can be passed on to the appropriate person.

The service desk may also monitor the mainframe systems to ensure availability. If a user calls in and says he cannot connect to an important system, this might indicate that for whatever reason the specific mainframe capability has ceased to function.

Web-enabled cell phones and personal data assistants (PDAs)—Many sites support these units in the same way as they do PCs. Medical staffs depend on the portability of RF-connected devices to provide information as they roam through the hospitals. Web-enabled telephones extend the PDA model into also providing web access. These devices have also replaced internal radio and pager systems for locating key staff anywhere in the facility.

[D] Building a Service Desk Team

With a list of the products that the service desk will be supporting and how well it will be supported, decide what sort of people will be answering the telephones. The skill level of the service desk staff depends on the level of service these individuals are expected to provide. Whatever they cannot answer must be passed up to the next level of expertise. Meanwhile, the customer is still waiting for an answer.

On one end of the support scale is the person who answers the phone and always dispatches someone to fix the problem. These people are cheap but do not save the IT department much time since they cannot fix anything and probably do not understand the business environment. On the other end is the highly paid technical person who can answer most questions but is bored because the work seems "easy."

With that trade-off in mind, consider these three general levels of service desk support.

Level I support takes the message and dispatches someone to address the problem. The advantage of this approach is that it is cheap to staff. It provides the immediacy of someone answering a call. Since they do not know how to repair anything, they refer to their list of who is available to address that type of issue at that moment. However, there is still a training issue. To know who to dispatch, this person must know the proper questions to narrow down the problem. Using Level I support means the caller can always expect a delay in obtaining results, even in an "emergency." The first call resolution rate will be very low.

A user stating, "the third-floor computers are down," might mean that there is a power outage or that the network connection for these devices has been broken. They may also be exaggerating the problem (imagine that!). Instead of sending an electrician to check the power grid, or instead of dispatching the network technician, the service desk staff must know the sort of questions to ask. In this example, the caller's PC could not start the desired program and was the only one that had a problem. In the caller's mind, the entire enterprise had stopped even though his problem was local and minor.

Level I support is often outsourced. The users call a toll-free number and have no idea where it is answered. The experience may seem familiar when trying to call a public utility. They cannot check anything while the customer is on the line and always dispatch someone to call the customer back and to look into the problem. A disadvantage of an outsourced service desk is that they will never learn much about how the facility is laid out or the internal terminology the company uses daily. This becomes frustrating to users when describing an urgent problem.

Some outsourcing arrangements involve sending the caller to an "off shore" company. This is done to save on labor costs. Companies have experienced mixed results when customers have difficulty understanding the technicians' questions and directions.

Level II support is similar to the mainframe console operators of days gone by. Level II service desks require a higher level of technical expertise and on-site training. Like Level I, they take the call but they can also resolve common problems while the customer is on the line. A common example is to reset passwords. This implies providing the service desk with security authorizations to set up accounts and change passwords (background checks are essential!).

Level II support handles routine questions for computer operations. They may include kicking off or killing mainframe jobs and monitor the running of critical jobs. They can check to see when long-running jobs have completed and the status of reports being printed. At some sites, Level II support may also be permitted to change the priority of mainframe jobs.

Providing Level II support implies that the service desk manager must establish a training outline when hiring new technicians. Level II technicians work on mainframe problems, simple network problems, and PC software issues—truly a wide range of issues. Few people walk in the door with this level of understanding, especially of site specific tasks. The service desk manager must develop a documented training program to ensure the new employee can learn to answer questions like the rest of the staff.

Level III service desk support normally cannot be reached directly by the end users. This small group supports the Level I or Level II service desk by taking calls they cannot resolve. Level III support might include such things as resolving network device problems, rebooting a server, or replacing a PC hardware component. It might also include the person who makes changes to the PBX (adds/deletes). Level III support can also be contracted through a third-party service. The IT department's service contracts typically provide Level III support. They require that only a few skilled IT staff named on a list can call them for help. Be sure to include the service desk staff on this list, or at least the service desk manager. The key to faster training is carefully documented procedures and technical documentation.

[E]   Service Desk Staffing Issues

One of the more valuable aspects of the service desk to the IT Manager is how it handles all of the routine calls that flow in. The service desk is a natural place to store forms for requesting user IDs and for later creating the new ID/passwords. Requests for user IDs, office moves (PCs and telephones), and all of the other routine paperwork can flow out from and into the service desk. The service desk staff must of course be trained in this and have guidelines to follow, but overall, this is routine work to fill their off-peak hours. Requests for security access to sensitive data or software will flow through the service desk but is handled by the IT staff as before.

Resetting passwords can be time consuming. If the company's security software forces periodic password changes (as it should), then the service desk staff will be called on to assist the people who forget them. The trick is to ensure that no one fools the service desk technicians into letting them into another person's account. An identity authentication procedure is essential.

> ## COMMENT
>
> Step-by-step work instructions are needed that will closely control who can reset a password and how they will authenticate who is calling. The service desk technician is not permitted to deviate from these steps.

Another time killer for the IT staff is restoring files that the user has deleted. The service desk can pick this task up and, depending on their size and complexity, run the reloads in their off-peak hours.

The industry standard for staffing service desks is roughly one technician per every 75 users. The size of the staff also depends upon other factors:

A. The expertise of users is a big driver for staffing. If the team is supporting a large number of novices, they can flood the service desk with many basic questions. This is more typical in sites that experience a lot of employee turnover or who hire seasonal workers. On the other hand, if the team is supporting a large number of engineers running high-powered workstations, a low-tech service desk is not of much use to them.

B. The stability of the systems being supported can also be a factor. If the systems are stable and behave in predictable ways, then it is easier to train the staff. If they employ cutting edge technology, then the staff must have the technical background to isolate the problems.

C. The number of technologies to support may guide staffing plans. The wider the range of technologies or things there are to know, the more likely that the staff will specialize or take longer to train.

D. In the long run, staff size can be reduced if the service desk manager proactively chases down recurring problems. This will result in fewer repeat calls (and happier users).

[F]   Service Desk Problem Tracking Database

Sometimes the service desk is quiet as a summer afternoon at the fishing lake. Other times it is a boisterous, hectic madhouse. In both cases there is a common problem of how to ensure that "no request is left behind." A very important service desk tool is a problem tracking database. As these calls are received, they are entered into a problem tracking and reporting database. The database will provide many essential functions:

A. Move problem tracking off a notepad and onto a shared database. This provides visibility of the problems encountered to the service desk manager and the potential for a wide range of management reports. Problem reports are less likely to be lost.

B. The tracking database keeps track of which IT person the call was escalated to, and when. The service desk manager will use this to follow up with the assigned IT person to ensure they complete the tasks.

C. The database tracks calls based on their priority. Each site devises their own scale for prioritizing problems. A priority system can be as complex as desired.

Some sites find a five-level system adequate:

1. Critical—This involves a system that prevents a critical business process from functioning. Assigned IT technicians drop what they are doing and help resolve this issue. An example would be if the facility's data network died. Notify the service desk manager immediately.
2. Important—This is an issue that impacts a number of users but the facility's critical functions are still operating. An example might be a failure in the e-mail system.
3. General support—A problem affecting a single user. This will be the majority of the calls.
4. Routine—Typically this is for new user IDs, office moves, etc. These requests need to be assigned and scheduled, but their urgency depends on how close they are to becoming due.
5. Information—These are questions that are escalated in a non-urgent fashion to the appropriate IT support person. An example would be a question as to how to build a pivot table in Microsoft's Excel. This type of question would be passed on to the software trainer.

COMMENT

Many companies automatically apply a "critical" priority to problem calls from top executives no matter how trivial the issue.

So how would a typical problem call database work? Starting at the beginning, the telephone rings! The technician sees who the caller is in the telephone instrument's caller ID window. He initiates a new problem report and answers the call. If the call involves an appropriate service desk issue, the technician decides if it is a "quick hitter" or a problem to be tracked. Sometimes the call involves a question such as how late the service desk will remain open that evening, the status of an open call, etc. These types of calls are recorded on a tick sheet as they take longer to add to the database than they do to resolve. It is useful to track overall call volume but entering these calls into the database would not serve any purpose.

If the caller has a problem to be tracked, their contact information is entered into the database. This can be read directly from the caller ID display. Most sites preload customer information that is automatically pulled into a new problem ticket based on the telephone number. More sophisticated sites also tie in their asset database so the service desk technician knows exactly what the caller is supposed to have on their desk.

Next the service desk technician asks the pertinent questions that will narrow down the issue to hardware, software, or user training. As he discusses the problem's symptoms with the user, the service desk technician enters notes in a problem description field. Don't be surprised if the user categorizes it as one thing and, upon questioning, the service desk technician concludes the cause is something else.

If the service desk technician escalates the call to the IT staff, he selects the appropriate person based on the chart of the primary and secondary support person for each technology. When the ticket is saved, copies are e-mailed to the requestor and the person assigned to the call. If the problem is urgent, the service desk technician will also call the IT support person to dispatch him directly to the problem site.

Most service desk databases use e-mail to notify the requestor whenever anything on their call ticket changes. The tickets typically maintain a history of date/time stamps so the responsiveness of the IT staff can also be monitored. This can be an important management metric for evaluating responsiveness and productivity. Sometimes technicians close a problem ticket even though the customer says the problem still exists. E-mailing a confirmation catches many of these discrepancies before they explode into larger issues.

[G] Communicating with Customers

Customers contact the service desk several ways. Some will send e-mail for non-urgent requests and a few will walk over and knock on the door. However, most will call on the telephone which can provide some powerful management tools. Giving priority to callers over walk-ins will reduce the number of people hanging around to chat with the service desk staff.

The first thing the service desk needs is a single number that all service desk calls funnel into. The number should be catchy and easy to remember. One company used a four-digit extension that spelled out HELP (4357). When that number rang, it could be picked up by any of several adjacent telephones. Each telephone could handle numerous calls all made into the single number.

On the telephone was an internal caller ID function. This provided the answering service desk technician a quick heads-up of who is calling. (Of course anyone could call from any unused telephone and the best joke was calling from the facility manager's phone.) The caller ID was also used to screen calls. Political reality is that the top executives approve the IT budget. If they call, they are usually answered first.

> ## COMMENT
>
> End users run the gamut from "I'm an expert," to the quiet ones who are afraid they will break the PC and be forced to pay for it. In between is the curious person who tinkers, the know-it-alls, and the ones "documenting everything that happens to them to cover their backsides." Unfortunately, every in-house lunatic feels it is their duty to call the service desk and offer their services for resolving problems!

If it is difficult to adequately staff to cover peak periods, provide callers with the choice of holding or leaving a voice-mail message. This allows those people with routine requests to leave their message and move on instead of endlessly waiting on hold.

It is essential that someone monitor the voice-mail box and begin addressing these calls in the order they were left (oldest first). If customers perceive that these voice-mail messages will not be answered in a reasonable time period, they will stop using this service. Consider a guideline that every message will be answered within two hours. Again, this is a matter of staffing during peak periods.

Spending the day with a telephone pressed against an ear can become quite uncomfortable. Equip each service desk person with his or her own telephone headset. This also reduces background noise and improves his or her ability to hear a faint voice over the hubbub around the service desk.

Another useful telephone tool for the service desk is to broadcast a system-wide announcement via voice mail to all telephones. Unfortunately, the message may not be relevant to all users, so use this sparingly. However, if a major component is broken and will remain so for some time, it will reduce the number of calls the service desk receives about it. The message should acknowledge what is wrong and a conservative time estimate of when it will be resolved.

[H]   Other Handy Service Desk Tools

The service desk staff needs tools close at hand to do their job. During busy times, the calls can come in fast and furious. Ready access to tools will increase the number of calls they can resolve without escalating the issue to the IS staff.

A.   **Reference manuals.** When the phone rings, there is no time to go searching for manuals to research questions. The service desk staff needs a set of technical manuals close at hand to investigate questions that arise. In addition to technical manuals they need a complete and current set of end-user instructions in both printed form and electronic form (to e-mail to new users). This will allow them to assist users of in-house developed systems with operational questions.

It is amazing how many users cannot read or refuse to follow instructions. Often a substitute worker in a department is not provided with adequate instruction so the service desk ends up walking them through the process. Before escalating a problem to a programmer, the service desk will walk them through the appropriate steps to ensure the user is correctly using the product. The service desk library might include a set of PC manuals for standard software. The service desk manager must set a limit for how much time they can afford to give one caller. At some point, these questions must be referred to the training staff to address.

During slack times, the service desk technicians can review this documentation to improve their skills. They can also review technical manuals of their key products.

B. **Asset lists.** A list of the assets assigned to each user is helpful. This gives the technician an idea of the type of workstation, the operating system, and the standard software loaded on it. It would also detail any unusual peripherals. If the IT department has a current asset inventory, identified by user, it may be possible to connect it with the client database and whenever a user's telephone number is entered, both their contact information and their asset information becomes available.

C. **Recall lists.** A matrix is needed that describes who on the IT staff supports what technologies. This list, in technology order, identifies the primary and secondary support person to call. The third one on the support list is always the IT Manager. Typically this list would include all known hardware and software. It would include back room technical staff such as the network team and the database administrators. When a problem occurs that must be escalated to the IT staff, the corresponding name is selected from this list. A second list is referenced for the contact information for that person. This includes their office telephone number, cell phone number, and home telephone number. It should have everything the service desk technician needs to know about contacting this person. When calling someone for a problem, make a note on the problem report of when they were called and if a message was left. Wait about 15 minutes and try again. After another 15 minutes, call the next level of support.

COMMENT

The service desk policy must include instructions that the technicians never provide anyone's home telephone number to anyone from their recall rosters. This violates the privacy policy in most companies. If a call is essential, they should dial it and then patch the requestor through to the person they want to call.

D. **Critical process matrix.** An important tool for the service desk is a matrix of which processes are critical, and the time of day they are most important to be operational. This matrix is normally maintained in a spreadsheet. This sheet combines critical processes and times they must be available (see Exhibit 16-1: Critical Process Impact Matrix).

EXHIBIT 16-1. Critical Process Impact Matrix

Critical Process Impact Matrix									
Date:				Critical Availability		Support		Customer Contacts	
System	Platform	Software	Priority	Days	Times	Primary	Backup	Primary	Backup

Fields on the matrix:

System name—This is the official and/or common name this system is known by.

Platform—The server or primary hardware platform this system normally runs on. If a problem requires that the AS400 be rebooted during the day, sort the list to bring all of the AS400 systems together and quickly see which customers must be notified when it is to go down, and when it is restored.

Software—This is the name of the software system as known to the IT staff. This may or may not be the same as the system name.

Priority—This is how important this device is to restore to service. Consider using the Green/Yellow/Red ratings. Use the "Critical" rating for all critical business function components.

Critical availability—The times this system must be available to support the facility. For example, if the order-entry staff only works Monday through Friday, and if this system died on a Saturday, the downtime is not a critical event. The problem still needs to be worked but no one will miss it until Monday.

A. *Time of day*—Use the 24-hour clock format.

B. *Day of week*

C. *Support*—When a problem occurs, the service desk must quickly determine who to notify.

D. *Primary*—Who on the IT staff is called first for a problem?

E. *Secondary*—Who on the IT staff is called second for a problem? Remember, the third level support is always to call the IT Manager.

F. *Customer contacts*—If the system must be brought down, who must be notified? When service is restored, who should be told first?

G. *Primary*—Which customer is to be notified first of a problem?

H. *Secondary*—Which customer is to be notified second of a problem?

To make this matrix even more powerful, add to the bottom of the spreadsheet all of the contact information for each person on the list. Individually highlight each cell in the Support and Customer contact columns and establish a hyperlink between the name and their telephone number. Of course this adds yet another list that must be maintained when telephone numbers change, but on a day-to-day basis, it is faster.

E. **Big marker board.** Most service desks maintain a large marker board within sight of the service desk technicians, which contains current information.

 1. Calendar of availability—Rather than fumble through the support list leaving messages that may never be returned, the service desk can refer to the board to see which IT technical staff members are scheduled to be out of the building that day. Staff members that call in sick can also be added to this list.

 2. Scheduled system activities—Sometimes the only way to clear a system problem is to reboot the server. This might be held off until late hours or set up to occur during lunch. The service desk is informed but the note is also posted on the board. Also posted are

notices of system/software upgrades scheduled with the date and time of planned implementation.

3. Telephone numbers for reaching key support staff not in the facility or at home. Examples might be visits to other company sites, or attending seminars.

F. **Tools.** The service desk can be a busy place and sitting all day answering the telephone can be tedious. Ensure the service desk technicians have comfortable, adjustable chairs. Lighting can be a problem in many offices so ensure there isn't glare on their screens for quick reference. Desktop space is important for spreading out manuals and for taking notes. The temptation is to fill all space with dedicated monitoring equipment and more PCs. Leave some room for reading and writing.

§ 16.04 THE PROACTIVE SERVICE DESK

[A] Overview

Service desks tend to fall into one of two operating philosophies: reactive or proactive. Reactive service desks pride themselves on how fast they can answer a call. When no one calls, they sit and pass the day doing whatever they are inclined to do. However, when the calls come in again they are slow to react since their focus is on however they are passing the day—not on their customers. Reactive service desks will rise to a basic level of competence and go no further. Their outlook is entirely defensive, and as any military strategist can explain, defensive tactics may prevent defeat but will not win the war.

Proactive service desks address the calls as they come in. But when the call volume slackens, they shift their focus to identifying common problems and eliminating them before they result in a call to the service desk. The difference between reactive and proactive is like sitting in a fire station. A reactive fireman waits for an alarm before doing anything. A proactive fireman also inspects buildings and stops situations before they turn into fires.

Service desk staffs are organized to provide a certain level of service during busy times. Providing enough people to handle calls during the busy time will result in staff members sitting around during the slack periods. This need not be! The laws of physics apply to objects as well as to people. People at rest tend to remain at rest. But if these same people are taught to remain in motion then they will automatically remain in motion. During these slack periods, assign tasks for the service desk to perform.

Service desk managers must address this problem early and decisively. If executives see the service desk team lounging at their desks or wandering around the facility they will be quickly marked for staff reduction. What a pity. The service desk is uniquely situated to make a major improvement in the IT department's service level—if they are properly led!

The real power of the service desk is to identify marginal processes or emerging systemic problems and focus the IT team on their prompt resolution. From its central point of problem collection, the service desk can "see the big picture" of what is happening with the facility's technology.

It is often the first person to detect a problem-reporting trend that indicates a computer virus. He needs to know what signs to look for and what damage containment actions to take until the IT staff swings into action. Fast action here saves a lot of work later.

[B] Managing by Metrics—Nothing but the Facts!

Some managers blunder through their business day by day. They lack vision, imagination, and are probably already promoted beyond their level of competence. These people consider it a bad day when the telephone rings a lot and a good day when things are quiet. They do not manage their work—their work manages them!

Others recognize that to take control of their work environment, they need to measure it. Measurements provide early indications of problems before they explode! A true saying is that managers cannot manage what they cannot measure. Are call volumes increasing or decreasing? Why? Has a department just skipped training their seasonal workers and told them to call the service desk for every minor question? Are there any departments or users who never call the service desk? Why? What products or departments or users or time of the day are causing the most calls? Is there more than one cause at play here? Take care, though. Managers will find that they will get what they measure, whether the end result is what was wanted or not.

Metrics can build a case for more staffing, perhaps based on the number of callers who hang up before someone can get to them. They can build a case for better tools, such as a network monitoring system to detect when segments are becoming overloaded or RF nodes blink off. Metrics can show which categories or specific items of equipment are causing the most problems so they can be targeted for replacement. The performance functions the service desk manager measures can tell a lot!

In addition to measuring the IT systems it supports, the service desk must also measure its own performance. Services provided by the service desk must be measurable and regularly analyzed. Measuring without analyzing is just going through the motions. The time to answer calls and the overall level of service desk performance will be a constant issue with customers. Some will complain if the telephone is not answered on the first ring and others will try to cut the "over-staffed" service desk!

There are two tools readily available to the service desk manager for capturing data on the team's operations: the telephone system and the problem tracking database.

Telephone system metrics

Most telephone systems will allow the service desk software to capture usage characteristics for calls. These telephone metrics are a useful complement to the problem database metrics. If the telephone system does not support these features, consider adding them during the next capital budget cycle.

Common telephone systems statistics are:

A. **Average time to answer.** On the average how long is it taking the service desk staff to respond to an incoming call? This shows how well the service desk is meeting its published service level standard.

B. **Average talk time.** How long is the tech spending on the call? Are they talking too long? Chatting with users is an important part of relationship building, but it should be confined to slack times. During busy times, this could add an intolerable wait to incoming calls.

C. **Number of calls received after working hours.** Do the service desk hours need to be extended? Based on automated caller ID, who and which departments are calling, at what times and day of the week?

D. **Abandonment rate.** This is for people who gave up waiting for the service desk to answer and hang up. There is always the odd call where the user's problem resolved itself while waiting for the service desk to answer the telephone, but this may also be an indication that staffing during this time period is too light.

Problem tracking database metrics

Most problems are reported to the service desk via telephone. However, there is still a small but steady flow of walk-in requests, e-mail, and voice mail requests that are missed in the telephone metrics. The big picture for this is the problem tracking database. Trends might include:

A. Identifying troublesome hardware and software. Are there a lot of calls for problems with a particular printer? Does a particular network device cease working every time a thunderstorm rolls in? Identify equipment for additional maintenance or replacement.

B. Identifying troublesome users. Is there someone who calls the service desk a lot? Does he have legitimate questions or is he lonely and want to chat with someone? If he is lonely, ask his supervisor to talk to him. If he has ongoing problems, could they be addressed with further training?

[C]   One Call—One Success

An important service desk metric is the number of problems resolved during the first call. The greatest customer satisfaction is derived from one request—one resolved problem. When you consider the time to record information, dispatch someone to assist them, to return calls, etc., resolving problems at the first call is a money saver for the company. There are a number of things that affect this:

A. **Technical expertise of the service desk technicians.** IT departments everywhere are under pressure to reduce their costs, and workforce expense is a major part of this. Highly skilled service desk technicians can use their experience and training to resolve calls quickly. Unfortunately many calls are for basic questions and do not require a lot of skill to resolve. This leads to boredom and high employee turnover.

Most service desks follow a model of technicians skilled in addressing the basic issues. These people can address many of the calls without passing them on. But to address the more difficult issue, the next level technician is standing by to receive calls transferred to them. This hand-off is done with the customer still on the line so they are not lost in the shuffle, and a call back is not necessary. A second level technical staff can hang on to the first call and improve the statistics.

B. **Technical difficulty of the call.** The first call metrics not only depend on the expertise of the service desk technician, but also depend on the technical difficulty of the problem. These calls are quickly passed on to second level support since the service desk technician lacks the expertise to address them.

C. **Time available to work through the issue.** In busy times, the phone calls seem to roll in constantly. It is not possible to spend much time resolving the call instead of passing it on. The longer time spent on working a single call means that many more people are sent to voice mail or give up waiting. In this sense, trying to improve the first call statistics will hurt the metric for the average number of minutes that an incoming call must wait.

D. **The service desk manager must regularly review the problem tracking database to identify the types of problems referred to the IT staff.** Then develop a strategy to train the IT staff, or acquire the tools so the service desk technicians can address these problems—if appropriate. To address this, the service desk manager examines the statistics of the types of calls and when they are reported. The types of calls are further broken down into the symptoms and solutions. Working with the second level technicians, the manager can develop a series of questions that can be used to localize problems and recommended solutions. Additional training by the IT technicians is also helpful. In the case of common problems, the solutions can be provided without passing the call on to the next level.

[D] Training End Users

The service desk is uniquely situated to identify end users who require additional training in using a product's basic functions. Most people would prefer to address their own problems rather than call for help. When the call volume slackens, the proactive service desk can take positive steps toward increasing user satisfaction while reducing call volumes.

A. **Refer people to the training staff.** If someone is struggling to learn the use of a product one command at a time (and calling the service desk each time), then refer them to the training staff for assistance. The trainers can schedule some desk side support on basic product usage until that person can sit through regular training. The service desk could also provide by e-mail or through their Web site, information on training classes available. An alternative trainer is that department's power user.

B. **Conduct mini-training courses.** Mini-courses are a chance to present and discuss one aspect of a product to a small group of people.

Mini-courses can be over lunch (or as a special, focused training orientation session for a department). Typically the approach is a lecture with a set of written instructions on how to perform that specific function (such as pivot tables in Excel, formatting text and pages in Word, or how to write a very basic database report).

C. **Create self-help sheets.** Volume software licensing saves companies money by providing a single copy of the software along with the right to make a specific number of copies. However, this means that printed user manuals will not be provided. The manuals are only available electronically. Yet the user must have a grasp of the product's terminology before the electronic document's topic search can be successful. To assist end users, the service desk can create self-help booklets and guidelines. After assisting a user with the electronic manuals, the service desk can send a follow-up copy of the help sheet for future reference. The service desk may keep a supply of help sheets for basic functions, such as electronic mail practices, a list of standard company word processing templates, and using voice-mail accounts. There may also be easy to follow pictures for how to use various telephone features. These tools will increase customer satisfaction and reduce the volume of trouble calls. These sheets are e-mailed or sent out via inter-office mail on request.

D. **Issue end-user documentation for in-house created systems.** Sometimes new or transferred employees are thrust into a job without adequate training. To ease this transition (and to reduce the volume of calls), the service desk can maintain an online library of end user documentation that can be issued via e-mail to employees. These may also be available on the intranet (if they do not involve confidential data systems).

E. **Compose a list of the best third-party self-help books for each of the standard products.** Often these books provide a clearer explanation of a product's features than do the manufacturer's manuals.

[E] Carry the Message to the Masses

A problem with the service desk is that it appears to the caller as a faceless voice—almost a non-person. Of course this is not true, but matching a face to a voice to a name helps to build personal credibility with end users. To do this, during the slack work times, the service desk staff must leave its back room and mingle with the masses in the facility.

The service desk manager has a responsibility to explain and promote the service desk to other departments. One way is to attend their staff meetings and provide a short overview of the service desk, how it conducts business, and what it is and what it is not. Take time to educate these people about the IT world while learning about theirs. As time permits, bring along available service desk technicians. These meetings allow the users to match a face to a voice. They also are useful for setting an expectation in the users' mind of the services they can expect from the service desk. Make clear to everyone that the service desk manager is always open to any questions or criticisms of the service desk operations. This provides a ready outlet for customer complaints and suggestions for improving service.

Discussion points at these meetings might include:

A. **Visit the various departments carrying the word.** Use these conversations to raise any problems they have had with the service desk in the past.
    1. Explain to people that denied requests are the result of good policy—not the service desk (don't shoot the messenger!).
    2. Hours of operation—does this cause them any problems?
    3. Staffing levels—do they have problems getting through to the service desk? Is it worse at certain times or days of the week?
    4. Are the answers provided by the service desk technicians clear and understandable?
    5. What are supported products and how are they selected?
    6. What should the service desk do differently?

B. **Publish articles in the facility's newsletter and on its general information web page.** Profile a service desk staff member. Keep each article non-technical, brief, and focused on a single topic.
    1. Frequently asked questions.
    2. Most common problems reported for the past month.
    3. News of impending upgrades.
    4. Security practices.
    5. Company policies on end-user computing responsibilities.

C. **Posters.** Posters are another communication tool for the service desk to keep its message in front of its customers. Posters should focus on a single message. The message should teach the reader about something new or remind them of something they should be doing.

    Posters have a useful life of about two weeks. At that time, rotate the posters among locations and introduce new ones. Otherwise, they become a fixture on a wall and their message is no longer reviewed in passing.

    Examples of poster topics include:
    1. Service desk hours of operations and services offered.
    2. Information to capture before reporting a problem to the service desk (error number, actions that lead up to the problem, etc.).
    3. How to sign up for training.
    4. URL for the service desk web page.
    5. Company policy on security and safeguarding passwords.

D. **Establish a service desk—with links to:**
    1. Online manuals for company developed software.
    2. Self-help guides for standard products.
    3. User FAQs.
    4. Company policies concerning IT and end-user computing.
    5. Information on scheduled system outages.
    6. IT forms.

7. Software vendor sites.
8. Third-party product use sites.

E. **Speak to training classes.**

Computing training sessions are excellent times to spread the service desk's message. Recently graduated students are likely to call for help. A few minutes discussing tips for reporting a problem can make their next call to the service desk far more productive. Explain how to identify error messages, how important it is to write them down, and how to describe the steps leading up to a technology failure.

A standard part of this presentation is a recap of the service desk service level goals—hours of operation and services offered. Other basic information of interest includes the process for ordering new equipment or software, anti-piracy policy, and good data backup practices.

[F] Hail and Farewell

In large companies, there is a steady trickle of employees joining the company and departing for other opportunities. Each group will place a set of demands on the service desk technicians that are easily organized into checklists that can be provided to the appropriate managers.

New employees

New employees arrive full of enthusiasm and more than a touch of apprehension. Each company has their own twist on how e-mail, voice mail, etc., is implemented. Instead of responding to the same series of requests floating in one at a time, the service desk can collect the most common new user setup issues into a single form. Time spent working with new users will reduce their frustration and the number of elementary calls made to the service desk.

The first sign of a new employee is a user ID request. This might trigger an e-mail memo (which they cannot see until the account is created) that will contain pointers to the knowledge base and specific documentation of immediate interest.

Stop by on an employee's first day and provide him or her with a user ID and password. Walk the employee through setting up voice mail and logging into the e-mail system for the first time. This is another opportunity to spread the good word of the service desk's stated service level and hours of operation.

New employees often take on responsibilities of a person who has departed the company. They may require access to electronic records and department specific systems. Include on the checklist questions about who this person is replacing and what systems they will require access to (and training for).

Departing employees

Employees leaving the company must have their user IDs disabled promptly. This protects the company against any departing mischief and the employee from unfair accusations.

An important part of disabling the user IDs is to identify who will be provided access to the e-mail, voice mail, PC files, and server files. Often this is the supervisor of the departing person. Later when a replacement appears, some of these may be shifted to the incoming worker. The idea is to capture this information early and have it ready to act on instead of requests dribbling in from the department as they think of things. This sheet provides a basis for setting up the file shares and permissions of their replacement.

[G]   Knowledge Base

Over time, service desks become a major storehouse of information on problems and their solutions. So why not share it? A knowledge base is a powerful tool for capturing the successful resolution of problems and saving time when a similar issue arises. As problems are resolved, their solution is recorded in the service desk tracking database. The trick is to make this information available in an easy to search and understand format, usually accessible from the service desk's web page. The result is a self-help tools for end users as well as the service desk staff.

During times of slack service desk demands, assign a technician to review the problem description and resolution. Clean up both (grammatically and factually) and add them to the knowledge base. Extraneous notes entered during the debugging process should be removed so that when someone searches for a problem, only the successful solution is presented. Before adding an entry to the knowledge base, it is important to ensure that its solution does not contradict an existing article. Knowledge bases can be internal or external. An internal knowledge base would only be accessible to the service desk staff. It would include topics such as working with company confidential systems and other security issues. An external knowledge base is for general company self-help. A knowledge base can also be purchased from a third party or accessed via the Internet. This is a tool for the service desk staff to use until their own knowledge base is brought up to snuff.

[H]   Power Users—The Service Desk's On-Site Helpers

Every service desk has to contend with end users who are skilled in some aspect of data processing. They may have held a data processing position in a previous company or may be a skilled hobbyist. Some departments create "stealth" data processing staffs to fill their requirements that the IT department cannot or will not meet. These people can ask some very detailed questions when requesting support. In general, these people are referred to as power users.

Power users handle their own simple problems themselves. They like to tinker with things and teach themselves about technology by reading books. They can be dangerous, ignorant know-it-alls, or very intelligent, knowledgeable people. In some cases, they can even be malicious. Power users are easier to manage if the IT department works with them instead of against them.

Power users scare some IT departments. They see them as an uncontrolled threat to their systems' stability. They publish piles of rules to curtail their activities and inevitably lose the fight. It is far better to reach out and make these skilled people an extension of the IT staff than to try and rub them out.

Most departments have someone on their team they normally turn to when they have system problems. As can be seen from the service desk logs, many of these questions are basic and easy to answer. Let the power users do this! Help them to reduce the service desk's workload and free them for seeking out the root cause of the more serious problems.

Power users are still restricted from doing certain things, but give them the freedom to handle simple issues. Things to do to promote their use:

A. Consider giving them their own service desk telephone number. Give them priority service for their routine requests. Many of the people in the user departments will see this and go to them with questions, most of which the power user could possibly answer.

B. Use them to review software and process changes for their department before they are implemented. They can also sign off on the adequacy of end-user documentation.

C. Provide them with priority seating for training classes pertinent to their area.

D. Consider forming a user council to provide feedback from the departments.

E. Consider hiring them into the IT department!

[I]   Customer Surveys—Closing the Feedback Loop

Customer feedback is an important tool for improving the service desk's products and services. Sometimes the feedback is freely offered, such as in formal complaints or compliments. Sometimes, the feedback is indirect by departments no longer calling for assistance. Many people are reluctant to suggest things that may be viewed as criticism so they will not offer anything. Instead of waiting for people to speak up, the service desk manager can institute an ongoing program of customer satisfaction survey. These surveys are a series of open ended questions that try to understand how the team's performance is viewed by its customers.

Surveys have two general goals. The first is sent randomly to anyone with a user ID. This is to solicit general comments. The other is as follow-up to service desk calls. This would provide information about the quality of the technician's response and the customer's service desk experience.

§ 16.05   THE SERVICE DESK IN A DISASTER

[A]   Overview

In an emergency, there is a lot of chaos. Imagine if the electricity went out in the building at this moment. The IT Manager may have some idea of what to do but the dark can be disorienting. Other people may not be so cool-headed and add to the confusion of all. Where should the IT staff go? What should they be doing? No one knows when a short-term calamity will strike. A proactively managed service desk will have predetermined actions developed and published so that in an emergency, the IT staff knows where to go, what to expect, and what to do until the IT director can form a plan of action.

Containing and recovering from major disasters is covered in a later chapter. In this section actions will be described for addressing short-term disaster containment and recovery efforts that typically last four hours or less. This category of business disruption requires a concerted effort to address but is typically resolved before the full IT disaster plan can be implemented.

[B]   The Service Desk's Role in the Crucial First Few Hours

Companies occasionally struggle with short-term disruptions to their operations. Power outages or brownouts, loss of data communications, loss of telephone communications, or a small fire in the facility are examples of interruptions that are usually resolved within a few hours. Meanwhile the company's workers need a central place to contact and be contacted from until the emergency is resolved.

During their normal workday, whenever people have a technical problem, they call the service desk. In a crisis, they will instinctively fall back on previous actions to cope with the situation. With some prior preparation, the service desk will be ready to handle this influx of traffic. These actions are not intended to replace the facility's security or maintenance coordination. They are to provide guidance to the IT staff and information for end users.

Each type of emergency calls for its own response. Examples of this are:

A.   A power outage will require someone to help recover unattended computers when they restart. Those systems on mini-UPS systems must be monitored or gracefully shut down. Does the service desk have a list of these machines and where they are located?

B.   Network outages may require that the facility switch to manual processing until the network is restored. The loading of this paper-coded data may be tedious and IT assistance important. For example, in a factory, materials will still be accepted and issued during the network outage but the inventory will be out of sync. Does each department have manual procedures for continuing work and collecting data until service is restored? Does the service desk have copies of them?

C.   During a telephone service outage, the company may ask employees to use cell phones to notify key customers of the problem and to provide company cell phone numbers for critical incoming calls. Some companies depend heavily on the ability to respond to customer requests instantly. For others, the telephone is a useful tool that they can work without. If the facility is a just-in-time supplier to another factory, loss of telephone communication may unnerve the customer. Have an alternate plan for establishing communication of all critical information.

D.   During a fire, the network and asset management team tries to determine what is in the affected area and stages repair materials for use in an area where those work spaces will be recovered and where rewiring will be required. A fire may burn wires and destroy equipment. It may be hours before that portion of the facility can be entered. The team could while away their time waiting for admission to the burned area or it could estimate what is damaged and begin assembling materials for the repairs.

With just these four examples, it is easy to see how useful the service desk will be. As a command center and place for all to meet, it reduces chaos so that plans can be made and action begun. The response to all emergencies is essentially the same:

A. Determine the scope of the problem.
B. Determine the impact of the problem.
C. Implement containment actions to prevent it from spreading.
D. Implement recovery actions to restore everything to full service.

General emergency actions for the IT staff and the service desk include:

A. All IT Managers report to the service desk to provide status reports and to formulate an initial plan of containment/recovery action.
B. Everyone in the IT department, excluding the service desk and the IT Managers, will report to a central area to provide a workforce pool for addressing the issue. The central area should be equipped with emergency lighting and be in the proximity of the service desk.
C. The IT director will predesignate one manager to oversee the service desk area and one to oversee the personnel pool.
D. Pre-designate teams for:
    1. Network and telephone system support.
    2. Systems recovery (after the emergency passes) to catch up data files, restart systems, and whatever else is required based on the emergency.
    3. End-user notification of the problem, suggested work around actions and for when the issue is resolved.
E. Report the dispatch and return of all teams to the service desk.
F. Report the status of each team's efforts to the service desk on the hour.

[C] The Service Desk as the Emergency Command Center

To carry out this mission, the service desk must have more than adequate emergency lighting. Emergency lighting is battery driven and comes on when electrical power is lost to the building. In addition, the service desk equipment must be on a UPS system to maintain its PC and mainframe connections.

Finally, the IT management team must have a standing order to automatically report to the service desk when a crisis erupts. This saves valuable time and reduces chaos.

The service desk has the tools in place that are essential for coordinating an emergency:

A. Communications—Telephones set up to handle a rush of calls into a single number. Also the ability to broadcast messages over e-mail and telephone voice mail. Two way radios and company provided cell phones provide links between recovery crews and the service desk.

B. A status board—The white board used to post absences, etc., is perfect for posting problem status. The service desk usually has a large marker board that can be used to indicate the progress of the recovery. This provides the same message to all readers.

C. A team accustomed to working under pressure—On site and ready to act.

D. System and department information—Staff recall lists, system documentation, copy of the full disaster recovery plan, etc.

E. Emergency power and lighting to continue operations during outages.

F. An emergency supply of flashlights, batteries, and extra two-way radios.

The service desk is most suited to short duration, contained problems. Most IT crises last less than four hours. For example, how many electrical blackouts has your site experienced and how long did they last? Fires can be major disasters but most are contained within a portion of the facility, and out within an hour.

In a large emergency, the IT director would shift his command center function to the facility identified in the company's disaster plans.

17

MANAGING IT ASSETS: IDENTIFY WHAT YOU HAVE

§ 17.01 OVERVIEW
  [A] Purpose and Scope
  [B] Critical Policies to Develop Based on This Chapter

§ 17.02 LAY THE GROUNDWORK
  [A] Overview
  [B] Asset Management Project Scope
  [C] Asset Manager Appointment
  [D] Asset Information Database
  [E] Asset Tagging
  [F] Idle Equipment Collection
  [G] Data Collection Forms

§ 17.03 CONDUCTING THE INVENTORY
  [A] Overview
  [B] Conducting the Count
  [C] Set a Hardware Strategy
  [D] Determining the Number of On-Site Spares Required
  [E] Developing a Service Strategy
  [F] Ongoing Asset Management

§ 17.04 SOFTWARE ASSET MANAGEMENT
  [A] Overview
  [B] Lay the Groundwork
  [C] Unauthorized Software
  [D] Conduct the Inventory
  [E] Crunch the Numbers
  [F] Ongoing Software Asset Management
  [G] Using Computers to Solve Computer Problems—Automated
       Asset Detection

§ 17.05 SOFTWARE ASSETS
  [A] Overview
  [B] Software Copyright Compliance Planning

§ 17.01 OVERVIEW

[A] Purpose and Scope

Asset management policies address both hardware and software. Well-defined and maintained asset management policies and procedures are financially rewarding, will fine-tune the company-wide information systems operations, and help avoid embarrassing litigation.

IT assets are poorly managed in most companies. An IT Manager looking for a way to reduce the department's costs without firing anyone should always look here first. Most IT people take their equipment for granted and neglect the administrative side of their business. Typically, the asset manager position is assigned based on personnel availability rather than aptitude.

IT management must formally direct the IT asset management policies and procedures throughout the organization. To be successful, IT management should:

A. Assume the stewardship of all IT assets in the company.
B. Inform all employees of the directives.
C. Explain the need for the policies and procedures.
D. Mandate that all employees use only company-owned hardware and software. Even if their intentions are honorable, no one is to bring in their own hardware or software.
E. Never permit the downloading of company-owned software to privately owned computers or secondary storage in any form.
F. Note infractions in the employees' records.
G. Emphasize that serious or repeated violation of asset management policies will be grounds for dismissal.

Bygone mainframe computing days seldom had asset management problems. Capital expense budgets funded new hardware and the software was developed in-house. The hardware was unique and bulky and depreciated over time. All of this activity came under the domain of the data processing department. Today, computer hardware is found throughout the company. Often there are no controls over purchase, standardization, or use. Software is even more problematic. It can originate from legitimate in-house development or purchase, or from questionable or illegal sources. This anarchy can appear insignificant because of undocumented direct expense, but the indirect repercussions can be great and the cost astronomical.

[B] Critical Policies to Develop Based on This Chapter

Using the material discussed in this chapter, create the following policies:

A. The asset management program for the IT department.
    1. Covers all IT-related assets within the facility.
        a. Hardware, such as PCs, servers, network devices, printers, and monitors.

    b. Software, including that which resides on network devices, telephone equipment, and computers of all sizes.

2. Applies to all employees, contractors, and visitors.
3. Creates position of Asset Manager and defines scope of responsibility.
4. Identifies the intended goals of the program.
    a. Reduce costs.
    b. Drive out obsolete technology.
    c. Proper scrapping of paperwork.
    d. Development of asset-tracking database.
5. Mandates an initial asset count and periodic department asset verification counts throughout the year.

B. Tagging equipment.
1. What will be tracked and what will not.
2. How it will be tracked.
3. Who will track it.
4. Essential data elements to track on each device type.
5. How the data for each item will be tracked, such as in a database or card file.

C. Collection of idle assets.
1. IT Manager is charged with collecting idle assets.
2. Ensures idle equipment is collected, tested, safeguarded, and redeployed.
3. IT Manager has the authority to confiscate idle assets even if they were purchased with a different department's funds.

D. Personal assets.
1. Employees are prohibited from bringing into the facility personal assets such as PCs, hardware, and software.
2. The IT Manager may confiscate personally provided assets because it is a major administrative burden to track who owns what.

E. Consultant and visiting technician assets.
1. Assets owned by a supporting company and used on the premises must be clearly marked.
2. Consultants visiting the facility must clearly mark their equipment and check it in (and out) with the security team by serial number.

F. Scrapping hardware.
1. All disks and persistent memory must be scrubbed to remove company data.
2. CD and diskette drives must be empty.

G. Software assets.
1. All software created using company assets or while in the employ of the company belongs to the company.
    a. Includes employees.
    b. Includes all contract workers.
2. All software will be tracked on asset database.
3. New systems will use standard software tools.
    a. Exceptions will be noted by IT Manager.
    b. Using standard tools implies IT support for coding.

4. Illegal/Unlicensed software policy.
5. Illegal files on PC.
    a. Gambling using company equipment and time.
    b. Pornography.
    c. Harassment.
    d. Other activities prohibited by the company's human resources policy.

Policies should always be developed based on the local situation. Successful managers cannot issue appropriate guidance if the policies are written with another company's or location's situation in mind.

§ 17.02 LAY THE GROUNDWORK

[A] Overview

Counting all of the IT devices and software packages in even a small company is a tedious and time-consuming task. In a large company, it seems like an insurmountable assignment. This is why most IT departments do not want to tackle the job. IT Managers know there is excess technology in the company but feel it is cheaper to leave it alone than to pay for the labor of a wall-to-wall count. Such managers work day to day and are not in control of their department.

This section explains the careful preparations that can reduce the cost of counting equipment. A sharply defined project scope identifies what to count and what to pass by. Each item has its own characteristics. Which ones should be gathered? What is the best way to tag assets for later database updates? All of these questions depend on the local situation, but must be locked in before proceeding with the count.

> **COMMENT**
>
> Test the technology counting process on the IT department first. This should work out the obvious defects in the process.

[B] Asset Management Project Scope

The first step in asset management is to identify what is to be managed—the scope of the project. There are many different IT assets to manage and it might be easier to tackle them separately. Also, be prepared for resistance, as some people will believe this is the first step in taking away their equipment. The types of assets to manage may include:

- Workstations and peripherals.
- Company-owned PCs in employees' homes.

- Network devices.
- Desktop telephone instruments and add-on devices.
- Servers in computer room and business departments.
- Data collection devices, such as bar-code scanners.
- Data output devices such as bar-code printers, CD writers, etc.
- Mainframe and server software.
- PC software.
- Personal data assistants (PDAs).
- Company-sponsored cellular telephones.

This list can go on and on. The point is that there is a lot to look at. Each type of device has its own unique data elements to collect so identify these before starting. Examples of unique data elements might be the size of the monitor screen, the firmware revision level of network devices, or a workstation's CPU speed. For most companies, the main effort centers on workstations since there are so many of them, they cost so much, and they are very visible to executives.

COMMENT

Using the 80/20 rule, an IT Manager can save time by only tracking the major items such as desktop units. Rapidly evolving technologies such as PDAs may not be worth the effort to track unless widely used.

Exclude some things from the project. Keyboards and PC mice are generally disposable and not worth the expense to track. Consider setting a lower limit based on cost, such as hardware under $100 is not worth the effort to track. (Due to software licensing issues, track all software.) Typically, all software is tracked because a single package has the potential to interrupt the operation of a wide range of systems.

[C]   Asset Manager Appointment

Asset management is a major IT responsibility. The company depends on the IT Manager to identify requirements, to redeploy idle assets, and to save the company money. Yet when it comes to getting purchase orders signed, all the executives see is a never-ending stream of requests for expensive new equipment. If an IT Manager has problems getting purchase requests approved, it is because the executives do not believe that IT is a good steward of the company's assets. Establishing an asset management program can be a step in the right direction.

To establish an asset management program, appoint someone as the asset manager (or coordinator). This can easily become a full-time job. In some companies this function resides in the IT operations team since it is a part of IT's routine efforts. In smaller companies, it is an additional duty for the PC coordinator. An asset manager should be someone good at paperwork and who pays attention to details. They should have a broad business and technical background so they know the difference between a terminal, a PC, and a network router.

To begin, the asset manager should:

A. Inventory assets (what's out there?).
B. Tag assets (easy identification in the future).
C. Establish and maintain an asset database (management reports).
D. Develop a three-year workstation planning strategy (what should we buy or retain?).
E. Control all future purchases (adhere to strategy).
F. Reevaluate asset repair (when to scrap the old).

There are many benefits to doing this:

A. Use the data to develop a long-term asset strategy to drive out variation and focus on "standard" equipment. Standardization saves money in training, staffing, and reduced operational complexity. Standardization may seem a simple dream with rapidly changing technologies, but the department can drive in that direction.
B. Evaluate the equipment repair strategy to move some categories to less expensive approaches.
C. Collect idle equipment for redeployment or disposal.
D. Provide management with asset data for informed decisions.

See Policy ITP-17-1 Asset Manager Assignment Policy as an example.

POLICY ITP-17-1   Asset Manager Assignment Policy

Policy #:	ITP-17-1	**Effective:**	03/18/09	**Page #:**	1 of N
Subject:	Asset Manager Assignment Policy				

1.0 PURPOSE

This policy assigns the Information Technology Manager as the company's custodian of all technology owned by the company.

2.0 SCOPE

This policy governs all technology owned by the company, to include (at a minimum):

A. Telecommunications (telephones systems, cell phones).
B. Data network.

C. PDAs and Blackberrys™.
D. Desktop equipment (computers, monitors, personal printers, scanners).
E. All network attached devices.
F. Mainframe computers and peripherals.
G. Servers and peripherals.
H. All software.

3.0 POLICY

The Information Technology Manager is assigned as the company's Technical Asset custodian of all technology owned by the company.
The Technical Asset Custodian will:

A. Standardize hardware and software to minimize complexity.
B. Reallocate equipment and/or software for company benefit irrespective of the budget that originally purchased it.
C. Administer service contracts to provide an acceptable level of support for both hardware and software.
D. Analyze, publish, and follow a five-year technology strategy to guide purchases and identify technologies for retirement. This plan is to be updated semiannually.
E. Plan and manage the migration of all software (both purchased and in-house developed) to new versions.

4.0 REVISION HISTORY

Date	Revision #	Description of Change
03/18/09	1.0	Initial creation.

5.0 INQUIRIES

Direct inquiries about this policy to:

Harold Jenkins, CIO
2900 Corporate Drive
Columbus, OH 43215

Voice: 614-555-1234
Fax: 614-555-1235
E-mail: hjenkins@company.com

Revision #:	1.0	Supersedes:	N/A	Date:	03/18/09

[D]   Asset Information Database

In its simplest form, an asset inventory count could just be a count of what you have. To move this forward into managing your assets, you need to gather descriptive information as to what you have, where it is, and how it is being used.

If IT has service desk problem-tracking software, it may already have an asset management module. Service desk software uses a key, such as the user's telephone number, to bring up a description of that person's workstation to assist in the troubleshooting process. If such a module already exists, examine the data fields it captures to see if it is adequate. Once the asset database is populated with data, the service desk will be its biggest customer.

COMMENT

Data collection and maintenance is expensive. While it only takes a moment to jot down a serial number or other characteristic, it takes more time to enter the data, update it, etc. Justify every data element collected to avoid gathering useless data.

For every field in the asset database, create a validation table of correct entries. This minimizes the number of free form fields and makes counting text fields easier.

An asset management database can be as detailed as the IT Manager wants to make it. However, the more fields there are to track, the more time will be required to keep it current. Track only those data elements that need reporting. The best place to start is an outline of the reports the IT Manager might use. Such reports might be:

A.   Total number of devices, subtotaled by model.
B.   Number of workstations, subtotaled by processor speed.
C.   Number of network devices, subtotaled by model and where they are located.
D.   Number of devices per department.
E.   Breakdown of processors by user type.
F.   When each item was purchased.
G.   Length of warranty (save in a date field indicating when it ends).
H.   Operating system (type, version, and service pack level).
I.   Hardware characteristics such as CPU type, RAM, and disk space.

COMMENT

How powerful is an asset database? If today a requirement came down to install software in all desktop units (and not notebook PCs), and this package required a minimum of 10 GB of disk along with 1.5 GHz processors and 512 MB of RAM, how quickly could a cost estimate be determined? How accurate would it be?

Each of these reports brings its own data collection requirement—and each could be quite useful. The more successful the asset management efforts are, the more the accounting department will ask for data—especially data elements that were not collected during the inventory count!

Refer to Exhibit 17-1 and Exhibit 17-2 for an example of a simple equipment-tracking spreadsheet. Below are examples of how data tables might look for tracking assets.

In this example, identify users by their telephone extensions and names. The department code is necessary if the report is to detail the amount of equipment in a given department. Other things to add might be the location by office number or factory column identification. The telephone extension number can be used to link to the equipment table. If the telephone is shared over multiple work shifts, this may not be a problem since the workstation usually is also shared. The database may track it under the first shift owner's name or allow for multiple owners.

EXHIBIT 17-1

Data Table 1.   User Information

User		Dept.
Telephone	Name	Code

EXHIBIT 17-2

Data Table 2.   Equipment Tracking

User Phone #	ID Tag	Device Type	Serial #	Maker	Model	Workstation Specific						Monitor Size
						CPU Speed	Hard Disk Size	RAM	CD RW	DVD	OS	

In this example:

User phone #:	This ties to the user name table.
ID tag:	Used if placing a company asset tag on the device.
Device type:	PC, network hub, AS400 terminal, etc. Pick from a list to ensure consistency.
Serial number:	Essential for tracking movement and for some service contracts.
Maker:	IBM, Compaq, Machines, Cisco, HP.
Model:	Gives some idea of what is in it.
CPU speed:	Important when estimating cost of upgrading software.
Hard disk size:	Not so important with 100+ GB drives.
RAM:	Important when estimating cost of upgrading software.
CD RW:	May or may not be important—great for making data backups.
DVD:	May not be important.
OS:	Type and version number are very important when planning software upgrades.
Monitor size:	Or any other relevant fields.

To this, add any number of other fields such as date purchased, warranty expiration date, date information was last verified, etc. Warranty is a nice way to reduce hardware repair costs, but requires time for record maintenance. Further complicating this—if a new motherboard is installed in an old PC, does the IT department need a mechanism to track its parts warranty separate from the PC's?

> ### Comment
>
> Warranty support usually requires shipping the unit back to the manufacturer for repair. Workstations cannot leave the premises for repair because of data security issues. Consider negotiating a no-warranty purchase. Usually, this covers the unit for the first 30 days (to address out-of-box failures). Beyond that, repair the unit as usual.

Depending on how sophisticated the asset-tracking system will be, consider linking the asset record to a repair record for any updates or to a table listing every item in the machine. Although this example used personal computers, this is equally useful for network equipment, printers, bar-code scanners, etc. The result is useful for identifying problem units and problem vendors.

[E]   Asset Tagging

Many companies have a capital item asset-tagging process in place. It is intended to deter theft, help keep track of asset location, and allocate overhead budget based on material used to support a department. Asset tagging is something to do correctly or not at all. It is a major labor investment to establish and maintain. If the resources to do this or the benefits derived are not present, then do not start it.

> ### Comment
>
> Asset tagging is a poor theft deterrent. One of the authors worked at a company that always stamped their name and logo on their hand tools. So many tools were stolen that it became something of a point of pride to have a complete set of tools at home with the company imprint on them. The removal of asset tags can mar the surface of an item that may reduce its resale value—but not by much. Stolen goods are usually sold cheaply.

Most equipment comes with a serial number from the manufacturer. However, these numbers vary widely in length, composition, and attached in some of the most inconvenient places. In addition, the longer the serial number, the greater the chance of incorrectly keying it into the database.

Therefore, most companies attach their own asset number to expensive equipment. This makes it easier to track individual items.

The most basic asset-tracking numbering system starts at 000001 and increases by 1 from there. Other approaches use the first two digits to identify the class of item and the remaining numbers to identify the individual item. Typical groups might be workstations, network hubs, printers, monitors, etc. Embedding a "device group identifier" in the serial number reduces the likelihood of someone swapping asset tags on equipment. The service desk also has an idea of what the device is by the serial number.

The general costs for asset tagging are:

A. Expense of printing or buying preprinted tags.
B. Expense of portable tag readers (if using RF-ID or bar codes).
C. Time to expand the database to accept the tag ID.
D. Time to gather information on each item and to attach the tag.
E. Time to update the asset database every time a tag moves.
F. Interruption of new equipment delivery to attach a tag.

What to tag. What needs tracking? Someone must decide what is going to be tracked. Do not attach tags unless the IT department is committed to tracking equipment. There is a labor cost for every device tagged and tracked. Base this decision on what will be done with the information. Is equipment tracked to maximize warranty coverage? Is the goal to gather capital item depreciation for accounting? The IT department may want to manage certain classes of equipment such as network cards or workstations. Anything the IT department wants to track the location of is a good candidate. Disposable items such as keyboards and computer mice are not worth the effort. Perhaps the decision of what to tag may be driven by its cost, whether it is leased, or under a service contract.

How to tag. The purpose of a tag is to read it later. At the same time, the less obtrusive it is, the less likely the operator is to remove it. After determining what to tag, establish a procedure of where to attach the tag. For example, the back of a PC is difficult to read since some PC system units are tucked deep under desks and held in place by too-short wires. A suggested place to tag PCs is near the bottom of the case on the side, such as the front lower corner of the right side of the case (when facing the unit). Network hub cards are usually in a rack in a locked closet. Attach the tag to the front panel if there is space.

For items that can only be reached by technicians (usually in locked cabinets), the asset tag can be attached to a paper tag which is tied to the device. However attached, take some pictures of the tagging points to standardize where it goes. Document the tagging procedure for each major type of equipment. Different devices may have different attachment issues, but always tag workstations in one general area, printers in another, and so forth.

Asset tags, by their nature, are permanent. Using an adhesive to attach them requires an idea of the object to which they will be stuck. The more permanent the glue, the fewer chances there are to attach it! All adhesives have solvents that will remove them (even if they seriously mar the surface at the same time). In some cases, attach tags with screws, but this is a bit of overkill for electronic equipment.

Which tag is best? The best tags have an RFID chip embedded in them. This way, the chip reader only needs to get close to the device and there is no need to move equipment during an inventory count. A less expensive approach is to use bar-coded labels. In both cases, when conducting subsequent item counts, a portable reader can quickly collect information.

Along with the bar code, include the same number in human readable format, in case equipment is moved without access to a bar-code reader. Also, include on the label a request prohibiting its removal, along with the company name. It may not stop everyone, but it will slow down the more honest ones. Bar codes and RF-ID chips pay off in subsequent inventory counts. They allow the IT asset manager to move quickly through a department scanning bar codes instead of reexamining every device to discover whose it is. Without bar code, someone must write down every tag number and even careful people make data transcription mistakes. See Policy ITP-17-2 Hardware Asset Management Policy as an example.

POLICY ITP-17-2   Hardware Asset Management Policy

Policy #:	ITP-17-2	Effective:	03/18/09	Page #:	1 of N
Subject:	IT Hardware Asset Management Policy				

1.0 PURPOSE

This policy provides guidance for the proper management of computer hardware assets. Its purpose is to minimize costs, drive out obsolete technology, provide the ready location of assets, and ensure that obsolete devices are disposed of properly.

2.0 SCOPE

This policy applies to all employees, contractors, and visitors. It covers all electronic hardware assets purchased or created by the company, to include:

A. PCs, servers, network devices, printers, monitors, Memory sticks.
B. Computer workstations of all sizes to include both fixed and portable, to include PDAs. Combination cellular telephones and PDAs are considered to be PDAs.
C. Computer servers in any location on company property.
D. Company-owned workstations and servers at employee homes, for use while traveling, at vendor sites, or at customer sites.
E. Video cameras except for combination camera/cellular telephones, which are considered to be primarily cell phones.

Excluded from this policy are:

A. Telecom devices and cell phones.
B. Devices purchased by employees with their own funds for their personal use, such as cellular telephones, PDAs, and cell phone/PDAs, are excluded from this policy.

3.0 POLICY

The following guidelines are established for using company hardware and software assets.

A. **Appointment of an IT Hardware Asset Manager.** The IT Manager will appoint a member of the Information Technology (IT) department as the company's IT Hardware Asset Manager. This person has the authority for implementing this policy.
B. **Acquisition.** The IT Hardware Asset Manager is responsible for selecting and acquiring computer hardware for use by the company. This person will:
   1. Publish a quarterly list of standard hardware approved for use.
   2. Coordinate with the hardware repair and support organization to ensure they can support changes to the standard hardware list.
   3. Review and approve all IT hardware purchase requests to ensure they conform to the approved standard equipment list.
   4. Review and recommend approval or denial to the IT Manager for the purchase of any non-standard devices.
   5. Maximize redeployment of idle equipment prior to purchasing new devices.
C. **Strategic planning.** The IT Hardware Asset Manager will monitor company asset usage and IT strategic plans and will annually develop a Three-Year Hardware Asset Roadmap that:
   1. Includes industry projections of new hardware technology releases for planning changes to the standard unit list.
   2. Synchronizes future requirements with the Software Asset Management Three-Year Roadmap to identify required hardware upgrades.
   3. Identifies the number of devices, by type, expected to achieve obsolescence for budgeting replacement purchases.

D. **Maximize utilization.** The IT Hardware Asset Manager identifies, collects, and safeguards idle IT hardware assets.
   1. The IT Hardware Asset Manager has the authority to confiscate idle IT hardware assets even if they were purchased with a different department's funds.
E. **Disposal.** The IT Hardware Asset Manager ensures that all pertinent corporate policies for the proper disposal of assets are followed. The IT Hardware Asset Manager:
   1. Creates and maintains a process for removing data from disks and persistent memory prior to the scrapping, sale, or donation of equipment.
   2. Coordinates with the company's environmental management department to ensure that all equipment and supplies declared as scrap are disposed of in accordance with current environmental regulations.
   3. Updates the appropriate accounting records concerning capital assets.
F. **Tracking database.** The IT Hardware Asset Manager creates and maintains an asset tracking database. This database will provide the essential data for tracking equipment from purchase to obsolescence, locating specific devices, and providing information for warranty or insurance claims. The IT Hardware Asset Manager will:
   1. Conduct an initial asset count and periodic department asset verification audits throughout the year.
   2. Report monthly to the IT Manager on the number and location (by department) of all IT hardware assets.
   3. Attach an IT asset tag to all hardware assets.
      a. Promptly tag new equipment entering the facility.
      b. Idle assets recovered and lacking a tag receive a reissued or new tag.
   4. Update the asset database whenever tracked assets are relocated.
G. **Security.** The IT Hardware Asset Manager safeguards company assets from theft.
   1. An equipment pass recorded with the facility security team must accompany all assets leaving the premises.
      a. The IT Hardware Asset Manager provides passes for equipment leaving the premises for repair.
      b. Issues a permanent pass to Notebook PC users.
   2. Assets owned by another company and used on the company's premises must be clearly marked as to their owner. The company's security team must check this equipment in and out of the premises, by serial number.
   3. Employees taking assets off site are responsible for their safe return.
      a. Damaged items will be investigated by the IT Hardware Asset Manager to determine if neglect caused the damage. If so, the report will be turned over to the IT Manager for resolution.

    b. Employees whose borrowed items are stolen must provide a copy of the police report or repay the company for the borrowed but never returned item.

H. **Acceptable uses of company computer network, workstations, and servers.** The IT Hardware Asset Manager publishes guidelines for the appropriate use of IT hardware. These assets are to be used solely for company use. Personal use is prohibited.

I. **Personal assets.** Employees are prohibited from bringing into the facility personal hardware assets such as PCs, peripherals, or any other hardware devices.

    1. The IT Hardware Asset Manager may confiscate personally provided assets since only company property is permitted on the premises except where written permission is provided by the IT Hardware Asset Manager and the device has been checked onto the premises by the security team.

    2. Devices purchased by employees with their own funds, and for their personal use, such as cellular telephones, PDAs, and cell phone/PDAs, are excluded from this policy.

J. **Violations.** Any employee who abuses the use of company owned assets is subject to corrective action including termination. If necessary, the company reserves the right to advise appropriate legal officials of any illegal violations.

4.0 REVISION HISTORY

Date	Revision #	Description of Change
03/18/09	1.0	Initial creation.

5.0 INQUIRIES

Direct inquiries about this policy to:

Harold Jenkins, CIO
2900 Corporate Drive
Columbus, OH 43215

Voice: 614-555-1234
Fax: 614-555-1235
E-mail: hjenkins@company.com

Revision #:	1.0	Supersedes:	N/A	Date:	03/18/09

[F]   Idle Equipment Collection

What is it? During the course of an asset inventory, someone will undoubtedly come across small stockpiles of equipment. Some of this equipment does not work. Some of it will be obsolete. Some is new and never been plugged in. Now is the time to set aside an area to receive this material.

Idle material is the result of a number of things. Usually, someone had a system problem and a replacement unit was installed. However, no one ever came back for the old device so it was shoved into a closet or under a desk in an empty office. Most companies are littered with disconnected keyboards, monitors, and computer mice. Walk around with a large cart and pick up all the obvious material. If the facility has a newsletter, encourage people to call the service desk to arrange for a pick up.

Another type of idle equipment is the private stashes of spare equipment. These are computers, scanners, network cards, monitors, and a wide range of devices that are in working order but kept hidden away as spares. (This is an indicator that people lack confidence in IT's ability to support them!) Expect considerable political pressure not to pick up these piles. Once identified, the company's accounting manager will be the IT Manager's biggest ally in confiscating this equipment. The problem is that all of these stashes cost money to establish. By consolidating these stashes into one place, the company saves money since fewer spare parts are needed. These types of stashes often contain new in-the-crate equipment. The warranty clock is ticking! Over time, these new items are worth less and less as better technology becomes available.

Safeguard it. Idle equipment must be stored in a locked room. Do not permit people to freely walk in and take whatever they want. Remember, IT is now controlling the assets, not just shuffling them around. If the asset room is viewed as a candy store, then the best equipment will quickly migrate to newly reestablished department stashes. In this room, install a large worktable, shelving for the equipment picked up, and a cabinet for individual circuit boards. A file cabinet for keeping records will be useful as will a kit full of basic tools. Ensure only a few people have keys to the doors. Establish a sign-out sheet for equipment taken from the room. (All devices can enter but few can leave!) The IT Manager must establish guidelines for removing equipment.

Tag and test. Purchase three types of colored tags (or stickers): green, red, and yellow. Also obtain a stockpile of cleaning supplies. If using stickers, the attachment point must be clean. Attach a yellow tag. Yellow is for caution, that the device has not yet been checked. Imagine a technician's feelings if he trucked a large monitor up 10 floors only to see that it does not work! Assume all incoming equipment is broken until proven otherwise.

Once all of the technology orphans have been collected, test every item to see if it works. Sort the equipment into piles according to its value (very old workstations versus newer technology). Test the obviously new items first. Old equipment may not be worth the time. It is difficult to thoroughly test every item. In most cases, just turning it on and trying to use it is test enough.

The best time to attach the yellow tag is when picking up the device. Write on the tag where it came from. This is most important for workstations that may hold important data on the hard disks.

Every item that seems in workable order should have a green tag attached. The tester should write his name and the date on the tag. This provides some traceability. Items that do not work get a red tag. Place them in one of two piles. One pile is the to-be-scrapped items. The other is the to-be-repaired items. Note on the red tag in which pile they belong.

COMMENT

When preparing a workstation disk for redeployment or scrapping:

- Set the unit aside for two weeks to see if someone wants a file from it.
- Make a full backup of the disk.
- Repartition and perform a sector by sector reformat for at least three passes.

The company's accounting department will provide guidelines to follow for scrapping equipment. They will need to know the asset tag number, serial numbers, make, model, etc. In most states, businesses pay a "property tax" on their assets and the accounting team will want to remove these items from the books. If the company has an environmental department, they can advise the safest way to dispose of the devices. There are other possible disposal outlets:

A. Call the company used to repair that type of device. They might buy the old equipment for use in their repair operations. This is the most common source of spare parts for old technologies.
B. Call a local vocational school to see if they want them for their students to dissect and/or repair.
C. Offer them to the local computer repair shop that might be able to reuse some of the parts.
D. If the equipment is still usable, consider a donation.

When scrapping PCs, most companies overlook recovering the software licenses. The rights conferred on the purchaser by each software company's license are different, but they typically allow a company to use one copy of a program on one machine. The right to use that program may be transferable within the company after discarding to PC. However, the company will need to show proof of a license, which is why the license notices of incoming software are collected and filed as "IT Vital Records."

Collect items needing repair in one place. If the pile is high enough, the repair service may come in to work on them rather than requiring the IT Manager to send them all out. Manufacturers often offer a flat rate repair for some items, such as bar-code scanners. The biggest problem will be the data on workstation hard drives. Track down the last owner if possible or ask the manager of the department to look at the data to see what they want to keep.

COMMENT

Never send out a workstation for repair with the hard drive still installed. If this is done, the company just lost security over that data. If necessary, install another hard drive in the unit before shipping it out for repair. (With a spot of luck, this might fix the problem!)

When redeploying PCs, reformat the hard disk and load it with the company's basic software load. Most people are reluctant to delete old programs and data off their disk. This can make for a surprisingly complex set of software baggage that builds up but never gets used. Users also will expect support for these obsolete "drag-along" programs. Reformatting removes the accumulated program fragments and DLLs. It also will improve the unit's performance.

Provide a list of working equipment to the IT Manager. Consider this equipment for redeployment whenever someone calls for a new purchase. Another use is to begin migrating older working equipment out of the offices by installing newer equipment from the idle equipment room. Who gets the best of the redeployable equipment is another political battle. In this way, the IT department can quietly exchange idle assets for the most difficult to maintain units.

Justifying taking equipment out of this room for an installation is the same process as for purchasing a new device. This equipment is not for providing "favors" to someone.

[G]   Data Collection Forms

The last step before beginning an inventory count is to create a data collection form to gather equipment information as the inventory team moves through the facility. The form should include all of the data elements in the database table. There are also some decisions to make:

A.   Will PC software be counted and tracked? Which ones? How is it recognized?

B.   Will circuit boards within PCs be counted?

C.   What about PCs with locks or passwords that prevent anyone from checking them unless the assigned operator is present?

D. Is there anything else to do during the count, such as detect illegal copies of software?

For the machine count, use a form to record idle equipment uncovered for later pickup. A floor plan is useful if there is a lot of area to cover. As rooms are completed, color them in on the floor plan. Use a sheet of small colored dots to mark the doors of completed rooms.

MANAGEMENT TIP

If the company has previously standardized one model, then by capturing the model name of the desktop units it is possible to fill in the hard drive, CPU, etc. from the standard equipment for that model.

§ 17.03 CONDUCTING THE INVENTORY

[A] Overview

Finally! It is now time to begin the inventory count. The goals here are to uncover idle assets, find hidden equipment stashes, and tag all hardware assets and to gather data on what is present in the facility. This is a lot of work, but for a big payback.

A technology count touches employees across the organization from the executives to the custodians. When it is finished, how will IT be perceived by the employees? Before launching this effort, debug the process first on the IT department and then on at least one more department.

Throughout the process, continuously communicate with everyone. Tell departments what will happen before arriving for the count. Tell departments already counted just what was found. As the database is populated, constantly monitor for problems in the data entry and readability of the data collection sheets to ensure high quality in the data.

[B] Conducting the Count

Take some time to get (almost) everyone on IT's side. Meet with the facility staff and explain the process. Issue a schedule of when the inventory team expects to visit each area. This might be over a weekend so that equipment is not moving around during the count. Schedule days and times after a department is counted for the employees to bring over their notebook PCs and PDAs for tagging.

Before the count begins, issue an announcement to the "target" department several days in advance. The IT Manager and that department's manager should both sign and acknowledge it. It should explain the material counting process. This is a good time to remind the department why this is good for the company. Ask people to remove any material they have placed around their equipment so its serial number can be checked. Also, ask everyone to put idle assets outside their office door. Pick these up before the count to save and count them later.

During the count, be sure to look in every closet and large storage cabinet. If locked, ask security to open them. Ferret out stashes of good equipment and forgotten broken equipment. Be very thorough. Look into large boxes, drawers of empty desks—anywhere keyboards, mice, modems, scanners, etc., could be stuffed.

MANAGEMENT TIP

Enter data sheets into the asset database *as soon as they are turned in*. A problem reading the data may require someone to revisit some areas to verify information. It is best to catch this problem early in the process.

Once the count and tagging is complete, run some summary reports. Provide these to the IT Manager and the accounting manager. After the data appears to be clean, provide business managers with a recap of tagged material in their department. Exhibit 17-3 is an example of a report that includes some accounting allocation assigned to each device. Some companies would use an asset report such as this to assign depreciation expense to their budget. The value of each unit may be a flat amount based on equipment type.

[C] Set a Hardware Strategy

Identify a minimum workstation configuration. Examine the total equipment counts by category. Clean up any data classification inconsistencies. Let us use personal computers as an example. Report them by category. What are the current operating system hardware requirements in CPU, RAM, and disk space? Does each of the workstations meet the minimum configuration? How about the recommended configuration? Look on the vendor's web site for this information. Some example products are:

Windows XP Pro, a Microsoft product, sets their hardware minimum as:
    CPU: minimum 233 MHz, recommended 300 MHz
    RAM: 64 MB minimum, 128 MB recommended
    Hard disk space: 1.5 GB

EXHIBIT 17-3. Asset Report by Department

Date: 9/11/2004

Dept. Name: Tech Support

PCs	$95,950	< 1 GHz 62	1–2 GHz 8	2–4 GHz 18
Notebook PCs	$6,969		2	
Monitors	$24,240	15″ 21	17″ 47	19″ 20
Inkjet printers	$2,345	HP 932c 7	Canon 5100 3	Epson Stylus 740 12
Laser printers	$3,214	LJ 5000 2	Lexmark 1855 1	LJ 1100 1
AS 400 printers	$2,780	4224 1	4230 1	
Telephones	$24,240	Lucent 6224 69	ATT 7406 23	
Fax machines	$1,295	Intellifax 1550 1		

Total Assets	$161,033
Monthly Charge	$4,473

Corel WordPerfect 2002 Standard
    CPU: minimum 166 MHz
    RAM: 16 MB minimum, 32 MB recommended
    Hard disk space: 165 MB, 250 MB for a typical install

Sun StarOffice 6.0 Office Suite
    CPU: Pentium compatible PC
    RAM: 64 MB
    Hard disk space: 250 MB

These of course are the manufacturer's minimal configurations required for the product to run. Consider doubling these requirements if users want it to run with acceptable response times. Using the survey together with the hardware capabilities recommended by the company's standard software, a minimal standard workstation configuration can be selected. Do not bother to repair workstations with less than this minimal configuration. Any equipment in the idle assets room that falls below this must be either upgraded or scrapped.

COMMENT

Some companies never upgrade hardware or software. Every three years (about when the hardware warranty ends), all of the hardware is replaced along with the latest version of software.

Based on the hardware survey, the IT Manager can now estimate the cost to raise all of the existing workstations to the recommended hardware capability. As new software upgrades are contemplated, there is now a data-driven basis to identify workstations in the business departments that are below the minimum; these are prime candidates for replacement by any of the more capable equipment recovered. Most companies have at least three desktop minimum configurations. Some workers use their equipment lightly and only need a minimal configuration. An office worker spends more time using a keyboard but his programs do not tax the equipment. The engineering team will often exercise every megahertz of their equipment with newer and more complex software. Consider establishing categories of capability for workstations. Some examples might be:

> **Minimal User:** E-mail, Internet communications, runs basic software
> > **Minimum configuration:** 1-GHz processor, 20-GB hard drive, 15-in monitor
>
> **Office Worker:** E-mail, word processing, spreadsheet, database
> > **Minimum configuration:** 2.5-GHz processor, 40-GB hard drive, 17-in monitor
>
> **Engineer:** CAD, e-mail, word processing, spreadsheet
> > **Minimum configuration:** 3.0-GHz processor, 80-GB hard drive, 21-in monitor

COMMENT

Hard disk storage space is cheap. However, some companies keep user disks small to force storage of files on the file servers, which are then backed up to tape.

Identify candidates to eliminate. Are there any pockets of very old technology to eliminate? Electronic technologies of all types seem to reinvent themselves every two years. If there are clusters of very old equipment, spare parts to repair them may no longer be available. If the company waits until they break, the IT Manager must make a decision during a crisis instead of at leisure today. However, before announcing the scrapping of someone's "old faithful" terminal, find out if there is a special requirement for that specific device. The older the technologies, the more likely it is that a specific device must be used to support a business function.

Another type of device to eliminate is anything on a lease. Some leases allow the early return of leased equipment—some are just disguised time-payment purchases. If the equipment can be returned, it will lower IT's monthly costs a bit (assuming they can be replaced with equipment from the idle asset room). If the equipment cannot be returned early, at least now the IT department knows where it is. Document a procedure for returning "scrap" devices that are on lease.

Make a projection of the hardware minimums anticipated for the next several years. This forms an important part of the Desktop Computer Three Year Plan. Assuming the company staffing levels remain the same during this time, how many units will become obsolete.

COMMENT

There are many things the asset database can be used for. An easy benefit is to develop a roadmap for replacing and upgrading the desktop and notebook units in the company. By sorting the computers according to their CPU (assuming it was a data element that was captured for each unit), then the number of units to replace every year can be estimated.

Use the same process for servers, network cards, and any other hardware device. Look at what the company has, estimate what may be needed next year and the year after, identify the weak, and project the capital needs to replace them.

The primary driver for upgrading hardware is a new software version. A close relationship with critical software vendors will provide substantial advance notice of expanded hardware requirements, in time to include them in the upcoming year's budget.

[D]   Determining the Number of On-Site Spares Required

The following steps will help you to set the correct spare equipment stocking level:

A.   Look at the total number of machines in each class.
B.   Determine how long it would take to get one repaired. Are they sent away for repair? Does the service person come into the building to fix them? Are they common items or rare?
C.   Estimate how often this device seems to break down.

Calculating the number of spares:

A.   How many devices of this type are in service?
B.   How many workdays between failures?
C.   Typically, how many days does it take to get that type of device repaired?
D.   How many workdays in a year (roughly)?
E.   Determine the mean time between failures.
F.   Determine the number of machines/days in week.
G.   Divide the number from Step D by the number in Step E.

Example:

> Say the company is using 200 PCs. The IT Manager estimates one hardware problem per unit, every two years. History shows that it typically requires five working days to get a PC repaired. Given vacations and holidays, a PC is in use 48 weeks per year times five days per week or 240 days per year. Therefore, if the company works 240 days per year, and a PC fails every two years, there is a mean time between failures (MTBF) of 480 days. In a given week (five days), if there are 200 machines running, the result is 1,000 machine/days per week. Divide the MTBF by the number machine/days in a week to see if the IT department needs to keep a bit more than two spares on hand. Round this number up to three as the minimal stocking level.

If there is less than the minimal stocking level on hand, order some equipment today! If there is more than the minimal stocking level, then redeploy that equipment in place of purchasing new equipment. Another option is to scrap broken machines instead of paying to repair older equipment to deplete the idle assets. Once the emergency spares stocking level is on hand, lock it up! People with marginally financed projects will try to use this equipment to make their projects look less expensive than they are. Do not use these machines for anything other than spares.

[E] Developing a Service Strategy

Let us return for a minute to the equipment count.

Identify all key devices. The first step in a service contract strategy is to identify which equipment is vital to the organization. Some machines must be operational at all times. If practical, store the spare parts for those machines next to that device. However, most machines can wait for an hour or so for repair. The operator may not think so, but it is usually true.

Ideally, critical machines have their backup device always online and in parallel with the primary unit. This allows for a quick changeover. No matter how stable the existing process is, never let the users convert the backup unit to any other purpose. If a process is not critical enough to protect the spare machine, then it really isn't that critical at all.

Service contracts. Here is another area where an asset management program shows its power. Compare the equipment totals with the company's service contracts:

A. Evaluate the company's coverage. Is everything on the contract that should be on it?

B. Is the company paying for service support for hardware that is gone? Is every serial number on the contract still in-house? Before canceling anything here, make another pass or two through the area to look for it.

C. Look at each device separately. Is the company paying for the proper level of service? Is that expensive 24/7 support still required? Always check with the users before lowering the service response time.

D. Evaluate the list of critical equipment. Is it properly covered? This is not the place to cut corners!

Look for ways to lower cost. If there are plenty of spares for a particular device type, consider establishing a quick swap/service center. In this approach, exchange one of the spares for the broken item to restore service.

The repairperson only needs to come in weekly to work on the accumulated broken equipment. Do service contracts cover any of the older technologies? How much is it costing per device? Often the older hardware is the most expensive to support. This helps to justify the expense to eliminate older technology.

[F] Ongoing Asset Management

After tagging and counting, maintain a vigorous effort to keep the database current. This requires updating the asset database anytime that equipment moves out of the idle assets room. Anything moved back to storage also is noted. Depending on their workload, the service desk can keep this up to date. Every time someone reports a problem, take a moment to verify the asset information. Technicians who move equipment can also update the asset records. Use Worksheet 17-1 Install, Move, Add, Change (IMAC) Form to help control the movement of IT assets.

Think for a minute about how far the asset management program has come! From running the business using "tribal knowledge," the IT Manager can now proceed based on the facts! When the annual budgeting cycle comes around, the IT Manager can better estimate equipment needs for the upcoming year. When software conversions become necessary, a data driven estimate of required hardware upgrades can be created.

As is apparent, conducting a full asset count is very time-consuming. Instead of doing this every year, audit one department every month since there are now bar codes or RF-ID tags on all of the machines. This plus other steps maintain the accuracy and usefulness of the database.

WORKSHEET 17-1.   Install, Move, Add, Change (IMAC) Form

<table>
<tr><td colspan="3" align="center">Install, Move, Add, Change (IMAC) Form</td></tr>
<tr><td colspan="3">Please complete this form and fax to x1234 or email it to imac@ourcompany.com. One form must be completed for each affected device. Incomplete forms or requests that do not comply with relevant IT policies will be returned for revision.</td></tr>
<tr><td>Date Requested:</td><td>Department:</td><td></td></tr>
<tr><td>Name:</td><td>Extension:</td><td></td></tr>
<tr><td>Date Required:</td><td colspan="2">☐ Install ☐ Move ☐ Add ☐ Change</td></tr>
<tr><td>Current Location:</td><td colspan="2">New Location:</td></tr>
<tr><td colspan="3" align="center">Hardware</td></tr>
<tr><td>☐ Desktop</td><td>☐ External Speakers</td><td>Other Approved Hardware:</td></tr>
<tr><td>☐ Laptop</td><td>☐ Desktop Printer</td><td></td></tr>
<tr><td>☐ Monitor</td><td>☐ Memory</td><td></td></tr>
<tr><td>☐ Keyboard</td><td>☐ Hard Disk</td><td></td></tr>
<tr><td>☐ Mouse</td><td>☐ External Hard Disk</td><td></td></tr>
<tr><td colspan="3" align="center">Software</td></tr>
<tr><td>☐ Windows XP</td><td>☐ Visual Studio</td><td>Other Approved Software:</td></tr>
<tr><td>☐ Windows Vista</td><td>☐ Active Sync</td><td></td></tr>
<tr><td>☐ Microsoft Office</td><td>☐</td><td></td></tr>
<tr><td>☐ Microsoft Outlook</td><td>☐</td><td></td></tr>
<tr><td>☐ Adobe Reader</td><td>☐</td><td></td></tr>
<tr><td colspan="3" align="center">Computer Replacement</td></tr>
</table>

Current Computer		New Computer	
Computer Name:		Computer Name:	
Model:		Model:	
IT ID:		IT ID:	
Service ID:		Service ID:	

<table>
<tr><td colspan="4" align="center">Approval</td></tr>
<tr><td>Supervisor:</td><td></td><td>Date:</td><td></td></tr>
<tr><td>IT Manager:</td><td></td><td>Date:</td><td></td></tr>
</table>

§ 17.04 SOFTWARE ASSET MANAGEMENT

[A] Overview

When most people think of asset management, they think in terms of physical property. For a long time, this was true of IT systems also. Software was expensive but the hardware cost much more. With improvements in manufacturing and lower prices, companies now have more money invested in software than in the equipment to run it. Software asset management is quite different from hardware management yet it also can be a place to save money in the IT budget.

[B] Lay the Groundwork

Expand the asset database. The software asset database table is typically linked to the hardware table since software exists to support a hardware device. In addition to the user information collected during the hardware inventory, it is useful to know the software's version number.

What information to collect?

A. **Purchased Software—PC.**
    1. Software name.
    2. Manufacturer's name.
    3. Version.
B. **Purchased Software—Server/mainframe.**
    1. Software name.
    2. Manufacturer's name.
    3. Version.
    4. Annual maintenance fee.
    5. Number of simultaneous users licensed.
    6. Restriction on the license, such as CPU size, number of CPUs, etc.
C. **In-House Developed Software.**
    1. Software name.
    2. Programmer's name.
    3. Version.

The difficulty in collecting software information is in deciphering which EXE is which program. An automated inventory program will know. There is software available that will check the networked PCs overnight or the next time they log onto the server. A nice feature about this type of software is that it can be set to re-inventory PCs at programmed intervals. There is also software on the market that will use the network to "visit" each workstation on the network. In addition, by catching units as they log on, it can capture data from notebook PCs when they return from the field.

> ## COMMENT
>
> Examples of this class of products are iInventory at *www.lanauditor.com* and Express Metrix at *www.expressmetrix.com*.
> The Business Software Alliance (*www.BSA.org*) has three evaluation tools available for download that can audit Windows and UNIX based systems to identify what programs are present in those systems.

A major benefit of this class of automatic software auditing is when preparing to roll out new software. It is easy to assemble a list of who might need the new version, and who might still be running an old OS version and require a double version upgrade.

[C] Unauthorized Software

The inventory team will likely find unauthorized software during their count and must be ready to address it. Searches of user hard drives may turn up anything from the company bowling team scores to pornography. Be sure everyone on the team understands what the company will permit before proceeding. Based on the company's policy on unauthorized software, copy the offending files to a secure library on the server and then delete them from the PC. Leave the offending operator with a copy of the policy.

Remove illegal software and report to the IT Manager. The problem with removing it is that the longer it is in place, the more ingrained in that department's operation it may become. Removing it is the right thing to do but, in the short term, it may hurt that department's operations. In that case, immediately purchase the necessary number of copies and assign the cost to that manager.

An exception would be computer games. Most companies have a policy of "death on sight" for computer games loaded onto their company PCs. Make sure of what is being deleted before erasing it.

> ## COMMENT
>
> Disk checks performed during a software inventory may uncover other unauthorized files on the PC such as gambling pools and pornography. Before beginning the inventory count, work with the Human Resources department to determine:
>
> - Exactly what is a violation.
> - How (and to whom) to report these violations.

> - How to gather and secure the "evidence."
> - Rules of conduct for the technicians during and after any incidents.
>
> Draft written instructions for what to do and train the team on what to do. A similar set of instructions should govern unauthorized software.

[D]   Conduct the Inventory

Making the rounds of all of the offices for the software inventory is just like the one for the hardware count—only more tedious. If an automated software inventory system is used, then compare its results to the hardware list to determine who was missed. The inventory must include every workstation, every server, and do not forget the all-important network software versions. Remember that notebook PCs and PDAs may not show up on the automated software count—or they may pop up over time as they reenter the facility and attach to the network. Schedule times with each department to bring in their machines for evaluation.

Although PCs have been used throughout this chapter as an example, it is important to know information about IT's other software. Typically, each IT section handles their own. They can continue to do so but including them in the database allows some upper management visibility. For example, the software on network devices does not change very often but, without an accurate list of what is there, there is no management oversight. Often the network manager does not know what is there either.

[E]   Crunch the Numbers

Roll up the numbers after the inventory is completed. Compare this number with the number of software licenses the company can prove it has purchased. Report the results to the IT Manager. Purchase needed copies immediately.

Now look for traces of "homegrown" department-written software. If someone writes a program for his own use, that is one issue. But if someone has written such a program and now it is in widespread use, then the IT department must step in and ensure it follows good data processing procedures (like all of the numbers add up), etc.

[F]   Ongoing Software Asset Management

Cleaning illegal software one time is a good first step, but unless the employees believe that IT is now monitoring their systems, it will all be back. Publish a clear policy explaining that installation of software not purchased by the company is forbidden and that people doing so will be disciplined.

See Policy ITP-17-3 Software Asset Management Policy as an example.

POLICY ITP-17-3.   Software Asset Management Policy

Policy #:	ITP-17-3	Effective:	03/18/09	Page #:	1 of N
Subject:	Software Asset Management Policy				

1.0 PURPOSE:

This policy provides guidance for the proper management of computer software assets. Its purpose is to minimize costs, drive out obsolete technology, provide the ready location of assets, and ensure that obsolete assets are disposed of properly.

2.0 SCOPE:

This policy applies to all employees, contractors, and visitors. It covers all software assets purchased or created by the company, to include:

- A. Software purchased for use by employees.
- B. Software created by employees to include (at a minimum):
    1. Programs of all types written by employees on company equipment, whether on premises or during off-site business.
    2. Programs of all types developed during paid working hours.
    3. Spreadsheets, document templates, personal databases, etc.
- C. Company owned software at employee homes, for use while traveling, at vendor sites, or at customer sites.
- D. Personal software installed on company equipment.

Excluded from this policy are:

- A. Software purchased by employees with their own funds for their personal use, such as for cellular telephones, PDAs, cell phone/PDAs, or personal music devices.

3.0 POLICY

To ensure all employees understand their responsibilities, the following guidelines are established for using company software assets.

- A. **Appointment of an IT Software Asset Manager.** The IT Manager will appoint a member of the Information Technology (IT) department as the company's IT Software Asset Manager. This person has the authority for implementing this policy.
- B. **Acquisition.** The IT Software Asset Manager is responsible for selecting and acquiring computer software for use by the company. This person will:
    1. Create and publish quarterly a list of standard software approved for use by the company.

2. Coordinate with the server support team and desktop support teams to ensure they can support any changes to the standard software list.
3. Review and approve all IT software purchase requests to ensure they conform to the approved standard equipment list.
4. Review and recommend approval or denial to the IT Manager for the purchase of any non-standard software.

C. **Strategic planning.** The IT Software Asset Manager will monitor company asset usage and IT strategic plans and will annually develop a Three-Year Software Asset Roadmap that:
1. Includes industry projections of new software technology releases for planning changes to the standard unit list.
2. Synchronizes future requirements with the Hardware Asset Management Three Year Roadmap to identify required software upgrades.
3. Identifies the number of software products, by type, expected to lose technical support for budgeting replacement purchases.

D. **Maximize utilization.** The IT Software Asset Manager identifies, collects, and safeguards idle IT Software assets. Collecting idle assets makes them available for redeployment.
1. Prior to reuse, verifies each product's license to ensure it can be legally transferred from one machine to another.
2. The IT Software Asset Manager has the authority to confiscate idle IT Software assets—even if purchased with a different department's funds.

E. **Disposal.** The IT Software Asset Manager follows all pertinent corporate policies for the proper disposal of software. The IT Software Asset Manager:
1. Updates the appropriate accounting records concerning capital assets.
2. Creates and maintains a process for removing data from disks and persistent memory prior to the scrapping, sale, or donation of equipment.
3. Coordinates with the company's environmental management department and outside sources to ensure that all equipment and supplies declared as scrap are disposed of in accordance with current environmental regulations.

F. **Tracking database.** The IT Software Asset Manager will create and maintain an asset tracking database. (Potentially incorporate this into the Hardware Asset Management database.) This database will provide the essential data for tracking software from purchase to obsolescence, locating specific products, providing information for support or insurance claims. The IT Software Asset Manager will:
1. Conduct an initial product count and periodic software verification audits throughout the year.
2. Report monthly to the IT Manager on the number and location (by department) of all IT managed software assets.
3. Promptly add software entering the facility to the asset database.

G. **Security.** The IT Software Asset Manager safeguards company assets from theft. Software is a unique product because it can be stolen while the original product remains intact.

H. **Personal assets.** Employees *are prohibited* from bringing into the facility personal software, whether purchased or acquired through the "public domain."

　1. The IT Software Asset Manager may confiscate personally provided software. Only company property is permitted on the premises except where written permission is provided by the IT Software Asset Manager.

　2. Software contained in personal devices such as cellular telephones, PDAs, and cell phone/PDAs are excluded from this policy.

I. **Violations.** Any employee who abuses the use of company owned assets is subject to corrective action including termination. If necessary, the company reserves the right to advise appropriate legal officials of any illegal violations.

4.0 REVISION HISTORY

Date	Revision #	Description of Change
03/18/09	1.0	Initial creation.

5.0 INQUIRIES:

Direct inquiries about this policy to:

Harold Jenkins, CIO
2900 Corporate Drive
Columbus, OH 43215

Voice: 614-555-1234
Fax: 614-555-1235
E-mail: hjenkins@company.com

Revision #:	1.0	Supersedes:	N/A	Date:	03/18/09

[G] Using Computers to Solve Computer Problems—Automated Asset Detection

Asset management is a time consuming process—finding things, counting them, categorizing them and then totaling them. It is boring and time consuming. Time is required for the original count and then to keep it current. Consequently it tends to be a special occasion when a count is taken and considerable effort expended. This "snapshot" is useful in the short term but, as time goes on, is less and less reliable. Since IT is in the automation business—of converting tedious manual effort into quick machine based tasks—why not use computers to do the work? How would such an automated solution work? Is it confined to servers and mainframes, or does it reach down into PCs, PDAS and other devices? How low will it go? As always, before selecting a solution, clearly define the problem.

There are several problems with attempting to manage software assets. Asset management often focuses on physical objects. Controlling physical objects is important but somewhat easier since they can be seen and counted. However, even the sharpest IT technician cannot look at a server and say what software is loaded on the disks. To identify the software, directories must be searched and someone must know what package each of the executables represents. Again, this approach is only suited to an inventory snapshot.

An automated tool can quickly pay for itself just through the efficient management of software licenses. Most IT shops are a jumble of old and new versions—heavily used software and "residual" packages that were just copied over from the old server. An automated tool can determine:

A. How many copies of software are on the many servers and workstations? This number is essential for:
   1. License compliance reporting.
   2. Estimating vendor maintenance costs.
   3. Has someone recently loaded a non-standard package?
B. Is this software still needed?
   1. Can any of the software be turned off? Existence of software may create maintenance costs for something that no one uses. This is tricky when some packages run in the background to support other applications. In many situations, it is so difficult to establish true need that system administrators leave these tools in place "just in case" they are needed. An expensive insurance policy.
   2. How much is something being used? Can some of the light users share fewer licenses?
C. What version and patch level are the various packages?
   1. How does a company ensure that all copies of a particular software package are at the same patch level? Sometimes a package supporting other software cannot be upgraded. For example, if software used SQL Server 2000, it may not be able to use SQL Server 2005.
   2. How does a company detect when an older version of a package has been recently loaded "somewhere"? The financial payback from a successful tool may be immediate. Turning off unneeded licenses can halt monthly maintenance expenses for services not needed. Further, this savings compounds over time. An automated check also reduces the likelihood of being caught "under-licensed" for a product.

The central problem is how to search through the various devices to collect what is there. This is accomplished by collecting the various directories and system files that detail hardware and software installed. The tools selected must accommodate all of the various technology types in a given IT department. Typically, this is Windows Server OSs, UNIX, Linux, Solaris, mainframe and workstation operating systems.

> ## Comment
>
> The content of the inventory database is highly confidential to the company. Some software has known vulnerabilities. If a hacker knows that a particular server is running behind on its patches, his focused attack will have a greater chance of success.

Automated inventory tools use a central collection server, and some way to gather the information. Gathering falls into agent based and agentless systems. Whichever approach is used, the primary obstacle is navigating through the company's data security processes so that all devices can be examined.

A. **Central Collection Server.** The central server receives inventory information from the various workstations and servers. The information is compared against a database of known applications to identify which software they represent, and which entries are data files. The result is a database of hardware and software detected in the IT system.

There may be a set of rejected entries that are either data files or unknown software, such as home grown programs. These must be added to the recognition database to avoid flagging them as unknowns in the future. The remaining unknown entries must be researched. This effort is heaviest when the software is first set up.

The database of known software is ever changing. As software vendors add versions, patches, etc., this information must be updated. Typically, automated asset reporting vendors will provide a weekly download. It may be easier for the collection server to connect to the vendor and request the file instead of permitting the vendor to directly send it down through the firewall.

B. **Agent based.** Agent based asset information collection installs a piece of software (the agent) on each device where data collection is desired. The agent collects data throughout the day (especially on software usage). Once per day, this data is sent to the central server and the local file is purged. Overall, the agent and file place little burden on the server or workstation.

The primary complaint about agent based systems is the cost of the agents plus the fact that a different agent must be purchased to execute on each of the various technologies supported (workstation OSs, server OSs, etc.).

C. **Agentless.** Agentless data collection uses the central collection server to check the many devices and collect the data. The collection server checks the various devices at a pre-set rate to collect the data. This works best in a small to medium sized environment. Large environments running an agentless system must tier their collection servers since a single server may lack the capacity if usage data is also collected.

Life being as it is, every time something is saved (by not loading an agent), something else is increased—in this case, the complexity of data security. Security is more of an issue with the agentless approach. Where an agent based system is sending data out of a server, security is less of a hurdle. However, for the central server of an agentless server to "touch" so many devices requires opening a lot of security doors that may be difficult to maintain.

D. **Reporting.** Once the automated inventory system is complete, the reporting part is easy. IT Asset Managers can now detect when something is loaded onto a server or workstation. They can provide a count of how many copies of a software package are installed and compare it to their license count. When a software package is eligible for an upgrade, an estimate of the work required and sites affected can be made.

This reporting is valuable for tying asset use to those who benefit from it. It may be that a product is so little used that it does not justify the cost of its monthly maintenance. Reporting is also valuable for providing ad hoc information about software usage so often requested out of the blue by company executives.

§ 17.05 SOFTWARE ASSETS

[A] Overview

The IT Manager will keep current with software developments in the IT profession and proprietary software development. If there is (IT or user) beta testing, the status and results will be reported to the members of the committee.

A. **Approved software.** Approved software sanctioned by the IT Manager will be found on the approved computer software list. The software has been used, tested, and approved by the IT programming unit and the information systems software committee. Being on the approved computer software list means it will be available to users or information systems staff. The only question is whether to charge the software to the information systems budget or a user budget. This question will be addressed by corporate policy.

B. **Requesting software.** Software licenses cost money to purchase, to support and sometimes in monthly licensing fees. The IT Manager must safeguard the company's interest and prevent casual purchases. The unit manager requesting the software sends a request to install the software on an identified computer or computers.

Typically, requests for exemption are for:

1. **Other software.** If software is not on the list and is needed, look for it on the asset management software database. If the software is available and approved to be used, it will be installed on the end user PC.
2. **Special software needs.** There can be a special need for software that is neither on the approved computer software list nor on the asset management software database. The end user is required to resolve any software problems with the vendor. If the software gains acceptance, it is placed on the approved computer software list and the service desk will support the software.

C. **Unauthorized software.** Employing unauthorized software can be a very expensive experience for the company. The IT Manager is responsible for policing all company computers for any unauthorized software whether it is in use or not. Just the software's presence on the hard drive can create a problem.

D. **Antivirus procedures.** To start an antivirus procedure, no software will be brought into the firm that does not belong to the firm. Even authorized disks will be checked for viruses before they can be brought into the firm's work area. This includes newly purchased software prior to its release to the users. The antivirus device will contain the latest version of virus protection. Downloading of any Internet information without specially granted permission is absolutely prohibited.

E. **Approved computer software list.** The approved computer software list contains software approved for user acquisition, including approved software operating systems and company-developed software. To discourage the use of any unapproved software, service desk support will not provide support to any unauthorized computer or user.

The asset management software database lists all software that is permitted to be in use and by whom. Proprietary software can be on the asset management software database (i.e., software developed by members of the firm and owned by the firm). Users who may have a problem with this software will contact the person(s) who developed it.

[B] Software Copyright Compliance Planning

Software not in compliance with the authorized ownership puts the company in jeopardy of lawsuits by the manufacturer of the software and/or its distributor. It is imperative the IT organization has the full support of top management to develop and maintain a policy of software copyright compliance. Document and publicize the plan throughout the company. This in itself will provide credibility; the company has a policy in place and will not tolerate any infraction. Maintain records of employees punished for knowingly violating the policy. Always hold offenders liable for costs incurred by their actions.

The IT software asset manager has responsibility for enforcing the unwarranted use of copyrighted software used illegally within the company. There are software packages on the market that can assist this process, and vendors who will undertake a continuous or one-time contract.

One easy way to control the number of copies of software is to retain the disks after loading the programs. Tag them with the name of the person whose machine they were installed on, along with its asset tag number.

COMMENT

Sometimes it is difficult for IT Managers to draft a policy that clearly states the company's position on unlicensed software. The fear is always that an audit will find the policy to be inadequate and little better than no policy at all.

The Business Software Alliance (*www.BSA.org*) provides sample policies covering this area that address *all* of the important points. It is found at:

www.bsa.org/resources/upload/Sample-Organization-Software-Policy.doc

A companion document is a memorandum for employees reminding them of the company's policies on unlicensed software.

www.bsa.org/resources/upload/SAM-Companion-Employee-Memorandum.doc

18

PERSONAL COMPUTERS: MANAGING THE DESKTOP SYSTEM

§ 18.01   OVERVIEW
    [A]   Purpose and Scope
    [B]   Critical Policies to Develop Based on This Chapter

§ 18.02   PC COORDINATOR
    [A]   Overview
    [B]   Responsibilities of the PC Coordinator
    [C]   In-House Consulting Service
    [D]   PC Training
    [E]   PC Newsletter

§ 18.03   PC ACQUISITION PROCEDURES
    [A]   Scope
    [B]   Hardware Acquisition
    [C]   Software Acquisition
    [D]   Communications Acquisitions
    [E]   Database Access Acquisition

§ 18.04   OPERATIONS PROCEDURES
    [A]   Overview
    [B]   Acceptable Use
    [C]   Personal Hardware and Software
    [D]   PC Security
    [E]   Operation Rules and Procedures
    [F]   Backup Procedures
    [G]   PC System Crash
    [H]   Peripheral Device Operations Procedures
    [I]   Accessories and Supplies
    [J]   Disposal of Excess Equipment

§ 18.05   END-USER TECHNICAL SUPPORT
    [A]   Overview
    [B]   The Resident Expert
    [C]   Computer Technician

[D] Software Support
[E] Computer Ergonomics Support
[F] Service Desk
[G] Maintenance Contracting

§ 18.01 OVERVIEW

[A] Purpose and Scope

Personal computers make up a major share of today's IT assets. In most offices, there is at least one PC per person and more when including PDAs and notebook PCs. The cost of personal computer software and data within it now overshadows the cost of the hardware. The proper management of these assets is critical if companies are to gain maximum benefit. The responsibility for maximizing PC utilization falls squarely on the information services department.

Current technologies make PCs seem like a series of interchangeable building blocks to be mixed and matched at will. This is definitely not true. Internal software drivers, ROM-based software, design assumptions, and interactions with other software makes introducing new components a tedious task. The PC coordinator will carefully select hardware components that are compatible with the installed base to ensure that they will work as envisioned.

To maximize the company's benefit and minimize its cost, the PC coordinator will recommend to the IT Manager a series of policies governing the purchase and use of personal computer assets. These policies will reduce the variation in desktop systems making their support and repair possible for lower cost and with fewer people.

[B] Critical Policies to Develop Based on This Chapter

Using the material discussed in this chapter, you will be able to create the following policies:

A. Duties of the PC coordinator.
   1. Standardization of hardware and software.
      a. Hardware, such as PCs, servers, network devices, printers, and monitors.
      b. Software, including that which resides on network devices, telephone equipment, and computers of all sizes.
   2. Workstation replacement strategy.
   3. PC training and troubleshooting services.
B. Acquisition policies.
   1. Approved hardware and software.
   2. Management of software licenses.
C. Operations policies.
   1. Acceptable use of computer equipment.
   2. Daily operations procedures.
   3. Backup procedures.
   4. How accessories and supplies are managed.
   5. Managing portable devices.
D. End-user computer committee.
   1. Responsibilities.
   2. Organization.
E. End-user technical support.
   1. Hardware and software support policy.

    2. Network support policy.

    3. Maintenance contracting.

Policies should always be developed based on the local situation. Successful managers cannot issue appropriate guidance if the policies are written with another company's or location's situation in mind.

§ 18.02 PC COORDINATOR

[A] Overview

The PC coordinator's duties and responsibilities will vary from one location to another, depending on needs. Whatever title this person has, the objective is to ensure that PC policies meet existing business needs and are enforced. Many companies create this assignment to provide a single point of contact for all activities and information pertaining to PCs. This provides a "single voice" that consistently issues the same information. The PC coordinator recommends policies relating to personal computers to the IT Manager for approval.

[B] Responsibilities of the PC Coordinator

The PC coordinator ensures that the company's investment in personal computers achieves its full potential. The person assigned the position of PC coordinator will have a wide range of responsibilities, including:

    A. Recommends a list of hardware and software for the company to standardize on based on its existing assets, its current business needs, and the strategic business direction of the company. Accompany each item with a note of why it was selected. All existing items in the same product class (such as word processors) will be grouped together with the recommended replacement. The narrative also should state which existing items in the company assets inventory it replaces.

    B. Creates and maintains a three-year workstation strategic direction list for hardware and software migration. The IT Manager approves the final list. Base the recommendation on the existing asset inventory, emerging technologies, and emerging business requirements. Update the plan annually.

    C. Processes requests for new hardware and software in a timely manner. (If the PC coordinator's review becomes a major delay in the process, people will find ways to avoid it.)

    D. Keeps abreast of the latest hardware and software technologies and problems through review of trade press and by attending trade shows.

    E. Provides an ongoing hardware and software troubleshooting service for users to handle day-to-day operating problems. This includes management of outside hardware repair services.

    F. Provides informal and formal training assistance for PC users.

    G. Enforces policies regarding PC hardware and software operations, to include actively seeking out and deleting unauthorized software.

   H. Provides backup service for critical PC data.

    I. Provides PC LAN service and/or supervision.

    J. Works closely with the service desk to detect systemic problems with PC processes and products.

   K. Publishes a newsletter detailing PC user successes, known problems and their workarounds, and tips for easier computing.

   L. Assists the IT Manager in identifying end-user applications for conversion into IT applications.

  M. Identifies critical end-user files that must be moved to the server for data backups.

[C] In-House Consulting Service

The PC coordinator is the in-house consultant for users of PC hardware and software. The person in this position assists users in understanding the capabilities of their systems and advising them how to use them for maximum performance. In this role, the PC coordinator constantly strives to demystify the technology by using nontechnical terms to describe technical functions.

The network manager identifies the standard for PC and network communications to ensure continuity and compatibility of the PC systems. The PC coordinator ensures that all workstations connected to the network use equipment approved by the network manager.

PC access to mainframe databases should require approval by the coordinator before contacting the database administrator and/or data manager. The PC coordinator should try to match requests to existing data views. End users should only access corporate databases in a read-only mode and are never allowed to update corporate databases.

The coordinator should maintain a daily log, which is the data source for monthly activity reports. Depending on cost accounting practices, users may be charged for the time they use. The daily log should record, by user charge code, time spent on the following items (travel time also will be included):

   A. PC hardware troubleshooting.

   B. PC software troubleshooting.

   C. Informal and formal training assistance.

   D. User consulting service.

   E. The coordinator's indirect (administrative cost) time can be kept in the following categories:

      1. Reading and other education methods used to keep up with current technology.

      2. Communication network services.

      3. Web site use and maintenance.

      4. Publishing newsletters and other information.

      5. User education and training preparation when not charged to a given department.

      6. General administration duties, etc.

> **COMMENT**
>
> Most sites use trouble tickets issued by the service desk instead of an activities log. Both serve the same purpose. This data can be used to demonstrate service levels, work load, problem trends, etc.

[D]   PC Training

The PC coordinator arranges for PC training on all company standard hardware and software. The goal of this training is to raise user productivity and satisfaction with the tools provided to them. It is a waste of company resources to drop off a new PC loaded with software on someone's desk and hope he can master it on his own. Training leverages the equipment investment by showing the basic as well as advanced features to all employees. Offer training on the standard products in three levels:

A. **Basic.** How to start and navigate through the basic features of the product.
B. **Intermediate.** How to manipulate data, import, export, and build complex reports. Most users stop at this point.
C. **Advanced.** A thorough explanation of all product features for those users who are constantly running this software.

Training is a time-consuming process. Not everyone is suitable as a trainer. Many people lack the patience to work through the issues with users who do not seem to understand the technology. Those people who do have the patience often find this position very rewarding. To accommodate employees' busy schedules, provide training in several ways:

A. **Read the manual.** Software comes with two basic types of manuals. The first type is for reference only. Use it to look up steps for performing specific functions. It is not very good for learning about the product. The second type is a training book that walks the user through the product from beginning to end. The problem with this second type of manual is that there is no one to ask questions and it may take a long time to find the answer.

> **COMMENT**
>
> Software is cheaper without the manuals. Many third party books are cheaper and easier to follow than the

> manufacturer's manuals. Set up an account with the local bookstore to provide manuals as requested. A $30 self-help book (from a list of recommended titles) costs about the same as a service call.

B. **Self-paced.** Some companies purchase self-paced software that users use to walk through the product at their own pace. This may be available to them in a central "walk-up" facility or they might start the software from their own desk. There is the same issue of who to ask specific questions about the product.

C. **Classroom.** This is the best way to instruct a group of people over a short period, but there is the added expense of an equipped classroom and an instructor.

COMMENT

> A fully equipped training center has many other uses. It can provide a test area for new software since the testers are within earshot. With additional telephone jacks, it can provide an emergency operations center for disaster recovery.

D. **One-on-one.** Personal tutoring is the typical way that executives learn how to use the features of their PCs. This is the most time-consuming method, but the PC support staff often provides personal mentoring on specific issues.

A major tool in the training program is a dedicated training room. This room should be equipped with one PC per student, plus a PC for the instructor. The instructor will require a projector to display the PC screen on the wall where all can follow along. The classroom should be isolated from the production network to prevent accidental corruption of corporate data. Reload the training room PC hard disks to the basic configuration at the end of every class.

Whenever the training room is not in use, anyone should be able to walk in and access self-paced training. However, the ideal way to access self-paced training is from the individual's desktop. This way they can do small portions of the training throughout the day. However, if there are too many interruptions throughout their day, they could use the PCs in the classroom.

The PC coordinator should manage the PC training room schedule. Anyone wishing to use the room for any purpose should schedule it through the PC coordinator. This avoids conflicts with scheduled classes.

COMMENT

A training center attracts strange classes. One author's training center was used for self-paced training for volunteer firemen!

Offer PC training in a variety of ways:

A. Purchase blocks of "tickets" to a local training facility and distribute them to people who require training. This has the added benefit of getting them off site and away from distractions. This is the best path for supporting non-standard products.

B. Hire a full-time training company. This works if there are many people to train, an equipped training room is available, and the training company has a pool of instructors who can cover all of the company's primary products. When the instructors are not in class, use them for one-on-one instruction. They may also develop courses on in-house developed software.

C. Hire college teachers on an as-needed basis. Most college instructors are available on an hourly basis for work outside the college. For most PC products, these people can teach the material they have already developed for use at the college! They may also develop training sessions for in-house-developed software or new PC software upgrades. Again, an equipped training room must be available to do this.

D. Promote training provided in the evenings by local colleges on the standard PC tools. Make schedules available and assist employees in filing claims for tuition reimbursement.

A major issue for providing training is when people reserve seats in a class and then do not show up. This prevents others from scheduling to attend training. Establish a training policy such that anyone who makes a reservation and does not show up (and stay for the class) still pays for their portion of the instructor's expense.

COMMENT

For training conducted on site, half-day classes seem to work best as it allows time for the students to address pressing matters in their normal jobs.

Training is the IT department's best tool for raising user productivity and satisfactions. Good training is the number one defense against a deluge of simple questions to the service desk. In addition, after the service desk solves a problem, they may recommend to the PC coordinator that specific people receive additional training or that specific topics need better coverage in class.

To back up the training, the PC coordinator should maintain a library of reference material for use on a walk-up basis. This allows the IT staff and end users to investigate issues and find better ways to do a task. This library should include a complete set of manuals for every approved product (past and present).

The PC coordinator's office should be near the training center and easily accessible to all users. It is important that users feel comfortable in approaching and discussing issues at any time during business hours. Obtain basic support equipment for a PC training operation:

- Whiteboard, which can double as a projection screen.
- PC projector.
- Tabletop lectern.
- Flip chart (floor model).
- VCR, DVD player, and monitor.
- Supply items: nonpermanent color markers, flip chart paper, camera supplies, and erasers.

[E] PC Newsletter

Most companies still create and distribute company newsletters. Most of the paper newsletters have shifted to a web-based format, which is cheaper to distribute. PC coordinators must maintain an open communication channel with users. This makes them more approachable by the "shyer" users.

A newsletter is a great place to spread the good news about maximizing desktop tools. It is also a valuable communications tool for the service desk to explain ways to address common and systemic problems. If many users experience the same problem, workarounds can be detailed here. This is a great outreach tool for proactive issues, such as pending upgrades. Let everyone know what is coming and when. Publish the training schedule so everyone knows what is available. Remember the target audience and keep the style conversational; stay away from technical jargon. If a dedicated newsletter is too burdensome, add articles to the facility's newsletter. In any event, keep the flow of communications consistent.

§ 18.03 PC ACQUISITION PROCEDURES

[A] Scope

PC coordinators are responsible for the inventory control of all PC hardware (desktop, notebook, and hand-held) and software acquisitions. They also assist users with all future hardware and software requirements.

Forward purchase requisitions for PC hardware, software, and service or consulting contracts to the information systems department's PC coordinator who approves the purchase requisitions, then forwards them to the purchasing department. Use purchase requisitions only for approved budgeted expenditures.

[B] Hardware Acquisition

The information systems manager sets the standards for PC hardware acquisitions. The fewer the variations in personal computer hardware there are in the company, the easier it is to maintain the existing base and to test new items for future use. The PC coordinator recommends to the IT Manager a list of hardware and software that meets the company's needs in the most reliable and cost-effective manner. Create a policy stating that all PC purchases must conform to the approved product list.

An approved products list allows companies to focus their buying power on a few products and drive down the price. It also simplifies support requirements since there are fewer products for the IT support staff to master and eases the testing and rollout of new products since the desktop units are similar.

To ensure purchases adhere to the list, the purchasing department should forward to the PC coordinator any requests for PC products they receive. Once the PC coordinator verifies that the product is on the approved list, return the purchase request to the purchasing department for processing.

There are many valid business reasons for deviating from the approved list. If a requested item is not on the list, the PC coordinator should call the requestor for an explanation. Sometimes there is a valid reason to purchase copies of very old hardware or software if the migration to newer technology is too expensive. Some departments, such as engineering, may require unique products to achieve their business goals. The approved product list is a guideline that should restrict the majority of users with the option that the IT Manager can make exceptions to meet business needs. Before approving an exception, the PC coordinator should explore standard solutions with the users to see if they fully understand the capabilities of approved products. All deviations to the list must include a plan for providing ongoing training and support for that item.

Hardware that deviates from the list must include an explanation of who will repair it and how much it will cost. If the device will support a critical function, then the user must pay for an on-site spare machine as a quick backup (a function that the PC coordinator provides for standard units). Once IT approves the purchase of non-standard hardware, they assume responsibility for maintaining it just like any other device.

Some PC coordinators take the stance that since they are unfamiliar with non-standard hardware they should not support it. This sounds like a spoiled child. The PC coordinator exists to support the customers in satisfying *whatever* might be their business needs. If their needs are for an unusual item, then the local IT staff should make a "best effort" to support that item and know who to call for help if the problem is beyond their technical abilities.

Suggested procedures for hardware acquisition include:

A. **Approved hardware purchases.** Departments with budget approval for hardware expenditures complete a purchase requisition and forward it to the PC coordinator, who checks the equipment against the approved hardware listing. If the equipment conforms to the current standard, the purchase should be approved. (Refer to Policy ITP 17-2, Hardware Asset Management.)

   If it is not on the approved list, the PC coordinator should call the requestor for clarification as to why an exception is needed (often they do not realize what is available). If the requestor cannot provide a satisfactory explanation and is adamant about the equipment desired, then the purchase requisition is forwarded to the IT Manager with a note explaining the problem.

B. **Hardware loans.** It is very handy to have equipment to loan as needed. It is a very unpopular job holding borrowers to their commitments to return it on time, and with all of its pieces. If departments frequently need to borrow equipment for things such as road shows, temporary offices, etc., then consider establishing their own pool of equipment. It is usually more cost effective to maintain a company owned equipment pool than it is to rent equipment.

   Departments requesting a loan of hardware from the PC idle assets room should send a memo or e-mail to the coordinator with the following information. (In the event of an emergency, a telephone call will do.)

   1. What is to be loaned? Include a checklist of accessories (consider a notebook PC and its charger cords as one kit), such as cables and power supplies that must come back with the unit; otherwise, there will be a delay before loaning it again. Be sure to include any important software beyond the standard office tools.
   2. Expected length of time for the loan. A firm return date is critical.
   3. Reason for the loan.
   4. The department and person requesting the loan.
   5. Where the equipment will be used.
   6. The person who will be using the equipment.

   The person to whom the equipment is released should complete an "out card" that shows the date, time, equipment loaned, serial number, and to whom it is loaned. This card should be signed by the receiving person and filed, by date, under the requesting department. When the item is returned, the card should be signed and dated by the person returning the item. The "out card" file should be reviewed once per month. Delinquent borrowers should be contacted. Cards for returned items should be held on file for one year.

   If the item is damaged, it should be noted on the card, which will become the source for a damage memo report completed by the PC coordinator. This memo should be sent to the department manager of the borrower. Arrangements should be made to repair or replace the piece of equipment. The PC coordinator should decide the cost, if any, that will be charged to the borrower's account for the repair or replacement and ensure borrowers have removed their data and reload the system's standard configuration promptly on its return before shelving it.

C. **Notebook and hand-held PCs.** Company-owned notebook and hand-held PCs are useful because they allow a user to take the computer to the problem. As prices have dropped and computing power increased, notebook PCs are now considered as alternatives to desktop units in many offices. Companies spend a considerable amount of time maintaining security on their premises. Once a notebook PC leaves this shelter, it becomes highly vulnerable to theft and damage.

Before allowing notebook PCs to leave the premises, determine whose insurance covers loss or damage. If a notebook PC is stolen from someone's car, whose insurance covers the theft? If a notebook PC is damaged (and they are quite fragile), who covers the repairs? How much responsibility does the user have for safeguarding the unit?

Besides the loss of the hardware, notebook and hand-held PCs also contain company data. This hits the company in two ways. Before a notebook or hand-held PC leaves the company premises, a safety copy of the data should be made and left inside the facility for the following reasons:

1. The loss of use of data will delay whatever work was being done.
2. Company-confidential data can be compromised. What seems to be a random theft may have actually been industrial espionage. Why break into a building with all of its guards and security cameras when the most sensitive files can be read by stealing the CEO's notebook PC at an airport?

COMMENT

There is security software available for the most sensitive notebook and hand-held PCs that encrypt everything on the hard disk every time a file is saved. This extra layer of software may slow system performance but keep the company's secrets off the front page of the newspaper.

D. **Peripheral Device Acquisition Procedures.** The policies and procedures for the acquisition of peripheral devices should give clear guidance on how these devices are brought into the organization. Areas that should be covered by such policies include:

1. **Budgeting procedures.** Specify the budget from which these devices are to be purchased. How are repairs and replacements handled?

2. **Requisition procedures.** How are requisition requests handled?
3. **Purchasing procedures.** Document the procedures for making the actual purchase.
4. **Receiving procedures.** How are the devices received in the organization and placed into inventory?

See Policy ITP-18-1 Peripheral Device Acquisition Procedures as an example.

POLICY ITP-18-1 Peripheral Device Acquisition Procedures

Policy #:	ITP-18-1	Effective:	03/18/09	Page #:	1 of N
Subject:	Peripheral Device Acquisition Procedures				

1.0 PURPOSE

This policy defines the process for the acquisition of non-PC electronic peripheral devices.

2.0 SCOPE

The policy applies to all portable peripheral devices that interface in any way with the corporate systems. This includes PDAs, cellular phones, USB flash drives, pagers, and any other device capable of storing corporate data.

3.0 POLICY

The following guidelines will be followed for managing peripheral data devices:

3.1 Budgeting Procedures

Peripheral devices are budgeted as part of each department's budget. Each department submits its expected needs for the following year's budget. This is based on the last year's budget plus inflation, replacement of old equipment, and new needs. It is supported by the use of the current equipment and forecasted use for the next budget year.

Budgets must be created for supplies and replacement of current equipment. Departments with their own hardware for one-of-a-kind use will require a budget for maintaining the equipment.

The information systems department will create a budget for general corporate support. This department creates a budget for capital expenses benefiting the whole company plus a replacement parts budget. In addition, a vendor service budget is required.

3.2 Requisition Procedures

Budgeted items must have a requisition issued. The requisition goes to the IT asset manager to confirm it meets standards or requires a standards waiver.

The need for the device is evaluated just as any new device that has access to the corporate network.

The requisition is approved and sent to the budgeting department so it can adjust the records. It is then sent to the purchasing department.

3.3 Purchasing Procedures

Purchasing receives the approved purchase requisition. If needed, they will take care of the competitive bids for the item. After the purchase order is sent to the vendor, a copy is sent to receiving and accounts payable.

3.4 Receiving Procedures

The agent for the asset manager or a special order item representative inspects the item for approval. After it is approved, a receiving notice is sent to accounts payable.

The asset manager's agent affixes a tag to the device and records the information. The information is sent to the asset manager.

4.0 REVISION HISTORY

Date	Revision #	Description of Change
03/18/06	1.0	Initial creation.
02/12/08	1.1	Modified section 3.4 Receiving Procedures

5.0 INQUIRIES

Direct inquiries about this policy to:

Harold Jenkins, CIO
2900 Corporate Drive
Columbus, OH 43215

Voice: 614-555-1234
Fax: 614-555-1235
E-mail: hjenkins@company.com

Revision #:	1.1	Supersedes:	N/A	Date:	02/12/08

COMMENT

The research firm IDC estimates that 68 percent of PDAs are bought by individuals or given as gifts. Only 10 percent were provided by an employee's company.

[C] Software Acquisition

It should be company policy that information systems management has control over all company software. To ensure system compatibility and to avoid interoperability problems, purchase all software from a list of approved products. The PC coordinator drafts the list for approval by the IT Manager. A standard software products list enables the support staff to focus on a few vendors for better price and support.

Unlike most hardware, software typically requires training for users to become productive with it. Standardize on a few software packages. This eases both training and employee mobility within the company since all departments use the same basic tools.

Larger companies may purchase a software license for a certain number of machines. A variation is purchasing a "site" license for unlimited copies at a single site. The PC coordinator will administer any per-seat or site-licensed software according to the terms of license, to include loading software on the appropriate systems and tracking the number of copies installed.

Departments must not bypass this process by purchasing their own software. Doing so introduces new support costs that were not apparent when the purchase was first considered. Controlling the purchase of software is an important part of a company's software license compliance (antipiracy) program.

Software may be developed in-house or acquired from an outside source. Only consider in-house software development if commercially available software cannot be found for less than the in-house cost. The availability of in-house programming personnel is also a consideration. The coordinator, who decides whether the actual programming effort is done in-house or contracted out, makes arrangements for any in-house-developed software. Charge the cost of this effort to the requesting user's department budget.

Software can be purchased for multiple users or a single user. Most software is purchased from vendors for a one-time cost, while some is only available for an annual fee. In addition, upgrades are generally available for a single user or multiple users. Purchased off-the-shelf software is available in two forms. One is for the horizontal market, for widespread use across many different kinds of firms. Examples would be word processing or spreadsheet software. The other is for the vertical market, that is, for applications pertaining to given industries. This kind of software may be more flexible because, in some cases, the source code is available, making it possible to alter the program to meet the user's own needs.

It is the coordinator's duty to seek newer and better software. (Refer to Policy ITP-17-3, Software Asset Management.) Maintain a published list of approved software, continually updated with equipment newly approved to respond to new needs. Only approved software may be used.

A part of the PC coordinator's technical advisor role is to include a budget for training, especially if software is for several people. It reduces the number of service desk calls, raises user satisfaction, and ensures the company's investment returns benefits as quickly as possible.

Suggested software acquisition procedures are as follows:

A. **Specially developed software.** A user requiring software that is not available by purchase works with the coordinator to define the needs. The coordinator then submits a memo to the person responsible for PC programming systems and provides enough information so that a project proposal can be developed and the cost estimated. (In some cases, the PC systems programmer and the coordinator may be the same person.) Project proposal information is reviewed with the user requesting the program. If time and money are available, a written request is issued by the user management. Program development is handled using the standard procedures for information systems program development. As long as no security problem exists, the new software is made available to other PC users.

B. **Purchased software.** The user sends a memo requesting the approved software to the coordinator who reviews the request and, upon approval, sends the software to the requesting party. An internal charge is made to the requesting department's account. If the software license is not available for reuse in the idle assets stock, the coordinator will issue a purchase requisition on behalf of the requesting department, which is forwarded to the purchasing unit. When the software is ready to install, send a copy of the class schedule to the requesting department along with the software manuals. Since this is from the approved software list, a class should be available. If no local classes are available, see if local colleges offer continuing education classes and forward their schedule and registration forms.

   It is critical that the PC coordinator maintain software licenses in a fireproof file cabinet, preferably off site. In case of a disaster, those copies can be used as authority to reload software into replacement PCs without repurchasing it (often the manufacturer will even send a "gold" disk if there is adequate documentation). This license file is a primary company defense in case of a software audit. It is evidence for buying upgrades instead of purchasing new software.

C. **Software registration.** All software registration will be collected, completed, and mailed by the coordinator in the company's name.

D. **Software library.** Copies of in-house-developed PC programs and the original licensed software, as well as backup copies of other purchased software, are maintained in a software library. Users with one-of-a-kind software are encouraged to store backup copies here as well. All software will be the most current version in use. Disks out of the shrink-wrap may require bug fixes. The library ensures the latest stable version is provided. The same applies to manuals' errata sheets. The library is under the control of the PC coordinator.

E. **Software demo disks.** Software demo disks will be provided to users requesting them. These can be provided by vendors or developed in-house, and are not charged to the user's account. Preferably these will run on a dedicated PC, as demos may introduce subtle configuration problems and not all software uninstalls cleanly.

The software library may provide an opportunity for potential users to try software before obtaining their own copies. The library also contains proper documentation and user instructions so that software may be tested. The PC coordinator may be called on to demonstrate software or demo programs to potential users.

[D]   Communications Acquisitions

The company's data network analysts will identify acceptable network cards to be used in personal computers. These cards will be selected based on industry reliability and data throughput reports. The network analysts also will document and forward to the PC coordinator the proper operating system and driver settings for these cards for each supported operating system. No user is permitted to change the operating system network settings.

PC communication systems require some planning, by both the potential user and the coordinator acting as resource person for acquisitions. The coordinator must maintain an information file of network hardware and software needed when considering future acquisitions or upgrading. There are a variety of network systems today including wired, wireless, and even one employing power supply lines as the transmitting media. Remote network users (mobile or home offices) use modems or the Internet to link with network systems.

For many years, the number of modems in companies grew and grew. Eventually, modem pools were established that could be accessed over the network. Most of this modem traffic has been replaced by virtual private network (VPN) communications over the Internet. If applications require modem communication, be sure there is an analog telephone connection at the point it will be used. Send a request to the PC coordinator along with an explanation as to for what it will be used. The user is supplied with "approved" modem hardware and software with the required (or a higher) transmission rate and installed by the coordinator.

Connectivity over the Internet is replacing information systems host-based systems. Remote connection to a network opens the door to viruses and hackers. Ensure safeguards are in place and that there are no backdoors to the system administration account that could be used to load unauthorized software, etc.

One of the remaining major areas for modem requests is for employees to remotely access their e-mail and network files while they are away from the office. People will require access through the firewall via a login process. Some companies automatically set this up in all notebook PCs assuming they will be used away from the office often.

[E]   Database Access Acquisition

Database access is an important part of personal computer management since most end-user-written PC programs are for report writing. Arrange database access through a database administrator to ensure the query is efficiently coded. All corporate database updates must be by way of IT developed or approved programs.

The coordinator also arranges for new PC users to access the database and provides them with training and an operations manual that explains the programs being used and what each of the data elements represent. Normally, database access front-ends are provided to prevent the uneducated user from "dimming the lights" with poorly designed queries. Including a data dictionary explaining the contents of a field will improve reporting. Ambiguous field names should never be used.

§ 18.04 OPERATIONS PROCEDURES

[A] Overview

PC (desktop, transportable, notebook, and hand-held) operations use recommended manufacturers' operations instructions as outlined in the manufacturers' manuals. These manuals should be supplemented with those provided by the information systems PC coordinator, which can be purchased or written in-house.

[B] Acceptable Use

Acceptable use policy explains the appropriate use of company assets. A personal computer is an incredibly versatile thing. It can be used to draft documents, add numbers, draw pictures, communicate over long distances, and on and on. A company's acceptable use policy outlines the activities that the company identifies as acceptable uses of its equipment. It also details activities it specifically forbids.

Acceptable use policies are an extension of the pre-computer days. In those times, gambling pools were kept on a pad of paper, pornographic pictures hung on the walls, or piles of personal catalogs might be on a desk. All were forbidden on company property as distracting employees from work.

Today, a PC can do all of that and much more. Companies must publish a policy to remind employees of the ways this tool can be used that are acceptable to the company's management. Publishing this policy and ensuring all employees read and understand it provides a tool in the event that abusing employees need to leave the company. See Policy ITP-18-2 Acceptable Use Policy as an example.

POLICY ITP-18-2   Acceptable Use Policy

Policy #:	ITP-18-2	**Effective:**	03/18/09	**Page #:**	1 of N
Subject:	Acceptable Use Policy				

1.0 PURPOSE

This policy describes the acceptable use of company computer equipment.

2.0 SCOPE

This policy applies to all users of information technology within the company.

3.0 POLICY

Employees are responsible for exercising good judgment regarding reasonable personal use.

    A. Physical security.
1. Employees are required to safeguard all company equipment assigned to their exclusive or shared use, and all company equipment within their work area.
2. Employees traveling with notebook computers will always carry them in carry-on baggage and not in checked baggage.

    B. Information security.
1. Data created on company systems remains the company's property. The company cannot guarantee the confidentiality of information stored on any network device.
2. Any information considered sensitive or vulnerable must be encrypted.
3. For security and network maintenance purposes, individuals authorized by the IT Manager may monitor equipment, systems, and network traffic at any time.
4. Secure all PCs, laptops, and workstations with a password-protected screensaver with the automatic activation feature set at 10 minutes.

    C. Self help.
All users of company equipment are expected to take charge of their own training:
1. Attend in-house classes provided by the IT department.
2. Review and become familiar with software documentation.
3. Take night classes at the local college on software use (reimbursable through the company's tuition assistance program).

    D. Unacceptable use.
1. Employees are never authorized to disable the anti-virus software on their work station.
2. Hacking systems and databases or acting to disrupt systems or cause unnecessary network congestion or application delays.
3. Use of remote control software on any internal or external host personal computers or systems not specifically set up by the IT staff.
4. Any use of computer equipment that violates state or U.S. law and regulations.
5. Creating or forwarding of chain mail regardless of content, sources, or destinations. Posting company information to external newsgroups, bulletin boards, or other public forums without authority.
6. Using company equipment for personal profit, political fundraising, gambling activity, non-business-related instant messaging or chat room discussions, and downloading or display of offensive material.

4.0 REVISION HISTORY

Date	Revision #	Description of Change
03/18/09	1.0	Initial creation.

5.0 INQUIRIES

Direct inquiries about this policy to:

Harold Jenkins, CIO
2900 Corporate Drive
Columbus, OH 43215

Voice: 614-555-1234
Fax: 614-555-1235
E-mail: hjenkins@company.com

Revision #:	1.0	Supersedes:	N/A	Date:	03/18/09

[C]   Personal Hardware and Software

It must be a firm company policy that no one is permitted to bring into the facility any hardware or software that was not purchased through the normal acquisition process. This is to prevent inadvertent damage to corporate systems from well-meaning but untested equipment or software. Along this same line, no one is permitted to load personal software on company-owned hand-held or notebook PCs, or to add any hardware upgrades to them. Enforcing this policy will reduce the likelihood of introducing software viruses or hardware incompatibilities into the company's processes.

[D]   PC Security

Theft of hardware is bad, but the cost to reproduce the data lost with the unit could be more than the value of the equipment. Locate desktop PCs or any stationary PC in a secure environment. Employees assigned mobile equipment assume full responsibility for safekeeping both the hardware and the software. Preventing unauthorized access to any PC system should be of utmost concern to all employees.

Due to their light weight and small size, notebook PCs are very vulnerable to theft. A special pass should be attached to notebook PCs with the owner's photograph on it so guards can easily check them out of the facility.

Physical location. The room where computers are kept should be locked when not in use. If not possible, seriously consider employing a cable lock to deter any removal of the desktop computer hardware. Keep portable computers in a safe place at all times, including when the hardware is in transit. Handle all portable computers as "carry-on luggage" while on public transit.

If a desktop PC is moved to a new permanent location within an area under the jurisdiction of the coordinator, the coordinator should be informed in writing within 24 hours of the move. If the new area is not under the jurisdiction of the current coordinator, the coordinator must approve the move before it takes place and inform the asset manager and the new area's coordinator. The PC coordinator ensures there is adequate electrical and network connection available in the new location prior to moving the equipment.

Access security. Stationary PCs with a modem or network and/or hard drives with any restricted information should be required to have one of the following:

- A lock.
- An access security board with a lock-slot so the board can use a cable security system.
- Personal access code software (in the event the PC does not have an available slot for an access security board) or use of a screen-saver password.

Software and data security. Software disks held centrally should be stored in a locked place. Data disks and backup tapes and disks should be stored in a PC media safe or other such comparable device if so warranted by the data administrator or coordinator. Where practical, data backups should be stored off site for protection. Encourage users to back up their data directories to the network, which will in turn be backed up daily and the media stored off site.

[E] Operation Rules and Procedures

The following are rules and procedures that apply to the operation of all PCs:

A. PCs should be rebooted at least once a week for reliable operation. Daily rebooting is recommended for critical systems.
B. In areas with a higher than normal amount of airborne dust, dust covers should be used for PCs, keyboards, monitors, and other attached devices when not in use.
C. No food or beverages on or near the hardware or software.
D. No smoking near the hardware or software.
E. A clean, cool, and dry air working environment is recommended for the computer.
F. Keep magnetic devices away from the computer, disks, and tapes.
G. Plug all computers and peripheral equipment into a surge protection unit. Do not permit other electric devices to be plugged into the surge protection outlet or into the same wall plug with the surge protection device. Use only grounded electrical outlets. Plug company-critical equipment into an uninterrupted power source (UPS) with a signal to shut-down the PC before the UPS batteries die.
H. Illegal copying of software is never permitted.
I. No hardware or software may be removed from the firm's premises without the coordinator's written permission for each occasion.

Portable computer systems used outside the workplace require a permission letter or ID card signed by the manager to be kept with the system at all times. The permission letter/ID card identifies who has permission to use and carry the authorized equipment and software. It also will contain the serial numbers of the units authorized and identifies the software contained in the system.

J. No hardware or (including portable equipment) software will be loaned to noncompany persons.

K. Removable media will be kept in their disk containers or storage unit when not in use.

[F] Backup Procedures

Backup procedures may vary within the same company. Not all data and software have the same value (although it is better to be safe if not sure). The following procedures are recommended:

A. **New software.** The PC coordinator who retains all the original media should install new purchased software. If subsequent upgrades require access to the media, they must be coordinated with the PC coordinator. This step is to reduce the company's liability of someone making illegal copies of the software that it owns.

B. **Hard drive backup procedures.**
   1. At the end of each workday, all new data should be backed up onto network drives or tape. Some active transactions (e.g., word processing, billing) will need to be backed up more often.
   2. A backup copy of the hard drive data should be maintained on the network disk or tape.

C. **Removable media data.** When data is kept on removable media (e.g., floppies, Zip disks, CDs) and not on a hard drive, the disk is copied for backup. The two copies of the data are never stored together. It is recommended that the backup copy be write-protected.

D. **Storage.** All data copies will be stored securely as soon as they are made.

COMMENT

The U.S. Post Office in Washington backed up its PCs daily. But when the ninth floor of the building burned, so did its PCs and the backups that were stored in the desks under the PCs.

[G]   PC System Crash

In case of a PC system crash, the operator writes down what occurred just prior to the crash and the time of the crash, and then calls the service desk for assistance. The machine should be left on, ideally with the error message displayed. Post a sign on the computer stating that the system has crashed and it is not to be used. Portable computers should be taken to the PC coordinator.

[H]   Peripheral Device Operations Procedures

Peripheral devices cover a wide range of applications and complexities. The total investment in these devices can be difficult to track and is not known in most companies. More important, the data kept on these devices is difficult to track and control. Meanwhile, most of these devices operate without a central sense of direction. Without the orchestration and guidance of information systems, their costs continue to grow while their efficiency diminishes. A major part of controlling these devices is the procedures set forth by an IT department within well-thought-out policies.

> **COMMENT**
>
> According to a 2006 report by Ipsos Insight, 28 percent of mobile phone users worldwide have browsed the Internet using their phone.

Information systems is responsible for maintaining and enforcing a company-wide software application policy for all supporting devices. The acceptable application software list should be maintained in the asset management software database and updated monthly by the information systems software committee. Installation of unauthorized application software should not be permitted. Service desk support should not be provided for unauthorized application software.

Most devices are configured by default to power on with no security. If supported by the device, a password must be entered when the device is powered on. The password should be the same as the password used by the user when logging into his personal computer or corporate network domain. Make sure the data is encrypted if supported by the device.

> **COMMENT**
>
> Roughly one out of five users lost a mobile device in 2005, according to a report published in Innovations (Winter, 2006).

See Policy ITP-18-3 Mobile Device Usage as an example.

POLICY ITP-18-3   Mobile Device Usage

Policy #:	ITP-18-3	**Effective:**	03/18/09	**Page #:**	1 of N
Subject:	Mobile Device Usage Policy				

1.0 PURPOSE

This policy defines the acceptable use of mobile devices within the organization, specifically the protection of important corporate data stored on such devices. This policy is also designed to protect the corporate network from being infected by any hostile software when the mobile computer returns. This policy also considers wireless access.

2.0 SCOPE

The policy applies to all mobile devices used by employees that are at any point connected to or share data with the corporate network. This includes laptop computers, PDAs, cellular phones, and portable data devices.

3.0 POLICY

The user of the mobile device will accept responsibility for taking reasonable precautions in protecting the data on the mobile device and agrees to adhere to this policy. The mobile device user will not be allowed to have administrative rights on the network unless granted special exception by the network administrator. The user of the mobile device agrees not to use the mobile device for personal business and agrees to abide by the organizational computer usage policy. Any device that is connected at any time to the corporate network must adhere to the following:

A. Devices connected to the corporate network must be determined to be a benefit to the organization rather than convenience by the designated IT manager.

B. Any mobile device that can store corporate data must support encryption of the data; corporate data on mobile devices must be encrypted at all times.

C. All mobile devices owned by the organization or allowed on the organization network must be identified by their MAC address to the IT department before being connected.

D. The mobile device operator must be identified by name and contact information to the IT department.

E. The mobile device operator must be familiar with the organization's acceptable use policy.

F. Devices not owned by the organization are subject to a software audit to be sure no software that could threaten the network security is in operation. All computing devices are subject to a software audit at any time.

G. Mobile devices capable of taking pictures are not allowed in sensitive areas of the company.

4.0 REVISION HISTORY

Date	Revision #	Description of Change
03/18/09	1.0	Initial creation.

5.0 INQUIRIES

Direct inquiries about this policy to:

Harold Jenkins, CIO
2900 Corporate Drive
Columbus, OH 43215

Voice: 614-555-1234
Fax: 614-555-1235
E-mail: hjenkins@company.com

Revision #:	1.0	Supersedes:	N/A	Date:	03/18/09

COMMENT

Not just PCs are vulnerable to hackers. Cell phone manufacturer Nokia reported in February 2004 that several of its Bluetooth-enabled phones were vulnerable to attack, which could result in a hacker gaining access to personal data stored on a targeted phone (as reported in *eWeek*, February 20, 2004).

A. **Personal Data Assistants**

A PDA is a small hand-held computer used to write notes, track appointments, contacts, and otherwise keep your life in order. Some PDAs require data to be input using a keypad with keys the size of Chiclets, but other models (e.g., the Palm Pilot or Palm PC) use a combination of pen-based input and character recognition software to accept user input. Many can also be used to send and receive e-mail and browse the Internet. Information in the PDA can be synchronized with data in PC-based applications such as Microsoft Outlook.

Information systems is responsible for determining the manufacturers and models of PDAs that should be supported. At no time should personally purchased PDAs be allowed to be used and supported due to security concerns.

COMMENT

The popularity of PDAs can prove a headache for corporate IS departments. Palm and Windows Mobile have long targeted enterprise customers, touting the benefits of employees connecting remotely to corporate databases of information via their hand-held computers. According to Ken Dulaney, vice president at Gartner Group, the influx of new products, designs, and technologies will add 10 percent in technical support costs.

Information systems is responsible for maintaining and enforcing a company-wide synchronization policy for all PDAs. A standard synchronization package should be selected that supports all the different PDAs in use at the company. The applications and data to be synchronized must also be determined. It is desirable to use synchronization software that can be administered from a single server to control what is being transferred to and from the PDA. Other items to consider include:

1. **Filtering of data**—Information systems must determine what subset of data records is to be synchronized with the PDA. Filter setting can protect sensitive data that should not be synchronized and can be used to save time by transferring only data that is actually needed.
2. **Field mapping**—This is used to map fields from the PC application to the PDA application. Information systems must create standards for which data fields can be synchronized and where they map between the PC and the PDA.
3. **Conflict resolution**—Data kept on both a PC and a PDA have conflicts when data is changed in one or both places. Establish policies to resolve these conflicts.
4. **Control at the server**—Some synchronization products allow settings to be controlled at a central server. This also makes it possible to synchronize over the LAN without being connected to a PC.

The use of PDAs makes good data backup procedures even more critical, as there are more opportunities for data to be changed inadvertently. Verified backups before the first synchronization are very important in case there is a problem during the synchronization process.

PDA users are notified that the data on the PDA is valuable and sensitive company information, and must be protected. All PDAs should be password-enabled with encryption turned on, if available, to prevent unauthorized access to the data if the PDA is lost or stolen. Some PDAs with remote access capability can now be erased remotely if lost or stolen—check to see if your devices support this feature.

COMMENT

Intellisync from Puma Technology synchronizes data from all Windows-powered Pocket PCs, hand-held PCs, and Palm devices with a broad number of PC-based personal information management (PIM), contact management, and groupware applications using advanced features such as conflict resolution, filtering, and field mapping. Intellisync supports Microsoft Outlook, Microsoft Schedule$^+$, Lotus Notes, Lotus Organizer, Novell GroupWise, Symantec ACT!, GoldMine, Meeting Maker, and other PC-based PIMs.

B. **Cellular Phones**

An Internet-enabled cell phone allows users to access the Internet using their cell phones. Information systems is responsible for maintaining and enforcing a company-wide usage policy for all cell phones. Use should be monitored periodically to ensure the phones are used for business-related purposes.

Cell phone users should be notified that the data on the cell phone is valuable, sensitive company information and must be protected. All cell phones should be password-enabled (if possible) to prevent unauthorized access to the data if the cell phone is lost or stolen.

Another issue to consider is the proliferation of cell phones that are capable of taking and transmitting pictures. These phones can be a huge security risk, especially in sensitive areas of the company. You may need to ban the use of cell phones in sensitive areas to protect against unauthorized images being taken using these devices.

COMMENT

According to Pointsec Mobile Technologies (now a division of Check Point), 60 percent of information theft results from lost or stolen equipment; only 25 percent from network

> intrusion. They have developed a picture-based password entry process that makes passwords easy to remember, yet discourages users from making a hardcopy of the password. Pointsec can be reached at *www.checkpoint.com*.

C. Wearable Computers

A wearable computer is a small computer that is designed to be mobile. The system is worn. This differs from a PDA, which is designed to be carried and used by being held in the hand. A wearable computer is normally worn on a belt, with optional peripherals including a wrist-mounted touch-screen display, voice-enabled headset, and a head-mounted monitor. They are sometimes integrated into a person's clothing. Wearable computers are especially useful for applications that require computer support while the user's hands, voice, eyes, or attention are actively engaged with the physical environment. Such applications include presentation of information to mechanics, military or paramilitary personnel, path-finding for the blind, real-time translation from one spoken language to another, and continuous medical monitoring.

Information systems is responsible for maintaining and enforcing a company-wide use policy for all wearable computers. Wearable computer users should be notified that the data on the wearable computer is valuable, sensitive company information and must be protected. All wearable computers should be password-enabled to prevent unauthorized access to the data if the wearable computer is lost or stolen.

Information systems is responsible for setting up processes for backing up data on all wearable computers. Procedures include standards for use of docking stations, connections to the LAN, and backing up data to a server. A directory on a server that is regularly backed up should be created for storing data and applications from the wearable computer. Instructions for backing up data and applications are created by information systems and provided to all users of wearable computers.

COMMENT

> IBM's Almaden Research Center is working on personal area network (PAN) technology, which uses the natural electrical conductivity of the human body to transmit electronic data. In the future, a user of PAN technology will be able to transfer information via touch rather than issuing typed commands or pressing buttons. For example, your computer might recognize you when you simply touch the keyboard. This capability could yield significant benefits in the areas of access control and data privacy.

D. **Flash Drives**

Flash drives have replaced the once ubiquitous floppy disk as the most common tool for copying and transporting files. They are inexpensive, easy to use, easy to transport, and hold large amounts of data. These attributes not only make them attractive to end users for legitimate transportation of computer files, but also cause a security headache for the security personnel responsible for protecting the organization's important data. The same device that allows a user to easily transport Word documents or PowerPoint files for work at home can also be used to carry viruses back to the office, or used to steal valuable corporate data.

Just as it is impractical to search everyone's lunch box as they exit a factory, it is impossible to search every employee and visitor as they leave the office. It is critical that the organization establish policies on the approved use of these devices to keep this risk to a minimum. These policies should include at least the following:

1. Define who is permitted to use flash drives and what types of data are permitted to be stored on these devices. Many organizations go so far as to prohibit the use of personally-owned flash drives with corporate-owned computers.
2. Procedures for copying files to and from flash drives.
3. Develop rules for vendors and visitors who want to use flash drives during presentations or visits to the organization.
4. Backup procedures for any data that is updated while on a flash drive.
5. Cover the use of flash drives as part of your virus and spyware policies for employees who use home or off-premise computers.
6. Create password and data encryption standards for flash drives. You may want to consider using biometrically protected flash drives for extremely sensitive data.
7. Institute a reporting procedure for notifying security in the event that a flash drive is lost or stolen.

COMMENT

One source of biometrically protected flash drives is Memory Experts International. They can be reached on the Web at *www.memoryexpertsinc.com*.

E. **Power Users**

A power user is a person who uses a particular device on a regular basis (usually daily) and becomes very knowledgeable about its operation. This person usually enjoys sharing information about using the device with others in the organization. Ask power users if they could be contacted if a new user needs assistance. If they agree, their names should be listed as power users with the instructions given to new users.

Power users should be able to operate and perform minor device adjustments. They should know how to replenish expendable stock items and perform standard housekeeping and preventive maintenance procedures. A power user can be walked through some of the malfunctions by the service desk or a maintenance person over the telephone. At the service desk, there should be a power user's location book with the power user's name, telephone number, and location listed. A second listing by location, with the power user's name and telephone number listed, is also helpful. This can be used to contact another power user who is close by for assistance when the nearer power user is not available.

F. **Peripheral Device Operations Procedures**

These are the operating procedures furnished to all device users. The IT service department or the systems and procedures department should furnish the operator procedure manuals. The manuals provide operator instructions, minor maintenance instruction, backup procedures, and procedures for troubleshooting. Minor preventive maintenance procedures should also be provided. If practical, the manual should be available on the company's intranet site.

The procedure manuals contain any manufacturer's furnished material helpful to clarify the device's operation. The illustrations used by the manufacturer could be beneficial to the operator. Close-up and wide-view photographs are helpful if included in the operator procedure manuals. A prototype manual should be developed and tested before it enters service. Use an unskilled person for the test. This should be done with more than one person. Avoid the brightest person in the area and any experienced operator for debugging the procedure manual.

[I] Accessories and Supplies

PC accessories can improve productivity, reduce fatigue, and improve morale. These accessories and supply items are on a "recommended" or "approved list" provided by the coordinator. The approved vendors will carry listed items. This information helps when ordering through the purchasing department. The approved list will be published, updated, and distributed by the coordinator.

PC supplies and minor accessories can, over the course of a year, amount to a large expense. Still, given the size of the items and the volumes, it is much easier to treat them as you would the pens and pencils in the office supplies. The PC coordinator should identify what items are acceptable (e.g., inkjet refills, toner cartridges) by brand and model, and purchasing will provide these items through their office supplies program.

Supply items can be purchased with the user's department petty cash fund or a budget requisition. They are requisitioned from the unit responsible for office or computer supplies according to standard operating procedure.

Accessories are classified in two groups: ergonomic devices and productivity aids. (The following items are not identified by brand name.)

A. **Ergonomic devices.** PC ergonomic devices are to help the human body interact with the PC system and function with the least amount of fatigue, error, and bodily harm. The following types of ergonomic devices are available on the "recommended list" provided by the PC store:
   1. Keyboard wrist rest.
   2. Mouse wrist rest.
   3. Footrest.
   4. Ergonomic keyboard.
   5. Arm support.
   6. Ergonomic, adjustable chair.
   7. Adjustable workstations for special employees.
   8. Radiation and/or glare monitor screen.

COMMENT

Remember to consider the requirements of the Americans with Disabilities Act when developing policies concerning ergonomic devices.

B. **Productivity aids.** The following, if used properly, have been known to increase productivity:
   1. Tilt-and-turn monitor stand.
   2. Copyholder (flex arm, attachable, or standard).
   3. Copyholder light.
   4. Diskette storage devices.
   5. Cartridge storage devices.
   6. Desktop printer stand and/or organizer.
   7. PC rollout keyboard system.
   8. Keyboard with mouse.
   9. Keyboard labels for F keys and/or other keys.

[J] Disposal of Excess Equipment

Office computer and other electronic devices contain hazardous materials such as lead, mercury and cadmium. Old CRT monitors are the worst offenders, containing up to five pounds of lead. With computer obsolescence accelerating, the volume of waste from discarded computers is growing at three times the rate of any other type of waste. It is projected that as many as 500 million computers were taken out of service between 2000 and 2007.

The Resource Conservation and Recovery Act (RCRA) was updated in 2004 to include guidelines regarding the disposal of computer monitors. The RCRA rules only apply if the equipment is disposed of in a landfill; they do not apply when recycling, donating the equipment or trading the equipment in when buying new.

> ## COMMENT
>
> Environmental regulations on disposal of computer equipment should not be taken lightly—in 2000, AT&T agreed to pay a penalty of $195,000 for not properly responding to an agency request for information about its computer-disposal practices.

Policies covering the disposal of surplus computer equipment should mandate that all such equipment be disposed of properly. Computer equipment may no longer be needed for a variety of reasons:

A. Worn out or damaged.
B. No longer utilized.
C. Technical obsolescence.
D. Maintenance costs are excessive.
E. Replaced with a newer model.

These policies should cover all computer equipment that is capable of storing data. This includes PCs, PDAs, external hard disks, cell phones, etc. The policies should also outline the approved processes for disposal of the equipment. Possible disposal options include:

A. **Redistribution**—Every effort should be made to redistribute the equipment to another use within the organization. This may require minor upgrades to the equipment such as additional memory or hard disk capacity.
B. **Recycling**—Some computer equipment can be recycled or disassembled for parts for reuse in other equipment.
C. **Disposal**—Equipment must be disposed of in compliance with local and federal regulations.

Procedures must also be developed when equipment has been identified for disposal. The procedures should provide for consistent tracking and handling of the equipment. Before any computer equipment leaves the control of the organization, the procedures must ensure that all company software and data has been removed from the system. If any licensed software is eligible for use on another device, the software license inventory should be updated to reflect the availability of the license for use on another device. The software and data on any physical storage device must be destroyed using a method appropriate for the type of hardware, operating system, and the sensitivity of the data.

See Policy ITP-18-4 Computer Equipment Disposal Policy as an example.

POLICY ITP-18-4   Computer Equipment Disposal Policy

Policy #:	ITP-18-4	Effective:	03/18/09	Page #:	1 of N
Subject:	Computer Equipment Disposal Policy				

1.0 PURPOSE

This policy mandates that all surplus computer equipment be disposed of properly. Computer equipment may no longer be needed for a variety of reasons:

    A. Worn out or damaged
    B. No longer utilized
    C. Technical obsolescence
    D. Maintenance costs are excessive
    E. Replaced with a newer model

2.0 SCOPE

This policy covers all computer equipment that is capable of storing data. This includes PCs, PDAs, external hard disks, cell phones, etc.

3.0 POLICY

There are three approved processes for disposing of excess computer equipment listed below. They are listed in order of preference:

    A. **Redistribution**—Every effort should be made to redistribute the equipment to another use within the organization. This may require minor upgrades to the equipment such as additional memory or hard disk capacity.
    B. **Recycling**—Some computer equipment can be recycled or disassembled for parts for reuse in other equipment.
    C. **Disposal**—Equipment must be disposed of in compliance with local and federal regulations.

The following procedures must be followed when equipment has been identified for disposal:

    A. The department with the surplus equipment will notify the help desk and schedule a time for the equipment to be picked up.

B. The help desk will assess the condition of the equipment and determine the appropriate means of disposal.
C. Based on the disposal process selected, the help desk will:
1. Notify the appropriate department that the equipment has been removed from inventory.
2. Arrange the transfer of the equipment to inventory is it is being redistributed.
3. Arrange for the equipment to be picked up by the approved disposal vendor if being recycled or disposed of.

Before any computer equipment leaves the control of the organization, the help desk must ensure that all company software and data has been removed from the system. If any licensed software is eligible for use on another device, the software license inventory must be updated to reflect the availability of the license for use on another device. The software and data on any physical storage device must be destroyed using one of the following methods:

A. Both Windows 2000 and Windows XP provide a mechanism for repartitioning and formatting the original hard drive before installation.
B. Utilize a Department of Defense approved data destruction software following DOD guidelines.
C. Destroy the hard drive in a manner that does not allow the drive to be rebuilt. Options include crushing or shredding of the disk drive.

4.0 REVISION HISTORY

Date	Revision #	Description of Change
03/18/09	1.0	Initial creation.

5.0 INQUIRIES

Direct inquiries about this policy to:

Harold Jenkins, CIO
2900 Corporate Drive
Columbus, OH 43215

Voice: 614-555-1234
Fax: 614-555-1235
E-mail: hjenkins@company.com

Revision #:	1.0	Supersedes:	N/A	Date:	03/18/09

§ 18.05   END-USER TECHNICAL SUPPORT

[A]   Overview

End-user technical support is available in several forms. The information systems organization provides some forms of support. Different vendors provide other end-user support.

Payment for support services depends on company policies. The payment can come from one central source and/or department budgets. Whichever method is used, a record system will be maintained. The following sections cover the various types of end-user support available in most organizations.

[B]   The Resident Expert

Every business department seems to have at least one person with an aptitude for all things technical. This person is usually looking over a technician's shoulder whenever they come to resolve a problem or to tune a system. Early on the PC coordinator can choose to fight this person (and lose) or enfranchise them as an extension of the IT staff. The resident expert concept means that they will be asked to handle all of the simple problems that arise in a department. They probably already do so. In exchange, they will be given priority service, first chance at new software classes that open, ready access to the technical library, and help with tougher problems. A thorough resident expert program will reduce the volume of simple user error calls and open a wide channel of business user feedback.

[C]   Computer Technician

Computer technician is the title of the IT person who provides desk-side help with end-user computer and equipment problems. PC technicians work under the direction of the PC coordinator. In either case, the person in charge of this unit reports to the manager of information systems. The service desk contacts this unit when they cannot solve a PC problem. The problem may be with hardware, software, or a supply item.

The computer technician is always dispatched by the service desk (users are never given their direct telephone number). The problem-tracking database provides utilization tracking. The computer technician should carry a cell phone or pager so they can proceed to their next call without always returning to their desk first. This communications path also allows them to "drop and run" when critical systems are having problems. If there are multiple PC technicians, consider assigning them to the primary support of specific areas to better understand the users' needs. They can still support other areas but will have deeper knowledge of specific departments. Another way is to assign them by technology but this will confuse users. By nature, a PC technician is a generalist.

Computer technician skill requirements. The computer technician has general knowledge of the users' PC hardware and/or software uses, including supply items. The hardware and software are identified under their respective approved lists. For large, complex organizations, there are specialists for lesser-used equipment. The computer technician is called by the service desk if the computer operator has a problem the service desk cannot walk them through. It could be a problem where the computer technician requested a call to them the next time it happened.

It is important that computer technicians have a good understanding of their users' business to recognize a priority call. This helps them focus on critical issues and less on "squeaky wheels." The technicians need patient temperaments so they can help users through basic and embarrassing mistakes without alienating them. Computer technicians are IT's primary trainers since they can provide a steady stream of tips to users with whom they are constantly in contact. The technicians who run calls must have a quick connection to someone they can refer to for priority resolution (who do I see next?) and for backup in a crisis.

Computer technician resource requirements. The computer technician will be provided with a toolkit to cover the kind of hardware they will need to resolve problems. This will be carried in an attached case provided by the company. There will be a minimum of space for spare parts. Supply items that are often used should be stored close to the computer operation. Other items needed may be obtained by someone else, from the source, to save the technician's time. The computer technician also will be provided with a pager or mobile phone.

Computer technician's responsibilities. The technician will maintain a daily activity log. The computer technician should perform the following computer tasks at the user's site:

A. Replace faulty computer parts.
B. Perform hardware upgrades.
C. Check connection cords.
D. Run a virus check and remove any viruses.
E. Check operation of modem.
F. Reformat hard drive.
G. Reload operating system.
H. Load new software and confirm it is operational.
I. Install hardware accessories.
J. Perform routine diagnostics.
K. Remove any unauthorized software from computer.
L. Disconnect and/or remove unauthorized hardware. Turn over the unauthorized hardware device to the PC coordinator.

At times there may be hardware problems requiring the user's computer or attached devices to be taken back to the repair shop. If the time the equipment is away from its operating area becomes a problem, the computer technician will arrange for a loaner unit to be provided. The loan will be only for the time the user's equipment is not available. If the loaner is the functional equivalent to the old one, then leave it. Expect loaners that are superior to the old unit to be difficult to get back. Given the time necessary to copy files from the loaner back to the old unit, it may not be worth the fight.

The computer technician's work log. While working on any workstation, the technician should look for any illegal software. Any such software found is deleted and recorded in the log. Unauthorized hardware attached to the desktop computer will be confiscated and delivered to the PC coordinator. It also will be recorded in the daily log sheet. The PC coordinator acknowledges acceptance of the equipment by signing the computer technician's daily log sheet.

Weekly computer technician's report. The charge time will be portal to portal. The charge time is summarized by user, user's unit, and other duties not charged to a user. Any administration or other nonuser charge time is prorated to service calls. If the company has an interdepartmental charge system, the end-user's department is charged for the service time for the maintenance. How these costs are handled will depend on the company's accounting practice.

The computer technician writes a short weekly report to the PC coordinator. The report notes any special hardware or software problems occurring during the week. Any operator problems needing resolution will be recommended. Can the operator problems be remedied with operator training, new operation manuals, or equipment? If the operator problem deals with an ergonomics issue, state what the problem is in the report

[D] Software Support

There will be software that is not on the current approved computer software list, but is in the asset management software database. Some of the end users using software will be assigned to a computer technician if the service desk cannot be of assistance. The technician will pull the software file folder for the programs and review the documentation before going to the end user's workplace.

Computer technicians are not expected to solve all the end-user problems they encounter. There will be special hardware and/or software technicians who are not generalists. When the service desk contacts the IT unit for computer support, they will provide information to have the proper technician answer the service call.

COMMENT

Consider an outside support contract for critical software the team cannot support. For example, two vocal users needed PageMaker to build company newsletters. It was not feasible to train or hire a support person for them. Instead, an open purchase order was arranged for outside support as needed.

The asset management software database has the inventory information of legally owned company software. All software on the approved computer software list is on the asset management software database. Not all asset management software database programs will be found on the approved computer software list. The technician will not resolve all software problems for these programs.

A. **End-user computer software.** The software for end users is found on the approved computer software list. The service desk and the IT technical support unit support this software.

B. **IT computer software.** The software for the IT units is on the approved computer software list. The IT programming unit supports this software. Obviously, games, football pools, questionable photographs, etc., are not a part of the company's business and can be removed.

C. **Company IT unit's computer software.** Other IT units using purchased packaged software may call on the IT technical support unit for assistance. If the IT programming unit developed the software, it should be contacted for support. This software is in the asset management software database but seldom found on the approved computer software list.

D. **Special computer software.** All software is required to be in the asset management software database. This software can include several types of programs and may be supported by information systems. The question will be asked: How did the user come into possession of the software? Some special computer software, not on the approved computer software list but on the asset management software database, can be identified as follows:

  1. **End-user software still in use.** End users can use software that is no longer available but is still supported. The software may no longer be available on the market or is about to be replaced. Often this software was on the hard drive of the last PC which was on the hard drive of the PC before it. Users do not know why it is there but are afraid to remove it.

  2. **Software for special applications.** This software is purchased for specially approved application and/or hardware. The department that arranged to acquire the software is responsible for obtaining the needed support.

  3. **Software testing.** Software purchased by end users for testing will not be supported. The person who acquired the program(s) will seek support from the vendor.

  4. **Turnkey software operations.** The vendor will support contracts drawn for vendor-developed turnkey-operated systems.

[E]   Computer Ergonomics Support

If the company has an environmental ergonomics unit, it should be available to assist the information systems department. If the service is unavailable, consulting firms are available for this kind of support. Most ergonomic problems do not require a consultant. Someone is selected in the end-user technical support unit and trained. College courses and short commercial programs on ergonomics are now available. Books and periodicals also are available.

> ## COMMENT
>
> The Human Factors and Ergonomics Society is a national organization with local chapters. They can be reached at *www.hfes.org*. AliMed publishes an excellent ergonomics and occupational health catalog. They can be reached at 1-800-225-2610 or at *www.alimed.com*.

[F]   Service Desk

A service desk provides a central point of contact for all users who are experiencing a problem. A well-run service desk is critical to user satisfaction. In years gone by, users "just knew" who to call. If they had a computer problem, they left a message on a specific person's phone (usually a programmer) and waited for that person to call back. If that person was on vacation or out sick, they had no way of knowing. If that person did not know how to solve the problem, it did not matter, as they would find someone for the user who did. This was very personal customer service but with hit-or-miss results.

A service desk acts as a buffer between the users and the IT department. The service desk should be informed who will be out of the office, and when. They should have a matrix of who to call for support for each system first, who to call next, etc. The service desk technicians should resolve all of the simple calls that used to interrupt the kindly but very busy programmer. In an emergency, such as a network outage, all users call the service desk to get updates instead of each user calling his favorite programmer.

An early decision is the level of service the service desk is to provide. Its staffing level will determine how quickly a call will be answered. Certain times of the day will be busier than others so use a call-tracking database to chart the time of day and the day of week when call volume peaks. The larger the staff, the quicker the telephone can be answered and problems addressed.

The second decision ties closely to the first in that now that the phone is answered promptly, can the technician resolve the call? How much technical depth should be required of a service desk technician? One strategy is to use nontechnical (low-paid) people to answer the telephone, ask a few questions to identify whom to refer the call, and then pass on the message. In this model, the customer twiddles their thumbs and awaits a call from a technician. Another approach is to use technical people to resolve the questions as they come in and refer difficult problems to the appropriate technician. Both approaches work but which one is right for the facility?

Another question is if the service desk resides in the local facility or is provided by an outside company. The advantage of the inside service desk is that the people learn about the facility's operations, insider jargon, who works where, and allows the technicians an opportunity to be on a more personal basis with end users. The service desk also can take walk-up requests. Using an outside provider allows them to staff for the peaks and valleys but the company loses a great deal of control over who is answering the telephone.

With this trade-off in mind, consider that the person answering the service desk telephone will have more one-on-one contact with IT users than anyone else in the department. A bad experience calling the service desk will translate into a black mark on the entire IT department no matter how many times it is explained that these people are a contracted service.

Service desk calls tend to come in waves. During the quiet periods, the technicians can get a bit of rest and monitor vital system activities. This monitoring of network volumes, mainframe job flows, and the pattern of incoming calls provide the IT Manager with some early warning of data system problems.

Some companies rotate their programmers and PC technicians through the service desk during peak periods so they can listen to some of the user calls. This is a valuable opportunity for the service desk staff to learn more about their systems and for the programmers to hear some of the problems their systems cause end users.

A key cost driver for contracted service desk services is the level of service provided. If all that is expected is taking a message and asking a few scripted questions, then just about anyone—anywhere—can take the call. The result is to dispatch a technician. This is the model used by most public utility companies. This approach is synonymous with a simple answering service. Another cost driver is the required response time—how many rings before the call must be picked up?

But if service desk staffers are expected to provide some level of problem resolution during the initial contact, they need the ability to access data systems for troubleshooting. This may require an on-site office or a dedicated high-speed data line.

Security also is a major concern. High-volume calls for service desks are password problems. Since the service desk technicians need access to change these, they may pose a security risk.

Vendor contracting. After the bid proposals are received, they are compared with each other. Lowest bidders do not always provide the best service. Beware of startup companies without verifiable experience. Calculate the costs for providing the service in-house. This provides a baseline to evaluate the bids.

Write a short-duration flexible contract when beginning a relationship with a new vendor. This provides information to both the vendor and the company about the contents of the final contract. The company's legal representatives review the contract and make recommendations before it is signed.

In-house service desk. An in-house service desk often starts as a pilot project. As the bugs are worked out, it can accommodate more internal customers. Start an in-house service desk with a lump-sum budget. Record the number of contacts by unit and the time spent per contact. This will be helpful for future planning.

There are several ways to operate an in-house service desk. The one best method depends on corporate culture, union concerns, etc. The following things should be considered when operating an in-house service desk:

A. **Operations.** Record conversations to provide an audit trail of the dialogue between the user and the service desk technician. This reduces and simplifies note-taking by the service desk staff. Use a voice-mail system to avoid busy signals or no answer when calling the service desk.

B. **Facility.** The service desk work area provides rapid access to information needs. It is ergonomically suitable for the tasks of the service desk staff. The job is confining and any ergonomic assistance would help reduce the burnout rate for this job. A regular change or rotation of duties also would prolong the life of the service desk technician.

A service desk is a built-in feedback mechanism for finding out how the company's systems perform. Use the data!

The service desk's demeanor is critical. Users' opinion of the department will be greatly shaped by the service desk; they are the ones users talk to most. The service desk staff must be able to work under pressure. Abusive callers should be forwarded to the service desk supervisor.

[G]   Maintenance Contracting

All hardware may not be maintained in-house. In some instances, vendor equipment service contracting for some devices might be a better solution. Some peripheral devices are best maintained using vendor contracts. Some leased items include service agreements. Contracts can specify an unlimited number of service calls or charges on a by-call basis. Contracts can provide for spare parts or parts can be charged as installed. Some vendors can offer an array of equipment they can service. Service can be provided for normal working hours or around the clock.

There can be one or more service vendors. There are firms providing a full-service blanket for most hardware. Other firms service one or more machines. Consider these options when deciding the service best for the company.

Before any maintenance contracts are signed, the legal representative of the company reviews them. Upon approval, the authorized management personnel sign them. Purchasing is contacted regarding such contracts. The procedure followed will be the corporate procedure for contracting services.

Some things must use outsourced repairs:

A. Parts availability—They will not sell them to anyone.
B. Technical expertise.
C. Warranty work—Usually only good if the equipment is packed up and delivered back to the factory or to a salesperson. This may not be worthwhile in the case of PCs unless they can be removed from service and sent away.

Equipment with moving parts (like printers) has a higher ongoing maintenance cost than solid-state devices.

Using an asset database, compare the cost of a maintenance contract to the cost of buying several spare devices. Use spare devices to replace broken equipment and then send the damaged material out for service on a time-and-materials basis.

A key component of maintenance contracts is the hours of coverage. Normal working hours coverage is cheapest and "24×7" is very expensive. Keep in mind that this is response time—not maximum resolution time.

19

NETWORKS: THE GREAT FACILITATOR

§ 19.01   OVERVIEW
          [A]   Purpose and Scope
          [B]   Critical Policies to Develop Based on This Chapter

§ 19.02   NETWORK SECURITY
          [A]   Overview
          [B]   Network Design
          [C]   User Authentication
          [D]   Routers
          [E]   Corporate Firewalls
          [F]   Personal Firewalls
          [G]   Virtual Private Networks (VPNs)
          [H]   Wireless Networks

§ 19.03   THE NETWORK COORDINATOR
          [A]   Overview
          [B]   Network Support Responsibilities
          [C]   Network Disaster Recovery Plan
          [D]   Documentation

§ 19.01 OVERVIEW

[A] Purpose and Scope

Corporate data communication networks are an essential IT service. In most cases, if the network fails all work stops. Users expect the network to be as reliable as electrical service—plug in and there it is! Network administrators are victims of their own success.

Networks are popular because they make so many things accessible to desktop workstations. They are doorways into all sorts of the data processing tools. Some of these capabilities include:

A. Mainframe/server access—Instead of a separate dumb terminal on a desk, PCs run terminal emulation packages and can speak to all of the mainframes and servers.

B. Print sharing—Allows the company to buy fewer and faster printers. It also frees space on desktops.

C. Sharing files and folders—A central repository for shared information sources, similar to a department's filing cabinet and bulletin board.

D. Groupware applications—Software that allows users to collaborate on projects using tools such as shared calendars, text and video conferencing, electronic whiteboards, etc.

E. Internet communications through high-speed lines—Research is quicker; applications can be more easily distributed.

F. E-mail—Enables quick and short messages that are easily broadcast to many.

This list could go on and on. The key element is the sharing of resources enabled by the use of a network. If the network does not work, then all resource sharing ceases. A data network is a hugely complex beast. When all the different components of a network are considered—each with its own potential to fail—the fact that they work together despite being made by different manufacturers is a truly amazing thing.

Like all good things in life, bad things can happen to networks. Problems that can occur include:

A. PC viruses—These spread quickly through a network. Just as fast as someone can send a file or open a program, viruses can spread. To protect equipment against PC viruses, ensure that all data traffic that originates from external networks passes through an antivirus firewall. Similar to a firewall in a building (which stops the spread of flames), a network firewall provides a barrier against incoming viruses.

B. Illegal uses—The faster the communications, the faster someone can make illegal software copies.

C. Access to confidential files—An electronic filing cabinet is much less secure than the metal cabinet in an office. Ensure that user-specific and departmental file folders require user authentication to keep out the curious and the malicious.

[B] Critical Policies to Develop Based on This Chapter

Using the material discussed in this chapter, you will be able to create the following policies:

A. Network management.
   a. Identify the network coordinator.
   b. Define responsibilities and authority.
   c. Develop and test the disaster recovery plan.
B. Firewall maintenance.
   a. Create baseline configurations and apply updates.
   b. Periodically search for updates.
   c. Monitor access logs to identify problems.
C. Unauthorized network connections prohibited.
   a. IT must approve installation of all wireless access points, routers, and hubs.
   b. Non-employees may not attach their equipment to the network.
   c. Employees must never attach their personal equipment to the network.
   d. IT must periodically scan for unauthorized equipment.
D. Wireless Networks.
   a. IT must approve installation of all RF routers and equipment.
   b. Wireless routers must be encrypted.
   c. IT must manage the company's use of the network spectrum.
E. Password Management.
   a. Minimum composition of passwords.
   b. Frequency of password changes.
   c. Security of passwords.
F. Documentation.

Policies should always be developed based on the local situation. Successful managers cannot issue appropriate guidance if the policies are written with another company's or location's situation in mind.

§ 19.02 NETWORK SECURITY

[A] Overview

Network security is a balance between making it easy for authorized users to use the network and preventing access to the network by unauthorized users. One source of security issues is the connection of unauthorized devices to the network. With cable jacks scattered throughout the organization and the proliferation of wireless devices, it is imperative that the network be proactively monitored for unauthorized devices. Network security policies must clearly state that no unauthorized devices may be connected to the network. Any device to be connected to the network must be approved and installed by the IT department. The policy must outline the process for requesting new devices to be connected to the network and the penalties for noncompliance.

Some organizations include the attachment of unauthorized devices to the network in the list of offenses for which an employee can be terminated.

The network administrator must have a policy in place that requires the periodic scanning of the network for unauthorized devices and access points. Periodic scanning also can ensure that devices connected to the network are communicating properly and using the proper ports and protocols. By reducing unnecessary traffic a more efficient use of network bandwidth will be achieved.

Any unauthorized connections must be immediately blocked until the device is found and its purpose determined. Unauthorized devices may compromise network security; at a minimum, they have already bypassed the externally facing firewalls.

[B]   Network Design

A properly designed network architecture optimizes throughput and provides a multi-layered security blanket. It speeds throughput by isolating segments against system-wide broadcasts that are not addressed to them. It protects against external intrusion and internal attacks as well as the problems introduced by mobile workstations.

The outer security layer consists of the externally facing firewall, an intrusion detection system, and a VPN concentrator. This provides several benefits. The first is to detect and prevent network intrusions. The second is to scan the traffic flow to validate authorized users and detect potential problems. The third is to provide on-demand access to the network via the Internet for authorized external users. An important attribute of the outer security layer is its ability to scan all incoming e-mail and attachments.

The middle layer is the division of the company's network into virtual networks or subnets. This prevents problems in one part of the network from bringing the entire system down. It also prevents intruders from within the company from accessing confidential data by requiring permission to access other subnets.

The inner layer protects individual workstations; this includes personal firewalls and the all-important anti-virus software. The inner layer security recognizes that workstations sometimes bypass the other security layers inadvertently. For example, third-party e-mail such as Hotmail and Yahoo bypass the corporate e-mail firewall. Instant messaging also can bypass security as can USB flash drives and CDs.

As with all security software, the challenge is to ensure that all security systems consistently receive timely updates against the latest threats. If not updated, yesterday's safe-and-secure system will be tomorrow's open target.

[C]   User Authentication

Most data processing user authentication depends on the tried-and-true combination of user ID and password. In the beginning, passwords were treated with little respect. They were considered something handy but worthless to remember so they were often found on scraps of paper taped to monitors.

Over time, a sense of security and urgency gradually arose and passwords have become more closely guarded.

As office systems proliferated, a typical worker may have had four or more passwords to connect to the mainframe, Windows, the AS400, etc. Keeping track of all of these special codes was challenging enough and then someone decided for added security, they should periodically expire—all at different times.

This resulted in a lot of very frustrated people. They have too many passwords to remember and track. To ease the burden, in most cases, users were allowed to create their own passwords; however, their choices were often easy to guess by a determined hacker.

COMMENT

Ali Baba was cutting wood in the forest when a troop of robbers rode up. Quickly he hid in a tree. The robber leader walked to some brush and shouted (his password), "Open Sesame," revealing a magical cave full of riches. When the robbers left, Ali used the password, entered the caves and removed many bags of gold.

—Arabian Nights, Ali Baba and the Forty Thieves

Despite the use of user IDs and passwords, hackers just became more persistent and inventive. When they uncovered a user ID, they would try common passwords to see if one worked. This included words like "password," the company's name, and popular proper names. If this failed, they resorted to more tedious methods, including trying every word in the dictionary (less than 10 characters long).

Several steps can be taken to reduce the success rate of hackers:

A. Strong passwords are passwords that are case sensitive; at least eight characters in length; and contain at least one capital letter, one lower case letter, one number, and one special character. This reduces the likelihood of guessing a password, but because the user can create his or her own password, it is not completely secure.

B. System-generated passwords can provide for better security, but completely random characters are often hard to remember and the user will more than likely write it down and hide it nearby (e.g., under the mouse pad). A variation on this is to build "random" passwords that resemble nonsense words. For example, "ZOOmT!c" uses zeroes for "O's" and an exclamation point for an "I." The password is easier to remember because it can be pronounced "zoom-tic."

C. Another approach is to provide a numeric password that changes every 60 seconds. This depends on an authentication "token" device that fits on the end of a key ring. The internal electronics are tied to the user's ID and in sync with an authentication server. When the user logs on, he waits for the number to change (providing him with a full 60 seconds) and then he logs on. The authentication server at the other end of the connection matches the number and either allows or rejects the user's request.

D. The future lies in the use of attached biometrics devices. Rather than require a password, biometric devices can be added to a computer to scan the retina or read the fingerprints of the user. Hardware manufacturers already offer biometric readers as alternatives for passwords. For example, IBM offers a fingerprint reader as an option on its notebooks PCs. The biometrics identifier is something that cannot be lost or forgotten; however, they are not 100 percent reliable. Biometric devices offer an alternative to, but not a perfect substitute for, passwords.

See Policy ITP-19-1 Password Policy as an example.

POLICY ITP-19-1   Password Policy

Policy #:	ITP-19-1	**Effective:**	03/18/09	**Page #:**	1 of N
Subject:	Password Policy				

1.0 PURPOSE

The purpose of this policy is to establish a standard for the creation of strong passwords, the protection of those passwords, and the frequency with which passwords should be changed.

2.0 SCOPE

The policy applies to all corporate information system and telecommunication networks. It applies to all users of the organization's network, using any device that has access to the network.

3.0 POLICY

The following password policies must be followed for access to the corporate network:

A. General Guidelines
    1. All user-level passwords (e.g., e-mail, web, desktop computer, etc.) must be changed at least every 60 days.

2. User accounts that have system-level privileges granted through group memberships must have a unique password from all other accounts held by that user.
3. Passwords must not be inserted into e-mail messages or other forms of electronic communication.
4. All user-level and system-level passwords must conform to the guidelines described below.

B. Use a strong password that has the following characteristics:
1. Contains both upper and lower case characters (e.g., *a–z, A–Z*).
2. Has digits and punctuation characters as well as letters (e.g., 0-9, ! @#$%^ & * ( ) { } | [ ] < > ? /)
3. Is not based on personal information, names of family, etc.
4. Is at least eight alphanumeric characters long.
5. Is not a word in any language, dialect, slang, jargon, etc.

C. Passwords must never be written down or shared with anyone. If anyone demands your password, report them immediately to your supervisor.
D. Never use the "Remember Password" feature of applications such as Internet Explorer.
E. Passwords must be changed every 60 days.
F. Do not use the same password for your corporate network account as any used for any personal accounts.
G. Do not store your password in any device such as a PDA without it being encrypted.

4.0 REVISION HISTORY

Date	Revision #	Description of Change
03/18/09	1.0	Initial creation.

5.0 INQUIRIES:

Direct inquiries about this policy to:

Harold Jenkins, CIO
2900 Corporate Drive
Columbus, OH 43215

Voice: 614-555-1234
Fax: 614-555-1235
E-mail: hjenkins@company.com

Revision #:	1.0	Supersedes:	N/A	Date:	03/18/09

[D] Routers

A network router is a special-purpose computer that connects two or more network segments. Routers provide policy-based control, broadcast management, route processing, and distribution. Routers pass their day monitoring traffic on the network. They determine whether incoming packets are addressed for one of the attached network segments. If they are, that packet is then passed through the router. If that address is not on the router, the packet is ignored.

When passing packets, routers forward them via the optimum routing based on network "layer" information and router tables. These are often constructed using routing protocols.

Routers can selectively isolate locally connected devices from other network equipment. This might be every network device in one building or just in a single critical department. In large organizations, there may be many local area networks (LANs) connected to form a wide area network (WAN). The standard rule for this is where 80 percent of the traffic is between workers locally connected and only 20 percent is nonlocal traffic. Instead of all network traffic touching each device, the router screens out the superfluous traffic to allow faster throughput on the "quieter" network segment. Each of the local networks is behind a router that separates it from the wider network.

LANs are primarily based on physical location. To gain the same performance benefit for workstations and servers located on different LANs, a virtual LAN (VLAN) can be established. Devices connected to a VLAN behave as if they were on the same LAN segment even though they are connected to different LANs. Because the connection is based on a logical connection rather than a physical connection, the devices can be physically moved without degrading network performance.

[E] Corporate Firewalls

A firewall is a special-purpose computer designed to filter access to a network segment. It is a critical tool for securing networks against unauthorized intrusion. Firewalls are a one-way barrier that prevents traffic from entering but not from exiting. This characteristic means that a firewall "faces" the direction it wants to protect against.

COMMENT

In an office building, a firewall is a windowless wall constructed of thick, inflammable material. It greatly inhibits the passage of a fire and heat from one section of the building to another.

Firewalls can be internal or external. An external firewall "faces outward" and attempts to keep undesirable traffic outside the company's network. Generally, this is to prevent access by unauthorized users on the Internet. An internal firewall protects a network segment from unauthorized intrusion by a user authorized to be on the network or who has bypassed authentication security. This might be to protect a company's payroll and accounts payable systems or other confidential areas where access should be limited.

Firewalls are a prime hacker target since they must be overcome for an attacker to reach any of the company's data. A firewall uses an operating system that has been stripped to the minimal possible configuration. Small programs are then added to monitor and filter packets attempting to enter the network. Firewalls provide network filtering that is more sophisticated than can be provided by a router. The minimal operating system and specialized programs use programmable logic called "policies." This logic can allow or exclude certain IP addresses or users from the protected network. For example, all access may be prohibited except from specific IP addresses. Another example is to exclude any traffic originating from a range of addresses known to belong to spammers. This provides fewer opportunities for hackers to attack the firewall.

Firewalls default to one of two states:

A. **Default deny.** Unless the user is identified and accepted, he or she is not permitted to pass. This provides a higher level of security but also requires a higher level of administration because new users must be added and curtailed ones removed. This is typical for a company firewall.

B. **Default permit.** Everyone is allowed to pass unless they are identified as excluded. This is typical of an online retailer who wants customers to have access, but still wants to exclude those who are problematic.

Company firewalls are only one component of a comprehensive company security strategy. A single dial-out modem that bypasses the firewall can be the back door that a hacker needs to gain access. This must never be permitted. Firewalls can only work on packets passing through them. If they are bypassed, the company may not realize why its networks are so polluted with unauthorized outside access.

[F] Personal Firewalls

Home computers are not immune from attackers and greatly benefit from a personal version of a firewall. Few homes would purchase a dedicated PC to monitor their network, so personal firewall software is configured to run on the home user's PC. The home firewall screens out unwanted sites and provides a log of access attempts.

In addition to a personal firewall, virus scanning software is an important tool for workstation protection. Working together, they are the most common protection for a personal workstation. Both of these technologies must be regularly updated to protect against emerging threats.

How is this relevant? Consider the number of sales staff, field engineers, and others who connect to the Internet while they are outside of the corporate firewall-protected network. As these portable units move around they must be protected from the networks to which they connect. Also, many people take their work home on disks to work on after hours. The cleaner these machines remain, the lower the likelihood they will be the source of a problem.

[G]   Virtual Private Networks (VPNs)

The greatest exposure for a user is when data packets are passed between the user's workstation and the server. Personal data, sensitive corporate data, and passwords may be passed between a workstation and a server. Any of this data could be intercepted and misused. To reduce the likelihood of this occurring, companies establish an encrypted communications link called a virtual private network (VPN). Firewalls are an important part of a VPN design. VPNs pass data packets between a workstation and a server as if they went through an encrypted tunnel.

To obtain a VPN session, the requester provides some sort of identification. The firewall interacts with an authentication service inside the perimeter. The client and the firewall negotiate an encryption key that is used to encode all traffic for the duration of that session. Your network policies should include the use of a VPN for all communication with the corporate network via the public Internet.

[H]   Wireless Networks

Wireless networks are a wonderful advancement. In the past, wiring and rewiring offices was a tedious process. An office network that exclusively uses wireless networking not only eliminates wiring, but makes workers readily mobile. Unfortunately, this advancement comes with a price because intruders may tap into the signal and monitor traffic.

Wireless networks must provide multi-layered security. The greatest threat is interception.

All wireless traffic should be encrypted, preferably using WPA2 (wi-fi protected access). SSID broadcasting should be turned off so that the name of the wireless network must be known before it can be used. Your policy should also include SSID naming conventions to follow.

A dark side of wireless networks is the ready availability of inexpensive wireless routers. Cheap to buy and easy to install, they can be silently added to the network. IT must regularly monitor the network to seek out these rogue wireless routers and remove them. Unauthorized access points may conflict with authorized network traffic and may permit nonsecure network access. In addition, there are many low-cost or free wireless sniffers available that intruders also may use to monitor network traffic.

If using a wireless network, the IT department also must manage the company's use of the radio spectrum. Many devices depend on the 2.4 GHz frequency band, including cordless telephones and remote controls. To avoid conflicts and interference from other devices, the IT department should investigate and resolve frequency conflicts to the company's best advantage.

Before installing or extending a wireless network, a radio frequency (RF) survey must be conducted. This involves monitoring the presence and strength of signals at various points in the facility. This will identify the areas with existing signals and "dead spots" in the existing RF network, thus allowing IT to evaluate whether to replace the sources or to work around them.

See Policy ITP-19-2 Wireless Network Policy as an example.

POLICY ITP-19-2   Wireless Network Policy

Policy #:	ITP-19-2	**Effective:**	03/18/09	**Page #:**	1 of N
Subject:	Wireless Network Policy				

1.0 PURPOSE

The purpose of this policy is to define the standards and procedures for the use on wireless networks with the company. It is designed to ensure reliable and secure operation of the wireless network, and to protect the security of the company's information resources and electronic communications.

2.0 SCOPE

The policy applies to all uses of wireless local area network (WLAN) technologies at all locations of the company. It does not apply to cellular wireless technology. All information technology policies that apply to standard wired networks also apply to all wireless networks.

3.0 POLICY

The CIO or his or her designee is responsible for establishing and enforcing all WLAN technology standards. Any WLAN installation or use that varies from this standard must be approved by the CIO.

The IT department will be the sole provider of design, specification, installation, operation, maintenance, and management services for all wireless access points. Employees may not independently install or operate WLAN access points in their departments.

Only company employees and authorized visitors may use the company WLAN; exceptions must be authorized by the CIO or designee. All company WLANs must be configured according to security standards established by the CIO. The IT security department will be responsible for managing the security of the company WLAN. All WLAN communications must be encrypted. All wireless devices using the company WLAN must be registered with the IT security department.

SSID broadcasting must be turned off on all wireless routers. In addition, the following SSID naming conventions must be followed:

A. Personal information or department identifying information must not be part of the SSID.

B. The SSID must contain both letters and numbers.
C. The SSID should be as long or nearly as long as the maximum length allowed.
D. Change the SSID every few months.

4.0 REVISION HISTORY

Date	Revision #	Description of Change
03/18/09	1.0	Initial creation.

5.0 INQUIRIES

Direct inquiries about this policy to:

Harold Jenkins, CIO
2900 Corporate Drive
Columbus, OH 43215

Voice: 614-555-1234
Fax: 614-555-1235
E-mail: hjenkins@company.com

Revision #:	1.0	Supersedes:	N/A	Date:	03/18/09

§ 19.03   THE NETWORK COORDINATOR

[A]   Overview

Every company has someone who supports its network. Large companies have large teams, while small companies may have one person who works part time. However the network is managed, that person (or the team) needs to be formally appointed, with his or her duties and authority clearly identified.

[B]   Network Support Responsibilities

The position of network coordinator is technical by nature and is responsible for network components and servers. In a small office, this position may be merged with that of the PC coordinator, which means he or she will manage both the network and the end users.

The network coordinator should have a detailed understanding of networking equipment capabilities and topographic design. He or she should be expected to monitor and troubleshoot network traffic throughput problems. The coordinator also should monitor network usage (internal and external traffic) to ensure adequate resources are always available and that anyone using an excessive amount of resources is investigated (it could be an early indication of a serious problem).

The network coordinator should establish and maintain the anti-virus firewall to ensure all traffic is properly filtered. This tool requires regular updates. In addition, the coordinator should schedule off-hours scans of the network servers to protect against "infected" files that may have been loaded onto the network by authorized users. The network coordinator also should establish and maintain trusted connections with other LANs in the company for the easy exchange of information.

At times, the company may be asked to open the firewall to allow access by a vendor to support some application or piece of hardware. The network coordinator should first evaluate the risk of granting these requests. If the risk is acceptable, the coordinator also must determine the best time for the temporary firewall drop, which will depend on network infrastructure limitations and the availability of resources.

Other network coordinator responsibilities should include:

A. Analyzing current usage and projecting future growth to ensure adequate hardware, network, and software capacity.
B. Providing information and service for users.
C. Being a source for operation documentation.
D. Providing needed backup hardware and software.
E. Being a knowledge source for user applications.
F. Ensuring the physical security of network components.
G. Establishing the security profile for all new users, making changes as required, and removing security access from departing employees.
H. Authoring the network portion of the disaster recovery plan.
I. Providing on-call support for after-hours problems.
J. Maintaining computer security procedures.
K. Maintaining an operation performance problem log.
L. Checking for unauthorized devices connected to the network.
M. Checking for unauthorized changes to device configuration.

[C]   Network Disaster Recovery Plan

As previously stated, a company's data network is an integral part of the company's daily activities. To assist in the prompt recovery of this vital service after a disaster, the network coordinator must create and maintain a network disaster recovery plan.

A disaster recovery plan is a narrative of the steps necessary to recover the network in a different facility in the event that the current company facility becomes unusable—or if it is partially or entirely destroyed. No plan can address every possible scenario, but it should outline the steps to be taken in any major emergency.

The plan must include a copy of the current network topology. Although a network recovery may likely be in a different facility with a different physical layout, the topology will form the basis for wiring the new spaces.

The network plan must include a list of the vendors needed in an emergency; all details necessary to invoke service contracts; and an after-hours number for each vendor listed so equipment and services can be started at any hour.

One section in the recovery plan should address firewalls. A list of the policies for each firewall should be maintained in the plan, making the recovery plan a highly confidential document that should be safeguarded from prying eyes.

[D]   Documentation

Network documentation is critical for the ongoing support and maintenance of your corporate network. A network documentation policy defines the level of network documentation required, such as which switch ports connect to what rooms and what systems. It should define who has access to read network documentation and who updates the documentation. It also defines how and who will be notified when changes are made to the network.

The IT networking and enterprise IT security staff normally have full access to all network documentation. Network coordinators for each area manage the updating of the network documentation for their area. Corporate service desk staff should have read access to the network documentation for their areas of responsibility.

The network coordinator must be notified when network changes are made. Changes that require notification include:

A.   The reboot of any network device including routers, switches, and firewalls.
B.   Configuration changes of any network device including routers, switches, and firewalls.
C.   Upgrades or additions to any software on any network device.
D.   Changes to any servers which perform significant network functions whether configuration or upgrade changes are made. These servers include:
   1.   DNS.
   2.   DHCP.
   3.   Domain controllers.
   4.   WINS.
   5.   E-mail and database servers.

The network coordinator will notify all groups affected by the network changes, such as service desk, server administration, and application developer teams, as well as IT management.

The network coordinator must ensure that network documentation is kept current by performing a periodic review of documentation or designating a staff member to perform a review. Any service desk requests made within the last period should be reviewed to help determine whether any network changes were made. Also any current or completed projects affecting network settings should be reviewed to determine whether there were any network changes made to support the project.

Network documentation is a critical corporate asset, and should be stored and managed as such following the corporate standards for asset disaster recovery planning. A minimum of two copies should be kept in separate facilities to ensure survival of at least one copy in the event of a disaster.

See Policy ITP-19-3 Network Documentation Policy as an example.

POLICY ITP-19-3   Network Documentation Policy

Policy #:	ITP-19-3	**Effective:**	03/18/09	**Page #:**	1 of N
Subject:	Network Documentation Policy				

1.0 PURPOSE

This policy helps to ensure network stability by requiring that documentation for all corporate networks is kept complete and current. Accurate documentation also reduces troubleshooting time by ensuring that appropriate personnel are notified when changes are made to the network. This policy complements disaster recovery planning by ensuring that documentation is available in the event that systems should need to be rebuilt after a catastrophic failure.

2.0 SCOPE

The policy applies to all corporate information system and telecommunication networks. The documentation is available only to approved network support and security personnel, and is not available to employees outside of IT. Any changes to the network must be reported to the area network coordinator.

3.0 POLICY

The following information concerning the corporate network infrastructure must be documented:

A. IP addresses of all devices on the network with static IP addresses.
B. Configuration information for all servers connected to the network.
   1. Operating system version.
   2. Services supported on the server.
C. Network drawings showing:
   1. The locations and IP addresses of all switches, routers, hubs, and firewalls on the network.
   2. The locations of every network drop and the associated switch and port on the switch to which it is connected.
   3. The interconnection between all network devices showing lines running between the network devices.
   4. The various security zones on the network and devices that control access between them.
   5. All subnets on the network and their relationships including the range of IP addresses on all subnets and subnet mask information.

      6. All wide area network (WAN) information including network devices connecting them and IP addresses of connecting devices.

  D. Configuration information on all network devices including:
      1. Routers.
      2. Switches.
      3. Firewalls.

  E. Configuration must include but not be limited to:
      1. IP address.
      2. Subnet mask.
      3. DNS server IP addresses for primary and secondary DNS servers.
      4. Default gateway.
      5. Any relevant WINS server information.

  F. Network connection information including:
      1. Type of connection to the Internet or other WAN including T1, T3, frame relay.
      2. Provider of Internet/WAN connection and contact information.
      3. Configuration information including subnet mask, network ID, and gateway.
      4. Physical location of where the cabling enters the building and circuit number.

  G. DHCP server settings showing:
      1. Range of IP addresses assigned by all DHCP servers on all subnets.
      2. Subnet mask, default gateway, DNS server settings, WINS server settings assigned by all DHCP servers on all subnets.
      3. Lease duration time.

4.0 REVISION HISTORY

Date	Revision #	Description of Change
03/18/09	1.0	Initial creation.

5.0 INQUIRIES

Direct inquiries about this policy to:

Harold Jenkins, CIO
2900 Corporate Drive
Columbus, OH 43215
Voice: 614-555-1234
Fax: 614-555-1235
E-mail: hjenkins@company.com

Revision #:	1.0	Supersedes:	N/A	Date:	03/18/09

20

TECHNOLOGY RELOCATION: SUCCESSFULLY MOVING YOUR IT OPERATIONS

§ 20.01 OVERVIEW
    [A] Purpose and Scope
    [B] Critical Policies to Develop Based on This Chapter

§ 20.02 BUSINESS ISSUES
    [A] Overview
    [B] What Can Go Wrong
    [C] Benefits of Outsourcing
    [D] Relocation Project Coordinator
    [E] Partners

§ 20.03 RELOCATION PROCESS
    [A] Benefits of Planning
    [B] Design Phase Activities
    [C] Implementation Phase Activities
    [D] Relocation Phase Activities

§ 20.01 OVERVIEW

[A] Purpose and Scope

Relocating a modern office is fraught with challenges. The infrastructure that supports the modern office worker is usually built up over a long period of time. Many firms have not relocated their offices for 10 or 20 years, which means that most of the technology being used in the office has been added over that period. Since the office was first established, new workstations have been purchased, new servers installed, network and communication cabling run and rerun, and phone systems installed and upgraded.

In an ideal world, each new addition or modification to the office infrastructure would be clearly documented. Each new system or upgrade would be seamlessly integrated with the existing technology. Unfortunately, what we normally end up with is a collection of technologies that are jury-rigged together and poorly documented. As long as the technology works, no one pays much attention to it, and as time goes on, the person who implemented the system moves on to another firm. This can happen with networks, servers, telephone systems, and cable and wiring. Worse yet, the configuration information that is part of the computer infrastructure is not always backed up as part of the backup process and often is not documented elsewhere.

Adding to the challenge of office relocation is the infrequency of such a project. Because moves are so infrequent, there is rarely someone on staff who has been through the relocation process.

Without proper planning, a relocation project will cause mission critical disruption in business services. In addition, hundreds of detailed tasks must be done properly in order to give you the amount of time you need to make the move a success. All of these tasks need to be executed *in addition* to all of the current daily requirements of keeping the business functioning.

If you have an existing disaster recovery plan (DRP), it can often times be extended to your relocation plan. It is often an excellent opportunity to test your DRP. If you do not have a DRP (shame on you!), then a relocation project provides an opportunity to collect the information needed to prepare one.

[B] Critical Policies to Develop Based on This Chapter

Using the material discussed in this chapter, you will be able to create the following policies:

A. When to outsource a relocation project.
B. Relocation processes.
   1. Planning requirements.
   2. Design requirements.

Policies should always be developed based on the local situation. Successful managers cannot issue appropriate guidance if the policies are written with another company's or location's situation in mind.

§ 20.02 BUSINESS ISSUES

[A] Overview

When faced with a technology relocation project, there are several issues to consider:

A. **Resources.** What resources are currently within the organization that can be used on this project? Are there enough people to perform all of the tasks required leading up to and including moving day? Who will be available at both the new and old locations for follow-up post move?

B. **Experience.** What level of experience do people within the organization have with a project of this type? Have they relocated a business prior to this move? Do they understand the move process? Can they think about the overall business process?

C. **Downtime.** A relocation project will be disruptive to operations. What are the company's vital processes and how long can it afford to have them unavailable? How much will it cost your business to be non-functional or impaired for one hour? For one day or longer?

D. **Cost.** There are numerous costs to be considered in a relocation project. In addition to the cost of the physical move, costs for outside resources, temporary furniture, last-minute glitches, etc., must be included.

Worksheet 20-1 is a questionnaire that can help during the planning process of a relocation project. The questionnaire can help the IT Manager determine the readiness of the organization for the move and highlight areas where outside support may be needed.

[B] What Can Go Wrong

Like most projects, a relocation project consists of many small tasks, most of which must be done correctly if the project is to be successful. You will of course want to have help in physically moving the furniture and equipment, but what else do you need to worry about? As you begin your planning for this project, think about the following aspects of the relocation process:

A. **Disruption of ongoing business.** In addition to employees having to pack and unpack their own belongings and personal contents, someone has to pack file cabinets, common areas such as kitchens and conference rooms as well as supply and storage areas. Someone also has to plan the physical move of such contents and infrastructure requirements such as telephones, local area network, and connectivity to the outside world.

B. **Relocation learning curve.** You have probably never managed a relocation project before, so you will be learning as you go along. The learning curve can be steeper than it looks. Organizing existing contents, furniture and technology and placing them properly onto new floor plans can be a highly complicated process.

WORKSHEET 20-1.   Relocation Information Questionnaire

Relocation Information Questionnaire

1. What is the impact of this project to the success of the organization?

   - ☐ Mission Critical
   - ☐ Very Important
   - ☐ Somewhat Important
   - ☐ Not Very Important

2. What is the reason the company is considering the move?

   - ☐ Current facility too big
   - ☐ Current facility too small
   - ☐ Consolidation of facilities
   - ☐ End of lease
   - ☐ Improved location
   - ☐ Cost reduction
   - ☐ Acquisition
   - ☐ Other

3. Are you moving or renovating into the following:

   - ☐ Constructing a new building
   - ☐ Existing site no renovation
   - ☐ Existing site with renovation
   - ☐ Renovation of you current site

4. Location information if moving:

   Moving from:

   Address: _______________________

   ____

   Sq. footage: _______________________

   Moving to:

   Address: _______________________

   ____

   Sq. footage: _______________________

5. Will this relocation affect daily operations?

   - ☐ Yes
   - ☐ No

6. Will this relocation affect critical projects?

   - ☐ Yes
   - ☐ No

7. Will this relocation affect the company's computer technology?

   - ☐ No
   - ☐ Yes
     - ☐ Workstations
     - ☐ Servers
     - ☐ Infrastructure
     - ☐ Internet connectivity
     - ☐ Other

8. Will other technologies be affected by this relocation?

   - ☐ No
   - ☐ Yes
     - ☐ Telephones
     - ☐ Building security
     - ☐ Time clocks
     - ☐ Other

9. What dependencies exist?

   - ☐ Construction schedule
   - ☐ Equipment schedule
   - ☐ Lease expiration
   - ☐ Personnel resources
   - ☐ Communications connectivity
   - ☐ Utilities connectivity
   - ☐ Other

10. Has a budget been established?

    - ☐ Yes
    - ☐ No

WORKSHEET 20-1.   (Continued)

Relocation Information Questionnaire

11. Has a schedule been established?

☐ No
☐ Yes

Start date: ______________________

End date: ______________________

12. Who is responsible for coordinating the move?

Name: ______________________

Title: ______________________

Phone: ______________________

13. Has a project team been created?

☐ Yes
☐ No

14. How are current IT needs supported?

☐ Internally
☐ Not support currently maintained
☐ Outsourced to a 3rd party

Who: ______________________

15. Do you have internal staff to provide follow up support after the move?

☐ Yes
☐ No

16. Do you have people on staff experienced in managing relocation vendors (construction/utility/movers, etc)?

☐ Yes
☐ No

17. Have you addressed any of the following?

☐ Choosing vendors
☐ Vendor management
☐ Communication to employees
☐ Establishing timelines
☐ Allocating resources
☐ Preparing the project plan
☐ Identifying the risks
☐ Controlling the budget
☐ No decisions have been made

18. Is the documentation of all the company's technologies current and complete??

☐ Yes
☐ No

C. **Downtime costs.** Just what are the costs you will incur if users are down after the move? What if they cannot use their workstations, or there is no connection to the Internet, or the telephones do not work and customers cannot reach you? What is the cost to your organization if one or all of these problems occur?

D. **Day-to-day work.** While you are planning for the move, employees still have their day-to-day tasks to perform. Does the IT staff have extra time to plan for the connectivity required at the new location and to work with all the service providers involved? Do your executives and department heads have time to manage additional responsibilities associated with the move?

E. **Things that can go wrong.** Many things can go wrong during the relocation. Some things to consider include:
   1. Internet or phone systems are not working and your customers cannot reach you.
   2. No one is managing the old site and you get charged with a clean-up bill.
   3. T1 lines stay connected at $1,300 per month in the old empty building.
   4. Improper installation of furniture, carpet, cabling, electric—pick your poison.
   5. Lost of productivity while looking for workstation or server parts.

COMMENT

The biggest problem areas in most moves are telephones and connectivity. Most of the problems are caused by language and timeline expectations. Start early, confirm repeatedly, and if necessary, respectfully demand resolution. If you can't speak the language, find someone who can as soon as possible!

[C]   Benefits of Outsourcing

There are many reasons why the IT Manager may want to consider outsourcing the management of a technology relocation project. Using a relocation expert can have the following advantages:

A. **Ability to focus on task.** As a Project Manager at your organization, you probably have multiple projects for which you are responsible at any one time. An outside person can focus 100 percent of his or her time on the relocation project, without the distractions of other activities within the organization.

B. **Availability as needed for project.** An outside Project Manager can more easily dedicate time to the relocation. Internal Project Managers still have other responsibilities, and have trouble dedicating the required time. Like many projects, technology relocation can take more time than originally estimated.

C. **Service provider connections.** Does any one person within the organization have connections with all of the service providers required to successfully complete the move? These service providers may include:

1. Movers.
2. Security/safety teams.
3. Property manager.
4. Technical furniture/cabinets specialists.
5. Equipment disposal companies.
6. Temporary office space.
7. Electrician/HVAC professionals.
8. Voice/data/video cabling.
9. Utilities.
10. Internet service providers (ISPs).
11. General contractor.
12. Architects/space planners/interior designers.
13. Off-site storage and alternative storage solutions.
14. Office furniture.
15. Hazardous waste removal.
16. Electrostatic.
17. Painters.

D. **Availability of qualified resources.** Do you have the necessary expertise in-house to assist with the relocation? You will need to work with multiple outside service providers for many of the required tasks and it helps to have experience working with these service providers. Experience has shown it takes an average of 8 hours per external vendor to coordinate a move. For complex systems (such as phones), it is not uncommon to spend over 160 hours with a vendor to guarantee services at the destination.

E. **Communications.** A central point of contact is integral to the success of the move. In addition, having the right person available, one who understands the escalation process of your vendors and suppliers and can speak their "language," may be the difference between service and no service come Monday morning.

F. **Can scale to meet needs of the project.** When it comes time to make the move, an outside service provider can bring the extra resources needed to help complete the project on time. Internal employees will be focused on getting back to the deadlines to take care of your customers and conduct "business as usual." External resources can supplement as needed.

G. **Past experience.** The organization does not move very often, so it is not likely there will be someone on staff who has experience with a project of this type. External relocation specialists will bring experience to your table and will benefit you in many ways.

H. **Facility planning**. Do you have someone who understands the construction and infrastructure of building as well as your business? Having someone with building experience in the pre-construction phase will help you plan your space more effectively and avoid many expensive change orders—often at $250 or more. This applies to cabling, telephone, plumbing, electric, etc.

COMMENT

I have experienced moves with two different corporations. The first chose to use a professional relocation firm. I left on Friday at my regular time and arrived at my new office Monday morning, sat down and began working immediately. *I didn't know how amazing that was until I experienced a move without a relocation team.*

My new employer did not outsource our relocation. Our business operations were significantly impaired for a full week. Amidst the file and content wreckage, PCs were in disarray, the phone system did not work correctly, and our nuclear camera as well as several printers were offline for weeks. I will not choose to go it alone again.

—A Medical Billing Director in Columbus, Ohio

[D]   Relocation Project Coordinator

One of the most important tasks of a relocation project is the selection of a relocation project coordinator. It should be someone with a broad knowledge of the company's operations. Even if an outside service provider will perform most of the relocation effort, there must be an internal person responsible for making sure the firm's objectives for the project are achieved. If this job is relegated to a person with low status within the organization, the relocation is guaranteed to be plagued with problems. The relocation project coordinator should be someone who can gain the willing cooperation of the team members and their supervisors. The type of person selected to lead this project will signal to everyone else in the company how serious the relocation project is.

The relocation project coordinator should be publicly assigned to this task with management's unqualified support. This is essential to overcome internal politics and to let everyone know their assistance is important and required. As the project moves forward, regular public displays of support are required if the project is to result in a smooth and trouble-free relocation.

Except in the smallest of companies, no one person knows all aspects of the operation. Supporting the relocation project coordinator will be a team of representatives from the various business units within the organization. These representatives are critical to building a viable relocation plan and are the source for the expertise needed to keep their area functioning and running efficiently before, during, and after the move. To a great degree, a team's success will depend on who is selected as the relocation project coordinator and how well he or she works with the team. The relocation project coordinator should be someone with good analytical, communications, and leadership skills that can keep the project focused. Therefore, the relocation project coordinator must be a skilled negotiator and able to reach consensus with the various company departments to gain the use of their key people.

The relocation project coordinator policy must spell out the responsibilities of the position:

A. Creates and maintains the master move plan, communication plan, and budget.

B. Accepts total responsibility for the relocation. This should be his or her main responsibility for the duration of the project.

C. Creates documentation. It is critical to document every aspect of the project. If the current environment is not well documented, the relocation project coordinator must lead the effort to get it updated. The layout of the new facility must be documented, as well as the move from the current facility to the new one.

D. Maintains service provider relations. Working closely with all of the various service providers is critical. This might be simply working with the outside relocation service provider or managing all the individual service providers if the project is managed in-house. A good rapport must be established with each service provider to ensure its cooperation as the project progresses. You never know when you will need one of them to put out some extra effort to get something completed on time or to accommodate last-minute changes.

E. Serves as the central point of contact for all communications. The relocation project coordinator should be the central source for information concerning the project. A relocation project requires the coordination of the services of multiple service providers and task requirements with the organization.

F. Provides leadership and direction. The relocation project coordinator must keep everyone involved focused on the successful completion of their tasks.

G. Has the authority to make quick decisions. No matter how complete the planning and attention to detail, many tasks will require last-minute adjustments or change orders. The relocation project coordinator must have the task and budget authority to get these things done in a timely manner to keep the project on schedule.

See Policy ITP-20-1 Technology Relocation Coordinator Policy as an example.

POLICY ITP-20-1.   Technology Relocation Coordinator Policy

Policy #:	ITP-20-1	**Effective:**	03/18/09	**Page #:**	1 of N
Subject:	Technology Relocation Coordinator Policy				

1.0 PURPOSE

This policy mandates that a project coordinator be appointed for any technology relocation that includes more than 25 users.

2.0 SCOPE

This policy encompasses all IT systems and technology that supports critical business functions.

3.0 POLICY

The IT Manager will designate a project coordinator for any technology relocation project that includes more than 25 users. The relocation project coordinator has the following responsibilities:

A. Creates and maintains the master move plan, communication plan, and budget.
B. Accepts total responsibility for the relocation. This should be his or her main responsibility for the duration of the project.
C. Creates documentation. It is critical to document every aspect of the project. If the current environment is not well documented, the relocation project coordinator must lead the effort to get it updated. The layout of the new facility must be documented, as well as the move from the current facility to the new one.
D. Maintains service provider relations. Working closely with all of the various service providers is critical. This might be simply working with the outside relocation service provider or managing all the individual service providers if the project is managed in-house. A good rapport must be established with each service provider to ensure its cooperation as the project progresses.
E. Serves as the central point of contact for all communications. The relocation project coordinator should be the central source for information concerning the project. A relocation project requires the coordination of the services of multiple service providers and task requirements with the organization.

F. Provides leadership and direction. The relocation project coordinator must keep everyone involved focused on the successful completion of their tasks.

G. Has the authority to make quick decisions. No matter how complete the planning and attention to detail, many tasks will require last-minute adjustments or change orders. The relocation project coordinator will have the task and budget authority to get these things done in a timely manner to keep the project on schedule.

4.0 REVISION HISTORY

Date	Revision #	Description of Change
03/18/09	1.0	Initial creation.

5.0 INQUIRIES

Direct inquiries about this policy to:

Tom Jones, CIO
Our Company, Inc.
2900 Corporate Drive
Columbus, OH 43215

Voice: 614-555-1234
Fax: 614-555-1235
E-mail: tjones@company.com

Revision #:	1.0	Supersedes:	N/A	Date:	03/18/09

[E] Partners

Few companies will have all of the resources required to successfully complete a relocation project. Most will require the assistance of several different service providers that specialize in some aspect of the project. As much as possible, IT should try to find service providers that have experience with technology relocation projects. The moving of servers and other delicate equipment is not the same as moving household furniture. These service providers may include:

A. **Movers.** No matter how sophisticated the technology, there will still be plenty of heavy lifting that needs to be done. These people have the skill, training, and muscle to get your equipment moved to the new location with a minimal amount of damage. That said, the "mover's" job is to move product from Point A to Point B. You need to fully understand your risk in this process.

B. **Security/safety.** The service providers should have security plans in place to ensure the equipment arrives safely and is not damaged or compromised during the move. The IT Managers must ensure access to corporate data is not compromised due to poor security during the relocation.

C. **Technical furniture/cabinets facilities.** New furniture and equipment cabinets may be required due to differences in the layout of the new facility as compared to the old one. Specialized HVAC, fire suppression and electrical requirements need to be planned and ordered 90 to 180 days in advance of the move.

D. **Equipment disposal.** A relocation is the perfect time to dispose of equipment that is no longer being used. Many areas have restrictions on placing old computers and monitors into the normal trash due to the high concentrations of toxic material within this equipment; therefore, a special disposal service may need to be contacted.

E. **Temporary office space.** If new construction is not completed when the move date arrives, you may need temporary office space for affected personnel.

F. **Cabling.** The new office will of course need network cabling installed to company specifications. Cabling is the least expensive component in the technology network, yet is expected to last the longest. Do you have engineers who have the talent to run new cable? Do they have the time and quantity of labor needed to complete the task?

G. **Utilities.** Companies require electricity, water, heating, cooling, etc., to operate a modern office. Independent contractors install most of these items and will require a central point of contact to coordinate their efforts.

H. **ISPs.** A corporate or department connection to the Internet will more than likely need to be up and available on day one. Dedicated connections to an application service provider also may be required if the company uses software applications delivered in this manner.

I. **General contractor.** Some businesses work with a general contractor who will ensure all the service providers can complete their tasks on time and on budget. When it comes to crunch time and the flooring guy is holding up the furniture guy who is holding up the cabling guy who is holding up the new phone system from being installed, the general contractor can keep the project moving along.

J. **Technology SPACE Planner.** If the new location requires extensive remodeling, an architect will be required to ensure the new facility is properly designed. Most architects and space planners do not normally deal with technology-specific issues. Therefore, IT should work with someone who understands and can identify the company's technology SPACE requirements for the new location. SPACE stands for:
    * **S**tructure and layout of your technology rooms and closets.
    * **P**athways to deliver and support technology throughout the facility.
    * **A**ir conditioning/humidity and other environmental concerns for sensitive electronics.
    * **C**abling and wiring.

- Electrical and lighting (many times the existing power and configuration is not adequate to support company-specific needs).

K. **Off-site storage.** Off-site storage may be required for certain equipment that cannot be immediately installed in the new facility.

L. **Office furniture.** System furniture (cubicles) needs to be ordered in advance of the installation date, which then needs to be coordinated with cable and electrical vendors. During a move, it is not uncommon for businesses to paint or reorganize file cabinets to make them all match within a department. Now is a great time to get rid of old, worn furniture rather than move it.

COMMENT

Firms that specialize in technology relocation are usually a division of a moving company or a technology consulting company. When using outside help, make sure they specialize in technology relocation. Don't forget to ask for success stories and testimonials!

§ 20.03 RELOCATION PROCESS

[A] Benefits of Planning

Just like any other major project, a relocation benefits greatly when it is well planned. Some of the benefits of planning include:

A. Resource needs are known ahead of time.
B. Problem areas are identified.
C. Follow-up support costs are lower.
D. Environmental problems are identified and cleaned up.
E. Other resource-intensive projects are consolidated.
F. Asset management can be initiated.
G. Project management is more efficient.
H. Disaster recovery/site guide can be developed.
I. Stress on employees is minimized.

As noted in Exhibit 20-1 by The Knowledge Group, a Columbus, Ohio–based consulting firm that specializes in planning integrated building technology, the earlier in the process decisions are made, the higher their value and lower the cost. If the IT Manager waits to make decisions, values diminish and cost rises sharply. A little pre-planning can result in huge savings.

EXHIBIT 20-1   Planning Cost/Benefit Analysis

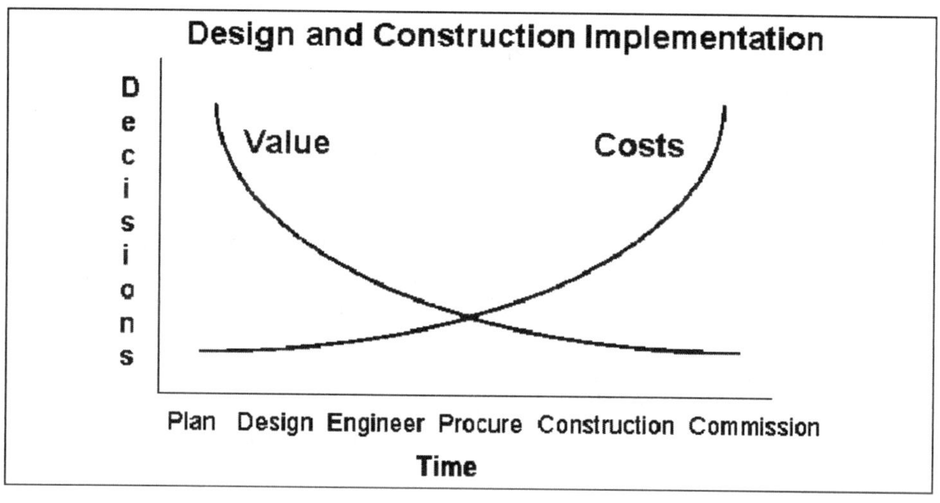

The results of not planning can include the following problems:

A. Lack of testing.
B. Longer project duration.
C. Possibility of theft.
D. Poor use of personnel.
E. Reduced time for daily support and other business projects during the relocation project.
F. Lost opportunity to save by shopping for services (especially local phone service).
G. Lost chance to upgrade or replace technology.

Numerous things can go wrong on this kind of project before, during, and after the move. Most, if not all, of them can be prevented with careful planning. Common omissions prior to move include:

- Forgetting to arrange copier (or other special equipment) move.
- Not having updated floor plans.
- Not having accurate inventory of furniture.
- Non-networked equipment not accounted for.
- Networked equipment inventory is incomplete.

During the move, problems that may crop up include:

- Theft due to improper security.
- No power at new location.
- No access or limited access to elevators.
- Telecommunications lines not installed as needed.
- Unorganized activities that can make work very inefficient.

After the move is complete, some problems that may occur include:

- Basic supplies missing.
- PCs cannot connect to network.
- Old telecommunications lines not cancelled.
- Lack of supplies in new facility.
- Fax machine will not dial out.
- Pictures need hanging.

A well-planned relocation project managed by an experienced Project Manager will take much less time and resources than a relocation managed by someone without experience. Exhibit 20-2 shows the results of research performed by Franklin Moves, a technology relocation firm, comparing moves managed by experienced versus inexperienced Project Managers. Franklin Moves' research shows that, although the experienced manager spends a little more time up front, this planning time pays big dividends later in the project. The small shaded area on the left side of the chart in Exhibit 20-2 shows the extra time spent by the experienced manager. The shaded areas at the top and right portion of the chart show a dramatic increase in the amount of hours spent by the inexperienced manager versus the experienced one. Proper planning allows the experienced Project Manager to complete the project more quickly, with fewer fires to fight after the move has taken place.

EXHIBIT 20-2   Experienced vs. Inexperienced Coordinator

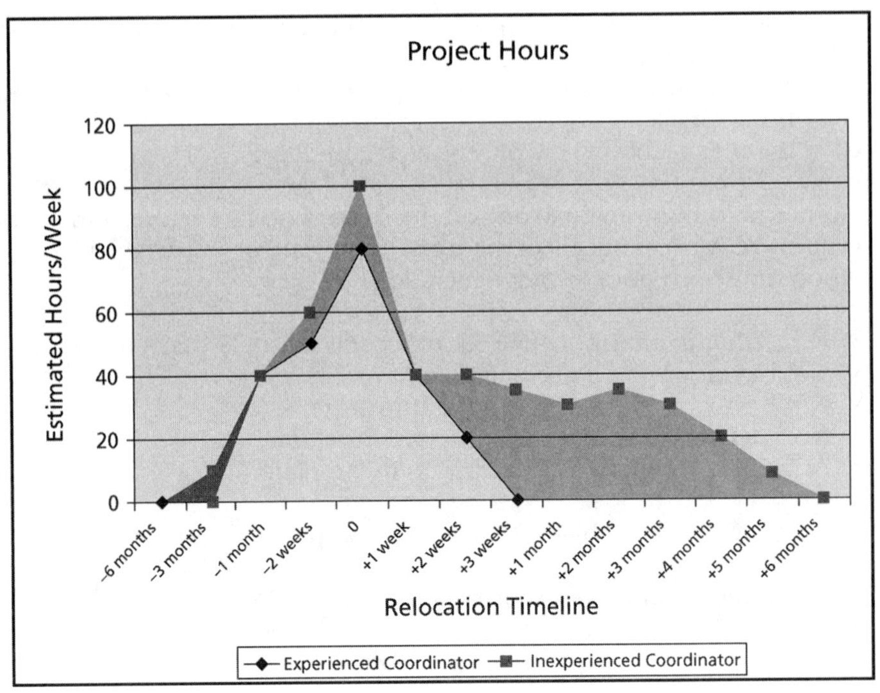

[B]   Design Phase Activities

Once the initial planning is completed, the IT Manager can begin designing the logistics of the relocation project:

A. **Select tracking tools.** Determine what tools and software will be needed for project tracking, budget tracking, and implementing the communications plan.

B. **Create a communications plan.** This will include a central repository for communications such as meeting minutes, budget status, and scheduled items to which both internal and external contacts can refer. A good communications plan will reduce miscommunication and the workload of the project coordinator.

C. **Develop a budget.** IT must have the necessary budget resources to complete the project effectively. Make sure there is a contingency fund for unexpected items that pop up at the last minute. This fund should be approximately 10 percent of the total budget.

D. **Collect data.** IT will need data on many areas of the organization in order to get it moved to the new location. Look for office diagrams, review floor plans, and develop checklists to make sure you have covered everything. Some areas requiring special attention include:
   1. General.
      a. Room dimensions and location of outlets and ports.
      b. Power and lighting.
      c. HVAC.
      d. Security.
      e. Floor coverings.
      f. Dedicated spaces for technical equipment.
      g. Backup batteries for computer and phone equipment.
   2. Networks.
      a. Document and assess current network architecture and applications.
      b. Review technology standards, policies, and procedures.
      c. Interview affected employees.
      d. Create a list of reusable equipment.
      e. Determine a budget for new local and wide area networks.
      f. Develop new local and wide area network architecture designs.
      g. Issue RFPs if outside service providers are required.
      h. Review RFP responses and provide recommendations if necessary.
      i. Coordinate with network service providers (wide area network only).
   3. Voice systems.
      a. Document and assess current voice communications architecture.
      b. Review technology standards, policies, and procedures.
      c. Interview affected user groups.
      d. Determine a budget for voice system.
      e. Develop a new voice network plan and specifications.

      f.　Issue RFPs if outside service providers are required.

      g.　Review RFP responses and provide recommendations if necessary.

   4.　Data centers.

      a.　Audit existing equipment to determine what can be used at new location.

      b.　Define equipment layout and cabling floor plan.

      c.　Issue RFPs if outside service providers are required.

      d.　Review RFP responses and provide recommendations if necessary.

   5.　Business continuity plan.

      a.　Develop a business continuity plan for move.

      b.　Determine possible points of failure and develop prevention and restoration plans.

      c.　Coordinate design of all systems to ensure connectivity.

      d.　Develop technology delivery schedule for new location.

E.　**Confirm lead times.** Many of the tasks that will be performed for the relocation must be done in a specific order. For example, cubicles cannot be placed until the carpeting is completed, inter-cubicle voice/data/electric cannot be run until the cubicles are in place, and computers cannot be reconnected on the desktops until all of the previous steps are completed. If one falls out of place, the whole schedule slides. There are typically 30- to 60-day lead times for many types of phone services.

F.　**Review new space.** IT should walk through the new facility and compare what is there to the diagrams the company was given. Special attention should be paid to wiring, door locations and swing, furniture size, and how the furniture will be delivered. Make sure the doorways are wide enough for the company's equipment and the equipment that will be used to move it. Hallways and elevators also should be noted.

G.　**Identify resources required.** Different types of resources will be required during the relocation project. Without the required resource levels and skill levels available, the project will suffer.

H.　**Finalize employee locations.** It is critical to know where everyone will end up at the new location and what infrastructure requirements they have. When planning for network drops, plan to have extra drops in case there are last-minute changes.

I.　**Develop timeline.** Work your way back from the relocation date to make sure there is enough time to complete the project.

J.　**Create and resolve post-move punch list.** This is the step that always gets dropped first and costs companies thousands of dollars. It is critical to address all remaining details to successfully complete the move.

K.　**Confirm project closure across all areas.** This includes facilities, technology, and internal employee communication. Once in the new facility, internal employees will be focused on meeting deadlines and taking care of customers. If project closure is not confirmed, there may be items that remain unresolved that can cause problems when addressing customers' needs.

Other items that need to be accounted for include:

A. Business cards.
B. Letterhead and envelopes.
C. Marketing materials (use up old stuff before the move; have new stuff delivered to new location).
D. Business contact notification (e.g., customers, service providers, partners).
E. Having calls automatically transferred to the new number.

If new construction is involved, work closely with the contractor. Be available to answer questions at any time during the project.

[C] Implementation Phase Activities

Once IT has planned and designed how the relocation will be executed, the plan can be implemented. The following are some of the tasks performed during the implementation phase:

A. Updating and maintaining project plan and schedule.
B. Managing the purchase, delivery, integration, installation, and configuration of equipment.
C. Defining labeling standards for new building.

> ## COMMENT
>
> The importance of labeling cannot be overstressed. Label computers, peripherals, boxes, binders, etc., with some kind of identification of the new location. In addition, designate a location to serve as a holding area for miscellaneous IT items.

D. Reviewing network and telecommunications plans.
E. Managing inventory logistics plan.
F. Managing change management system.
G. Managing project budgets.
H. Creating acceptance test plan.
I. Conducting quality audits.
J. Facilitating project status meetings.

Other things to consider during this phase include:

A. Packing nonessential items early and identifying temporary storage locations.

B. Making sure plenty of moving materials are available (e.g., boxes, packing material).

C. Checking employee vacation schedules and other reasons to be absent.

> **COMMENT**
>
> It is a good idea to give every user a large plastic, resealable bag for all the smaller items, such as cables and mice. Have the users label the bags and their equipment with the location of their new desks.

[D] Relocation Phase Activities

Finally, the company is ready to move. The following tasks are performed during the relocation phase:

A. Developing a final relocation plan.
B. Developing a relocation contingency plan.
C. Establishing a relocation service desk.
D. Managing and coordinating the relocation of systems.
E. Conducting acceptance testing of new and relocated systems.
F. Completing final documentation of new facility.
G. Creating and resolving a post-move punch list.
H. Confirming project closure across all areas.

Follow-up support after the move is critical to success. No matter how well-planned the relocation, minor issues are sure to pop up that will need attention. A quick resolution of these items will ensure that everyone affected by the relocation is back to work and productive as soon as possible.

> **COMMENT**
>
> Do not forget to have phone services, T1 lines, etc., disconnected at the old location after the move is completed. Forgetting to do so simply wastes money.

21

GREEN COMPUTING: EARTH FRIENDLY IT

§ 21.01 OVERVIEW
[A] Purpose and Scope
[B] Critical Policies to Develop Based on This Chapter

§ 21.02 A TIME TO STOP
[A] What Is Green?
[B] Stop Wasting Energy
[C] Stop Wasting Equipment
[D] Stop Polluting the Planet
[E] Policies Implement Strategies

§ 21.03 PUT ENERGY-HOG EQUIPMENT ON A DIET
[A] Overview
[B] Energy Star
[C] Electronic Products Environmental Assessment Tool™ (EPEAT™)
[D] Advanced Configuration and Power Interface (ACPI)
[E] Restriction of Hazardous Substances (ROHS) Directive
[F] Virtualization
[G] Is Thin Client the Answer?

§ 21.04 WHAT CAN YOU DO?
[A] The Basics
[B] Create a Power Usage Baseline
[C] Telecommuting
[D] Enable Software-Controlled Power Management
[E] Buy Some Power Strips
[F] Save Trees and Toner
[G] Substitute One Piece at a Time

§ 21.05 SAFE DISPOSAL
[A] Overview
[B] Reuse Surplus Equipment Elsewhere
[C] Recycling Old Technology
[D] Tossing Equipment onto the Scrap Heap

§ 21.01 OVERVIEW

[A] Purpose and Scope

Climate change is a socially disruptive issue. Many people have opinions as to whether it is caused by or is accelerated by human activities. One of the significant questions involves the emission of greenhouse gases that are a result of fossil fuels burned to create electricity. The concept of Green Technologies begins with the responsible use of electrical energy. However, the more companies explore how they use energy, they see that from their perspective it is more about the cost-efficient use of resources.

A key resource used in the modern office is electricity. If you think of it as a material, much like steel or plastics, then it is easier to understand material waste. Imagine buying a small tree just to create one wooden pencil. Imagine buying half of a cow just to eat one steak. These may seem like exaggerations, but they are not far off. Consider the desktop workstation that is never turned off. It runs 24 hours per day seven days per week (including vacations and holidays). For all of that electricity purchased, it is used about 25 percent of the time. The rest of the time is wasted running and contributing nothing to the company's profits.

Another issue is the proper disposal of obsolete electronics. Old computers, printers, cell phones, network devices, telephone instruments, and so on require proper disposal. Improper disposal may result in companies paying for expensive landfill clean-ups. There is also an emerging body of laws governing how electronic devices may be scrapped.

[B] Critical Policies to Develop Based on This Chapter

A Green Technologies policy is both an opportunity to save money and necessary to avoid legal entanglements. It explains how the company will reduce the amount of energy it consumes while maintaining its current level of service. It also details the approved process for disposal of obsolete electronic assets.

This policy will also identify by position title required actions by IT managers. This clarifies who must complete what actions and at what time. A series of periodic reports provides executive management with assurance that the savings gained through a well-considered Green Technologies strategy are not lost through staff inattention.

Using the material discussed in this chapter, you will be able to create the following policies:

A. Purchase of New Electronic Equipment
B. Utilization of Data Center Assets
C. Equipment Disposal

Policies should always be developed based on the local situation. Successful managers cannot issue appropriate guidance if the policies are written with another company's or location's situation in mind.

§ 21.02   A TIME TO STOP

[A]   What Is Green?

Green Technologies are the efficient use of computing resources in an environmentally friendly manner. They provide economic savings, demonstrate corporate social responsibility, and minimize environmental impact. Green Technologies also reduce energy consumption. Given the rising cost of energy of all types, these savings can be significant. Green Technologies are a collection of things:

   A. **They are the efficient use of electricity to support computing.** Efficient use minimizes wasted energy that does not contribute to a company's business. Typically this is energy lost through heat to power equipment no one is using and the use of inefficient electronic devices. Green Technologies also encompass using energy sources with a minimal environmental impact, such as solar or wind power.

   B. **They maximize existing equipment utilization.** For many years, it was far easier to add another server and more disks than it was to properly manage system capacity. As existing systems became more powerful, yet more lightly used, their hardware was rarely swapped out for something smaller. Another issue was the many copies of large databases and files kept online "just in case" they are needed. All of this added up to high energy usage to power and cool servers and disk drives that added nothing to the bottom line.

   C. **We live in a throwaway society.** Many things we use, especially electronic devices, are cheaper to discard than to repair. A repair is minimally one-half hour of bench time (technician and tools at about $100 per hour) plus parts. Given the amount of surface-mounted components used on electronic circuit boards, a repair may not be practical. Entire circuit cards must be exchanged. This may lead to a multiweek delay. Given the time delay, labor, and price of a replacement, it is often cheaper to buy a replacement and discard the old item.

Climate change is a socially disruptive factor. As nations search for ways to reduce their greenhouse gas emissions, they are turning their attention toward the carbon footprint created by modern technology. There is no need to wait for this unwanted governmental interference. Green Technologies do not require that companies sacrifice performance or features. It is just a different way to provide the same things.

[B]   Stop Wasting Energy

Computing equipment is the main user of energy in most companies. There is a desktop workstation for every office worker. Data centers are always "on." Servers are running and disk drives are spinning even during holidays and weekends when no one is around. Many applications are only used occasionally, but the equipment still draws power around the clock. All of this adds up to a large amount of electricity that is spent "just in case" something is needed.

This is compounded by the number of desktop units that run around the clock, even when no one is present to use them.

Think about it. Are your office lights left on around the clock, every day of the year? Is the heat or air conditioning for the offices always held at the most comfortable temperature over long winter weekends? You carefully manage the other electrical wastes, why not this one? How about saving some money? Consider:

A. Reduced energy to power IT equipment has an immediate financial payback to the company.

B. Reduced power usage will reduce the amount of air conditioning required.

C. Cooler-running equipment extends its useful life.

D. If no one is present to use the computer, then who is inconvenienced?

[C] Stop Wasting Equipment

Over the years, companies kept adding technology but not managing its efficiencies. It is far easier to add a new server and slap in additional disk drives than it is to rebalance the load across existing units. Equipment is plentiful and becoming more powerful with every new model. Disks regularly drop in price, and there was plenty of storage to support the sloppiest system design. It was much easier to purchase new equipment than to argue with someone.

Purchasing a new server for each application meant that some applications, though important, only ran for a short time every day. The rest of the day, that server and its disk drives were powered up but idle. Eventually, data centers began to fill up. This idle equipment used electricity and generated heat that had to be cooled, requiring even more energy.

Another waste of equipment is through online storage. Everyone wants all of their files, along with their many versions, to be available online all of the time. This is a waste of energy and resources. Some databases keep multiple copies of the same data online for recovery and to potentially ease trouble-shooting later. All of this takes disk space, energy, and cooling. Most of it is never accessed.

[D] Stop Polluting the Planet

Large companies often follow a three-year equipment refresh cycle to match the manufacturer's warranty coverage. Items older than three years are replaced with newer and faster units. These old components are either sold on the used-equipment market or sent away as scrap. Consider the pollution this still-useful equipment creates in a landfill, and the additional pollution produced while creating its replacement.

Electronic equipment usually includes small amounts of toxic materials. Old hardware improperly thrown in landfills may release toxic elements into the environment. This can be addressed by purchasing equipment that does not include toxic materials, by using electronics longer than a few years, and by proper disposal. Of course, to buy equipment without these toxic materials, manufacturers must first offer it at a reasonable price.

COMMENT

The transition from traditional IT processes to Green Technologies has its roots in the chemical industry. Over time, chemicals have been reformulated and manufacturing processes modified to reduce the amount of toxic materials used and discarded. Many newer chemicals are now biodegradable or recyclable.

[E]   Policies Implement Strategies

A Green Technologies policy must explain to all employees the company's executive guidance for implementing the Green Technologies program. The policy must address every area of the company involved. Some companies focus on electronic devices while others also include paper recycling and waste water management. Manufacturing facilities should not combine their Green Technologies and manufacturing environmental programs to avoid confusion.

A company's Green Technologies policy must reflect its strategy. Companies approach this issue various ways. A common theme is that this is an issue that must be addressed for economic and social reasons. Before drafting a policy, select the strategy you intend to implement. The different strategic approaches are:

A. The "From Here on Out" approach is to apply the policy to future purchases where practical. This can be implemented as an official purchasing policy or even quietly by the person specifying which new equipment to purchase. This may also be attached to a company's social responsibility initiatives. This approach takes time before it can show any measurable results. The cost of energy and equipment disposal is added to the company's normal ROI calculation.

B. The "Company Differentiator" approach is for organizations that want to use their Green credentials to differentiate their company and attract or retain customers. They see it as a way for their business to stand out as more socially responsible than those of competitors. Rather than wait for equipment to expire, this organization seeks out and replaces the most inefficient offenders. The principles of Green Technologies are applied across the organization to include all sources of energy waste and disposal concerns such as copiers, fax machines, refrigerators, vehicles, etc.

C. "Thoroughly Green" seeks to reorganize the way that technology is used in a company from top to bottom. Over the years, many companies have rushed to automate everything without a full understanding of what is needed—or if something else is already in place to do that function. Eliminating low value or duplicate systems reduces the need for equipment (which is better than using it efficiently). Examples of this are multiple copies of mirrored data, insistence on keeping rarely used data in online storage instead of offline, and maintaining a larger number of generations of online data than needed (need is determined by the frequency of access). Thoroughly Green encompasses new building construction using on-site, nonpolluting renewable energy sources. Social factors are on an equal level to financial considerations.

See Policy ITP-21-1 Green Computing Policy as an example.

POLICY ITP-21-1. Green Computing Policy

Policy #:	ITP-21-1	**Effective:**	03/18/09	**Page #:**	1 of N
Subject:	Green Computing Policy				

1.0 PURPOSE

This policy requires employees to consider all significant environmental and cost factors in the purchase, use, and disposal of electronic equipment. It ensures the consistent, efficient, and effective implementation of environmentally friendly operations across the organization.

2.0 SCOPE

The policy applies to all technology devices and their operation within the company. Specifically this includes all equipment purchased for the collection and processing of data throughout the organization as well as all telecommunications devices to include telephones, cellular telephones, and fax machines.

3.0 POLICY

This policy provides for the efficient use of electronic equipment in terms of energy management and fuller utilization. It applies to all employees and identifies specific duties for the IT Manager, Facilities Manager, IT Desktop Support Manager, Data Center Manager, and Purchasing Manager.

A. Purchase of new electronic equipment
    The purchasing manager will ensure that all technology hardware purchases include an energy usage comparison between the new item

and the item it is replacing—or the last similar item purchased. The power supply of new equipment must have an Energy Star Plus 80 rating. If the price difference between the "Plus 80" item and least cost alternative is within 10 percent, then the Plus 80 item will be purchased.

Incoming equipment must be compliant with European Union's directives 2002/95/EC (Restriction of Hazardous Substances directive, or ROHS). This will ease the disposal of equipment at the end of its useful life.

The Vice President of Technology is authorized to approve any deviations to this policy.

B. Utilization of data center assets

   1. The data center manager will semiannually review equipment utilization for the previous 12 months and report:

      a. Review all databases in the data center and submit a report that the minimum number of data copies are maintained in online storage, or identify the excess number of copies in use.

      b. Verify that all data in online storage is accessed at least once every three months or is moved to offline storage media.

      c. Create a baseline report of estimated electrical usage (or request a special meter to monitor data center use) for the data center. Provide a comparison of electricity used over the past 12 months and detail specific actions to reduce it.

      d. Identify servers that are not required for 24 X 7 operations and the impact of shutting them down on evenings, weekends and holidays.

      e. Identify batch reports suitable for conversion to online review instead of printing the entire document.

   2. The data center manager will create and maintain a document:

      a. Detailing the electrical utilization of each piece of data center equipment as a cost factor used for calculating when to replace existing equipment.

      b. Listing efforts to reduce the amount of cooling required.

   3. The System Administrator will review all servers and identify units that could be combined using virtualization. A proposal and action plan for migrating servers used less than 30 percent during working hours to a virtual environment.

   4. The Desktop Support manager will create and maintain a document detailing the electrical utilization of each model of desktop and portable computing items used in the company. The amount of energy required for a particular piece of equipment will be considered as a cost factor used for calculating when to replace it.

      a. Create a baseline report of estimated electrical usage for the desktop equipment to include shared printers. Report semiannually on estimated power usage.

      b. Ensure all power converters are on a power strip so they can be turned off.

     c. Remind users to turn off equipment when leaving for the night.

     d. Turn on and prevent user changing of power saving options on each company computer, monitor, and printer.

5. The Facilities Services Manager will create and maintain a document detailing the electrical utilization of each model of copier and fax machine. The amount of energy required for a particular piece of equipment will be considered as a cost factor used for calculating when to replace existing equipment.

C. Equipment Disposal

The IT Manager is responsible for the proper disposal of all electronic devices from the desktop, the data center, telecommunications systems, and company-owned telephones. The Facilities Services Manager is responsible for the proper disposal of all copiers and fax devices.

The first choice for technology disposal is resale or donation to someone who can continue its useful life. If that is not an option, then return it to the original manufacturer for disposal. If a third-party company is used to manage equipment disposal then the IT Manager and the Facilities Manager must visit the disposal facilities every six months to ensure the equipment is properly broken apart and toxic materials are sent on for proper disposal or recycling.

4.0 REVISION HISTORY

Date	Revision #	Description of Change
03/18/09	1.0	Initial creation.

5.0 INQUIRIES

Direct inquiries about this policy to:

Tom Jones, CIO
Our Company, Inc.
2900 Corporate Drive
Columbus, OH 43215

Voice: 614 555 1234
Fax: 614-555-1235
E-mail: tjones@company.com

Revision #:	1.0	Supersedes:	N/A	Date:	03/18/09

§ 21.03 PUT ENERGY-HOG EQUIPMENT ON A DIET

[A] Overview

Green Technologies focus on hardware. The amount of energy it demands every day and generally around the clock is substantial and ever increasing. If someone offered to sell you a new computer server for 20 percent more cost than everyone else was paying, would you buy it? If the taxes on data centers went up 20 percent would your company react? If the price of gas for your car went up 20 percent, would you be angry? When will energy prices level off? Isn't it time to take a fresh look at your organization's energy usage and eliminate areas of waste?

Computing equipment wastes electricity. It wastes a lot of electricity, and that translates into money spent for doing nothing. Green Technologies is about minimizing the amount of energy that is wasted by computing hardware that is doing . . . nothing.

Have you ever seen coworkers who never turned off their workstation—even before leaving on vacation, because they did not want to wait while it started from a power-off state? If you asked this person why, he or she will provide a long list of reasons—none of which compares to the money lost for powering unused equipment. Funny thing is, this same person will likely turn out the office lights every night . . . to save electricity.

The traditional reason given for not turning off equipment is that the spike of electricity when it is turned back on slowly wears down the electronic components. This is true, but the impact is minimal. It would take so many more years of daily off-and-on switching to cause a failure that the equipment would not still be in service.

A similar situation occurs in data centers. In this case, it takes time to power down and then restart servers. Many system administrators fear (no better word describes this) that if turned off, they will not restart properly. Given the amount of time required to power down and restart the many servers, does it makes sense to even look here for savings?

COMMENT

When you drive your car to work, you stop to put gas into it. You see how much it costs and how the price has risen, so you adjust your driving habits and usage accordingly. Data center managers rarely see a company's electric bill. While the facilities manager strives to reduce usage, the IT Manager's goals are maximum availability. A company's reward system and feedback system need to change.

Computing equipment is powered by electricity. To create this energy, power companies use coal-fired plants, nuclear energy, and hydroelectric power generation. Each of these has its own drawbacks. As the world's requirements for electrical energy increase, so does the number of power plants, which further adds to greenhouse gases in the atmosphere, which some people believe increase the natural cycle of global warming. As nations strive to fulfill their treaty promises to reduce greenhouse gases, businesses can expect increased governmental pressure to use less energy.

Government initiatives have emerged over time to encourage various aspects of Green Technologies. Often these guidelines overlap or are based on previous standards. Government initiatives are either guidelines to be followed voluntarily or legal mandates.

[B] Energy Star

Electronic devices that plug into a wall outlet use a "power supply" module to connect to a power source. This device filters line noise and power fluctuations, and converts the incoming power to the voltage levels required for that device. A typical power supply is about 70 percent efficient. For example, it takes 100 watts of incoming power to provide 70 watts of usable power in the device. The rest of the energy is lost as heat.

In 1992, the U.S. Environmental Protection Agency (EPA) created "Energy Star" as a program for promoting energy-efficient technologies. It began as a voluntary labeling program to promote energy-efficient computers and monitors and later expanded to encompass office equipment and residential climate control equipment. Over the years, Energy Star has contributed to the use adoption of (light-emitting diode) LED traffic lights, power management for office equipment, and minimal standby power usage for a wide range of devices.

In 1996, the Energy Star program was extended to encompass major appliances, lighting, home electronics, new homes, and commercial and industrial buildings. Today, Energy Star is a joint effort of the EPA and the U.S. Department of Energy.

COMMENT

Obtain the latest information about Energy Star at: http://www.energystar.gov.

Energy Star was revised in 2007 to tighten efficiency goals and introduce a tiered rating system. Existing equipment designs can no longer use the logo unless they are requalified. Energy Star's latest specifications for computers apply to a variety of products, including desktop and notebook computers, integrated computer systems, desktop-derived servers, and workstations.

The latest Energy Star version introduced a power supply certification called "80 Plus." This means that a power supply has 80 percent or greater AC power supply efficiency at rated power. Qualified products must now meet energy use guidelines in standby, sleep mode, and while computers are being used:

A. Desktops, integrated computers, and desktop-derived servers must use less than 2 watts of power when the device is switched off, and no more than 4 watts when in sleep mode.
B. Notebook PCs must use less than 1 watt of power when the device is switched off, and no more than 1.7 watts when in sleep mode.
C. Internal power supplies must switch to sleep mode within 15 minutes of inactivity.
D. External power supplies must switch to sleep mode within 30 minutes of inactivity.

The new computer specification is expected to save consumers and businesses more than $1.8 billion in energy costs over the next five years and prevent greenhouse gas emissions equal to the annual emissions of 2.7 million vehicles.

Power management of monitors is an easy place to save money. The older cathode ray monitors (non-flat panels) use a lot of power. Even the newer flat-panel models need power to operate. A popular notion is that turning a monitor off and on several times a day (through power management) will damage it. The power surge on startup does wear on the components, but problems will take about 20 years before they are apparent.

The first step in power management is to place the monitor in sleep mode. This is a reduced power consumption state ordered by the computer. The screen wakes up when a key is pushed or some other recognized user interaction occurs.

The least power is used when the monitor is turned off. Typically, this means the monitor is still drawing a small amount of power. To stop this power leak, plug the monitor into a power strip and turn it off at the power strip and not the monitor power switch.

COMMENT

Screen savers do not save power because the program running to display the image requires CPU resources.

[C] Electronic Products Environmental Assessment Tool™ (EPEAT™)

EPEAT™ is a tool that evaluates how "green" a product is prior to its purchase. It was created by the Green Electronic Council in cooperation with major electronic component manufacturers. EPEAT™ provides an independent standard for purchasers of electronic devices. It includes self-declaration of equipment conformance to the standard. These claims are randomly audited. EPEAT™'s criteria are based on the EPA's Energy Star requirements for PCs, IEEE 1680 Standard for Environmental Assessment of Personal Computer Products, and the "sensitive material" criteria requiring companies to meet the European Union's tough standards for limiting the hazardous chemicals and components used to make them.

COMMENT

Obtain the latest information about EPEAT™ at: www. greenelectronicscouncil.org.

Executive Order 13423 requires all U.S. federal agencies to use EPEAT™ when purchasing computer systems. Ninety-five percent of electronic products procured by federal agencies must meet EPEAT™ standards, as long there's a standard for that product.

EPEAT™'s 23 mandatory and 28 optional evaluation criteria cover such things as:

A.   Energy conservation.
B.   Recycling and disposal.
C.   Packaging materials.
D.   Reduction of environmentally sensitive materials.
E.   Design for end of life.

EPEAT™ evaluates electronic products according to three tiers of environmental performance—bronze, silver, and gold. A product must meet all the required criteria in order to qualify for EPEAT™ bronze. Manufacturers may pick and choose among the optional criteria to boost their EPEAT™ "score" to achieve a higher level.

A.   Bronze—Meets all 23 required criteria.
B.   Silver—Meets all required criteria plus at least 14 optional criteria.
C.   Gold—Meets all required criteria plus at least 21 optional criteria.

[D]   Advanced Configuration and Power Interface (ACPI)

ACPI was developed in 1996 by a group of major hardware and software manufacturers as an open industry standard. It defines the hardware and software interfaces that enable operating systems to configure and manage a device's power usage. Previous standards used the hardware to determine power management switching, and the results were sometimes unpredictable.

ACPI uses the Basic Input Output System (BIOS) chip on a computer to control the low-level hardware details under the control of the operating system. ACPI first appeared in Windows 98. An example of this is the "Power Option" module in the Windows™ Vista™ operating system. ACPI is also found in Linux and FreeBSD.

ACPI's power management language called ACPI Machine Language (AML) is embedded in the BIOS's firmware. It includes power event interruptions that are controlled by the operating system. The goal is to provide code that will run in all operating systems. However, ACPI must run with full privileges. This means that buggy or hacked code can easily damage a computer's data. Two power management modes are supported:

A. **Sleep mode.** A Windows PC can be set to sleep mode (or standby mode) after a period of inactivity. In this condition, the disk drives are stopped and the system state is maintained in RAM by a small amount of electricity. Take care! If total power is lost, so is everything in RAM. While in sleep mode your monitor draws about 5 watts and your PC about 2 watts. The savings are about the same as if the equipment was turned off for the night. The advantage is that when you wake it up, the machine is ready for work much faster than starting it from a cold state as everything is already in RAM.

B. **Hibernate mode.** Hibernate mode copies the computer's state to disk before shutting down. This is commonly used in notebook PCs. However, it takes noticeably longer than sleep mode to recover to full readiness. It also requires the same amount of free disk space as it has RAM. If a hibernating PC loses power, everything is still safely stored on disk for recovery.

[E]   Restriction of Hazardous Substances (ROHS) Directive

Among the strictest regulations on the computer industry is the European Union's Restriction of Hazardous Substances directive, or ROHS. This directive covers hardware sold in the European Union countries, although many other countries have also adopted it. ROHS restricts the sale of equipment with more than the permitted levels of:

A. Lead—found in solder, printed-circuit foil, and rechargeable batteries.
B. Cadmium—found in rechargeable batteries.
C. Mercury—found in high-intensity light bulbs, batteries, and high-voltage rectifier tubes.
D. Hexavalent chromium—found throughout electronic circuitry.
E. Polybrominated biphenyl (PBB)—a flame retardant.
F. Polybrominated diphenyl ether (PBDE)—flame retardants used in plastics.

In the United States, ROHS is a component of the EPEAT™ standards. The United States competes in global markets, and meeting global standards ensures that its products will be welcome in those markets.

[F] Virtualization

Past practice has been to purchase a new server to support each new application. This created more heat in the data center and consumed floor (or rack) space. This server also consumed electricity around the clock. In many cases, a server was used for less than an hour a day. This was compounded when servers were replaced with newer and more powerful equipment during the typical three-year equipment refresh cycle. Old servers that were lightly used are updated to even more powerful servers, which resulted in yet more idle time per day.

A popular solution is to let a collection of small applications share the same server. This reduces electrical usage because fewer servers are in operation. Consequently, this reduces energy required for cooling and frees floor space in the data center. This is accomplished by moving small applications on physical servers to virtual servers.

Virtualization is not new. It originated in mainframe computers decades ago and was more recently reintroduced into servers (themselves much more powerful than the long-gone mainframes). Virtualization creates a set of virtual machines within the operating environment of a server. Each virtual machine thinks that it is a physical device when it is actually a partition in RAM. If a virtual server needs to be restarted, just that partition is initialized while the rest of the physical server keeps running.

The cost of the software to create and manage these virtual environments is offset by the savings on buying servers and their licenses. There are additional savings on energy and cooling over what would have been the server's service life. Additionally, there is the energy savings.

> ## COMMENT
>
> For every watt of power used to power something in the data center, another watt is expended to cool it.

[G] Is Thin Client the Answer?

Another power-savings approach is the use of "thin client" devices instead of personal computers on desktops. The term "thin client" can mean many things. It is easier to explain by first describing a "fat client" device.

Basically, a fat client is a full-function personal computer. It pulls data out of the data center as needed and then processes it. A fat client has a hard drive for storing data and programs, etc. The problem with a fat client is that data on its drives are not backed up to offline media. A disk crash means data are lost. If software must be patched, then the changes must be tested against a wide range of applications and local operating system settings. Also, they must be scheduled around each end user's schedule. Also, if a fat client PC is broken, that worker is hindered until it is repaired, as his or her workspace is stored on the device.

A thin client contains just enough software to interact with a server that performs most of the processing. A thin client device is rather small and may be included in the same case as the monitor or the keyboard. If it breaks, then it can be easily swapped out because no data are stored within it.

With their smaller size and lack of a hard drive, thin clients need much less power than a PC. Some operate on as little as 5 watts. Part of this is due to the absence of a hard drive. Also, because the data are in the data center, there is no need for CD drives, floppy drives, and so on. A thin client usually has an embedded operating system stored in flash memory. Most offices have one PC per desk. Many of these have 300- to 500-watt power supplies in them. Consider the savings in energy usage by swapping them all for 5-watt units.

Of course, this only shifts the load from the desktop to the data center. Thin clients require a significant server support and a robust network along with space in the data center. There are many advantages to thin clients, notably the amount of control over programs run on the equipment. However, from a Green Technologies perspective, running a few servers requires less electricity than powering hundreds of PCs that spend much of their day idle.

§ 21.04 WHAT CAN YOU DO?

[A] The Basics

Sometimes companies are slow to act. There are things that you can do with your own desktop or department, ranging from the simple to the extreme. The tipping point is where more time is spent saving energy than is saved by reducing power usage. Also, few companies can afford to swap out all of their power hogs, so improvements are made one step at a time.

Energy waste is sometimes easy to spot. Power adapters attached to electrical outlets continue to draw electrical power even if the attached device is turned off. It seems like anything you use outside a PC's chassis has yet another power transformer. Each of these continues to draw power even when the device is turned off.

Another sign of waste is heat. Devices that are warm to touch indicate a loss of energy converted to heat. Not only does the heat represent wasted electricity but it increases the building's cooling load.

[B] Create a Power Usage Baseline

A clear baseline or starting point is important to show the progress you will make in your conservation program. It is difficult to use the company's electric bill to show less usage because so many things impact it, such as seasonal highs and lows of heat or air-conditioning use, addition of new equipment, and so on. It is easier to claim savings based on the power rating of devices and hours of nonuse saved.

Begin by gathering the power rating of each device in use. Yes, this will take a long time, but the Internet can speed this along. Also, there will be many devices that are the same (such as standardized purchase of PCs from one manufacturer), which minimizes the number of devices to research. This baseline is a measurement of where you are today. It will allow you to demonstrate the benefits provided by your Green initiative. Otherwise, the disconnect between the one who pays the bill and the ones who use the electricity will continue. Also, as you reduce, other departments may be piling on. Take the following steps:

A. Obtain an inventory of all equipment in the data center, on the desktop, and in between on the network. If such a list does not exist, then create one.
B. After you know what is in service, look up the devices on the manufacturer's site or e-mail them for the devices' rated power consumption, standby power usage, and cooling requirements. Note next to each item on the list its rated usage.
C. Identify the biggest electrical and cooling users. It is not always the biggest physical devices. These devices are warm to touch when in operation. These are targets for elimination.
D. Identify the cost per kilowatt for your facility.
E. Estimate the cost of cooling to be the same wattage as used to operate something. If you have doubts as to how much heat a personal computer generates, shut off the ventilation to a closed training room for a few hours and then step inside.

With this information in hand, you can now compare future purchase requests to existing usage to ensure the energy needed goes down with each purchase. Also, as you evaluate devices for updating your standard equipment list, you can select those with the smallest requirements.

[C]   Telecommuting

Telecommuting, or working virtually, is where office workers do their work from home. Now that high-speed networks are generally available, people can sit at home and do most of their daily work. Some companies offer their employees the chance to work from home one or two days every week.

Company savings from telecommuting include reduced electricity and cooling (because you are not there and your desktop unit is off). However, the savings to the environment are significant. Imagine the amount of air pollution saved if no one drove to work for two days per week! Employees with company-provided notebook PCs and cellular telephones can work from nearly anywhere.

Many people welcome the opportunity to work from home one day per week. Just the time saved from not commuting to work is reward enough! Companies that depend on a primarily virtual workforce can reduce their expensive office space and bring in each team for meetings one day per week. This maintains personal contact while dramatically reducing pollution from long commutes to work.

[D]   Enable Software-Controlled Power Management

Something you can do today is to turn on the power management settings on as many devices as possible. Operating systems include a Power Management module. This software sets a timer and, after a specified period of inactivity, will place the device into "sleep" mode. After an additional length of time, the device is completely turned off. As a way to save power, many companies set the sleep and power-off timers and then lock that module so only system administrators can change it.

> ## COMMENT
>
> Setting power management timers to a low value is a sure way to gain enemies. Be sure that the power settings take into account the length of a typical lunch break or office meeting.

Power management can be enabled on many different office devices. Printers, copiers, and fax machines typically have their own sleep mode and power-off settings. Take the time to learn about each to set them, or require the company supplying them to set it for you.

In many cases, if a device is to be idle for more than 16 minutes, it should switch to sleep mode. At that point it costs less energy to turn something back on than is used for it to consume electricity doing nothing. Consider how much your time is worth. If it takes a long time to shut down the computer and then restart it later, the value of your time will probably be much greater than the value of the amount of electricity you will save by turning off the computer.

> ## COMMENT
>
> Modern PCs are solidly built. They will become obsolete long before the effects of being switched on and off multiple times cause noticeable damage. Also, electronic devices produce heat, so turning them off reduces building cooling loads.

[E]   Buy Some Power Strips

Many devices arrive with a power transforming device that is plugged into the wall. Cell phone chargers are a good example. These devices remain active and drawing electrical power even when the device they are attached to is turned off. The amount of power consumed may be significant. Some larger devices also have a similar arrangement where they continue to consume electrical power even through the power switch is off.

Where possible, connect all of these devices to a power strip and then connect that power strip to the wall. At the end of the day when this equipment is no longer needed, turn off the power strip. That will completely disconnect everything from the power grid. If this is done for all desktop computers across the company, the savings will be noticeable. Refer back to your equipment inventory and add up the standby power that is no longer drawn by these devices.

[F]   Save Trees and Toner

An ongoing tragedy is the trash cans sitting outside a data center. Some people have mounds of paper printed and then use it little or not at all. Reports are picked up and much of the paper simply tossed away. Sometimes it is printed "just in case" the data center has a problem and then tossed at the end of the day. This can be reduced by providing reports online to everyone, and on CDs for those who "must" have a hard copy.

Printing is expensive! Printers use a lot of energy. They are physical devices with many moving parts. Add to that the ink or toner that hits the paper. Finally, there is the cost and time to dispose of the now unneeded paper. Because it is hard to tell what might violate security guidelines, many companies hire someone to come in and shred it all before disposal.

Therefore, online viewing of reports is an all-around time and money saver. Users receive their reports through e-mail or pull them out of an online directory. Report-viewing software permits selected pages to be printed or saved on a local hard drive.

[G]   Substitute One Piece at a Time

When compiling the energy usage baseline list, some of the devices will stand out as significant electrical consumers. Liquid crystal displays (LCD) use less than half of the electricity consumed by old, bulky cathode ray tube (CRT) monitors. However, select replacement models carefully. Sloppy design can result in a sleek-looking LCD using almost as much power as the CRT it replaced. The most efficient LCD monitors are those that use LED for backlighting.

Watch the trade press for technology trends toward more efficient equipment. For example, in notebook PCs, flash memory is becoming (an expensive) substitute for fixed disks. This lightens the weight and reduces battery drain. Solid state electronics are also more reliable than mechanic disk drives. As the cost for large-scale flash memory comes down, this will become more common.

Power stepping enables a CPU to adjust its power consumption based on demand. If there is less computing demand, the power used may drop by 30 percent. In some units, if the processor detects excessive heat, it will automatically switch to low power instead of damaging itself.

> **COMMENT**
>
> AMD's "PowerNow!" technology allows operating systems to dynamically adjust processor power states, voltage, and clocking frequencies depending on workload. Tests indicate this can reduce up to 75 percent of the CPU's power consumption.

Some devices just need to be available all of the time, such as network components (hubs, switches, etc.). In these cases, the goal is to replace existing devices with more energy-efficient equipment. Review all aspects of the network design to remove layers that may no longer be necessary. In most companies, networks have grown over time. Adding people here, moving departments there, and even work areas temporarily created may have left underutilized components strewn about.

§ 21.05 SAFE DISPOSAL

[A] Overview

Companies declare equipment to be surplus for a number of reasons. Some companies dispose of servers and desktop units when the three-year warranty expires. This way they hold down their repair costs. Also, the older the device, the more frequently its hardware will fail. The belief is that the newer hardware is significantly more powerful and reliable.

There are three categories of disposal: reuse elsewhere, recycle, or scrap. Each of these options has many variations. The key is to minimize the company's expense in proper disposal while ensuring that toxic materials are not introduced into the environment.

> **COMMENT**
>
> California's Electronic Waste Recycling Act of 2003 established a state-wide recycling program for obsolete computer and consumer electronics equipment. Retailers collect an electronic waste recycling fee at the point of sale of certain products. Distribution of recovery and recycling payments to qualified entities covers the cost of electronic waste collection and recycling. This law further recommends environmentally preferred purchasing criteria for state agency purchases of certain electronic equipment.

[B] Reuse Surplus Equipment Elsewhere

A part of your company's Green Technologies policy must include the collection of surplus electronic devices for disposal. Establish a collection point where everyone can drop off surplus items. Provide a set of tags that can be attached as they are dropped off. Usually this is a green tag for known good, yellow if it works but has minor problems, and a red tag for known bad.

Much of this hardware has plenty of useful life remaining in it. Where possible, it should be sold on the used-equipment market or donated to local charities. Technical schools can use older equipment to illustrate lessons on how to repair hardware. Used equipment vendors will snap equipment up for resale as a unit or to sell the individual parts.

[C] Recycling Old Technology

Recycling generally means to overhaul and then reuse something again (e.g., rebuilding a car engine is expensive but cheaper than purchasing a new one). The same is true for recycling printer supplies. Inkjet printer cartridges, laser printer toner cartridges, toner cartridges for copiers, and other devices can often be recycled. In many cases, a company will purchase the old cartridge from you. Some companies sell their empty cartridges to finance their annual Christmas party.

Computing hardware, such as monitors and personal computers, may have traces of valuable materials, but for the most part, the best way to recycle them is to assign them to a new purpose through donation or sale on the used equipment market.

[D] Tossing Equipment onto the Scrap Heap

If the device cannot be reused in this way, then disposal must be properly handled. Green Technologies ensures that electronic components, with the toxic substances used to create them, are properly disposed. Surplus equipment that is of no further use to the company (including defective circuit cards and components) must be properly broken apart through verifiable channels. This fulfills the company's responsibility to ensure the environmentally friendly demise of equipment.

There are various places that accept computing equipment for disposal:

A. Manufacturer sites.
B. Local government collection sites.
C. Private disposal companies.

Design for end of life is a concept in which the original design of a piece of hardware acknowledges that the item will someday become scrap. It minimizes the amount of toxic materials used in the manufacture of the equipment. Further, those toxic materials that are used will be easy to isolate from the nontoxic parts of the item.

So how big an issue is this? Computing equipment contains leads (in the solder), cadmium, mercury, hexavalent chromium, and polybrominated fire retardants. These serious pollutants must be excluded from the normal waste stream. Up to 50 million tons of surplus computing and cellular telephone equipment are dumped annually across the globe.

COMMENT

Proper disposal of nonvolatile memory, such as disk drives and static RAM storage, is important to ensure the security of company data. Companies must ensure that the data on all equipment leaving for disposal or reuse is properly deleted according to Department of Defense standards.

Many major manufacturers have long recognized the problems with improper disposal of equipment. Two of the popular programs are:

A. Hewlett-Packard accepts equipment from consumers no matter what brand it is. It sorts incoming devices for reuse or to recapture materials used to create it. The latest information and guidelines for HP's extensive program can be found at: www.hp.com/hpinfo/globalcitizenship/gcreport/productreuse.html.

B. Dell computers offers the "Dell Earth" program, which provides consumers free recycling of Dell-brand computer equipment. You may also recycle the computing equipment from other manufacturers if it is together with the purchase of a new Dell computer. Dell offers its Asset Recovery services to companies for recycling their old equipment at: www.dell.com/assetrecovery.

22

DOCUMENT MANGEMENT: CAPTURING CORPORATE KNOWLEDGE

§ 22.01   OVERVIEW
          [A]   Purpose and Scope
          [B]   Critical Policies to Develop Based on This Chapter

§ 22.02   CAPTURE AND STORAGE
          [A]   Capture Options
          [B]   Storage Options
          [C]   Indexing
          [D]   Retention, Compliance, and Legal Issues
          [E]   Security

§ 22.03   RETRIEVAL AND COLLABORATION
          [A]   Document Access
          [B]   Annotation and Redaction
          [C]   Workflow

§ 22.04   PRINTING AND ARCHIVING
          [A]   Legal Requirements
          [B]   Long-Term Storage
          [C]   Disaster Recovery

§ 22.05   DESIGNING A SOLUTION
          [A]   Gathering Business Requirements
          [B]   Technical Requirements
          [C]   Planning for Implementation

§ 22.01 OVERVIEW

[A] Purpose and Scope

While the paperless office has not yet arrived, document management solutions available today are a big step in making the paperless office a reality. An appropriate document management system will not only reduce the number of trees killed to support your business but will also help you to meet legal requirements, such as Sarbanes-Oxley and HIPAA, and support your disaster recovery plan.

A document stored electronically has many advantages over a printed piece of paper. The advantages include:

A. A single copy is available to more than one person at a time without physically making copies.
B. Backups of the document are easy to create and retrieve if needed.
C. Electronic documents are harder to lose—they cannot easily be lost by misfiling.
D. They can be found using computerized search technologies.
E. They can be processed by a workflow system and quickly routed to the appropriate person.
F. They are much cheaper to store than paper.

Document management encompasses all systems and processes used to capture, store, manage, and print information that either originates physically on paper or that is created using document-creation software such as Microsoft Office. This includes the storage of paper or microfiche in file cabinets and the storage of documents in electronic formats on a computer system. When evaluating an existing or proposed document management system, consider the following questions:

A. What are the documents that are critical to my business?
B. What is document collaboration?
C. Why not just put documents in a file cabinet?
D. What about my offsite storage?
E. How much can we afford to spend?
F. What regulations do I have to follow?
G. How long do I need to keep documents?
H. Can I incorporate my existing documents into this system?
I. Is the system easy to use?
J. When can I get started?

[B] Critical Policies to Develop Based on This Chapter

Using the material discussed in this chapter, you will be able to create the following policies:

A. Document Management Policy Scope.
B. Document Retention Policy.

   C. Document Capture Procedures.
   D. Document Management System Implementation Procedures.

Policies should always be developed based on the local situation. Successful managers cannot issue appropriate guidance if the policies are written with another company's or location's situation in mind.

§ 22.02 CAPTURE AND STORAGE

[A] Capture Options

A document management system must make it easy for documents to be captured and stored in the system. For paper-based documents, the capture process must be a fast, simple, and reliable way to capture the valuable information stored on paper and convert it into a digital format that can be efficiently stored and made available to those who need it.

Source documents come in many flavors. They might be on paper or stored in a computer using the native file format of the application that created the document. Paper documents come in many different sizes, including (in inches) $8\frac{1}{2} \times 11$, 11×17, 17×22, 22×34, and 34×44. The International Organization for Standardization (ISO) has created a standard paper size system specifying a number of formats; the most common formats and their uses are:

   A. A0, A1—technical drawings, posters.
   B. A1, A2—flip charts.
   C. A2, A3—drawings, diagrams, large tables.
   D. A4—letters, magazines, forms, catalogs, laser printer and copying machine output.
   E. A5—note pads.
   F. A6—postcards.
   G. B5, A5, B6, A6—books.
   H. B4, A3—newspapers, supported by most copying machines in addition to A4.

Of course, most documents created in the modern office start out as an electronic file; many never see physical paper. Popular electronic file formats include:

   A. .doc—Microsoft Word 2003 and earlier.
   B. .docx—Microsoft Word 2007.
   C. .html—web page.
   D. .pdf—Adobe portable document format.
   E. .rtf—rich-text format.
   F. .tiff—used for images.
   G. .txt—plain-text file.

H. .xml—Extensible Markup Language; a standard for creating markup languages that describe the structure of data.

Documents can also arrive at the organization through e-mail attachments or via a network fax server. When reviewing document capture options, consider the following:

A. How many documents will you need to capture?
B. How often will the system be utilized?
C. What condition are the documents in? Documents in good condition can be scanned using an automatic document feeder; older or worn documents may have to be scanned by hand on a flatbed.
D. What are the dimensions of the documents? Larger documents such as blueprints or architectural drawings may require a large flatbed device.
E. Can the system be centrally administered? Centralized administration can lessen the burden on the service desk by reducing configuration errors caused by users in remote locations.
F. How well the system scale? As your needs change and increase, will the system be able to handle future volumes?
G. Does the system support batch processing of documents? Batch input of documents is important when source documents arrive in batches.
H. Can documents be easily grouped together?

Most organizations will want to consider using a scanner with an automatic document feeder. This allows a stack of documents to be scanned at one time, rather than having each page placed by hand on the flatbed of the scanner. The most important consideration is that the scanner be able to handle the size and condition of the majority of paper documents to be scanned by the organization.

[B] Storage Options

Two questions need to be addressed concerning document storage options: how will original paper documents be stored and how will electronic documents be stored? There are basically three options for dealing with original paper documents:

A. **Store in file cabinets.** You may need to store the original documents in a readily accessible location if quick access to the original is a business requirement. The main disadvantage is the cost of file cabinets and storage space required.
B. **Use a professional document storage company.** This option eliminates the need for onsite storage but does come at a cost. Access to the physical document may require several hours for the document to be retrieved and delivered. This is a good method for storing e-mail if the SEC is a potential auditor.
C. **Shred documents after scanning**. For most documents the original copy is not required, so the paper can be shredded and

recycled. Shredding can be done onsite or the documents taken offsite to be shredded.

COMMENT

Companies that provide offsite storage include Fireproof Records, Global Relay, and Iron Mountain.

There are several options for the storage of digital documents:

A. **Magnetic media (hard drives).** This is the storage media used by the typical computer. This type of storage is becoming increasingly cheaper and allows for fast access to digital documents. Technologies such as storage area networks (SANs) and network attached storage (NASs) support scaling your storage requirements to whatever is needed. Its main drawback is that it contains a large number of moving parts that are subject to failure.

B. **Compact disks (CDs).** These are small disks used to store digital information. Their main advantages include low cost, durability, and ubiquitousness. The CDs main disadvantage is the limited amount of storage available per disk (650 MB).

C. **Digital video disk (DVDs).** A DVD is essentially a larger CD. Like a CD, it is very durable and ubiquitous but holds up to eight times as much information as a CD.

An electronic document management system must not only reliably store digital documents today but must also support new technologies developed in the future. To increase the chances of the system supporting future technologies, nonproprietary file formats for both scanned documents and documents created by software applications should be used. This will help ensure that a move to a new and improved system in the future will not require documents to be converted from a no-longer-supported file format. The two most common and oldest standard file formats are ASCII for text and TIFF for images. It is a good bet that future systems will continue to support these formats.

[C] Indexing

Indexing of documents when they are captured make it easier to find the document later. Common indexing processes include:

A. **OCR/pattern matching.** OCR (optical character recognition) translates printed characters into alphanumeric characters recognized by a computer. This allows the document to be stored not just as a picture but as the words in the document. OCR cannot usually translate handwriting or characters created with ornamental fonts. Pattern matching provides the capture of data on a form based on a desired pattern. For example a Social Security number is in the pattern of xxx-xx-xxxx. Pattern matching will look for this pattern and translate the result (using OCR) into an index field.

B. **Full-text indexing.** Full-text indexing is used in conjunction with OCR to allow the entire text of a document to be searched. The usefulness of full-text indexing depends upon the accuracy of the OCR process and the power of the search logic. There are several search options that make full-text indexes more useful:

   1. Soundex—This is a phonetic algorithm for indexing names by their sound when pronounced in English. This allows for words with the same pronunciation to be encoded to the same string so that matching can occur despite minor differences in spelling.

   2. Fuzzy logic—Allows for minor differences in spelling of words to still return a match during a search. The helps compensates either for words that were misspelled in the source document or for errors in the OCR process.

   3. Wildcards—Allows for the use of special characters in a search to match portions of a word. Common wildcard characters are the asterisk (*), used to match any character or characters ("comp*" would find the words "computer" and "company"), and question mark (?) for matching any single character ("d?g" would find the words "dig", "dog," and "dug").

   4. Proximity—Used to find occurrences of words used within a specified number of characters or words from each other.

C. **Metadata.** Metadata is the use of index field information stored about a document that makes a search quick and easy. For example, you might associate in an index the date the document was created, the author, a subject, etc. You can then use this metadata index to quickly find the document. This is especially helpful if the metadata does not occur within the text of the document.

D. **Electronic folders.** By creating electronic file folders, search time can be reduced by only searching specific folders. It also allows users to browse a folder that contains documents of the type they seek. A flexible electronic folder system also eases the transition from a paper-based file system to an electronic one by having the electronic folders mimic the paper-based system.

[D] Retention, Compliance, and Legal Issues

Most documents have a shelf life. Few documents need to be kept forever, so it is important to have a document retention policy to provide guidance on when a document should no longer take up valuable shelf or disk space. A document retention policy should make your organization more efficient while avoiding litigation due to the improper destruction of documents. Federal and state laws dictate how certain documents should be handled and stored, and the method of their destruction.

It is vitally important to follow the document management process that you have put into place. If a scanning solution is implemented but the paper document is retained, a court of law may ask for the original paper-based document. In this case having the electronic document does you no good. But if your process is to scan the paper document then destroy the original, a court of law must recognize the electronic document as the best evidence. In this case the metadata and index search become more powerful.

COMMENT

The trial and collapse of Arthur Andersen made clear the importance of a well-thought-out document retention policy.

Your document retention policy should address the following:

A. What documents will be maintained?
B. How long should each type of document be kept?
C. What process should be used to destroy each type of document?
D. Who is ultimately responsible for retention activities?
E. When and how will retention policies bee tested.
F. How is the destruction of documents to be tracked?

The following types of documents should be covered in your document retention policy:

A. **Accounting documents.** This includes gross receipts, expense receipts, and other business transactions. Often this is the most paper-intensive area in a business.
B. **Business records.** This includes articles of incorporation, bylaws, capital stock, copyrights, and trademark registration and patents.
C. **Tax records.** This includes any documentation to support deductions and well as federal, state, and local tax returns.
D. **Personnel records.** Employment records are critical for dealing with lawsuits from current and former employees. This includes resumes, applications, performance reviews, and employment contracts. Employee records should be kept at least five years after the employee leaves the company.
E. **Legal records.** Documents such as customer and supplier contracts, intellectual property, and corporate records must be retained.
F. **Electronic records.** E-mail is becoming a critical means of business communication and is subject to discovery in legal proceedings. Other forms of electronic communication such as instant messaging and web pages may also need to be retained.

Exhibit 22-1 lists the generally recommended retention period for different types of documents. These are only guidelines; please consult the advice of your organization's legal and accounting advisors for specifics that may apply to your type of business and your legal jurisdiction.

EXHIBIT 22-1.   Generally Recommended Document Retention Period

Type of Document	Retention Period
Most financial records	4 years
Auditor's reports	Permanent
Annual financial statements	Permanent
Payroll records	6 years
Business records	Permanent
Insurance records	6 years
Tax records	Permanent
Pension and profit sharing records	Permanent
Personnel records	6 years
Press releases	Permanent
Legal documents	10 years
Sales and marketing documents	3 years
E-mails	Depends on subject

All paper documents are to be destroyed at the end of the retention period using a licensed and bonded third-party document destruction company that can bring the destruction equipment onsite. This will allow the destruction of the documents to be monitored.

COMMENT

The latest information on tax record retention can be found at the IRS Web site at www.irs.gov.

See Policy ITP-22-1 Document Retention Policy as an example.

POLICY ITP-22-1.   Document Retention Policy

Policy #:	ITP-22-1	**Effective:**	03/18/09	**Page #:**	1 of N
Subject:	Document Retention Policy				

1.0 PURPOSE

The company views documents created and received by the company as an asset of the company to be managed and protected. The law requires the certain types of documents be maintained for a specified period of time; failure to do so may subject the company and any responsible employees to lawsuits and fines.

2.0 SCOPE

This policy encompasses all documents in all their forms and throughout their lifecycle. This includes documents such as memos, contracts, account information, e-mails, instant messages, etc. The following types of documents are covered by this policy:

- A. Accounting documents. This includes gross receipts, expense receipts, and other business transactions.
- B. Business records. This includes articles of incorporation, bylaws, capital stock, copyrights, and trademark registration and patents.
- C. Tax records. This includes any documentation to support deductions and well as federal, state, and local tax returns.
- D. Personnel records. Employment records are critical for dealing with lawsuits from current and former employees. This includes resumes, applications, performance reviews, and employment contracts. Employee records should be kept at least five years after the employee leaves the company.
- E. Legal records. Documents such as customer and supplier contracts, intellectual property, and corporate records must be retained.
- F. Electronic records. E-mail is becoming a critical means of business communication and is subject to discovery in legal proceedings. Other forms of electronic communication such as instant messaging and web pages may also need to be retained.

The CEO will appoint a person to be responsible for implementing all aspects of this policy.

3.0 POLICY

The company has established a retention and destruction policy for documents received or created by the company to ensure compliance with legal requirements and to protect the company's intellectual property. The retention policy for each type of document is listed below:

Type of Document	Retention Period
Most financial records	4 years
Auditor's reports	Permanent
Annual financial statements	Permanent
Payroll records	6 years
Business records	Permanent
Insurance records	6 years
Tax records	Permanent
Pension and profit sharing records	Permanent
Personnel records	6 years
Press releases	Permanent
Legal documents	10 years
Sales and marketing documents	3 years
E-mails	Depends on subject

All paper documents are to be destroyed at the end of the retention period using a licensed and bonded third-party document destruction company that can bring the destruction equipment onsite. This will allow the destruction of the documents to be monitored.

4.0 REVISION HISTORY

Date	Revision #	Description of Change
03/18/09	1.0	Initial creation.

5.0 INQUIRIES

Direct inquiries about this policy to:

Tom Jones, CIO
Our Company, Inc.
2900 Corporate Drive
Columbus, OH 43215

Voice: 614-555-1234
Fax: 614-555-1235
E-mail: tjones@company.com

Revision #:	1.0	Supersedes:	N/A	Date:	03/18/09

[E]   Security

Security is critical to the success of a document management system—you don't want the wrong document to fall into the wrong hands at the wrong time. In addition, the system's security should ensure that legitimate users are able to do their job and not compromise the integrity of the underlying database, file system, and network. The document management system should provide multiple levels of security, including the authentication of users, the proper assignment of what the user is authorized to do, and the logging of activity in an audit trail.

The system must balance access and security through the control of access to the system and control over what each user is able to do once in the system. Access to the system is done through some sort of authentication process, which might include any combination of the following:

A. **Username/password.** The user gains access by providing a username and password.
B. **Login levels.** Access to certain features and functions is based on the user's login level.
C. **Biometric.** Access is controlled by scanning a fingerprint or by voice recognition.

Once authenticated into the system, the user is allowed to perform activities based on the rights set up by the system administrator. There are several basic types of rights that the system should support:

A. **Individual/group rights.** Rights can be assigned to each user individually or as a member of a group.
B. **Access rights.** Rights are assigned to specific objects in the system, such as folders and documents.
C. **Feature rights.** Determines what actions a user can perform, such as view or read/write.

The security system should also support the logging of all system activity and the generation of audit trails. It should include who used the system and when and what actions were performed. Especially important is logging unsuccessful attempts to access content or to make unauthorized changes to documents.

§ 22.03 RETRIEVAL AND COLLABORATION

[A] Document Access

Access to the right information stored in the right document by the right person at the right time is the ultimate purpose of any document management system. Another strength of a document management system is the ability of multiple users to access a single document at the same time. The system should support the following process for getting documents into user's hands:

A. **Online access.** Most document management systems include an application that is run on the user's workstation to support searching and managing documents.
B. **Intranet and Internet.** This allows the user to access documents using a web browser on the organization's intranet or via the public Internet.
C. **Print and fax.** The system should support common printers and fax systems.
D. **CD and DVD.** CDs and DVDs are common ways to send large volumes of documents that might be too much for other methods.
E. **E-mail.** E-mail has become the most common form of communication in business today; e-mail makes it possible to distribute documents widely at a very low cost. The system should allow the e-mailing of documents such that the recipient does not require any special software to read the document.
F. **Portable folders.** This allows users to synchronize important documents between their laptop and the document management system, so that they have copies when needed on their laptop when they are not connected to the system.

[B] Annotation and Redaction

Annotation is the mark up of documents without altering the original. Common annotations include highlighting a portion of text, using special stamps such as "draft" or "secret," and adding comments and redaction (using blackout or whiteout to hide text). A document management system's security should allow the administrator to control who can annotate documents and what annotations are visible to what users. All annotations should be overlays that in no way alter the original document. In this way the original document can still be printed or viewed by those with the proper security.

[C] Workflow

Workflow can have a major impact on the efficiency of an organization by automating the routing of work documents from one person to another. An example is a purchase order that is created then routed to the appropriate people for approval and payment. Rules can be created so that the purchase order goes through one series of steps if the amount is below a certain threshold, and a different series of step if it is above a specified amount. Workflow can be of two different types:

A. **Serial or linear.** The document flows in a single path from one person or department to another until the workflow is complete. At a single step only one person can route the document to the next task.

B. **Parallel or group.** The document can be routed to the next step by more than one person. For example, a purchase order is approved for payment if any one of three different accounting clerks approves it for payment. Or, a proposal may require the approval of two different managers in a single step before going on to the next step.

A workflow system also helps to eliminate bottlenecks by giving management visibility into the status of any document at any time. The system can also notify users if a document has been waiting for some action past an acceptable amount of time.

§ 22.04 PRINTING AND ARCHIVING

[A] Legal Requirements

As regulatory requirements continue to increase, a document management system becomes an increasingly critical tool to ensure the organization is in compliance with regulations at the local, state, and federal level. A properly implemented system can help ensure compliance by enforcing the consistent application of document policies and procedures and by providing a verifiable audit trail of all actions taken surrounding a document.

While legal requirements will differ in the details, two major features must be supported to fulfill the basics requirements of most regulations:

A. **Storage media cannot be altered.** All activities performed on a document from creation to destruction must be tracked in a way that cannot be altered.

B. **Information must be set in time.** All activities performed on a document from creation to destruction must be time-stamped in a way that cannot be altered.

In addition to the items above, other features that the document management system should support to meet legal requirements include:

A. Documents can be retrieved and printed as needed.
B. Indexes should be used to allow for quick retrieval.
C. Documents are stored on appropriate media.
D. Documentation on how the system works must be available and up to date.
E. Cross-referencing of other systems should be allowed.

F. Controls should be in place to detect and prevent the deterioration of documents.

While following the processes just listed should keep you in compliance with most legal requirements, a local attorney should be consulted for any specific local requirements.

[B]   Long-Term Storage

All document management systems do a good job of storing documents for today's software and hardware environment, but what about long term? Many vital records must be kept in perpetuity; will you have the hardware and software available to retrieve these documents 50 or 100 years from now? There are several issues to consider that can affect your ability to access documents in the future:

A. **Media failure.** All media will eventually fail; hard drives, CDs, DVDs, and tapes do not last forever. The only way to avoid media failure is to periodically read and refresh the data to new media.
B. **Software failure.** All software has bugs; it is possible that a bug in the software could damage a document.
C. **Obsolete data formats.** Software for creating documents gets updated to "new and improved" file formats or may at some point be no longer available.
D. **Site failure.** If all your documents are stored in one place, will they survive a fire or natural disaster?
E. **Organizational failure.** If an organization ceases to exist, what happens to the important documents being stored?

COMMENT

While the tapes containing the data on how to build a Saturn V rocket still exist, there are no longer any machines available to read the data. And even if you could read the data, the software to turn that data into useful information is no longer available!

[C]   Disaster Recovery

One of the most important aspects of a document management system is its support for your disaster recovery plan. The digital archiving of documents simplifies the disaster recovery planning by making it easy to store important documents offline in a secure location. Backups of entire document repositories can easily be made to portable media such as CD, DVD, and tape and stored in a secure location. The documents can then be easily restored if the active documents are lost. The document management system should provide software to allow viewing of the documents stored on the backup media.

§ 22.05 DESIGNING A SOLUTION

[A] Gathering Business Requirements

The first step required in a document management project is the documentation of all of the business reasons for doing this project. As cool as the technology might be, it only exists to help us meet one or more requirements of the business. This is true not just in document management projects, but for any project that will change how the organization functions. This activity will include the following steps:

A. Determining the primary business objective.
B. Documenting the secondary business objectives.
C. Determining the financial value of meeting the business objectives.
D. Understanding your organization's technical and user environments.

There are always more projects than there are funds available in almost any organization. Your document management project is just one of many projects that management will be asked to fund.

The first step in designing a document management system is the determination of the business objectives of the project. There are many good business reasons why an organization would consider implementing a document management system. Maybe the organization is looking to implement a disaster recovery plan. Maybe there is some regulatory compliance issue related to your industry that requires you to be able to efficiently retrieve documents. Your employees might be asking for a better way to share documents. Or maybe it's just that the number of filing cabinets is overwhelming and there is no end in sight to the growth. It seems that every new business day we discover that another document or set of documents is lost or missing.

All of these business needs are found throughout every conceivable type of business, whether your business is one person in your basement or a Fortune 500 corporation with operations in several countries. Everyone deals with paper and filing paper and the problems that paper generates.

So the issue here is that one of these needs or maybe several of these needs are the reason why a company would want or need to implement a document management solution. Defining the most critical needs is to define your business objectives.

Business objectives will vary from organization to organization. But the primary function of a document management system is to store information in an organized fashion and to make that information available to end users in such a manner that they are able to enter key points or indexes about the document, and the result is what they need to work with. The information must also be sharable across the network or maybe even the entire world if the information is public in nature. The document management system end user must also be able to print any document on demand or have the ability to e-mail or distribute the document if the need arises. Additionally, the document management system must be able to accommodate multiple file types and the existence of electronic files along with digital images.

All of these aspects are and will be business objectives that need to be met in order for a document management system to be implemented. A particular business may have only one of these items as its objective, or a business may have all of them. But at least one of the mentioned items will be present in order for a document management system to be necessary.

While there are usually many objectives for a project, the primary business objective oftentimes is the only reason for purchasing and implementing a document management solution. Once the primary objective is met, then and only then will you be able to move on to secondary and ancillary business objectives. However, often we find that multiple objectives are met because of the overlapping nature of documents.

As an example, ABC Company was having a hard time storing dispatch records. A technician would complete work at a customer's site and the ensuing record or document would be stored in a traditional steel filing cabinet. With the ever-growing set of documents to track service technicians' hours, it was time to digitize the documents and store them electronically. This electronic storage of the documents was the primary business objective.

A secondary business objective was discovered at the same time. Once the documents were electronic, searching for a particular item was shortened often from days or weeks to seconds. Once an operator knew what he or she needed to search for—technician name, ID number, or a word-text search—the result was displayed on the computer screen in seconds.

This secondary objective was discovered only after the initial objective had been met. The financial windfall was that both objectives were met with the same initial investment in the application.

Determining financial benefits is a very complex process, and it is very often difficult to get an exact answer. If a company or department is doing research, then the paper copy is invaluable and a price cannot be put on preserving the data forever. In a real estate environment where many different parties have a copy of the same document, it might be a matter of simply making an electronic copy and moving on. The cost to have someone photocopy the document and ship a new version is considerably lower than having to re-create a research document from scratch.

Financial benefit is determined by the value of the data on the paper and what goes into storing the ever-growing amount of paper. Here are some items to consider when evaluating financial benefit of a document management solution:

A. What is my current cost to store paper?
B. What is the long-term storage requirement?
C. What is the relative value of the data on the paper?
D. Can I easily recreate the paper?
E. Does someone else own a copy of the paper document?
F. Is there some regulation forcing me to preserve the data?

At this point in the discussion you must stop and ask yourself: how do I store paper for my office? Several questions come to mind when determining the current physical storage and also determining the eventual physical storage once you start to store some or all of the documents digitally:

A. What is the physical environment available to house all of the documents that are used during the normal course of business?
B. How many pages need to be stored (weekly, monthly, and annually)?
C. What sizes of documents need to be stored?

Remember to consider different sizes of documents used in various departments, such as small invoice documents in accounting. Accounting departments are full of many different sizes of paper—check stubs, invoices, receipts, cash register receipts, etc.

Part of the discussion must also be centered around documents that are never on paper. Accounting applications can print reports to an electronic file. Resumes are routinely written and then e-mailed from recipient to recipient until they are either eventually printed or stored electronically. A good, usable document management application should be able to have electronically created documents stored right alongside scanned paper documents.

[B] Technical Requirements

Once the business requirements are understood, the requirements can be compared against available hardware and software to design a solution that fits the organization. A document management system will require at least a personal computer. In many cases the system will be installed on a network file server and then be distributed to end users by way of their personal workstation. A workstation can be directly connected to the file server either by way of a network cable or over a connection through the Internet.

The most important aspect of the technical environment is the amount of hard disk space that will be required to store the paper images. What a document management system will do first and foremost is store electronic images of paper documents. Vast amounts of paper documents exist in today's business climate, and this usually makes up the bulk of the information that will be stored in the system. So we need to be aware of the number of pages and take into consideration size of paper and whether any of the documents need to be scanned in color.

Another issue of a technical nature is what different types of systems will be delivering information into the system. This includes scanners, AS400 mainframes, digital copiers, existing PDF images, and business software applications such as AutoCAD and accounting and practice management applications.

Network infrastructure is vitally important to the end users who are using the document management system. A good infrastructure is necessary to move the large amounts of data that are found within a document management system. If the network infrastructure is not adequate, once a large number of documents are scanned the whole system will begin to run slower and or halt business productivity. One of the many reasons to implement a document management system is to increase productivity. If productivity is diminished because of poor execution of the network infrastructure, then you are not better off. This argument is true of any software application but is even more important for a document management system due to the nature of a scanned image. In a pure database application a weak network infrastructure may be usable for several years because the data being entered are placed within a database. A document management system uses the database as well, but the existence of the image magnifies the weak network infrastructure and a network slowdown or failure will be imminent.

Workstation and server hardware should be fairly new and robust. Many document management systems require the use of a fat client. A fat client is software loaded on the local workstation that connects with the server component. Other document management systems will store the documents on an Internet-connected server and only require a web browser to attach to the server. This will allow older equipment at the workstation or even appliance terminals to be used as the client workstation. However, with newer software it is advisable to stay current on the workstation hardware. Upgrades to hardware and software should be considered every year and completed when productivity begins to decrease due to old or outdated hardware and software.

The same discussion about the workstation is also true of the server. Servers purchased from most hardware suppliers and manufacturers usually carry a three-year warranty. The hard drives in the server may have a five-year warranty. The technology is upgraded so fast that more often than not the server will need to be upgraded at every three years, and it is advisable to upgrade at least within five years of purchase.

Of equal importance with computer hardware is the scanning hardware used to convert paper documents into digital ones. Devices used to scan paper documents fall into the following categories:

A. **Scanner only.** Scanning is the only function the device performs.
B. **Multifunction devices.** The device performs functions besides scanning, such as copying and printing documents.
C. **Desktop scanners.** A small device the sits on a desktop and is typically used by a single user at a single workstation.
D. **Workgroup scanners.** A larger device that is connected to multiple users via the local area network.

[C]   Planning for Implementation

Implementing a document management solution is similar to any other IT project. An internal project leader must be assigned to see the project through to completion. The project leader will also be responsible for managing the activities of outside vendors used, especially the selected document management solution vendor. Planning is critical for the success of the project and should include the following:

A. **Organize the project team.** The team should include representatives from the user community as well as IT.

B. **Develop a detailed work plan.** Break the project down into manageable phases with clear deliverables at the end of each phase.
C. **Hold regular status meetings.** Review project progress on a regular basis.
D. **Develop a communication plan.** Be sure to keep all important stakeholders informed of progress as well as any issues that come up.
E. **Develop a support plan.** The long-term success of the project will depend on the quality and level of support available to users. The plan should include service level agreements and how issues are to be handled.

End-user training is critical for the success of a document management solution. Training should be performed onsite if possible so that the users' training experience is as close to what they will experience on the job as possible. Make sure that all end users understand the following:

A. How does a user get access?
B. What is the scan procedure?
C. What is the retrieval procedure?
D. How is tech support supplied?
   1. Via Web site?
   2. Via telephone?
E. Who is the onsite expert?
F. Is follow-up training available?

23

THE INTERNET: MAKING IT PRODUCTIVE

§ 23.01   OVERVIEW
    [A]   Purpose and Scope
    [B]   Policy Objectives
    [C]   Critical Policies to Develop Based on This Chapter

§ 23.02   METHODS OF INTERNET ACCESS
    [A]   Overview
    [B]   Individual Access
    [C]   Corporate/Networked Internet Access

§ 23.03   INTERNET SECURITY POLICY
    [A]   Responsibility
    [B]   Firewall Usage
    [C]   Internet Usage Control
    [D]   Internet Training

§ 23.04   INTERNET E-MAIL USE POLICY
    [A]   Overview
    [B]   Tracking Internet Usage
    [C]   Internet and E-mail Use Guidelines
    [D]   E-mail Etiquette
    [E]   E-mail Marketing
    [F]   E-mail Archiving

§ 23.05   MESSAGING AND BLOGGING POLICY
    [A]   Instant Messaging (IM)
    [B]   Blogging
    [C]   Peer-to-Peer Applications

§ 23.06   ACCEPTABLE USE AGREEMENT
    [A]   Overview
    [B]   Sample Acceptable Use Agreement

§ 23.07   SOFTWARE AS A SERVICE
    [A]   Overview
    [B]   Definition
    [C]   Application Outsourcing Policies

§ 23.08 SAAS VENDOR SELECTION PROCESS
    [A] Overview
    [B] Request for Proposal
    [C] Evaluating SaaS Vendors' Proposals

§ 23.09 SAAS VENDOR MANAGEMENT
    [A] Overview
    [B] Service Level Agreement

§ 23.01 OVERVIEW

[A] Purpose and Scope

Internet and e-mail policy formalizes standards for how the company connects to the outside world through the Internet and e-mail, and how these services are used by employees. While the Internet provides access to a wealth of valuable information and facilitates communication, it also exposes the company to a number of dangers. Some of the issues that cause problems for a company when employees use the Internet include:

- Productivity—uncontrolled access to the Internet can drain away employee time and irresponsible use reduces network resource availability for critical business operations.
- Inappropriate content—employees who view inappropriate content while on the job leave the company open to potentially damaging litigation.
- Exposing proprietary information—a connection to the Internet opens the potential for others to access the company's valuable proprietary information.

The Internet and e-mail policy covers all types of connections to the outside world through the Internet. The types of connections include:

- An individual computer using a plain old telephone service (POTS) connection through a modem (wired or wireless).
- An individual computer or workgroup server using wireless access over a cellular network.
- A workgroup server using an ISDN, DSL, T1/T3, or cable modem connection.

The policy also covers all activities performed while using the Internet, including but not limited to browsing (viewing Web pages), using e-mail, Instant Messaging (IM), blogging (using Web logs), and transferring files using file transfer protocol (FTP).

[B] Policy Objectives

Policies developed for Internet and e-mail use should provide guidelines to ensure the secure, proper, and reliable use of the Internet. Policy objectives should be flexible enough to cover new methods of Internet connectivity and technologies as they become available.

The company's Internet and e-mail use policy should be part of the new employee orientation process. All new or existing employees should sign an acknowledgment that they have received a copy of this policy and that they will abide by it. The Internet and e-mail use policy should also appear in the employee handbook. An online message, appearing when the user logs onto e-mail or the Internet, is helpful to remind employees of this policy. The company should offer training sessions on proper Internet and e-mail usage.

> **Comment**
>
> Research in 2002–2004 by IDC found that companies lose up to $3,000 per year per employee due to non-business related Internet activity, and that 30–40 percent of Web access had nothing to do with the employee's job, resulting in lost productivity and an increased risk of legal liability.

[C]   Critical Policies to Develop Based on This Chapter

Using the material discussed in this chapter, you will be able to create the following policies:

A. Internet Usage.
1. Appropriate use defined.
2. Inappropriate use defined.
B. Electronic Mail.
1. Appropriate use defined.
2. Inappropriate use defined.
3. Privacy.
4. Prohibit use of third-party e-mail systems on company computers.
C. Internet Security.
1. Downloading of files is prohibited.
2. Disabling installed firewalls and anti-virus software is never permitted.
3. Peer-to-peer music swapping programs are forbidden on company equipment.
D. Instant Messaging.
1. Appropriate use defined.
2. Inappropriate use defined.
E. Web Logs (Blogging).
1. Appropriate use defined.
2. Inappropriate use defined.

Policies should always be developed based on the local situation. Successful managers cannot issue appropriate guidance if the policies are written with another company's or location's situation in mind.

§ 23.02   METHODS OF INTERNET ACCESS

[A]   Overview

There are several methods to connect to the Internet from an individual workstation. Each individual workstation might have its own connection to an

Internet Service Provider (ISP) or be connected through the corporate network. The connection itself can be on-demand or continuously connected to the Internet. Each method has its own set of advantages and disadvantages. The IT Manager is responsible for developing policy on how corporate computer systems are connected to the Internet.

[B] Individual Access

The simplest method technically to connect to the Internet (usually done by the smallest organizations) is for each individual PC to connect directly to an ISP using a modem and a POTS line. The user's PC connects to the local ISP using dial-up networking (if using Microsoft Windows) and uses a browser to view content on the World Wide Web.

The IT technical support unit develops the procedure for connecting to the Internet through individual PCs. The technical support unit also determines the browser software used and may need to install the browser on the user's PC if not preinstalled.

An advantage of this method is there is less direct exposure of the network to the outside world if any existing network connection is unplugged. Another is the user's PC is exposed for only the time it is connected. This gives hackers less opportunity to gain access to the user's PC. Personal firewall software should be used as a form of protection while connected to the Internet.

A disadvantage of individual connections to the Internet is the lack of centralized monitoring or control. Usage standards cannot easily be enforced, and virus protection is left up to the user. Speed is severely limited when using a modem and POTS line. Anytime there is an Internet connection, that machine and any subsequent machine behind it are subject to unauthorized access.

Policies using the Internet via an individual connection should include the following procedures covering:

- Personal firewall software must be installed and active.
- Any network connections must be unplugged.
- Virus-scanning software must be installed and active.

COMMENT

Examples of personal firewall software include ZoneAlarm and WinProxy. ZoneAlarm from Zone Labs costs less than $30; see their Web site at *www.zonelabs.com* for the latest information. WinProxy 3.0 from Ositis is a personal firewall and proxy product. They can be reached at *www.winproxy.com*.

[C]   Corporate/Networked Internet Access

In most organizations employees have access to the Internet and e-mail from their workstations through the local area network. The network connects to the Internet through a router and/or proxy server; this acts as a firewall to protect the network from unauthorized access. The user's PC uses a browser to view content on the World Wide Web.

The IT technical support unit develops the procedure for connecting to the Internet through the corporate network. The IT technical support unit also determines the browser software used and may need to install the browser on the user's PC if not preinstalled.

An advantage of this method is Internet use can be centrally monitored and controlled. Also, a centralized firewall (either software or hardware) is used to protect the network from unauthorized access. Virus protection software is centrally installed and kept up to date.

A disadvantage of Internet access through the corporate network is there is a single point of failure protecting the network from the outside world. The connection is normally up 24/7, which gives hackers more opportunity to test your protection.

When using the Internet via the corporate network, the following procedures should be included in your policy:

- Firewall software or hardware is installed at the point of connection to the Internet and updated daily.
- Virus-scanning software is installed and updated daily. All downloaded files and e-mails are scanned for viruses.
- The IT technical support unit generates a weekly report that shows the most frequently visited web sites and total time connected to the Internet for each user.

COMMENT

Losses related to Distributed Denial of Service (DDOS) attacks in early 2000 that shut down several popular Web sites came to more than $1.2 billion, according to a report from the Yankee Group.

See Policy ITP-23-1 Internet Connection Policy as an example.

POLICY ITP-23-1.   Internet Connection Policy

Policy #:	ITP-23-1	**Effective:**	03/18/08	Page #:	1 of N
Subject:	Internet Connection Policy				

1.0 PURPOSE

This policy is designed to ensure that connections to the Internet by corporate computer systems are safe from intrusion by malware such as viruses that may be brought into the network by users using the Internet. It is also designed to prevent unauthorized and unprotected connections to the Internet that may allow a variety of unsafe content to enter the organizational network and compromise data integrity and system security across the entire network.

2.0 SCOPE

The policy applies to all corporate computer systems that are connected to the Internet. This includes connections made via the corporate network, modem connections using telephone lines, and wireless connections of any kind.

3.0 POLICY

All physical Internet connections or connections to other outside networks must be authorized and approved by your IT coordinator. Most users will access the Internet through the corporate network connection provided for their area by the IT department. Any additional connections must be approved by the IT department. These additional connections include but are not limited to:

A. Modem connection from a computer or communication device that may allow a connection to the network.
B. Any multipurpose printing or fax machines that have both a phone and network connection must be examined and approved for use by the IT department.
C. Wireless access points or devices with wireless capability are not allowed unless approved by the IT department. If any computers or other devices have wireless capability, the wireless capability must be turned off before connecting to the network unless it is approved for wireless operation by the IT department when connected to the network.

Any additional Internet connections not provided by the IT department must be reviewed and approved by the IT department. Typically any additional connections from the corporate network to the Internet or other outside networks will require:

A. An IT department approved firewall operating at all times and properly configured.
B. Some communications through the connection may require encryption subject to a review of data to be transmitted by the IT department.

Any devices connected directly to the Internet without going through the corporate proxy servers must adhere to the following:

A. Personal firewall software must be installed and active.

B. Any network connections must be unplugged.

C. Virus-scanning software must be installed and active.

4.0 REVISION HISTORY

Date	Revision #	Description of Change
03/18/08	1.0	Initial creation.

5.0 INQUIRIES

Direct inquiries about this policy to:

Tom Jones, CIO
Our Company, Inc.
2900 Corporate Drive
Columbus, OH 43215

Voice: 614-555-1234
Fax: 614-555-1235
E-mail: tjones@company.com

Revision #:	1.0	Supersedes:	N/A	Date:	03/18/08

§ 23.03 INTERNET SECURITY POLICY

[A] Responsibility

The chief information officer should assign the responsibility for Internet security to the IT Manager. Internet security policies are critical for protecting corporate systems while connected to the Internet. The IT unit responsible for the corporate Internet connection develops and enforces security procedures protecting corporate systems while connected to the Internet.

A connection to the Internet not only connects a computer to systems all over the world, but also with all computers currently running on the company network. The Internet was not designed to be very secure, as open access for research purposes was a major design consideration. Other factors making an Internet connection a possible security problem include:

A. **Vulnerable TCP/IP services.** A number of the TCP/IP services are not secure and can be compromised by knowledgeable intruders; services used in the local area networking environment for improving network management are especially vulnerable.

B. **Ease of spying and spoofing.** The majority of Internet traffic is unencrypted; e-mail, passwords, and file transfers can be monitored and captured using readily available software. Intruders can then reuse passwords to break into systems.

C. **Lack of policy.** Many sites are configured unintentionally for wide-open Internet access without regard for the potential for abuse from the Internet; many sites permit more TCP/IP services than they require for their operations and do not attempt to limit access to information about their computers that could prove valuable to intruders.

D. **Complexity of configuration.** Host security access controls are often complex to configure and monitor; controls that are incorrectly configured often result in unauthorized access.

[B] Firewall Usage

A firewall is a computer server providing security to a network. A firewall includes a number of technologies such as policy, network arrangement, and technical controls and procedures. The firewall protects the network from probing by unauthorized users and allows only authorized access to the system.

Management first defines the type and level of security desired for the Internet connection for the protection of company information resources. Issues to consider for policies concerning firewalls include:

A. Dial-in policy.
B. VPN connections.
C. Which Internet services the organization plans to use (e.g., Telnet, FTP).
D. Assumptions about security versus usability (When does a service become too risky to use?).
E. Access to internal resources from the Internet.
F. Restriction of access to approved sites only or restrict only certain sites.
G. Use of chat programs such as AOL Instant Messenger and Windows Messenger.
H. Use of streaming audio and video.

There are two types of access control—explicit denial and explicit approval. Explicit approval restricts access to approved sites only and denies all other services by default. This is the more secure method, but more difficult to implement and maintain. Explicit denial restricts only certain sites and is easier on users, but new services that become available may expose the network to security problems.

The firewall installed should have the following features:

A. The firewall should be able to support a "deny all services except those specifically permitted" design policy, even if this is not the policy used.
B. The firewall should support the company's security policy, not impose one.
C. The firewall should be flexible and able to accommodate new services and needs if the security policy of the organization changes.
D. The firewall contains advanced authentication measures or contains the software hooks for installing advanced authentication measures.

E. The firewall employs filtering techniques to permit or deny services to specified host systems as needed.

F. The IP filtering network language should be flexible, user-friendly to program, and should filter on as many attributes as possible, including source and destination IP address, protocol type, source and destination TCP/UDP port, user, and inbound and outbound interface.

G. The firewall uses proxy services for Internet services such as FTP and Telnet, so advanced authentication measures can be employed and centralized at the firewall. If services such as NNTP, http, or gopher are required, the firewall contains the corresponding proxy services.

H. The firewall contains the ability to centralize SMTP access, to reduce direct SMTP connections between site and remote systems. This results in centralized handling of site e-mail.

I. The firewall accommodates public access to the site, so public information servers can be protected by the firewall but segregated from site systems not requiring public access.

J. The firewall should contain the ability to concentrate and filter dial-in access.

K. The firewall contains mechanisms for logging traffic and suspicious activity and contains mechanisms for log reduction, so logs are readable and understandable. Mechanisms for alerting someone when suspicious activity occurs are also important.

L. A firewall requires a secured version of the operating system, with other security tools as necessary to ensure firewall host integrity. The operating system should have all security patches installed.

M. The firewall is developed so its strength and correctness are verifiable. It should be simple in design so that it can be understood and maintained.

N. The firewall and any corresponding operating system are updated with patches and other bug fixes in a timely manner.

See Policy ITP-23-2 Firewall Usage Policy as an example.

POLICY ITP-23-2.   Firewall Usage Policy

Policy #:	ITP-23-2	Effective:	03/18/08	Page #:	1 of N
Subject:	Firewall Usage Policy				

1.0 PURPOSE

This policy is designed to ensure that connections to the Internet by corporate computer systems are safe from intrusion by unauthorized individuals from outside the organization. It is also designed to prevent unauthorized and unprotected connections to the Internet that may allow a variety of unsafe content to enter the organizational network and compromise data integrity and system security across the entire network.

2.0 SCOPE

The policy applies to all corporate computer systems that are connected to the Internet. This includes connections made via the corporate network, modem connections using telephone lines, and wireless connections of any kind.

3.0 POLICY

All networks or systems connected to the public Internet must be protected by a firewall that is configured using the following default settings:

A. All valid outgoing packets are let through regardless of their type.
B. All valid incoming packets "related" to the outgoing packets are allowed.
C. All outgoing TCP connections to port 80 (HTTP) are allowed.
D. All incoming ICMP packets of types 0 (ping response), 3 (MTU), 8 (ping), and 11 (TTL exceeded) are allowed.
E. All incoming packets from a trusted machine are allowed.
F. All other (incoming) packets are blocked.

All requests for modifications to the above default policy settings must be approved by the IT Network Administrator.

4.0 REVISION HISTORY

Date	Revision #	Description of Change
03/18/08	1.0	Initial creation.

5.0 INQUIRIES

Direct inquiries about this policy to:

Tom Jones, CIO
Our Company, Inc.
2900 Corporate Drive
Columbus, OH 43215

Voice: 614-555-1234
Fax: 614-555-1235
E-mail: tjones@company.com

Revision #:	1.0		Supersedes:	N/A	Date:	03/18/08

[C]   Internet Usage Control

An Internet usage control system should be used to control access to inappropriate web sites as well as to improve your network efficiency. It can also assist in enforcing your Internet acceptable usage policy and ensure relevant regulatory and legislative compliance by monitoring and controlling Internet content into and out of your organization. Features to look for in an Internet usage control system include:

A.   Easy to use user interface.

B.   Comprehensive reporting that allows you to easily and effectively monitor web activity throughout your organization.

C.   Allows you to identify sites to be avoided during key periods of the day.

D.   Enforces policy through MIME and file types—manage/restrict access to different content types (e.g., video, music, images) and file types (e.g., MP3, AAC, MP4, and VBS).

E.   Provides ability to configure the administrator e-mail alert policy.

F.   Enforces URL and user management policy—controls access to Web-based e-mail, defines acceptable URL categories, protects against anonymous proxies that re-route traffic to inappropriate destinations, and controls access by unauthorized groups or users.

G.   Configures the service with user and group level settings, using existing directory information on specific user level details.

H.   Prevents accidental exposure—protects against inadvertent access to bad URLs and compromised sites.

 I.   Flexible user interface—creates different access policies, customizes block messages, and builds rules for recreational Internet access.

J.   Support for multiple content categories.

K.   Flexibility that allows and blocks lists.

L.   Scalable across multiple sites.

M.   Real-time advanced content analysis.

COMMENT

Suppliers of Internet usage control systems include Message-Labs at *www.messagelabs.com*, Wavecrest Computing at *www.wavecrest.net*, and Websence Inc. at *www.websense.com*.

[D]   Internet Training

Training for connecting to the Internet and for using the e-mail system should be provided by the information system's IT training unit. If the site does not have an IT training unit, training material can be made available by the local training unit. If unavailable, the company information systems organization can provide the training material.

Internet connection and e-mail system use training should be available as individualized training. The material should be loaned to the user and then returned to the unit that provided the material. The training provided should be in one of the following forms:

A. **Tutorial.** Users learn via a tutorial. This allows them to learn how to connect to the Internet and use the e-mail system at their own pace and as time is available. Users are provided with a learning guide with step-by-step instructions that assumes basic knowledge of the computer's operating system. After all items in the learning guide are completed, the tutorial is returned to the training unit.

B. **On-the-job training.** An experienced Internet user may be assigned to provide on-the-job training (OJT). The OJT instructor has a learning guide provided by the information systems organization. The IT organization provides the user with a copy of the learning guide via the instructor.

The OJT instructor follows the learning guide when working with the student. Training proceeds as time and the student's learning skills permit. A skill test is provided with the learning guide to gauge the student's mastery of the material.

§ 23.04 INTERNET E-MAIL USE POLICY

[A] Overview

Use of the Internet and e-mail makes business and communication more effective. However, Internet service and e-mail are costly corporate resources. Irresponsible use reduces their availability for critical business operations, compromises corporate security and network integrity, and leaves the company open to potentially damaging litigation. An Internet use policy in the employee guidelines defines how the Internet is used as a corporate resource.

COMMENT

According to a December 2006 study by Cyber Source Corporation, online shopping jumps noticeably about 10 a.m. and builds up through noon; online buying then drops noticeably between noon and 1 p.m., then rises again between 3 p.m. and 5 p.m. as the workday concludes. The highest volume of online shopping occurs on Mondays and Tuesdays, with the lowest volumes on Saturdays and Sundays.

[B] Tracking Internet Usage

The company should establish a mechanism for tracking all Internet usage by employees. Employees are notified of this policy through the use of an Internet/E-mail Acceptable Use Agreement (see § 23.06 ACCEPTABLE USE AGREEMENT). This enables the company to manage its Internet and e-mail resources in a cost-effective manner and to manage its network more efficiently for future technology expansion.

> **COMMENT**
>
> Many states and the federal government are considering requiring firms to notify employees if their Internet and e-mail use is being monitored, with stiff fines imposed for not doing so.

The intention is to monitor the existence of the traffic being generated, much like a telephone bill tracks the calls made, the numbers called, the time of the calls, but not the content. In this manner the company will be aware of how its resources are being used, where they are needed, where new capacity is required, and other infrastructure management issues. Additionally, because of the vulnerability to litigation over inappropriate conduct in the workplace environment, it is the company's responsibility to ensure that its resources do not support inappropriate activities.

> **COMMENT**
>
> Software from Fatline Corp. *(www.fatline.com)* allows users to monitor their own Internet usage, which some firms have found to be an effective way to reduce non-work-related Internet use.

[C] Internet and E-mail Use Guidelines

To ensure all employees understand their responsibilities, policies covering the use of the Internet and e-mail should cover the following guidelines:

A. **Acceptable uses of company e-mail and Internet access.** Describe what uses of the Internet and e-mail are considered acceptable at your company.

B. **Unacceptable uses of company e-mail and Internet access.** Describe what uses of the Internet and e-mail are considered unacceptable at your company.

C. **Communications.** Remind employees that e-mail is just as serious a communication tool as is the printed page, and must not be treated lightly.

D. **Personal e-mail accounts.** Personal e-mail accounts are prohibited as a potential source of viruses and as a potential compliance issue with government regulations for corporate recordkeeping.

E. **Software.** Downloading of unapproved software poses a serious security threat.

F. **Firewalls and Anti-Virus software.** These tools must not be tampered with or disabled for any reason.

G. **Copyright issues.** Transmission of company secrets is a serious violation of company policy.

H. **Security.** Make sure they understand how the use of the Internet and e-mail affects network security for the company.

I. **Spam.** While this should be obvious, remind employees that sending unwanted e-mails is not acceptable.

J. **Violations.** Describe the penalties for violating the policy.

See Policy ITP-23-3 Internet/E-mail Acceptable Use Policy as an example.

POLICY ITP-23-3. Internet/E-mail Acceptable Use Policy

Policy #:	ITP-23-3	Effective:	03/18/08	Page #:	1 of N
Subject:	Internet/E-Mail Acceptable Use Policy				

1.0 PURPOSE

This policy defines the acceptable use for the company's Internet and e-mail services.

2.0 SCOPE

The policy applies to all uses of company owned e-mail and Internet access.

3.0 POLICY

3.1 Acceptable Uses of Company E-mail and Internet Access

The company provides Internet and e-mail access for business usage. Every staff member has the responsibility to maintain and enhance the company's public image and to use company e-mail and access to the Internet in a responsible and productive manner that reflects well on the company. The company recognizes that there will be occasional personal use on lunch breaks and during non-working hours (with the approval of management), but this shall not be excessive or unreasonable.

3.2 Unacceptable Uses of Company E-mail and Internet Access

The company e-mail and Internet access may not be used for transmitting, retrieving or storage of any communications of a discriminatory or harassing nature or materials that are obscene or "X-rated." Harassment of any kind is prohibited. No messages with derogatory or inflammatory remarks about an individual's race, age, disability, religion, national origin, physical attributes, or sexual preference shall be transmitted. No excessively abusive, profane or offensive language is to be transmitted through the company's e-mail or Internet system. Electronic media may also not be used for any other purpose that is illegal or against company policy or contrary to the company's best interests. Solicitation of non-company business, or any use of the company e-mail or Internet for personal gain, is prohibited.

3.3 Communications

Each employee is responsible for the content of all text, audio, or images that they place or send over the company's e-mail and Internet system. No e-mail or other electronic communications may be sent that hides the identity of the sender or represents the sender as someone else or someone from another company. All messages communicated on the company's e-mail and Internet system should contain the employee's name.

Any messages or information sent by an employee to another individual outside of the company via an electronic network (e.g., bulletin board, online service, or Internet) are statements that reflect on the company. While some users include personal "disclaimers" in electronic messages, there is still a connection to the company, and the statements may legally be tied to the company. Therefore, we require that all communications sent by employees via the company's e-mail and Internet system comply with all company policies and not disclose any confidential or proprietary company information.

3.4 Software

To prevent computer viruses from being transmitted through the company's e-mail and Internet system, there will be no unauthorized downloading of any unauthorized software. All software downloaded must be registered to the company. Employees should contact MIS if they have any questions.

3.5 Copyright Issues

Employees on the company's e-mail and Internet system may not transmit copyrighted materials belonging to entities other than this company. Please note that non-adherence to this policy puts the company in serious legal jeopardy and opens the company up to significant lawsuits and public embarrassment. All employees obtaining access to other companies' or individuals' materials must respect all copyrights and may not copy, retrieve, modify, or forward copyrighted materials, except with permission. Failure to observe copyright or license agreements may result in disciplinary action up to and including termination. If you have questions about any of these legal issues, please speak with your manager or MIS before proceeding.

3.6 Security

The company routinely monitors usage patterns in its e-mail and Internet communications. The reasons for this monitoring are many, including cost analysis, security, bandwidth allocation, and the general management of the company's gateway to the Internet. All messages created, sent, or retrieved over the company's e-mail and Internet are the property of the company and should be considered public information. Notwithstanding comments above regarding our present intention not to monitor content, the company must reserve the right to access and monitor the content of all messages and files on the company's e-mail and Internet system at any time in the future with or without notice. Employees should not assume electronic communications are totally private and should transmit highly confidential data in other ways. E-mail messages regarding sensitive matters should warn that such communications are not intended to be secure or confidential. This is just good business sense.

3.7 Violations

Any employee who abuses the privilege of company facilitated access to e-mail or the Internet will be subject to corrective action up to and including termination. If necessary, the company also reserves the right to advise appropriate legal officials of any illegal violations.

4.0 REVISION HISTORY

Date	Revision #	Description of Change
03/18/08	1.0	Initial creation.

5.0 INQUIRIES

Direct inquiries about this policy to:

Tom Jones, CIO
Our Company, Inc.
2900 Corporate Drive
Columbus, OH 43215

Voice: 614-555-1234
Fax: 614-555-1235
E-mail: tjones@company.com

Revision #:	1.0	Supersedes:	N/A	Date:	03/18/08

[D]   E-mail Etiquette

As e-mail has not only replaced paper-based communication, but also become a substitute for having a conversation, the proper use of e-mail etiquette has become increasingly important. Communication received in an e-mail does not easily convey the mood and emotions of the communicator. Most messages come across harsher than intended. The following are useful guidelines for communicating by e-mail (most also apply when developing policies covering instant messaging (IM)).

A.   **Be brief.** E-mail messages should be concise and to the point. It is helpful to think of e-mail as a telephone conversation that is typed instead of spoken. Always make the main point as quickly as possible (within the first two or three sentences). Many software programs used for reading e-mail allow for a preview mode, where only the first few sentences are displayed. Many people receive hundreds of e-mails a day and use this preview mode to determine which e-mails they will read completely. E-mails that take several sentences to get to the point may not be read at all.

COMMENT

Thank you for sending me a copy of your book—I'll waste no time reading it.

—Moses Hadas (1900–1966), book reviewer.

B.   **Use the subject line wisely.** An accurate and specific subject line is helpful for determining which e-mails merit closer attention by those who receive mountains of e-mail, but be careful not to earn a reputation for over-hyping a message in the subject line; otherwise really important messages may not get read.

C.   **Use grammar and punctuation correctly.** Poor grammar and punctuation reflect poorly on the sender. Do not overuse exclamation points (sometimes called "bangs") in an attempt to emphasize the importance of your message. If something is important, it should be reflected in the text, not in the punctuation.

D.   **Use special formatting sparingly.** Avoid the use of fancy HTML formatting or "wallpaper" backgrounds. What looks great using e-mail client software may look like gibberish to the recipient. Stick to commonly available fonts, and realize that the spacing as displayed by the recipient may be different from that in which the message was sent, especially when displaying columnar data. Many users turn off HTML formatting to help prevent malicious code from being executed on their system.

> ## COMMENT
>
> Consider the use of software tools that allow standard e-mail disclaimers to be created and attached to all outgoing e-mail messages.

E. **Abbreviations.** Abbreviation use is rampant with e-mail and IM. In the quest to save keystrokes, users have traded clarity for confusion (unless you understand the abbreviations). Avoid using abbreviations not normally used in paper-based communication.

F. **Salutations.** Each situation will be different, but in general, use the same salutation as you would in a business letter. Some form of salutation should be included in every e-mail as a common courtesy.

G. **Signatures.** Do not rely on the return e-mail address to inform the recipient who sent the e-mail. Sign e-mail messages in the same manner as a business letter. Include full name, title, company name, and telephone number and e-mail address. Avoid using quotes or images at the end of your e-mail.

H. **Printing e-mail.** Avoid printing a paper copy of e-mails received unless absolutely necessary. Most e-mail systems allow the creation of folders for storing old e-mails if a copy will be needed later.

> ## COMMENT
>
> According to a 2006 American Management Association survey, 26 percent of employers have terminated employees for e-mail misuse.

I. **Privacy.** E-mails are not private. The company should reserve the right to monitor e-mail content ensuring that the e-mail system is used for appropriate purposes. Also, no security is 100 percent hacker-proof; someone outside the company may intercept and read e-mail. Routing of e-mail is not without errors; someone other than the intended recipient may receive the e-mail. Do not send anything by e-mail that should not be placed on the company bulletin board.

J. **Other.** Remember, all recipients may not read e-mail immediately. While the e-mail usually arrives quickly, this is not always the case. E-mail is not designed for immediacy (that is why people have telephones); it is designed for convenience. Do not use e-mail to schedule a meeting the same day or for anything requiring an immediate response. Other tips to keep in mind:

1. Avoid using e-mail to deliver bad news. Questions cannot be answered when a person reads the e-mail.
2. Do not include confidential or embarrassing information in an e-mail, as you have no control over someone forwarding it.
3. Avoid filling up other people's inboxes with "Thank You" or "You're Welcome" messages unless the sender requires an acknowledgement.
4. If an e-mail is received that causes a strong personal reaction, avoid responding to it immediately. Use the telephone to clear up any possible misunderstanding.
5. Make sure you have actually attached attachments when you say you have.
6. Using all capital letters in an e-mail is the equivalent of SHOUTING.
7. Never send a blank e-mail with attachments; make sure the subject line or body of the e-mail explains what the attachment is about.
8. When replying to an e-mail, either leave the old message as part of the new one or clearly reference your response. Do not assume the reader knows exactly what is being talked about.

COMMENT

The consequences of e-mail content were highlighted in the Microsoft antitrust trial, where the government used e-mails written by Microsoft executives to undermine their credibility. Statements made by executives in e-mails contradicted their public statements.

[E]   E-mail Marketing

Although e-mail can be a cost-effective way for a company to reach existing and potential customers, the abuse of e-mail by "spammers" has caused an outcry against unsolicited e-mail. In response, Congress passed the Controlling the Assault of Non-Solicited Pornography and Marketing Act of 2003 (CAN-SPAM). This law, which took effect in January 2004, requires that companies maintain opt-out lists for people who do not want to receive e-mail from the company. The act allows for fines of up to $2 million against companies that violate the act. IT staffs will need to stay up-to-date on further CAN-SPAM developments and be attentive to the compliance efforts of the company, including the potential creation of a national "do not e-mail" list.

COMMENT

According to Nucleus Research, a Massachusetts based consulting group, the average annual cost of spam per employee in 2004 was $1,934. This figure does not include the expense of IT personnel, software, CPU hardware, and bandwidth hogged by spam. The figure also doesn't account for the less visible layer of costs associated with spam, like the negative impact of virus-triggered network outages on customer satisfaction or increased corporate exposure to harassment suits.

According to the CAN-SPAM Act, spam is defined as any communication that does any of the following:

A. Accesses a protected computer without authorization and intentionally initiates the transmission of multiple commercial electronic mail messages from or through such computer.
B. Uses a protected computer to relay or retransmit multiple commercial electronic mail messages, with the intent to deceive or mislead recipients, or any Internet access service, as to the origin of such messages.
C. Falsifies header information in multiple commercial electronic mail messages and intentionally initiates the transmission of such messages.
D. Registers, using information that falsifies the identity of the actual registrant, for five or more electronic mail accounts or online user accounts or two or more domain names and intentionally initiates the transmission of multiple commercial electronic mail messages from any combination of such accounts or domain names.
E. Falsely represents the right to use five or more Internet protocol addresses and intentionally initiates the transmission of multiple commercial electronic mail messages from such addresses.

COMMENT

Also according to Nuclear Research, nearly 6 months after the passage of the CAN-SPAM Act, the costs of spam doubled from the year before: The average e-mail user received 29 spam messages daily, as compared with the average of 13 messages reported before the passage of the CAN-SPAM Act.

The IT department is responsible for developing policies and procedures to work with their marketing department to ensure compliance with CAN-SPAM. All e-mail marketing sent out by the company must do the following in order to meet the requirements of CAN-SPAM:

A. The subject line must be accurate.
B. E-mail recipients who opt-out must be removed from the e-mail list within 10 business days.
C. The header information in the e-mail (originating e-mail address, domain name, and IP address) must be correct and accurate.
D. The return e-mail address must be accurate and active for at least 30 days after transmission so recipients can opt out.
E. The postal address of the sender must be included in the e-mail.
F. The e-mail must be identified as an advertisement or solicitation.

COMMENT

Go to *http://thomas.loc.gov* and search for "S.877" and "108th Congress" to see the exact text of the CAN-SPAM Act.

[F] E-mail Archiving

With the ever-increasing amount of business communication being done via e-mail, it is critical that the organization has an effective and efficient process for archiving this communication. An e-mail archiving system can reduce the amount of active data stored on the network file system and can be important in satisfying regulatory and legal requirements for the retrieval of e-mails.

While e-mail archiving can be done manually, it is much more efficient to use an automated program. Consider the following when creating an e-mail archiving policy:

A. How long should e-mails be retained?
B. Should users be able to easily view archived e-mails?
C. Can users delete personal e-mails before they are archived?
D. Will other items such as tasks and calendar items also be archived?

See Policy ITP-23-4 E-mail Archiving Policy as an example.

POLICY ITP-23-4. E-mail Archiving Policy

Policy #:	ITP-23-4	Effective:	03/18/08	Page #:	1 of N
Subject:	E-mail Archiving Policy				

1.0 PURPOSE

In order to manage the ever increasing volume of e-mail, calendar items and tasks, and to facilitate their retrieval, the company has implemented an enterprise-wide automated e-mail archiving system. The e-mail archiving system also reduces the amount of active data stored on the network file system and satisfies regulatory and legal requirements for the retrieval of e-mails.

2.0 SCOPE

The policy applies to all users of the company owned e-mail system. It applies to permanent and part-time employees, as well as contractors.

3.0 POLICY

This policy authorizes the implementation of an automated e-mail archiving system. The system automatically archives all company e-mail, calendar items and tasks older than 45 days. All e-mails, calendar items and tasks related in any way to company business must be archived. E-mail users are encouraged to delete personal e-mails from their mailbox before they are automatically archived after 45 days. Archived e-mail will be retained for a period of 10 years.

4.0 REVISION HISTORY

Date	Revision #	Description of Change
03/18/08	1.0	Initial creation.

5.0 INQUIRIES:

Direct inquiries about this policy to:

Tom Jones, CIO
Our Company, Inc.
2900 Corporate Drive
Columbus, OH 43215

Voice: 614-555-1234
Fax: 614-555-1235
E-mail: tjones@company.com

Revision #:	1.0	Supersedes:	N/A	Date:	03/18/08

§ 23.05 MESSAGING AND BLOGGING POLICY

[A] Instant Messaging (IM)

Instant Messaging (IM or chat) is one of the most popular and most interactive services on the Internet. Using an IM program such as Windows Messenger, Trillian, or AOL Instant Messenger enable users to chat instantly with anyone anywhere in the world. Many companies find IM to be a useful tool for communicating with coworkers and customers. If someone is on the phone, a message can be sent that pops up instantly on their screen. IM has great potential for becoming an important business communication tool. It is a great tool for facilitating ad hoc discussions between workers in different locations.

But the capability to interrupt concentration—much like a ringing telephone—makes IM very disruptive in the office. Many IM programs will not work through a firewall and can be difficult to monitor. The use of external servers to distribute the messages can present a security issue, as no data security exists for consumer IM tools nor are enterprise management tools available. The informal nature of IM encourages the creation of informal practices that are outside the formal communications channels of the firm. Key decision makers without access to IM may be left out of important discussions by users of IM.

The IT Manager is responsible for developing policies and procedures for using IM programs. All guidelines listed in Section [C], "Internet and E-mail Use Guidelines," apply to the use of IM. Additional guidelines to consider concerning IM include:

- Employees must be specifically authorized to use IM.
- Only company approved IM software should be used.
- Employees will be assigned a unique IM identifier (also known as a nickname or handle) by the company. This identifier belongs to the company and its use by the employee is terminated when the employee leaves the company.
- Company business cannot be conducted from non-company IM accounts.
- As with e-mail, a retention policy for storing IM messages must be established.

COMMENT

The Securities and Exchange Commission's Rule 17a-4, which governs the financial services industry, requires companies to record, log, index, audit, and retrieve electronic communications. This includes IM messages.

If there are pockets of IM use already within the firm, consider using those groups as pilots for implementing an enterprise IM solution. Use the lessons learned in the pilot to develop enterprise-wide policies for IM use.

Because of the difficulty in verifying the identity of the person at the other end of an IM conversation, companies involved in financial services, health care, and legal services may want to totally ban the use of IM in their organizations.

[B]   Blogging

Web logs, or blogs, have become a popular way to express personal opinions about current issues and subjects of general interest. Some blogs even attract a faithful following of readers.

Employees using blogs on company time, equipment, or connections must ensure that their comments adhere to the company's policies on e-mail. Employees publishing blogs on their own time, using their own equipment and resources, should understand that their comments will still be constrained by the same e-mail policies.

Free speech is a legal freedom in most countries. However, in business, it is difficult to call someone an imbecile in public and then expect that person to retain the same working relationship in the office. When a comment is published, it assumes a different character than when it is voiced to a small group. Companies do not want to assume liability for misplaced company remarks that may be attributed to an official company action or prevailing attitude. A web log policy should outline clearly what the company's position is on the use of web logs by employees both at work and outside of work.

See Policy ITP-23-5 Email Archiving Policy as an example.

POLICY ITP-23-5.   Internet Blogging Policy

Policy #:	ITP-23-5	Effective:	03/18/08	Page #:	1 of N
Subject:	Internet Blogging Policy				

1.0 PURPOSE

This policy defines the organization's position on employee participation in the communication and sharing of information in the public Internet through such mediums as personal Web sites, web logs (blogs) and networking sites.

2.0 SCOPE

The policy applies to all forms on information publication and communication via the Internet, including but not limited to web logs (blogs), social networking sites such as Facebook and MySpace, and professional networking sites such as LinkedIn and Plaxo.

3.0 POLICY

While the company respects the right of employees to use personal Web sites and web logs as a medium of self-expression, you must not be identified as an employee of the company while using such mediums without the prior approval of the corporate communications department. The following guidelines must be followed to ensure that readers will not view you as a de facto spokesperson for the company:

A. You must make it clear to readers that any views you express are yours alone and that these views do not necessarily represent the views of the company. If there is any chance that you could be identified as an employee of the company when expressing personal views, you must provide the following notice in your communication:

   The views expressed on this Web site/blog/network are mine alone and do not necessarily represent the views of my employer.

B. You must not disclose any information that is confidential or proprietary to the organization or to any customer or vendor that has disclosed such information to the company. Review the company's policy on confidential and proprietary information for guidance.

C. Any communication occurring in a public forum such as those identified previously in this policy must be respectful to the company, fellow employees, our affiliates, and our business partners.

D. As outlined in your employment agreement, any concepts or discoveries that you produce that are related to the company's business are property of the company and should not be discussed in a public forum with expressed written permission of the company. Consult your manager if you have any questions about topics that may be covered by this policy.

E. The company may request at any time that you cease any communication concerning the company in a public forum or require you to block access to such communication of the company believes that such action is necessary to ensure compliance with government regulations or other laws.

F. Do not use the company's trademarks on any personal communication or reproduce any company material.

4.0 REVISION HISTORY

Date	Revision #	Description of Change
03/18/08	1.0	Initial creation.

Direct inquiries about this policy to:

Tom Jones, CIO
Our Company, Inc.
2900 Corporate Drive
Columbus, OH 43215

Voice: 614-555-1234
Fax: 614-555-1235
E-mail: tjones@company.com

Revision #:	1.0	Supersedes:	N/A	Date:	03/18/08

[C]   Peer-to-Peer Applications

Peer-to-Peer (P2P) applications are used to allow individual PCs to share files. These applications are mostly used for sharing music and video files. Examples include KaZaa, Morpheus, and Audiogalaxy. The use of these applications should be strictly forbidden on company-owned systems. P2P applications can introduce significant gaps into the corporate network, allowing viruses and worms to be introduced. P2P applications can be used to allow third parties to obtain the user's IP address, or allow access to data on the user's computer and the corporate network. Many P2P applications have been known to include "spyware" or "malware," which can allow others to monitor the user's Internet browsing or to take control of a PC's system resources.

P2P applications can also be a significant drain on the company's Internet bandwidth, especially when large files are downloaded. This problem is made worse when other users on the P2P network connect to the employee's PC and download files to their PC. This uses bandwidth that should be available for legitimate company purposes, such as e-mail, web browsing, and e-commerce. Employee productivity also can be adversely affected by the use of P2P applications, as time is taken from business related duties. Support costs may increase if the P2P application causes problems with business related software on the employee's workstation.

§ 23.06   ACCEPTABLE USE AGREEMENT

[A]   Overview

An acceptable use agreement must be put in place ensuring all employees understand and agree to the company's Internet use policies. The employee's immediate supervisor reviews the policy with the employee ensuring that the employee understands the seriousness of the policy.

[B]   Sample Acceptable Use Agreement

Exhibit 23-1 is a sample e-mail and Internet user agreement that is to be signed by all existing employees and by all new employees at orientation. The employee receives a copy and another copy is placed in the employee's personnel file.

EXHIBIT 23-1.   E-Mail/Internet User Agreement

Employee Agreement:

I have received a copy of XYZ Company's E-Mail and Internet Acceptable Use Policy # _______________, dated _____________. I recognize and understand that the company's e-mail and Internet systems are to be used for conducting the company's business only. I understand that use of this equipment for private purposes is strictly prohibited.

As part of the XYZ organization and use of XYZ's gateway to the Internet and e-mail system, I understand that this Acceptable Use Policy applies to me. I have read the aforementioned document and agree to follow all policies and procedures that are set forth therein. I further agree to abide by the standards set in the document for the duration of my employment with XYZ Company. I understand that e-mail and Internet usage may be monitored by the company to ensure compliance with the Acceptable Use Policy.

I am aware that violations of this Acceptable Use Policy may subject me to disciplinary action, up to and including discharge from employment. I further understand that my communications on the Internet and e-mail reflect XYZ Company worldwide to our competitors, consumers, customers, and suppliers. Furthermore, I understand that this document can be amended at any time.

___________________________	___________________________
Employee's Printed Name	Date
___________________________	
Employee's Signature	
___________________________	___________________________
Manager's Signature	Date

§ 23.07   SOFTWARE AS A SERVICE

[A]   Overview

Software as a service (SaaS), also sometimes referred to as on-demand software, is becoming a significant component of managing an organization's software infrastructure. With the increasing shortage of skilled workers to operate software systems in-house, more companies turn to SaaS to manage and maintain their software infrastructure. It is critical that the information systems group manage the selection and use of SaaS, ensuring the company receives the value the SaaS vendor was hired to provide. SaaS policies formalize standards for how SaaS vendors are used and managed within the organization.

The most likely software applications to outsource to a SaaS vendor are everyday applications that every organization in an industry uses, or functions such as security that require specialized personnel to support properly. Such services are also appropriate when an organization does not have the time, technical resources, or money to buy, build, maintain, and support a software application. Requirements for future scalability can also be a consideration, as a SaaS vendor can usually scale up more quickly if additional resources are required to support more users.

COMMENT

Almost one-third of survey respondents are already using SaaS, and another third are currently considering it, according to a Fall 2005 Cutter Consortium survey.

[B]   Definition

A SaaS vendor is a supplier who makes software applications available over the public Internet, usually on a subscription basis. The SaaS model has grown out of the ashes of the ASP offerings during the dot-com bubble and works similarly to the time-sharing systems used in the 1960s and 1970s. SaaS vendors typically provide access to the following types of applications:

- Supply chain management.
- Voice-response systems.
- Virus protection on a VPN.
- Hosted contact center.
- Enterprise resource management.
- Security.
- Data warehousing.
- Industry specific vertical applications.
- E-purchasing.
- Human resources.
- Recruiting.
- E-mail.
- Document and workflow management.
- Customer relationship management.
- Group scheduling.
- Service desk.
- Secure collaboration communities.

A SaaS vendor can also combine service offerings traditionally not offered by one company. The four primary ingredients are the following:

A. **Packaged software applications.** Licenses to products developed by ISVs are sold for a sizable up-front fee, on a subscription basis or on a per-use basis.

B. **Data centers and connectivity.** Data-center services are offered by hosting companies (e.g., Jumpline), hardware companies (e.g., IBM), and telecom providers (e.g., Qwest). Telecom and business Internet service providers (ISPs) provide connectivity.

C. **Application monitoring and ongoing support.** Firms such as Infocrossing, Digex, and Jumpline typically offer application monitoring. System integrators (SIs) or ISVs typically provide second-level support.

D. **Systems implementation and integration.** Systems integrators (SIs) or the service arms of ISVs traditionally offer these services.

The SaaS vendor is used to provide access to a single application or can be used to replace the entire user desktop.

COMMENT

International Data Corp. (IDC) estimates that SaaS sales will grow by at least 26 percent annually from $2.1 billion in 2002 to $8.1 billion in 2008.

[C] Application Outsourcing Policies

Corporate and IT management must have a clear set of long-term goals and objectives for the outsourcing of applications. SaaS vendors can be used:

- For operations difficult to manage and staff. SaaS vendors can reduce headcount needs.
- To avoid hardware and software obsolescence.
- To improve focus on core competencies. Most companies do not include IT as part of their core competency.
- To supply talent and/or resources unavailable in the organization.
- To reduce internal operation costs.
- To make applications available to a mobile, distributed workforce.
- For their ability to scale rapidly.
- To make IT cost more predictable.
- For turnkey solutions. The role of general technology contractor shifts from the company to the SaaS vendor.

- To free resources for other efforts.
- To bring systems up and running faster. SaaS vendors can generally deliver software to a customer more rapidly than in-house resources or an external software developer can.

Establish guidelines for how the organization's relationship with SaaS vendors is to be managed. See Policy ITP-23-6 SaaS Vendor Policy as an example.

POLICY ITP-23-6.   SaaS Vendor Policy

Policy #:	ITP-23-6	Effective:	03/18/08	Page #:	1 of N
Subject:	SaaS Vendor Policy				

1.0 PURPOSE

This policy defines the framework by which SaaS vendors will be managed. SaaS vendors are any vendors of software where the software and data is stored by the vendor.

2.0 SCOPE

The policy applies to all software applications that are managed and hosted by a third-party provider.

3.0 POLICY

The following guidelines will be followed for managing a SaaS vendor:

A. The areas for which a SaaS vendor is used will be budgeted annually.
B. Contracts that expire within the next budget year require a new contract proposal 3 months before the cutoff for budget consideration.
C. If the current SaaS vendor's performance or new proposal is not satisfactory, an RFP will be sent to no fewer than two other vendors.
D. SaaS vendor proposals must include the following items:
   1. A copy of their Business Continuity Plan along with a log of when and how it was tested.
   2. Compliance with government regulations.
   3. Credentials of firm.
   4. Former and current customer references.
   5. Documentation clarity and completeness.
   6. User-training and implementation resources available.
   7. Process to ensure data security and availability.
   8. Reliability of service.
   9. Scalability of service.
   10. Availability of support.
   11. Quality of support (credentials of staff, average length of service, etc.).

12. Security of connection.
13. Physical security of data center.
14. Next expected release of software.
15. Types of reports issued detailing application access and use statistics.
16. Management of software upgrade process.
17. Dedicated or shared server.
18. Storage space available per user and cost.
19. Backup and redundancy resources available.
20. Customization options available, if any.

4.0 REVISION HISTORY

Date	Revision #	Description of Change
03/18/07	1.0	Initial creation.

5.0 INQUIRIES

Direct inquiries about this policy to:

Tom Jones, CIO
Our Company, Inc.
2900 Corporate Drive
Columbus, OH 43215

Voice: 614-555-1234
Fax: 614-555-1235
E-mail: tjones@company.com

Revision #:	1.0	Supersedes:	N/A	Date:	03/18/07

§ 23.08 SAAS VENDOR SELECTION PROCESS

[A] Overview

Selecting a vendor to provide application services requires the use of stringent evaluation procedures. Not only must the applications themselves be evaluated, but hosting facilities, bandwidth, and support capabilities must also be carefully considered. The relative newness of the SaaS market and the volatility of the stock market upon which they rely for funding make the selection of the right SaaS vendor extremely important. Betting an organization's technology infrastructure on a company that may experience a sharp drop in its stock price may cause trouble. If its stock price drops, the company may not have the money to invest in research and development, which may impact its ability to service its customers.

In addition to technical considerations, constantly reevaluate with whom the company does business. Have a company-wide agreement on the criteria for choosing a technology vendor. Get involved in a professional network of chief technology officers (CTOs) who can meet on a regular basis to discuss technology providers' performance. Bet the infrastructure on a combination of established and newer companies. The best SaaS companies, and the ones most likely to stay in business, are those that have formed a technology and business alliance with an established company such as IBM, Microsoft, or Oracle. These more established companies have done their own evaluation of technology providers and found them credible partners. A small sample of SaaS vendors is listed below:

Company	Product	Web site
Sage Software	Customer relationship management	*www.sagecrm.com*
Google	Word processor	*www.google.com*
Trim Path	Spreadsheet	*www.numsum.com*
Smart Online, Inc.	Small business software	*www.smartonline.com*
Zimbra, Inc.	Enterprise messaging and collaboration	*www.zimbra.com*

[B] Request for Proposal

When IT management is ready to receive vendor proposals, a formal request for proposal (RFP) letter is sent to all possible candidates. The RFP defines the format of the proposal ensuring that a responding vendor can be evaluated and compared easily with others. The RFP should cover the following items:

A. Type of applications to be outsourced.
B. Minimum performance requirements and evaluation criteria.
C. Reliability level required.
D. Level of integration with other systems required.
E. Any required reporting capabilities.
F. Service volume expandability.
G. Vendor contact person.
H. IT contact person.
I. Vendor maintenance, training, and operation support.
J. Current users of the SaaS vendor's systems.

The RFP is for an ongoing service contract, with a given time limit. The service is billed monthly at a flat rate or prorated by transaction or user volume.

All items in the contract with the SaaS vendor are negotiable. A 3- to 5-year contract is typical. Standard support is usually 12/5 (12 hours a day, 5 days a week) with 24/7 support available at an additional cost. Systems with a small number of users are typically placed on a shared server with other customers of the SaaS vendor. Dedicated servers are available for an additional cost. The base fee per user normally covers the infrastructure at the SaaS vendor (but not the cost to connect) and any software licenses required. A fixed amount of hard-disk storage space is usually included, with 100MB per user typical. Carefully evaluate what users need and try to ensure as much as possible is covered in the standard agreement. As with any major purchase, add-ons can significantly add to the cost of the service.

The method by which the company connects to the SaaS vendor is also an important consideration. A dedicated frame relay connection to the SaaS vendor is the most secure and reliable, but more expensive than connecting over the public Internet. A connection over the Internet can be much less reliable, as overall Internet traffic can impact your performance. Using a dedicated frame connection, a good rule of thumb is 10 users for a 64K line, 20 users on a 128K line, and 50 to 60 users on a full T1 connection. For the same connection over the Internet, about one-half to two-thirds as many users can be supported as on the frame connection.

For each vendor selected to receive a copy of the RFP, assign an internal IT person the task of liaison between that vendor and the company. That person's job is to manage the communication between the vendor and the company and to encourage the vendor to provide its best response to the RFP. Encourage the vendor to put the maximum effort into its response, especially if the vendor suspects that a competitor may have an advantage. Even if another vendor is selected, any attractive items in the losing vendors' proposals can be used as negotiating points with the vendor ultimately elected.

[C] Evaluating SaaS Vendors' Proposals

All proposals received should be analyzed using a predetermined set of criteria. The elements compared should be in the same sequence on each proposal. Copies are given to each evaluator, and a date and time are selected to meet and discuss them.

Vendors providing clear and complete information requested in the RFP and meeting preliminary evaluation standards are selected for more detailed analysis. Those who do not will be removed from further consideration.

The vendors' proposals should address the specification elements noted in the RFP. Clear statements should be made by the vendor to address the following items:

A. A copy of their Business Continuity Plan along with a log of when and how it was tested.
B. Compliance with government regulations.
C. Credentials of firm.
D. Former and current customer references.
E. Documentation clarity and completeness.
F. User-training and implementation resources available.

G. Process to ensure data security and availability.
H. Reliability of service.
 I. Scalability of service.
 J. Availability of support.
K. Quality of support (credentials of staff, average length of service, etc.).
L. Security of connection.
M. Physical security of data center.
N. Next expected release of software.
O. Types of reports issued detailing application access and use statistics.
P. Management of software upgrade process.
Q. Dedicated or shared server.
R. Storage space available per user and cost.
S. Backup and redundancy resources available.
T. Customization options available, if any.

Current and former customers should be contacted to discuss their experiences with the vendor. The following questions are helpful for obtaining useful information:

A. Would you use the same vendor again? If so, why? What has been the major problem with the vendor? Do you know other users of the vendor's product? Are they generally happy? If so, why? Who are the other users? What are their names and telephone numbers?

B. How long does it take for the vendor to respond to problems? Are the people who respond knowledgeable and friendly? Has the vendor ever lied? Has the vendor had the resources to resolve your problem(s)?

C. Does the application satisfy your needs? Follow up with questions about how long they have had the system and how often it has gone down. Ask about its expandability and upgrading possibilities.

D. Do the users like the service? Ask to talk to users and confirm this. Ask users what they liked and disliked about the service and why.

E. Ask how long it took to put the application into operation. Did they receive adequate training? Are the user manuals easy to understand and follow?

F. Is the service provided better than they could do themselves, and why? Is the service worth the cost?

G. Were there any unexpected or hidden costs? What was the nature of these costs? Were the costs reasonable? Was the vendor confronted about this? If so, what was the reaction?

H. Were the vendor's employees easy to work with? Did their salesperson follow up after the sale was made? Does the vendor seem to have a genuine interest in the success of the service?

 I. If you were starting all over, what would you do differently?

> **COMMENT**
>
> "This coming 'services wave' will be very disruptive... Services designed to scale to tens or hundreds of millions will dramatically change the nature and cost of solutions deliverable to enterprises or small businesses."
>
> —*From an internal memo from Bill Gates, Microsoft Chairman, October 30, 2005.*

§ 23.09 SAAS VENDOR MANAGEMENT

[A] Overview

Managing a long-term SaaS project is not an easy task. Some of the reasons for difficulty include:

A. Pricing and service levels established at the beginning of the contract do not contain meaningful methods for measurement and improvement of service.

B. Expectations and assumptions of both parties change over time. Most contracts cannot anticipate changes in technology, personnel, and business processes, etc.

C. Cultural differences between the two companies can cause misunderstandings and mistrust.

D. Differences in the goals and objectives of the two companies can cause problems.

E. Lack of management oversight may cause priorities to become out of sync with the reasons for entering into the contract in the first place.

[B] Service Level Agreement

Information services and affected business units must work together to determine the service level requirements for the applications that are outsourced to the Saas vendor. These service levels must be determined at the outset of the agreement and used to measure and monitor the supplier's performance. The service levels are written in an SLA. The SLA defines the consequences for failing to meet one or more service levels.

The SLA should include the following sections:

A. A precise definition of key terms.

B. Specific service levels for all key categories (e.g., system availability, service desk responsiveness, security administration, change management).

C. Frequency of service level measurement (usually monthly).
D. Guarantee that all security breaches are reported.
E. Responsibility for sensitive data.
F. Weighting by importance of key service levels.
G. Calculation of credits for missing service levels.
H. Calculation of credits for frequency of missing service levels (increased frequency of missed service levels might increase the service credit by some predetermined factor). The performance factors specified in the SLA not only provide an objective measure of the vendor's performance, but can serve as a basis for termination of the service if threshold service levels cannot be met. Other non-key performance levels can be specified to add to the case for termination if warranted.

Typical credit for failure to meet routine service levels ranges from 5 to 15 percent, with penalties for severe service failures reaching 20 to 25 percent. Force majeure clauses excuse a party's failure to perform if the failure resulted from an act of nature, such as an earthquake or other natural disaster beyond the party's control. The SaaS vendor will attempt to include as much as possible in this category; the IT Manager will define it as narrowly as possible. Under no circumstances should a force majeure clause absolve the vendor completely from its responsibilities.

The SLA might also include provisions for vendor rewards for any additional value-added services provided. Make sure these services will really add value before agreeing to payment.

Negotiating and designing an SLA is difficult and time-consuming, but a fair and comprehensive SLA is critical for a successful SaaS relationship. During the negotiation, both parties learn a lot about how their future partner approaches various aspects of their relationship.

24

WEB SITE USABILITY: BUILD IT SO THEY WILL COME

§ 24.01 OVERVIEW
- [A] Purpose and Scope
- [B] Policy Objectives
- [C] Critical Policies to Develop Based on This Chapter

§ 24.02 WEB SITE USABILITY
- [A] What Is Usability?
- [B] Why Usability Is Important
- [C] Consistency and Commonality
- [D] Internet Standards
- [E] Elements of Usability-Based Design
- [F] Effects of Technology Advancement on Usability

§ 24.03 WEB SITE USABILITY POLICIES
- [A] Overview
- [B] Usability Testing Policy
- [C] Content Policy
- [D] Organizational Policy
- [E] Physical Layout Policy
- [F] Visual Design Policy
- [G] Homepage Policy
- [H] Features to Avoid

§ 24.01 OVERVIEW

[A] Purpose and Scope

A web site usability policy formalizes standards for how the company designs web-based applications. The Internet has become a preferred medium for customers and supply chain partners to gather information, transact business, and request support on the company's products and services. Well-designed web sites make it more efficient for customers and supply chain partners to do business with the company, making it more likely that the company will keep that business. This policy should have the endorsement and support of the CEO or head of the organization.

The web site usability policy should cover all software applications that are based on Internet technology, specifically web-based applications. This includes Internet, intranet, and extranet applications. The user software application interface for using these applications is a web browser, typically Microsoft Internet Explorer, Safari, or Firefox.

[B] Policy Objectives

This policy provides guidelines to ensure all web-based applications are "usable" by the intended user; that is, the application is capable of being utilized by the intended user to accomplish a task in an effective and efficient manner. Policy objectives should be flexible enough to cover new types of software and tools that may become available for developers of web-based applications.

The policy should also include a general chronological ordering of the design process. Though there are often looping or reoccurring steps in the process, a general order should be established. Section 24.03 of this chapter provides a general chronological framework for you to consider and adapt to your own situation.

[C] Critical Policies to Develop Based on This Chapter

Using the material discussed in this chapter, you will be able to create the following policies:

A. Web site usability objectives.
    1. Guidelines for consistency and commonality.
    2. Usability design standards.
B. Web site design standards.
    1. Usability testing policies.
    2. Content policies.
    3. Organizational policies.
    4. Physical layout policies.
    5. Visual design policies.
    6. Homepage policies.

Policies should always be developed based on the local situation. Successful managers cannot issue appropriate guidance if the policies are written with another company's or location's situation in mind.

§ 24.02 WEB SITE USABILITY

[A] What Is Usability?

Usability is primarily about understanding user needs and how to effectively make your web-based application seamlessly support those needs.

The application must not hinder the user during the task that the application is intended to address. That is to say, when a user is accomplishing a task, the focus will be on the task and not on the application or how to use the application. Confusing or poorly designed applications require the user to analyze the application itself. This takes attention away from the task and creates a "cost" of time, energy, and focus for the user. The best application will allow the user to complete a task with the least cost. The application then becomes seamless to the user, allowing the application to provide the purpose for which it was intended.

Every "product" (whether the product is an actual application, presentation, meeting, or physical device) should have usability as a key consideration. A product is not useful if it is not designed and presented in a way that meets user needs and expectations.

COMMENT

A non-web example of poor usability is assembly instructions. Everyone makes jokes about an experience in which they purchase an item that required assembly, but after hours of confusion they were still unable to understand how to put it together! This is a very broad example of where usability has obviously failed—to the point that it has become a common frustration.

Usability as an academic discipline is referred to as *usability engineering, human factors,* or *cognitive engineering.* This discipline has a strong focus on psychology, which is not surprising given the people-oriented focus of this field. Human factors professionals are used in many fields. Some of these fields include: automobile dashboard configuration, industrial equipment controls, ergonomics, web site structure, data analysis and presentation, and software development.

[B] Why Usability Is Important

Investing in web-based application usability is a smart business practice and can provide a strong return on investment. Some of the return on investment includes:

    A. Savings internal to the organization:
        1. Increased user productivity.
        2. Decreased user errors.

    3. Decreased training costs.

    4. Savings gained from making key changes early in the product's development life cycle.

B. Savings external to an organization:

    1. Increased sales.

    2. Decreased customer service costs.

    3. Decreased training costs.

C. Usability has become a key differentiator in many product lines. Many ad campaigns highlight how much easier their product or service is to use over their competitors (e.g., AOL, camera phones).

COMMENT

"The importance of having a competitive edge in usability may be even more pronounced for e-commerce sites, which commonly drive away nearly half of repeat business by making it difficult for visitors to find the information they need." (Manning, 1999)

There are few "great" web sites. There are many "poor" web sites. Experts say that nearly two-thirds of corporate web sites contain common mistakes. For example, many include too much marketing jargon and their navigational structure is often confusing. The techniques and guidelines outlined here should put your organization well on the way to being one of the "good sites," which will be preferred by users and profitable for you.

[C] Consistency and Commonality

Consistency and commonality are important aspects of usability. Users have many expectations about web site structure and navigation. The more an application, device, or process matches the behaviors the user has experienced with other such web sites, applications, devices, or processes in the past, the easier it will be for the user to embrace it and begin to make effective use of it.

Non-Internet examples where consistency plays a strong usability role include things like street signs. Street sign standards have been put in place so that people looking at them instantly understand what they mean and react appropriately. Imagine a scenario where street signs varied between cities or across state boundaries!

COMMENT

"More than 83 percent of Internet users are likely to leave a web site if they feel they have to make too many clicks to find what they are looking for." (Arthur Anderson, 2001)

[D]   Internet Standards

"Standards" for the Internet are largely unwritten and evolve with technology. However, users have a large set of expectations built from experiences with all of the web sites and applications they have visited. Consistency and commonality play just as important a role in the Internet as they do in the more traditional usability fields.

The Internet by its very nature tends to allow companies or individuals to express themselves in their own unique way. So there will most likely never be fully defined or fully enforced web-based standards. However, in many areas of the web, de facto standards have evolved and are being documented by people like Jakob Nielsen (see www.useit.com). It definitely benefits web designers to consider these de facto standards if they want a web site that has high usability. Jakob's book *50 Web Sites Deconstructed* outlines, with strong statistical backing, conventions and expectations that users have come to expect from a web site. Deviating from those standards can cause the user confusion. This confusion at best diminishes the user's effectiveness within your web site. At worst, it causes the user to lose confidence in you as a vendor or service provider and results in the user leaving the web site for one that feels more "comfortable."

Examples of common web site conventions that should be followed to leverage users' expectations about consistency and commonality:

A. Logos should appear in the upper left. It should be a hyperlink and should take the user back to the homepage.
B. Do not use frames (this causes confusion when book-marking a page).
C. Do not use music (if used, allow user to silence any audio).
D. Do not use splash pages.
E. Include a search option.
F. Include sections called "About Us" and "Contact Us."

In building a web site, designers should leverage and exploit this "transfer of learning." Creativity should be used in those aspects of a web site that are unique to a given product or service and should *not* be used to modify common web site conventions.

> ## COMMENT
>
> Jakob's web site is *www.useit.com*. It contains a significant amount of web usability research results, views, and opinions around web site usability.
>
> Another useful site is *www.trainingfoundation.com/standards*. It contains point-by-point categories to consider regarding the usability of your site.

Usability is an even greater factor in the Internet than it is in the brick-and-mortar world. For example, if you have spent the last hour driving to your favorite store to find a product—ducking orange barrels, traffic, and detours—you will most likely put up with a reasonable amount of unusable store layout and work pretty hard to find the item you came looking for. In the point-and-click world of the Internet, if you find a web site that is not organized well and gets in the way of your finding the item you are looking for, you can simply point and click out of the web site (and to a competitor) in seconds. Your barrier to exit is much lower in the electronic world. To take this analogy a step further, in the physical store you will be able to ask for the assistance of a clerk for help. When navigating through a web site the user is alone, thus the "search" option becomes a substitute for the store clerk.

> ## COMMENT
>
> Research has shown that users give a web site about 10 seconds before they either look deeper or abandon the site in search of another that serves the same purpose.

There are evolving Internet standards for creating web sites that meet the needs of users with disabilities. These standards are currently required for all federal web sites and may be required by other web sites in the future. The accessibility standards follow the W3C Web Accessibility Initiative (*www.w3.org/WAI*). Another informative resource is A List Apart (*www.alistapart.com*), which is a leading example in the combination of accessibility standards and eye-catching design.

> ## COMMENT
>
> "The power of the web is in its universality. Access by everyone regardless of disability is an essential aspect."
>
> —Tim Berners-Lee, W3C director and inventor of the World Wide Web

These standards include considerations as enabling the font size to be increased by browser settings, providing text equivalents for all non-text elements (via "alt," "longdesc," etc.), and ensuring that information conveyed with color is also understandable without the use of color.

[E]   Elements of Usability-Based Design

What are the elements of usability-based design? The needs of both the business and the user must be taken into consideration. But the user is the most critical element. Exhibit 24-1 illustrates the usability design process.

User-centered design follows a model where the user is at the center of the design process. The object of user-centered design is to enable users to accomplish their goals with the least amount of effort possible. User-centered design plays a strong role early in the life cycle of a project and goes hand in hand with the requirements or user needs analysis phase of a project.

EXHIBIT 24-1.   Usability Design Process

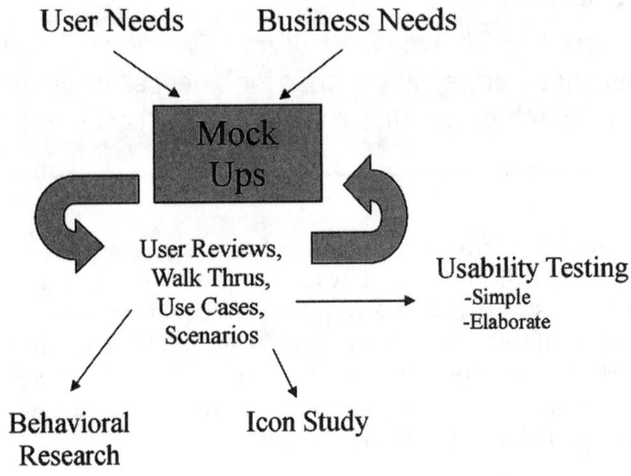

Use cases and scenario-based design are a common way of defining user needs. There are several techniques and tools available to follow a use case model for system definition. Unified Modeling Language (UML) is commonly used for this purpose. Rational Software from IBM is an example of a comprehensive tool suite for following this type of process. Use cases basically document the expected scenarios an application or product must support for it to be of value, or useful.

Understanding your target audience, and their preferences, is critical in user-centered usability planning. Some questions to consider are: What technologies are they familiar with? Do they have a preferred way of accessing information, and can you utilize that medium in your web site? What is their level of experience with the Internet? What design elements do they prefer or expect? Once you understand your user, you are equipped to begin using case studies and scenario-based testing within this demographic.

> ## COMMENT
>
> "You can design for all of the people some of the time. You can design for some of the people all of the time. But you can't design for all of the people all of the time." (William Hudson with apologies to Abraham Lincoln (*www.wdvl.com*).)

Use cases and scenario-based designs typically are highly iterative and include mock-ups to confirm user expectations as early in the process as possible. The goal is to make sure the requirements are accurate early, before actual code gets written, tested, documented, trained on, and deployed.

> ## COMMENT
>
> "Once a system is in development, correcting a problem costs 10 times as much as fixing the same problem in design. If the system has been released, it costs 100 times as much relative to fixing in design." (Glib, 1998)

Usability design techniques also include usability testing. Usability testing can be formal or informal. Formal techniques include a dedicated usability test lab, with two-way mirrors, video equipment, and instrumented code to capture timing through the system. Informal methods can be simple walk-throughs of the application with just a few typical users. Early confirmation of a system by actual users is the goal. The informal usability approaches, which are relatively inexpensive to set up and run, are usually good enough to identify the major problems with an application.

[F]   Effects of Technology Advancement on Usability

Advances in technology typically hinder usability improvements for some period of time. Things like animation, music, splash pages, frames, flash, and lots of graphics all came into vogue when each new technology became possible. Many web site designers jumped on the bandwagon by incorporating these new elements, only to find significant usability issues with many of them.

In some cases, the new element found an appropriate, usable niche (use of flash in some cases is completely appropriate and graphics can certainly add interest to a web site if used appropriately). In other cases, the technology was almost totally abandoned (splash pages, music, frames).

There are usability considerations to take into account depending on the type of technology used in making a web site. These include:

- Download times are affected by things like the loading of images, Java applets, and size of script files.
- Not all features (e.g., ActiveX controls, Java applets) are equally supported across browser types (e.g., IE, Safari, Firefox). The audience of your web site or web application must be taken into consideration when making technology choices that impact their overall user experience.
- Some technologies such as Flash and PDF files require browser plug-ins to be installed and configured, potentially causing user confusion, usability issues, and mis-configurations.

The web also brings a different metaphor to the user. Traditional applications run on the user's desktop. The model for these types of applications to fit into is a *desktop metaphor*. This metaphor is centered on the concept of simulating a physical desktop. A desktop includes folders. In those folders are files. The user owns the file and the content. The user is in control of when the content gets updated and/or shared with other users.

A web user interface brings a *network model metaphor* to the users. The content is stored "out there" on a server. Content is updated in a collaborative environment, where many people can add to or update information. The user is presented with a series of pages that are linked together in a network or "web" of linkages.

These two metaphors are very different. For instance, users expect to click once on a web page. They expect text that is underlined to be a hyperlink to another page. They expect the back and forward buttons of the browser to move them through the application. Users in a more traditional application expect to double-click on options and they expect the File, Edit, Help menus across the top. They expect to use the navigation provided by the application, typically a menu structure, to allow them to move through the application.

A common mistake is placing what is essentially a desktop application in the middle of a browser page. This applies a desktop metaphor to a web-based application and causes user confusion. This happens quite frequently with Java-based applications that use the web mainly as a deployment mechanism, completely missing the metaphor differences that will significantly impact the user's effective operation of the application.

> ## COMMENT
>
> *Top Ten Web Design Mistakes*
>
> 1. Bad Search Engine.
> 2. PDF Files for Online Reading.
> 3. Not Changing the Color of Visited Links.
> 4. Non-Scannable Text.
> 5. Fixed Font Size.
> 6. Page Titles With Low Search Engine Visibility.
> 7. Anything That Looks Like an Advertisement.
> 8. Violating Design Conventions.
> 9. Opening New Browser Windows.
> 10. Not Answering Users' Questions.
>
> Source: *Jakob Nielsen's Alertbox (www.useit.com/alertbox)*.

§ 24.03 WEB SITE USABILITY POLICIES

[A] Overview

It is important to establish the policies to be followed for all web-based applications designed for the organization. This ensures that the applications are usable for their intended purpose by the users of the application. These guidelines are listed below in chronological order. Notice that you will work in the reverse order of a user's experience (e.g., the homepage is the last aspect you define, although it is the first aspect the user encounters). There will be some repetition of these guidelines as needed during the project. As you increasingly define your web site, you will want to go over these categories repeatedly to be sure that your web site is still meeting all the requirements.

[B] Usability Testing Policy

If you want a great web site, you need to get user feedback through usability testing sessions. Even a small set of users (less than five) can provide significant important feedback to the usability of your web site. Develop several steps in your usability testing—early, midproject, and upon completion. In the early steps of usability testing, this will involve defining and understanding your target audience.

> ## COMMENT
>
> Jakob Nielsen and Tom Landauer have shown that testing five users tends to uncover 85 percent of a site's usability problems (*Jakob's March 2000 Alertbox* column, "Why You Only Need to Test with 5 Users" at *www.useit.com*).

Your usability testing policy should include the following items:

A. Define your user group or target audience.

B. Testing with a few users early in the project is significantly more valuable than testing many users near the end of the project. Usability testing must be planned for from the beginning and what you learn from it put to use.

C. Usability testing is an iterative process. Retest key sections of your site after modifications to confirm improvements.

D. Lightweight usability testing that does not require expert users (just typical users), a usability test lab, or excessive cost has proven invaluable in the development of a highly usable web site.

[C] Content Policy

Your content policy should cover the general content of each page of the web site. Your content policy should include the following:

A. Less is more. Steve Krug's Third Law of Usability says "Get rid of half the words on each page; then get rid of half of what's left" (from the book *Don't Make Me Think*).

B. Most users do not read web sites; they only skim them. Content, style, and organization must facilitate skimming.

C. Keep messages clear, crisp, useful, and simply stated. Avoid "fluff," marketing lingo, and clever phrases.

D. Use customer-focused language. Use words your customers will relate to.

E. Avoid exclamation marks and words spelled in all upper case.

F. If an interactive form is provided (e.g., submission form, registration form, or "contact us" form), make sure to include an appropriate Privacy Statement to assure users that you will not distribute their personal information.

[D]   Organizational Policy

Your company's organizational policy should cover what pages are on the web site and how they are organized. Items in your organizational policy that must be followed are:

A.   All web sites should incorporate top-level navigation that includes Home, About Us, and Contact Us.

B.   Data presented within the web site should be consistently and cleanly organized. Similar information should be grouped together. A web site is of little value if users cannot find the data they are looking for. Major categories should have titles that mean something to the visitor, not the web designer.

C.   If the site is at all complex, it should include a site-wide search function. The search function should appear consistently on each page of the site, typically in the top area of each web page.

D.   Site navigation should be located either across the top of the page and/ or on the left-hand side of each page.

E.   Visited links within the site should be marked so the user knows he has traversed the link.

F.   Users should be provided with feedback through highlighting, bread-crumbs, or other visuals of where they are within the web site at all times.

G.   If a link does not go to another web page (e.g., a PDF, e-mail form), tell the user what will happen when the link is clicked.

See Policy ITP-24-1 Web Site Organizational Policy as an example.

POLICY ITP-24-1   Web Site Organizational Policy

Policy #:	ITP-24-1	Effective:	03/18/09	Page #:	1 of N
Subject:	Web Site Organizational Policy				

1.0 PURPOSE

This policy mandates what pages are on company Web sites and how they are organized.

2.0 SCOPE

This policy encompasses all Web pages on company-owned Web sites developed in-house or by outside vendors. The IT Manager is responsible for implementing all aspects of this policy.

3.0 POLICY

The following Web pages must be on every company Web site and organized as follows:

A. All Web sites must incorporate top-level navigation that includes Home, About Us, and Contact Us.
B. Data presented within the Web site must be consistently and cleanly organized. Similar information must be grouped together. Major categories must have titles that mean something to the visitor—not the Web designer.
C. If the site contains more than 20 pages, it must have a site-wide search function. The search function must appear consistently on each page of the site in the top area of each Web page.
D. Site navigation must be located across the top of each page.
E. Visited links within the site must be marked so the user knows they have traversed the link.
F. Users must be provided with feedback through highlighting, breadcrumbs, or other visuals of where they are within the Web site at all times.
G. If a link does not go to another Web page (e.g., a PDF, e-mail form), tell the user what will happen when the link is clicked.

4.0 REVISION HISTORY

Date	Revision #	Description of Change
03/18/07	1.0	Initial creation.

5.0 INQUIRIES

Direct inquiries about this policy to:

Tom Jones, CIO
Our Company, Inc.
2900 Corporate Drive
Columbus, OH 43215

Voice: 614-555-1234
Fax: 614-555-1235
E-mail: tjones@company.com

Revision #:	1.0	Supersedes:	N/A	Date:	03/18/09

[E]   Physical Layout Policy

Physical layout policy should guide the design of the physical properties of the web site. Your physical layout policy should include the following:

A.   Design to the broadest anticipated screen size and resolution. In the absence of marketing data for your anticipated customer base to the contrary, assume a screen real estate of 800 by 600 pixels minus the real estate taken up by the browser menus. This typically leaves about 770 pixels for the page width.

B.   Avoid horizontal scrolling on all pages.

C.   Vertical scrolling is acceptable, assuming the vertical scrolling is three pages of information or less. Keep the most important information on any page "above the fold" (in the first page of text as viewed in 800 by 600 resolution). Avoid vertical scrolling completely on the homepage, however.

D.   Keep page load times under 10 seconds on the assumed connection speeds of your anticipated visitor community. Faster is always better.

E.   Logos and taglines should appear in the upper left of the page. Copyrights and privacy policy statements should appear in the footer of each page.

[F]   Visual Design Policy

Visual design policy guides the design of the visual elements that make up the web site. Elements of visual design that must be followed are:

A.   Carry the corporate visual design to the web site. Keep marketing material, brochures, stationery, and other branding elements consistent with your web site and vice versa. Use the web site to help extend your brand recognition. That recognition gets diluted if there is no consistency.

B.   Keep graphic resolutions appropriate for web displays (72 dpi). Higher resolutions are typically wasted on the web and cause longer download times.

C.   Avoid watermark graphics. These are background images with text on top of them. Watermark graphics make the page text difficult to read.

D.   Limit the number of different font styles, sizes, and colors used on the web site.

E.   Always use relative text sizes that make it possible for a user to increase or decrease the text size via browser settings.

F.   Make sure there is a high contrast between text and background colors to maximize readability.

G.   Use animation sparingly. While technologies such as Flash can provide some interest to a site, they become tedious on repeat visits. Animation should only be used for a specific, focused purpose that enhances the effectiveness of the overall site. Typically animation should be used only to help explain a complex process and should be avoided altogether on the homepage.

[G]   Homepage Policy

The homepage is the first visited page of any site and must instantly attract a wide population of visitors. This is the page to spend considerable time fine-tuning. Homepage policies that must be followed are:

A.   The homepage should quickly convey what the site is, what it is for, and why someone would want to visit the site.

B.   The homepage should establish top-level navigation and provide an overview of the content that can be found on the site.

C.   The content on the homepage should change frequently to keep users coming back and increase popularity with search engines.

D.   The homepage is typically the place to put special notices—like an upcoming seminar, a special deal, or a new product announcement.

[H]   Features to Avoid

Many techniques available for the creation of web sites are a source of usability problems. To help ensure that the organization's web sites are usable, avoid the following features:

A.   Do not use splash pages on web sites. Splash pages are appropriate for desktop applications, but not web-based applications.

B.   Do not "lock" a user into your site and disable the back button. Taking away user control in your web site is one sure way to have them never return again.

C.   Avoid pop-up windows whenever possible. Most of these types of windows will be blocked by pop-up blockers.

D.   Do not use frames.

E.   Do not use music that plays automatically.

25

DATA MANAGEMENT: TAKING CARE OF YOUR INFORMATION

§ 25.01   OVERVIEW
          [A]   Purpose and Scope
          [B]   Critical Policies to Develop Based on This Chapter

§ 25.02   ISSUES RELATING TO DATA
          [A]   System of Record
          [B]   Ownership of Data
          [C]   Legal Obligations

§ 25.03   ACCESS TO DATA
          [A]   Data User Roles
          [B]   Data Retention
          [C]   Handling of Restricted Data

§ 25.04   PROTECTING EMPLOYEE DATA
          [A]   Overview
          [B]   Privacy Officer
          [C]   Collection of Personal Data
          [D]   Use of Personal Data
          [E]   Security of Personal Data
          [F]   Access to Personal Data

§ 25.01 OVERVIEW

[A] Purpose and Scope

Data is a critical corporate resource that must be managed properly as well as protected from unauthorized disclosure or modification. Corporate data must be managed in a controlled environment to ensure the integrity and accuracy of the data. As new systems are developed or purchased, they should be integrated into the existing corporate data environment and not implemented as standalone systems. The sharing of data in a secure environment requires that the appropriate policies and procedures be in place.

Data management policies cover all data created and used by the organization. This data includes, but is not restricted to:

A. Human resource data.
B. Customer data.
C. Memos.
D. Strategic plans.
E. Planning data.
F. Emails.
G. Financial data.
H. Best practices.
 I. Facilities data.
J. Employee data.
K. Policies and procedures.
L. World Wide Web pages.

All of this information must be protected and managed properly; the appropriate policies and procedures help ensure that each employee understands his role in protecting the organization's valuable data.

[B] Critical Policies to Develop Based on This Chapter

Using the material discussed in this chapter, you will be able to create the following policies:

A. Define system of record.
B. Define ownership of data.
  1. Belongs to the organization if created by the organization.
  2. Includes data in all forms; databases, spreadsheets, unstructured data.
C. Define the roles and responsibilities of those who create or have access to sensitive data.
D. Protecting sensitive employee information.

Policies should always be developed based on the local situation. Successful managers cannot issue appropriate guidance if the policies are written with another company's or location's situation in mind.

§ 25.02 ISSUES RELATING TO DATA

[A] System of Record

Data is factual information, in particular, information organized for analysis or to make decisions. Organizations create a tremendous amount of data, all of which must be managed properly just as you would any other valuable asset. Data includes every piece of factual information created by the organization. There are numerous systems within the typical organization that create and manage this data. These systems include:

- A. Accounting/finance.
- B. Customer relationship management (CRM).
- C. Enterprise resource planning (ERP).
- D. Order entry.
- E. Human resources.
- F. Customer service.
- G. Intranet/extranet.
- H. Document management.

In an ideal world, each data element used by the organization would only exist in one place and would not be duplicated in different systems. The reality is that specialized systems from various vendors are implemented in most organizations that require copies of different data elements. For example, your CRM system may not interface with your Accounting system, so you end up with customer information in both systems. The larger the organization, the more likely you are to have multiple special-purpose systems that require their own copy of important data. It is critical to identify which system will be the definitive source of important information.

A "system of record" is an information storage system (usually a computer system) which is the definitive data source for a given data element or piece of information. We go to the system of record when we need to know the "truth" about a particular item of data. All other systems are considered incorrect if their copy of the data does not match the system of record. Ideally, these secondary systems do not edit the data for which they are not the system of record, but instead receive updates from the system of record for these data elements. For example, you may determine that the CRM system is the system of record for basic customer information such as name, address and contact information. This basic contact information is also needed by your Accounting and Customer Service applications. Any changes necessary to basic customer information should be made only in the CRM system. The Accounting and Customer Service applications should receive updates on a regular schedule of this basic customer information.

In selecting which system should be the system of record for a particular data element, consider the following criteria:

- A. Scope—How widely is the system used throughout the organization?
- B. Value—How much impact does the system have on the core economics of the business?

C. Influence—How important is the sponsor of the system within the organization?

D. Activity—How much raw data is being fed into the system by high-volume, mission-critical transactions?

The higher a given system rates using the criteria listed above, the more likely it is to be a good candidate for being the system of record for the data elements used within the system. A system of record policy is necessary to ensure that a single "version of the truth" exists for all important data used throughout the organization. See Policy ITP-25-1 System of Record Policy as an example.

COMMENT

According to a 2007 study conducted by research firm IDC for information infrastructure company EMC Corporation, 161 billion gigabytes (or 161 exabytes) of digital information was created or copied worldwide in 2006; this number is expected to rise six-fold to 988 billion gigabytes in 2010. This represents a compound annual growth rate of 57 percent.

POLICY ITP-25-1.   System of Record Policy

Policy #:	ITP-25-1	**Effective:**	03/18/09	**Page #:**	1 of N
Subject:	System of Record Policy				

1.0 PURPOSE

The company views corporate data as an asset of the company to be managed and protected. While multiple versions of data may necessarily exist due to the existence of specialized computer systems, this policy mandates that a system of record be identified for all data created and maintained within the organization. The system of record is to be considered the definitive and authoritative source of truth for a given data element.

2.0 SCOPE

This policy encompasses all data in all its forms and throughout its lifecycle. The IT Manager is responsible for implementing all aspects of this policy.

3.0 POLICY

The IT Manager is responsible for defining a system of record for all corporate data. In addition, the IT Manager is also responsible for the following:

A. All points of data collection for the system of record must be defined and documented.
B. Data entered into the system of record must be accurate and timely.
C. Systems that capture data that update the system of record must include the appropriate validation and security to ensure the integrity of the data.
D. Processes used to update the system of record must be documented and auditable.

Users of copies of data from a system of record are responsible for managing the refresh of the data copy from the system of record to ensure that accurate information is used in all systems.

4.0 REVISION HISTORY

Date	Revision #	Description of Change
03/18/09	1.0	Initial creation.

5.0 INQUIRIES

Direct inquiries about this policy to:

Tom Jones, CIO
Our Company, Inc.
2900 Corporate Drive
Columbus, OH 43215

Voice: 614-555-1234
Fax: 614-555-1235
E-mail: tjones@company.com

Revision #:	1.0	Supersedes:	N/A	Date:	03/18/09

[B]   Ownership of Data

Your data management policies should make it clear that all data created by the organization is owned by the organization, and not by any individual within the organization. This includes both structured and unstructured data, and any metadata about that data. Structured data is data that is formatted in an organized way for easy retrieval from computer systems, such as data in a database or in an XML file. Unstructured data is typically data created by a human being for personal use, such as word processing documents and spreadsheets. Metadata is information about the data, such as field names, file layouts, version control information, etc.

The Data Custodian (see section 25.3[A] Data User Roles for a definition of Data Custodian) is responsible for ensuring that the appropriate policies and procedures are in place to protect the data under his stewardship. These policies must document how access to the data is obtained, who has access to the data, and the retention period for the data.

[C] Legal Obligations

There are several federal and state laws and regulations such as the Family Rights and Privacy Act (FERPA), the Sarbanes-Oxley Act (SOX), the Health Insurance Portability and Accountability Act (HIPAA), the Electronic Communications Privacy Act (ECPA), the Gramm-Leach-Bliley Act and the Freedom of Information Act (FOIA) that affect various aspects of data within the organization. These laws are quite complex and have been modified from time to time. It is critical for the organization to ensure that the legal obligations with respect to the organization's data are kept current. These obligations require the following actions:

A. All managers are expected to stay informed on any local, state and federal laws and guidelines that affect how the organization's data is stored and managed. This can be done through participation in professional organizations, subscriptions to appropriate periodicals, or thorough participation in Internet listservs. Where appropriate, this can be delegated to members of their team. Processes must be in place to disseminate important changes to others within the organization that may be impacted.

B. Senior staff meetings should include on their agenda a discussion of recent changes to laws and regulations that affect the handling of data within the organization.

C. All managers are responsible for ensuring that their staff members are informed about changes in the legal environment and that corporate policies on the handling of data are being followed.

D. Employees are responsible for staying current on applicable laws and policies that affect their job. They must attend any training opportunities that apply to the handling of data in their area of responsibility.

§ 25.03 ACCESS TO DATA

[A] Data User Roles

To ensure that everyone understands their role in the proper management of data, your data management policies should outline the different roles associated with the handling of data and the responsibilities of the people in those roles. These roles and their responsibilities include:

A. **Data Owner**—The organization is the owner of all data that originates within the organization.

B. **Data Custodian**—A member of senior management of the organization who is ultimately responsible for ensuring the protection and use of the organization's data. His responsibilities include:

   1. Identifying what data belongs to the organization and determining the system of record for the data.
   2. Identifying and documenting what roles are allowed access to the data and the level of access they have.
   3. Determining and documenting the process for authorizing individuals to access the data.
   4. Implementing processes that maintain the integrity and accuracy of the data.
   5. Ensuring that the data is protected and that applicable laws are followed concerning handling of the data.

C. **Security Administrator**—This role is responsible for the security of the data and systems that store the data. The responsibilities of this role include:

   1. Providing access to the users that are approved by the data custodian.
   2. Protecting the data from unauthorized users.
   3. Ensuring that appropriate disaster recovery procedures are in place.

D. **Data User**—This role is designated by the data custodian to have permission to access and use the data. The responsibilities of the data user include:

   1. Being accountable for all data access made with his user account.
   2. Ensuring that all use and distribution of data is only for approved purposes.
   3. Not disclosing data to unauthorized people.
   4. Keeping his password secret.

E. **IT Department**—This role is responsible for supporting the data systems infrastructure. The responsibilities of this role include:

   1. Documenting and supporting the structure of the organization's data.
   2. Supporting the use of standard data definitions throughout the organization.
   3. Facilitating the sharing of data and integration of data between the organization's systems.

[B] Data Retention

It is important to establish a data retention policy for all data in your organization for two reasons: to meet legal and business requirements, and to prevent data overloading your storage systems. Various state and federal regulations require data to be retained for some minimum period of time; some examples include:

A. Information relating to the manufacture, processing and packaging of food—two years.
B. Patient medical records—up to two years after the patient's death.
C. Information relating to the manufacture, processing, and packaging of drugs—three years.
D. Information relating to the manufacture of biological products—five years.
E. Records relating to the audit process, including emails—seven years.
F. Trading account records—six years after the termination of the account.

Some organizations will want to save virtually every bit of data they create to be on the safe side; others will weigh the expense of storing all of this information with the possible costs of legal action caused by data not being available. The organization's legal department and senior management are responsible for creating the data retention schedule; it is then up to IT to enforce and conform to the policy in the most efficient way possible.

[C]   Handling of Restricted Data

While all data is important, special care must be taken when a user is in possession of data that is confidential or restricted in some way. Restricted data is data whose use is restricted by law, is confidential to the organization, or data that has been designated as protected from general access or modification. Types of restricted data include, but are not limited to, personnel data, financial data not for use outside the organization, and data to which unauthorized access, modification, or loss could seriously or adversely affect the organization, its partners, or the public.

COMMENT

The cost of lost data is high: in early 2006, one IT worker at Providence Health System in Portland, Ore., was fired and three others quit following the theft of computer tapes that held sensitive patient information, including addresses, phone numbers, and social security numbers. Employees at Providence routinely brought home tapes used to back up the data on systems there. Predictably, the tapes were stolen from a van parked outside one of their homes. A company official told the local paper that the loss was expected to cost the company more than $7 million, not including any costs of litigation.

The following are basic practices that employees must follow when handling restricted data:

A. **Systems should not include restricted data unless absolutely necessary.** Examples of restricted data include social security numbers, employee personal information, financial information such as credit card numbers or bank account numbers, and responses to a Request for Proposal (RFP) before a decision has been reached.

B. **Restricted data should not be stored on workstations, laptops, or other portable computing and storage devices unless absolutely necessary.** Restricted data should only be retained on a temporary basis on such devices. Protective measures such as encryption must be used to safeguard the confidentiality or integrity of the data in the event of theft or loss of the equipment. Permanent copies of restricted data should never be stored for archival purposes on workstations or portable equipment.

C. **Avoid transferring or storing restricted data.** Proliferation of data greatly increases risks of unauthorized access, particularly when the data is stored in ad hoc analysis tools such as spreadsheets and desktop databases. When data is copied for analysis or research, restricted data should be deleted whenever possible. When use and storage of restricted data must occur, provide appropriate security, following the organization's security protocols and the security requirements.

D. **Never email restricted data.** Since email is not a secure form of communication, restricted data should never be part of an email, either in the body of the email or in an attachment.

E. **Do not leave restricted data on a printer unattended.** Documents printed with restricted data must be removed immediately from the printer.

F. **Printed documents with restricted data must be shredded when no longer needed.** Never dispose of restricted documents in the regular trash.

G. **Delete personal information.** Any personal information such as gender, ethnicity, credit card numbers, etc., must be deleted from all systems when there is no longer a business need for the information.

H. **Make sensitive data easily identifiable.** When designing data structures, use naming conventions that make it easy to identify sensitive information.

§ 25.04   PROTECTING EMPLOYEE DATA

[A]   Overview

While all data is important to the organization, data concerning the employees of the organization is of a special nature. The handling of employee data is indicative of the relationship between the organization and its employees, and establishes the level of trust the employee has in the organization. It is critical that this trust be maintained by protecting the privacy of personal data about the employee and his/her family that is collected by the organization from any source before, during, and after employment.

Your policy for the management of employee data should include the following:

A. Define the personal data the company collects from the employee and from other sources.
B. Describe how the data is used and disclosed.
C. Document the security measures used by the company to protect the employee's information.
D. Define who has access to the employee's information and the purposes for which it will be used.
E. A process for access by the employee to his personal information and how corrections can be made.
F. Procedures for notifying the company of possible improper disclosures of personal information.
G. How and under what circumstances an employee can opt out of disclosing certain personal information and the consequences of doing so.

The policy should also state that it applies to all entities controlled by the organization, and to any subcontractors that receive personal information. The policy does not imply any privacy rights for communications by the employee using company resources, such as emails, instant messages, telephone calls, etc.

[B] Privacy Officer

A member of senior management must be designated as ultimately responsible for the protection of personal employee information. This is usually the head human resources person with the organization. The person will be responsible for the following:

A. Ensure that all systems and processes comply with the employee data privacy policy.
B. Assess on a regular basis (at least annually) the compliance status of all systems with applicable laws and regulations.
C. Report to senior management the results of each assessment in writing.

[C] Collection of Personal Data

Personal data about employees is typically collected during the application and hiring process, and during their term of employment. This information may include:

A. Background checks.
B. Results of personality tests.

    C. Drug test results.
    D. Medical insurance enrollment information.
    E. Applications for participation in certain benefit programs.

Personal employee data that is collected may include, but may not be limited to, the following:

    A. Individual information such as name, gender, date of birth.
    B. Contact information such as home address, phone numbers, email addresses.
    C. Identification numbers such as driver's license number and social security number.
    D. Background information such as education, work history, military status and criminal record.
    E. Work history and training attended.
    F. Medical and health information.
    G. Compensation information such as salary, commissions, stock options, and 401K plan account information.

[D] Use of Personal Data

The personal information collected is to be used only for the purpose required, and may be shared with service providers or other organizations where required. Personal data may be disclosed under the following situations to:

    A. Internal personnel who need to receive the information to perform their jobs, such as managers and finance personnel for budgeting purposes.
    B. Service providers of benefit programs, such as health plans and 401K plans.
    C. Potential buyers of the business unit that the employee is a part of.
    D. Customers to whom the organization is providing services.

Personal information is disclosed only to the extent necessary to perform the activity. Home addresses and personal contact are typically not disclosed, without the prior approval of the employee except in emergency situations. Outside firms that are given access to personal employee information are required to sign a written confidentiality agreement before the personal information is disclosed. Employee personal information is never disclosed or sold for marketing purposes.

Employees should also be aware that the company may be required to disclose personal data by law in situations such as the issuance of a search warrant, a court order or subpoena, or for other legal reasons by government agents or agencies.

[E] Security of Personal Data

The company will maintain reasonable and appropriate physical, electronic, and procedural safeguards to protect the personal information of its employees. Personal data will be protected against misuse, modification, unauthorized access, and improper disclosure. Each employee of the company is required to sign an employment agreement that contains an obligation to protect the confidential information of the company, which includes personal information of fellow employees. Employees in the Human Resources department may be required to sign an additional confidentiality agreement before gaining access to sensitive personal data. All new employees are required to attend a training course within the first 30 days of employment that covers their obligations to protect company information.

[F] Access to Personal Data

All employees will have access to personal data that is stored by the company to ensure the accuracy of the information. Access is available during regular business hours, and notice must be given at least 24 hours in advance to allow Human Resources to schedule access to the information. Each member of the employee's immediate family will also be allowed access to any information stored about them (but not the employee) during regular business hours, with at least 24 hours notice.

If the employee or family member feels that the data stored by the company is inaccurate, a request can be made in writing to have the information changed. The appropriate data custodian (usually the Human Resources Manager) must respond within 48 hours confirming that the information has been changed or explaining why the change will not be made. If the change is not made, the employee may submit written information to be stored with the data in question explaining why he feels the data is inaccurate; this most commonly occurs in the case of information concerning performance reviews.

26

END-USER SYSTEMS: DO IT YOURSELF COMPUTING

§ 26.01   OVERVIEW
          [A] Purpose and Scope
          [B] Critical Policies to Develop Based on This Chapter

§ 26.02   THE PROBLEMS WITH END-USER COMPUTING
          [A] Overview
          [B] The Evolution of End-User Computing
          [C] Reasons End-User Computing Is Popular
          [D] Examples of End-User Programming
          [E] Some of the Pitfalls
          [F] Sharing
          [G] IT Strikes Back!

§ 26.03   PERSONAL COMPUTING vs. CORPORATE COMPUTING
          [A] Overview
          [B] When End-User Programs Should Fall under IT Control
          [C] Moving End-User Authored Programs to Production

§ 26.04   MANAGING A PROACTIVE END-USER COMPUTING PROGRAM
          [A] Overview
          [B] What to Do?
          [C] End-User Development Training
          [D] Cultivate the Power Users
          [E] Appoint IT Staff Members to Mentor End Users

§ 26.05   END-USER POLICIES
          [A] Overview
          [B] End-User Software Policies
          [C] System Documentation

§ 26.01 OVERVIEW

[A] Purpose and Scope

End-user computing is the creation of computer applications by someone internal to the company but outside of the IT department. These applications can be developed in a wide range of computer language formats, from traditional languages such as C or BASIC to the embedded formulas in spreadsheets. The challenge to the IT Manager is to ensure that those who create such applications understand and adhere to good data processing practices using effective policies and procedures.

Long have end users complained about the slowness of traditional IT application development. In their view, simple requests to the IT department take weeks or months. As personal computers became more powerful, software became easier to use. Non-IT employees knew how to use them both, and end-user computing emerged as a force. Today personal computing classes are routinely required throughout the national education system.

Initially managers of the various departments thought they now had a quick way to develop their own applications. They gradually came to realize that they had grabbed the proverbial tiger by the tail and could not let go!

The individual department managers were relearning the lessons painfully learned by IT over the years. End user computing policies must be in place to ensure that end users do not create more problems than they solve when they take matters into their own hands.

[B] Critical Policies to Develop Based on This Chapter

Using the material discussed in this chapter, you will be able to create the following policies:

A. Permissible end-user systems.
   1. What type of systems are permitted.
   2. Who is responsible for maintaining systems.
   3. How systems are implemented.
B. IT involvement.
   1. Level and degree of support.
   2. When support should be taken over by IT.
   3. Documentation requirements.

Policies should always be developed based on the local situation. Successful managers cannot issue appropriate guidance if the policies are written with another company's or location's situation in mind.

§ 26.02 THE PROBLEMS WITH END-USER COMPUTING

[A] Overview

The IT staff works with technology every day. They likely have several years of technical college training as well as years of experience designing, implementing, and supporting data systems of various types. During this time, some basic principles of the art of data processing became ingrained in their actions and work plans. In short, they do things automatically that will ensure their systems are reliable, efficient, and always available.

Business managers focus on the problems found in their own department. End-user programming for them is something of a diversion. If something provides the results they seek, then it is a success. Little time is wasted polishing the code or checking results. That work is for another time.

Most end-user problems result in subtle errors. A slightly inaccurate total here, a missing record there, slightly out of date tables used, etc. If a value is blatantly incorrect, then something is done about it. However, if the numbers appear to be plausible the report is issued.

Regardless of the source, end-user computing generated reports are relied upon by management for decisions that impact corporate strategies, regulatory compliance, and customer relationships. The integrity of the data and the accuracy of this processing are no less important than that provided by the IT department.

[B] The Evolution of End-User Computing

In times long gone by, punch cards were the primary tool for controlling computers. Each card held an 80-character line of data or programming code. Developing programs was a tedious process involving the building, debugging, and maintaining of sequences of punch cards in a series of trays.

Around the late 1970s, from the ranks of electronics hobbyists emerged personal computers. These machines could perform simple tasks but were mainly a curiosity. Sometime around 1978, the early personal computers emerged. Among these machines were the Commodore PET, TRS-80 Model I, and the Apple II. An important feature of these devices was that they contained a small version of the BASIC programming language on an 8K ROM. BASIC was easy to learn and could perform simple tasks. Data was stored on cassette tapes and later on floppy disks.

These devices initially lacked powerful, easy-to-use software. As the software emerged, so did demand for the machines. Word processing programs drove early demand. Up to this point, professionals used typewriters to create lengthy documents or paid someone to type them. Back and forth went draft copies with pen changes until finally the document reached its final form. Each document revision required typing the entire text from the beginning, which introduced more errors. The productivity improvement justified the purchase for many secretaries' desks, although the printers that were used closely mimicked electric typewriters.

A popular package of this early era was WordStar, which provided many formatting features. Limited as it seems today, this package encouraged more people to buy PCs for home and the office. Still, PCs were a novelty the users thought of as playing with an oversized calculator.

> ## COMMENT
>
> Around this time special-purpose word processing worksta-
> tions appeared in many secretarial areas around companies.
> The refinements made to this software made their way into
> PC software and these stations disappeared.

In 1981, IBM introduced their first personal computer. This greatly increased the credibility of PCs as office tools and opened the gates to purchase by large corporations. Along with the new computer came a new type of software called VisiCalc. This product introduced the concept of an electronic spreadsheet and, together with new word processing software, spurred the widespread use of office personal computers—and along with it end-user computing.

The combination of word processing and spreadsheet programs provided sufficient value to move PCs from secretary stations onto managers' desktops. Now, instead of asking a secretary to type a simple memo, they did it themselves. (Many of their peers would sniff that they do not want to learn how to use a PC as "they do not type.")

Up to this point, end-user written programs in BASIC or Pascal were primarily for engineering purposes. Saving programs and data to cassette tapes was quite slow. Although the IBM had a tape storage option, it was rarely seen as everyone used the 160K, single-sided floppy disk drive (power users had *two* floppy drives). PCs were still expensive and only found on selected desks.

Most company data was in the form of reports. These reports display the summation of the individual data elements but the elements themselves and the calculations used to create them are not visible to the reader. Reports compiled in an office included the names of the people creating and typing them. Mainframe-generated reports were meticulously developed. However, VisiCalc spreadsheets allowed anyone to create financial reports that appeared like the tediously created, manually assembled reports.

Soon, the first end-user introduced problems appeared. These reports depended on the accuracy of the formulas embedded in the spreadsheet cells, and the data that was entered. They were recognizable by the simple dot matrix printers that created them. Still, the strong reputation of mainframe-generated reports gave these documents unwarranted respect.

In a short time, easy-to-use database packages, more programming languages, and faster hardware rolled in. Desktop units gradually contained as much raw computing power as mainframe computers. Windows with its GUI interface shielded users from the coldly impersonal DOS and provided a visually attractive interface for programmers. Merge this with recent college graduates who worked with computers in school and the mix was right for business departments to write their own data systems.

Aware of the benefits and tired of delays in getting needed systems from IT, end-user departments began to establish "shadow" data processing operations. Programmers hid behind titles like "data coordinator" with a job description that read like something right out of the IT department. "Power users" emerged as recent college graduates, familiar with personal computing tools, entered the offices. Some offices began to resemble PC repair stations complete with stacks of spare parts and piles of tangled cables.

COMMENT

One author worked for a company whose IT director routinely sidelined program requests and bragged of the money saved by not performing "low value" work. Unfortunately, the only person whose value judgment he listened to was his own.

So here we are today. In every business department are users with enough technical sophistication to create complex data systems, write reports against major databases, and develop sophisticated spreadsheet analysis all without IT involvement. Is this a good idea or are there problems lurking under the surface?

[C]   Reasons End-User Computing Is Popular

Personal computing, as its name implies, is computing done by and for a single person. Although playing a game is a form of personal computing, this term usually refers to programming "something" to do work. In a home setting, personal computing is not much of an issue. If a student's spreadsheet has an error, then their grade suffers. If their database search of an encyclopedia fails, then they reap the consequences.

In an office setting, end-user computing can be more rewarding or create its own consequences. End-user computing—the creation of data systems (big or small) by others than the IT department—carries with it far more responsibilities than most people are aware of, or are willing to take on. Regardless of the source, the reports generated by end-user computing tools for decisions affecting corporate strategies and customer relationships. The integrity of the data in these documents is no less important than the data stored in the corporate databases.

The widespread use of end-user computing attests to its popularity. Some of the reasons end-user computing remains popular include:

A. **Productivity**—Documents of all types are created and stored electronically. Changes are quickly made and printed. Word processing allows typing memos instead of writing them out and sending them back and forth for revisions.

B. **Agility**—In a fast-paced business environment, there is no time to wait for a bureaucratic IT department to waddle through their justification processes simply to estimate the cost of a request. By then, the opportunity is gone.

C. **Timeliness**—Small requests take far longer to explain than for a trained user to create them.

[D] Examples of End-User Programming

End-user developed programs primarily automate the tedious and repetitive tasks on a worker's desk. Examples of this are:

A. **Reporting**—Roughly half of the requests to IT involve developing new reports or modifying existing ones. Many requests are for single use reports where the end user only has a vague idea of what he wants. Rather than perform exhaustive data systems analysis and design process, IT should provide easy-to-use tools to allow end users to create their own reports. These tools must have limits to prevent a poorly written database query from dragging down the entire server. A common check is to limit end user queries to a maximum of 5,000 records.

> **COMMENT**
>
> End-user computing has long been a mainframe function. Some programs such as Information Builders' FOCUS system and Business Objectives Crystal Reports have provided the tools for generating reports from the core mainframe databases with a minimum of keystrokes.

B. **Web pages**—This powerful communications medium is useful for internally publishing information. Rather than print reams of paper and then walk around distributing it, a department can post the information on a web page. Examples of information include daily reports, business performance metrics, policy manuals, etc. IT limits are usually to publish a policy about acceptable content in a department's Web page. IT also locks the page to internal usage only while policing all pages to keep confidential data off the web.

C. **Spreadsheets**—A great tool for listing and totaling numbers for budgets, expense tracking, quality statistical analysis, etc., spreadsheets manage very large lists through sorting and pivot tables. The rapid graphing of data (instead of tediously graphing by hand) is also a great tool for quickly examining data. The text formatting capabilities of spreadsheets make them a quick way to develop simple forms.

D. **Word processing**—Many programs provide a capability to create data entry forms which only allow data to be entered into specific fields. People who complain about the time it takes to perform basic work in a word processing program never had to suffer through the various tab settings, line spacing settings, and other mechanical aspects of setting up an electric typewriter to build a document. Not only is the software easier to use, but it makes the creation of newsletters with graphics and pictures an easy desktop task.

E. **Database**—Great for collecting data or reporting from lists too large for a spreadsheet. All end-user created databases must be maintained on the department's server file share to ensure they can be backed up. Multi-user databases (except for read only) must be created and managed by the IT department.

F. **Graphics**—Computer-aided design (CAD) software did for draftsmen what spreadsheets did for accountants. It has taken the engineering world from drafting tables to the desktop and saved countless hours redrawing and copying blueprints and component designs.

[E] Some of the Pitfalls

A long list of problems can arise from end-user computing. They are quite familiar to IT workers who have been struggling with the same issues for years. The key to end-user computing is to identify the risks from these issues at the local site, to educate end users on how to minimize the risk, and to support them in these mitigation efforts. IT Managers have found that addressing the issues in advance is far easier than "firefighting" the problems as they arise.

End users do not differentiate between sensitive company data and all of the other data they work with. "Sensitive data" requires protection due to the risk and magnitude of loss or harm which could result from inadvertent or deliberate disclosure, alteration, or destruction of the data.

Some of the end-user computing pitfalls include:

A. **Data**

Data, the object of end-user computing, is also its central point of failure. End users do not apply the necessary controls to ensure data accuracy going in and its correct summation coming out. The result can damage a company in several ways.

1. Incorrect management decisions, based on incorrect reports.
2. Improper disclosure of information, due to poor security.
3. Fraud, since the person controlling the data can also control changing it.

End users who create their own database systems risk the data being out of date with the rest of the company's data.

> ### COMMENT
>
> One author worked at a company where the freight traffic manager kept detailed records of all shipments in a spreadsheet. It included items such as what was sent to where, how much it weighed, the amount bid by the carrier, the class of service ordered, etc. The following month when the freight bills were submitted, this sheet was validated to reconcile the bills and stop numerous attempts at overcharging. It also provided data for filing missing freight claims.
>
> This spreadsheet automated a routine task that concerned no one else. However, the data was critical to protecting the company from freight overbillings and enhanced their ability to file successful claims. Overbillings frequently ran $10,000 per month or more. To protect this important company information, the file moved from the creator's never-backed-up PC to a computer file server.

The problem arises when departments create their own set of data parallel to the IT databases. These files and databases are beyond the standard IT data integrity safeguards. Although quick to report from and easy to manipulate, these parallel data stores may provide misleading results. IT should develop department databases to ensure they contain accurate data. On request, IT can reload the database with the latest data. Problems that may arise with end-user created data files include:

1. The corruption of data due to a lack of program edits for data entry or correction.
2. Errors may take a long time to become apparent with bad output embedding into other files.
3. A loss of critical company data due to poor program controls, lack of storage management, or poorly written programs that corrupt files.
4. Failure to retain data according to regulatory requirements places the company at legal risk. This is true even if the end user created the file solely for his personal use. Since these files are out of the IT department's sight, their existence may not be known to the company until an inopportune moment.
5. When an end user downloads corporate data or builds his own database, he assumes personal responsibility for its security. This is something that few users think about since IT has always handled this quietly in the background. The simplest way to protect data is to store it on a network server where the user accesses it through his

own user ID security access. Unfortunately, with the proliferation of notebook PCs, this has become more of a challenge.

6. In a report, old data often looks just like new data. To ensure that the data in the file is the current version, consider displaying the latest date in a data field on the report, reading the directory for the file creation date.

7. Notebook PCs and portable computing devices present double problems since both hardware and data can be lost at the same time. Portable computing devices should contain a minimal amount of sensitive data. If used for data collection, periodically copy the information to a server for protection.

Another issue surrounds who "owns" the data. If an end user creates a file or database from scratch, then, in his mind, he controls use of this file. Of course, the company owns all data and the IT Manager represents the company in all technical matters. Still, some users use databases as part of their ongoing turf battles.

MANAGERS BE WARNED

Spreadsheets and other end-user developed software used in the preparation of company financial information may be audited under the Sarbanes-Oxley Act. IT managers must find these programs and bring them under IT quality control. Controlling these programs includes controlling access to them and locking cells to prevent unauthorized changes. Be sure to keep an adequate number of data generations in archive.

B. Software

Unlike hardware problems, software defects have no physical appearance. They require tedious effort to identify and resolve. Sometimes the problem only occurs in that rare moment when several circumstances converge at once and may be very frustrating to figure out. Normal IT testing uses a wide combination of data and logic branches to test for such errors.

End-user programs employ a wide range of languages. The most common type of programming is the formulas embedded in spreadsheets. Each formula in a spreadsheet represents another opportunity for an error. Problems with end-user coding include:

1. Managers do not thoroughly question the code developed by their clerks as they lack coding skills themselves (the danger of managing what someone does not know). However, they can cross-check the

totals on reports with reports from other sources to see if they are consistent.

2. If a program problem arises after an employee leaves the company, then managers are on their own to address it. Yet they often lack the technical skills to review or update the code. In a crisis, expect a call to the IT department requesting a bail out. This is caused by:
   a. Employees leaving the company.
   b. Consultants or college interns writing something and then leaving.

3. Programs often lack a clear identification or version number. As copies float about, no one knows who has what code. Often the various copies look the same but are actually different versions and provide different results. Updates are not carefully distributed. Consequently, in the eyes of the users, the same programs are giving different results for the same data!

4. End-user programmers often lack a standard naming convention for programs, files, or program variables, which make them difficult to track or debug.

5. Half-hearted programming attempts that are pressed onto IT a half-built program for upgrading as a production system. This circumvents the cost/benefit analysis that screens out the low value work.

C. **Lost productivity**

A business manager writing his own programs is similar to the IT department hiring their own accountant instead of using the accounting department. A few people thrive on writing their own programs. They find it a useful outlet for their talents and gradually spend more and more of their workday (and personal time) writing and supporting these programs. Gradually, their regular job suffers and they realize that this new "hobby" is ruining their normal work performance. At this point, their supervisor often steps in and reminds them that their assigned work always takes precedence over their optional (computer) work. Although they may entertain notions that IT will "discover" them and hire them as a programmer, this very rarely happens.

Problems that occur include:

1. These programs are not free. The ratio of maintenance time to development time is approximately 10 to 1. Every program that is created and used adds an ongoing time burden to that department.

2. End users generally underestimate the complexity of a task and time required to develop the programs. They save time by skipping such things as data entry edits.

3. Time is lost to the company when employees build parallel databases that may be out of sync. If the data exists in the data center, that is where to use it. Assuming responsibility for a database containing the same data doubles the cost to the company.

4. Similarly, data downloads are a one-way trip. Never send a download back to the main corporate database. This would bypass the edits buried in the data entry screens and could result in corrupted files.

[F]   Sharing

A single program used by its author is not the problem. This person knows the underlying assumptions and can correct code errors as they move on. In its truest sense, this is "personal" computing. The problem is when friends share programs and the code seems to take on a life of its own. The more useful the program, the faster it moves from hand to hand through the facility. As defects are uncovered and repaired, no one knows where all of the copies are. The original author is held responsible for any problems that arise and calls are made to his desk expecting support for the program, just as if IT provided it. After a few weeks of fending off calls and complaints made to their boss, most end users learn their lesson and never share code again!

COMMENT

The authors have seen homegrown code seemingly proliferate all by itself. An example of this was a complex spreadsheet built to track overtime hours for union members in a large factory. This was a very useful tool for each department. The IT department snubbed the spreadsheet as "too controversial and low payback." Yet each end user saved a considerable amount of time every day using these sheets. The result was a lack of management for important plant application. As different versions of the same sheets floated around, the union members were paid grievances for improper solicitation of overtime.

[G]   IT Strikes Back!

From IT's point of view, all of this end-user computing amounted to unnecessary chaos. IT occasionally receives panicked calls to figure out why an important program did not work that was used to generate critical data. Sometimes this involved languages that were far different from the IT standard and no one knew where to begin. Also, "foreign" hardware appeared connected to standard workstations that were also dumped on IT to support. To deflect criticism and avoid future problems, IT took the offensive!

The first stage is denial. The IT department denies any obligation to support these technologies and tells the user he is on his own. This lasts as long as it takes a complaint to reach the executive level and then some poor soul in IT is dispatched to "figure it out before going home tonight." Denying a department support for its homegrown systems may be the fair way to treat the problem but the company is stuck in the middle. On one hand, they have paid for this "nonstandard" system and need it to work. On the other hand, IT has worked diligently to standardize units to save money and now someone is demanding support for something else. If the floodgates were opened, the IT department would be required to support every rickety amateur system cobbled together on obsolete or oddball hardware by anyone whose intentions far exceeded his abilities.

The second stage is locking down the operating system on everyone's workstation to prevent anyone from adding software or hardware tools to his unit. Supplement this barrier by terse company policies forcing all hardware and software requests to flow through the IT department, which lacks the resources to answer any request in a timely manner. A common action is to establish a system administrator account on each workstation and to severely limit user rights, such as:

A. The system administrator locks down the operating system stopping the installation of driver programs without IT involvement. Non-standard hardware is forbidden.
B. Restrict end-user computing by "outlawing" most programming languages. Remove software development tools from all workstations. Lock the operating system so that only the system administrator can load software.
C. Only the IT Manager can grant exceptions to this policy, and the answer is always a terse but polite "no."
D. Issue an executive directive that department managers are responsible for the accuracy of end-user computing created and used in their departments. The IT department will only assist with debugging it on an as-available basis.
E. IT will confiscate any non-company computing hardware that appears.
F. Data may not be taken to use on home computers outside of IT control, since data security may be compromised.

The second stage of reaction solves IT's problem of support requests for strange technologies at all hours, but it deprives the company of the productivity gains of these tools, reducing the value of personal computers to that of stand-alone word processing stations. As a department, IT lacks the time to support all of the service requests as it is. After locking down the workstations, expect the number of requests to rise since users can do little themselves. In a short time, IT will be viewed as more of the problem than a solution.

To gain executive support for locking down workstations, the IT Manager will list all of the problems and service calls that will go away since users can no longer cause these types of problems. This often accompanies a promised reduction in IT staffing with fewer calls anticipated. What they fail to realize is that all of the small things that the "well behaved" users did for themselves now become urgent requests for IT support. IT becomes a broken record repeating this or that cannot be done—or that it is not allowed. Instead of saving the company money, it adds another level of complexity. IT becomes the place that all departments love to hate.

The second stage only lasts as long as it takes the company's executives to realize that IT is the problem and not the solution. The next IT Manager will focus on the company's greater interests, and end-user computing policies will move on to the next stage.

The third stage strikes a compromise between the open environment and the totally closed environment. In this situation, users are "certified" as competent by attending specific training classes (typically two hours in length or less) that explains the IT development standards for testing, documentation, exchange of software, why standards are a benefit to them, etc. After this, they are free to use approved software tools to develop systems for their own use or use in their departments, so long as they adhere to the company policies for end-user computing.

In the third stage, IT's cost of supporting an expanded tool set is balanced against the productivity gains for the company from using these tools. The IT team facilitates the proper use of technology by making it the easiest path to follow.

See Policy ITP-26-1 End-User Computing Policy as an example of an end user computing policy.

POLICY ITP-26-1.   End-User Computing Policy

Policy #:	ITP-26-1	Effective:	03/18/09	Page #:	1 of N
Subject:	End-User Computing Policy				

1.0 PURPOSE

This policy provides guidance for the proper development and management of software created outside of the IT department. It is intended to ensure that all software used by more than one person, or software that provides a critical company function, adheres to good programming practices. The result will be software that operates in a predictable manner and consistently provides correct calculations.

End-user programming refers to any software developed by someone who does not work in the IT department. Software developed within the IT department is subject to the IT department's policies for software quality, documentation, change control, and testing.

2.0 SCOPE

This policy applies to all employees, contractors, and visitors. It pertains to software developed outside of IT to support critical business functions or that is shared among two or more employees. At a minimum, it includes:

A. Programs.
B. Spreadsheets.
C. Databases.
D. Document templates.
E. Report queries.

Excluded from this policy is software developed by an employee to assist in their work duties, and that is not required to perform a critical business function, and that is not shared with other employees.

3.0 POLICY

Computers can be found in every work area of the company. An important component is the software that runs inside of them to perform work. Often this software can be used to organize or automate daily office tasks. This is the "personal" in personal computing. Examples are spreadsheets, single user databases or even document templates. Some of this software can also be used to build complex programs.

The problem arises when this software is used to build software that becomes critical to a department or that is used to provide data for use in executive decisions. Where the IT department will extensively test and validate the output of its software, programs developed by non-IT employees may not be as rigorously proven accurate or reliable. In some cases, they may provide inaccurate data that will be used as the basis for management decisions.

3.1 Employees

Employees are permitted to use software provided by the IT department to develop programs for use in their normal duties. They are not permitted to purchase software for developing programs without IT management approval.

    A. Employees may not distribute copies of software that they have created to other employees unless it has been validated by the IT department.

    B. Personally developed software used in their normal work tasks must be documented for use by others in their absence. One time use software is excluded.

    C. As described in the Software Management Asset Policy, employees may not bring in software from home or other sources to develop personal use software.

3.2 Managers

Managers are required to safeguard the company's continued effective and efficient operation by ensuring that all software developed by end users is properly managed. They will:

    A. Monitor the work tasks for critical company tasks to ensure that any software developed for them will be properly documented and, where appropriate, submitted to the IT Manager for review.

    B. Identify and submit to the IT Manager employee developed software candidates for shared use.

    C. Keep employees focused and not permit their responsibilities to evolve into a full-time software developer or maintenance function.

    D. Require reports generated by personally developed software to include a notation in the heading indicating the person creating the document.

3.3 IT Manager
The IT Manager will:

A. Annually inform all business managers concerning this policy.
B. Provide ongoing advice to all company departments on managing end-user computing to the maximum benefit of the company.
C. Identify a standard set of software for use by end users to develop software.
D. Promptly respond to requests to review locally developed software.
E. Provide team members to advise all departments on the proper use of end-user programming tools, and to answer technical questions as they arise. These people are not provided to write code or to debug programs.
F. Maintain an online catalog of locally developed software supported by the IT department.
G. Ensure that the data output of any end-user developed programs may not be loaded back into any corporate database.

4.0 PROCEDURES

Software deemed of value to other departments or that is critical to the operation of the company must be validated by the IT department. Candidates are forwarded to the IT Manager for consideration after the end user inserts all of the updates and features that they require in the final product.

This review is not a bypass of the company's normal software development qualification process. Software is evaluated and accepted on an "as is" basis. Mandatory updates and additional features will be processed through the normal software upgrade request process.

The originating department manager will provide:

A. One copy of the software and any required data files.
B. A verbal description of the software's function, to include its inputs, outputs, frequency of use, and any situational variables required for the software to function.
C. Examples of correct input files and reports and/or output files.
D. Name of the person who wrote it and their contact information.
E. List of data that feeds the program and where the output is used.
F. Assurance that no changes are made to the software during the review process.

The IT Manager will assign a Business Analyst to:

A. Communicate with the manager who submitted the code and keep them apprised throughout the evaluation process.
B. Review the code and provide an estimate to bring it up to IT standards.
  1. If more than 20 hours of code re-work is required, then the evaluation is passed over to the new development review process.
  2. Additional work may be required by the requesting department in the area of user documentation.

   C. Ensure that the software does not duplicate an existing function.
   D. Validate that all outputs are correct given the data input.
   E. Review all code to ensure it conforms to standard IT naming conventions.
   F. Estimate the resources required to bring the code up to IT standards.

After acceptance of software by the IT department, the original author can no longer change it. All changes must be made by the IT department through its change control process.

5.0 REVISION HISTORY

Date	Revision #	Description of Change
03/18/09	1.0	Initial creation.

6.0 INQUIRIES

Direct inquiries about this policy to:

Tom Jones, CIO
Our Company, Inc.
2900 Corporate Drive
Columbus, OH 43215

Voice: 614-555-1234
Fax: 614-555-1235
E-mail: tjones@company.com

Revision #:	1.0	Supersedes:	N/A	Date:	03/18/09

---

§ 26.03 PERSONAL COMPUTING vs. CORPORATE COMPUTING

[A] Overview

At some point, someone is going to want to borrow a copy of a program that an office worker has written. In exchange for the program, the borrower promises to accept it "as is" and never call for assistance in using it. Perhaps it automates some sort of tracking database. Perhaps it generates reports on some department metric. Whatever it is, end-user programs are shared and control of versions has just been lost. The person who "borrowed" the program may later provide it to another person and on and on. Meanwhile the original author has found and repaired several bugs in the code (one of them critical) and added more features. However, to the casual observer, there is no identifiable difference as the interface screens look the same in both the new and old versions. Since the program is written for his or her own use, the office worker has not mentioned these changes to anyone else.

[B]   When End-User Programs Should Fall under IT Control

End-user programs are those that have impact on a single person—truly personal computing. An end-user developed program becomes corporate computing and may fall under IT control if the program crosses any of these "lines in the sand":

A. The application uses or creates sensitive data as described by the company or government regulatory agency. To protect the company against government actions, the IT department must take immediate control of the program and data. The user still has access to it, but any software changes must pass through the IT department and the data must be stored on a computer room server.
B. All multi-user systems or multi-user files are corporate systems due to their complexity and impact on operations. For end users, this usually involves many people sharing the same data file.
C. All company applications or data files must be under the control of the IT department. Each company creates their own criteria for what a critical system is, but in general, it is any application that impacts the company's cash flow or regulatory compliance.

[C]   Moving End-User Authored Programs to Production

Just because the idea and design for a program originated outside of the IT department is no reason to invoke the "Not Invented Here" response. There are many advantages of starting programs in user departments. The program already has:

A. Proven worth so a cost-benefit analysis is quickly completed.
B. The end-user developed program acts like a prototype. The basic logic flow has already been defined and there are committed users ready and interested in the finished products.
C. Much or all of user-developed code can be included in the final product.

Moving an end-user program into normal corporate production involves running it through the same development process as with other programs. The time savings comes from the portions of the work already done by the original developer. All of this assumes that the production version will have essentially the same features as the end-user developed version.

Of course there are some pitfalls in this process:

A. End users will want IT to add features and functions that were never in the original design.

B. The end user will be impatient and not understand the complexities or delays. He or she may even try to pull the program back from the IT developers.

C. The end user will chafe at the questions asked to build the project scope and system design documentation. They may mistake these questions as criticism, so phrase them carefully.

D. The program is now locked and the source code maintained by IT, and the end user has lost the freedom to change it at will. He or she may try to circumvent the IT change control process by not deleting all copies of the program.

E. End users may try to circumvent the normal software development process by creating a half-baked program and use this conversion process to have it more quickly completed. Only working programs should be considered and the production version should have the same features as the original.

PROCEDURE FOR MOVING END-USER PROGRAMS TO IT CONTROL

Software deemed of value to other departments or that is critical to the operation of the company must be validated by the IT department. Candidates are forwarded to the IT Manager for consideration after the end user inserts all of the updates and features that they require in the final product.

This review is not a bypass of the company's normal software development qualification process. Software is evaluated and accepted on an "as is" basis. Mandatory updates and additional features will be processed through the normal software upgrade request process.

A. The originating department manager will provide:

Procedures for moving end-user programs to IT control which should include the following:

1. One copy of the software and any required data files.
2. A verbal description of the software's function, to include its inputs, outputs, frequency of use, and any situational variables required for the software to function.
3. Examples of correct input files and reports and/or output files.

> 4. Name of the person who wrote it and his or her contact information.
> 5. List of data that feeds the program and where the output is used.
> 6. Assurance that no changes are made to the software during the review process.
>
> B. The IT Manager will assign a Business Analyst to:
>
> 1. Keep the manager who submitted the code apprised throughout the evaluation process.
> 2. Review the code and provide an estimate to bring it up to IT standards.
>   a. If more than 20 hours of code re-work is required, then the evaluation is passed over to the new development review process.
>   b. The requesting department may be required to provide or rewrite end-user documentation.
> 3. Ensure that the software does not duplicate an existing function.
> 4. Validate that all outputs are correct given the data input.
> 5. Review all code to ensure it conforms to standard IT naming conventions.
> 6. Estimate the resources required to bring the code up to IT standards.
>
> After acceptance of software by the IT department, the original author can no longer change it. The IT department through its change control process will manage all future changes.

§ 26.04 MANAGING A PROACTIVE END-USER COMPUTING PROGRAM

[A] Overview

It is difficult to resist an idea whose time has come. End-user computing is one such idea. The key for the IT Manager is to maximize the good that the company derives from this idea while minimizing its costs. It is also an opportunity for the IT Manager to show some leadership. This end-user computing thing is not going to go away. The best course of action is to shape the course of events for maximum IT benefit at minimal cost.

It is said that "nature abhors a vacuum." If the IT Manager does not take the initiative to control events, then the events will control the IT Manager! By providing leadership in this area, IT is seen as a facilitator of technology instead of a spoiled child who must be dragged into the modern era, kicking and crying every step of the way.

The IT Manager is ultimately responsible for the company's end-user computing program. They see a clear distinction between corporate computing and personal computing. However, if the IT Manager were to ask any executive about this, he will find that supporting *any* technology in the company is the responsibility of the IT department. In most cases, it is better to step forward and take up the assignment than wait until it is a mess and be told it was the IT Manager's job all along!

Never lose sight that IT provides a service to the company by supporting their fellow employees in the various departments. If this linkage is enhanced, then the status of the IT department, in their opinion, will be enhanced. If IT becomes irrelevant to their efforts, they will find less and less support for their activities—and IT will never have a clue why!

Managing the efforts of so many end users can be akin to herding cats. Focus the IT support team's energies on managing a few of them closely and the rest of the herd will drift off in all directions. End users cannot be kept tightly together but at least they can be moved in the same general direction. With a well-thought-out and properly supported program, the IT Manager can shape an end-user computing environment that is controlled, consistent, and secure and that will enhance the productivity of end users.

[B] What to Do?

The IT Manager can take some basic steps to energize and focus the company's end-user computing efforts with these simple actions:

A. Develop guidelines for users to follow. Most employees will strive to do things "the right way"—if they know what the "right way" is. These guidelines are usually stated as company policies. People cannot be faulted for breaking rules that do not exist. Craft a set of clear expectations of what end users and their managers should be doing to ensure data accuracy and security. Then begin an employee awareness program to explain these policies to them. The sooner this begins, the fewer bad habits that will need to be broken later.

B. Educate users, managers, and IT staff members on their respective roles. End-user computing is just like anything else in a company. Whether it is filling in an expense statement or scheduling vacation, there is a right way and a wrong way to do it. But just like filling in an expense statement, the IT Manager can make it easy to comply or difficult to understand, resulting in an ongoing stream of questions from frustrated users. Education is an ongoing process to make people aware of the policies and then to periodically remind them what should be done. It is far easier and cheaper to work with people than to police them. The policing still needs to be done, but fewer problems will be uncovered.

C. Provide software training and support for end users on the tools the company wants them to use. The IT staff must understand its role in providing this support. In some companies, end-user support groups allow employees to help their coworkers and cut down on IT support requirements. The IT Manager's goal is to make it easier for end users to comply than to go their own way.

D. Appoint one or more IT staff members to assist users in program development and management. This group must not write programs. They help end users over the "rough spots" in their own code. These must be patient people who can explain complex issues in easy-to-understand terms.

E. Develop a "power user" program to help users to help themselves. These people act as a "force multiplier" for the IT staff by addressing many of the simple issues in their department without calling IT for help.

F. Periodically solicit employees for end-user developed programs to consider converting into company systems. A part of their cost/benefit analysis will be how widespread the program's applicability is.

G. Monitor workstations to ensure the company is in compliance with its software licenses. If employees are free to load anything they want to—they will! If an IT staff member is asked to assist on an unlicensed program, he or she must immediately take firm action to remove the offending software.

H. Every IT team member acts as the enforcer of company computing policies. Any time he or she encounters a violation, he or she must make an on-the-spot correction. The explanation can teach the user and eliminate the problem. Although an unpopular task, this will be accepted by end users if it is applied in a tactful, fair manner.

I. Work with the company's internal audit department to conduct periodic reviews of departments to ensure that policies and procedures are adequate to properly control the environment and that all end users consistently follow them.

[C] End-User Development Training

Time spent training end users will save much more time later undoing their poor work because no one told them how to do it any differently. The following people should be trained:

A. **Train the users**

Some IT workers get a sort of thrill in making computing appear as something just shy of magic. Although entertaining, an effective end-user computing program requires just the opposite approach. IT processes work the way they do for a reason. Often they are the result of a specific problem that was found to be avoidable. When working with end users, take every opportunity to demystify IT practices. Point out why each policy exists and how adhering to them will reduce the likelihood of problems later.

All employees will benefit from end-user computer training. For most, this is just basic word processing and spreadsheets. Others will want more technical training on databases and mainframe reporting tools. All classes should include a section to increase employees' awareness of data security risks, vulnerabilities, and the appropriate preventive controls. An understanding of the "big picture" will help the details in the IT policies to make sense.

Some companies provide end-user training in an internal facility which allows full control of the class environment and curriculum. A training facility is an expensive investment since it ties up a number of desktop units (usually 12 to 15). However, the classroom provides other capabilities for the IT department such as a disaster recovery command center and a place to test software.

An important adjunct to formal classes is to make self-help material readily available. This includes manuals, related third-party "how-to" books, and self-paced instructional materials. The cost of books can be lowered by bulk purchases. Many companies provide third-party books to anyone who attends a class, as the employee may reach for the book in the future instead of calling IT for basic problems. Often these books are easier to understand than the manufacturer's manuals.

B. **Train the department managers**

The key to controlling end users is through their supervisors. Few managers will admit that their departments are so over-staffed that they have time to develop their own programs. Create a training session that explains to these managers the pitfalls of end-user computing and the negative side of minor software development in their department. The better that these managers understand the issues involved in managing technology, the fewer problems that IT will be called in to clean up.

Much of this information is common sense. The manager of each business department is responsible for ensuring that all of his employees know, understand, and adhere to all company policies governing end-user computing—just as he ensures his employees follow the policies issued by human resources, accounting, etc. In this sense, end-user computing is the same as any other office process he oversees.

Manager training is important since they are the ones who stand to lose the most from a poorly run program. Inaccurate reports will be angrily tossed back by executives. Disgruntled employees may leave on short notice leaving the manager to figure out a way to update programs that no one else knows how to read.

The department managers should conduct their operations as if the company's auditor may walk in the door tomorrow—as well he may! Even if an audit is scheduled, there may be considerable effort required to "clean up" the end-user systems. The easier task is to ensure that all systems adhere to company policies as they are being developed instead of delaying this work until some time later.

> ## COMMENT
>
> One author worked for a major manufacturer who decided to outsource their materials warehouse. The materials director carried end-user computing to a different level by negotiating the outsourcing contract that included warehouse management software without involving the IT department in the discussions. They then ordered almost a quarter of a million dollars of custom program modifications (which they thought the outsourcing partner would absorb but did not), only to find out after the money was spent that they had not even purchased the base software license. The software and the changes all belonged to the programmer!

[D]   Cultivate the Power Users

Every department has at least one person that all workers come to with their computing problems. This local computing expert is often known as a "power user." Power users are recognized by their supervisors as master PC tool smiths and may evolve into full-time support for that department. Managers like this since they can control their priorities and align the power user's support efforts to the department's priorities. Part of their value is their understanding of the department's processes and how to apply technology to address their issues. In short, it places a small "IT shop" under the department manager's control.

The IT Manager should encourage this process by providing a high level of support to power users. Power users must understand that this is a two-way street. In exchange for them addressing simple issues in their departments, the IT department will support them with a full set of reference materials and priority support from the service desk.

Being power users does not exempt them from the limitations placed on end-user computing. They still are restricted on the types of tools that can be used and must document all of the code they develop. In a sense, they are held to a higher standard than other users since their coworkers may violate a rule out of ignorance, whereas the power user would have known better.

[E]   Appoint IT Staff Members to Mentor End Users

Appoint one or more IT staff members as internal computing consultants. This team provides instruction on proper computing practices and technical advice for end users of computing equipment and software. The role of internal computing consultants includes advising end users on the true capabilities of equipment and helping them match business needs to the appropriate, cost-effective equipment.

An internal computing consultant's responsibilities might include:

A. Helping people through the IT bureaucracy. IT procedures have a purpose, but to outsiders prone to fast action, they may appear as worthless obstacles. The internal computing consultants can assist with this paperwork by ensuring the forms are correctly filled in and sent to the right person. They must not, however, shortcut the IT process or assume the role of filling in requests for end users. They are to help the process to work, not teach people how to cheat it.

B. Providing informal and formal training for end users. Often these are 30-minute one-on-one sessions addressing a single issue, for example, how to debug a spreadsheet or create a pivot table.

C. Coordinating with the service desk to identify problem areas for proactive problem solving. Again, this team helps end users with service desk issues and demonstrates how to work through the "IT system."

D. Maintaining a web site for end-users' self-help, to share tips and success stories, and to record their concerns with the end-user computing program. Often, the most effective teachers are coworkers.

E. Coordinating formal training on standard software tools. Ensure that classes are "tuned" to include local issues and working preferences.

COMMENT

End User's Computing Pledge

- I will use personal computing tools to automate the routine tasks on my own desktop.
- I will keep all company assets and data safe from theft and secure from unauthorized access.
- I will not copy for others software or sensitive company data files.
- I will only use software authorized and installed by the company.
- I will back up the routine files on my PC to the network server at least once per week.
- I will maintain all critical data on the server, and make copies daily if it is on a notebook PC or PDA.
- I will safeguard all user ID and password codes and never divulge them to others—to include writing them down in an easily accessible place.

- I will be patient and understand that major IT problems take a long time to resolve.
- I will not bring home computing questions to work as this takes time away from the company's business.
- I will identify all critical applications on my workstation so they can be included in the department's business continuity planning.
- I will develop user documentation for all programs I create that are routinely used or that are critical to my work assignments.
- I will identify all programs that I create with version number and "last changed" dates according to IT guidelines.

§ 26.05   END-USER POLICIES

[A]   Overview

The "personal" in personal computing implies a great deal of autonomy from the central IT organization. However, this autonomy does not allow end users the freedom to create unreliable or inaccurate code. They must follow the company's policies and procedures to reduce the likelihood of misleading information, avoid lawsuits, and avoid public embarrassment.

Department managers are responsible for all aspects of their operations including end-user computing. The needs of each department vary as does their ability to support independent data systems. A wise manager follows IT policies governing this area to avoid many of the problems that may arise.

A successful end-user computing program is a team effort. Team members contribute according to their skills and abilities. Use end-user computing policies to educate both the end users and the IT department about how both parties can work together for the company's benefit.

End-user responsibilities echo standard IT practices for good computing. This is a two-step process. First, make each standard as simple to understand and easy to comply with as possible. The second step is to convince users that these actions are in their own self-interest. The easier a task is to perform and the more that the participant believes in the value of the outcome, the less enforcement that will be required. Enforcement takes valuable IT time and usually results in ill feelings. If a good reason for an end-user policy cannot be explained in simple terms, then it is likely that the policy is not needed.

> ## COMMENT
>
> Make good computing practices a habit in your organization. Military uniforms in all countries include hats. Yet the prevailing fashion in Western countries for decades has not included hats. Is the military that far behind in its fashions? The answer is that aside from fashion, military uniforms are built for utility. They include a hat because the military wants to *ingrain* in its members to always put something on their head whenever they venture outside. In a war zone, this would be a helmet for their protection. The goal is to make that action habitual.

[B]   End-User Software Policies

End-user policies are a way for the IT Manager to identify and communicate specific actions to ensure the security of data and that all programs follow prudent IT practices. Phrase end-user policies in a nontechnical, straightforward fashion that details what is to be done, as well as why it is important. Base policies on existing IT policies. Polish the language to improve clarity for the intended audience.

A. **Data security**—When data is stored in the data center, the IT organization controls who can access it. This not only safeguards it from competitors, but ensures the company is in legal compliance with a wide range of government regulations from such agencies as the Securities and Exchange Commission, Internal Revenue Service, and a wide range of federal laws governing personal data privacy. The protection of data stored on a user's PC becomes that person's responsibility.

B. **Information contained in computer files is to be accessed or used for authorized business purposes only.** Casual browsing through computer servers for personal reasons is strictly prohibited. This policy reminds users that rummaging through files is like rummaging through someone's desk and not permitted.

C. **Asset protection**—Hardware, software, and data are all company assets and must be safeguarded. The first line of defense is the person using the equipment. Losing a notebook PC is a double hit—loss of the hardware and loss of the data in the unit.

D. **Ownership of software**—Software created using company time or equipment belongs to the company and not to the person who wrote it. It may not be removed from the premises or sold by its author. Many companies require that a copyright notice be added to all software created by end users.

E. **Anti-piracy**—It is illegal and against company policy to create unlicensed copies of software. In some cases, this may include the libraries used to develop the code. End-user computing developers must be aware of the license restrictions of any purchased modules incorporated into their systems. For example, a compiled program may require a run time module to execute. It may or may not be permissible to distribute this with copies of the compiled program.

> **COMMENT**
>
> A published policy and documented enforcement is a company's best defense against lawsuits for software piracy.

F. **Software forms a large part of IT's initial and ongoing expenses.** Most companies delegate the authority to control the purchase of *all* software to the IT department. This allows for the management of software licenses, upgrades, and a measure of cost control. Departments may purchase their own software but only if it is on the list of software the IT department supports.

G. **Data backup**—It is the responsibility of the workstation user to make safety copies of the unit's data whenever it has changed significantly. This is typically accomplished by copying the data to the network server, or copying it to a CD which is stored in a place far removed from the unit.
   1. Storing critical files on a server—it is the end user's responsibility to store the primary or backup copy of their critical data on network-attached servers. This provides a safety copy to restore inoperable machines. Backups must be accomplished based on the volatility of the data, but usually daily.
   2. Data backups from workstations should be automatic and completed without end-user assistance. However this will require preparation. The goal is to only back up data and not a copy of every workstation's operating system. This also implies checking periodically to see if a workstation's backup is not occurring and find out why.
   3. Provide storage space on the network for personal files and department data sharing. Educate and periodically remind end users why this is in their own self-interest.

> **COMMENT**
>
> One author worked with a freight traffic manager who created and maintained detailed shipping records on an extensive set of spreadsheets. All of this data resided on his PC. Its

> existence only came up in casual conversation and the user never thought about saving the data on a network server. Yet the loss of this data would seriously damage the company's ability to audit its extensive freight bills—and cost it valuable cash.

[C]   System Documentation

System (or user) documentation is an explanation of how to use a particular program. It includes such simple things as how to start it, the data to enter, types of results to expect, options to select or commands to issue, etc. In essence, it tells "the story" of the software.

System documentation is not written for the people who wrote the software. They already know all of this stuff. It is written so that others can use the program. Therefore, it must be straightforward with sufficient visuals so that someone familiar with the department but relatively unfamiliar with the program can run it and correctly use its options.

System documentation is required in ISO compliant shops. All experienced managers require it since every employee takes vacations, has the occasional sick day, or leaves the department. Good documentation provides a way to train new employees and/or allow a substitute to stand in during an absence. Without documentation, the manager is faced with a period of time without the benefit of that program until someone can figure out how to use it.

Therefore, it should be an IT end-user computing policy that every end user who develops software for company purposes provide a written explanation of the system before it is deployed. The documentation must be simple enough to understand so that the system may be run by anyone familiar with the general business function but unfamiliar with that program.

An electronic copy of all end-user system documentation (and subsequent updates) must be filed with the IT service desk. This will provide a reference file in the case of future problems. The service desk will not provide copies of this documentation to anyone outside of the originating department without the IT Manager's permission.

At a minimum, system documentation should include the following elements:

A.   An author's identification section to include the author's name, date of the program's last update, and the date of last update to the documentation. (Some sites prefer to use version numbers instead of the last date of update.)

B.   The program's name (or identifier) and a brief description of its purpose.

C.   An explanation of any assumptions used when developing the code. This will be useful when researching a problem.

D.   A list of all edits applied against incoming data.

E.   The details of every formula and data transformation used in the code.

    F. A list of error messages generated by the program and what may cause them. Exclude error messages generated by the software tool (such as programming language) since these are included in that product's manual.

    G. The series of commands to initiate the application, to include the path and filename.

    H. An explanation of the data sources used or referenced, such as electronic downloads, data entered, validation tables, database files, etc.

    I. Samples of output documents such as forms, reports, and data entry screens. Any formulas used to create these documents must be explained.

    J. Schemas of the database file structures to include the name of each field and the data type and length. Also include access keys for each table along with their relationships to other tables.

    K. The developer will display a version number somewhere on the program's first screen so that a user can readily identify which version of the program he is using.

See Policy ITP-26-2 End-User Systems Documentation Policy as an example.

POLICY ITP-26-2. End-User Systems Documentation Policy

Policy #:	ITP-26-2	Effective:	03/18/09	Page #:	1 of N
Subject:	End-User Systems Documentation Policy				

1.0 PURPOSE

This policy provides guidance for the proper documentation of software created outside of the IT department. It is intended to ensure that all software used by more than one person, or software that provides a critical company function, is well documented so that the system may be run by anyone familiar with the general business function but unfamiliar with that program.

End-user programming refers to any software developed by someone who does not work in the IT department. Software developed within the IT department is subject to the IT department's policies for software quality, documentation, change control, and testing.

2.0 SCOPE

This policy applies to all employees, contractors, and visitors. It pertains to software developed outside of IT to support critical business functions or that is shared among two or more employees. At a minimum, it includes:

    A. Programs.

    B. Spreadsheets.

   C. Databases.
   D. Document templates.
   E. Report queries.

Excluded from this policy is software developed by an employee to assist in their work duties, and that is not required to perform a critical business function, and that is not shared with other employees.

3.0 POLICY

An electronic copy of all end-user system documentation (and subsequent updates) must be filed with the IT help desk. This will provide a reference file in the case of future problems. The help desk will not provide copies of this documentation to anyone outside of the originating department without the IT Manager's permission.

At a minimum, system documentation should include the following elements:

A. An author's identification section to include the author's name, date of the program's last update, and the date of last update to the documentation. (Some sites prefer to use version numbers instead of the last date of update.)

B. The program's name (or identifier) and a brief description of its purpose.

C. An explanation of any assumptions used when developing the code. This will be useful when researching a problem.

D. A list of all edits applied against incoming data.

E. The details of every formula and data transformation used in the code.

F. A list of error messages generated by the program and what may cause them. Exclude error messages generated by the software tool (such as programming language) since these are included in that product's manual.

G. The series of commands to initiate the application, to include the path and filename.

H. An explanation of the data sources used or referenced, such as electronic downloads, data entered, validation tables, database files, etc.

I. Samples of output documents such as forms, reports, and data entry screens. Any formulas used to create these documents must be explained.

J. Schemas of the database file structures to include the name of each field and the data type and length. Also include access keys for each table along with their relationships to other tables.

K. The developer will display a version number somewhere on the program's first screen so that a user can readily identify which version of the program they are using.

4.0 REVISION HISTORY

Date	Revision #	Description of Change
03/18/09	1.0	Initial creation.

5.0 INQUIRIES

Direct inquiries about this policy to:

Tom Jones, CIO
Our Company, Inc.
2900 Corporate Drive
Columbus, OH 43215

Voice: 614-555-1234
Fax: 614-555-1235
E-mail: tjones@company.com

Revision #:	1.0	Supersedes:	N/A	Date:	03/18/09

27

CHANGE MANAGEMENT: KEEPING EVERYTHING UP TO DATE

§ 27.01   OVERVIEW
           [A]   Purpose and Scope
           [B]   Policy Objectives
           [C]   Critical Policies to Develop Based on This Chapter

§ 27.02   CHANGE MANAGEMENT POLICY
           [A]   Overview
           [B]   Definition of Change Management
           [C]   Change Management Scope
           [D]   Change Management Process

§ 27.03   PATCH MANAGEMENT POLICY
           [A]   Overview
           [B]   Policy Objectives
           [C]   Asset Inventory
           [D]   Process Overview
           [E]   Risk Assessment
           [F]   Patch Testing
           [G]   Capability Maturity Model as Applied to Patch Management

§ 27.04   PATCH MANAGEMENT TOOLS
           [A]   Overview
           [B]   Basics of Patch Tool Selection
           [C]   Sources of Additional Information

§ 27.01 OVERVIEW

[A] Purpose and Scope

Managing change within the IT environment of an organization is critical to ensure that a high level of service quality is maintained. It is also important for ensuring compliance with various regulatory requirements such as Sarbanes-Oxley and for maintaining ISO certification. An effective change management policy can also reduce risk to the IT department and to the rest of the organization, as any change to the IT infrastructure introduces an element of risk. Items that must be included in a change management policy are:

A. **Defined approval process.** A formal, well-defined approval process is critical to ensure that changes are successful and do not cause disruptions.
B. **Up-to-date and accurate documentation.** This makes it easier to identify systems and processes that are affected by the proposed change.
C. **Scope.** Identify in the change management policy what areas the policy will cover. All major systems and processes that affect the organization's ability to perform its mission should be included.
D. **Oversight.** A Change Advisory Board (CAB) should be established to review all proposed changes. The CAB should include members from all critical areas of the organization.

Change management applies to changes to both hardware and software used to operate the organization. In this chapter we discuss not only change management in general but also specific concepts that apply to the patching of the software applications used in the organization.

[B] Policy Objectives

The primary objective of a change management policy is to ensure that changes made to the organization's IT infrastructure do not interrupt the functions of the organization (i.e., do not make things worse than before the change!). It does this by providing a thought-out, standardized process and procedures for making changes. IT governance models such as ITIL and COBIT require a defined change management process as a foundational element of the model. An effective change management policy also helps to satisfy Sarbanes-Oxley corporate governance audit requirements. Objectives for your change management policy include:

A. Reduce the risk associated with the introduction of changes.
B. Reduce the impact of changes on the organization.
C. Create clearly defined best practices for introducing changes into the IT environment.
D. Define a process for the approval of changes with multiple levels of review.

    E. Improve communication about changes through notification and escalations, ideally through the use of automated tools.

    F. Create a central data repository for all changes and their affect on the IT infrastructure.

The strategic objective of a company's change management program is to create a consistently configured environment that is effective, meets the needs of the organization, and is secure against known vulnerabilities in operating system and application software.

[C] Critical Policies to Develop Based on This Chapter

Using the material discussed in this chapter, you will be able to create the following policies:

A. Change management policy.
1. Establishment of the CAB.
2. Identify changes within scope.
3. Process for making changes.
B. Patching Policy.
1. Identify the person (or position title) who is responsible for patch management.
2. Develop a process to determine how promptly a patch must be applied.
3. Determine who must monitor the patching sites and how often.
4. Require mandatory testing prior to rollout.
5. Develop a process for evaluating risk of implementing a patch.
6. Develop a process for forcing out patches.
C. Policy mandating an asset inventory of all hardware and software.
1. Create and maintain inventory.
2. Standardize products to minimize configurations for easier testing.
3. Restrict use of nonstandard software as it will be difficult to patch.
D. Policy for assignment of patch priority.
1. Develop guidelines for when a patch may interrupt production.
2. Develop a process for assigning a risk score to a patch.

Policies should always be developed based on the local situation. Successful managers cannot issue appropriate guidance if the policies are written with another company's or location's situation in mind.

§ 27.02 CHANGE MANAGEMENT POLICY

[A] Overview

An organization's change management policies formalize the process of keeping its IT infrastructure up to date. That process starts when a request for a change is first made and ends when the change has been satisfactorily implemented. This request for change includes both planned changes, such as the implementation of a new software version, and unplanned changes, such as the patching of software to protect against a newly discovered vulnerability. Given the impact on the company and the urgent nature of some changes, its change management policy must have the endorsement and support of the CEO or head of the organization.

[B] Definition of Change Management

IT change management is the process of making any change to the organization's IT infrastructure. It typically includes the following steps:

A. A request for a change is made.
B. The change is analyzed for its potential impact on the IT infrastructure.
C. The change is approved or rejected by a change oversight committee (typically called the CAB).
D. If the change is approved, an implementation plan is created for the change. If the potential impact of the change is significant, the implementation plan should also be reviewed by the CAB.
E. The change is implemented.
F. The results of the change are documented.

The CAB should include members from all critical areas of the organization. Any area that has a stake in the functioning of the IT infrastructure should be represented. Members typically include:

A. User managers.
B. Business manager to represent the organization's customers.
C. IT Manager.
D. Security Manager.

Other individuals may be required to participate on the CAB for some changes; other possible members used as needed may come from the following areas:

A. Network infrastructure support.
B. Customer support.
C. Service desk.
D. Applications development.

The CAB is lead by the Change Manager, who is responsible for managing the change management process. The implementation of each individual change is managed by the Change Coordinator. See Policy ITP-27-1 Change Advisory Board Policy as an example policy for creating a CAB.

POLICY ITP-27-1. Change Advisory Board Policy

Policy #:	ITP-27-1	**Effective:**	03/18/08	**Page #:**	1 of N
Subject:	Change Advisory Board Policy				

1.0 PURPOSE

This policy authorizes the establishment of an information technology change oversight committee to be called the Change Advisory Board, or CAB. This committee is responsible for overseeing all changes made to information technology systems throughout the organization.

2.0 SCOPE

The Change Advisory Board authority encompasses all IT systems and technology that support critical business functions. The CAB operates under the authority of the CIO, and is responsible for any changes made to any of the following:

- A. **Software applications.** Any changes to software used in production, such as installations, patches, and version upgrades. This includes operating systems, business applications, and device control software.
- B. **Hardware.** Addition, removal, or relocation of computer hardware such as servers and desktops.
- C. **Data.** Any changes to databases such as changes in the table structure or changes in source data, or changes to the database software.
- D. **Schedule changes.** Any changes to the schedule of periodic or batch processes, such as backups, file transfers, accounting updates, etc.
- E. **Telephony.** Any changes to the main telephone equipment such as relocating the PBX, adding new hardware, etc.

3.0 POLICY

The CIO will appoint a Change Manager, who is responsible for managing the change management process and heads the Change Advisory Board. The CAB will include members from all critical areas of the organization. The following areas must designate a member to serve on the CAB:

- A. Administration
- B. Production
- C. Sales
- D. IT Manager
- E. Security Manager

Other individuals may be required to participate on the CAB for some changes; other areas to provided representatives as needed include:

- A. Network infrastructure support
- B. Customer support
- C. Service desk
- D. Applications development

4.0 REVISION HISTORY

Date	Revision #	Description of Change
03/18/08	1.0	Initial creation.

5.0 INQUIRIES
Direct inquiries about this policy to:

Tom Jones, CIO
Our Company, Inc.
2900 Corporate Drive
Columbus, OH 43215

Voice: 614-555-1234
Fax: 614-555-1235
E-mail: tjones@company.com

Revision #:	1.0	Supersedes:	N/A	Date:	03/18/08

[C] Change Management Scope

It is important to define those types of changes that are covered by the organization's change management policy and those that are not. The organization's change management policy covers any change that can materially
impact the ability of the organization to perform its mission. Changes to the
following items are typically within the scope of the change management
process:

A. **Software applications.** Any changes to software used in produc-
    tion, such as installations, patches, and version upgrades. This includes
    operating systems, business applications, and device control software.
B. **Hardware.** Addition, removal, or relocation of computer hardware
    such as servers and desktops.
C. **Data.** Any changes to databases such as changes in the table structure
    or changes in source data, or changes to the database software.
D. **Schedule changes.** Any changes to the schedule of periodic or batch
    processes, such as backups, file transfers, accounting updates, and
    so on.
E. **Telephony.** Any changes to the main telephone equipment, such as
    relocating the PBX, adding new hardware, and so on.

While there are no "insignificant" changes in an IT environment, there are
a number of changes that do not require the full attention of the CAB. These are
typically changes that are performed repeatedly during the course of operating
the business and have established policies in place defining how these changes

are to be performed. Changes outside the scope of the change management policy include:

A. Password resets.
B. User adds/changes/deletions.
C. System reboots.
D. Security group changes.
E. File permission changes.
F. Changes to nonproduction systems.
G. Disaster recovery plan updates.

The CAB should periodically review production problem reports to see if items not currently within the scope of the change management policy should be within its scope. Special circumstances within the organization may require that seemingly minor changes be reviewed because of their potential impact on the organization.

[D]   Change Management Process

The organization's IT change management process must ensure that changes to the IT environment are done efficiently while minimizing the risk to the business. This is best facilitated by the use of a change management software application.

> # COMMENT
>
> Change management software can be purchased from several vendors including SunView Software (www.sunviewsoftware.com), bmc software (www.bmc.com), and IBM's Rational Software division (www-306.ibm.com/software/rational).

No matter what system is used to document the change management process, the following steps are necessary:

A. **Enter change request.** All requests for changes to the IT environment must be made using the organization's change control system. The organization should have a Change Coordinator to work with the person requesting the change to bring some consistency to the process and to make sure all relevant information is captured. The Request for Change (RFC) should include the following information:
   1. **Contact information.** The requestor's name, position, and contact information.
   2. **Description.** A description of the change, including the nature of the change and a description of the item(s) to be changed.

3. **Reason.** The reason for the change, including a cost-benefit analysis and any budgetary approvals required.
4. **Priority.** A suggestion of the priority and category of the change based on the information currently available. Priorities for changes can vary between organizations, but typically include:
   a. **Emergency.** A change that will cause significant damage or risk of damage to the organization if not implemented immediately, such as major security patches.
   b. **High.** A change that is important and should be implemented soon, such as software changes required to meet regulatory requirements.
   c. **Medium.** A change that provides benefits to the organization, such as an enhancement financial planning system.
   d. **Low.** A change that is "nice to have" but not needed immediately and has a low impact.
5. **Category.** A suggestion of the category of the change based on the information currently available. Categories for changes can vary between organizations, but typically include:
   a. **Major.** The change affects a large part of the organization, such as a department or division.
   b. **Significant.** The change affects a smaller portion of the organization, such as a group with a department.
   c. **Minor.** The change affects a small number of users.
6. **Implications of not making the change.** Include financial impact and any impact on service level agreements (SLAs).

B. **Assess the change.** Someone from IT (the Change Coordinator if that position exists) assesses the urgency and impact of the change on the organization as a whole, considering the scope of the change and its impact on user productivity. This should include:
1. Impact of the change, including how users and the organization will be affected.
2. Risks involved in making the change.
3. Risks of not making the change.
4. Suggested implementation plan.
5. Description of the change backout plan.
6. Impact of the change on disaster recovery plans.

C. **Approve the change.** For minor changes, approval is granted by the Change Coordinator or IT Manager; major changes are reviewed by the CAB for approval or rejection.

D. **Plan for the change.** This includes documenting the steps required to make the change, taking into account the technical requirements of the change. The plan should be optimized to minimize the impact on the IT infrastructure. For major changes the implementation plan should be reviewed by the CAB. The plan must also include steps required to back out or reverse the affects of the change if the change does not have the desired effect.

E. **Implement the change.** Implement the change following exactly the steps outlined in the implementation plan.

F. **Document the results.** A review should be made to determine if the change had the desired affect on the IT infrastructure or system changed. Document what went well and what did not; this will help in planning future changes.

See Policy ITP-27-2 Change Management Policy as an example.

POLICY ITP-27-2.   Change Management Policy

Policy #:	ITP-27-2	Effective:	03/18/08	Page #:	1 of N
Subject:	Change Management Policy				

1.0 PURPOSE

This policy governs the process used to make changes to the organization's IT infrastructure and systems, and is designed to ensure that changes to the IT environment are done efficiently while minimizing the risk to the business.

2.0 SCOPE

The Change Management Policy encompasses all IT systems and technology that support critical business functions. This includes changes made to any of the following:

A. **Software applications.** Any changes to software used in production, such as installations, patches, and version upgrades. This includes operating systems, business applications, and device control software.
B. **Hardware.** Addition, removal, or relocation of computer hardware such as servers and desktops.
C. **Data.** Any changes to databases such as changes in the table structure or changes in source data, or changes to the database software.
D. **Schedule changes.** Any changes to the schedule of periodic or batch processes, such as backups, file transfers, accounting updates, etc.
E. **Telephony.** Any changes to the main telephone equipment such as relocating the PBX, adding new hardware, etc.

3.0 POLICY

The following steps must be followed when making changes covered under this policy:

A. All requests for changes to the IT environment must be made using the organization's change control system. A Change Coordinator will be assigned by the Change Advisory Board to work with the person requesting the change to bring some consistency to the process and to make sure all relevant information is captured. The Request for Change (RFC) must include the following information:

1. Contact information. The requestor's name, position, and contact information.
2. Description. A description of the change, including the nature of the change and a description of the item(s) to be changed.
3. Reason. The reason for the change, including a cost-benefit analysis and any budgetary approvals required.
4. Priority. A suggestion of the priority and category of the change based on the information currently available. The following priorities are to be used:
   a. Emergency. A change that will cause significant damage or risk of damage to the organization if not implemented immediately, such as major security patches.
   b. High. A change that is important and should be implemented soon, such as software changes required to meet regulatory requirements.
   c. Medium. A change that provides benefits to the organization such as an enhancement financial planning system.
   d. Low. A change that is "nice to have" but not needed immediately and has a low impact.
5. Category. A suggestion of the category of the change based on the information currently available. The following categories are to be used
   a. Major. The change affects a large part of the organization, such as a department or division.
   b. Significant. The change affects a smaller portion of the organization, such as a group with a department.
   c. Minor. The affects a small number of users.
6. Implications of not making the change. Include financial impact and any impact on service level agreements (SLAs).

B. Assess the change. The Change Coordinator assesses the urgency and impact of the change on the organization as a whole, considering the scope of the change and its impact on user productivity. This should include:
1. Impact of the change, including how users and the organization will be affected.
2. Risks involved in making the change.
3. Risks of not making the change.
4. Suggested implementation plan.
5. Describe the change backout plan.
6. Impact of the change on disaster recovery plans.

C. Approve the change. For minor changes, approval is granted by the Change Coordinator or IT Manager; major changes are reviewed by the Change Advisory Board (CAB) for approval or rejection.

D. Plan for the change. This includes documenting the steps required to make the change, taking into account the technical requirements of the change. The plan should be optimized to minimize the impact on the IT infrastructure. For major changes the implementation plan should be reviewed by the CAB. The plan must also include steps required to backout or reverse the affects of the change if the change does not have the desired effect.

E. Implement the change. Implement the change following exactly the steps outlined in the implementation plan.

F. Document the results. A review must be made to determine if the change had the desired affect on the IT infrastructure or system changed. Document what went well and what did not; this will help in planning future changes.

4.0 REVISION HISTORY

Date	Revision #	Description of Change
03/18/08	1.0	Initial creation.

5.0 INQUIRIES

Direct inquiries about this policy to:

Tom Jones, CIO
Our Company, Inc.
2900 Corporate Drive
Columbus, OH 43215

Voice: 614-555-1234
Fax: 614-555-1235
E-mail: tjones@company.com

Revision #:	1.0	Supersedes:	N/A	Date:	03/18/08

§ 27.03   PATCH MANAGEMENT POLICY

[A]   Overview

A company's patch management policy formalizes the process of keeping software up to date. If these patches were merely to repair defects in programs, life would be much simpler. The existence of viruses and worms requires that software be patched on a regular basis to repair security vulnerabilities as they are discovered. The lack of an effective patch management process compromises corporate security and network integrity. It also leaves the company open to potentially damaging losses. Given the impact on the company and the urgent nature of some patching, this policy must have the endorsement and support of the CEO or head of the organization.

COMMENT

The most famous worm was the one created by Robert Morris at Cornell that shut down many Unix computers on the Internet in 1988. It successfully propagated itself on more than 6,000 systems across the Internet.

An operating system follows a predicable series of actions as it executes. It is this predictability that allows the smooth interface with other programs. It is also this predictability that allows a virus to insert itself and take control.

In the beginning, a virus was passed in an executable file format, so antivirus programs were created to look for those file types. As defenses against this approach improved, viruses began appearing in macro files for word processors and spreadsheets. The "Winword Concept" was the first of the multiplatform viruses because it could infect any operating system that could run that word processing program.

COMMENT

An excellent source of information on computer viruses and how to address them can be found at the Symantec Web site (*www.symantec.com*). Symantec defines a computer virus as:

"A computer virus is a small program written to alter the way a computer operates, without the permission or knowledge of the user. A virus must meet two criteria:

1. It must execute itself. It will often place its own code in the path of execution of another program.
2. It must replicate itself. For example, it may replace other executable files with a copy of the virus infected file. Viruses can infect desktop computers and network servers alike."

The best defense against the various forms of viruses is a vigorous prevention program. To defend against these types of attacks, software manufacturers analyze their programs and issue software patches to plug the gaps in the code. The problem is that, like any change to corporate software, it should be extensively tested to ensure that the cure is not worse than the disease. However, the longer the patch installation is delayed, the greater the likelihood that the company's computers will be infected. To address this, "Patch Management" has emerged as an IT process and, in some cases, its own IT team.

Patches themselves might involve only a few lines of source code. However, these few lines of code cannot be distributed by themselves. They must be compiled into the program in which they reside, and that entire module must be downloaded to correct the problem. At times, the patch may touch multiple modules. Therefore, in some cases, a single patch to a user's PC may require moving tens of megabytes of data to that machine. Multiplied over the number of units in service in a company, it is easy to see how a single patch can dramatically impact a company's workflow. Multiply this number again over the number of products supported in a PC, and it is easy to see how time-consuming the management of patches can become.

A company's patch management policy covers all types of hardware connected to the outside world through the Internet. The types of hardware might include:

- Workstations.
- Servers.
- Routers.
- Switches.
- Firewalls.
- Internet-enabled cell phones.
- PDAs.

Any device connected to the network is a potential target of worms and viruses. While workstations and servers are the most frequent targets, future worms and viruses that may attack PDAs, cell phones, or other network-connected devices should not be overlooked.

Many of these security flaws are identified and fixes developed before exploits are unleashed by virus creators. However, the time window available to apply and test patches is becoming shorter and shorter.

COMMENT

The Holy Grail for malicious program and virus writers is the "zero day exploit." A zero day exploit is an exploit that is created on or even before the same day as the vulnerability is discovered by the vendor. By creating a virus or worm that

> takes advantage of a vulnerability the vendor is not yet aware of and for which there is not currently a patch available, the attacker can wreak maximum havoc.

Also complicating matters is that workstations are now the targets of the attack as much as servers. Because workstations far outnumber servers, stamping out an infection becomes more difficult. In addition, when mobile users reconnect to the network, they are likely to become reinfected. Although Microsoft Windows gets much of the press, viruses and worms have also been known to target switches, routers, and firewalls. Unix and Linux systems are also not immune to virus infections. As Linux becomes more popular, expect to see more viruses targeted to these systems.

Unfortunately, patches can have bugs too. Many administrators are reluctant to apply new patches without learning—either by testing or by reports through informal sources—how they will affect systems. If the company cannot test adequately, make sure the vendor does.

[B]   Policy Objectives

Most companies manage security patches in the same manner that they control other software upgrades—through their change management process. This allows for the orderly and controlled implementation of changes. The change management process ensures that quality verifications are performed by the appropriate teams before the patch is implemented. It ensures that patches are processed expeditiously while the potential for negative impact on the company is minimized. It is doubtful that a patch management system can be successful if it is not integrated into the IT department's change management process.

The company's policy provides guidelines to ensure all software is up to date and has all known security vulnerabilities repaired. It must also ensure that existing applications still function properly after the patch is applied. Policy objectives should be flexible enough to cover new types of software that may become a target for viruses, worms, or other malicious code.

COMMENT

According to research by Eric Hemmendinger of Aberdeen Group, "[w]orldwide, enterprises spend in excess of $2 billion annually to investigate, prioritize, and deploy patches for security vulnerabilities. The trend is upward, with no end in sight for IS decision makers."

The strategic objective of a company's patch management program is to create a consistently configured environment that is secure against known vulnerabilities in operating system and application software.

[C] Asset Inventory

The first step toward a coherent corporate patch management program is an assessment of what the company has to protect. A comprehensive asset management program can determine if all existing systems are accounted for and considered when processing patches. This requires a thorough inventory of all of the company's hardware and software.

The asset inventory should identify what is to be protected and where it is located. At a minimum, the inventory should identify:

A. All types of equipment in service.
B. All operating systems in service, their versions, and their patch levels.
C. All applications software installed, their versions, and their patch levels.
D. Where all equipment, systems, and software are located.
E. Who the primary user or primary support person is for each device.

Next, the current patch level recommended by the manufacturer for each of the operating systems and applications should be determined. Comparing this to the inventory results will indicate the company's current vulnerability to an external threat.

A side benefit of a company-wide inventory is to identify anyone who is already patching any of this equipment. Different subdivisions may be doing things differently—with uneven results. The contact information for each device will speed questions to the problem area.

What will undoubtedly become clear from the asset inventory is that patch management will be greatly simplified if software and equipment are standardized. The fewer the configurations to protect, the faster patches will be tested and the more stable the corporate technical environment will be. This implies that only standard company software should be loaded onto PCs as each additional product becomes another patch source to track—which is another reason companies should make their prohibition of unlicensed software clear to all users.

Another useful data application is "system discovery" tools. These programs help to identify when additional (rogue) equipment has been added to the network, often without prior approval. Once identified and located, the equipment can be checked for security compliance and brought up-to-date.

COMMENT

A source of inexpensive systems discovery tools is the System Center Tools Home page at *www.systemcentertools.com*. These tools work with Microsoft's SMS and MOM systems.

[D]   Process Overview

An effective patch management process requires that the company have the following in place:

A. An asset inventory of all devices connected (or that might be connected) to the network.
B. An asset management process to collect changes as they occur.
C. Well-defined change management process.
D. Guidelines for prioritizing how critical each application is.
E. Communication plans to alert users of pending changes.

A well-defined change management process documents what was changed and how. Unless the company has the resources necessary to patch every system right away, a patch coordinator will need to determine which systems are most critical and deserve attention first. A good communications plan enables the IT team to efficiently use the resources available for applying the necessary patches.

The change management program must include a patch cycle for the application of routine patches. The routine cycle can be based on the calendar or on the release of an important update. Critical updates are processed differently and should be based on the company's exposure to the identified threat.

In either event, the process normally unfolds in the following manner:

A. **Identify a new patch requirement.** This can occur through notification by the software vendor or through the intelligence-gathering efforts of internal or external sources. The patch management policy must identify who is responsible for the identification of new patches.

   In either event, the process normally unfolds in the following manner:

COMMENT

Vendors of security vulnerability intelligence include:

Cybertrust   *www.cybertrust.com*

IBM Internet Security Systems *http://xforce.iss.net*

Symantec Corp.   *http://enterprisesecurity.symantec.com*

B. **Assess exposure to the organization and risks involved.** The urgency for applying the patch should be determined by the level of exposure the security risk poses to the organization and the risks involved in applying the patch (see § 27.02[D], "Risk Assessment").

IT should determine the likelihood of a security breach if the patch is not applied versus the potential impact on mission-critical systems if applying the patch causes other problems.

C. **Determine whether patch should be applied.** Based on the potential threat and level of risk, IT must determine whether the patch should be applied immediately or during the next scheduled software update cycle.

D. **Create a plan to apply the patch.** IT should treat the application of patches like any other important project. Before rushing in to apply the patch, IT should take time to plan out the most effective steps to apply the patch and determine the impact it may have on other software applications.

E. **Test patch before it is applied.** New software is not installed without testing and neither should patches. IT should create a test environment that is isolated from the production network where workers can test for any unintended consequences. Again, there will be fewer configurations to test if the environment is standardized.

F. **Apply patch to systems.** Once satisfied with the testing, IT may apply the patch to the affected systems.

G. **Validate that patch was correctly applied.** Once the patch is applied, check the affected systems to ensure the patch was correctly applied.

H. **Document results.** IT must document lessons learned, problems solved, and unforeseen problems encountered so the next patch will go more smoothly.

COMMENT

According to The Gartner Group, 40 percent of cyber attacks in 2008 will be motivated by financial gain.

[E] Risk Assessment

To patch or not to patch, that is the question (apologies to Shakespeare). Many system administrators have bad memories of patches that caused more problems than they solved, especially with Microsoft Windows 2000. While vendors have gotten much better about the quality of the patches they release, they still cannot guarantee the patch will work with all possible combinations of hardware and software. The patch management process must include a thorough analysis of the risks involved in either applying the patch or not.

Before establishing a patch management plan, executive management must determine their corporate risk tolerance toward patching. Maximizing security might impact productivity if production systems are shut down every time a relevant patch becomes available. On the other hand, some patches may be so vital as to overcome objections. A policy guideline that addresses this situation will reduce the guesswork.

Of course, in practice such extreme measures are rare. The point is that patch management must be viewed as one component of the overall corporate risk management program.

To assess the risk of applying a patch, the following questions should be considered:

A. What is the probability of a vulnerability being exploited if the patch is not applied?
B. If the vulnerability is exploited, what is the probable severity of the damage?
    Consider the likelihood of physical damage to information, any legal ramifications, the possible financial impact, and how news of the incident will affect the company's reputation.
C. Which is the greater problem—downtime while applying the patch or security breaches from not applying the patch?
D. What effects will the patch have on mission-critical applications?
E. Is the patch really necessary for the company's systems?
F. What will indicate whether or not the patch was successful?

Some risks inherent in the patch management process include:

A. Missed patches.
B. The approval of risky patches.
C. A poorly designed patch application process.
D. A failure to perform adequate testing.
E. No identification of the issues created by the application of the patch.

To make a rough calculation of the severity of the risk involved with a patch, the following formula can be used:

$$\text{Risk Score} = \text{Threat Probability} \times \text{Criticality} \times \text{Effort Required}$$

Threat probability is scored from 1 to 10 and includes an assessment of the risk to the organization and the likelihood that the vulnerability will be exploited.

Criticality is scored from 1 to 10 and includes the importance of the system affected and the amount of damage that can be done.

Effort required is scored from 1 to 10 and is an estimate of the number of labor hours that will be required to complete the entire patch application process.

A very high risk score indicates the need for an immediate patch, while a low score indicates the patch may be applied during the next change management process update. For values that do not meet either of these levels, the risk score should enable IT to prioritize when each patch should be applied.

[F] Patch Testing

All patches must be tested prior to installation to ensure that they will function as expected and be compatible with other systems. Patches must be tested for compatibility with the production operating system environment and with other applications. Testing must also be done to ensure that the patch does not expose vulnerabilities that were previously corrected or create new ones. A separate testing environment must be created for testing patches before patches are applied in the production environment.

The application of patches is similar to any other change made to production software and should follow the same change control procedures. Once a patch has been applied in the production environment, additional testing must also be performed to check for unanticipated problems.

The inventory of software systems must be kept updated with information about the latest patch level. A history of patches must be maintained to ensure that if a system has to be rebuilt, software patches can be reinstalled in the proper order. A backup of the patched software should be made after each patch is applied to facilitate rollback or recovery to a previous version if necessary. See Policy ITP-27-3 Patch Testing Policy as an example.

POLICY ITP-27-3.   Patch Testing Policy

Policy #:	ITP-27-3	**Effective:**	03/18/08	**Page #:**	1 of N
Subject:	Patch Testing Policy				

1.0 PURPOSE

This policy is designed to ensure that software patches are properly tested before being released into the production environment.

2.0 SCOPE

This policy encompasses all IT systems and technology that support critical business functions.

3.0 POLICY

The IT manager will designate a patch management coordinator who ensures that all software patches are handled as follows:

A. A separate testing environment must be created for testing patches.
B. All patches must be tested prior to installation.
C. New patches must be tested to ensure new vulnerabilities that were previously corrected are not exposed and that new ones are not created.
D. Patches must be tested for compatibility with the production operating system environment and with other applications.

   E. Application of patches must follow the same change control procedures as any other change to the production systems.

   F. An inventory of software systems must be kept updated with information about the latest patch level.

   G. A history of patches must be maintained to ensure that if a system has to be rebuilt, software patches can be reinstalled in the proper order.

   H. A backup of the patched software should be made after each patch is applied to facilitate rollback or recovery to a previous version if necessary.

   I. Once a patch has been applied in the production environment, additional testing must also be performed to check for unanticipated problems.

4.0 REVISION HISTORY

Date	Revision #	Description of Change
03/18/08	1.0	Initial creation.

5.0 INQUIRIES

Direct inquiries about this policy to:

Tom Jones, CIO
Our Company, Inc.
2900 Corporate Drive
Columbus, OH 43215

Voice: 614-555-1234
Fax: 614-555-1235
E-mail: tjones@company.com

Revision #:	1.0	Supersedes:	N/A	Date:	03/18/08

[G] Capability Maturity Model as Applied to Patch Management

The Capability Maturity Model (CMM) was developed by Carnegie Mellon University in 1991 to measure the efficiency and effectiveness of organizations who develop software (see Exhibit 27-1). The CMM has been widely used and adopted to other technical areas, including patch management. The chart in Exhibit 27-1 can be used to determine which level the organization is at and compare it to the desired level for patch management. A comparison of where an organization is today versus where it would like to be will help IT to create an appropriate patch management process.

EXHIBIT 27-1. Capability Maturity Model for Patch Management

Level	CMM Attributes	Patch Management Attributes
1	Initial—the environment is unpredictable and reactionary.	Patches are not being applied.
2	Repeatable—controls are in place, but not used consistently; no formal training or communication processes in place.	No formal process in place or responsibility assigned for patch management; patches are downloaded directly from vendor web sites; patches applied by hand using removable media.
3	Defined—controls are well documented and communicated; no monitoring of control activities.	Patches are obtained from known good sources; individual groups have assigned responsibility for patch management; patch process is documented but not consistent between departments; patches deployed using script files or Windows Update.
4	Managed—controls are standardized and tested on a regular basis; automated tools are not well integrated into the process.	Patch management is centrally coordinated and a common reporting process used; standard builds are updated with required patches; patch deployment is performed using software tools such as SMS or PatchLink.
5	Optimizing—an effective continuous improvement process is in place; integrated automated tools allow for quick action.	Patch deployment responsibility is centralized and fully automated; central responsibility is assigned for managing the patch management process.

§ 27.04 PATCH MANAGEMENT TOOLS

[A] Overview

Patching software is a time-consuming process. In the past, a technician may have scurried around to each PC with a floppy disk loading the patch on machines. However, with the hundreds or thousands of devices in use by a typical company today, this is no longer practical. Manual patching is time consuming and error prone (due to missed devices). Given the time required to locate every device and then to load the patch, it is quite likely that a second patch will be required before the first patch is applied everywhere.

The solution to this problem is the use of software tools that can distribute approved patches. These updates can then be controlled to be applied at the same time everywhere or selectively, and to confirm the installation was successful.

[B]   Basics of Patch Tool Selection

A key consideration in developing a patch management program is the tools that are used to implement it. Many software tools are available to manage the patch application process. These tools follow one of two technological approaches:

A. **Agent-based.** Agent-based tools require that a software component be installed on each device to be managed. This can be a challenge due to differences in configurations and when a system administrator is required to answer screen prompts during installation. In addition, the agent may require remote administrative rights.

   The advantage of an agent-based approach is the speed with which patches can be applied. A single patch management server can service thousands of workstations at one time.
B. **Agent-less tools.** The agent-less approach is based on a patch management server that controls the network server to identify and push required patches. The success of this approach depends heavily on the network: pushing large patches to a number of units may swamp the corporate network.

The appropriate choice of patch management tools for an organization depends on a number of issues, including:

- The number of platforms supported.
- The number of systems to be patched.
- The existing expertise and amount of personnel involved.
- The availability of existing system management tools.

Portions of the patch management process may need to be automated because of:

- The increasing frequency of patches that are released and the systems they affect.
- The complicated interrelationships among installed software, patches, and service packs.
- The need for deployment speed.

> **COMMENT**
>
> On average, Microsoft issues a new security patch every 5.5 days.

Patch management software should include the following features:

A. Identification of which patches are required. The software also should be able to determine which patches are required before other patches are installed.
B. Automatic deployment of mandatory patches.
C. The ability to roll back to the previous version of the software.
D. The ability to deploy multiple patches.
E. Comprehensive reporting capabilities that can identify which patches are needed by which systems.
F. Patch compliance monitoring to ensure patches are not removed due to backup restoration or the installation of a new application.
G. Secure patch delivery through encryption.
H. Continuous enforcement of security policies to help ensure systems stay patched. Some patch management systems also can ensure that anti-virus software is always running and that the virus definitions are current. Some also can check to make sure users do not make configuration changes that could make their PCs vulnerable.
I. The ability to support all the platforms on the corporate network. (Many systems only support Microsoft Windows workstations and servers.)
J. Accurate, up-to-date information and analysis of current security patches.

> **COMMENT**
>
> Patch management software vendors:
>
> | | |
> |---|---|
> | PatchLink Corporation | *www.patchlink.com* |
> | BigFix, Inc. | *www.bigfix.com* |
> | Shavlik Technologies | *www.shavlik.com* |

[C] Sources of Additional Information

Patch management depends on accurate, timely, and pertinent information to know what is needed, when, and why. Locating and assessing patches is a never-ending administrative challenge. The trick is to know all of the sources useful in gathering this information for evaluation.

The easiest information source to identify is the vendor that supplied the software or network components. These companies often have an invitation-only web site to distribute updates to their customers. They also may include an automatic notification system to inform registered customers of a new release.

In addition to web sites that provide information about security alerts, there also are lists of fake alerts. These bogus warnings are usually passed around in e-mails. Although harmless to the company's systems, it can require a considerable amount of patch management time to calm excited users. Some web sites to monitor include:

Symantec Hoax List	*www.symantec.com/avcenter/hoax.html*
Microsoft Security	*www.microsoft.com/technet/security/ default.mspx*
McAfee	*www.mcafee.com*
Infraguard (an FBI/business consortium to address security threats)	*www.infragard.net*
U.S. Department of Energy— Office of Cyber Security	*ciac.llnl.gov/ciac/index.html*
U.S. Department of Energy— Office of Cyber Security Hoax List	*hoaxbusters.ciac.org/*
Computer Associates Virus Information Center	*www3.ca.com/securityadvisor/virusinfo/ default.aspx*

28

SYSTEMS ANALYSIS AND DESIGN: PLANNING FOR SUCCESS

§ 28.01   OVERVIEW
    [A]   Purpose and Scope
    [B]   Policy Objectives
    [C]   Critical Policies to Develop Based on This Chapter

§ 28.02   SYSTEMS DEVELOPMENT AND PLANNING
    [A]   Project Planning
    [B]   Analysis of Requirements
    [C]   Estimating Resource Requirements
    [D]   Risk Analysis
    [E]   Avoiding "Scope Creep"

§ 28.03   SYSTEMS ANALYSIS
    [A]   Overview
    [B]   Pre-analysis Survey
    [C]   Initial Business Unit Visit
    [D]   Information Gathering Interviews
    [E]   Document the Interviews
    [F]   Work-Sampling Studies
    [G]   Final Report

§ 28.04   SYSTEMS DESIGN
    [A]   Overview
    [B]   Systems Design Specifications
    [C]   Utilization of Resources
    [D]   Final Systems Report
    [E]   The Acceptance Presentation

§ 28.05   SYSTEMS PROTOTYPING
    [A]   Overview
    [B]   Prototype Development
    [C]   Prototyping Methods

§ 28.06   SYSTEMS IMPLEMENTATION
[A]   Implementation Prerequisites
[B]   Implementation Procedures

§ 28.07   SYSTEMS MAINTENANCE
[A]   Modify or Redesign?
[B]   Types of Maintenance Projects
[C]   Requirements and Responsibilities
[D]   Control
[E]   Revision Conventions

§ 28.01 OVERVIEW

[A] Purpose and Scope

Most projects start at the beginning, with an initial project planning stage, and then progress logically through each succeeding phase. However, some projects are not that neat and tidy, and begin later in the process. Either way, it is the responsibility of the project leader or systems analyst to make certain that the project has had the required planning.

Systems analysis and project management are complementary processes. Systems analysis identifies the "what" that is to be accomplished. It includes the system's logic flow and all of the elements that must be accounted for. Project management details the "how" it will be done, by whom and by when.

A plan is required to manage any project in the most efficient manner. It provides a "roadmap" to the journey toward project completion. Without a good map, you will not know where you are or where to turn next. Establishing a policy to guide the format and development of project plans will allow others to pick up a project if you must move on, since everyone uses the same basic approach.

A properly written project plan keeps management informed on the status of each project with periodic progress reports, starting with the first phase, and following through to the end. The plan should aim for those results that are achievable with the resources allocated by management. Remember that a project plan is a written document—not something simmering in the back of your mind. A project plan also is a communications tool between the Project Manager and the team members, the project's sponsor, and any other interested stakeholder.

Project planning is reviewed in greater detail in Chapter 6, "Project Management: Getting It Out on Time."

[B] Policy Objectives

The policy objectives governing project development should include the following:

A. Organize systems projects into manageable major phases.
B. Establish a timetable that specifies both chargeable and calendar time.
C. Stipulate the format for progress reporting, which can be arranged by task phases to be completed or by target completion date.
D. Create an overall plan containing the principal ingredients required for an acceptable undertaking. These are:
   1. **Economic feasibility.** Will the new system pay for itself in its expected lifetime?
   2. **Organizational feasibility.** Will the system operate within the current organizational structure?
   3. **Technical feasibility.** Will the proposed system actually work?
   4. **Operational feasibility.** Can the system work within the environment for which it is designed? If applicable, will it successfully operate outside the firm?

[C]   Critical Policies to Develop Based on This Chapter

Using the material discussed in this chapter, you will be able to create the following policies:

A.   Systems analysis and design procedures.
1.   Process for gathering requirements.
2.   How to document user interviews.
3.   How to perform work sampling studies.
4.   Format of final report.
B.   System prototyping.
1.   How and when they are used.
C.   System implementation procedures.
D.   System maintenance procedures.
1.   Requirements and responsibilities.
2.   Revision convention.

Policies should always be developed based on the local situation. Successful managers cannot issue appropriate guidance if the policies are written with another company's or location's situation in mind.

§ 28.02   SYSTEMS DEVELOPMENT AND PLANNING

[A]   Project Planning

The system project's organization must have standard procedures to ensure proper planning, control, and status reporting. These defined procedures provide standards to: (1) assess a project in progress, (2) assess the merits of one project over another, and (3) provide a tool when reviewing employees for merit rewards.

The following tasks are included in project planning:

A.   **Definition of project goals.** How will we measure the success of the project? Typical goals might include:
1.   Systems output.
2.   Data manipulation processes.
3.   Systems throughput process.
4.   Systems control mechanism.
5.   Systems requirements.
6.   Implied major tasks.
7.   Calendar time needed to complete project.

If any of these areas can be subdivided into measurable milestones for reporting, it should be done. (For example, throughput processing may entail more than one manual procedure or computer program.)

B. **Project plan preparation.** A brief plan and schedule are developed outlining the requisite tasks and timetable to accomplish the project goals. These include:
   1. Identify the work necessary to accomplish each of the project's goals. This includes tasks applicable to projects not initially identified as work to be covered in planned goals. These should be divided into measurable units or milestones. Break down tasks into functional requirements small enough that you can identify the resources required and the length of time necessary to complete them. Beware of the overlooked or hidden technical requirement!
   2. Develop detailed database, file, report, and program specifications.
   3. Establish a budget to implement your plan. State every cost assumption you use.
   4. Assign responsibilities. To a great extent, time estimates are based on the expertise of the person working on the task. Most projects involve people "loaned" from other departments and who bring with them their usual workload. The sharpest people will be the hardest to get.
   5. Prepare workload schedules.
   6. Prepare appropriate project documentation. This can be time-consuming but essential when looking back to see the basis used to make a decision. It will also provide some actual performance history useful in planning your next project.
   7. Develop Gantt charts from project schedules for planning and reporting the status of project tasks. If possible, use a project management software package to build these charts, identify resource conflicts, and help to track the project's progress.
   8. Prepare a format and schedule for project status reports.

[B] Analysis of Requirements

The project leader or lead systems analyst works closely with the project sponsor to ensure that the systems requirements are defined and understood, and that the user does not expect system revision in the near future. It is a rare business manager who knows exactly what he or she wants. Business managers need software developed to meet specific business goals. Take time to understand what they want to achieve and what they visualize it will look like. During these meetings, the IT Manager also should educate them on technical capabilities and cost. They may feel that specific features are "nice to have" but have no idea of the cost to develop them. Separate the essential project elements from the "nice to have" features. The smaller the project is, the more likely it is to succeed. Add nonessential features to later releases of the product.

A number of techniques exist to ensure that all systems requirements are precisely defined. These are:

A. Determine capabilities of project team to achieve given system objectives.
B. Establish operating parameters.
C. Organize all pertinent data elements.
D. Define processing requirements.

    E. Determine output requirements.
    F. Determine required database or file needs.
    G. Determine required data input requirements and method of input.

To ensure all requirements are defined prior to the systems design phase, use a checklist similar to the one shown in Worksheet 28-1.

WORKSHEET 28-1. Systems Development Checklist

Systems Development Checklist	
A. Data Input Editing	
1. Does editing look for missing data?	Y / N
2. Does editing include verification of format?	Y / N
3. Does editing include verification of codes through the use of drop-down lists?	Y / N
4. Will editing be completed field by field as the data is entered?	Y / N
5. Will all data rejection messages clearly state why a field was rejected?	Y / N
6. Will there be a supervisor bypass procedure?	Y / N
B. Database and File Updating	
1. How frequently are backups done?	
2. Are partial updates done?	Y / N
3. Must source data be corrected prior to update procedures?	Y / N
4. Are files purged periodically?	Y / N
5. Are there legal data retention requirements?	Y / N
6. Are purged data files transferred to inactive files?	Y / N
7. Will a transaction backup file be online?	Y / N
C. Output Preparation	
1. Is the output viewable online?	Y / N
2. Is the data real time or updated periodically?	
3. If the output is hardcopy, how many copies are needed?	
4. Is the hardcopy output a regular report or only provided on demand?	
5. Do the reports contain summaries and intermediate summaries?	Y / N
6. Will output be made available over a network or the Internet?	
D. Error Correction	
1. Will the error correction routines require rewriting the source document?	Y / N
2. Is it possible for uncorrected data to enter the processing system?	Y / N
3. Can an error be corrected after it has been placed in a file or database? How?	Y / N

> ## COMMENT
>
> You can't get there from here! Always beware of the implied tasks to accomplish a goal. The more detailed your analysis is, the more of the "implied tasks" you will uncover. For example, if the request was to develop software for use in a warehouse, there may be an implied task to run electricity and network connections to distant places. Another example might involve an implied requirement to maintain a database in sync with another database on a different hardware platform and software application.

[C] Estimating Resource Requirements

A resource estimate, prepared for each project, is used to allocate resources and provide a basis for project financial control. Estimates may also provide a basis for preparing user service charges. The person in charge of planning should:

A. Estimate the worker-hours required for analysis and programming. This estimate may be revised as programming proceeds. If you did a thorough job extracting system characteristics from the project's sponsor, you will know what is needed in terms of people, expertise, equipment, and time. It is not unusual to miss an item or two but always hope they were small ones. Establishing good worker-hour estimates is an art since different people have different productivity levels. Therefore, time estimates are either based on a job description (anyone with these qualifications should be able to work at an estimated rate) or based on specific people. If you are using contract workers yet to be hired, then the job description approach is used. If the team member is already on staff, ask him to estimate a time. Where possible, use the actual hours required from previous projects of similar complexity.

After all of the time estimates are rolled up, add a percentage for contingency time to each task, depending on similar past experience and/or the past performance of the person assigned the task. The contingency time for each task is then summed and tracked as a separate task. If the project covers an extended calendar time period, this becomes even more important. This can help avoid a possible late or over-budget project. If a project is late or over budget, as most projects are, this budgeted extra time will be welcome. Convert the worker-hours needed into dollars. If the project finishes ahead of schedule and/or under budget, this can reflect well on the project leader.

Use a software package to prepare Gantt charts for the worker-hours required, indicating the calendar time when personnel will be available since not all project personnel are available full time. Set milestones within each Gantt chart to identify the status of each project task. This status can be plotted against the budgeted allotted time to determine whether the task is on schedule.

B. Most project-tracking software packages also will provide a financial report on the project's status. This report compares the amount spent to date to the budgeted amount at any given point in the project.

C. Identify and estimate all equipment, software, and service costs required for the new system. A dollar contingency amount should be added to cover any unforeseen expenses.

COMMENT

Contingency times should be held in reserve by the Project Manager and not handed out to the workers. Some people will act as if the contingency time is something to be frittered away at the beginning of the task and only begin work when time is short (similar to the student who only studies for a test the night before). Then if a problem arises, the time set aside for them to deal with the issue is gone and tasks will always run over in spite of contingency time.

[D]   Risk Analysis

All IT projects involve some degree of risk. Risk management should be a proactive process, part of the overall project. Risk is not to be avoided, but managed. To manage risk proactively, identify and analyze risk continuously in the normal course of the project. The following steps can be used to manage the risk in a project:

A. **Identify the risk.** Discuss risks early in the project. The sooner risks are identified, the sooner solutions can be found.

B. **Analyze the risk.** Determine how risk can impact the project. What effect will the risk have on cost, project duration, or the ability of the project to satisfy the user's requirements?

C. **Prioritize.** Determine which risks deserve the most attention and which risks can be safely ignored.

D. **Mitigate.** Identify and implement action steps to reduce the likelihood of the threat occurring or its impact if it is unavoidable.

E. **Follow up.** Keep track of all risks and what is being done to mitigate their impact.

F. **Control.** By making risk management part of day-to-day project management, you control the risk, rather than it controlling you.

> ## COMMENT
>
> A CEO study by the Gartner Group reveals that change initiatives are most likely to fail because of such problems as resistance to change, lack of sponsorship, and unrealistic or unknown expectations.

There are several areas of risk that can influence an IT project:

A. **Economic.** Economic fluctuation can change the value of the project to the firm or affect funding available for the project.
B. **Government.** Changes in government regulations can impact the cost or utility of the project.
C. **Marketplace.** If the project is meant to support a new product, consumers' acceptance or changing needs can affect the project.
D. **Technology.** A project's technology may not work as advertised or may change during the course of a long project.
E. **Organizational.** Lukewarm management support, changes in management, unrealistic expectations, etc., can all adversely affect the project.

Worksheet 28-2 is an example of a form used to track and manage the risks identified in a project.

WORKSHEET 28-2.   Risk Analysis Form

			Risk Analysis		
ID	Description	Severity	Probability	Value	Plan
1	Database designer with required skills not available when needed.	8	.2	1.6	Work with DBA group to make sure resource is available when needed.
2	Learning curve for new version of report writer steeper than expected.	5	.4	2.0	Send member of team to training before start of project.

WORKSHEET 28-2.   (Continued)

			Risk Analysis		
ID	Description	Severity	Probability	Value	Plan
3	User resource not available when needed.	9	.5	4.5	Work with senior management to ensure resource availability.
				0.0	
				0.0	
				0.0	

ID—A unique identifier for the risk.

Description—A description of the risk.

Severity—The effect on the project on a scale of 1 (low) to 10 (sever).

Probability—The probability the risk will actually have an impact on the project: 0.0 (none) to 1.0 (certain).

Value—Severity × probability. Used to rank the risks.

Plan—How are we going to deal with this risk?

[E] Avoiding "Scope Creep"

The scope of a systems project is typically identified by its constrained elements (its boundaries). First, the relevant activities of the project establish limits confined by time, dollar resources, required changes, and/or systems or organizational boundaries. Second, the subject itself can identify and restrict the project scope. If expanded beyond its subject area, the project loses its frame of reference, unallocated resources are likely to be expended, and the objective of the project becomes less clear. Therefore, containing the scope of a project is essential to its success.

Begin every project with a written scope statement. This is a summary of what this project is supposed to achieve. A well-written scope statement is used to develop a list of "success criteria" (or features) that the project is intended to achieve. Together, the scope statement and success criteria provide an anchor for your project. Anything beyond what is in these statements is to be considered an expansion of the project and requires additional resources. The project plan is the roadmap for how these features will be created. These statements must be approved by the project's sponsor before the plan can be written.

> ## COMMENT
>
> Many IT or systems managers attribute late, over-budget, or uncompleted projects to wandering into unrelated areas of user needs. Objectives and careers are jeopardized if control of a project and resources is not retained. This lack of control may help explain some of the management turnover in the information technology profession.

§ 28.03 SYSTEMS ANALYSIS

[A] Overview

Systems analysis is the process of gathering and analyzing user requirements in preparation for developing a new or enhanced software application. It can be the most critical part of any software development effort, as a system that does not meet the requirements of its intended users has no reason to exist. Some new to systems analysis and others who do not want to allocate resources and/or costs to this effort avoid it or limit its scope. This lack of analysis leads to a process of "code and fix," whereby coding begins before user requirements are fully known, and accounts significantly for new system failures. It is common for established consulting firms to relegate this task to their lower-priced help, with predictable results. There also can be a problem of "paralysis through analysis," spending too much time on this phase. But this is seldom the case.

This section on analysis provides the traditional, proven procedures. Knowing the steps will not guarantee success, but knowing and practicing the procedures can produce the desired results.

[B] Pre-analysis Survey

Before attempting to contact the user for an analysis of the current system, gather as much knowledge about the business unit as possible. A feasibility study is a good place to start.

Identify the business unit's head and subordinates, if possible, from an organization chart for large units. Many firms employ organizational charts with pictures to go along with the names and titles. Try to remember the names of personnel and their respective titles. Also, know the corporate hierarchy. Any information about personalities and the unit's organization status that can be discovered beforehand can help. Become aware of the unit's corporate politics; any hidden power structures can be a minefield, delaying the system's progress.

Examine current procedural documentation. This provides the systems analyst with the formal procedures of the current operation. Later, the analyst will have an opportunity to confirm if the procedures are still valid, and, if not, what has changed. The operating procedures should include forms used. If it does not, obtain copies. They will help you understand their role in the operation.

[C]   Initial Business Unit Visit

Call the business unit's head for a first meeting in his or her office. If he or she is not in, leave a voice-mail message to return the call.

COMMENT

Prepare for the visit. Dress in a manner appropriate for management. If the area being visited is the manufacturing operation's spray-painting section, do not wear your best suit.

During your first contact, the art of listening becomes important. It has been said, "You cannot be a listener with your mouth open." Ask about the operation, the unit's problems, and the unit's people. If time and conditions permit, include a little social chatter, along with a cup of coffee. Later, have the person introduce you to the employees. Set up "the best time" for the return visit. If this person cannot see you within a reasonable time, ask to speak with someone lower on the organization chart, or start with the first person in the unit working with the current system.

[D]   Information Gathering Interviews

It is wise not to spend too much time on the first visit with any one person. Speaking with a person six times for 10 minutes each is better for the systems analyst than a single one-hour visit because the analyst will learn more and also develop a closer relationship with that person. Remember, when conducting an interview:

A.   Start at the beginning of an operation flow.
B.   Interview the person at his or her place of work or meet at a neutral place.
C.   If the person is ill or has a problem, come back later.
D.   Develop good listening skills.
E.   Do not repeat rumors; sidestep any local office politics or personality clashes.

F. Interview all the people in the unit, if possible. No one will be seen as a favorite and more will be learned. Even if several people perform the same job, each may see it from a different perspective. One may contribute something the others overlooked. Each person will add something that leads to another question for someone else.

G. Be open with your note taking. Shorthand pads work well.

H. Do not jump to conclusions.

I. Listen carefully for what each person really means.

J. Leave your information technology jargon at the door.

K. Be aware of the interviewee's body language.

L. Look for content, not style of delivery of information.

M. Do not assume anything.

N. Avoid playing favorites with workers.

O. Define what tools are employed (e.g., hardware, software, files accessed).

P. Ask questions, but be aware of who may have a stake in or have developed the current system.

Q. Give people time to answer correctly.

R. Collect copies of documents and ask:
    1. What is the daily volume of forms, reports, and so on?
    2. From where do documents come?
    3. Who originates the first inside document?
    4. Why is the document used?
    5. How is the document completed?
    6. Where are the documents filed?

S. Also ask questions:
    1. Has a worker come up with his or her own procedures to make things work?
    2. How often and when are backups done?
    3. What is the security procedure?
    4. What problems are there with operating instructions?
    5. Who do you contact for help?

T. Conclude the interview by thanking the person.

[E]   Document the Interviews

After the interviews are over, analyze the information gathered. Draw flowcharts from the data collected (see Chapter 13 "Documentation: Getting Everyone on the Same Page") and document the user requirements. One effective method for documenting the user requirements is to create use cases. Use cases are created by defining the "actors" who will be using the system and, for each actor, the "goals" that he or she wishes to accomplish by using the system. This is done in language that the business user will understand, with a minimum of technical jargon. There are a number of different formats for creating use cases; Exhibit 28-1 is an example of a two column use case with the user actions in the left column and the system actions on the right.

EXHIBIT 28-1.   Sample Use Case

Company, Inc	Version 2.11
Widget Services Application	Date: May 1, 2008

1.1 Add Company Screen 4.3.A

User adds a new company.

1.1.1 Flow of Events

User Actions	System Actions
Open Screen	
1. User selects "Add Company" on Main Menu (Screen 4.1.A)	2. System opens the Add Company screen (Screen 4.3.A). The data controls are empty.
Create New Company	
1. User enters data	
2. If User presses the Add Company button	3. System ensures the new ID is a valid key. If not, a message is displayed informing the user, and control returns to the user.
	If Company Name text box is empty, system displays a message informing the user that a name is required and returns contr ol to the user.
	Otherwise, system creates a new company record in the database and saves the entered data.
	The Company Bar at the top of the screen is updated with the new company's name and code. The new company becomes the select-ed company.
	System closes this screen and displays the Main Menu (Screen 4.1.A); all items are available for selection.
4. If User presses the "Cancel" button	5. The entered data is thrown away. The data controls are empty.
Cancel	
1. User presses the Cancel button.	2. System clears all data controls.

EXHIBIT 28-1.   (Continued)

Close Screen

1. User selects "Main Menu"   2. If data has been entered into the
                                          controls, the system prompts the
                                          user to press either the Add
                                          Company or Cancel button.
                                          Control returns to user.

                                          Otherwise, system closes this
                                          screen and displays the Main
                                          Menu (Screen 4.1.A); all items are
                                          available for selection.

1.1.2 Business Rules

1. Each Company must have a unique Company ID.
2. Each Company must have a name.
3. The Company ID can not contain any of the following characters: /, *, :, <, >, ?, \, |, ",

1.1.3 Additional Information

The Notes field can contain a maximum of 1000 characters. This is a varchar field which only consumes the disk space needed to store the data actually entered into the field.

1.1.4 Special Requirements

None.

1.1.5 Pre-conditions

None.

1.1.6 Post-conditions

None.

1.1.7 Notes

The "Status Yr," "Age Correction," Billing Contact Name, Phone and e-mail and the Company Contact Name, Phone and E-mail fields in the old Widget application will not be in the new application

No contact information is maintained. Company stores this data in Outlook and Peachtree. If stored here, it would be redundant and difficult to ensure it was updated every time a change was made in either of those programs.

It is also helpful in most situations to create screen prototypes to help the user visualize how the system will work. If used, add references to these in your use cases.

Return to the business unit and authenticate the flowchart(s) and use cases by observing the actual people doing the jobs. If necessary, send a follow-up memo verifying approval of the documented information by the person or persons interviewed.

Document present procedures to be included in the final systems report. Prepare the final documentation and make necessary copies. See Policy ITP-28-1 System Analysis Documentation Policy as an example.

POLICY ITP-28-1.   System Analysis Documentation Policy

Policy #:	ITP-28-1	Effective:	03/18/09	Page #:	1 of N
Subject:	System Analysis Documentation Policy				

1.0 PURPOSE

This policy defines the systems analysis documentation necessary for the successful development of new or revised computer systems.

2.0 SCOPE

The policy applies to all software development projects with a budgeted cost of more than $20,000. It applies both to systems developed in-house and to systems developed by outside vendors.

3.0 POLICY

The following documentation must be completed before software development can begin on a new or enhanced system:

A. Logical flowcharts of all major components must be created conforming to corporate policy standards.
B. Use cases created documenting all user interaction with the system.
C. User interface prototypes of all major forms.
D. Report layout prototypes of all major system output.

Sponsor signoff on all system analysis documentation is required before software development can begin.

4.0 REVISION HISTORY

Date	Revision #	Description of Change
03/18/09	1.0	Initial creation.

Direct inquiries about this policy to:

Tom Jones, CIO
Our Company, Inc.
2900 Corporate Drive
Columbus, OH 43215

Voice: 614-555-1234
Fax: 614-555-1235
E-mail: tjones@company.com

Revision #:	1.0	Supersedes:	N/A	Date:	03/18/09

[F] Work-Sampling Studies

Work sampling is a tool used by the systems analyst to find out how people spend their time at work. Since labor costs are a significant part of operating cost, it is essential to know how that time is spent. To justify the cost of new procedures or system investments, work sampling is used to study a current operation. It is a simple procedure and, when properly used, can reveal the areas that require further study.

For example, take the question, "Should the company integrate document imaging into the billing support process?" The systems analyst performs random observations of the billing support team to determine the hours spent on the various activities performed during the day. These hours represent dollars: the cost of an employee working on each task represents real cost to the company. The daily cost per employee divided by the number of items processed gives you the cost per item processed. This cost can then be compared to the increase in productivity if document imaging is implemented to determine the payback period for implementing the new technology. This information helps management decide whether to make the purchase.

Another focus of this work-sampling information might be the time of people who use the billing documents at a later time. Ask people who use these documents if having them available online would increase their productivity. If so, this will decrease the payback period of implementing document imaging in the billing support process.

This is a very simple example. More complex studies yield other kinds of information. One undercover study in a department of 16 people revealed that each person was spending 35 percent of the time doing no work at all. The reason was a lack of supervision.

Another study was set up in an engineering support unit of a Fortune 500 firm to find out how people spent their time, and what new equipment was needed to reduce the heavy overtime. The result of the study showed that employees were not working as hard or as efficiently as they could, because they enjoyed the overtime income too much. These findings enabled the company to eliminate Saturday overtime costs.

Other information can help address specific problems. In one instance, discovery of a new government regulation that required a ratio of hours to workers that equaled three persons made it possible to cost justify these three people quickly and cheaply.

A work-sampling study involves the following:

A. **Observation times.** Observations of the work area studied are performed at random times and dates. Random numbers can be generated by computer software, taken from a random number table in a math book, or drawn out of a hat. It is suggested that two sets of observation times be drawn: a small sample of 50 to 100, and a larger sample later. The specific sample size is dependent on the number of items and people observed. About a hundred observations per item type observed is typical. There are formulas available used by industrial engineers to compute the number needed for the required confidence level.

B. **Preliminary observations.** Compose a list of tasks for the preliminary study of the initial observations. Personal time and miscellaneous should always be included. "Out of the area and available, but no work" may in some cases be selected, too. These tasks are posted to the tally sheet for observations (see Exhibit 28-2). The observations are performed only by the systems analyst and no one else, especially not the boss. People are not usually identified by name. The observations are taken in a split second and tally marked (e.g., a mark is made for each observation; four in a row, with the fifth mark across the other four). The tallies are counted and posted in the total column on the right-hand side. After the tallies are posted, each total value is divided by the total number of observations. For example, with a preliminary observation of 50, divide each task total value by 50 to get the percent of time spent with that task. Added together, the percent values will total approximately 100 percent.

C. **New tally sheet.** Using the results of the preliminary observations, add or delete items from the final observation study. Those with less than a five percent tally are normally deleted from the final study. When the miscellaneous category is very high—more than 20 percent—try to identify a category or categories to be removed and placed under their own tasks. Then construct a new tally sheet for the final study.

D. **Final observation study.** The final observation study is made at the random times and dates selected. Complete the tally sheet as explained in Item B. Then divide each task total by the total number of observations to get the task percentage. The total number of observations for the final study, as shown in Exhibit 28-2, will be no less than 10 times the number of observations in the preliminary study.

EXHIBIT 28-2. Completed Sampling Tally Sheet

Date(s) _1/10 – 1/20/03_ By _Mary Smith_
Unit observed _Billing Support_ Number of people _4_

Task	Tally	Total	%
Filing	||||‖ |||| |||| |||| |||| ||||	30	30
Telephone	|||| ///	8	8
Reading	|||| |||| /	11	11
Writing	|||| |||| |||| |||| /	21	21
Personal	|||| ||||	10	10
Misc.	|||| |||| |||| ||||	20	20
	TOTAL NUMBER OF OBSERVATIONS	100	100

COMMENT

People tend to act differently if they feel they are being observed or their work output evaluated. The more often you are seen in a department, the less of a stranger you will be and the less this effect will be apparent. Most workers will view work sampling as something that will change their environment for the worse and may exhibit negative behavior toward you.

[G]   Final Report

Place the procedure text and flowcharts in a binder with a cover sheet titled Final Analysis Study Report, and a name to identify the study. The cover memo summarizes the study, including any recommendations and any additional comments the analyst may make. This memo should not be placed in the report binder, but sent to the project leader, along with the feasibility study and the report. The dates and hours expended on the analysis should be reported in the format required by the project leader.

When the final analysis report is submitted, the project's sponsor will issue a decision to proceed with the project or to drop it. Dropping a bad project is a good thing to do. Proceeding with a bad project will generally result in failure at some point in the project so this is the best time to "keep it or kill it."

§ 28.04   SYSTEMS DESIGN

[A]   Overview

The objective of systems design is to take the systems parameters as defined in the development and planning phase and create a system to the degree allowed, given the allocated resources and timeframe. The defined scope of the project determines the resources and time limitations. If a systems analysis final report is available, use it as an information base in designing the new system. The systems analyst synthesizes the elements of several design alternatives and compares them with the design criteria. Compare them with each other and with the current system. The system closest to achieving the defined objectives, with the best utilization of resources, is the best choice. This decision is not the systems analyst's alone; management and/or the user will have an impact on the final selection of the "best" solution. The analyst may design the alternative systems, but management and the user have to live with the selection long after the analyst has moved on to other projects.

The procedure steps required to achieve optimal design are:

A. Establish detailed system design specifications for the selected design.
B. Determine proper utilization of software, hardware, assigned personnel, and contract services.
C. Prepare the final systems report supported with documentation and system flowcharts.
D. Gain acceptance of the proposed system from requesting authorities and users.

[B]   Systems Design Specifications

The development of systems design specifications includes any refinements incorporated into the design as requested by users and the requesting authority. Final design documentation will include input, output, database, and software specifications to meet the design requirements. Above all, backup and recovery procedures, along with security requirements, are a must.

   A. **System specifications.** The details for this phase are determined by what is needed to communicate the system requirements to programmers or software vendors. Following are guidelines for developing these specifications:

      1. **Develop output requirements.** These are first based on user report or workstation display needs. Use prototyping tools to create example screens and reports. This helps the customer to visualize what he or she is asking for. Remember that the desired outputs are what drives the inputs needed and the processing steps in between.

      2. **Develop file specifications.** Develop an Index of Table Field Names—the names used in databases, programs, and input/output locations. The specifications include all data elements required for present or anticipated needs, and a data dictionary to provide their specifications. Most installations already have a standard naming convention for you to follow.

      3. **Define the input layouts.** This is the format of all data to be captured for use by the system. This input can be source documents coming into the information systems data entry unit or input received as captured data from outside the computer operation. The source of captured data received by the system is input from terminals or other, non-keyed data, and is of major concern to the systems analyst who must ensure that only the required input gains entry to the system. This will include all required user security and data edits.

      4. **Develop the processing requirements.** Describe in detail the processing operations required by the software. In addition, general guidelines may be required for some functions, such as:

        a. Procedures for entry of corrections.

        b. Controls to monitor out-of-balance conditions (e.g., a negative payroll check or inventory balance).

        c. Editing routines for missing or incorrect data entering the system for the first time.

        d. Proper restart procedures for the user.

   B. **Manual procedures.** All data processing begins and ends with a person. The computer sits in the middle digesting what the input person tossed in and spitting out the result on the other side. If you ignore the people part of your process, you are ignoring two-thirds of the process and the best-made system will fail. Clerical tasks are included to:

      1. Review data to ensure it can be entered. Bad data will make a good program act in unusual ways.

      2. Correct input data. At any place where someone is entering or scanning data, validate each field as it is entered. If the data is not valid, immediately send a message to the operator as to why it was rejected.

3. Change data already in the system.
4. Hold or dispose of input data. Some data source documents must be retained for business or legal reasons.
5. Distribute output (printed, CDs, or LAN file). If you understand how the output is being used, then you can better determine the media to deliver it on. You cannot annotate a CD, but if it is used only for reference, a CD saves storage space.

[C]   Utilization of Resources

Understanding the availability of hardware, software, and personnel resources is essential to preparing the system design specifications. Analyze these to determine their adequacy to fulfill the systems objectives. If any of the three is inadequate, changes are required. If the resources cannot be changed, it may be necessary to alter the system's scope or objectives.

Often, the availability of scarce resources is contingent on when the project will begin. If a project's approval is delayed for a significant amount of time, or if other critical projects have begun since the original estimate was made, the assumptions used for estimated resources required should be reviewed.

[D]   Final Systems Report

The proposed system design is documented in the form of a final systems report that defines objectives and states how the proposed system design meets them. The scope of the undertaking is defined, along with a proposed timetable for installing the new system. It contains proposed costs and return expected, in both tangible and intangible benefits, for the resource investment. Its purpose is to inform and gain acceptance of the proposed system. The report should be hand-carried to the proper individuals one to two weeks before the verbal presentation is to be made.

The report should contain the following:

A. Summary of the full systems study.
   1. Overview of events leading up to the study.
   2. Subject of study.
   3. Objectives and scope of the proposed system.
   4. Statement of recommendations and justifications for the proposed system.
B. Body of report.
   1. Description of the current system, including:
      a. Brief description of the current system and its use.
      b. Purpose of current system.
      c. Problems with the current system (if any) and rationale for the new system.
   2. Description of proposed system, including:
      a. Overview of proposed system.
      b. Scope of project.
      c. Exhibits of all reports and screen displays.

     d. System flowcharts.
     e. Systems documentation of proposed system and any vendor-supplied material that provides additional information.
     f. Summary of proposed recommendations.
     g. Summary of assumptions that recommendations are based on.
     h. List of personnel needs:
        i. Personnel required to install the new system.
        ii. Personnel required to maintain the new system.
     i. Proposed timetable for installing suggested system and work-hours required to complete project.
     j. List of special equipment or software that must be purchased for the project.
  3. Financial information section, including:
     a. Present system operating cost.
     b. Proposed system operating cost.
     c. Installation cost of new system and its estimated useful life.
     d. Tangible and intangible benefits of proposed system.
  4. Proposed system summary: A positive statement of rationale for installing the proposed system, the summary also contains any concerns that exist about timetable, funds, software, hardware, outside contractors, or personnel available.
A. Appendix.
  1. Prior reports.
  2. Memos and letters.
  3. Other supporting documents not included in body of report:
     a. Sample documents and forms.
     b. Charts.
     c. Graphs.
     d. Gantt charts.
     e. Tables of data.
     f. Vendor literature.

[E] The Acceptance Presentation

Gaining acceptance is the last step before system implementation. All concerned should be brought together for a verbal and visual presentation. Everyone attending should have had enough time to read the report. This presentation is used to confirm that the proposed system will meet its objective and stay within the defined scope. Although not requisite, the presentation to gain final acceptance can be just as important as the final written report that serves as a basis for the verbal presentation. However, reading the report itself is not enough. Therefore, a different approach must be adopted to resolve any problems, whether political or technical. It is very important that the presenter know the attitudes, political positions, and status of all those attending the presentation. Not everyone present may be supportive; some may object to possible added demands on their areas, loss of present control, or loss of operations.

Suggestions on how to sell a proposal include:

A. Be relaxed. Otherwise, people may think you are trying to hide something.
B. Gain approval by seeking support from people before the meeting. If possible, contact each of the key managers before the meeting to discuss any questions they may have about the report. This will allow you time to send out any clarifications before the meeting.
C. Decide whether you want credit for your innovation or acceptance. You may not get both. This is corporate politics.
D. Do not expect others to think like you.
E. Never have surprises at this presentation. People do not like them. Address all known problems before the meeting begins.
F. Never expect that people want change or innovation simply because they may have indicated they did in the past.
G. You may have a compelling story to tell but keep the entire presentation to under an hour. If someone wants to know more, they will ask you.

Well-planned audio and visual aids help to create a positive impression on the audience. Flip charts or PowerPoint slides particularly add visual interest by providing step-by-step information with graphs, flowcharts, and text materials. You can write notes on the edge of each page to assist you if using flip charts.

In-house graphic arts departments may be of help in producing the visual aids required. They may have a PC or notebook PC and a portable projector for running your presentation using PowerPoint or similar software. Vendors may be a source of visuals, too.

Make sure you are comfortable with whatever materials you use. New, untried hardware or software can spell disaster. Check out the room the day before and have a dry run if possible. To ensure everything is ready on the day of the presentation, arrive no less than one hour before the presentation. Test any equipment to make sure it works. Your high exposure may not spell a promotion, but a disaster is something you may have to live down.

The presentation should help gain as much support for and acceptance of the new system as possible. In some cases, it may even wrap up the sale. Following is a basic presentation outline:

A. **Introduction.** The introduction consists only of preliminary descriptions: Introduce yourself and the subject. Explain how the system study began and progressed and how the presentation will be made, including:
   1. A statement defining the need for a new system. Gain their interest!
   2. An explanation about how alternative systems were reviewed before selecting the one being presented.
   3. An explanation of the format that follows the introduction.
B. **The body.** The body is the heart of the presentation. Use terminology familiar to your audience, especially management and users. Those

attending will be more interested in what is done than how the technology works. Emphasize the benefits of the new system and not its hardware or software. Have a positive attitude about the benefits (such as faster processing or response time, better accuracy and control, and, maybe, reduced costs). Reliable information and honesty about any drawbacks are necessities. The body should:

1. Briefly describe the current production system.
2. Describe the proposed system and any alternate proposals.
3. Present economic information:
    a. Current system operating costs.
    b. Proposed system operating costs.
    c. Cost of installing proposed system. (Be conservative with cost claims.)
    d. Intangible benefits and/or requirements imposed by customers, vendors, or government.
4. Provide recommendations for proposed selection.

C. **Summary of the presentation.** All tangible and intangible benefits of proposed system should be stressed.

D. **Discussion**
    1. Open the meeting for questions.
    2. Keep discussion going; call on people who support proposed system for input. You do not have to answer every question yourself if some attendees helped provide that technical aspect.
    3. Be aware of attitudes of people and have a strategy ready to handle any negative comments.

E. **Conclusion.** End your presentation on a positive note.
    1. Summarize areas of agreement brought up during open discussion.
    2. Make a positive statement as to what will happen with project and how those involved will be kept informed of its progress.

§ 28.05 SYSTEMS PROTOTYPING

[A] Overview

This section covers ideas and procedures for using prototyping to design a working systems model. Prototyping is an analysis and design technique involving end users in defining the requirements and developing the system according to their needs and desires. It helps define the end-user requirements more quickly than the traditional analysis and design approach. A complex system can involve a number of (modular) prototypes.

Prototypes can be hand drawn (see the dataflow diagrams in Chapter 13, "Documentation: Getting Everyone on the Same Page") or developed with computer software tools that are available for PCs. Computer-aided systems and software engineering (CASE) technologies automate the analysis and design process using modeling tools and other techniques.

Another useful technique is Joint Applications Development (JAD). The JAD methodology requires that the user be heavily involved in the design and application development processes. If you plan to use JAD, start with a "safe" project, one that has very little chance of failure with the following characteristics:

A. The user is skillful and cooperative.
B. The application is a one-user and/or simple application.
C. Minimum of hardware/software changes are needed.
D. A top-quality team is assigned to the project.
E. There is an adequate budget.

COMMENT

A well-selected user is essential for an effective JAD session.

The systems analyst working with the user can develop an iterative series of prototypes that can be viewed and revised interactively. This reduces both the calendar and chargeable project time.

Prototyping is best suited for developing systems that are not well defined, or for exceptional, smaller systems applications. It allows for the visualization and conversation required for quick systems development. All too often users request something they cannot define, or cannot see how changes will satisfy their needs. This type of situation would be a candidate for a prototyping effort.

The characteristics of systems that are likely candidates for prototyping are:

A. User requirements are difficult to define.
B. The application has few users—often only one.
C. The application may be ad hoc or even parochial in nature.
D. The application has a low volume of input and/or output.
E. The application requires a minimum of editing controls.
F. User(s) may only require a stand-alone PC using their own files or database.

[B] Prototype Development

The systems analyst needs to consider what kind of system requires development since not all undertakings are suitable for prototyping. A traditional system that cuts across two or more departments would probably be a poor candidate. Another poor candidate would be an order-processing or payroll system. Rather, single-user, novel, and/or complex applications, and semi-structured or even unstructured applications are all good candidates for this kind of approach.

The systems analysis management also must evaluate the environmental conditions where the systems analyst will operate. The political climate and the user's personality play a major role in the success or failure of this kind of undertaking.

The lead systems analyst maintains a prototype project folder, containing all papers related to the project, and an activities diary for which a shorthand pad can suffice. The diary should be hand-posted while the information is still fresh and should contain such information as the day's activities, time spent on each activity, and any other information the analyst deems relevant. The diary is not for publication; it is only a reference record to be placed in the prototype project folder after the effort is completed.

The procedure for prototyping is as follows:

A. **Estimate project expense.** Both direct and indirect costs are computed. This includes the chargeable time of systems analysts and programmers, along with other development costs. Software and hardware costs are generally considered indirect costs, but a one-time-use software package required for the project is a direct cost.
   1. The information system's personnel define the calendar timeframe, as well as the estimated worker-hours. If costs and time requirements are agreeable to the user and information systems management, the project will proceed. The costs may be charged directly to the requesting user's budget or applied to an information systems budget for such projects.

B. **Develop manageable modules or objects.** Module or object size is reduced to a manageable level so that each one can be built separately from other system or subsystem objects. Each is also designed to allow other objects to interact with its features. This development is done in concert with the end user(s) and the systems analyst.

C. **Build the prototype.** As the systems analyst gathers information about the user's requirements for the application, he or she assesses user feedback about the developing prototype to better visualize the systems requirements. Successful prototyping depends on early and frequent end-user feedback to the developing process. User changes made early in the development process will reduce costs and total project development time.

   The systems analyst illustrates to the user(s) as early as possible how parts of the system actually accomplish their objectives. This early construction of an operational prototype allows early user feedback so the systems analyst can gain valuable insight into the direction of the prototype construction.

   To develop the prototype as quickly as possible, the analyst uses whatever special tools are available, such as personal, workgroup, or even organizational databases, computer software, and other prototype design tools. Access to databases, other than personal ones, will require the permission of the data administrator and/or the database administrator. Rapid prototyping development reduces the chance of changes imposed by the user. The longer it takes to develop a system, the more the system is susceptible to changes imposed by the user and/or the operational environment. Rapid prototyping development safeguards against over committing resources to a project that could eventually become unworkable.

> # COMMENT
>
> The saying "strike while the iron is hot" applies here. The hotter the iron is, the easier it is to work. The longer a project is stretched out, the less chance it has to succeed.

D. **Complete the prototype.** The prototyping is complete when the user has what he or she wants and the systems analyst is willing to sign off on the prototype. The sign-off can take two forms:

1. **Scrap the prototype** when the user(s) is not satisfied with the finished product or the requirements are beyond what can be reasonably provided. The systems analyst is the representative of the systems department, the database administrator, and the data administrator. These areas require limited access by the end users. The systems analyst is required to police the needs of users so that they do not violate any policies or procedures that are in place for these areas.

2. **Accept the prototype.** Operationally completed prototypes require sign-off by both the user(s) and the systems analyst. This might be a joint memo from both to the users' management and the head of the systems department. The user(s) by this time will have been trained in the operation of the prototype system, and an operations manual will have been completed and put in place. This training and documentation is the responsibility of the lead systems analyst assigned to the project. The lead systems analyst sends a final project memo to the systems manager within a week after the prototype has been signed-off. This allows for follow-up to confirm that all went as planned. The memo is a summary report on the effective utilization of information systems resources on behalf of the prototype effort. The report may end with an editorialized summary by the analyst responsible for the prototype. The prototype project folder and its diary are sources of information for this report.

[C]   Prototyping Methods

Due to different needs, a single "all-in-one" prototype model is not realistic. However, there are four tools available to the systems analyst. All four follow the same prototype development procedures as outlined in § 28.05[B], "Prototype Development." They are:

A. **First-of-a-series prototype.** A pilot prototype is developed as a full-scale system, can be made up of subsystems, and is a "true" prototype (e.g., one that is developed and debugged at one site). The following prototypes are modified to further improve the system. The first prototype is volume tested after it is debugged, ensuring that the prototype can be replicated at other sites with a minimum of effort and problems.

B. **Modular prototype.** This prototype does not contain all the attributes that the final system version will have. This allows for the rapid development of less complex prototypes. After the first has been developed, another similar-featured one is developed and joined to the first to construct a finished product. There can be any number of designated prototypes connected to complete a final version.

C. **One-shot prototype.** This prototype does not have to be efficient because it will be used only once. (It could be used later, but seldom is.) Such a prototype can afford to be inefficient, as long as the development cost is less than what would be gained from a more efficient operating model. The retrieval, storage, and computation can be primitive, if workable. If this type of prototype were popular, time and effort to develop a "user/request" form would make sense. This form will save time for both the user(s) and systems analyst or programmer analyst.

D. **Input-output prototype.** This is a scale model prototype, without an operating program, used to save the cost of developing an expensive process program. This prototype has well-defined input and output formats, like those used for a model car. Management may gain enough information from this scale model to determine that the cost of the process development is worth it. A software tool used for this prototype could simply be a good word-processing program. Of all the prototype methods, this is the one least used.

COMMENT

A simple input-output prototype observed by one of the authors was one constructed by a group of students working on a systems project. The students were asked to write a COBOL program that would produce a printed report. Instead of having the program perform the calculations, they hand-calculated the results from input test data and then used WordPerfect, a word processor to print the report. There was no operating program, just an output prototype.

§ 28.06 SYSTEMS IMPLEMENTATION

[A] Implementation Prerequisites

There are several steps that should be followed to ensure a successful implementation of the proposed system. This is the most challenging task of any information systems undertaking. Develop a list of tasks that must be completed before a system is implemented and approved as operational.

While technical and business people can be impatient to implement a new or revised system, time spent carefully reviewing the system before implementation can save a tremendous amount of time and resources later. A poorly implemented system is almost always worse than no system at all. See Policy ITP-28-2 System Implementation Prerequisites Policy as an example.

POLICY ITP-28-2.   System Implementation Prerequisites Policy

Policy #:	ITP-28-2	Effective:	03/18/09	Page #:	1 of N
Subject:	System Implementation Prerequisites Policy				

1.0 PURPOSE

This policy defines the required prerequisites necessary for the successful implementation of new or revised computer systems.

2.0 SCOPE

The policy applies to all new computer systems at the company. It applies both to systems developed in-house and to systems purchased from outside vendors.

3.0 POLICY

The following tasks must be completed before beginning the implementation of any new or enhanced software application:

A. The documentation must conform to corporate standards.
B. A system walk-through must be performed. The purpose of a systems walk-through is to prove the logic of the system with another systems analyst or with users. It must be proven that data records are compatible between operations and/or programs. Technical documentation is referenced, updated, and corrected at this point. The walk-through starts with input and is followed through to the required output. This is the last chance to catch system problems before functional users begin to report bugs and lose confidence in your project.
C. Input requirements for walk-throughs include:
   1. Raw data or machine-usable input.
   2. Batch or online input.
   3. Control totals or record counts.
   4. Database elements chosen or generated to provide realistic test data.
D. Review all anticipated logic flows. This includes the process steps required to provide output of data or update of the database or files.

E. Review all anticipated outputs. These are normally classified into categories and followed through to ensure all the data elements are available in the forms required. The following are possible actions that should be taken:
   1. Total record counts, units, dollars, or other data are checked against expected values.
   2. Contents and format of monitor displays and reports are checked against stated requirements and pre-computed results.
   3. Error criteria and messages are identified for those items expected to be rejected by system.
   4. Output data elements that will become input to other systems are checked for compatibility.

4.0 REVISION HISTORY

Date	Revision #	Description of Change
03/18/07	1.0	Initial creation.

5.0 INQUIRIES

Direct inquiries about this policy to:

Tom Jones, CIO
Our Company, Inc.
2900 Corporate Drive
Columbus, OH 43215

Voice: 614-555-1234
Fax: 614-555-1235
E-mail: tjones@company.com

Revision #:	1.0	Supersedes:	N/A	Date:	03/18/09

[B] Implementation Procedures

Policies and procedures must be created to ensure that new or revised systems are implemented consistently throughout the organization. Best practices should be developed with the business and technical environment of the organization in mind. Develop a list of activities that must be performed to help ensure that the implementation of a new system goes smoothly. See Policy ITP-28-3 System Implementation Procedures Policy as an example.

POLICY ITP-28-3.   System Implementation Procedures Policy

Policy #:	ITP-28-3	Effective:	03/18/09	Page #:	1 of 2
Subject:	System Implementation Procedures Policy				

1.0 PURPOSE

This policy defines the required procedures to follow to ensure the successful implementation of new or revised computer systems.

2.0 SCOPE

The policy applies to all new computer systems at the company. It applies both to systems developed in-house and to systems purchased from outside vendors.

3.0 POLICY

The following actions are taken as part of the implementation of a new or revised software system:

- A. Develop implementation plans, estimates, and conversion procedures.
- B. Review and update systems specifications to reflect requirements developed during programming.
- C. Develop test data for program and systems testing.
- D. Evaluate results from program tests, systems tests, volume tests, and any parallel testing operations. This is done with users to ensure that test specifications and system requirements have been met.
- E. Update schedule changes.
- F. Develop training procedures for systems operations and user personnel. Give everyone systems documentation to refer to as they are learning the software.
- G. Confirm that all operational procedures and manuals are in place.
- H. Confirm that all operational personnel have been trained.
- I. Request systems operations and/or user sign-off.
- J. Perform any tests that auditors have requested.
- K. Follow up very quickly on end-user questions and defect reports.

4.0 REVISION HISTORY

Date	Revision #	Description of Change
03/18/09	1.0	Initial creation.

5.0 INQUIRIES

Direct inquiries about this policy to:

Tom Jones, CIO
Our Company, Inc.
2900 Corporate Drive
Columbus, OH 43215

Voice: 614-555-1234
Fax: 614-555-1235
E-mail: tjones@company.com

Revision #:	1.0	Supersedes:	N/A	Date:	03/18/09

§ 28.07   SYSTEMS MAINTENANCE

[A]   Modify or Redesign?

Before a request for any maintenance is approved, the system must be examined to determine if it should be modified or redesigned. The presence of any of the following five factors tends to favor redesign instead of modification:

1. The cost of maintenance of a project exceeds 30 percent of the actual development costs.
2. The existing system has been patched extensively or modified over a period of two to three years.
3. The existing system lacks proper documentation and there is sufficient factual information to justify redesign of the system.
4. Portions of the source code are missing or use an obsolete language.
5. The program depends on obsolete objects called from the operating system.

[B]   Types of Maintenance Projects

Maintenance efforts may originate from one or more of the following sources:

A. Change in policy.
B. Change of operation requirements.
C. Change in procedure.
D. Change of operating system.
E. Change of system flow.
F. Change in hardware.
G. Change of program instructions.

[C] Requirements and Responsibilities

The systems manager defines the responsibility for coordinating requirements for system maintenance and establishes tasks to be performed.

A. **Review and estimate of work required.** The standard task list is reviewed to determine which tasks are necessary to satisfy the maintenance request.
   1. Identify problem to be solved by maintenance project.
   2. Define scope and limitations of maintenance effort.
   3. Rewrite operational procedures as required.
   4. Redesign input-output documents, files, or database requirements, and monitor displays or reports as required.
   5. Correct Index of Table Field Names, as needed.

COMMENT

No change is too simple to test. The results of a programmer's decision not to test a "too-simple revision": It cost the programmer his job and the firm more than $1 million! Always test revised programs.

   6. Designate programs and procedures that require modification.
   7. Make needed program changes.
   8. Test revised programs.
   9. Document revisions.
   10. Perform system tests.
B. **Management and/or user approval.** Management and users are responsible for the following tasks:
   1. Approve intent and objectives of system modification.
   2. Help develop test data for system modification.
   3. Review and approve test results.
   4. Make operational personnel available for any retraining required.

[D] Control

Control checkpoints are established for each maintenance project. Their purpose is twofold: to ensure the quality and completeness of the maintenance project and to make sure the changes made to the system do not alter policy or degrade the system's present performance.

Minimally, controls should be at the following points:

A. Completion of program testing.
B. Completion of system testing.
C. Completion of changed documentation.

    D. End of maintenance (for confirmation that policies have not been changed).

[E] Revision Conventions

These revision practices should be followed:

    A. All binders for revisions are updated at the same time to avoid any documentation conflicts.

    B. A revision information cover page, with revision number and date, is completed and inserted into each binder.

    C. Obsolete documentation is labeled "obsolete," date posted, and documentation filed or destroyed according to the records retention procedure.

    D. The revision number is posted on the top right-hand side of each new page of documentation.

SOFTWARE DEVELOPMENT: SOLID PRACTICES

§ 29.01 OVERVIEW
    [A] Purpose and Scope
    [B] Critical Policies to Develop Based on This Chapter

§ 29.02 SOFTWARE DEVELOPMENT PROCESS
    [A] Why IT Is Important
    [B] Ownership of Computer Software
    [C] Review of Software Specifications
    [D] Reusable Component Identification

§ 29.03 PROGRAMMING METHODOLOGIES
    [A] Systems Development Methodologies
    [B] Waterfall
    [C] Spiral
    [D] Rapid Application Development
    [E] Extreme Programming

§ 29.04 PROGRAMMING CONVENTIONS
    [A] Coding Conventions
    [B] Controls

§ 29.05 SOFTWARE ACQUISITION
    [A] Overview
    [B] IT Purchased Software
    [C] Other Unit Software Requisition Procedures
    [D] Contract Programming
    [E] Contract Programmers
    [F] Evaluation of Packaged Software
    [G] Beta Software Testing and Evaluation

§ 29.06 PROGRAM TESTING
    [A] Test Planning
    [B] Test Preparation
    [C] Test Analysis
    [D] Operating Program Maintenance
    [E] Testing
    [F] Audit Review

§ 29.07   SOFTWARE INSTALLATION
          [A] Overview
          [B] Review and Acceptance of Test Results
          [C] Review and Acceptance of Documentation
          [D] Acceptance of Contracted Software
          [E] Development Programmer Sign-Off
          [F] Selection of an Implementation Day

§ 29.08   PROGRAM MAINTENANCE
          [A] Types of Program Maintenance
          [B] Responsibilities and Controls
          [C] Conventions
          [D] PC Software Developed by End Users
          [E] End-User Testing Training
          [F] Stealth Systems
          [G] Hidden Programming Staffs

§ 29.01 OVERVIEW

[A] Purpose and Scope

A company's software is a reflection of its ever changing and complex operations. Creating or buying software is more than a question of resources and cost; it is also a question of remaining competitive. Software and the services it provides can give a company a competitive advantage; poorly designed software acts as a drag on the business. IT policies covering software development and acquisition help ensure that the organization receives the desired benefits from its software.

Creating computer software is expensive, and a company that employs its own programming staff has invested a considerable amount of money into processes to support its business. Ideally, this provides the company with an operating efficiency or other business advantage. To protect this investment, the company must have a clearly defined policy that stipulates that all programs written using company resources (such as time, equipment, utility software, books, and so on) are the company's property. Without this protection, a company may find its internal software processes being used by a competitor or generally available in the marketplace.

[B] Critical Policies to Develop Based on This Chapter

Using the material discussed in this chapter, you will be able to create the following policies:

A. The company possesses title to all software created using its resources.
    1. Include a clause in agreements with contract programmers that logic flow, Web screen designs and code created while in the pay of the company belong solely to the company.
    2. Employees must understand that software created while on the job or while using company resources belongs to the company.
B. Version control and authorized upgrades.
    1. Change control guidance to ensure all software changes are properly tested prior to implementation. All changes proposed should include a detailed back-out plan.
    2. Patch management to track pending ignored and implemented patches for such areas as security and bug fixes.
    3. Include in the policy a prohibition from downloading and applying patches or upgrades to programs that have not been tested and approved.
C. Purchasing software.
    1. The IT department will publish a list of the software that it can support:
        a. For development.
        b. Through the service desk.
    2. All software purchases must be approved by the IT department.
D. Beta and test software.
    1. Test copies are accompanied by permission from holder.

    2. Beta software is only loaded onto company data systems with executive approval.

    3. Beta proposal must detail the scope, schedule, and budget for the test.

E. Uniform coding practices.

    1. Standard naming convention for data elements, programs, and objects.

    2. Before implementation, all programs will be accompanied by a test plan and test data to exercise each logical branch within the program. Subsequent changes to the software will require updating the test plan and data.

F. Adequate documentation must be provided whenever implementing a major software change.

    1. End users—How to use the data system to include examples of all screens and a nontechnical explanation of each field. Include a list of edits applied.

    2. Technical support—Used by future programmers to quickly locate and repair problems. Also a starting point for system enhancements.

    3. Service desk—A cross between the technical support and user documentation (and sometimes contains both). This reference allows for quicker customer response and fewer calls to the programmers.

G. Software change control.

    1. All new software and system updates must be approved by quality control prior to roll out.

    2. All system changes should be applied on Thursday evenings.

H. Use of non-standard programming languages and software tools.

    1. The policy must prohibit introducing any software technologies without executive IT approval. This must specifically include databases, operating system, system utility programs, and programming languages.

    2. All purchase proposals for non-standard software must include funds for training the programming staff in its use and for consultants to mentor the department until the staff masters its use.

I. Unlicensed software.

    1. Loading demo programs onto company equipment is prohibited unless specifically approved by the IT Manager.

    2. Copying software purchased by the company is prohibited unless specifically permitted by the terms of the software license agreement.

    3. Bringing personally owned software onto the company premises or loading onto company equipment is prohibited.

Policies should always be developed based on the local situation. Successful managers cannot issue appropriate guidance if the policies are written with another company's or location's situation in mind.

§ 29.02 SOFTWARE DEVELOPMENT PROCESS

[A] Why IT Is Important

Proper policy guidance makes the software development process more efficient: the longer it takes to develop software, the greater the chance that problems will occur. Creeping user requirements are the result of trying to build software to meet dynamic and ever-changing business requirements. It is simple; a company's business environment (competitive, legal, and environmental) is constantly changing.

Anyone who has been involved with software development for any length of time knows that the majority of all software development projects run over budget or are cancelled before completion. Even those that are completed rarely totally meet the user's original requirements.

> **COMMENT**
>
> Research by the Standish Group finds that almost 30 percent of IT projects will be cancelled; 52 percent of projects will cost 189 percent of their original estimates. Only 16 percent are completed on time and on budget. In larger companies, the news is even worse: only 9 percent of their projects come in on time and on budget.

Capers Jones, in his book *Assessment and Control of Software Risks* (Prentice Hall PTR, 1994), identified no fewer than 50 major problems affecting software development. While technology has advanced since this book was published, our ability to complete projects successfully has not. He notes, "Few projects have more than 15 software risk factors at any time, but many projects have half a dozen simultaneously." He points out the "five most frequently encountered risk factors for large IT shops":

1. Creeping user requirements.
2. Excessive schedule pressure.
3. Low quality.
4. Cost overruns.
5. Inadequate configuration control.

Application project overload and the deterioration of programming quality play havoc with programmer productivity. The prudent IT Manager not only has effective programming policies and procedures in place, but makes certain they are observed.

> ### COMMENT
>
> All developers are encouraged to read *Code Complete, A Practical Handbook of Software Construction* by Steve McConnell. The sections on commenting code and code reviews are particularly important.

[B] Ownership of Computer Software

Policy should be created to ensure that employees understand that all software developed by employees during the hours they are being paid by the company and/or using company equipment is the exclusive property of the employer. Many companies cover this under their employment agreement concerning development of patentable items. Be sure software ownership rights are specifically included in company employment agreements. Employees must also be aware of their responsibilities in honoring the terms of the license agreement for purchased software.

Purchased software. Purchased software and software documentation may only be copied as specified by the vendor. No versions of any purchased software are permitted beyond the number the firm has purchased. This applies to everyone in the company.

> ### COMMENT
>
> Purchased software provides only a license or permission to use a product under the conditions detailed in the license. The terms of this license will be violated if the purchaser makes more than the stipulated number of copies of the software. If the agreement is violated, the copyright holder may file a lawsuit for damages. They may also reclaim all of the licenses purchased from them.

Unauthorized software. Personnel may not purchase or write their own software for use in the organization without authorization. They may not bring into the organization any software, in any form, that is not the property of the organization. The downloading of any unauthorized software to company-owned hardware at any company site also is not permitted.

See Policy ITP-29-1 Ownership of Computer Software as an example.

POLICY ITP-29-1.   Ownership of Computer Software

Policy #:	ITP-29-1	Effective:	03/18/09	Page #:	1 of N
Subject:	Ownership of Computer Software				

1.0 PURPOSE

This policy defines the ownership of computer software developed using the company's time and resources.

2.0 SCOPE

The policy applies to all software applications developed at the company. It applies both to applications developed by the IT staff and to software developed using end-user tools such as Microsoft Excel or Access by non-IT staff.

3.0 POLICY

All software developed by employees or contractors during the hours they are being paid by the company and/or using company equipment is the exclusive property of the company. Salary-exempt personnel have no proprietary interest in programs they develop. All programming effort and documentation is the exclusive property of the employer as long as the hardware/software used belongs to the firm.

Personnel may not purchase or write their own software for use in the organization without authorization. They may not bring into the organization any software, in any form, which is not the property of the organization. The downloading of any unauthorized software to company-owned hardware at any company site also is not permitted. Any violation of this policy subjects the offender to immediate discharge and/or the reimbursement of all costs associated with such action.

4.0 REVISION HISTORY

Date	Revision #	Description of Change
03/18/07	1.0	Initial creation.

5.0 INQUIRIES

Direct inquiries about this policy to:

Tom Jones, CIO
Our Company, Inc.
2900 Corporate Drive
Columbus, OH 43215

Voice: 614-555-1234
Fax: 614-555-1235
E-mail: tjones@company.com

Revision #:	1.0	Supersedes:	N/A	Date:	03/18/09

COMMENT

Computer technicians appreciate the difficulties of keeping all the loaded systems software in "agreement" so that one program does not "crash" another. The introduction of additional software not previously tested and approved for company use exposes stable systems to a potentially destabilizing influence. Other issues include the ability for the unapproved software to exchange files with other systems as well as the ability of the company to provide cost-effective support to users.

[C]   Review of Software Specifications

The initial step in program development is a review of the system's software specifications to ensure there is no misunderstanding of specification requirements between the systems analyst, the requesting business sponsor, and the programmer(s). The following steps should be taken before any software is written:

A. **General review.** With the purpose and scope of the programs understood, the next step is to determine their relationships in the total system. When reviewing each program:
   1. Review the program's place in the system.
   2. Check the functions of programs preparing input for programs under review. Include the sequence of input elements and contents of element sets. In addition, check the purposes of the program(s) that will use the output of this program.
   3. Resolve any questions regarding system or programming requirements.
B. **Detailed review.** To ensure a complete understanding of the requirements for the program(s), consider the following items:
   1. Data element specifications determine the precise record formats for files and the data dictionary specifications for database systems. For example, are the "year" data elements four-numeric character

       fields, or is there some other solution that was used to resolve the Y2K problem?

2. Data element flexibility to handle impending or likely field expansions. Examples of this are the size of currency fields, foreign currency conversions, additional tax requirements, or even an expansion of the Social Security number field.
3. Processing specifications determine calculations and comparison tests of data.
4. Systems specifications are reviewed to resolve any ambiguities or problems.

[D]   Reusable Component Identification

Reusable components are those having identifiable commonalities across programs of a given project. The project must be large enough or consist of several smaller projects in the same general domain to justify a reuse strategy. For reuse to pay off, a specific plan must be developed before program coding starts. Reuse planning prior to coding a new system will help organizations avoid the error of thinking about reuse too late.

A taxonomy system is needed to identify modules or objects for reuse. No single taxonomy system will apply to all reusable component libraries.

Program module commonalities include common data, common constants, common formula process, common tables, and/or reiteration processes. Because models are built prior to coding the actual program modules, potential reuse is greater.

One word of caution: Make sure the module or object works. There is nothing worse than having reusable code that has a bug placed into your library. A list should be maintained of each object location in case errors are detected later, as well as for future update requirements. At some installations, a comment line is added to the top of each object identifying each program that uses it. When the object is changed, these programs must also be updated and tested.

§ 29.03   PROGRAMMING METHODOLOGIES

[A]   Systems Development Methodologies

A software development methodology (also known as a systems development life cycle, or SDLC) is a set of rules and practices used to create computer programs. It describes the stages involved in a software development project, beginning with the initial feasibility study through the maintenance of the completed application. Various methodologies have been developed over the years to guide the processes involved, including the waterfall model, rapid application development (RAD), joint application development (JAD), agile, code and fix, spiral, and many others. Most software teams will use a combination of these models, using the attributes from each that work best in their particular environment. In many cases it is not so much the particular model that is used that is important for project success, but more that the chosen model is followed consistently.

Most practitioners divide the various software development methodologies into one of two camps: heavyweight and lightweight. A heavyweight methodology has many rules, practices, and documents. It requires discipline and time to follow correctly. A lightweight methodology has only a few rules and practices or ones that are easy to follow. Whatever methodology is used, most follow the steps below:

A. The existing process or system is evaluated. This is usually done by interviewing users of the existing process.
B. The requirements of the new system are documented.
C. The new system is designed. The design should take into account the hardware and operating system requirements, security issues, and communication processes.
D. The new system is developed. Users of the system are trained. Any adjustments due to user requirements or performance issues are made.
E. The new system is implemented and integrated into the existing processes.
F. The system is maintained and modified as needed.

Popular development methodologies are described in the following sections. You must create policies that ensure that whatever methodology you use, it is consistently followed by all members of your development team.

[B] Waterfall

The Waterfall methodology is one of the oldest software development processes. It looks at a software project as a sequential series of phases, which each then consists of a series of activities and tasks. Each phase must be complete and accurate before the next phase can begin. The phases typically consist of the following:

A. System concept.
B. System requirements definition.
C. Software design.
D. Detailed design.
E. Code and unit test.
F. Integration and system test.

While all software development projects consist of these phases in one form or another, the Waterfall methodology treats each phase as distinct and separate. The project progresses in an orderly fashion from one phase to the next, much like water flowing downstream from one waterfall to the next. It provides an orderly sequence of development steps, which helps ensure that documentation and design reviews are completed before coding begins. This helps to guarantee the quality, reliability, and maintainability of the developed system.

Most software development teams today do not follow a strict Waterfall methodology, as it is seen as having too much overhead and being too slow for today's fast moving environment. But the Waterfall process does illustrate the steps necessary to successfully complete a software development project, with many of the basic concepts living on in the newer methodologies.

[C] Spiral

The demands for reducing the time to develop a usable software system make it difficult to strictly follow the Waterfall methodology. The Spiral methodology allows for multiple deliveries of usable software to the user by compressing the phases of the Waterfall method to deliver some portion of the ultimate system to the user while then working on the next portion.

Rather than attempting to deliver a complete system all at once, the desired user functionality is broken up into portions that can be incrementally delivered to the user. Each portion is then developed in turn using the basic Waterfall process and delivered as completed. User feedback from delivered portions of the system can then be incorporated into portions yet to be developed. In this way the user gets his hands on usable software early in the process, which helps to ensure that the system being developed is what the user required.

The Spiral methodology also benefits from the fact that most users really do not know what they want until they see it, and many times ask for features they really do not need. By delivering the system in smaller pieces with minimal functionality, the user can provide valuable feedback to the developers early in the process. The Spiral method should still be planned methodically, with tasks and deliverables identified for each step in the spiral.

[D] Rapid Application Development

Rapid Application Development (RAD) is a systems development methodology created to radically decrease the time needed to design and implement information systems. RAD relies on extensive user involvement, Joint Application Design sessions, prototyping, integrated CASE tools, and code generators. The RAD approach is most appropriate for projects that do not have to be 100 percent right the first time, but that can be refined as the software is used. Project scope, size, and circumstances all determine the success of a RAD approach. RAD is appropriate for projects with the following attributes:

A. The scope of the project is narrow and well defined.
B. There are a limited number of people that are involved in design decisions.
C. Users are available for questions at all times.
D. The data for the project is well defined and already exists.
E. The technical architecture is defined and in place.
F. The project team is small; preferably six people or less.

G. The technical requirements of the system are reasonable and well within the limits of the technology being used.

The major difference between RAD and other development methodologies is in the management techniques used. These techniques are:

A. Rapid prototyping—Software usable by the user is created as quickly as possible to enable the user to provide feedback. This requires close cooperation between the developers and the users, with emphasis on relationship management and change management. Knowing when to start prototype development is an important skill.

B. Iteration—There must be a commitment to make changes often based on user feedback. Development becomes an incremental process based on constant refinement.

C. Time boxing—This is a management technique that forces delivery on a set schedule. The scope can be changed for an iteration but the delivery schedule cannot.

RAD works well when the user community and the software development team have established an environment of mutual respect and trust.

[E] Extreme Programming

Extreme Programming, also known as XP, is an approach to software engineering first developed in the late 1990s by Kent Beck, Ward Cunningham, and Ron Jeffries. Kent Beck authored the first book on the topic, *Extreme Programming Explained,* which was published in 1999. XP is the most popular of several so-called agile methods that make an effort to reduce the complexity of the development process.

The XP process is intended to improve the efficiency of software development. It does this by delivering solutions early and often, keeping things simple, and recognizing that change is an inevitable part of the process. The fundamental characteristics of XP are:

A. **User Stories**—The planning process in XP is a joint effort of the customer and the developers. User stories are written on 4×6 cards and are used to communicate the desired outcome. Each user story is given a name and an overall description of what the customer wants. The development team then estimates the amount of time and effort required to deliver the requirements of the story. Each story must fit within the iteration time frame established by the team.

B. **Simple Design**—The design of any part of the system must be as simple as possible and still get the job done. Nothing is added that does not meet the requirements of the current story. No planning for the future is done, as the future is difficult to predict with accuracy.

C. **System Metaphor**—A consistent, organizing metaphor must be developed using a common terminology so that communication between the development team and the customer is error free.

D. **Coding Standards**—Coding standards are enforced to ensure consistency throughout the system. Two other XP practices, pair programming and refactoring, help to enforce coding standards.

E. **On-Site Customer**—An on-site customer ensures that the development team stays on track. The rapid nature of the XP development process requires that a customer be available at all times to answer questions and provide feedback.

F. **Small Releases**—Small releases allow the development team to put the system into production early, and to update it frequently. Each update cycle adds a few new features, and allows the team to get feedback from the customer much sooner.

G. **Continuous Testing**—Programmers using XP develop customer approved test plans before writing any code. The developer then knows when they are done—when the test plan executes cleanly, the code is complete. Once that is done, future changes can be more easily validated using these test plans. The use of automated testing tools greatly improves this process.

H. **Refactoring**—Refactoring is the process of continuously improving existing code. The goal is to keep the code as clean and simple as possible, most often by removing any duplicate code. By using the test plans completed for each part of the system, you can ensure that any changes made by refactoring do not introduce errors.

I. **Pair Programming**—In XP, all production coding is done in pairs with two developers using a single machine. This causes all code to be reviewed while it is being written, which is much more effective than trying to review code after the fact. Pair programming also encourages the sharing of best practices throughout the team.

J. **Collective Code Ownership**—Not only do developers work in pairs, but the pairs are reassigned on a regular basis, as are the parts of the system to be worked on. This ensures that no one person "owns" any part of the system, and it allows changes to be made without waiting for any one person.

K. **Continuous Integration**—All changes are integrated into the complete system. This helps eliminate integration problems since they are caught earlier in the process.

L. **Forty Hour Work Week**—Tired programmers tend to make more mistakes. XP considers overtime to be a sign of a poorly managed project.

These 12 characteristics of XP are derived from software development principles that are known to be good, and are taken to an extreme in XP:

1. **Communication**—Communication and interaction between the customer and the developers is good. Therefore, an XP team should have a customer on site that answers questions and helps to prioritize the work.

2. **Learning**—Learning is good, so have the developers work together in pairs to more easily spread the group knowledge. As a manager, you also get quicker feedback on new team members.
3. **Simple Code**—Simple code is more likely to work. Therefore, in XP, you only write the code you need today to meet the customer's requirements. You also rewrite any code that becomes too complex.
4. **Code Reviews**—Reviewing code is a good practice. XP programmers work in pairs, sharing one screen and keyboard (which also improves communication) so that all code is reviewed as it is written.
5. **Testing**—Testing code is good. In XP, tests are written before the code is written. The code is considered complete when it passes the tests. The system is tested regularly using all automated tests to ensure that it works.

COMMENT

Excellent sources of additional information on XP include the *Manifesto for Agile Software Development* (*www.agilemanifesto.org/*), Ron Jeffries' Web magazine at *Xprogramming.com—an Extreme Programming Resource* (*www.xprogramming.com/*), and the *Extreme Programming Roadmap* at *http://c2.com/cgi/wiki?ExtremeProgrammingRoadmap*.

Two of the more controversial aspects of XP from a project manager's perspective are the concepts of pair programming and refactoring. To a project manager experienced with other software development methodologies, pair programming looks like two people doing the job of one; and refactoring looks like fixing something that is not broken.

Pair Programming. Pair programming is probably the most controversial practice in XP. The typical reaction of management is that two people are getting paid to perform one job. Pair programming is—as the name implies—two programmers at a single workstation. One programmer is at the keyboard "driving," while the other is helping to solve problems and review the code as it is being written. The programmers take turns at each task. The pair collaborates on the design, coding, and testing of every line of code written.

Objections by management include:

A. Having two people at one workstation cannot be very cost effective.
B. If two people are doing the work of one, it is going to take twice as long.
C. That is not the way we have always done things around here.

Programmers who have never tried pair programming are not usually excited about trying it. Most programmers have been trained to work alone. Objections by programmers include:

A.   Working with another person will slow me down.
B.   I am used to working by myself; I need peace and quiet to think.
C.   That is not the way we have always done things around here.

While all of these objections seem intuitively obvious, studies that have looked at XP have shown numerous benefits for the Project Manager and the members of the team. Benefits for the Project Manager include:

A.   Improved team training.
B.   Knowledge sharing is built into the process as pairs are switched.
C.   Positive peer pressure increases productivity and rate of learning.
D.   Quality is improved through greater defect prevention and defect removal.
E.   All production code has been tested and reviewed.
F.   Improved design, coding, and testing.
G.   Faster and more accurate feedback on new team members.

Benefits for the team members include:

A.   Less time is wasted being stuck on a problem.
B.   Feedback on ideas is immediate.
C.   Better able to solve problems due to the synergy created by working in pairs.
D.   Greater exposure to different parts of the application.
E.   Empowered to try new things without worrying about breaking the system.

In order for pair programming to work, each person must understand his or her role and responsibilities to make the pairing a success. In an XP pair, the person using the keyboard is called the "driver," and the other member of the pair is called the "observer." Both have to do their job correctly to make the pair work. The role of the driver is to:

A.   Control the keyboard and mouse to actually enter the code or design.
B.   Discuss options and ideas with the observer.
C.   Brainstorm as required with the observer and others.
D.   Think tactically about how to implement the solution.

The role of the observer is to:

A.   Actively observe the work of the driver.
B.   Watch for defects.
C.   Discuss options and ideas with the driver.
D.   Think strategically about the direction the solution is going.

While the benefits of XP are many, it can be difficult to introduce the practice within an existing team. Some of these difficulties include:

A. Resistance from team members.
B. Personality conflicts within pairs.
C. Egos getting in the way.
D. Driver not accepting advice.
E. Observer not actively participating.
F. Selling the idea to management.
G. Negative attitudes from team members such as:
   1. Not wanting to be a team player.
   2. Being defensive toward suggestions.
   3. Cowboy mentality.
   4. Impatience with less knowledgeable teammates.
   5. Fear of others discovering your lack of knowledge.

So how do you get started using XP with your team? The first step is to educate all of the team members on the process and the benefits it can provide. A small initial project works best, where a few members of the team can get their feet wet with pairing. It will take some time before the team becomes comfortable with XP, but 90 percent of programmers who have tried XP actually prefer it to other methodologies.

Some keys to successfully using pair programming include:

A. Play nice.
B. Check your ego at the door.
C. Do not take criticism too seriously.
D. Clean up your mess.
E. Share everything with your partner.

Refactoring. To the uninitiated, refactoring looks a lot like fixing things that are not broken. But the reality is that as a system evolves, changes made to the code at least indirectly affect all the code in the system. Refactoring is taking the time to review code that has not been changed recently to ensure that it is still the most appropriate code to support the current state of the system. When a change is made to the code, refactoring does not just look at what needs to be changed, but also looks at how the code can be improved or simplified. Constant refactoring improves the design of existing code, and helps to prevent unintended side effects from causing problems later.

One of the main goals of refactoring is to keep the code as simple as possible. Nothing is added to the code that is not needed *now*. Code should be refactored when:

A. A new function or object is added.
B. Code is reviewed.
C. A bug is being fixed.
D. There is redundant code.
E. The code becomes complex.
F. New functionality is added.

§ 29.04 PROGRAMMING CONVENTIONS

[A] Coding Conventions

There may be a different format coding convention for each programming language used. RAD and CASE tools conventions, depending on the vendor, may not be similar to other language tools. In any case, conventions should be used consistently. Some suggestions for creating policies specific to your environment are listed below:

A. Program coding.
   1. Coding format is restricted by compiler language specifications.
   2. All program source code should have programmer's name, program title, page number, and date at beginning of each source module or object.
B. Character representation.
   1. Special care should be exercised in coding to distinguish alphabetic uppercase O and numeric zero (0). To avoid confusion, never use a zero in a field name—only as a number.
C. Comments or notes.
   1. Comments or notes should be used to explain special mathematical or programming techniques at that point in the program where these techniques appear. Use them freely—especially before each major section of code.
D. Names used in programming.
   1. Data element names and variable names should be related to the type of data being stored.
   2. Size of names used is limited by the naming conventions of the language.
   3. Procedure names used for programming should correspond to names of those procedures used in program flowcharts.

COMMENT

One popular naming convention is "Hungarian notation," invented by Microsoft's chief architect Dr. Charles Simonyi, and is widely used by Microsoft. It became known as Hungarian notation because Simonyi is originally from Hungary and the prefixes give the variable names a non-English look. Documentation on the use of Hungarian notation can be found on Microsoft's Web site at *http://msdn2.microsoft.com/en-us/library/aa260976(VS.60).aspx*. This notation ties the data element to its originating field making it easy to trace data elements back to their source.

E. Error messages embedded within a program should clearly describe what the problem is and *where* in the program it occurred. You should also include instructions to the user as to what to do. For example, to troubleshoot this error, the PC must be left as-is until the programmer examines the program, or it could direct the user to reload the data file, etc. This assists the user because he or she knows if and how to proceed.

[B]   Controls

It is the programmer's responsibility to incorporate into a program the controls specified by the program supervisor, systems analyst, or auditor. Programmers should identify any additional controls necessary for the proper processing of data through the system. These controls may focus on such details as:

A. Specifying the use of standard labels.
B. Sequence checking input files.
C. Validating vital input elements not checked by a previous program.
D. Showing specific control totals to be accumulated within program.

§ 29.05   SOFTWARE ACQUISITION

[A]   Overview

The decision to purchase software is typically made when in-house development cost is prohibitive or programming talent is unavailable in the timeframe required. It is a waste of money to write software already available as an off-the-shelf, shrink-wrapped package. One type of packaged software, known as horizontal software, is widely available for PCs, such as word processors, spreadsheets, or personal database programs. The other type of packaged software, vertical software, has a much more limited market. It is used for specific procedures by organizations that have common needs, such as a billing system for hairdressers.

If a shrink-wrapped program is not available, you can contact outside software contractors for bids. Contractors can work at their facilities or yours. How much control the company wants over product development will govern where the contractors work. Different procedures for requesting a purchasing order and for payment of the invoice will be required, depending on where the work is done.

[B]   IT Purchased Software

The IT Manager should delegate the job of coordinator of IT software purchasing. This person is responsible for ensuring that all software requested is on the approved software list. The coordinator is also responsible for ensuring that the software inventory is kept current and that all licenses are accounted for. He or she should generate a periodic report informing the IT Manager of all purchases, budget status, and software license status. See Policy ITP-29-2 Acquisition of Computer Software as an example.

POLICY ITP-29-2. Acquisition of Computer Software

Policy #:	ITP-29-2	Effective:	03/18/09	Page #:	1 of N
Subject:	Acquisition of Computer Software				

1.0 PURPOSE

This policy defines the process for purchasing computer software.

2.0 SCOPE

The policy applies to all software applications purchased by the company. It applies both to the IT department and to software purchased by end users.

3.0 POLICY

The IT Manager will designate an IT staff member to be the coordinator of IT software purchasing. This person will oversee the purchasing of all software used at the company. The following procedures must be followed when purchasing new software.

IT software requisition procedure. The coordinator of IT software purchasing is sent a memo listing the software requested, the reason for the request, and the date by which the software is needed. The coordinator checks the approved software purchasing lists by name and kind of software. The coordinator then prepares a purchase requisition. If the coordinator can approve the requisition, information will be extracted for the monthly software report before the requisition is sent to purchasing. If not, it will be forwarded to the IT Manager for his or her approval.

The IT Manager will approve or deny the request, note the decision on the requesting memo, sign and date it, and return it to the software coordinator.

The coordinator will take the approved requests and issue purchase requisitions. Information will be extracted for the monthly software report before the purchase requisitions are sent to purchasing. The IT Manager must sign the requisitions before they are sent on to purchasing. The IT Manager, providing any information as to why the request was denied, will answer the unapproved requisitioning memos. The original requesting memos, requisition copies, and reply memos will be filed in the form of hardcopies or scanned and saved.

IT monthly software report. The software coordinator should report the following information to the IT Manager by memo on a monthly basis:

A. Cumulative expenditures to date for software.
B. Balance of budget to date.
C. Name and cost of software purchased.
D. Total amount spent to date by kind of software purchased.
E. Name of software purchased by each organizational unit and dollars spent.
F. Total spent to date by each unit.
G. Monthly license maintenance fee per product (if any).
H. Expiration date for each software license (if applicable).

Payment of invoice. For purchase orders to be paid, the IT software coordinator has to confirm the software has been received. If there are any problems, the coordinator should notify accounts payable to hold up payment to the vendor. If the software is returned, purchasing and accounts payable should be notified. If the vendor will not accept the returned software, and there is a problem with it, this information should be given to the IT Manager. If the vendor requires a rewrapping charge, the original purchase order is canceled and a new requisition written for the rewrapping charge, which will have to be applied to the software expense list and identified as such.

4.0 REVISION HISTORY

Date	Revision #	Description of Change
03/18/07	1.0	Initial creation.

5.0 INQUIRIES

Direct inquiries about this policy to:

Tom Jones, CIO
Our Company, Inc.
2900 Corporate Drive
Columbus, OH 43215

Voice: 614-555-1234
Fax: 614-555-1235
E-mail: tjones@company.com

Revision #:	1.0	Supersedes:	N/A	Date:	03/18/09

> **COMMENT**
>
> The addition of new software technology to an IT department increases the technical requirements on an IT staff. Each new tool comes with an implied requirement for software maintenance support, staff training, documentation, etc. This may be easier to say than to do. One CIO made a rule that for every new tool added to the data center, one had to leave. Despite this, four years later the number of software tools had risen by 10 percent.

[C]   Other Unit Software Requisition Procedures

Other business units that have their own budget for software should use the same procedures as for other purchases. The information systems unit should publish a list of approved software they support. Training costs time and money. There is far more software in the world than there is time to learn it. If someone sneaks around and installs non-standard software, it will be difficult for the IT staff to assist him or her. If the person calls for help, there is no point in denying the request, but it will not be a high priority. In these cases, IT may purchase some service desk support time from the vendor, but funds from the customer's department should be used.

The small print on a software package lists restrictions in force unless the vendor guarantees something else in writing. License restrictions should be reviewed before the seal is broken on the program disk container since it is usually impossible to return opened software. If the seal is broken and the software does not perform as expected, ask the purchasing department to contact the vendor. Send a memo to accounts payable instructing a hold on payment of the invoice until the problem is resolved.

[D]   Contract Programming

Purchasing contract software is governed by the organization's policy for contracting outside services. The purchase order should contain a statement describing an acceptable program as noted in § 29.05[G], "Beta Software Testing and Evaluation." In addition, if this software is written exclusively for your company, a clause should be included in the purchase that specifies the company will have complete ownership of the software copyright. (It is unsettling to see a contract programmer selling on the open market the software you paid to have him develop. When in doubt, refer to your legal counsel concerning copyright ownership.)

The vendor must provide the source code that will be converted to executable code and tested, as well as the software documentation. These results will be compared with the vendor's test output to ensure it is the same. The vendor will be provided with test data that has been approved and/or generated by the user, and a copy will be used for the final (in-house) source code test.

Once the software has been purchased, there is little leverage to get corrections made (assuming the firm is still in business when corrections are needed). Therefore, the prudent IT Manager sends the contract and/or purchase order specifications to the organization's legal department before signing any commitments.

[E]   Contract Programmers

Contract (temporary) programmers may or may not work in-house, but are paid by the hour to work on assigned projects. When contract programmers start, the person they are reporting to should give them a short introduction to the staff, a tour of the facilities, and information about the company's established policies and procedures for programming and documentation. Giving them samples of previous project efforts to review would be helpful. Contract persons working at the firm's IT site should be provided with a desk and required tools. Other information about working with contract programmers is provided in Chapter 12, "Vendors: Getting the Goods."

The contract person should be monitored closely during the first week or two to ensure proper job performance, in addition to the regular progress reports filed weekly by all programmers. Any personality problems with staff or users also should be noted and addressed promptly.

[F]   Evaluation of Packaged Software

There are some major issues to address when purchasing packaged software that can apply to almost any type of software supplier. Use the list below to develop policy specific to your organization on how packaged software is to be evaluated.

A.   Will the vendor be in business next year?
B.   What warranty will be provided?
C.   Will the software integrate with other software used by the company?
D.   Will the software adapt to the company's information systems standards?
E.   How flexible is the software package?
F.   Is current company hardware compatible with the proposed software?
G.   Will documentation provided be user-friendly?
H.   What type of training is offered?
I.   What other expenses will be required?
J.   Can the vendor provide modifications to the software?
K.   Is there an upgrade planned in the near future?
L.   Is there a vendor service desk?
M.   What is the vendor's reputation?
N.   How many will use software?
O.   Is there a users' support group?
P.   Will the vendor supply names of current users? If answer is yes, contact him or her and ask for names of other users to contact.
Q.   What is the major business focus of the vendor?

To discover how difficult or easy it will be to implement the proposed software, the following issues should be addressed:

A. How complex is the installation procedure, including the initial data load?
B. Will the vendor provide installation assistance?
C. How easy is the software to maintain?

To evaluate vendor-supplied software, ask current or former users the following:

A. Would they buy from the same vendor again?
B. Did the software perform as promised?
C. Was the training of value?
D. Was the documentation easy to follow and complete?
E. Were there any implementation problems?
F. Did installation or operation have any hidden costs (to find real cost of installation and data conversion)?
G. Would the referenced user allow a visit to his or her site to see how the software is working and talk to operations personnel?

New packaged software must be evaluated, whether for new applications or for placement on the "approved purchase list," especially if this purchase commits the company to buy in volume. Depending on the software being evaluated, consider using the following procedures.

General use software evaluation. A person or formal committee will be responsible for general-use packaged software evaluation. A request for such evaluation can come from a user, a systems analyst, information systems management, or the party performing the evaluation. The person or committee responsible will be a source for packaged software information consulting services. Worksheet 29-1 is a sample form used for software evaluation.

Whenever possible, more than one vendor should be evaluated for the same kind of software. Computer publications and Web sites, as well as their advertisements, are good sources of evaluation information. Keep an information folder for each type of packaged software evaluated.

Client/server and vertical software evaluation. Client/server and vertical packaged software will require a preliminary operations hands-on test followed by controlled client/server prototype operations testing. Users' evaluation also will be required. The time required for each controlled group prototype test will vary with the complexity of the software operation and the number of planned future users. The more users, the safer the software should be (e.g., free of bugs). The time required for testing also would be limited by the vendor, the time limit on returning the software, or when the invoice has to be paid.

[G] Beta Software Testing and Evaluation

In their quest for a competitive advantage, some companies reach out to the leading edge of technology. Often, this involves assisting in the testing of

WORKSHEET 29-1.   Software Evaluation Worksheet

<table>
<tr><td colspan="5" align="center">Software Evaluation Worksheet</td></tr>
<tr><td>Software Title:</td><td></td><td>Version:</td><td></td></tr>
<tr><td>Vendor:</td><td></td><td>Description:</td><td></td></tr>
<tr><td>Vendor Address:</td><td colspan="3"></td></tr>
<tr><td>Contact Person:</td><td></td><td>Phone #:</td><td></td></tr>
<tr><td>PO #:</td><td></td><td>Date:</td><td></td></tr>
<tr><td>Date(s) Software Tested:</td><td></td><td>By:</td><td></td></tr>
<tr><td>Copied to Server:</td><td></td><td>Date:</td><td></td></tr>
<tr><td colspan="2">Rights Are Assigned/Flagged (list rights):</td><td colspan="2"></td></tr>
<tr><td colspan="4">Software Copied to Other Servers (list):</td></tr>
<tr><td colspan="4">Software Evaluation (attach extra pages and documents):</td></tr>
<tr><td colspan="4">Documentation Evaluation (attach extra pages and documents):</td></tr>
</table>

products that are still in development. This is known as beta testing (alpha testing is done by the programmers). Beta testing agreements commit the company to apply some of its hardware and personnel resources to further debug a product. The advantage to the company is to gain in-depth knowledge of a leading-edge product or technology and how to best use it before it is released to the general marketplace.

However, the cost to a company can be high. One or more technical people must be dedicated for a considerable amount of time to learn a product that is still changing. The product being tested can crash at any time, corrupt company files, and even lock up the hardware platform it is running on. There is no guarantee that the final commercial version of the product will even possess the key functions the company desires.

In general, IT policy should discourage beta testing products. Technical people by nature enjoy working with the latest technologies and tend to quickly volunteer for such programs. A firm policy against this will inhibit the flow of beta requests. The policy also must strictly forbid the installation of any beta products without the IT Manager's approval.

Any beta commitments should require the prior approval of the head of information systems or a designated agent. Any commitments to use beta testing should be limited to pilot operations not part of the corporate information systems operation. No beta operations should be planned beyond the time limit specified by the vendor.

Beta testing should not have access to the corporate system or database at any time but will be limited to client/server, workgroup, or stand-alone PC systems. It should not have contact with any processing or database that is under the domain of the auditors.

All costs associated with a beta testing operation should be monitored and reported monthly to the head of information systems. In addition, a final report should be submitted after beta testing is complete. The following should be reported:

A. **Personnel time.** Personnel time used should be kept for IT staff, user employees, and other workers. The total time for each group should be reported. If required by the head of IT, the dollar cost by each group, the total cost, and any overtime incurred because of beta testing should be listed and identified in the report.

B. **Other costs.** Costs, other than personnel, also should be reported. This covers such items as: supplies, postage, telephone calls, costs of outside services rendered, any charge-back services (computer, copies made, etc.), and expense account reimbursements.

C. **Beta operating problems.** Any beta testing and/or operating problems occurring during the month should be reported, with the estimated total cost of each occurrence. It should be noted if any problem has occurred before and, if so, how often.

D. **Vendors' contact documentation.** Copies of correspondence sent to vendors, telephone call notes, and e-mail sent or received should be attached to the report. The person writing the report should summarize comments addressing these issues.

E. **User reports.** Copies of beta testing memos or e-mail concerning the project should be attached to the report. The person writing the report should summarize comments addressing these issues.

F. **Report summary.** The person writing the report should summarize the status of the beta testing. Any changes the vendor plans to make that would benefit the future use of the software should be noted. Any recommendation as to continuing or discontinuing the beta testing or any other comments worth noting should be included. Also, the question of whether the beta shut-down date will create any problems should be addressed.

G. **Final report.** A final report should be submitted after beta testing has been completed. Attached to the final report should be a copy of all completed Software Evaluation Worksheets (see Worksheet 29-1). Benefits derived from the beta test project should be reported in detail. The report also should include a summarized cost-benefit analysis and what final action was taken based on the beta testing.

§ 29.06   PROGRAM TESTING

[A]   Test Planning

Software written by IT programming staff or contract programmers, or contracted with an outside firm, will require program testing according to the procedures presented here. All new and updated programs require testing, the magnitude and complexity of which may be determined by the auditors. User acceptance should not be overlooked. Everyone concerned in the company may be happy with the test results, but unless the user is satisfied, operation problems may occur later. A formal test plan should be composed of the following:

A. **General information.** This section contains pertinent information needed to identify a program and the project with which it is associated. The following information is included:
   1. Project number.
   2. Programmer(s).
   3. Program identifier(s).
   4. Scheduled completion date.
   5. Date.
   6. Language in which program is written.
B. **Test plan.** This section describes the steps required for testing individual segments of each program's logic. The information includes:
   1. Program identifier.
   2. Function to be tested.
   3. Test number.
   4. Test priority.
C. **Approval.** This section contains the signature blocks required to approve the test plan and authorize the testing. The program supervisor or Project Manager also will use this part of the program test to indicate the type of testing to be conducted.

1. **Unlimited.** The programmer may test until completion without additional review and/or approval.
2. **Limited.** A specific number of tests is permitted before approval expires and a review to approve further testing is required.
D. **Test results.** This section reflects the progress of the program during testing, including date of the first test, systems tests, and volume test. If tests are run for the auditors, the date the auditors' presence is required will be noted.

[B]   Test Preparation

To ensure test data is representative, all conditions shown in the program flowcharts must be included. The flowchart can be reduced to a decision tree, showing only the decision points and the conditions for the decisions. This makes it easy for users or auditors to follow the decision conditions.

Another tool for test preparation is a decision table. (See Worksheet 29-2 for a Decision Table Structure.) The box labeled "title" contains the procedure title. The area labeled "condition stub" lists all possible conditions tested. The "action stub" area lists all actions that can take place. Under "decision rules" are listed "condition entries," the actual conditions that determine

WORKSHEET 29-2.   Decision Table Worksheet

Decision Table Worksheet									
TITLE	DECISION RULES								
	1	2	3	4	5	6	7	8	
CONDITION STUB			CONDITION ENTRY						
ACTION STUB			ACTION ENTRY						

how the data will be treated, and "action entries," the actions that determine which course to follow predicated on the entry conditions. A sample procedure for credit approval is shown in Exhibit 29-1. A decision table with an "else" rule is shown in Exhibit 29-2. For best results, someone other than coding personnel should prepare the test data. ***Never use live data for testing!*** Make a copy of it and, if possible, run all tests on similar but separate platforms. The developer may conduct preliminary testing, as long as someone else does the final test development. This procedure and use of the decision table enhance the potential for detecting errors.

Test material is retained and kept current for later use in testing systems and program specifications. Following are specifications for preparing test data:

A. The requirements outlined in the system specifications must be clearly understood.
B. The logic and major routines requiring testing must be reviewed and the findings documented.
C. The test data must be filed in the library or project folder. This material is considered part of the documentation and must be maintained during the life of the program.

The analyst or program supervisor responsible must review all system modifications to determine if any changes are required in the test data. When a

EXHIBIT 29-1. Sample Decision Table

Decision Table Worksheet								
CREDIT APPROVAL	DECISION RULES							
	1	2	3	4	5	6	7	8
ON APPROVED LIST	Y	N	N	N	N			
PAST EXPERIENCE OK	—	Y	N	N	N			
APPROVED CO-SIGNER	—	—	Y	N	N			
SPECIAL APPROVAL RECEIVED	—	—	—	Y	N			
APPROVE ORDER	X	X	X	X	—			
RETURN ORDER	—	—	—	—	X			
GO TO TABLE A5	X	X	X	X	—			
END OF PROCEDURE	—	—	—	—	X			

EXHIBIT 29-2.   Sample Decision Table With Else Rule

Decision Table Worksheet		
EMPLOYMENT	**DECISION RULES**	
	1	ELSE
COLLEGE DEGREE	YES	—
3 YEARS EXPERIENCE	VISUAL BASIC	—
APPLICATION FORM	GET ONE	—
INTERVIEW	SCHEDULE	—
DISPOSITION	—	REJECT

change is made, the programmer or test preparer conducts tests with the pertinent data to ensure the modifications are correct and have not affected other processing areas.

[C]   Test Analysis

Once the test cases have been prepared you are ready to test the software. Your testing policy should include the following items that should be carefully checked to avoid testing errors:

Input/Output

   A.   Proper heading format, line spacing, spelling, and punctuation of reports.
   B.   Correct data element size and content.
   C.   Report output matches expected specifications.
   D.   Correctly keyed-in data.

Problem Analysis

   A.   Original specifications are understood.
   B.   Flowcharting does not have logic errors.

C. Coding errors are not present.

D. No software revision errors exist.

[D] Operating Program Maintenance

Only maintenance programmers should have access to the software and be allowed to copy it for maintenance. The maintenance of running programs should be forbidden without the approval of the operations manager, and auditor if required. A violation of this procedure is grounds for dismissal.

After the required maintenance is completed, the program(s) should be tested. The procedures described in § 29.07[B], "Review and Acceptance of Test Results," should be repeated in order for the changes to become part of the production system.

[E] Testing

The purpose of testing a coded program is to detect syntax and logic errors. Syntax errors are detected while compiling a source program into an executable program and commonly occur when program-coding rules for the language being used are not followed. The compiler will identify the statement that contains the error by producing syntax error messages. In some cases, an executable program is not generated because of syntax errors. After all syntax errors are corrected, the compiler generates an executable program.

Use the test data prepared in desk checking (reviewing your code) to generate input data to test the program's functions. Several types of errors often are made by programmers and can be detected and corrected with the proper testing procedures. These errors are classified as:

A. Clerical errors.

B. Logical errors.

C. Interpretation or communication errors (these occur due to misinterpretation or misunderstanding of program requirements).

D. Data type errors.

There are tools available to automate testing. Some automated testing environments include:

Java programming	Junit	*www.junit.org*
Web development	e-Tester	*www.scl.com*
Windows development	TestComplete	*http://automatedqa.com/ products/testcomplete/index.asp*

Maintain a copy of the test plan with the program documentation. This will be handy the next time a quick change is made and a test is needed to verify the software.

> **COMMENT**
>
> Just how expensive can bad software be? In December 2005, the Tokyo Stock Exchange reported that a bug in its trading system software contributed to a trade mistake that caused an investment bank to lose $346 million. A trader entered an order to sell 610,000 shares at 1 yen each, when what he meant to do was sell 1 share at 610,000 yen. When they tried to cancel the order, they discovered that the system was not designed to allow a sell order to be cancelled while processing buy orders.

[F]   Audit Review

Rare indeed is the company that is not heavily dependent on computer technology. As business objectives and processes evolve, so must the data systems. Data systems audits are necessary to ensure that the computer systems in use continue to run properly and accurately.

Management bears the ultimate responsibility for having an IT audit policy that can assure them of the validity and integrity of financial and reporting programs. Auditors determine the actual audit procedures, and either internal or external auditors perform the actual audit.

Computer-related fraud is now an everyday possibility. Because of the disturbing rise in unauthorized access to databases, computer fraud, mismanagement, and lawsuits, IT managers and auditors have to be more security-minded than ever before.

Auditors approve and oversee financial programs. They also are very concerned with data's accuracy. IT managers should seek the auditor's approval to confirm reliability of financially related systems and programs. Audits are intended to:

A. Review all corporate computer programs under development or have maintenance performed to ensure that adequate and reliable audit controls are built into the system and program software.

B. Determine that specified controls are reliable within operational system programs.

C. Confirm that access to operating programs and databases by remote or network access is continually governed by security policies and technologies to prevent unauthorized access.

D. Confirm that established accounting standards have been met and employed by all information systems using them.

§ 29.07 SOFTWARE INSTALLATION

[A] Overview

Transferring a software program from developmental to operational status follows standard review and approval procedures. These procedures apply to programs developed by IT programming staff or contract programmers, or contracted with an outside firm. Purchased or completed beta tested software will follow the same procedures whenever possible. The conversion can begin only after the software or system passes all testing procedures.

Installation or conversion is placing into operation the tested software or system, which either replaces existing programs or is completely new. When discontinued software is replaced by a new system, the options are:

A. **Phased.** The new system can be installed in modular fashion or in phases. When one phase is identified as operational and accepted, the next part of the installation can begin.

B. **Direct.** Direct installation can be a complete, one-time conversion or installation. The old system will be replaced completely by the new. Operations has to be totally involved with the installation and operation of the new system software.

C. **Pilot installation.** The new system can be installed as a prototype operation in one safe location. After this operation is running properly, it may be installed in other locations. This type of installation is ideal for workgroups or independent PC operations.

D. **Parallel conversion installation.** This type of installation is most often used with corporate IT computer operations. It is the safest and most preferred method of installing a new software system, but also the most costly as it requires the business user to enter data twice—once into each system. If, after comparing output results and the database status of both systems, the results are compatible, the new installation is considered complete.

When no existing software is being replaced, new software installation can occur as phased, direct, or pilot installation. The other procedures for software installation are the same whether a new system is replacing an old one or not.

[B] Review and Acceptance of Test Results

To ensure that correct results are obtained from extended program testing, a review should be conducted with users, and auditors, if they are involved. Now is the time to bring to everyone's attention any concerns by the people who will be using this product. Acceptance should be confirmed by memo from involved users and/or auditors directed to the system Project Manager or the program supervisor. A vendor who is involved with the project should receive this information from the system manager and/or programming supervisor.

[C]   Review and Acceptance of Documentation

Technical and end-user documentation should be prepared according to established specifications. Any changes or additions should be conveyed by e-mail or hardcopy memo to the appropriate person in charge of documentation approval. Its acceptance should be conveyed by memo to the heads of programming and systems.

Documentation should be approved by the intended audience. The end users should verify that the instructions are clear and understandable by the technical level of their workers. Technical documentation will be accepted by the program manager if it is complete and conforms to the staff's normal document flows. Computer operations and service desk documentation focus on actions these teams must perform to support this product.

[D]   Acceptance of Contracted Software

The installation of contracted software should follow the same installation procedures as in-house developed software programs. Acceptance of purchased software as operational includes informing accounts payable via memo or e-mail that the invoice can be paid. The note should contain the vendor's name, item name and description, and purchase order number. If, on the other hand, the software does not meet the standards specified in the purchase order, a memo or e-mail is sent to the purchasing and/or accounts payable departments so informing them; the purchasing department will then inform the vendor.

[E]   Development Programmer Sign-Off

After the installation of the software is completed and accepted, the development programmers will no longer have access to the production system software. The source and object code is moved to an in-production library. This library cannot be changed without performing the routine change control turnover process. Access to this library is usually restricted to the maintenance programmers.

[F]   Selection of an Implementation Day

The first day that the revised program is to be run is very important. Some companies have a policy that all changes will go in on the same night of the week, such as Thursday. Then, on Friday, they are on alert to any problem arising from the change. This also allows time to alert the service desk so they can promptly call the programmer if anything unusual or unexpected is reported for that system during the rollout day.

A very good business policy is for the programmer to walk through the program with the business department who uses the code to obtain first-hand information of any start-up problems and to explain to the business users how to benefit from system changes.

§ 29.08 PROGRAM MAINTENANCE

[A] Types of Program Maintenance

Program maintenance tasks, maintenance responsibility, and maintenance conventions are required for program maintenance.

A. Program revisions are changes made that do not require a major logic change. Examples are:
   1. Updates of constants and other variables.
   2. Increases in dimensions of tables, arrays, or work areas.
   3. Implementation of hardware features.
   4. Inclusion of new software by recompiling a program.
   5. Correction of minor processing deficiencies.
   6. Conformation to programming standards.
B. Program modifications are changes involving the redesign of program logic or the relationships of the subprograms or components. They are required to accommodate changes in input or output specifications.

[B] Responsibilities and Controls

Policy should be developed that defines the responsibilities and controls of software in production. It should include the following items:

A. Testing or program maintenance will not be performed on any production software under the control of IT computers or workgroup systems. This will be done offline on a separate "test system," with no access to the production system software.
B. Testing or program maintenance should verify that changes have been made properly and that other sections of the program were not affected by the changes.
C. The programmer and program supervisor will review the final test output and documentation for correctness and completeness.
D. User management or IT computer operations management will require a sign-off before the modified software is placed into production. Once this occurs, the maintenance programmer will no longer have access to it. However, in case of an emergency the programmer may regain access under supervision and with the permission of user management or IT computer operations management.

[C] Conventions

In addition to the conventions outlined below, those established for program development (as found in § 29.03[A], "Coding Conventions") should be followed in performing program maintenance.

A. **Changes to flowcharts.** Flowcharts should be modified in the following manner:
   1. A new chart is drawn using the software used to draw the original flowchart. The changes are noted on the new chart, dated, and initialed by the programmer. Both old and new charts are filed.

    2. Additional pages added to flowcharts because of changes require off-page connectors to direct the flow to the inserted pages.

B. **Changes to reports.** Always retain one copy of the original report layout in the documentation.

    1. Include in your documentation an example report that illustrates all of the totals derived.

    2. Include screen prints of options the business user has to select reports, such as by date range or other criteria.

C. **Changes in program coding and testing.**

    1. A source program is copied into a new file before extensive changes are made. After testing is complete and the updated program put into production, the old source program may be saved to an archive directory or erased after 90 days.

    2. When testing program changes, the entire program must be checked, not just the routines that were inserted, deleted, or changed. Those segments not changed are tested to ensure the program will continue to function properly. The test data becomes part of the program documentation.

[D] PC Software Developed by End Users

Personal computers have evolved from glorified calculators to powerful machines. Fueling this change is a wealth of powerful software that is easily customized by the person using it. This can lead a manager down a dark and slippery path. Amateur programmers lack the depth of experience to include safeguards of data integrity in their programs. They change them on a whim without adequate testing. They are even friendly to a fault and pass around copies of their handiwork without tracking versions or who has copies of the program. When bugs are repaired, only the programmer's copy is updated. In short, this can create havoc if it is not closely controlled. Policy must be created to keep this under control. See Chapter 26, "End-User Systems: Do It Yourself Computing" for policy suggestions.

[E] End-User Testing Training

IT departments spend a considerable amount of time ensuring the accuracy of the reports and data issued to the business departments. Because of this, some people assume that any computer-generated report is accurate and do not question how it calculated the data or where the data came from. This can lead to faulty business decisions based on bad data.

If someone develops a spreadsheet or small database for his or her own use, it is his or her business. He or she knows where the data came from and how it works. But as soon as he or she begins using this report away from his or her own desk, you begin to see problems.

When training new users in the company, include instruction on data validation, editing, and how to cross-check results against samples of the input file. Most people care about the quality of their work and will appreciate this instruction.

[F] Stealth Systems

It is rare an IT department can address every business user request for new software or additional features in existing systems. This sometimes leads to a well-meaning but hazardous growth of stealth systems throughout the company.

Stealth systems are PC code written by someone for his or her own use to address a specific business problem. These will range from a department's home-grown vacation schedule to a Materials Management System. IT Managers cannot stop these systems from occurring. Instead, when it is reported that a PC system has become an integral part of a department's operations, or has jumped to another department, the IT department must evaluate its validity. The IT Manager must decide if there is a compelling business case for supporting such a system. If so, then that system must be removed from end-user control and subjected to the IT validation checks and safeguards. It becomes a production system just like any other. Further user changes are not permitted.

[G] Hidden Programming Staffs

Sometimes, end users frustrated with attempts to obtain data processing support within their company will hire their own programming support staff under other titles. These might be college interns or others who are trained in the basics of PC programming. The problem is the loss of IT policy control of these people.

There are two basic approaches to this—accept it or kill it.

Accepting this "secret IT staff" normally involves establishing the following policies:

A. The creation of a separate computing environment for these people to work in, typically on their own network and server. This reduces the likelihood that their efforts will bring down your more reliable production systems.

B. They are permitted to download data from the corporate files but never to upload anything to prevent them from adding back in bad data.

C. They are not permitted to write any software for anyone outside of their department and must adhere to IT policies concerning software piracy, antivirus protection, etc.

D. A requirement that all code be fully documented to the same standard as that maintained by the IT department. A copy of this documentation must be maintained in the IT library.

Quashing a secret IT staff means that the IT department must determine what business need this staff meets and then fulfill it. These people were brought in to meet a user requirement. If you take them away, the requirement is still there so IT must step up and fulfill it. The easiest way to do this is to take technical control of the people but leave their work assignments to the business department. The business department will continue to carry them under their budget. Since they are under your technical control, you can better ensure their code and data integrity meets your standards and can easily move the code around to other departments as required.

GLOSSARY OF IT TERMS

802.11 An evolving family of specifications for wireless local area networks (WLANs) developed by a working group of the IEEE.

ACTIVEX This Microsoft-based technology is designed to link desktop applications to the World Wide Web from within a browser. Activex allows software developers to create interactive Web content for their applications

ADWARE A software application that can display advertising banners while the program is running or via some other triggering mechanism. This is sometimes installed as part of a free program as a way to generate advertising revenue for the creators of the software.

AMERICAN NATIONAL STANDARDS INSTITUTE (ANSI) Organization devoted to the voluntary development of standards. It has worked with the computer industry to develop standards for languages such as FORTRAN and COBOL.

API (APPLICATION PROGRAM INTERFACE) A method of allowing an application to interact directly with certain functions of an operating system or another application.

APL (A PROGRAMMING LANGUAGE) A high-level language used for programming scientific or mathematical applications.

APPLET A Java program that can be embedded in a Web page.

APPLICATION A term referring to a software program that accomplishes a certain task.

APPLICATION LAYER The layer of the OSI model concerned with application programs such as electronic mail, database management, and file server software.

APPROVED LIST A list of computer software and/or hardware for which the IT department provides user support.

ARCHITECTURE A system's architecture is described by the type of components, interfaces, and protocols it uses and how these elements fit together.

ARCHIVAL BACKUP A procedure to back up or copy files in secondary storage onto another secondary storage device.

ASCII (AMERICAN STANDARD CODE FOR INFORMATION INTERCHANGE) A standard for encoding characters (including the upper- and lowercase alphabet, numerals, punctuation, and control characters) using seven bits. The standard set is 128 characters; IBM expanded this to 256 by adding an eighth bit to each existing character. This expanded set provides graphic, mathematical, scientific, financial, and foreign language characters.

ASP (ACTIVE SERVER PAGE) A Web page that has one or more ASP scripts embedded in it.

ASP (APPLICATION SERVICE PROVIDER) An older term for SaaS.

ASP.NET A set of Web development tools offered by Microsoft.

ASP SCRIPT A small computer program that runs when an ASP-based Web page is accessed.

AUDIT TRAIL A means of locating the origin of specific data that appears on final reports.

BACKUP A copy of a file, directory, or volume placed on a separate storage device for the purpose of retrieval in case the original is accidentally erased, damaged, or destroyed.

BAR CODE A printed pattern of vertical lines used to represent alphanumerical codes in a scannable reading form.

BENCHMARK A standard measurement used to test the performance of hardware or software.

BETA TESTING Using and testing software not yet put on the market by the vendor.

BI (BUSINESS INTELLIGENCE) A broad category of application programs and technologies for gathering, storing, analyzing, and providing access to data to help enterprise users make better business decisions. BI applications include the activities of decision support, query and reporting, online analytical processing (OLAP), statistical analysis, forecasting, and data mining.

BIA (BUSINESS IMPACT ANALYSIS) A systematic analysis of a company or business unit to identify its critical business functions and the impact to the company if these functions ceased to function. These business functions are linked to the IT systems that support them (lose the IT system, and that function cannot continue). Risks to the most valuable processes are identified along with mitigation actions to reduce the likelihood or impact of these risks. In the event of a disaster, the BIA indicates how much is lost per hour or per day for the length of the outage.

BIT A binary digit; must be either a zero (on) or a one (off). The smallest possible unit of information in a digital system.

BLOG A short form for weblog.

BLUETOOTH A wireless technology that enables communication between Bluetooth-compatible devices; used for short-range connections between two electronic devices.

BRIDGE A device used to connect LANs by forwarding packets across connections at the media access control sublayer of the data link layer of the OSI model.

BROADBAND Refers to high-speed data transmission in which a single cable can carry a large amount of data at once.

BROWNOUT A period with low voltage electric power because of increased demands.

BROWSER A program used to access the World Wide Web. It interprets HTML code including text, images, hypertext links, Javascript, and Java applets. Also referred to as a Web browser.

BUG A programming error causing a program or a computer system not to perform as expected.

BYTE Eight continuous bits representing one character in memory.

CALENDAR TIME The actual duration of a project, from the date it starts to the date it is completed. This includes both work and nonwork days.

CHANGE ADVISORY BOARD (CAB) A committee tasked with reviewing changes to be made to an IT system.

CHANGE COORDINATOR An individual designated to oversee the management of the change control process.

CHANGE MANANAGEMENT A general IT term that under ITIL identifies the process for ensuring changes do no harm on installation.

CHAT Another term for instant messaging.

CLIENT A computer that accesses the resources of a server. See Client/server.

CLIENT/SERVER A network system design in which a processor or computer designated as a server, such as a file server or database server, provides services to clients' workstations or PCs.

CLIP ART A collection of graphic images available for use with desktop publishing.

COBIT™ (CONTROL OBJECTIVES FOR INFORMATION TECHNOLOGY™) A framework of IT management best practices that assists companies in maximizing the business benefits of their IT organizations.

COMPILER A program that reads high-level program coding statements (source code) and translates the statements into machine executable instructions (object code).

COMPUTER STORE An IT support unit of information systems providing company employees with the opportunity to view and try out approved hardware and software.

CONTROL OBJECTS Used to maintain control of some aspect of IT. It might be security access to customer data; it might be read access to the payroll file, ability to manipulate data before or after processing, or even the ability to intercept data that should be confidential. COBIT has 215 specific control objectives.

COPY PROTECTION The inclusion in a program of hidden instructions intended to prevent unauthorized copying of software.

COST-BENEFIT ANALYSIS A projection of the costs incurred in and benefits derived from installing hardware, software, or a proposed system.

CPM (CRITICAL-PATH METHOD) A process used in project management for the planning and timing of tasks relying on the identification of a critical path. The time needed for the series of tasks along the critical path determines the total project completion time.

DAT (DIGITAL AUDIO TAPE) A popular tape backup format.

DATA DICTIONARY A list of data elements used in database management programs. Each data element contains information about its use, its size, its characteristics, who can use it, who can alter it, who can remove it, and who can only view it.

DATA ELEMENT A field containing an element of information used in records found in database management systems. Examples would be FICA number, name, part number, etc.

DATA INDEPENDENCE Data stored in such a way that users can gain access to it in a database system without knowing where the data is actually located.

DATA MANAGER A person responsible for the management of all corporate data. The database manager may report directly or indirectly to this person.

DATA PROCESSING The preparing, storing, or manipulation of information within a computer system.

DATA RECORD A complete addressable unit of related data elements expressed in identified data fields used in files and database systems.

DATA REDUNDANCY The same data stored in more than one location.

DATABASE An organized collection of information, in random access secondary storage, made up of related data records. There can be more than one database in a computer system.

DATABASE MANAGE-MENT PROGRAM A data application program providing for the retrieval, modification, deletion, or insertion of data elements. Database systems tend to reduce unnecessary "data redundancy" by providing a central location for accessing data.

DATABASE MANAGE-MENT SYSTEM (DBMS) The operating software system that provides for the access and storage of data.

DATABASE MANAGER The person responsible for managing the corporate IT database. This person reports to the manager of corporate information systems, but can report to the corporate data manager, too.

DATABASE SERVER The back-end processor that manages the database and fulfills database requests in a client/server system.

DATAFLOW DIAGRAMS A method of showing data flows all on one page. It starts at the lowest detail level, which is the system level. Corresponding process parts are all shown in more detail, each on its own page. Dataflow diagrams have their own flow-charting symbols.

DDOS (DISTRIBUTED DE-NIAL OF SERVICE) Denial-of-service attacks are attacks whereby a hacker floods a network server with data in an attempt to crash the system. A distributed denial-of-service attack uses multiple computers to attack at the same time.

DEBUGGING The procedure of locating and correcting program errors.

DECISION TREE A graphic representation of all possible conditions or processing alternatives and end results. It resembles the branches of a tree growing out from the main trunk.

DEDICATED FILE SERVER A file server that cannot be operated as a user's server work station. See File server.

DE FACTO STANDARD A standard based on broad usage and support.

DEFAULT A value or option that is chosen automatically when no other value is specified.

DINGBAT Stock symbol, such as a star, triangle, dot, or arrow, usually used for visual emphasis.

DISK DUPLEXING A method of safeguarding data whereby the data is copied simultaneously to two hard disks on separate channels. If one channel fails, the data on the other channel remains unharmed. When data is duplexed, read requests are sent to whichever disk in the pair can respond faster, decreasing the file server's response time.

DISK MIRRORING A method of safeguarding data whereby the same data is copied to two hard disks on the same channel. If one of the disks fails, the data on the other disk is safe. Because the two disks are on the same channel, mirroring provides only limited data protection; a failure anywhere along the channel could shut down both disks and data would be lost. See also Disk duplexing.

DOCUMENTATION The instructions and references providing users with the necessary information to use computer programs and systems or alter them at a later date.

DOCUMENT FLOWCHART A flowchart constructed all on one page showing the flow of documents used in a given system. It shows the documents traveling from left to right across a page from one user to another. Each user is in its own vertical column.

DOMAIN NAME The name that identifies a Web site (e.g., Microsoft.com).

DOMAIN NAME SERVICE HIJACKING A hack in which inquiries seeking one domain are routed to another domain without the user's knowledge. Such attacks on the Internet's control structures could make packets of information undeliverable, quickly snarling traffic on the network.

DNS (DOMAIN NAME SERVICE) A service on the Internet that translates a Web site name (e.g., www.microsoft.com) into the actual IP address for the Web site (e.g., 207.46.19.190).

DSL (DIGITAL SUBSCRIBER LINE) DSL is a modem technology that transforms ordinary phone lines (also known as "twisted copper pairs") into high-speed digital lines for ultra-fast Internet access.

DVD (DIGITAL VIDEO DISK) A high-density compact disk for storing large amounts of data, especially high-resolution audio-visual material.

ELECTRONIC MAIL (E-mail) A network service enabling users to send and receive messages via computer from anywhere in the world.

EMOTICON Common name for the small text-based symbols, such as the familiar smiley: :) used in e-mail to represent emotions.

EMULATOR A computer program that makes a programmable device imitate another computer, producing the same results.

ENCRYPTION The scrambling of information for transmission over public communication systems. The receiver requires the same technology key to unscramble the coded information.

END USER A person who benefits directly or indirectly from a computer system.

ERGONOMICS The science of designing hardware, tools, and the working environment taking into account human factors so as to enable people to interact more comfortably and more productively.

ERP (ENTERPRISE RESOURCE PLANNING) A software application that integrates departments and functions across a company into one computer system.

EXPERT SYSTEM A computer program containing the knowledge used by an expert in a given area that assists non-experts when they attempt to perform duties in that same area.

EXTREME PROGRAMMING A lightweight programming methodology that focuses on frequent testing, integration, and user review.

FAULT TOLERANCE Resistance to system failure or data loss.

FEASIBILITY STUDY A study to determine the possibility of undertaking a systems project.

FILE A name given to a collection of information stored in a secondary storage medium, such as a tape or disk.

FILE ALLOCATION TABLE A table on a disk recording the disk location of all the file parts.

FILE SERVER A computer providing network stations with controlled access to shareable resources. The network operating system is loaded on the file server and most shareable devices, such as disk subsystems and printers, are attached to it. The file server controls system security. It also monitors station-to-station communications. A dedicated file server can be used online as a file server while it is on the network. A non-dedicated file server can be used simultaneously as a file server and a workstation.

FILE SHARING The ability for multiple users to share files. Concurrent file sharing is controlled by application software, the workstation operating system, and/or the file server/database server operating system.

FLOWCHART Analysis tool consisting of a diagrammatic representation of a system process or abstract relationship, normally made up of labeled blocks or keyed symbols connected by lines.

FTP (FILE TRANSFER PROTOCOL) A protocol used to transmit files between computers on the Internet. An anonymous FTP is a file transfer between locations that does not require users to identify themselves with a password or log-in. An anonymous FTP is not secure, because it can be accessed by any other user of the Internet.

GANTT CHART A project scheduling tool using graphic representations to show start, elapsed, and completion times of each task within a given project. It can also show the planned scheduled (S) time and the actual completed

(C) time. The Gantt chart indicates the status of a given project at any point. A Gantt chart employing dollars can also illustrate money budgeting for given tasks vs. money spent.

GATEWAY A device providing routing and protocol conversion among physically dissimilar networks and/or computers.

GIGABYTE (GB, G-BYTE) A unit of measure of memory or disk storage capacity; two to the thirtieth power (1,073,741,824 bytes).

HACKER A technically knowledgeable computer enthusiast who enjoys programming but is not usually employed as a programmer.

HTML (HYPERTEXT MARKUP LANGUAGE) The authoring software language used on the Internet's World Wide Web. HTML is used for creating World Wide Web pages.

ICANN (INTERNET CORPORATION FOR ASSIGNED NAMES AND NUMBERS) A nonprofit corporation that is responsible for allocating IP addresses and managing the domain name system.

IEEE Institute of Electrical and Electronics Engineers, Inc. Develops standards for the design and use of technology, including computer-related technology.

IM (INSTANT MESSAGING) A form of communication over the Internet which involves immediate messages between two or more users who are online simultaneously.

INCIDENT MANAGEMENT An ITIL term for a controlling the resolution of a service disruption.

INFORMATION SYSTEMS The department within a company that is responsible for computer information systems processing and the storage of all centralized data.

INFORMATION TECHNOLOGY (IT) The different techniques required to perform the task of information systems processing. The technology units within the information systems organization are required to be orchestrated by the information systems manager.

IN-HOUSE Denotes that the task is done within the company.

INPUT DEVICE Peripheral hardware that inputs data into a computer system.

INTELLIGENT WORKSTATION A terminal containing PC processing capability that runs independently or in conjunction with a host computer.

INTERFACE A shared boundary between two systems, such as between data communications (terminating) equipment and data terminal equipment (DTE). Also a boundary between adjacent layers of the ISO model.

INTERNAL IT AUDITOR A person representing the company with internal information technology auditing. He/she follows the guidelines provided by the CPA firm's auditors. He/She is concerned with computer systems audit trails and the security of the hardware, software, and data.

INTERNET The largest network in the world. Successor to ARPANET, the Internet includes other large internetworks. The Internet uses the TCP/IP protocol suite and connects universities, government agencies, businesses, and individuals around the world.

INTERNETWORK Two or more networks connected by bridges and/or routers; a network of networks.

IP ADDRESS A code made up of four numbers separated by three dots that identifies a particular device on the Internet. Every device on the Internet requires an IP address to connect.

ISO 20000 The international standard for IT governance, based on ITIL.

ISP (INTERNET SERVICE PROVIDER) An ISP is used as your local connection to the Internet. It provides other companies or individuals with access to, or presence on, the Internet.

ITIL (IT INFRASTRUCTURE LIBRARY) An integrated set of best-practice recommendations with common definitions and terminology. ITIL covers areas such as Incident Management, Problem Management, Change Management, Release Management and the Service Desk.

KED (KNOWN ERROR DATABASE) A database where information for all known errors is maintained.

KNOWN ERROR An ITIL term for a known IT service problem that will be repaired later, and where the customer has a documented work around to maintain service.

LASER PRINTER A high-resolution printer that uses electrostatic reproduction technology, like electrostatic copy machines, to fuse text or graphic images onto plain paper.

LEASED LINE A full-time link between two or more locations leased from a local or inter-exchange carrier.

LIBRARY A collection of programs and data files for a computer system's offline storage.

LOCAL AREA NETWORK (LAN) The linkage of computers within a limited area so users can exchange information and share peripherals. This linkage can be wired or wireless.

MAINFRAME A large computer, generally with high-level and multiprocessing power and the capacity to support many users at once.

MALWARE (MALICIOUS SOFTWARE) A generic term covering a range of software programs and types of programs designed to attack, degrade, or prevent the intended use of a computer or a network. Types of malware can include viruses, worms, Trojans, malicious active content, and denial of service attacks.

MEGABYTE (MG, M-BYTE) A unit of measure for memory or disk storage capacity; two to the twentieth power (1,048,576 bytes).

METADATA Data about data. It may describe how the data was created, who created it and why, how it can be modified and accessed, and how it is formatted.

MILESTONES Used with Gantt, CPM, and PERT charting to show when measurable units of task(s) have been completed. With Gantt charts, the actual milestones can be drawn on the charts.

MODELING An analytical process based on mathematical network behavior formulas called models used to predict the performance of product designs.

MODULAR PROGRAMMING A style of programming requiring that program functions be broken into modules. It is a form of program segmentation and is the correct way to code procedural programs. This is also a good way to write reusable code. Quick BASIC and Visual BASIC programming require this type of program coding.

MSP (MANAGED SERVICE PROVIDER) Another term for a SaaS vendor.

NETWORK A series of points connected by communications channels. Public networks can be used by anyone; private networks are closed to outsiders.

NETWORK ADMINISTRATOR A local area network manager who is responsible for maintaining a network.

NETWORK INTERFACE CARD (NIC) A circuit board installed in each network station allowing communications with other stations.

NONDEDICATED FILE SERVER A file server that also functions as a workstation.

OBJECT CODE The machine-readable instructions created by a computer or assembler from source code.

OBJECT-ORIENTED PROGRAMMING A type of programming in which the data types and the allowed functions for a data type are defined by the programmer.

ONLINE DEVICE A peripheral device externally attached to a computer or available to other computers on a network.

PASSWORD A security identification used to authorize users of a computer system or given program.

PC (PERSONAL COMPUTER) Smaller computers employing microprocessor chip technology. These can come in various configurations, such as PDAs, mini-notebooks, notebooks, laptops, transportable desktop workstations, and microcomputers.

PC COORDINATOR An end-user person responsible for the coordination and operation of an end-user PC operation. The person can have full- or part-time responsibility for this duty, and can be hourly or salaried, union or nonunion.

PC MANAGER A person responsible for managing and providing support to and training for users of PCs. This person reports to IT management. Since this position is almost always a full-time responsibility, it is advisable it be filled by a salaried worker.

PDA (PERSONAL DATA ASSISTANT) A small hand-held computer used to write notes, track appointments, and otherwise organize your life. Early PDAs required data to be input using a keypad with keys the size of Chiclets, but more recent models (e.g., the Palm Pilot) use a combination of pen-based input and character-recognition software to accept user input. Many can also be used to send and receive e-mail and browse the Internet.

PEER-TO-PEER A network design in which each computer shares and uses devices on an equal basis.

PERIPHERAL A physical device (such as a printer or disk subsystem) that is externally attached to a workstation or directly attached to the network.

PERT (PROGRAMMED EVALUATION REVIEW TECHNIQUE) A planning and control tool for defining and controlling the tasks necessary to complete a given project. The PERT chart and CPM charts are one and the same. The only difference is the manner in which task time is computed. The CPM chart uses only one expected time. With the PERT system, the time required for each task is computed as follows: The longest expected time, the shortest expected time, and four times the expected time are totaled and divided by six. This gives the expected time needed.

PHISHING A form of identity theft in which an authentic-looking e-mail is used to trick recipients into giving out sensitive personal information, such as credit card, bank account, or Social Security numbers.

POTS Plain old telephone service.

PRINCE 2™ A project management technique developed in the UK. PRINCE2 is a highly structured "gate" approach good for large or complex projects but a bit too administrative for smaller efforts.

PRINT SERVER A device and/or program for managing shared printers. Print service is often provided by the file server, but can also be provided from a separate LAN microcomputer or other device.

PROGRAM RUN BOOK Operating instructions for the benefit of those who run a given program, including any restart procedures in case of program failure. Most often used by mainframe computer operators, but can also be provided for minicomputer operators and PC users.

PROJECT SLIPPAGE Occurs when a project's critical path milestone finish date is not met. The critical path of a PERT or CPM chart determines the project completion time. Projects that are not using PERT or CPM technology can have project slippage, too. It is first recognized when it becomes obvious that the project finish date will be later than planned. See CPM.

PROTOCOL A formal set of rules setting the format and control of data exchange between two devices or processes.

RECOMMENDED LIST A list of software that the IT department recommends and for which it provides user support. The list can also contain recommended IT hardware for users.

RECORD LOCKING A data-protection scheme preventing different users from performing simultaneous writes to the same record in a shared file, thus preventing overlapping disk writes and ensuring record integrity.

RELEASE MANAGEMENT An ITIL term for the area that controls the release of approved changes.

REQUEST FOR CHANGE (RFC) The process of proposing a modification to any component of an IT infrastructure or any aspect of an IT service.

ROUTER Hardware and software routing data between similar or dissimilar networks at the network layer of the OSI model.

RPO (RECOVERY POINT OBJECTIVE) The point where data was last backed up. The time between that point and the point of a disaster indicates how much data may be lost. This is determined by a BIA.

RTO (RECOVERY TIME OBJECTIVE) The amount of time that a company can be out of service due to a disaster before its survival is threatened. This is determined by a BIA.

SAAS (SOFTWARE AS A SERVICE) A process where software is deployed, hosted, and managed to multiple parties from a centrally managed facility. The applications are delivered over networks on a subscription basis. This delivery model speeds implementation, minimizes the expenses and risks incurred across the application life cycle, and overcomes the chronic shortage of qualified technical personnel available in-house. Sometimes referred to as on-demand software.

SAO (SELECTIVE APPLICATION OUTSOURCING) See SAAS.

SCANNER A PC input device that copies documents into computer memory.

SCHEMA Schema and sub-schema are the tools used to define the structure of a database.

SERVER A network device providing services to client stations. Servers include file servers, disk servers, and print servers. See Client/server.

SERVICE LEVEL MANAGEMENT The primary interface between the customer and IT. It negotiates cost effective service level agreements with customers and then works within the IT organization and external vendors to ensue the desired level can be provided. The agreed services and support levels are detailed in the service catalog which is created and maintained by Service Level Management.

SHIELDED TWISTED-PAIR CABLE Twisted-pair wire surrounded by a foil or mesh shield to reduce susceptibility to outside interference and noise during network transmission.

SIMULATION A technique for evaluating the performance of a network before downloading it. Simulation employs timers and sequences as opposed to mathematical models to reproduce network behavior.

SITE LICENSING Procedure in which software is licensed to be used only at a particular location.

SIZE SNOWBALL EFFECT The larger the project size and/or the longer the required project calendar time, the more likely that additional time and effort will be needed to complete the project. As more time and effort are required, these snowball, which in turn extends the finish date and increases the final cost. The user's needs change over time. The longer a project takes, the more the user can justify changes to the final product, and the number of changes will snowball. In addition, the changes that are required for a useable product also take even more time to install, which can justifiably require more changes.

SLA (SERVICE LEVEL AGREEMENT) A formal agreement between an outsourced service provider (such as a SaaS) and customers to provide a certain level of service. Penalty clauses typically apply if the SLA is not met.

SOA (SERVICE-ORIENTED ARCHITECTURE) A collection of services that communicate with each other. The services are self-contained and do not depend on the context or state of the other service. They work within a distributed systems architecture.

SOURCE CODE Written program code before the program has been compiled into machine instructions.

SPAM Common term for unwanted or unsolicited e-mail. To 'spam' someone is to send massive amounts of unwanted e-mail.

SPYWARE A general term for a class of software that monitors the actions of a computer user. It is usually installed without the user's knowledge, typically as part of software that the user downloaded from the Internet.

SURGE PROTECTOR An electrical device that prevents high-voltage surges from reaching the computer system.

SYSTEM OF RECORD The data source for a given piece of information. The system of record for any given data element is the single "version of the truth" for that data element.

THIRD-PARTY VENDOR A firm marketing hardware for manufacturers.

TURNKEY SYSTEM A system in which the vendor takes full responsibility for complete system design and provides the required hardware, software, operations manual, and user training.

TWISTED-PAIR CABLE Wiring used by local telephone systems.

UNSTRUCTURED DATA Data that is typically created by a human being for personal use, such as word processing documents and spreadsheets.

UPS (UNINTERRUPTED POWER SOURCE) A device providing electric back-up power to a computer system or other devices when the normal electric power fails. This occurs so quickly that the operation of devices that depend on electricity is not interrupted.

USE CASE A description of how end-users will use a software application. It describes a task or a series of tasks that users will accomplish using the software, and includes the responses of the software to user actions.

USER-FRIENDLY A computer system easy for persons with no computer experience to use, causing little or no frustration.

VISUAL BASIC A more advanced form of programming than Quick BASIC, available from Microsoft. Program operation is screen-driven, which makes the program user-friendly.

WALK-THROUGH A technical review of a newly designed program or system. The review is conducted by interested parties such as programmers, systems analysts, users, and/or auditors. Program walk-throughs are conducted by peer programmers to detect program errors. In a walk-through, people play the role of devil's advocate in reviewing another person's/team's effort.

WAN (WIDE AREA NETWORK) Any network extending more than a few miles. It can use more than one form of message carrying.

WAP (WIRELESS APPLICATION PROTOCOL) A standard used by mobile phones and other hand-held devices to access the Internet.

WEB BROWSER See BROWSER.

WEBLOG A journal stored on the Internet that is frequently updated and available for public access. Usually referred to as a blog.

WEBMASTER The person in charge of maintaining a Web site.

WEB PAGE An HTML document that is designed to be read by a Web browser.

WEB SITE A collection of Web pages.

WEP An acronym for "Wired Equivalent Privacy." WEP is a security protocol designed to create secure wireless (Wi-Fi) networks. It was the first widely used security protocol for Wi-Fi networks and has declined in use as more secure protocols have become available.

WI-FI Refers to wireless network components that are based on the IEEE 802.11 specifications.

WIKI A Web site that allows users to add and update content on the site using their own Web browser.

WIRELESS NETWORK A LAN system that does not require physical connections—information is transmitted through the air. Commonly referred to as a WLAN.

WLAN See WIRELESS NETWORK.

WORK SAMPLING Consists of a large number of random observations of predetermined tasks that an employee or group of employees perform. Data collected by the work sampling observations identifies the amount of time spent on each task.

WORLD WIDE WEB A subset of the Internet that consists of pages that can be accessed using a Web browser.

WORM A program that replicates itself repeatedly. A worm capable of penetrating networks could quickly overload the Internet.

WPA An acronym for "Wi-Fi Protected Access." WPA is a security protocol designed to create secure wireless (Wi-Fi) networks. It is similar to the WEP protocol but offers improvements in the way it handles security keys and the way users are authorized.

XML (EXTENSIBLE MARK-UP LANGUAGE) Used to define documents with a standard format that can be read by any XML-compatible application.

ZERO DAY EXPLOIT A malicious computer attack that takes advantage of a security hole before the vulnerability is known. So called because the software developer has zero days to fix the security problem before the first attack is made.

INDEX

References are to sections, exhibits and policies.

A

Accounting department
 project closeouts and,
  6.05[C]
 vendor relationships and,
  12.03[E]
Asset management
 generally, 17.02[A]
 data collection forms,
  17.02[G]
 hardware asset management
  policy, Pol. 17–2
 hardware strategy, 17.03[C]
 idle equipment collection,
  17.02[F]
 information databases,
  17.02[D]
 inventory
  generally, 17.03[A]
  conducting, 17.03[B]
  hardware strategy, 17.03[C]
  ongoing management,
   17.03[F], 17.04[F],
   Pol. 17–3
  on-site spare requirements,
   17.03[D]
  patch management,
   27.02[B]
  reports, Exh. 17–3
  service strategy, 17.03[E]
  software assets, 17.04[D]
 manager assignments,
  Pol. 17–1
 managers, 17.02[C]
 ongoing management,
  17.03[F], 17.04[F],
  Pol. 17–3
 on-site spare requirements,
  17.03[D]
 policy, 17.01[B]
 project scope, 17.02[B]
 purpose of, 17.01[A]
 scope of, 17.01[A]
 service strategy, 17.03[E]
 software assets. *See* Software
  assets
 tagging, 17.02[E]
 tracking equipment,
  Exh. 17–2
 user information, Exh. 17–1
Audits
 COBIT, 3.02[E]
 computer operation audits

generally, 8.06[B]
 computer room controls,
  8.06[C]
 data library controls,
  8.06[E]
 input data controls, 8.06[F]
 objectives, 8.06[A]
 output controls, 8.06[G]
 reporting, 8.06[D]
contingency planning, 8.08
data networks
 generally, 8.07[A]
 scope of, 8.07[C]
 security, 8.07[B], 8.07[D]
disaster recovery planning,
 8.08
ITIL, 2.03[B]
IT management audits
 controls, 8.02[C]
 financial analysis, 8.02[D]
 organization of IT, 8.02[B]
 purpose of, 8.02[A]
 sample policy, Pol. 8–1
legal mandates, 8.03[A],
 8.03[B]
policy, 8.01[C]
programming activities
 control
 generally, 8.05[A], 8.05[C]
 database management,
  8.05[D]
 post-implementation
  reviews, 8.05[E]
 standards, 8.05[B]
purpose of, 8.01[A]
record retention, 8.03[A],
 8.03[C], 8.03[D]
resource management
 personnel resources,
  8.04[C]
 scope of, 8.04[A]
 technical resources,
  8.04[B]
scope of, 8.01[A]
survival strategies, 8.10
types of, 8.01[B]
workstation audits, 8.09

B

Background checks, 10.02[J]
Backups
 generally, 15.03[A], 15.05[A]

Database Manager
 responsibilities, 15.03[C]
data mirroring, 15.04[B]
data retention, 15.07
designs for
 generally, 15.04[A]
 data mirroring, 15.04[B]
 data retention, 15.04[D]
 journaling, 15.04[C]
destruction of old media,
 15.05[D]
inspections, periodic,
 15.05[C]
IT Operations Manager
 responsibilities, 15.03[B]
legal mandates, 15.07
marking media for ready
 identification, 15.05[B]
Network Manager
 responsibilities, 15.03[E]
PCs, 18.04[F]
policy, 15.01[B], Pol. 15–1
purpose of, 15.01[A]
recovery of data. *See*
 Recovery of data
scope of, 15.01[A]
Shop Floor Systems Manager
 responsibilities, 15.03[F]
Software Manager
 responsibilities, 15.03[D]
station backups, 15.06
Telecommunications
 Manager responsibilities,
 15.03[G]
Beta software testing and
 evaluation, 29.05[G]
BIA. *See* Business impact
 analysis (BIA)
Business continuity planning
 generally, 7.02[A], 7.03[A]
 adding to, 7.04[C]
 "already available," 7.04[A]
 assumptions in planning,
  7.02[D]
 certification for, 7.06[B]
 checklist, 7.06[D]
 contact information,
  7.04[C]
 critical processes,
  identifying, 7.03[B]
 employee skills matrix,
  7.04[K]
 executive business
  continuity plans, 7.03[F]

experts, 7.02[B], 7.02[E]
interim copies, distributing, 7.04[B]
keys, 7.04[D]
policy, 7.01[B]
publications on, 7.06[A]
purpose of, 7.01[A]
reasons for, 7.02[C]
relationships, Exh. 7–1
restoration priorities, 7.04[I]
risk identification, 7.03[c], 7.03[D]
risk mitigation, 7.03[E]
scope of, 7.01[A]
service contracts, 7.04[E]
software asset lists, 7.04[H]
toxic material storage, 7.04[J]
training for, 7.06[B]
up to date plans, 7.05[F]
vendor contacts, 7.04[F]
walk-around asset inventory, 7.04[G]
web sites on, 7.06[C]
writing a plan
generally, 7.05[A]
contents of, 7.05[C]
need for, 7.05[D]
scope of plan, 7.05[B]
testing, 7.05[E]
up to date plans, 7.05[F]
Business impact analysis (BIA)
generally, 4.05[A]
benefits of, 4.01[C]
data collection
generally, 4.03[A]
business function description, 4.03[C]
glossary, 4.03[B]
identification block of questionnaire, 4.03[C]
IT applications supporting process, 4.03[C]
loss of business function, impact of, 4.03[C]
non-dollar issues, impact of on company, 4.03[C]
vital equipment, 4.03[C]
vital records, 4.03[C]
data collection planning, 4.03[D]
department meetings, 4.03[D]
interviews instead of questionnaires, 4.03[D]
questionnaire issuance, 4.03[D]
questionnaire recipients, 4.03[D]
respondent stratification, 4.03[D]
trials, 4.03[D]
data crunching
data gathering, 4.04[A]

initial reports, 4.04[B]
business unit, 4.04[B]
department, 4.04[B]
work group, 4.04[B]
defined, 4.01[B]
evergreen
business updates, 4.06[A]
IT updates, 4.06[B]
organizational chart, Exh. 4–1
project nature of, 4.02[A]
purpose of, 4.01[A]
recovery point objective, 4.05[C], 4.05[D]
recovery priority, 4.05[B]
recovery time objective, 4.05[C]
risk analysis, 4.05[E]
scope of, 4.01[A]
senior executive sponsorship, 4.02[B]
team building, 4.02[C]

C

Canadian Budget Measures Act, 14.04[K]
Capability Maturity Model, 27.02[F], Exh. 27–1
Change management, generally, 27.01
advisory board policy, Pol. 27–1
defined, 27.02[B]
patch management, *See* Patch management
policy, 27.01[B], 27.01[C], 27.02, Pol. 27–2
process, 27.02[D]
scope, 27.02[C]
CMMI, 1.02[A]
COBIT, 1.02[A]
generally, 3.02[A], 3.03[A]
Acquire and Implement domain, 3.03[C]
audit guidelines, 3.02[E]
changes in, 3.01[B]
computer security, 14.04[G]
control objectives, 3.02[D]
COSO and, 3.01[B]
Delivery and Support domain, 3.03[D]
executive summary, 3.02[B]
history of, 3.01[B]
implementation, 3.04
implementation toolset, 3.02[F]
ISACA and IT Governance Institute, 3.01[C]
management guidelines, 3.02[G]

Monitoring and Evaluation domain, 3.03[E]
operational framework, 3.02[C]
Planning and Organization domain, 3.03[B]
purpose of, 3.01[A]
scope of, 3.01[A]
College recruiting, 10.02[G]
Commodity vendors, 12.02[G]
Communication plans, 6.03[F], Exh. 6–3
Computer equipment disposal, 21.05
Computer operation audits
generally, 8.06[B]
computer room controls, 8.06[C]
data library controls, 8.06[E]
input data controls, 8.06[F]
objectives, 8.06[A]
output controls, 8.06[G]
reporting, 8.06[D]
Computer security
anti-virus policy, Pol. 14–1
Canadian Budget Measures Act, 14.04[K]
COBIT, 14.04[G]
COSO, 14.04[f]
disaster recovery planning, 14.03[G]
encryption, Exh. 14–3
FACTA, 14.04[I]
Gramm-Leach-Bliley Act, 14.04[D]
HIPAA, 14.04[B]
Instant Messaging, 14.03[I], Pol. 14–2
internal threats, 14.02[A]
ISO 17799, 14.04[J]
network design, 14.03[D]
objectives, 14.01[B]
passwords, 14.03[E], Exh. 14–2
people security, 14.02
physical security, 14.03[F]
PIPEDA, 14.04[H]
policy, 14.01[C]
process security
disaster recovery planning, 14.03[G]
Instant Messaging, 14.03[I], Pol. 14–1
network design, 14.03[D]
passwords, 14.03[E], Exh. 14–2
physical security, 14.03[F]
planning, 14.03[B]
software development, 14.03[C]
testing, 14.03[H]
threat analysis, 14.03[A]

purpose of, 14.01[A]
Sarbanes-Oxley Act, 14.04[C]
scope of, 14.01[A]
SEC rules, 14.04[E]
social engineering, 14.02[B]
software development,
14.03[C]
Consulting. *See* Temporary
personnel services
Contingency planning, 8.08
Continuing education,
10.05[C]
Continuity planning. *See*
Business continuity
planning
Contract employees and
project closeout, 6.05[F]
Contract programmers,
29.05[E]
Contract programming,
29.05[D]
Copyrights, 17.05[B]
Corporate firewalls, 19.02[E]
COSO, 1.02[A], 14.04[f]
Customer service. *See also*
Customer surveys
generally, 9.03[A]
applications support, 9.03[E]
communication, 9.02[E]
level of, 9.02[B]
metrics
generally, 9.04[A]
collection policy, Pol. 9–1
quality and, 9.04[B]
typical metrics, 9.04[D]
what to measure, 9.04[C]
operational *vs.*
developmental activities,
9.02[C]
opinion *vs.* fact, 9.02[A]
overhead, 9.03[F]
perceptions, 9.02[D]
policy, 9.01[B], Pol. 9–1
purpose of, 9.01[A]
scope of, 9.01[A]
separation of responsibilities,
9.03[D]
staff level requirements
generally, 9.06[A]
allocation of staff, 9.06[D]
performance goals, 9.06[B]
ratios, 9.06[C]
sample policy, Pol. 9–2
stand-by staffing, 9.03[B]
technical experts, 9.03[C]
voice of the customer,
9.02[F]
Customer surveys
generally, 9.05[A]
baselines, 9.05[C]
contents of, 9.05[B]
form, 9.05[D]
results, evaluating, 9.05[E]

service desk, 16.04[I]
team performance, 9.05[F]

D

Data backups. *See* Backups
Databases
access acquisition, 18.03[E]
asset management, 17.02[D]
ITIL configuration
management
generally, 2.02[D]
creation, 2.02[D]
up to date, keeping, 2.02[D]
programming activities
control, 8.05[D]
Dataflow diagrams, 13.08[F],
Exh. 13–5 to 13–8
Data management
legal obligations, 25.02[C]
ownership of data, 25.02[B]
policy, 25.01[B]
privacy. *See* Privacy of data
purpose of, 25.01[A]
record system, 25.02[A], Pol.
25–1
restricted data handling,
25.03[C]
retention of data, 25.03[B]
scope of, 25.01[A]
user roles, 25.03[A]
Data mirroring, 15.04[B]
Data network audits
generally, 8.07[A]
scope of, 8.07[C]
security, 8.07[B], 8.07[D]
Disaster recovery
Network Coordinators and,
19.03[C]
planning, 8.08, 14.03[G]
Disasters and the service desk,
16.05
Document management,
generally, 22.01
access, 22.03[A]
annotation and redaction,
22.03[B]
capture, 22.02[A]
designing a solution, 22.05
indexing, 22.02[C]
policy, 22.01[B], Pol. 22–1
printing and archiving,
22.04
disaster recovery, 22.04[C]
legal requirements,
22.04[A]
long-term storage, 22.04[B]
retention, compliance and
legal issues, 22.02[D]
retrieval and collaboration,
22.03
security, 22.02[E]

storage, 22.02[B]
workflow, 22.03[C]
Documentation
generally, 13.04[A], Pol. 13–2
access, 13.04[C]
desk reference
documentation, 13.05[D]
end-user systems, 13.05[B],
26.05[C], Pol. 26–1
flowcharts. *See* Flowcharts
formats
generally, 13.03[A], Exh.
13–1
knowing the audience,
13.03[B]
new user accounts,
Exh. 13–2
readability, 13.03[C]
management, *See* Document
management
Network Coordinators,
19.03[D], Pol. 19–3
operations reference
documentation, 13.05[C]
policy
generally, 13.02[A],
13.01[B], Pol. 13–1
objectives, 13.02[B]
process overview, 13.05[A]
program testing reference
documentation, 13.05[F]
project documentation,
13.06, Pol. 13–3
purpose of, 13.01[A]
quality enforcement,
13.04[B]
scope of, 13.01[A]
software installation,
29.07[C]
storage, 13.04[C]
system reference instructions
desk reference
documentation, 13.05[D]
end-user reference
documentation, 13.05[B]
operations reference
documentation, 13.05[C]
process overview, 13.05[A]
program testing reference
documentation, 13.05[F]
technical reference
documentation, 13.05[E]
systems analysis
documentation
generally, 13.07[A],
Pol. 28–1
binder, 13.07[B]
product specifications,
13.07[D]
recommendations,
13.07[H]
risk assessment, 13.07[F]
schedule, 13.07[E]

scope, 13.07[C]
stakeholders, 13.07[G]
systems analysis interviews,
  28.03[E]
technical reference
  documentation, 13.05[E]
version control, 13.04[D]

E

Education information
  booklet, 10.06[E]
E-mail
  generally, 10.07[C], 23.04[A]
  archiving, 23.04[F]
  etiquette, 23.04[D]
  Instant Messaging, 23.04[F]
  marketing, 23.04[E]
  messaging and blogging
    policy, 23.05
  peer-to-peer applications,
    23.04[G]
  policy, 23.04, Pol. 23–3, Pol.
    23–4
  tracking Internet usage,
    23.04[B]
  use agreements, 23.06, Exh.
    23–1
  use guidelines, 23.04[C], Pol.
    23–2
  web logs, 23.04[H]
Employees. *See* Staffing
Encryption, Exh. 13–3
End-user systems
  generally, 26.02[A],
    26.04[A]
  documentation, 13.05[B],
    26.05[C], Pol. 26–2
  evolution of, 26.02[B]
  examples of, 26.02[D]
  IT "strikes-back," 26.02[G]
  management objectives,
    26.04[B]
  mentors, 26.04[E]
  personal computing *vs.*
    corporate computing,
    26.03
  pitfalls of, 26.02[E]
  policy, 26.01[B], 26.05, Pol.
    26–1
  popularity of, 26.02[C]
  power users, 26.04[D]
  purpose of, 26.01[A]
  scope of, 26.01[A]
  sharing, 26.02[F]
  software maintenance,
    29.08[D], 29.08[E]
  software policy, 26.05[B]
  training, 26.04[C]
Energy reduction for
  equipment, *See* Green
    computing

Enterprise system flowcharts,
  13.08[C]
Environmental IT issues, *See*
  Green computing
Estimating factors in project
  management, 6.02[F]
Executive steering committee,
  6.06[E]
External opportunity
  postings, 10.02[E]
Extreme Programming,
  29.03[E]

F

FACTA, 14.04[I]
Firewalls
  corporate firewalls, 19.02[E]
  Internet security, 23.03[B]
  personal firewalls, 19.02[F]
  usage policy, Pol. 23–2
Firing employees, 10.04[F]
Flex-time, 10.10[C],
  Pol. 10–4
Flowcharts
  dataflow diagrams, 13.08[F],
    Exh. 13–5 to Exh. 13–8
  enterprise system, 13.08[C]
  global system flowcharts,
    13.08[B]
  IDEF, 13.08[J], Exh. 13–11
  procedure flowcharts,
    13.08[E], Exh. 13–3, Exh.
    13–4
  program flowcharts,
    13.08[H], Exh. 13–10
  purpose of, 13.08[A]
  supplemental dataflow
    conventions, 13.08[G],
    Exh. 13–9
  system flowcharts, 13.08[D]
  unified modeling language,
    13.08[I]

G

Global system flowcharts,
  13.08[B]
Gramm-Leach-Bliley Act,
  14.04[D]
Green computing
  generally, 21.01, 21.02,
    21.03, 21.04
  Advanced Configuration and
    Power Interface (ACPI),
    21.03[D]
  definition, 21.02[A]
  Electronic Products
    Environmental
    Assessment Tool (EPEAT),
    21.03[C]

energy reduction, 21.02[B],
  21.03
Energy Star, 21.03[B]
equipment reduction,
  21.02[C], 21.04[G]
  disposal, 21.05
  paper, 21.04[F]
  policy, 21.01[B], 21.02[E],
    Pol. 21–1
  pollution issues, 21.02[D]
  power usage, 21.04[B],
    21.04[D]
Restriction of Hazardous
  Substance Directive
  (ROHS), 21.03[E]
safe disposal, 21.05
telecommuting, 21.04[C]
"thin client," 21.03[G]
toner, 21.04[F]
virtualization, 21.03[F]

H

Hardware acquisition,
  18.03[B]
Help desk. *See* Service desk
HIPAA, 14.04[B]

I

IDEF, 13.08[J], Exh. 13–11
Instant Messaging (IM),
  14.03[I], 23.04[F],
  Pol. 14–1
Intellectual property
  ownership, Pol. 12–2
Internal opportunity
  postings, 10.02[D]
Internet
  generally, 23.01, 23.02
  acceptable use agreements,
    23.06, Exh. 23–1
  access, 23.02
  blogging, 23.05[B]
    policy, Pol. 23–5
  connection policy, Pol. 23–1
  corporate access, 23.02[C]
  e-mail. *See* E-mail
  individual access, 23.02[B]
  instant messaging (IM)
    policy, 23.05[A]
  network access, 23.02[C]
  objectives, 23.01[B]
  policy, 23.01[C], 23.04,
    23.05, Pol. 23–3
  purpose of, 23.01[A]
  SaaS vendor management,
    23.09
  SaaS vendor selection
    process, 23.08
  scope of, 23.01[A]

security, 23.03
software as a service, 23.07,
 Pol. 23–6
tracking Internet usage,
 23.04[B]
training, 23.03[D]
usage control, 23.03[C]
use agreements, 23.06,
 Exh. 23–1
use guidelines, 23.04[C],
 Pol. 23–2
Interns, 10.02[H]
Interviews
 business impact analysis data
  collection, 4.03[D]
 staffing, 10.02[I]
 systems analysis, 28.03[D],
  28.03[E]
Inventory of assets
 generally, 17.03[A]
 conducting, 17.03[B]
 hardware strategy, 17.03[C]
 ongoing management,
  17.03[F], 17.04[F],
  Pol. 17–3
 on-site spare requirements,
  17.03[D]
 patch management, 27.02[B]
 reports, Exh. 17–3
 service strategy, 17.03[E]
 software assets, 17.04[D]
ISACA, 3.01[C]
ISO 17799, 14.04[J]
IT Governance Institute,
 3.01[C]
ITIL, 1.02[A]
 "all or nothing" approach,
  2.06[A]
 auditable results, 2.03[B]
 availability management,
  2.03[C]
  new technology, 2.03[C]
  system resiliency, 2.03[C]
 books poorly written and
  inconsistent, 2.06[C]
 budgeting, 2.03[B]
 capacity management,
  2.03[D]
 certification, 2.04
  Foundations, 2.04[B]
  Practitioner, 2.04[C]
  Service Manager, 2.04[D]
  training and exams, 2.04[A]
 change management, 2.02[E]
  approval, 2.02[E]
  completeness of change
   package, 2.02[E]
  post change review, 2.02[E]
  scheduled changes, 2.02[E]
 coherence of model, 2.06[B]
 configuration management,
  2.02[D]
  database, 2.02[D]

database creation, 2.02[D]
database up to date, 2.02[D]
last working configuration,
 2.02[D]
relationships, 2.02[D]
 cost recovery, 2.03[B]
 financial management for IT
  services, 2.03[B]
  auditable results, 2.03[B]
  budgeting, 2.03[B]
  cost recovery, 2.03[B]
  history of, 2.01[B]
 implementation, 2.07
 configuration management
  database (CMDB), 2.07[C]
  leader, 2.07[B]
 incident management,
  2.02[B]
 new technology, 2.03[C]
 problem management,
  2.02[C]
 processes are artifact-centric,
  2.01[C]
 as a published standard,
  2.01[D]
 purpose of, 2.01[A]
 release management, 2.02[F]
 scope of, 2.01[A]
 service continuity
  management, 2.03[E]
 service desk, 2.02[A]
 service level management,
  2.03[A]
 Service Manager, 2.04[D]
 standards, 2.05
  British standard, 2.05[B]
  international standard
   organizations, 2.05[C]
  need for, 2.05[A]
 system resiliency, 2.03[C]
 training and exams, 2.04[A]
IT management audits
 controls, 8.02[C]
 financial analysis, 8.02[D]
 organization of IT, 8.02[B]
 purpose of, 8.02[A]
 sample policy, Pol. 8–1

J

Job descriptions, 10.02[B]
Job postings
 external opportunity
  postings, 10.02[E]
 internal opportunity
  postings, 10.02[D]
Job-sharing, 10.10[B]

L

Legal mandates
 generally, 8.03[A], 8.03[B]

backups, 15.07
computer security. *See*
 Computer security
data management, 25.02[C]
vendor contract reviews,
 12.03[C]
Low-volume vendors,
 12.02[H]

M

Manuals
 headers and footers, Exh. 5–1
 maintenance of, 5.04[D]
 organization, 5.02[A]
 page layout, 5.02[D]
 page numbering, 5.02[B]
 printing, 5.02[C]
 type styles, 5.02[B]
Mentors, 10.03[C], 26.04[E],
 Pol. 10–2
Metrics, 6.06[H]
 customer service
  generally, 9.04[A]
  collection policy, Pol. 9–1
  quality and, 9.04[B]
  typical metrics, 9.04[D]
  what to measure, 9.04[C]
 service desk, 16.04[B]
Models of governance,
 1.02[A]
 CMMI, 1.02[A]
 COBIT. *See* COBIT
 COSO, 1.02[A]
 ITIL. *See* ITIL
 PMBOK, 1.02[A]
 PRINCE2, 1.02[A]
 TickIT, 1.02[A]
 TOGAF, 1.02[A]

N

Network audits
 generally, 8.07[A]
 scope of, 8.07[C]
 security, 8.07[B], 8.07[D]
Network Coordinators
 generally, 19.03[A]
 disaster recovery, 19.03[C]
 documentation, 19.03[D],
  Pol. 19–3
 responsibilities, 19.03[B]
Networks
 generally, 19.02[A]
 coordinators. *See* Network
  Coordinators
 corporate firewalls, 19.02[E]
 design, 14.03[D], 19.02[B]
 Internet access, 23.02[C]
 passwords, Pol. 19–1
 personal firewalls, 19.02[F]

policy, 19.01[B]
purpose of, 19.01[A]
routers, 19.02[D]
scope of, 19.01[A]
user authentication, 19.02[C]
virtual private networks, 19.02[G]
wireless networks, 19.02[H], Pol. 19–2
New employee orientation
first impressions, 10.03[A]
mentors, 10.03[C], Pol. 10–2
orientation packages, 10.03[B]

O

Offshore staffing, 10.02[F]
Operations reference documentation, 13.05[C]
Outsourcing, 12.04[E]
relocation of technology, 20.02[C]
software as a service, 23.07[C]
training, 10.06[F]
Ownership of data, 25.02[B]
Ownership of software, 29.02[B], Pol. 29–1

P

Passwords, 14.03[E], Exh. 14–2, Pol. 19–1
Patch management
generally, 27.03[A]
asset inventory, 27.03[C]
Capability Maturity Model, 27.03[G], Exh. 27–1
policy, 27.03[B]
process, 27.03[D]
risk assessment, 27.03[E]
testing, 27.03[F], Pol. 27–3
tools, 27.04
Peer reviews, 10.04[D], Pol. 10–3
Peer-to-peer applications, 23.04[G]
Performance evaluations
generally, 10.04[A]
conducting, 10.04[B]
documentation, 10.04[E]
employee termination, 10.04[F]
peer reviews, 10.04[D], Pol. 10–3
periodic reviews, 10.04[C]
Personal Computer Coordinators
generally, 18.02[A]
in-house consulting service, 18.02[C]

newsletters, 18.02[E]
responsibilities of, 18.02[B]
training, 18.02[D]
Personal Computers
generally, 18.03[A], 18.04[A]
acceptable use, 18.04[B], Pol. 18–2
accessories and supplies, 18.04[I]
backups, 18.04[F]
communications acquisition, 18.03[D]
computer technicians and, 18.05[C]
coordinators. See PC Coordinators
database access acquisition, 18.03[E]
disposal, 18.04[J], Pol. 18–4
end-user technical support, 18.05
ergonomics, 18.05[E]
hardware acquisition, 18.03[B]
maintenance contracting, 18.05[G]
mobile device usage policy, Pol. 18–3
operation rules and procedures, 18.04[E]
peripheral device acquisition, 18.03[D], Pol. 18–1
peripheral device operations procedures, 18.04[H]
personal hardware and software, 18.04[C]
policy, 18.01[B]
purpose of, 18.01[A]
resident experts, 18.05[B]
scope of, 18.01[A]
security, 18.04[D]
service desk, 18.05[F]
software acquisition, 18.03[C]
software support, 18.05[D]
system crashes, 18.04[G]
Personal firewalls, 19.02[F]
PIPEDA, 14.04[H]
PMBOK, 1.02[A]
Policies and procedures
generally, 1.01[B]
acceptance criteria, 5.04[C]
annual policy review, 5.04[E]
approval process
generally, 5.04[A], Pol. 5–2
acceptance criteria, 5.04[C]
annual policy review, 5.04[E]
creation of policy, 5.04[B]
manual maintenance, 5.04[D]

sunset clause, 5.04[F]
asset management, 17.01[B]
audits, 8.01[C]
backups, 15.01[B], Pol. 15–1
business continuity planning, 7.01[B]
compared, 5.01[B]
computer security, 14.01[C]
creation of policy, 5.04[B]
customer service, 9.01[B]
data management, 25.01[B]
documentation
generally, 13.02[A], Pol. 13–1
objectives, 13.02[B]
policy, 13.01[B]
end-user systems, 26.01[B], 26.05, Pol. 26–1
establishment of policy authority, Pol. 5–1
format, sample of, Exh. 5–2
implementation, 5.03[C]
Internet, 23.01[C]
management authority, 5.03[A]
manuals
headers and footers, Exh. 5–1
maintenance of, 5.04[D]
organization, 5.02[A]
page layout, 5.02[D]
page numbering, 5.02[B]
printing, 5.02[C]
type styles, 5.02[B]
networks, 19.01[B]
patch management, 27.01[C]
PCs, 18.01[B]
policy, 5.01[C]
project management, 6.01[B]
purpose of, 5.01[A]
relocation of technology, 20.01[B]
responsibility for, 5.03[B]
scope of, 5.01[A]
service desk, 16.01[B], Pol. 16–1
software development, 29.01[B]
staffing, 10.01[B]
strategic planning, 1.03[B]
sunset clauses, 5.04[F]
systems analysis and design, 28.01[C]
vendors, 12.01[B]
web sites. See Web sites
PRINCE2, 1.02[A]
Privacy of data
generally, 25.04[A]
access to personal data, 25.04[F]
collection of personal data, 25.04[C]

Privacy Officer, 25.04[B]
security of personal data,
  25.04[E]
use of personal data,
  25.04[D]
Problem tracking database,
  16.03[F]
Procedure flowcharts,
  13.08[E], Exh. 13–3, Exh.
  13–4
Productivity of individuals
generally, 10.9[A]
employee productivity,
  10.9[C]
management productivity,
  10.9[B]
Program flowcharts, 13.08[H],
  Exh. 13–10
Programming activities
  control
generally, 8.05[A], 8.05[C]
database management,
  8.05[D]
post-implementation
  reviews, 8.05[E]
standards, 8.05[B]
Program testing, 13.05[F],
  29.06
Progress measurements,
  6.04[E]
Project closeout
generally, 6.05[A]
accounting department and,
  6.05[C]
contract employees and,
  6.05[F]
contractual issues, 6.05[F]
customers and, 6.05[D]
final report, 6.05[G]
sponsor and, 6.05[B]
team members and, 6.05[E]
Project documentation,
  13.06, Pol. 13–3
Project management
generally, 6.04[A]
basic rules, 6.04[C]
closeout. *See* Project closeout
definition of "project,"
  6.02[B]
estimating factors, 6.02[F]
hardware delivery, 6.02[G]
plans. *See* Project plans
policy, 6.01[B]
progress measurements,
  6.04[E]
project definition, 6.02[A]
Project Manager, 6.02[C]
purpose of, 6.01[A]
resources, 6.02[E]
scope changes, 6.04[B]
scope of, 6.01[A]
software delivery, 6.02[G]
sponsor's sign-off, 6.02[H]

task completion, 6.04[D]
Project management office
  (PMO)
generally, 6.06[A]
establishment, 6.06[B]
executive steering
  committee, 6.06[E]
metrics, 6.06[H]
policy, Pol. 6–1
project backlog
  management, 6.06[G]
resource management,
  6.06[D]
standardized project
  initiation, 6.06[F]
tool set establishment,
  6.06[C]
Project Manager, 6.02[C]
Project plans
generally, 6.03[A]
communication plans,
  6.03[F], Exh. 6–3
creation of, 6.02[D]
resources, 6.02[E]
risk assessments, 6.03[B],
  6.03[C]
risk mitigation plans, 6.03[D]
stakeholder analysis, 6.03[E],
  Exh. 6–2
Purchasing, 12.02[E]
Purpose of IT governance,
  1.01[A]

R

Rapid Application
  Development, 29.03[D]
Records
retention, 8.03[A], 8.03[C],
  8.03[D]
training, 10.06[C]
Recovery of data
generally, 15.02[E]
lifecycle of backups, 15.02[B]
recovery point objective,
  15.02[D]
recovery time objective,
  15.02[C], Exh. 15–1
types of backups, 15.02[A]
Recovery point objective,
  4.05[C], 4.05[D], 15.02[D]
Recovery priority, 4.05[B]
Recovery time objective,
  4.05[C], 15.02[C], Exh. 15–1
Recruiting, 10.02[A], 10.02[G]
Recruiting bonuses, Pol. 10–1
Rehiring former employees,
  10.10[D], Pol. 10–5
Relocation of technology
generally, 20.02[A]
cost/benefit analysis, Exh.
  20–1

design phase activities,
  20.03[B]
implementation phase
  activities, 20.03[C]
outsourcing, 20.02[C]
partners, 20.02[E]
planning, 20.03[A]
policy, 20.01[B]
problems in, 20.02[B]
Project Coordinator,
  20.02[D], Pol. 20–1
purpose of, 20.01[A]
relocation phase activities,
  20.03[D]
scope of, 20.01[A]
Requests for proposal
generally, 12.05[A]
bidder's conference, 12.05[E]
evaluating, 12.05[D],
  12.05[F]
preparing, 12.05[C]
project startup, 12.05[B]
SaaS vendor selection
  process, 23.08[B]
Resource management
personnel resources, 8.04[C]
project management,
  6.02[E], 6.06[D]
project plan resources,
  6.02[E]
scope of, 8.04[A]
systems development and
  planning, 28.02[C]
technical resources, 8.04[B]
Restoration priorities, 7.04[I]
Risk assessments
business continuity
  planning, 7.03[C], 7.03[D]
business impact analysis,
  4.05[E]
patch management,
  27.02[D]
project plans, 6.03[B],
  6.03[C]
systems analysis
  documentation, 13.07[F]
systems development and
  planning, 28.02[D]
Risk mitigation
business continuity
  planning, 7.03[E]
project plans, 6.03[D]
Routers, 19.02[D]
Rumor board, 10.07[D]

S

SaaS
generally, 23.07, Pol. 23–3
vendor management, 23.09
vendor selection process,
  23.08

Sarbanes-Oxley Act, 14.04[C]
Scope of IT governance, 1.01[A]
SEC rules, 14.04[E]
Security
computer security. *See* Computer security
Internet, 23.03
networks. *See* Networks
PCs, 18.04[D]
Service contracts, 7.04[E]
Service desk
generally, 16.03[A], 16.04[A]
"carry the message to the masses," 16.04[E]
communicating with customers, 16.03[G]
critical process impact matrix, Exh. 16–1
customer surveys, 16.04[I]
customer's voice, 16.02[A]
disasters and, 16.05
end user training, 16.04[D]
"hail and farewell," 16.04[F]
knowledge base, 16.04[G]
metrics, 16.04[B]
"one call – one success," 16.04[C]
on-site helpers, 16.04[H]
PCs, 18.05[F]
policy, 16.01[B], Pol. 16–1
power users, 16.04[H]
problem tracking database, 16.03[F]
products supported, 16.03[C]
purpose of, 16.01[A]
reference documentation, 13.05[D]
scope of, 16.01[A]
service levels, 16.03[B]
staffing, 16.02[B], 16.03[E]
team building, 16.03[D]
tools, 16.03[H]
working under pressure, 16.02[C]
Skills inventory, 10.05[B]
Social engineering, 14.02[B]
Software acquisition
generally, 29.05[A], Pol. 29–2
beta software testing and evaluation, 29.05[G]
contract programmers, 29.05[E]
contract programming, 29.05[D]
evaluation of packaged software, 29.05[F]
IT purchased software, 29.05[B]
PCs, 18.03[C]
requisition procedures, 29.05[C]

Software assets
generally, 17.04[A], 17.04[B], 17.05[A]
automated asset detection, 17.04[G]
copyrights, 17.05[B]
inventory, 17.04[D]
lists, 7.04[H]
number crunching, 17.04[E]
ongoing management, 17.04[F], Pol. 17–3
problem solving, 17.04[G]
unauthorized software, 17.04[C]
Software development
coding conventions, 29.04[A]
computer security, 14.03[C]
controls, 29.04[B]
Extreme Programming, 29.03[E]
ownership of software, 29.02[B], Pol. 29–1
policy, 29.01[B]
process
importance of, 29.02[A]
ownership of software, 29.02[B], Pol. 29–1
reusable component identification, 29.02[D]
specifications, 29.02[C]
purpose of, 29.01[A]
Rapid Application Development, 29.03[D]
scope of, 29.01[A]
Spiral methodology, 29.03[C]
systems development, 29.03[A]
Waterfall methodology, 29.03[B]
Software installation
generally, 29.07[A]
acceptance of contracted software, 29.07[D]
documentation, 29.07[C]
implementation day selection, 29.07[F]
programmer sign-off, 29.07[E]
results, 29.07[B]
Software maintenance
controls, 29.08[B]
conventions, 29.08[C]
end-user systems, 29.08[D], 29.08[E]
hidden programming staffs, 29.08[G]
responsibilities, 29.08[B]
stealth systems, 29.08[F]
types of, 29.08[A]
Software policies for end-user systems, 26.05[B]

Software support for PCs, 18.05[D]
Software testing, 29.05[G], 29.06
Spiral methodology to software development, 29.03[C]
Sponsors
project closeout and, 6.05[B]
project management sign-off, 6.02[H]
Staffing
allocation of staff, 9.06[D]
background checks, 10.02[J]
college recruiting, 10.02[G]
customer service. *See* Customer service
development of employees
generally, 10.05[A]
consultants, 10.05[E]
continuing education, 10.05[C]
plans, 10.05[D]
skills inventory, 10.05[B]
training. *See* Training
e-mail, 10.07[C]
employee burnout
causes of, 10.08[B]
company assistance, 10.08[C]
responsibility, 10.08[A]
signs of, 10.08[D]
employee skills matrix, 7.04[K]
external opportunity postings, 10.02[E]
flex-time, 10.10[C], Pol. 10–4
internal opportunity postings, 10.02[D]
interns, 10.02[H]
interviews, 10.02[I]
job descriptions, 10.02[B]
job-sharing, 10.10[B]
level requirements
generally, 9.06[A]
allocation of staff, 9.06[D]
performance goals, 9.06[B]
ratios, 9.06[C]
sample policy, Pol. 9–2
memos, 10.07[C]
new employee orientation. *See* New employee orientation
offshore staffing, 10.02[F]
performance evaluations. *See* Performance evaluations
performance goals, 9.06[B]
policy, 10.01[B]

productivity of individuals
generally, 10.9[A]
employee productivity,
10.9[C]
management productivity,
10.9[B]
purpose of, 10.01[A]
ratios, 9.06[C]
recruiting, 10.02[A],
10.02[G]
recruiting bonuses, Pol. 10–1
rehiring former employees,
10.10[D], Pol. 10–5
rumor board, 10.07[D]
scope of, 10.01[A]
selection of, 10.02[C]
service desk, 16.02[B],
16.03[E]
staff meetings, 10.07[B]
student interns, 10.02[H]
telecommuting, 10.10[A]
temporary personnel
services. See Temporary
personnel services
training. See Training
Staff meetings, 10.07[B]
Stand-by staffing, 9.03[B]
Strategic planning
generally, 1.03[A]
policies and procedures on
submitting, 1.03[B]
Student interns, 10.02[H]
Supplemental dataflow
conventions, 13.08[G],
Exh. 13–9
System flowcharts, 13.08[D]
Systems analysis
generally, 28.03[A]
documentation
generally, 13.07[A], Pol. 28–1
binder, 13.07[B]
product specifications,
13.07[D]
recommendations,
13.07[H]
risk assessment, 13.07[F]
schedule, 13.07[E]
scope, 13.07[C]
stakeholders, 13.07[G]
initial business unit visit,
28.03[C]
interviews, 28.03[D],
28.03[E]
objectives, 28.01[B]
policy, 28.01[C], Pol. 28–1
pre-analysis survey, 28.03[B]
purpose of, 28.01[A]
reports, 28.03[G]
scope of, 28.01[A]
tally sheet, Exh. 28–2
use case sample, Exh. 28–1
work-sampling studies,
28.03[F]

Systems design
generally, 28.04[A]
acceptance presentation,
28.04[E]
objectives, 28.01[B]
policy, 28.01[C]
purpose of, 28.01[A]
reports, 28.04[D]
resource utilization, 28.04[C]
scope of, 28.01[A]
specifications, 28.04[B]
Systems development and
planning
project planning, 28.02[A]
requirements analysis,
28.02[B]
resource estimates, 28.02[C]
risk analysis, 28.02[D]
scope creep, 28.02[E]
software development
methodologies,
29.03[A]
Systems implementation,
28.06, Pol. 28–2, Pol. 28–3
Systems maintenance
control, 28.07[D]
modifications and redesigns,
28.07[A]
requirements, 28.07[C]
responsibilities, 28.07[C]
revision conventions,
28.07[E]
types of projects, 28.07[B]
Systems prototyping
generally, 28.05[A]
development, 28.05[B]
methods, 28.05[C]

T

Technical experts
resource management,
8.04[B]
staffing, 9.03[C]
Technical reference
documentation, 13.05[E]
Telecommuting, 10.10[A]
Temporary personnel services
generally, 12.04[A]
outsourcing. See Outsourcing
PC coordinator, 18.02[C]
rules for engaging, 12.04[D]
types of, 12.04[B]
utilizing, 12.04[C]
Terminating employees,
10.04[F]
TickIT, 1.02[A]
TOGAF, 1.02[A]
Toxic material storage,
7.04[J]
Training
generally, 10.05[C]

consultants, 10.05[E]
education information
booklet, 10.06[E]
employee recognition,
10.06[D]
end-user, 10.06[B]
end-user systems, 26.04[C]
Internet, 23.04[I]
outsourced training, 10.06[F]
PCs, 18.02[D]
records, 10.06[C]
reports, 10.06[G]
service desk, 16.04[D]
strategy, 10.06[A]

U

Unified modeling language,
13.08[I]

V

Vendors
generally, 12.02[A], 12.03[A]
accounting's role, 12.03[E]
acquiring goods and services,
12.02[D]
budgets driving purchases,
12.03[F]
business continuity
planning, 7.04[F]
commodity vendors,
12.02[G]
contracts, 12.03[C]
expertise of purchasing
department, 12.03[B]
intellectual property
ownership, Pol. 12–2
key vendors, 12.02[F]
legal review of contracts,
12.03[C]
low-volume vendors,
12.02[H]
management policy,
Pol. 12–1
personnel augmentation,
12.02[C]
policy, 12.01[B], Pol. 12–1,
12–2
purchasing, 12.02[E]
purpose of, 12.01[A]
receiving the goods,
12.03[D]
requests for proposal. See
Requests for proposal
SaaS vendor management,
23.09
SaaS vendor selection
process, 23.08
scope of, 12.01[A]
selection of, 12.02[B]

temporary personnel
  services. *See* Temporary
  personnel services
Virtual private networks,
  19.02[G]
Virtual teams
  generally, 11.01
  career management, 11.03[F]
  communications, 11.03[C]
  company as, 11.02, 11.02[A]
  home office security,
    11.03[D]
  international issues, 11.05[F]
  leading, 11.05
  pitfalls, 11.02[D]
  policy, 11.01[C], Pol. 11–1
  work area, 11.03[B]
  worker as, 11.02[B], 11.03
  workforce strategy, 11.04

W

Walk-around asset inventory,
  7.04[G]
Waterfall methodology to
  software development,
  29.03[B]
Web logs, 23.04[H]
Web sites
  generally, 24.03[A]
  commonality, 24.02[C]
  consistency, 24.02[C]
  content policy, 24.03[C]
  definition of usability,
    24.02[A]
  design, 24.02[E]
  design process, Exh. 24–1
  features to avoid, 24.03[H]
  homepage policy, 24.03[G]
  importance of usability,
    24.02[B]
  objectives, 24.01[B]
  organizational policy,
    24.03[D], Pol. 24–1
  physical layout policy,
    24.03[E]
  policy, 24.01[C]
  purpose of, 24.01[A]
  scope of, 24.01[A]
  standards, 24.02[D]
  technological
    advancements, 24.02[F]
  testing policy, 24.03[B]
  visual design policy,
    24.03[F]
Wireless networks, 19.02[H],
  Pol. 19–2
Workstation audits, 8.09